A Celebration of Young Poets

New York – Fall 2007

Creative Communication, Inc.

A Celebration of Young Poets
New York – Fall 2007

An anthology compiled by Creative Communication, Inc.

Published by:

CREATIVE COMMUNICATION, INC.
1488 NORTH 200 WEST
LOGAN, UT 84341

Copyright © 2008 by Creative Communication, Inc.
Printed in the United States of America

ISBN: 978-1-60050-148-7

Foreword

The poets between these pages are not famous...yet. They are still learning how language creates images and how to reflect their thoughts through words. However, through their acceptance into this publication, these young poets have taken a giant leap that reflects their desire to write.

We are proud of this anthology and what it represents. Most poets who entered the contest were not accepted to be published. The poets who are included in this book represent the best poems from our youth. These young poets took a chance and were rewarded by being featured in this anthology. Without this book, these poems would have been lost in a locker or a backpack.

We will have a feeling of success if upon reading this anthology of poetry each reader finds a poem that evokes emotion. It may be a giggle or a smile. It may be a thoughtful reflection. You might find a poem that takes you back to an earlier day when a snowfall contains magic or when a pile of leaves was an irresistible temptation. If these poems can make you feel alive and have hope in our youth, then it will be time well spent.

As we thank the poets for sharing their work, we also thank you, the reader, for allowing us to be part of your life.

Thomas Worthen, Ph.D.
Editor
Creative Communication

WRITING CONTESTS!

Enter our next POETRY contest!
Enter our next ESSAY contest!

Why should I enter?

Win prizes and get published! Each year thousands of dollars in prizes are awarded in each region and tens of thousands of dollars in prizes are awarded throughout North America. The top writers in each division receive a monetary award and a free book that includes their published poem or essay. Entries of merit are also selected to be published in our anthology.

Who may enter?

There are four divisions in the poetry contest. The poetry divisions are grades K-3, 4-6, 7-9, and 10-12. There are three divisions in the essay contest. The essay division are grades 4-6, 7-9, and 10-12.

What is needed to enter the contest?

To enter the poetry contest send in one original poem, 21 lines or less. To enter the essay contest send in one original essay, 250 words or less, on any topic. Each entry must include the student's name, grade, address, city, state, and zip code, and the student's school name and school address. Students who include their teacher's name may help the teacher qualify for a free copy of the anthology.

How do I enter?

Enter a poem online at:
www.poeticpower.com
or

Mail your poem to:
Poetry Contest
1488 North 200 West
Logan, UT 84341

Enter an essay online at:
www.studentessaycontest.com
or

Mail your essay to:
Essay Contest
1488 North 200 West
Logan, UT 84341

When is the deadline?

Poetry contest deadlines are August 14th, December 4th, and April 8th. Essay contest deadlines are July 15th, October 15th, and February 17th. You can enter each contest, however, send only one poem or essay for each contest deadline.

Are there benefits for my school?

Yes. We award $15,000 each year in grants to help with Language Arts programs. Schools qualify to apply for a grant by having a large number of entries of which over fifty percent are accepted for publication. This typically tends to be about 15 accepted entries.

Are there benefits for my teacher?

Yes. Teachers with five or more students accepted to be published receive a free anthology that includes their students' writing.

For more information please go to our website at **www.poeticpower.com**, email us at editor@poeticpower.com or call 435-713-4411.

Table of Contents

Fall 2007 Poetic Achievement Honor Schools

* Teachers who had fifteen or more poets accepted to be published

The following schools are recognized as receiving a "Poetic Achievement Award." This award is given to schools who have a large number of entries of which over fifty percent are accepted for publication. With hundreds of schools entering our contest, only a small percent of these schools are honored with this award. The purpose of this award is to recognize schools with excellent Language Arts programs. This award qualifies these schools to receive a complimentary copy of this anthology. In addition, these schools are eligible to apply for a Creative Communication Language Arts Grant. Grants of two hundred and fifty dollars each are awarded to further develop writing in our schools.

Akron Middle School
  Akron
    Mrs. Keppel*

Avon Middle School
  Avon
    J. Hussar*

Bellport Middle School
  Bellport
    Christine Napolitano*

Bishop Ford Central Catholic High School
  Brooklyn
    Sr. Mary Towers*

Bronx Academy of Letters
  Bronx
    Ms. Battaglia*

Bronx High School of Science
  Bronx
    Mr. Brown
    Olivia Byun
    Joseph Gazzola
    Dermot Hannon

Bronx High School of Science
  Bronx (cont.)
    Helen Kellert
    Ms. Kress
    Mr. O'Brien
    Mr. Rubin
    Polly Schoenfeld
    Irma Weiss
    Holly Weiss

Camillus Middle School
  Camillus
    Ms. Rossi
    Diane Stukey*

Clarence High School
  Clarence
    Mary Sorrels*

DeSales High School
  Geneva
    Doreen DeSain*
    Beryl Tracey*

Eastplain School
  North Massapequa
    Jennifer Andes
    Christine Imbesi

Edward J Bosti Elementary School
Bohemia
    Karen Feinstein
    Joanna McManaman

Granville Elementary School
Granville
    Kim Bean
    Kathleen Casey
    Mrs. Glasier
    Faith Halnon
    Alicia Marcy
    Cara Pilch

Harold D Fayette Elementary School
North Merrick
    Christine Campisi
    Joyce Kelley*
    Ms. Porter

Harris Hill Elementary School
Penfield
    Joanne Gorman*
    David Hershey

Helen B Duffield Elementary School
Ronkonkoma
    Mrs. Alway
    Kay O'Rourke

Holy Cross School
Albany
    Janice Smircich*

John Bowne High School
Flushing
    Miss O'Sullivan*

John Hus Moravian School
Brooklyn
    Leila Baird
    Hortense Morgan

John T Waugh Elementary School
Angola
    Kathy Dole*

Leptondale Elementary School
Wallkill
    Mrs. Psilopoulos
    Joseph R. Zupan*

Long Beach Middle School
Long Beach
    Anita Bickman*
    Gwen Panoff*

Marie Curie Institute
Amsterdam
    Jerilynn Einarsson*
    Theresa Featherstone
    Linda Sawicki
    Shannon Loveland*

Massena Central High School
Massena
    Mr. Violi
    Elaine Whitcomb*

Most Precious Blood School
Walden
    Margaret Torres*

New Hyde Park Memorial Jr/Sr High School
New Hyde Park
    Mrs. Caruso
    Bryan DiScala*
    Mrs. Mirecki
    Inna Shapiro

Norman J Levy Lakeside School
Merrick
    Susan Molloy*

North Tonawanda High School
North Tonawanda
    Louis Colaiacovo
    Sarah Lazewski
    Jennifer Sommer

Northeast Elementary School
Brentwood
Ms. Betzold
Mrs. Bloom
Ms. Chu
Mrs. Correa
Mrs. Dale
Mrs. Ferro*
Ms. Giancaspro*
Mrs. Hanlon
Marge Leonard
Alison Maggio
Mrs. Martin*
Robert Melo
Lisa Patrick
Ms. Smith
Ms. Tapen
Mrs. Tejada

Oyster Bay High School
Oyster Bay
Marjorie Vigliotti*

Public School 114 Ryder
Brooklyn
Elaine R. Rowe*

Public School 124Q
South Ozone Park
Mrs. DeSena
Kate Marino
Ms. Posillco
Ms. Sadofsky

Public School 148 Ruby Allen
East Elmhurst
Lois Ricupero*

Public School 152
School of Science & Technology
Brooklyn
Mrs. Aris
Ms. P. Dong
Ms. Lutjen
Mrs. McGuire
Christina Romeo
Anna Randisi*

Public School 2 Alfred Zimberg
Jackson Heights
Ms. Eliodromytis*

Public School 205 Alexander Graham Bell
Bayside
Fran Bosi
Meri Naveh

Regis High School
New York
Mr. Lardner*
John Russo*

Robert Moses Middle School
North Babylon
D. Cerrito*
Ms. Kampf
Ms. Spath

Sewanhaka High School
Floral Park
Kathleen Dehler*

Shelter Rock Elementary School
Manhasset
Mr. Collyer*
Mrs. Lawrence*
Mrs. Mitchell
Joyce Rappaport*
Mr. Sirof
Patricia Siver*

Smithtown High School West
Smithtown
Christopher Gunsel
Michael Nolan

Solvay Middle School
Syracuse
Cece Kulak*

Southern Cayuga Middle School
Poplar Ridge
Bill Zimpfer*

St Benedict Joseph Labre School
    Richmond Hill
        Andrea Mastrandrea
        Miss Santos

St John School
    Goshen
        Arlene J. Melillo*

St Mary's School
    Waterford
        Tami Farron*

St Mary's School
    Staten Island
        Mrs. Depasquale
        Ken Parlatore*

Staley Upper Elementary School
    Rome
        R. Pezzulo*

Townsend Harris High School
    Flushing
        Mr. Babstock
        Ilsa Cowen
        Charlene Levi
        Aliza Sherman*
        Adam Stonehill
        Georgette Wallace
        Mr. Wamsteker

Warwick Valley Middle School
    Warwick
        Debra A. Leporati*

William B Tecler Elementary School
    Amsterdam
        Karen LaPlante*

Language Arts Grant Recipients 2007-2008

After receiving a "Poetic Achievement Award" schools are encouraged to apply for a Creative Communication Language Arts Grant. The following is a list of schools who received a two hundred and fifty dollar grant for the 2007-2008 school year.

Acadamie DaVinci, Dunedin, FL
Altamont Elementary School, Altamont, KS
Belle Valley South School, Belleville, IL
Bose Elementary School, Kenosha, WI
Brittany Hill Middle School, Blue Springs, MO
Carver Jr High School, Spartanburg, SC
Cave City Elementary School, Cave City, AR
Central Elementary School, Iron Mountain, MI
Challenger K8 School of Science and Mathematics, Spring Hill, FL
Columbus Middle School, Columbus, MT
Cypress Christian School, Houston, TX
Deer River High School, Deer River, MN
Deweyville Middle School, Deweyville, TX
Four Peaks Elementary School, Fountain Hills, AZ
Fox Chase School, Philadelphia, PA
Fox Creek High School, North Augusta, SC
Grandview Alternative School, Grandview, MO
Hillcrest Elementary School, Lawrence, KS
Holbrook School, Holden, ME
Houston Middle School, Germantown, TN
Independence High School, Elko, NV
International College Preparatory Academy, Cincinnati, OH
John Bowne High School, Flushing, NY
Lorain County Joint Vocational School, Oberlin, OH
Merritt Secondary School, Merritt, BC
Midway Covenant Christian School, Powder Springs, GA
Muir Middle School, Milford, MI
Northlake Christian School, Covington, LA
Northwood Elementary School, Hilton, NY
Place Middle School, Denver, CO
Public School 124, South Ozone Park, NY

Language Arts Grant Winners cont.

Public School 219 Kennedy King, Brooklyn, NY
Rolling Hills Elementary School, San Diego, CA
St Anthony's School, Streator, IL
St Joan Of Arc School, Library, PA
St Joseph Catholic School, York, NE
St Joseph School-Fullerton, Baltimore, MD
St Monica Elementary School, Mishawaka, IN
St Peter Celestine Catholic School, Cherry Hill, NJ
Strasburg High School, Strasburg, VA
Stratton Elementary School, Stratton, ME
Tom Thomson Public School, Burlington, ON
Tremont Elementary School, Tremont, IL
Warren Elementary School, Warren, OR
Webster Elementary School, Hazel Park, MI
West Woods Elementary School, Arvada, CO
West Woods Upper Elementary School, Farmington, CT
White Pine Middle School, Richmond, UT
Winona Elementary School, Winona, TX
Wissahickon Charter School, Philadelphia, PA
Wood County Christian School, Williamstown, WV
Wray High School, Wray, CO

Young Poets
Grades 10-11-12

Note: The Top Ten poems were finalized through an online voting system. Creative Communication's judges first picked out the top poems. These poems were then posted online. The final step involved thousands of students and teachers who registered as online judges and voted for the Top Ten poems. We hope you enjoy these selections.

Top Poem Grades 10-11-12

Make a Difference

I want to write a poem that can talk to you,
And that you'll feel comfortable around with,
Like an old friend if you know what I mean,
Where the words can be your companions,
And the metaphors and similes are your little "inside jokes,"
I want to write a poem that you can relate to,
Twenty minutes, twenty Tuesdays, twenty years from now.
Something that you'll remember for the rest of your days.
Where a bond so tight forms that even
The wittiest hyperboles cannot describe.
I want to write a poem that is melodious to your soul,
With harmonizing syllables and dreamy rhymes,
Where each stanza is a new movement in this
Symphony of words and thoughts and feelings.
Just give me a pencil and a freshly crisp sheet of white paper,
Because I want to write a poem, this poem, some poem, that
Can make a difference.

Linda Chu, Grade 10
Bronx High School of Science

Top Poem Grades 10-11-12

The Moon: Her Spotlight

She struts down the streets of New York,
Shoulders tossed back, neck arched, the free bird,
And she opens her mouth to sing her song,
So all of Manhattan can hear her thoughts, her dreams, her voice,
She struts down the streets of New York,
The moon: her spotlight,
Fretful city men glancing at wrists,
Skinny boys with baggy clothes and headphones, oblivious
And me
As her audience,
I can see her from here,
Her flushed cheeks,
Crimson from the bitter breeze,
Shining through the blackened cloak,
And she looks at me,
Eyes dancing like sky-scraping flames,
And she smiles mid-tune,
With teeth that absorb the stars,
She struts along the streets of New York,
With only the moon: her spotlight.

Marion Distante, Grade 11
Tappan Zee High School

Top Poem Grades 10-11-12

Fake Is the New Best Friend

"I will always be beside you and I will never let you fall,
I am always here if you need me, no task is too big or too small."
When was the last time I heard this? Honestly, I can't even recall.
People in this modern day world, have no remorse or compassion at all.
Whatever happened to the real friends who, no matter what, held you close?
Whatever happened to those people you can honestly say, you loved the most?
"A stranger is a friend in progress," is what my mother would always say.
And I would listen to her words carefully, then think that everything would be okay.
Though her words would soothe and comfort me, her theory was still unfortunately wrong;
Because teenagers will not even talk to you, unless you are in the clique in which you belong.
Our news channels are now filled with tragedies, everything from massacres, terrorism to fights;
Whatever happened to the sacredness of life and most importantly, our God given rights?
Everything today is based on rivalry, who can make it and who doesn't have what it takes;
But who needs tournaments, competitions or contests, if all the players were actually fakes?
Whatever happened to the people you could lean on, when times were rough and you didn't know what to do?
What happened to the friends you could trust who, no matter what, stayed true to you?
I miss those friends who won't abandon you, in your desperate times of need.
And I'm frustrated by those who replaced them, those who are overcome with envy and greed.
But I have finally come to the conclusion that I will never once comprehend;
Why people have changed so dramatically and why fake is the new best friend.

Akela Francis, Grade 12
Academy of Mount St Ursula

Top Poem Grades 10-11-12

Pretend

I remember Rocky Horror on Saturday nights,
while the foam leaked from the cuts in your car seats.
Half-burnt burgers digested in our stomachs,
and buzzing streetlights replaced trails of bread crumbs home.

Poisoned apples became paperweights to cluttered desks,
while pens and pencils enchanted into mythical swords.
When a tiny pea buried beneath a forest of mattresses
became the happy thought that helped us all fly.

A scaly-backed teacher blew fire down our throats,
while a freckle-faced dragon helped us pick out our library books.
Lunchroom buddies met to discuss political frailties,
and the round-table sat empty as knights enjoyed their recess.

The long whine of another day's school bell
became the next monotonous voice of a passing phony.
Our busses transformed to new steeds of gallant strength
and cliques met while Machiavelli twined through their heads.

A scary thing it is, to tally our years,
and easing thing it is to forget them.
But in the end, like Holden, Peter, and Arthur,
we do all we can to play pretend.

Ariel Goldberg, Grade 12
Ward Melville High School

Top Poem Grades 10·11·12

Undecided

Many possibilities run through my head
But ultimately, I am still undecided.
My heart yearns to find my one true passion.
Is it art? Is it history? I know it's not fashion.

Some tell me I don't have to decide right now,
To let myself explore I should allow.
They tell me I am in the majority
And to ignore any feelings of inferiority.

So then I'm at peace and finally okay.
When asked I say, "I'm undecided," without delay.
Out of this others make such a big issue.
Why should it matter if it is what is true?

I could easily make something up instead
And say that I am going to do pre-med.
I could bask in the oohs and ahs of their praise,
But I feel my very self that betrays.

A barrage of questions of what I'm going to do
Reopens my wounds and makes them sting anew.
Why do they contribute to my insecurity
When I reveal a natural feeling of uncertainty?

Pauline Lu, Grade 12
Dominican Academy

Top Poem Grades 10-11-12

Ocean Blue

The rolling, capricious deep ocean blue
With waves constantly pushing fro and to.
Reflecting the sky poised above it all,
The curves keep rising, 'til they finally fall.
Her water and mist, of salty taste,
Her graceful motions always traveling in haste.
A great filled abyss, with wonders unknown —
What human has seen all that can be shown?

It was then that I saw what Nature had meant
To give the sea all her blue content:
The roaring sound of a tremendous din,
Her giant swells pouring out, then in.
A queen who has her tempestuous days,
But otherwise, calm and serene, she stays
Controlled by the moon, a goddess who
Keeps her waves rolling, the ocean blue.

Irene Martinez, Grade 10
Preston High School

Top Poem Grades 10-11-12

Painted Plaster Sky

Morning light is blinding, though my curtains all are drawn,
as if I wish the night would linger past the coming of the dawn.
My throat is slowly sinking through the hollows of my chest,
and I wheeze a hopeless murmur underneath a dogged breath.
For fear of drifting into dreams, I lift my sleepy eyes
to contemplate the nothing of a painted plaster sky.
My fingers trace each grainy arc — the sunbursts wont to fading
I wonder how each swooping stroke achieved its perfect shading.
Such effects seem so inviting, and so pleasing to the touch;
all I've wanted is to reach my sky, o, I've wanted it so much —
but as I draw in closer, I fall back onto my bed.
O! my unassertive beauty is nothing, nothing — dead.
I have run my palms across it, picked away the chipping paint
I've forgotten I could reach such height, and left my sky to wane.
Morning light is blinding, but still I simply lie
beneath my limitations and my painted plaster sky.

Chelsea Mixon, Grade 12
Cato Meridian Sr High School

Top Poem Grades 10-11-12

A March for Peace?

What does it mean
to see men marching?
They wear the color of death, proudly.
Must they kill to create Peace?
I can hear from their mouths
chants of anger and pain.
Are they symbols of Peace,
or fading ghosts of our future?
Icons of Hope,
or messages of hate?
I wonder as I watch
which men will not return.
Who are these men?
In what direction are they marching?

Jamie Schefen, Grade 10
Plainview Old Bethpage/JFK High School

Top Poem Grades 10-11-12

A Flower's Paradox

Back when I was like other marguerites,
A snow-white flower of perfect radial symmetry,
Whom the sun lent its streaming rays,
Whom the moon turned its lustful gaze,
I would whisper to the purring wind,
"Set me free, set me free."

It was not until spring floated in,
Until my sisters unraveled such pearly wings
And bared their innocent hearts of gold
To the fumbling of strange rough hands
That crushed their leaves, twisted their petals,
Did I see the evil in what I wished.

By and by, leaves have rusted into copper red
And many summer skies have tapered into distant lines.
Here I am, clinging to my browning sun dress,
Letting my wrinkled forehead nod into a somber dream.
Rooted in the jaundiced garden of fruitless age,
I whispered to the earth soil to take me away.

Sadness yes, but alas, that sudden flood of relief!
I can do no better justice to my name than dying —
Pure.

Daisy Tang, Grade 11
Jericho High School

Top Poem Grades 10-11-12

Waiting

In these chairs, countless souls
young and old, have told their stories.
The chairs still hold their secrets safe.
They know the sounds of trumpets and strings,
of horses and children — of wind and waterfall.
Sometimes they shake when people sitting in them
laugh till tears roll down their cheeks.
They've heard the old man tell lovingly of how
he first danced with his wife.
Tired cooks have fallen into a strong green embrace,
to feel a cool breeze, while in their minds,
they silently taste their next creation.
Just last night, two friends sat here and shared a secret
that these chairs will never tell.
And under the sparkling canopy of the Milky Way,
a young man weeps for love he has lost,
his tears dropping silently on gentle green arms.

Kathryn Utter, Grade 11
Byron Bergen Jr/Sr High School

The Race

Who's the best?
Well the race will tell,
Seabiscuit against War Admiral.
A story of David and Goliath.
Around the last turn they go.
Only worry: to finish first.
Down the stretch they come.
Flash photo shows who's the best.
No one believes it,
Seabiscuit has won.
He defeated the odds,
And proved that outsiders could win.

Kaili Collins, Grade 12
DeSales High School

Hate You

I love you
and always will
if only from nothing but habit

Broken Freedom Fighter
with laughter pealing from your lips
and anger
darkening your brow

together always
how regret draws me in
you found someone

shunned aside, my time divided
while you are joined with another

how strange, the color green
it tints everything a shade

all is yours now,
everything

good fortune, good life, good love
I hate you

Alycia Askew, Grade 11
Greenwich Jr/Sr High School

Free Will

We all think we want to be the same
That's why we're playing human games
But I will dare to be different
I will stand out from this crowd
I will raise my voice
I will be proud
I will let my dreams soar
Soar like clouds in the sky
I won't worry about their dreams
I'll anticipate mine

Elizabeth LaBarge, Grade 10
Massena Central High School

The Enlightenment Influence

The foundations of our country can be attributed to
The enlightenment thinkers including Locke, Voltaire, and Montesquieu.
Immanuel Kant exclaimed "Dare to know!"
And the rest of the world did exactly so,
Voltaire rallied for freedom of speech,
For religious tolerance did he preach,
Cesare Beccaria fought for man's right to trial,
And what Locke wanted was a government, republic style.
So when Thomas Jefferson wrote the Declaration of Independence,
When the Continental Congress was in attendance,
He borrowed certain ideas from that thinking crew,
Like "All men are created equal," cited from Rousseau.
Jefferson was influenced by Jonathon Locke when he,
Included "Life, Liberty," and the right to be happy.
Enlightenment thinking allowed Americans to be,
Allowed us to be incredibly free.

Pearl Bhatnagar, Grade 10
Townsend Harris High School

Is It Only Me?

Look Jesus, look. Do You see what I see?
A land of hatred, just another branch off that old knowledgeable tree
Do You hear that Jesus, do You hear what I hear?
Little baby Samantha crying in the dumpster, waiting for Mommy to appear.
Jesus, Jesus, Jesus! Do You smell what I smell?
That foul stench of the man in the train station preaching words from hell.
Do You see those clothes he wears every day?
That black and that gray, make my eyes turn away.
Jesus, Jesus! Can You feel what I feel?
That cocaine, driving through my veins like a mad taxi driver, easing my pain.
Jesus, do You see that man with that knife?
That 14 year old girl, with her stomach full of life
Jesus, do You know where justice lies?
It lies on its stomach with the worms and the snakes.
Jesus, the world is Yours to reprimand, why do you allow such things to be?
Jesus, there are 6 billion pairs of eyes just like mine, so I know it's not just me!

Lemuel Gardner, Grade 11
Bishop Ford Central Catholic High School

Empty Arms

I said "yes," I don't know why I would compromise my life like this.
I wish you wouldn't have given me the choice of self sabotage.
I said "yes" and referred to you as my "lover," I felt so loved.
I was never so happy, only one other time I have felt this way.
But it never ended the way this will.
I was happy yet, uncomfortable.
Not knowing what to do, but neither did you.
You came up behind me and put your arms around me.
I felt loved for the first time, well, in a different manner from what I was used to.
I re-thought everything; you, me, life, death, love, hate, everything.
I came to the horrid conclusion, that I don't want to be touched, by anyone.
It's not you it's me.
I know you only wanted to express you cared.
To you the touch was not empty.
But for me, it was, though the love was there.
My arms felt empty.

Stacy Baughman, Grade 10
North Tonawanda High School

Overcoming Two Thousand Years
"Everything has beauty, but not everyone sees it."
Confucius' philosophy has been around
For over two thousand years,
But it will take another two thousand
To reach the ones who still spell the word 'ugly'

"Real knowledge is to know the extent of one's ignorance."
Confucius' philosophy has been around
For over two thousand years,
But it will take another two thousand
To reach the ones who call themselves a genius

"To see the right and not to do it is cowardice."
Confucius' philosophy has been around
For over two thousand years,
But it will take another two thousand
To reach the ones who say nothing when they see something
Ayumi Kano, Grade 10
Townsend Harris High School

The Civil War
Definition; war between Union and Confederate States,
A war between brothers fought with so much hate.
The North said slavery was wrong,
Unjust and it had been in the world too long.
Abe led the Union into the war,
Without knowing what was in store.
The South said let there be slaves,
Anyone who disagrees is a knave.
The Confederate's were led by Robert Lee,
Who won a series of victories.
But that all changed in 1863,
When the Union controlled the Mississippi.
At the Appomattox court house in 1865,
The Confederate's took a nosedive.
The North had won and the South had lost,
But the Country was left in exhaust.
Many soldiers had been killed,
And the nation was left to rebuild.
Sarah Aliahmad, Grade 10
Townsend Harris High School

Ice Cold Foe
With every brush I eradicate tears,
And comes to surface the ever lurking fears.
To force to me see to what I once was blind,
To force me to search for what I never thought to find.

So I replenish my heart with a glaze of flame,
And plunge back into the ice that I am entailed to tame.
And with every stroke I further expose my core
But simultaneously destroy the frigidity I so deplore.

And the canvas becomes alive with pieces of me,
Outwardly displayed for the world to see.
And only then will I feel the long-coveted heat,
That arises from concluding such a phenomenal feat.
Nushrat Hoque, Grade 10
Middletown High School

Life
Life is sometimes hard and not very nice
Life brings challenges and we should take them
Because I believe life is too short.
We need to live our life to the fullest,
And always be happy.
Let every day teach you something new
And fill you with joy.
Sometimes we feel like life is unfair,
But we need to take the good with the bad
And smile when we can.
We need to believe in God and trust Him to help us.
Nobody said life would be easy
God's just trying to prove that to us.
Life is full of beauty and wonderful things
We need to cherish them each and every day.
Give your love and you shall get love in return,
Also have pride in everything you do.
So when we start to get down on ourselves
Just remember we have love and God to help.
Also we have our family that cares,
Without them life just would not be the same.
Alyssa Liberatore, Grade 12
DeSales High School

The Wordsmith
The wordsmith wakes one long breath takes
To clear his mind and soul
He looks unto the rising sun
And beauty does extol

At desk he sit with humble wit
And takes his pen in hand
The marriage of ink and tablet
Make reality disband

And what a thing to see him sling!
His mind from common world
And enter one all of his own
Where fantasies unfurled

He makes the breeze he grows the trees
Draws the hills out from the land
He sculpts the world in his mind
With every wave of hand

The wordsmith smiles cast off his trials
And looks over the sheet
He scans the page and hints a grin
His work is now complete
Kathryn Miller, Grade 12
Warwick Valley High School

Amada Tierra

It began with a simple memory, of the times we head off from,
Being able to laugh, play, and cry freely, without constraints or regrets.
It was these emotions that drove us back to what we once had,
Far away from the infinite blows of the desert, the surging warmth of the tropics,
or the winds from the heights of the Andes,
We came to meet on this land, from seemingly different existence's of our pacha mama (mother earth,)
Seeking to find one voice, one identity, one tale,
In this story that is ours, bits of whom we are is enclosed,
Whereas we fought to be heard, to oppose the oppression that held us down,
Now we struggle to have our voices heard, to proclaim the truth that bonds us,
We are connected by our experiences, and our right to decide — it can either bloom
with the power of our will, or wither with our arrogance, that remains for us to choose,
What do you notice when you look into that woman's eyes, what is it you see?
Do you see her barefoot, dancing to her beloved huaynito, following the rhythms of her *tayta's queña?*
Can you see her as a young girl she was, working relentlessly in the fields of her *pueblo,* gathering the corns at harvest time?
Hunching as the rain drops feel upon her pale back.
Even now with the smile that graces her face, the reminiscent of her past empowers here to hope,
one day surely she knows she will return to her *amada tierra* (beloved land.)
One day I know I will return

Fiorella Diaz, Grade 11
Sewanhaka High School

What I See Through My Window

The things I see through my window are all unknown faces with unknown lives, and unknown secrets that lies deep in their souls.
I see forgotten faces with forgotten lives, I see men who have run out of time, I see heroes who have fought and died.
I also see the beauty in this world it lies peacefully, and undisturbed even by time, I've seen poets cry and lovers dream.
When I look through my window I see all of the heavens, and also hell I've seen people ask Saint Peter why is life like this.
And in their sacred moment all of their questions were hushed, but not a word was spoken to them.
I've seen soldiers who have fallen battle and say to Saint Peter one more soldier reporting for duty sir just tell her that I love her.
Now what you see is a beautiful world you have just been blinded by lies of men who know not what's right but wrong.
I hope you realize it's a beautiful world as I have realized, and when you look out your window I bet you'll see the same as me
a beautiful world full of unknown faces.

Thomas Sharp, Grade 11
Forestville Central High School

A Lost Smile

It's weird to see you in the hall because you were the one to make me fall.
You told me how much you loved me on my notebook.
Now you can't even look at me.
We would look into each other's eyes and wouldn't care about time.

Your gaze is burned in the back of my skull.
I messed with the bull and I got the horns.
You left me on my own and left me torn between what I was and what I should be.
It was the tragedy of you and me.

You said you couldn't live without me but you're doing just fine.
You just went to the next girl in line.
I'm supposed to put that smile on your face but you abandoned me without a trace of what we were.
There's no words to tell what just occurred.

I was head-over-heels and now it's over my head.
I'd like to say that you're dead to me but I can't say that yet.
I want to get over you but our memories won't let me.

Madison Morency, Grade 10
Hudson Falls High School

Rose

The twilight brings forth a peripheral dawn
The sun dances its way 'cross the lawn
The first kiss of light, on dew ridden petals
Gives way to the rainfall last night
But raindrops weren't the only things falling
For tears had escaped him as well
His heart had been broken unfixable
He held a rose; waiting for time to tell
Rain drops
Washing away
Everything that hadn't been said
Rain drops
Washing away
Everything, but the things that are dead
The twilight, hides the pain
Rain drops
Of everything during the day
Rain drops
Pouring down his face
The rose petals close, along with his eyes
Neither expects to see dawn any ways

Angela Post, Grade 11
DeSales High School

Agent Orange

The horrors of Agent Orange
Still plays its role today.
There are still many challenges
Facing the victims, to their dismay.

You'd think there are enough of proofs,
Yet still the government remains aloof.
In the Vietnam War, the chemical was sprayed
Over the forests, in order to aid.

The U.S. soldiers couldn't see past the vegetation,
Therefore on the herbicide, their battles were planned.
Twenty million gallons of this poisonous potion
Covered three point six million acres of land.

And twenty years later, what have they gained?
Nothing except the victims' healths all waned.
Three million mutated Vietnamese, plus a few soldiers,
Like Ken Dobbie, have more than one life dangers.

Sclerosis and pancreitis, and brain atrophy,
And ten other diseases are all found in Ken.
These men should be compensated for this catastrophe!
And what have the government done? Nothing, again.

Eva Fu-Yun Fan, Grade 10
Townsend Harris High School

The Light of Racism

I am a light that never stops shining.
I come to destroy humanity and justice.
I take my darkness and destruction with me wherever I go.
I am the reason behind anguish and depression.
I cause millions of people to die with my hatred.
I am the reason behind the Holocaust and Civil War.
I segregate the Black from the White,
the Christian from the Jew.
I become a mother for Hitler and the Nazis.
I become a father for early southern America.
I become food for insecure people,
who lost the right to be called human beings
when they welcomed me into their lives.
I interfere whenever I can,
in the middle of the desert or in the heart of a city.
I help to make the Earth as full of hatred as hell below.
No one can block my rays for…
I am the Light of Racism!

Ifza Riaz, Grade 10
Bronx High School of Science

The Light of Coincidence

Sweet heart, aching stomach
lungs filled with no air
You have me breathless,
unaware, eyes wandering from the attachment of your hair
to the grouped shyness of your toes
Captivated, within your stare
nervous laughter, a covered face
hiding from the enchantment of your curled lips
the innocence of your selective placement, beside me

Sipping your phrases, swallowing your words whole
Digesting the remainder of your aggressive pull
on the strings that encase my blood filled muscle
Goose bumped skin, crawling
Your touch ignites sensations unworthy of their complacence
I am caught,
tangled in this web of pure infatuation

Samantha Inesti, Grade 11
Stella Maris High School

Love

A snake's scaly skin is softer than my love;
Her touch is cold like a ghastly ghoul's blow;
If masked inside was a beautiful white dove;
Then kill me now because I will never know.
If I could stare forever frozen eternity at one;
If I had chanced to cut your tongue full of lies;
I won't be reluctant, to do it at a run.
If she ever inspired me to paint a masterpiece;
All the colors would mix and blend terribly;
A woman would appear ugly, disgusting, and obese;
But, yet again, you are my sweet darling Amy.
How I wish we could have collided yesterday,
And fallen in love and let our hearts run away.

Brian Ng, Grade 12
Staten Island Technical High School

The Immortal

Pope Urban II and his friends
Laid their cause to rest in 1204.
It wore the mask of a holy war
The truly righteous pillaging.
803 years later, I wonder
Will there ever be a change?

Lindsay Sovern, Grade 10
Townsend Harris High School

Free

she throws her arms up and
runs
to the train tracks
she's been there before
always waiting
holding back
afraid to take the next step on board
and see where it leads her
but now?
it's different
so much has happened
so much has changed
she's ready now
free at last
This is where her life begins
where she takes the pencil
erases her past
and writes her future.
Finally
She's starting over.

Liz Mauch, Grade 10
Massena Central High School

Entrapped

Help! Help! Oh, who ev'r will help'eth?
In this poem I'm entrapped'eth!
It's Shakespearean, as you see,
And it has such a hold on me
That although I may cry and howl
And shout and curse and yell and yowl,
Claw and dig and shovel and scrape.
I just cannot seem to escape.
Oh, who wilt assist, I beg you?
Must I languish one year, or two?
I know not how it came to be
That a poem ought imprison me.
I am but a poor miscreant,
A mere traveler on word's rant.
How long shall this all persevere?
Is there way out, door or lever?
Why is a poem a jailer, too?
And what now can ever ensue?
Prithee, prithee! Ah, me! Ah, me!
Should you need me, here I shall be.

Colleen Wilson, Grade 12
Our Lady of Mercy High School

Life

Life is the hardest thing you can endure.
When you're up there's always something there
To pull you down
Sometimes you feel so alone not knowing what
Way to go or what to choose
Forced to make decisions you don't want to
Knowing life can be worse but you never lived a life more trying than yours
What hurts you makes you stronger but I don't want to hurt to be strong
Life is something to think about.

Brittany Diggs, Grade 10
Middletown High School

Gone

In many ways you are held deep in my heart,
Like a river flowing you are soft and a blessing to see,
But when you're gone I can't deal with us being a part,
because my body begins to feel apart from me.

You've left to the other side of the Earth,
Willing to fight and serve,
In many ways I feel like this is your rebirth,
So by our government you can be curved.

Curved into an image they're proud to call their own,
Their own…I thought this was the country of the free,
But they're scared so they keep what they know,
And because of our country no one wants us around…so we flee.

I become scared because I know what's to come,
Your death and then you're done.

Valerie Lopez, Grade 11
Urban Assembly Media High School

Love

I keep hearing that you exist.
People say they see you — they touch you.
They say you help them when depressed, sad and lonely.
They say you keep people together — forever.
Some even say you do not work all the time;
You have a tendency to fade away — only for a short time however,
For you can return to set things back to norm. I'm curious — love.
Do you really return? — Do you really fade away?
Do you really keep people together — forever?
Do you really console the depressed, sad and lonely?
For I am sad, lonely and depressed.
Will not you help me? — Why ignore me? — Or forget me?
Why listen to what others have to say about me?
I tried to reach for you too — you just could not see.
For sadness, depression and loneliness kept you blind;
Blind from watching my hands reach for you…
You fell — long gone — never came back.
Do not worry — I keep hearing that you exist.
Tis' true? —
Do you really —
Exist?

Richard-Olivier Marius, Grade 12
Frank Sinatra School of the Arts

Not Just a Smile

When you see me I smile so you would think I'm okay
But depress and pain is where my heart lays
I smiled so you thought I was happy and nothing hurt inside
I smiled so that you couldn't see the loneliness in my eyes

I smiled to make you feel better I forgot about myself
But deep inside I was screaming out for your help
The last time I smiled — pain wouldn't let me —
But I remember the day I cried because I was happy

Reema Crews, Grade 11
Amityville Memorial High School

Coming Home

Sitting around or working hard,
Awaiting that one point in time.
Staring out that one, fogged window
Anxious to see a familiar face.
But yet you know, you are afraid
And nervous of who will pass next.
Having barely any sleep and nearly no food
Just makes the time drag out longer.
Until that one hectic day, where it is
Either life or death; heaven or hell.
You become frightened, but also excited
And unsure of what will come next.
Then after everything is over,
You get the good of it,
Even though nothing will ever be the same again.
And as you walk away from it all,
You find yourself starting over;
Never truly home.

Nicole Zito, Grade 11
Sachem High School East

The Invisible Line of Agony

A country divided.
Brothers and sisters torn from their ties.
The sun had turned away its shining face.
The land called for change.
Tanks rolled and the infantry advanced,
They pushed forward and retreated backward,
Both with the support of overlooking allies.
A feeble attempt to unite the country.
Innocence quivered in the battle trenches.
A never-ending shower of bullets.
A soldier turned to see a gun pointed at him,
By one of his race, forced to kill the enemy.
A country still divided.
Brothers and sisters on the other side,
Never to be seen again.
The land still calls for change.
The stains of blood
Of those who fought remain,
In the very minds of today's people.
A fiery flame never extinguished.
We will never disregard the 38th parallel.

Jun Jeong, Grade 10
Townsend Harris High School

Summer

Summer is every teenager's dream
There's no school, just fun in the sun
Summer is the warmth of the sunshine hitting your face
Rebirth of trees, plants, and flowers comes in summer
We celebrate our freedom on Independence Day
There's so much that can happen in summer
You can fall in love, and have a summer romance
You can have summertime adventures or tan on the beach
We change over the summer, and become different
In the summer we can make fun memories
When we travel to beaches, amusement parks, and states
In the summer we relax causing no stress
Girls shop for cute clothes at the mall, getting happy
Some of us exercise by biking, hiking or swimming
Others get a summer job to earn money and become happy
On our birthdays we get surprised
Sometimes we have barbecue to have a
Celebration, fun, parties, or surprises
To me summer is the best season of them all
There's so much to do! parties, shopping, jobs, and more
Summer is the best season of them all

Charlene Scism, Grade 10
Saugerties Jr/Sr High School

The Journey of Napoleon

The little corporal of a little kingdom
Took a huge burden on his hands:
To change the European freedom
Into a dictatorship of France.

Inspired by Josephine, his wife, so charming,
He looted Italy on their honeymoon;
In Egypt, trounced the Mamelukes army;
And turned to Northern Europe soon.

He crossed the Alps to strike on coalition.
To finish its defense, he had to do it fast.
He conquered lands accomplishing his mission,
And turned into an emperor at last.

His new empire soon grew bigger.
He added Germany and Spain,
And with self-confidence and vigor,
He did not stop on Russian lanes.

What was he thinking? Utterly unsighted
By his good fortune, triumph and fame,
He entered Russia uninvited
To find his dreadful end with shame.

Sophia Pinkhasova, Grade 10
Townsend Harris High School

A Lonely Prayer

Dear God,

It's funny how my fears can drive me into tears.

It feels like my imagination is messing with my brain; it's driving me insane.

It's scary knowing where my life is going now; never know if I'm headed up or down.

I'm tired of giving people attitude for caring and trying to take care of me

because I'm confused on where I want to be.

It feels like I bottle up my common sense and place it on a shelf.

I need to stop making excuses; I have no one else to blame but myself.

I am confused between the things I want and what I really need —

I need to *freeze* and just *breathe*.

God, You're right. I do have it good and should be grateful for my life.

And I am — but why do I cry lonely tears at night?

Why can't I see things aren't going back to the way they used to be?

My Nana belongs in my heart and that's where she should stay,

but sometimes I get really upset and pray and wish she had never died away.

I know I need to look into the future and let go of my past

because I'll never know when it came because it went by *so fast*.

I guess I need to open my eyes and realize what I have and enjoy each and every day like it's my last.

I want my Nana to be proud and see her grand kids grow up to successful ladies and men.

So I'm going to end this prayer with an Amen!

Javonnie Mack, Grade 10
Baldwin High School

With Just One Luck

It's crazy how lives just go down the drain, especially all these kids going through pain

All they feel is pressure inside, being put down and losing their pride

They feel like they're worthless and have nothing to give, they're living a life with no prerogative

They always leave and they're never around, they're getting beat up and some shot to the ground

Thinking they got it good but really living in hell, will they ever be happy, it's hard to tell

With just one luck we hope to find, that they pick up the pieces they once left behind

So that maybe one day you hear a knock on your door, hoping it's your son but you're really not sure

As you open the door your heart skips a beat, as you see your son kneeling down to your feet

Crying hysterical and saying in your ear, Mommy I love you as you break down to tears

You finally realize that life is like a light, when it's off it's pitch dark but when it's on it shines bright

As he holds you close and wipes your tears away, he says Ma today for us is a brand new day

He closes the door and says I know I ran on the wrong track, but I'm just happy that I'm finally back

Katiria Davila, Grade 10
Bronx Academy of Letters

Heaven's Newest Angel*

People would look at this young man who lay before us and begin to judge and assume,

but little did they know about him, Were they there to see him bloom?

Not like the flowers but like the thorns that are attached,

He came off as a different person, but his heart and smile was beautiful, in fact,

The bravery of a soldier, The strength of a lion untamed Dependable he was, anytime you needed something he came,

Hip Hop, that's another word that will be remembered when thinking of this young one,

Always with a pen and paper expressing thoughts, Chances of not seeing that, Slim to NONE,

Talented and Gifted there was much success to come but unfortunately that word does not arrive often for some,

"Time To Go, Time To Go" I imagine the man upstairs saying to himself "Time to go to heaven, where there's everlasting love, life and wealth"

So lovely ones down below, those with tears in your eyes, Wipe them away and just think...Heaven's Newest Angel has arrived

Briana Greenidge, Grade 12
Blessed Sacrament-St Gabriel High School
**Dedicated to my deceased cousin*

Combustion

What is going on?
I'm not tagging along.
This is getting too old.
Now the only way I feel is cold.
I'm so sick of the treatment
Anyone deserves better
Especially because I did nothing
You call yourself a friend even something more?
What happened?
Will someone bring me healing?

Whatever, I don't care anymore.
It's over and done with, I can't do it anymore.
I've got my savior.
So there's nothing more I need.
I'll take it all I've got
I won't fall down, and be forgot.

My heart still pounds
It's all so confusing.
I thought everything was perfect
What went wrong?

Sarah Doucette, Grade 10
North Tonawanda High School

Ghost Ship and Pale Monsters

Rows upon rows of fluffy white fields.
Too much for this weak body to take.
Sunburn on my neck, callus on my hands.
From dawn to dusk I toil away.
And if I stop, the pale monster appears.
With each blow, I hear a CRACK.
With each infliction, I feel the pain.
With each time, I see more scars.

In my memory, I see a ghost ship.
The terror of which haunts my dreams.
The darkness consumed us in thousands.
In its stomach, it stank of foul odors and ailment.
The clinking of chains sounded,
As I shifted to my left.
Only to my horror, a limp body laid.

I was famished and confused.
Yearning for my homeland of Niger.
But I found myself standing on alien soil.
Seeing pale faced monsters who spoke unknown words.
And now I am here in this fluffy white field.
Working for the pale face whom I call "master."

Amanda Liew, Grade 10
Townsend Harris High School

Since the Start

I never evolved like a butterfly out of a cocoon
Heart been frozen
Since I departed my mother's womb,
She said, "Son, hold your head
I know things'll be good soon,"
And this world, "I don't love you"
Never cared
That my whole life's been a struggle,
Multiple arrests
Got me lookin' at jail time trouble
Remember no man's untouchable,
Bullets'll rush you
Make a wrong livin' police'll bust you
But on life goes
Tears tend to drop
When caskets begin to close.

Brendy Flores, Grade 10
Williamsburg High School for Architecture and Design

I Can Make a Difference

I can make a difference by being loving and kind,
By being helpful and not being mean,
I can make a difference by being in my right mind,
By feeding the weak and the lean,

I can make a difference by spreading the word,
"Make love, Not War!"
Say it loud and be heard,
This issue is serious and not a bore!

I can make a difference by taking care of the old,
I can make a difference by being me,
By being strong and bold,
If I can make a difference then so can we.

Róisín Reid, Grade 10
New Hyde Park Memorial Jr/Sr High School

7.00.01

A river acting as forgiveness
cannot flow backwards as
wrongs cannot be changed to rights in people's lives
Things shall not be forgotten like
the lost loved one that passed at yet 19
Captive is the soul
that says yes not no
Feeling is the hurt
that has suffered its endless pain
Dying is what she feels when
she says no and is ignored
truth is the story
life was hers
now yet trapped in another's
But life, what she had tried so hard for
and yet asked for that second chance
The party ended at 7 PM
but her life just a second after

Jennifer Hartmann, Grade 10
Connetquot High School

Beary

new and puffy
soft and snuggly
light as a gentle breeze
squished and squeezed
tossed and caught
taken anywhere you please
best buddy from the start
crib to floor
out the door
everywhere in between
he never argues
he lets me always be right
never doubts never shouts
just loves unconditionally

Lauren Silvestro, Grade 11
Lancaster High School

Depression

Depression hurts,
Depression kills.
It kills the soul inside,
It hurts the people around.
It sneaks up on you,
It engulfs you in a cloud.
The cloud blurs your sight
Of the good in your life.
To get free you need
Friends and family.
Never let Depression control your life.

Kayla M. Lalonde, Grade 12
Massena Central High School

What We've Been Through

I made my mistakes
And he made his
He forgave me
And I forgave him
Hearts were broken
And tears kept falling
Feelings were hurt
And yet emotions
Were still torn
Fight after fight
Our friends were still there
Telling us don't let each other go
Because where would you go?
Laughter and insiders were always there
Never wanting to go anywhere
Our hearts unbend
And we let each other in
We fell in love
And now I can say
I found
My one true love

Angela Aponte, Grade 10
Bronx Academy of Letters

My Blanket

When I was born it greeted me warmly,
Made by loving hands just for me,
I came to love the smell and touch so much that we could never part.
To the church we went the whole family there,
In this blanket tightly wrapped for my baptism.
The next few years we stayed good friends,
Through peek-a-boo, hide and seek, and my dress up wedding veil,
From every sleepover until after prom, no one thought it would last this long.
High school is ending and college is near,
I know I will pack my favorite piece of home,
My blanket to greet me warmly.

Ashlee Williams, Grade 12
DeSales High School

Infinity

The 28th day of October is my birthday,
In 1992, 8:58 a.m. was the minute I came,
Infinity is the number of times I'm thankful for that.
To my mother, infinity is how much I thank you for not giving up on me.
2 was my age when I moved from one house to another,
And I was about 5 when I stopped talking to my father,
Infinity is the number of times I wonder if he still cares.
To my father, infinity is how much I'll think about family I could have had.
August 26, 2005 was the day my grandmother went to heaven,
My grades dropped because the fight with grief I just couldn't win,
Infinity is the number of times I miss her.
To my grandmother, infinity is how long you'll be in my heart.
I have 12 half brothers and sisters, I really do,
But 3 is how many I actually talk to,
Infinity is how long I will love them.
To my siblings, infinity is how long I'll wonder if we'll ever meet.
Being a sophomore in grade 10,
I wouldn't be here without my friends,
Infinity is how long I'll remember them.
To all my friends, infinity is how long I'll love you.
Infinity.

Savannah Thompson, Grade 10
Massena Central High School

Them

People say it's like the perfect sunset, it's the perfect moment in time.
But when you realize it, it can crush you. The feelings, so different from before,
make you say and do things you never thought you were capable of.
When you wear what he's given you, you feel like it's his mark on you.
But that's not necessarily a bad thing. It's just that eventually,
You get used to being with him. You know what he'll do, what he'll say.
You want something new, but don't want to lose what you have with him.
So you know of a great person, another, to have. He wants you too.
He doesn't care about the First. When you're with him,
you hide away what the other has given you; it feels like he's watching.
When you're with him, the first, the original, the One, he looks at you,
and you know, you can see, you're the only one in his eyes.
But meanwhile, you are thinking about both of
Them.

Kaelen Austin, Grade 11
DeSales High School

Why Am I Here?

Fire from the sky blankets the canopy of the jungle.
Like roaring beasts, helicopters slice through the smoke.
Screams of agony and fear sweep across the swamp.

I wait until they're gone. I hear silence, only silence.

I am lost in this awkward place.
Only 17, I wonder…
Will I die in Vietnam?

Sam Frankel, Grade 10
Oyster Bay High School

White Wicker Chair

She sits placid, serene
Detached from the world
In her white wicker chair
She sits on her porch facing the ocean day after day
She sees no one, no place
Alone in her home
Breathing in the salty air
Every week she buys a postcard of a place far away
She dreams someday, sometime
She will leave this town
Go beyond the ocean's edge
She has never been past the railroad tracks on Traverse Drive
She was cautious, wary
Her house was her home
Since the day she was born
Her life passed her by until she reached seventy-five
She sits seasoned, contrite
Until her last breath
In her white wicker chair

Jessica daSilva, Grade 12
DeSales High School

Woodstock '69

As the music filled the ground,
The world itself seemed to pause.
Sensations of excitement were all around.
As peace and love were the only laws.
Angels and demons played their part,
Causing an abundance of ruckus.
Yet the peace lovers never grew apart.
There was enough to make the crowd restless.
And although love can cancel out hate,
The music was there to enlighten.
People here could not forget the world's fate.
Three days was this musical titan.
They helped Jimmy Light his fire,
As good as they've been to the world.
400,000 as one choir,
As the smoke around them twirled.
There are those who don't remember,
Came home with someone else's clothes.
But you can always feel an ember,
In Max's field when the wind blows.

Samantha Frangos, Grade 10
Townsend Harris High School

Beneath the Lone Wolf

She gazed at the vivacious boughs
of an oak befriended in a field.
She gazes at its bleak remnants now,
And vaguely remembers the prizes it yields.
There was once a boy, an insecure friend,
Partners in a winning team,
Who together found treasure at the map's end
Nestled in a crook in this tree.
Gone are the flowers that beleaguered the stem,
Gone are the paths trodden beneath bare feet.
Contrary to chance, the tree remained stable.
Salvation for education was the chanted creed
Among youthful companions at a stone table.
The Lone Wolf is much like herself,
She knows, proud, sole, endearing.
But still, she feels the pain it once felt,
The forgotten one, left to die in the clearing.
Accomplishments from when she was a girl
To now all seem so meaningless.
For she has all the time in the world,
But nobody to share it with.

Jessica Noviello, Grade 10
Smithtown High School West

Euphoria

Sensing your presence
Paralysis takes over my body
And renders me incapable of moving

Hearing your voice
Sends euphoria through my head
I'm unable to breathe when you speak

My eyes feel graced
Incapable to take in the fact
That you're here, in front of me

As you drift through my veins
My heart pumps faster
Longing to spread you throughout my entire body

Feeling your touch
Sends shockwaves throughout my spine
I dive into heaven each time

You're the closest thing to perfect
And the farthest thing from me
And I can't help but wonder
Why the hell do you love me?

Diana Mallayeva, Grade 10
North Shore Hebrew Academy High School

Moving On

None of them saw it coming, none of them knew why
somebody please tell them why he had to die
he was there, right there healthy as an ox in October
then came November, he was gone and they were burying him in a box
his family gathered together to grieve, most of them still couldn't even believe
She was the only one who spoke at his funeral, the only one strong enough to
she felt as if she had to be the rock of the family instead of being little boo
a year has past but to her it feels like just yesterday, she watches as the ones close to her move forward and move on
while she still doesn't want to believe he's gone
since he has left everything has fallen apart
secrets have come out, abuse that had disappeared through the years has returned
they don't come home to a paradise, instead a nightmare
what goes on behind closed doors is not to be shared
when no one is around she begs for an angel to come down and heal her broken heart
over and over again she is told to try to move forward and move on
but that's impossible when your hero is gone

Dara Radtke, Grade 10
Sachem High School East

Longing to Be Free, an Irish Tale

We numbered many, we were one.

Home, it has been in my mind for last past days and I think to myself how much happiness I had, where grass lay green and the sky never ended. How I wish, how I yearn to go back home.

Yet tonight, as I think of home I watch the stars, the starry hosts laying claim of the heavens. I miss home.

The fun times, the quiet moments, and the memorable ones.

The pains, the toils, and hardships of home are nothing compared to this, having to see my friends die.

It brings back memories of when I fought in the Easter Rising.

It seemed as if I would die every moment I was on there racing the enemy face to face, but luck had been with me and I've survived through all.

I wonder if I'm the next, next to die for my friend.

Even as I sit on this mound of snow and feel the coldness run down my legs, the ambition, the need, the inspiration to keep on fighting drives me. I feel no sleep and my heart urges me to fight on the good fight.

War has truly changed me forever. However I can't wait for the world to change I must change the world and it is my duty to serve, a privileged honor and thus when duty calls I'll be ready, I'll be there for Ireland.

We may number many, but we are one.

Stanley Soman, Grade 10
Sewanhaka High School

Down

Down, down and under sinking to the bottom of the sea
Prior to reality
Down, down to the pitch of darkness
Where your voice cannot be heard, where your thoughts are blank
Down, down, down to the cold corner of fears
Where hopes and dreams are like nails digging in your mind
Down, down to the empty shell that once held you but now is just a broken wing of hope
Down, down to the nothingness of fears
Where the heavens crumble for stability and where the tears are shed by those of a thousand wings
Down, down to the empty tunnel with no ending
Where fears are faced and where heartbreak lives
Down, down to the screams of agony
Where your tears flow like a river
Down, down to the drain depth of life
Down, down, down

Debbie Jean Jacques, Grade 12
Midwood High School

The Essence of Greed

Below the thin horizons of human compassion,
Lies the foul odor of mistrust and greed
The fake smiles and the orderly fashion
Gives rise to the birth of the horrible breed.

We smile and speak articulately
But underneath, it bickers and sneers.
We, its host stand still and stoically
As it takes our heart and steers.

This horrible, ill-hearted species
Knows not of anything but for its need
Lurks about waiting for the object to seize
That satisfies its ravenous greed.

We kiss its hands and hold it lightly
And blemish ourselves with its horrible deeds
It then takes hold of us ever so tightly
And sucks our hearts which bleed.

We transform so quickly and silently
And let this creature control our outer shells
And quietly it does but violently
take the hearts that it compels.

Aysha S. Sultan, Grade 12
Ward Melville High School

Vitraux Masquent (Stained Glass Mask)

Looking through a b-r-o-k-e-n window
  I see a darling flitting shadow of a lonely soul
  Masquerading on her own
  A lovely mask she wears
  It complements the light
  As she wanders through the night
  Does no one hear her cry?
  Stained glass under the moon
reveals her thoughts within the room
    So delicate and weak
What gives her strength to walk through the street?
  The Stained Glass Mask
    it s h a t t e r e d
        pretty
By then it should have shown the truth
  But by now the point is moot
This, she found in bits and pieces
    Herself, just changed
    Cracked here and there
Glittering shadow of her heart
        On that strange poetic night
Lauren Post, Grade 12
DeSales High School

The Night Sky

Dark and wanting
Scared and dreary
But as I look to the night sky…
I see what matters most to all humanity

It may seem like you'll never be near…
But, in truth you are, we all are
No matter how much pain you feel
The help you need is right there in
The night sky

A place I hope to go when darkness comes
Where the angels dwell in love
The place I look often —
The night sky.
Elizabeth R. Hansen, Grade 11
Bishop Ford Central Catholic High School

Confused

I can't take what you're puttin' me through
I love you and my love is true
but I don't know what to do
I'm tired of feeling like I'm dirt
and always being hurt
my mind's tellin' me to let you go
but my heart's tellin' me no
confused between the two
I think what's the best thing to do
to have a heart break
and a little ache
or keep you
and always feel blue.

Amanda Miller, Grade 10
Randolph Academy

Nothing

To feel like nothing is to feel like a broken heart,
To be nothing is never to finish where you start.
To be nothing is being a plant and always gettin' stepped on,
To feel like nothing is the words to an incomplete song.
To hear nothing is to hear silence and quietness,
To breathe nothing is to be breathless.
To live as nothing is to be a tree which stands still,
But yet that tree of nothing provides us medicine for the sick.
Why is it that many of us feel like nothing,
Is it because nothing is something.
Nothing is a descriptive and unique word,
Many days we are nothing, if that is what we prefer?
To be nothing is bizarre and strange,
But yet feeling like nothing is like being trapped in a cage.
We want to be set free and begin from the start,
This may be hard since nothing is deep in our heart.
Nothing is just a descriptive word.
But describing ourselves as nothing, is what many prefer.
To feel like nothing is to feel like a broken heart,
But not if you become something and take nothing apart.
Shalana Ford, Grade 10
Clara Barton High School

I Stand Alone

I stand alone in the path of freedom
Not to be ruled by the body of the past
Not to be hanged
To set aside my tortured
To forget my problems
To stay alive with my clan
The problems of me standing alone
to see the world from another angle
I shall stay alive by standing alone
Brittany Windham, Grade 10
Bronx Academy of Letters

Hero

In the end
The hero always rides off into the sunset
If this is true,
Then why am I so afraid?
It is time for me to disappear
Not only do I fear for myself
But I fear for you
I fear for us

I am leaving what I know
I am leaving what I love
I wish that I could be your hero
I wish I had my sunset
Jerome Bass, Grade 12
Clarence High School

Perfect Night

The warm summer night
clear skies, stars bright.
Walking arm in arm,
sharing one beat, one heart

I promised you my love
for all the years to come.
My words are strong and final
for you to carry on.

No care in the world,
no memories of present or past
Its just, us right now
as we walk this amazing path.

I didn't think I could feel this way
but now I understand.
All I needed was you baby,
to be here and hold my hand.

As we come to a stop,
we breathe for the last time.
We say our last vows,
and kiss for the final time.
Paul Cho, Grade 11
Nyack Sr High School

Don't Fall too Far

the wind forces melodies
making instruments of chimes and trees
and the bass, it shakes the windows
I could never make such a symphony
when I was a kid I never learned to whistle, I only learned to scream

and all hope dies
because the sky if only full of shooting satellites
the moon's a fraction just off full
well maybe that's what makes the wolves howl
see, it's not just you and me
that cry ourselves to sleep

now leaves fall like confetti kicking off the calendar's finale
I wish I could fall as gracefully as a helicopter seed
come on someone dance with me
like the windshield wipers' captive leave
this has got to be, some kind of poetry
the words all rhyme but they don't quite sound right
we collect used cigarettes
we found on the ground, half burned out

and there's a tire swing on a tree that's been struck by lightning
I'm sure this is a metaphor for something
Michael Cauvel, Grade 11
DeSales High School

The Light at the End of My Tunnel

What do I do now?
For the light at the end of my tunnel has burned out
No one meant more to me in life
When she left, it was as if I was stabbed in the heart with a knife
Why do I feel this misery within?
It is as if my heart is numb, never to beat again
Tears run down my face, in this world I do not have a place
The skin on my body has been ripped off
She is my protector and she is gone
Every time I think of her I can't breathe
She is the one person in my life I need
No one can understand the sadness
That flows throughout my body
The day she left and went away
Was the day I found it would not be the same
What is the point of living now?
For she is no longer in existence
My mother, my life
I must not cry, for now I am the light
Continuing the flame
That my mother once was
Eva Rajan, Grade 10
Briarcliff High School

I Have Sinned

Dear God for I have sinned
Forgive me for the trouble I've been in
Pain flows through the back of my head
As I lay down to rest in my bed
This life You call cruel is no where for me
Being with the girls is a lot of fun
But left alone, the only thing I had to do is run
God give me the strength to live the day
God I know my parents love me with all their hearts
But when I go and do sin
All it does is tear us apart
I fear for my life when I go out at night
Whether or not I'll survive the next fight
But now a days I have to learn to watch my own back
When I listen to music
I'm reminded of my Grandpa, my backbone, my heart
I wish he could of had 80 more years
But when I look back at it all it just brings back more tears
As I close my prayer and let you in
So you may forgive me your Heavenly Father
For I have sinned

Julianna Benjamin, Grade 12
Martin Van Buren High School

Who Is He?

By the way He feels to me
Soft, caring, and unseen to me
Most powerful, almighty king to me
But who could it be?
His love over shines all things
I praise Him; for Him my heart sings
He's above, above, beyond it all
Not physically, but mentally, is there when I fall
Keeps existence real and sane
But do you know His name?
He's the leader of all that is good
Who is He you ask?
You want to know, I figured you would
You can't get His love at a high bidding price
He's the Father of our Lord Jesus Christ.

Staci Abbot, Grade 11
Bishop Ford Central Catholic High School

Her Silky Hair

The wind's blowing through her silky, brown hair,
A caramel shade, so sweet you can taste.
It's as sweet as the candies at the fair.
Her eyes shine so much, it can't be a waste.
Lips of this girl are pink as the roses.
She moves like a swan when she walks the streets.
Her hypnotizing smell fills the noses
Of boys; they follow her, just so they meet.
Her skin is so golden, all go loco.
Honey colored, with a hint of mocha.
Indeed she is pretty, but it's hidden with her devilish heart.
Her evil heart — that is hiding beneath her beauty of art.

Christina Lee, Grade 12
Staten Island Technical High School

I Don't Want to Love You/I Love You*

I don't want to love you,
it has nothing to do with you
its just everything I have been through
that made it impossible to do.

Each day we get closer — more and more
but I got to be careful not to get too close
because I think I'm falling for you
and that a fact I have to ignore

Now we are closer than ever
and will always stand by each other —
through the good and bad weather…

I fell in love with you
and I'm glad I moved on from the past
and gave you a chance
because I love you
and hopefully
we will forever last

Toni Bradberry, Grade 10
Randolph Academy
*Dedicated to Nate Parkhurst

Teenage Nature

The words cannot be chosen
to describe the thoughts in motion
I want to live forever here
as a saint among the crowd.

The lively emotions are dying down
in an apathetic concern to change the world.
Standards aren't at all what they were,
but does beauty still stand within our eyes alone?

The absence of immortality
seeps into this nighttime sky
and with the twilight overhead
all I can do is try.

This lack of interest grows
from a mind that learns to know
the dangers of the world
and the cruelty of them all.

I was wrong to doubt my bravery,
but it let me sleep at night;
by letting my fears take hold
I dreamt in a whole new light.

Panayiota Theodorou, Grade 12
Division Avenue High School

A Note to an Angel

With tears in my eyes,
With love in my heart
I dedicate these words to you
The way you cared,
Loved, and cried
Was nothing more than true
They say you never realize
What you have until it's gone

Those words seem all too real to me
And I wish it weren't so
I need you now more than ever
I wasn't ready to let go
The night I didn't say goodbye,
I always will regret
But you'll always have a place
In my heart
And of you,
I never will forget.

Jennifer Brogna, Grade 10
Sewanhaka High School

Spring Breeze

The wind blows gently;
the cherry blossoms rustle,
and then all is still.

Julia Galea, Grade 10
Kellenberg Memorial High School

Dusty Words

Your words are crystal clear:
With an occasional bruise,
That I try not to see.

Each syllable and noun,
Vibrates with fear;
So much that I try to look away.

With the command of a playmate,
And love of a friend:
That sometimes disappears,

These words slide off your tongue:
And mix with the dust in the air.
So they're old when they reach my ear.

I too reply with words,
Hidden beneath layers of dust
So that they've lost their initial meaning.

I look into your eyes;
And desperately hope:
And we will someday clean the air.

Sabina Smajlaj, Grade 10
Bronx High School of Science

Delicate

follow me; we will slip into spring unnoticed,
steal cherry blossoms from their mothers,
and grasp the delicately virgin buds in our lined and sweaty palms.
we will come home, place the buds in a book
of memories through flowers, beside last autumn's leaves,
brittle and lackluster.
we will press the pages together, clutch them to our chests,
and wait for the fragility of an end.

Anna Olkovsky, Grade 10
Hunter College High School

My Childhood…Gone

My purest thoughts
When the world was great
Everything so humane
Wrapped in my own worlds my own fantasies
The most beautiful moments of my life
Everything so warm so carefree
A symphony of sunshine and rainbows
My most happy times to ever occur
I try to cling to these moments
Desperately seeking the things that bring me back when I stray
The most wonderful wonders I keep close to my heart
I yearn the sweet innocence that used to define me
Struggling against the butcher of my childhood
I am weak against this monster of adultness
It has stolen these things from me
I am left destitute
Void of happiness
A melancholy being with a smile

Elisheva Davis, Grade 10
Hebrew Academy of the Five Towns and Rockaway High School

I Am Victor Frankenstein

I am intelligent yet crazy.
I wonder how life begins to grow.
I hear the buzz people are talking about my son.
I see the wickedness of the creature.
I want to raze the creature.
I am intelligent yet crazy.

I pretend that I'm a father but have no son.
I believe that the creature was born good but turned evil.
I touched the life of my son when I abandoned him.
I feel fearful because the creature is coming after what I love.
I worry for my own life plus the life of others.
I cry over Elizabeth's death.
I am intelligent yet crazy.

I understand that God is the only one who can create life.
I say that life is short yet long just like the time you have with loved ones.
I dream that some day I will be with the beloved Elizabeth.
I hope the creature will realize what he has done.
I am intelligent yet crazy.

Sarah Goldberg, Grade 11
Maria Regina High School

God's Love

God's love…
Is infinite;
It lasts for eternity.

God's love…
Is the only love that can be trusted
Without doubt

God created us out of goodness,
Love, hope, and kindness
Wanting us to carry out all these deeds,
Helping those who are in need
God created each individual with
a purpose, a moral, a reason.

We are all like flowers
Growing very beautifully,
Then awaiting death.
Like the soil in the ground, we must be replaced,
Reason being why we must make the best of
Every breath
Every laughter,
Every smile,
Because God can call on us whenever.

Kimberly Sanon, Grade 11
Bishop Ford Central Catholic High School

Modern World

12:00 p.m…The sirens are roaring, the portal is closed.
What was found is now lost, knowledge has been deposed.
The predator is creeping, its eyes a broken mirror.
The hunted is twitching like a child in fear.
The lock has been broken, the prisoners flee.
The anchor has spiraled into the salt-red sea.
The virus has awakened, the needles are dull.
The static is screeching, it pierces our skulls.
The windmill is spinning, the blades so dark.
The raven is calling, it's leaving its mark.
The chessboard is shaking, the faces are grim.
Disaster is spinning, like a tire's chrome rim.
The mother is crawling, she lets out her cry.
The child is gone, and she doesn't know why.
The antidote is gone, these lives are forsaken.
Power and control, our status was mistaken.
No person is on duty, but the beds are all full.
Salty red sickness, pain is paying the toll.
Take a deep inhalation, what is it you take in?
It's the cold, dry staleness of 9,000,000 sins.
Exhale…we live in this modern world…12:01 p.m.

Tyler Stepp, Grade 10
BOCES/Alt Ed Program

Perception of One's Self

There lies a pain within ourselves that cannot be suppressed.
It seemingly has no connection
With the past, or the present, but burns mysteriously inside.
You are trapped in a cage within yourself
A cage which has no exit
But taunts you with the outside world
Which is skewed through the tinted glass of the cage.
Any light filtering in becomes instantly dark.
It is the cage of the perception of one's own self.

Victor Jimenez, Grade 11
Townsend Harris High School

Face It…It's Preparing You for Tomorrow

Without a trial there is no triumph;
Without a test there is no testimony;
Without a cross there is no crown;
Without pain there is no gain;
Without an obstacle there is no opportunity;
Without victimization there is no victory;
Without bitterness there is no betterment;
Without waiting there is no winning;
Without pressure there is no pleasure;
Without "I WILL TRY" there is no "I CAN;"
Without opposition there is no ovation;
Without shunning there is no shining;
Without goal there is no gold;
Without fighting there is no finding;
Without heeding there is no heading;
Without mistake there is no measure;
Without difficulty there is no development;
Without enduring there is no elevation;
Without problems there is no progress;
Without practice there is no perfection;
Without tough times there are no tough experiences!

Antwi Prince, Grade 10
Frederick Douglass Academy

To Walk the Worlds

Forgive me father, for I have sinned,
Becoming an iconoclast of two worlds.
I choose, nay want to descend,
So I can follow one of two worlds.
Being in transition smites me,
But such is life.
The battle to reach salvation and serenity,
Is one of interminable strife.
Though there are no shadows, I fear all evil.
They tempt me to give up all,
And some day when I become ill…
It will be awhile before I fall.
Forced to suffer in both realms,
Endlessly like Sisyphus and Tantalus
With absolutely no dreams,
All because my soul was my stylus.
Let me walk among 2 worlds, despite sin and guilt.
I wish to do good, and have this world rebuilt.

Matthew Sands, Grade 11
Staten Island Technical High School

Independent

When you're independent
You're by yourself or alone
That may be the definition
But when you're independent
You're not always by yourself
You have you and your confidence
To do anything you dream to
As long as you're strong you
Can do anything by yourself
That's when you're independent

Ashley Brousseau, Grade 10
Ketchum-Grande Memorial School

Tears of Life

Tears are falling
Falling into waves of emotion
Emotion of joy
Waves crashing
Falling into whirlpools of joy
Joy of love
Whirlpools spinning
Falling into oceans of love
Love of life
Oceans flowing
Falling into ponds of life
Life of tears
Staying still
Tears are falling

Andreia DeVries, Grade 11
Briarcliff High School

Red

It consumed the forest
It consumed the trees
It drank the water
It ate the leaves

The fire grew
Consumed the Earth
It ruled the land
With growing girth

It built up armies
It scorched the land
We were the fire
Torch in hand

And then we realized
The Earth was ours
Our home was dead
On to the stars!

We consumed the forests
We consumed the trees
We drank the waters
And ate the leaves

Joe Tannenbaum, Grade 10
Seaford Sr High School

We Can Make a Difference

Look out in the world and what do you see?
War and turmoil throughout the seven seas.
People fighting and killing one another.
The plant's dying and everyone's blaming one another.
We live in this world that is on the road to its demise.
And all we can think of is if that money is mine.

We have to man up and take responsibility.
This world is ours and we have to make it last for an eternity.
We all can make a difference and need to make it now.
We have to change this world of ours.
We have to stop fighting and start thinking of a better way.

We all can make a difference, every last one of us.
We can make a change,
We can save ours world,
All we need to do is ask our selves what can I do?
How can I help?
What is needed to be done?
When everyone starts to think of change then we will have a change.
Our world can be different,
It can be better.
All it needs us, because we all can make a difference.

Akash Balaggan, Grade 10
New Hyde Park Memorial Jr/Sr High School

Shattered Pieces

The glass shattered. The walls fell. The love you possessed.
Shattered and fell.

I mended the glass. I rebuilt the walls. The love I possess.
Mended and rebuilt.

Everything in my heart points to you. Why can't you point to Me?
Don't we have the same feelings?
We did in the past. Why can't we now?

Now it seems more like an obsession. A dream or a fantasy.

Your glass lay shattered right where you left it.
The walls, in pieces near by.

Why can't you pick them up?
Mend them! Rebuild them!
Pick up right where we ended.

This obsession, This dream, This fantasy,
Lies on the ground,
Exactly where you left it.

Jaimie Stickle, Grade 12
Fallsburg Jr/Sr High School

I Am the Creature

I am repulsive yet intelligent
I wonder why my master abandoned me
I hear the peoples outcries coming from nearby
I see their eyes lacking despair as though they didn't even care
I want to know why they are doing this
I am repulsive yet intelligent
I pretend to be insincere like a hunter hunting a deer
I believe they shun me because of my looks
I touch a leather book as coarse as an iron hook
I feel that I am feared by people that is what I discovered
I worry that my face should be covered
I cry when my master dies
I am repulsive yet intelligent
I understand why he left
I say I should fear my own death?
I dream that I may appeal
I hope the people can love me with zeal
I am repulsive yet intelligent
Caterina DiPaola, Grade 11
Maria Regina High School

Life

Sometimes, life comes at us fast
we wonder if there is any hope
for the future,
Sometimes, we cry and weep and say
why me?
Sometimes, even the best of friends
may turn to strangers,
Sometimes, it may seem like life is cruel,
and has not else but troubles to offer,
Sometimes, I feel that way but one thing helps,
I remember the gift of life.
I remember that "where there is life, there is hope,"
Usually, it helps to smile and move on,
Try that it helps…
Ayomide Balogun, Grade 11
Huntington High School

Nothing Is What It Seems

Her heart is aching spirits are breaking
Nothing is what it seems
Her hands are shaking his for the taking
He captures all her dreams
With so much power she quivers in cower
She cries with such disgrace
She watches each hour as he looks with such glower
She can never leave this place
He lifts his hand and leaves his brand
She keeps her head so still
Hope hanging by a strand he wins in such demand
This is not God's will
He cannot believe her life on his sleeve
He falls with such dismay
Nothing to achieve he suffers in grieve
His life the price to pay
Jacquelyn Redington, Grade 12
DeSales High School

Making a Difference

I can make a difference by
Keeping a smile and never sigh
Although it may be hard I'll try
But sometimes I may wonder why

I can make a difference for
My mom and clean the kitchen floor
And for the weak hold open the door
And respecting elders so much more

I can make a difference when
I save a child among groups of men
And I'll gladly do it over again
Because I feel the same now and then

I can make a difference where
I visit old folk homes to care
And tell good stories and give a prayer
Because unlike some I am aware

I can make a difference because
I am not who I once was
And I want to help if no one does
Because making a difference is a good cause
Jaebee Kim, Grade 10
New Hyde Park Memorial Jr/Sr High School

Choice Black

Black is a color of choice,
It's classic for a dress
Combines with white a timeless photograph,
Out of a pen and onto paper we call it literature,
It's a choice of what to choose it for.

Some call it evil,
The color of rebels,
The suits of mafia men,
Sure blacks all that but it's also more,
It's just common sense.

It's powerfully graceful,
A never-ending dance,
For those who choose to adore it,
The color of choice always gives a chance,
Black is the color for those who choose it,
For they realize it's everything,
Versatility,
Classic ability,
Its greatness.
Devon Ross, Grade 11
Clarence High School

I Can Make a Difference By....
The blues and greens of the Earth,
Are constantly shifting with dabs and flashes.
The streaks of red that discolor our world,
Pollute serene beauty into a mottled disappointment,
As God stares down at the debauchery of his finest race.
Brothers betray each other with armaments and weaponry,
While ancient prejudices segregate the family of humanity.
Quickly do infants forget their inlaid morality,
As the seasoned living think carelessly about spreading their disease,
Infecting like a plague all save the strongest.
To fight our affliction it will take an iron-willed effort
Where our media stops endorsing war for publicity,
Where we stop using violence as entertainment,
And Racism is no longer a comedy subject but a mark of betrayal to our fellow man.
If we are to cast off this tradition we must do it as one,
As any dark values quickly corrupt the lighter among them.
If we restore the Earth's luster of purity,
Then God may begin speaking to us once again.

Justin Weiss, Grade 10
New Hyde Park Memorial Jr/Sr High School

Charmed Childhood
As a child, the world is your playground.
Above the shallows you fly, soaring with wild innocence against dreamy purple skies.
Like fairies, you ascend toward the sun.

You slowly descend —
Dreams of candy clouds and towering castles are no more.
Skimming the shores of adulthood,
Your wings disappear,
Left to float adrift upon the surface.
But time is of the essence!
What will you do with your life?

You stare up at the fey children with desire,
Not willing to let go of your charmed existence.
In spite of your longing, a decision is made.
There are no escapes from adulthood, responsibilities…

I long for my childhood —
Innocent.
Untarnished.
Charmed.

Ariana Shields, Grade 10
Oyster Bay High School

Dedication
Day in day out players around the world can be seen practicing their skills.
In rain or shine they have dedication, desire and love for their sport.
Game day comes and players give it their all.
Family and friends come to support.
Whistles, words of encouragement and the swoosh of the ball hitting the net can be heard.
It's soccer season.

Brittany Norris, Grade 12
DeSales High School

A Cruel Choice

Walking, emaciated skeletons
Their tortured faces
Show how much they've witnessed
And how much they've lost
They come towards you
Begging, pleading for even a morsel of food
Denying them breaks your heart
They'll die with it
They'll die without it
An impossible choice to make
To deny food to the tortured
Is a tragedy like no other
There is no choice
They'll die with it
They'll die without it
The immense guilt you feel
You denied food to the starving
There will never be a reprieve in your mind
Walking, emaciated skeletons
Their stories must live on
Or it will happen again

Rachel Mayo, Grade 10
Townsend Harris High School

Like a Ghost

Like a ghost you disappear
Leaving me nothing to hold onto but this empty pier
Finding nothing where you were
Seeing nothing more but a shadowed blur

So many summer days spent terribly alone
My feeling spiraling downward into a cyclone
Where you were now haunts me
Fixing no way, to describe you in any degree

Turning peaceful dreams into a nightmare
Always catching me in my deepest despair
Your voice once so light and calming
Now hits me like a suicidal bombing

The knowledge that you're there to provide
Gives me major fright so I will not stand but I do not hide
And yet I cannot ignore you or your attendance
As it slowly destroys my deep independence

Now I hope you do not see
There is no way for me to be free
You were there but now you're gone
As I lay down at a very quiet dawn

Kassie Rose Cole, Grade 10
North Tonawanda High School

Light's Task

Light.
A barely considerable amount
is being swarmed by an immaculate darkness.
Apparently hopeless in its struggle
the light constantly attempts to break through;
Tries to play David versus Goliath.
But violently fails to break through its overwhelming oppressor.

After decades of this constant struggle
with the light being unceasingly thrashed,
It gives up.
And gives into a life of pathetic despair.

Living life incessantly deprived,
of the light it so desperately craves
Its depression reaches unbearable heights.
Hope and desire to live rapidly fade into the blackness.
And life, becomes a worthless effort in their listless eyes.

Mike Indiano, Grade 11
Churchville Chili Sr High School

Shooting Star

I'm waiting to be released from this place
Like a shooting star.
Because my dreams fuel my insides, and all systems are go.
And all my pain will be released
Shooting into the air, streaking across the sky
Showing what beauty is possessed through its freedom.
And all the wishes and promises we made,
All just distant memories that link.
I will never think of them again.
As long as we both shall live.
You no longer hold me
You no longer keep me here
I'm off into the night sky
Bringing beauty to those who need me most.

Michelle Ortiz, Grade 12
Preston High School

Careful It's Hot: Your Medium Decaf. Cup of Life

Life is a sidewalk Café
People
In
Out
Rushing lumbering wandering pacing
Some stay
Throughout the day,
Slowly sipping
Sipping,
Sipping,
On the hot espresso.

While others, quick-paced and late
Go in and out like a breeze.

Each choose their flavor that suits them,
Some are mocha with a hint of chocolate
Not knowing where their cup will end.

Kimberly Hahn, Grade 11
Clarence High School

Paradox

Some are short
Some are long
Some rhyme
Some don't
They can be epic
Or even dramatic
A vision of the future
Or the rambling of a madman
There is no language they do not speak
No nation they do not reach
For poems are timeless
Breathless
Priceless
And this one ends now
Matthew Faherty, Grade 12
DeSales High School

Halloween

Crunch through leaves.
Battle crisp winds.
Ring the bells
of web-encrusted houses.
Say the magic words,
and candy appears.
To add to
the happy loads we carry.
Costume-encumbered kids
and candy-addict adolescents
all join in.
Spread the kindness
with candy to share.
Cries of "Thanks!"
will fill the air.
If you decide to stay inside,
listen, and start to wonder why.
Emily Grazia, Grade 11
Wellington C Mepham High School

I Can Make a Difference...

I can make a difference
I can change the world
I can, I can

Start a foundation
And feed the hungry
I can, I can

Clean up the town
Picking up the garbage
I can, I can

Serve the community
And really, really do it
I can, and I will!
Justin Miata, Grade 11
Sewanhaka High School

Competition, Compassion

The competition, the compassion.
The game, the love.
The struggle, the heart.
The competition; two, fight for it all.
The compassion; two, think they have the right to win it all.
The game; rules are set and cross words are spoken.
The love; the love of victory can leave spirits broken.
The struggle; some fight some get hurt.
The heart; with the heart to win, you're more alert.
The struggle needs the heart.
Otherwise it's a finish without a start.
The game needs the love.
Otherwise it's a push without a shove.
The competition needs compassion.
Otherwise it's a game without a win.
In a struggle you win with heart.
In the game, love is a big part.
Just like if you win, it involved,
Competition, Compassion

Bob Corona, Grade 11
DeSales High School

What Is Government?

Government is nothing but a myth.
It leads us to believe that people who are in power deserve it.
We believe that they earned it,
But we don't know their purpose.

Government is religion,
Not separated from the state.
The president is a figure head,
Representing everything we hate.

But government is a riddle, hard to figure out.
Full of reverse-psychology and things we don't understand.
So we look the other way and never raise a hand.
Never dare to question, or read between the lines,
But then again how could we, when the government controls our minds?

Deano Kritikos, Grade 10
Townsend Harris High School

Red Walls

a cloud is bearing down.
I'm suffocating!
Like a dark mass, shrouding —
I turn to leave, I crash —
I open my mouth to speak, choke on the words,
the fist, the hand smothering my voice —
there is no sound, I cannot make a sound.
I cry out, no one hears —
I am trapped, this is a cage, its walls bright yellow —
be happy, hypocritical, like a holograph, looking from an angle —
the bars are red, the red of love, the red of blood.
The love is seeping blood!
Blood on my hands, so undeserving — so cold,
I am willing to be good, willing to try, give me life!

Lydia Aimone, Grade 11
The Waldorf School of Saratoga Springs

School

A place to learn what we need to know.
To live, and learn, to gradually grow.
Those hallowed halls, built upon the sod.
Where myriads of growing children have trod.
Kids from all walks of life.
Kids who have known peace and strife.
Kids of different beliefs and ways.
Kids who look and act in varied ways.
Rooms of desks where books have rest.
Where Teachers teach with special zest.
Chambers echoing with voices a chant.
Math, English, History, studied, or teachers rant.
Halls of lockers, row upon row.
Bearing many marks, no longer aglow.
Soccer, Football, Baseball too, fields of green,
Rough tumble sports, they have seen.
Twelve years of lessons, we must do.
Then we get our diploma, a reward that's due.
We go on to colleges and/or jobs,
Some with smiles, some with sobs.

Mary-Kate Kraeger, Grade 12
Holy Cross Academy

I Gave Her Everything for Nothing

There was a girl named Shaynna that I really loved
Honestly she was an angel from above
She told me that she loved me when she looked into my eyes
But as time went by it was all just lies
She never really cared for me
And then she made me really see
That we were never meant to be
Because she broke my heart in front of me

Jose Rodriguez, Grade 11
Bronx Academy of Letters

New Day

As I finally left that house
I learned that breathing
Was not a task for the lungs but for the soul

The sun gazed and glowed on my skin
Warming my cold heart to a new adventure
Colors brightened
No more shades of grey
New life
I was on my own

I would no longer taste the bitter salt of my own tears
The bruises of the past no longer troubled my mind
I would no longer listen to the yells of hate thrown at me

Walking tall
With courage strengthening my bones
Pride pumping in my heart
And hope filling my soul
I walked away. I changed my life.

Danielle Esposito, Grade 12
Clarence High School

Snow Day Wish

The weatherman forecasts some snowfall
My anticipation builds
Tomorrow could be a snow day
I'm already excited and thrilled
He mentions our small area
And the possibility for a few inches
My parent's frown and pray for the opposite
They've always been snow day "grinches"
I call a friend; she's as excited as me
We both don't want that quiz in history
And hopefully there's not test on that English book
I still haven't read about the mysterious fry cook
I count on the snow to cancel school
I look out my window for covered roof tops
I finally do the snow day dance
Say my prayers and my stomach flip flops
I lay in bed hoping there's no school
The clock strikes twelve and I'm still awake
I doze off slowly, the alarm starts to ring
There's no snow on the ground
Not doing my homework was a big mistake

Sheila Robeniol, Grade 11
Sewanhaka High School

Trapped

The venomous sensation comes over me
When I know that there is no way out
My mind is blurred and empty
I'm trapped without a doubt

My silent screams are piercing
But no one seems to hear
And I slowly begin to wonder
If there is anybody near

I wonder if in this moment
A split-second before the chord snaps
Someone will come to rescue me
Save me from complete relapse

If they'll hold me in front of them
With strong and knowing eyes
That melts away this feeling
Free from pain, from scars, from lies

So I'll wait in aching silence
For this emotion to find a way out
Although I know deep, down in the darkness
That I am trapped without a doubt.

Danielle Brogna, Grade 10
Sewanhaka High School

My Neighborhood

He lived three houses down from mine, not more than a couple of meters away.
I thought him living three houses down would be as good as he living with me
With his long, muscular, dark legs, it would probably take him 10 steps to reach my house
However, the 10 steps I wish he took were taken by me to get to him
The house that met my nose with the smell of warm, buttery mashed potatoes with gravy,
cornbread, and BBQ chicken made by his mother roamed in the air
The smells of gel in the air also roamed from my aunt doing her girlfriends' weave
lingered into my small sensitive nostrils.
Strolling into his room, boxes were packed
Nothing in the room besides posters of his, twin MJ that abused the walls
Not noticing the audience behind me was he, I fell to the floor on my knees,
looked up to God for an answer to the unfortunate news that would torment my ears.

I looked his way; he nodded his head in agreement saying he was leaving
I did not understand, why he stood there eyes glued to mine bewildered.

I took 10 steps back to my house to cry myself to sleep in the arms of a woman who I
now call mom and dad.

Janelle Joseph, Grade 12
Baruch College Campus High School

Heart Beats and the Crowded Bus

I wake up in Times Square among the subway car and the standing souls.
In this light filled city I can walk for miles and work with the wanderers that somehow know me so well.
And as dawn begins to break, I'm sitting on the train with a heavy heart and a useless ticket to nowhere.
I'm colder than most should be and the talents of many are wasted on bustling passengers that are worried about getting to the
jobs they could honestly care less about, and those who believe living life to its fullest is more fiction than fact.
I am sitting above the horizon in a city that is told to be greater than it is, one that is a legend.
And I want to know what it's like to feel a touch complete in place that moves as fast as this.

Brittany Mishler, Grade 12
Nyack Sr High School

How to Break a Blameless Girl's Heart

Ignore the questions.
Ignore the IMs on AOL.
Ignore the rhetorical txt messages.
Ignore the love notes put into your locker.
Ignore the comments shouted across the halls.
Ignore the hand-written letters sent by mail to your home.
Ignore the Post-Its in the halls with just one word asking: WHY?
Leave her alone. Leave her heart.
Leave those eyes that only you think are truly beautiful.
Leave that lonely girl who no one talks to in the whole school besides you.
Leave the awkward conversations about her mother's depression.
Leave this unwanted girl who you secretly want.
Stop the love. Stop the exploration of her gentle mind.
Stop the milli-second looks in the halls.
Stop the only person preventing you from going insane because of the SAT's, a history test, or a pop quiz.
Stop the calls at three in the morning saving you from a terrible nightmare.
And all this to escape the guy in the locker room
Who mocks you for talking to a geeky girl who he called ugly, that only you think is cool
When you are alone. Break her down.
She is crying on the floor with stain marks on her carpet. It hurts her to cry.
Block her out of your life. You will regret this in two months.

Aviram Shoshany, Grade 11
North Shore Hebrew Academy High School

The Fairy Fantasy

I knew there was something about you
Something I couldn't yet see
Those hours of board games and cookies
They always meant much to me

My feelings soon came to the surface
I was sure we could never be
I didn't know just what to say
I was fearful you would disagree

You uncovered my secret
My worst fear came true
Awkward were those eight months
I couldn't help feeling blue

My eyes then could not meet yours
You always kept your distance
Your presence made me shiver
But you had yet to notice my existence

Then all seemed to be a dream
You said you admired me too
I felt so whole inside again
I knew there was something about you

Diana Monno, Grade 11
Douglas MacArthur High School

An Untimely Departure

A beautiful soul, she once was;
Her essence rests in a body
weakened by the world.
A constant tick-tock in her ear
pushes her to be all she can…
time's running out.
A love for her fills me up
but she must leave soon.
Fate is whispering in her ear,
"It's time to go now, dear,"
and reluctantly, she agrees.
A sinking feeling dusts onto
every part of my body
like confectioner's sugar sprinkled on a cake,
but with quite the adverse effect.
She'll be gone soon, as will part of my soul,
but love never dies.
Feelings harbored remain the same,
And though her earthly host has failed her
she will forever live in the eternal catalyst
which is my heart.

Gabriella Therese Ali-Marino, Grade 10
Stella Maris High School

Dad

Why do you make everyone's life miserable?
You hurt me so much,
But you don't realize it.
You never will,
Dad you won't realize it,
Until you don't have me.
You need to give it up.
It's not making your life any easier,
You know that right?
Dad even though you do what you do,
I want you to know,
I still love you.
I pray that one day,
You can see what I see,
Then see who you were…
Before all this.

Ashley Konton, Grade 12
Cairo-Durham High School

Twisted Reality

A twisted reality,
A snow globe upside down,
Where right is wrong and wrong is right.

Here inner beauty is just a pleasant idea
That no one glances at twice.
Everyone is too busy admiring the swirly sparkles
And the picture behind is forgotten.

The good are punished and the bad rewarded,
It's the inevitable truth.
All the true wonders are hidden on the inside
Where no one bothers to look.

Celine Li, Grade 10
Clarkstown High School North

Losing Control

You can't take it,
You're all confused,
Everything's a mess!
Your starting to lose it,
Not knowing what's what,
Not knowing what to do or say.
You try to calm down,
But it doesn't work,
Then you get angry and mad at the world!
You don't wanna talk,
You just wanna leave!
You think no one understands,
But your wrong.
Nobody's perfect!
No one can do everything right!
Everyone loses it,
Some even breakdown,
But you have to tell yourself,
That your not alone.

Samantha Garguilo, Grade 10
Christ The King Regional High School

Love

Love is more than a physical thing
Love is more than a thought
Love can never be bought
But when love is truly understood
Love could bring an everyday smile
Love could light a passionate fire
Love can bring happiness
But at the same time love can bring pain
Don't ever use love in vain
You must think
"Will my love bring sunshine
Or just bring rain"
Love is more than a physical thing

Taija Lewis, Grade 10
Lansingburgh Sr High School

Football

F ootball is the sport to play.
O n the field every day.
O ne game every week.
T he focus is to keep the streak.
B y ourselves we will not win.
A s a team, our journey begins.
L ooking downfield for every block.
L ast play before the clock.

Brendan Wingrove, Grade 10
North Tonawanda High School

A Glowy Black

She felt so small, so helpless.
Entering a large black hole.
But she could do nothing,
As it engulfed her.
She was paralyzed,
With the blackness,
Of the huge hole.
She could not even,
Put up a good fight.
Finally!
A glowing,
White light came.
Her mother,
Her angel,
She saved her.

Brandie Kieffer, Grade 12
Clarence High School

Creative

C ollaborate
R edesign
E mphasis
A rt
T alent
I nspiring
V ariety
E limination

Craig Frank, Grade 10
North Tonawanda High School

A Helping Hand

I'm not an average person; I'm different from them all,
I make a difference daily, no matter big or small.

I help kids in the school, study or do work,
I help my mom and dad, even when they cook.
I make a difference every day; I do whatever I can,
Because that one small action, will help my lifelong plan.

To help the poor, to help the young, in each and every way,
I act on plans, I do the work, and I don't just sit and pray.
A helping hand will do a lot, for a child in dire need,
To lift him up, to make him smile, this will help him succeed.

I clean my room, I make my bed, and I help take care of my pet,
These small, meaningful tasks will lift them up, and they surely won't forget.
The birds, and the bees, will live peacefully across the land,
To help out the environment, that effort would be grand.

I can pick up all the garbage, the cans and waste in the park,
Maybe these small efforts will help bring about a spark.
A spark of helpful efforts to make a difference around the globe,
I can make a difference; we should all make this our new job.

Joseph Weiss, Grade 10
New Hyde Park Memorial Jr/Sr High School

A Lost Autumn

Once, I saw a beautiful tree
in the midst of Autumn,
And at that first glance,
with its splendor, the crimsons, the scarlets, those rusted yellows,
I knew it for a queen amongst trees.

But as I passed that tree,
I refrained from pausing,
from chancing to take the time
to admire those short-lived vestments of nature.
Those brilliant hues, the magnificent deathbed, could wait.
I took that miracle for granted.

Autumn has long since passed
those leaves, those peculiar blots of color — gone.

I never appreciated that tree with the little leaves.
I was always thinking, hoping, wishing,
that they'd be there the day after.
They're not.

Forevermore will there be autumns,
but never my tree.

Matthew Chu Cheong, Grade 11
Douglas MacArthur High School

Wishing You Would Change

Cancerous chills send me wishing
You would change.
The moon doesn't wait for the sun before it surfaces.
You don't catch your breath
Before finding the next best poison to play with.

Hope can be so vague when
Your head is far from your shoulders.
But I wouldn't know.

Sandpaper hearts break first
And it always hurts.
Under all that snow I've lost
Your smile, and your eyes.
What a shame.

Melanie Hoffman, Grade 11
East Meadow High School

Where Is He?

God is everywhere; that's what they say
And I think it is true because I saw Him just yesterday.
He came to me
In my dream, that is.

God said to me, I will always be there.
I said how can this be?
If you are here, you can't be there.
God said surely this isn't true
Because when I am with everyone, I am also with you.

Now I see, I said to God.
You will always be here
And You will always be there.
Yes my child, He then replied.

God is everywhere, that's what they say
And now I *know* because I saw Him just yesterday.

Quescilla Brooks, Grade 11
Bishop Ford Central Catholic High School

Copper Lines

I'm copper lines, colliding, sending
shivers down your spine
and these words are binding
keep in mind
the metal heats and burns in time
and initials etched in gold will fade
so time dulls the quickest
blade to cut out the birch's heart
a soundproof day, a nameless art
set four of the alphabet apart
'til a carnivorous wind erased my name
my piece of mind
a simple frame
my lover and I, we were copper lines
temperature sensitive and undermined

Shannon Straney, Grade 11
West Canada Valley Middle/Sr High School

Where Does the Time Go?

I can never go back
Only forward each day
They say enjoy childhood
Don't throw it away

I wait for its end
and at times it flies by
then I remember
there's only one try

Each day I grow older
I get close to the day
When games come less often
blue skies look more gray

So why do I race
and wait for the close?
When I run too fast
I don't smell the rose

And one day I'll find
all those years have flown past
And I'll pity myself
'cause I grew up too fast

Marnina Sherman, Grade 11
Bat Torah Girls Academy

Heart Surgery

There I was without a face and it touched me.
The trials, tribulations, triple bypasses
All in front of me,
A line of dominoes waiting to collapse into each other.
Collapse into me.
Break my chest plate,
Let the pieces fall,
A broken dish,
It scatters along the floor.
Collapse into me;
Pass the broken bones and tattered skin,
That's paper between your fingers.
Collapse into my heart,
Burst the veins and pink tissue
That is so much like a wet pillow;
I want to scream in it,
As if it was a pillow on my bed.
Collapse out of me,
Leaving behind an empty vessel,
A crumbling wall,
A shell of a person.

Keara Kulaya, Grade 10
Bronx Academy of Letters

Silver Threads

The wind is blowing inspiration as I sit upon this wall,
Its silver hands weave silver webs as the sun begins to fall,
Silver threads of inspiration turn to silver cloth of new ideas,
As the silver coated moon climbs into the sky's frontier,
And in the silence of the night,
Those silver hands weave poetry by the placid silver light
As the dusk gives way to dawn, and the silver moonlight fades,
Those silver threads of inspiration often will remain.

Michael Dixon, Grade 12
Amityville Memorial High School

Are Tears the Only Cure for an Old Wound

Speaking the same language doesn't mean there is understanding

The day is night, the night is day.
The brightness attracts the dark.
At times it's best to listen
to that which you don't understand.
Listening to that which you do understand,
can wound you deeper than any sword, any gun,
any stone.

Eyes that don't see, a heart that doesn't beat.
Your eyes are closed, are you still in pain?
Never healing wounds that make a soul cry.
Wounds that make one feel like the sun at night.

The old wise winds have seen, heard, and presence all.
These old wise winds have many stories to tell those who don't listen.

Why doesn't it speak to me?
Are tears the only cure for an old wound?

Daynelis Vargas, Grade 10
Bronx Academy of Letters

Zephyrus

Society groups and labels
the masses.
They tell us how to live our lives, but
I will break away from this trend —
I will be
my own free spirit.
I will not allow labels to be put
upon me.   I will
become the god of the wind.
No one will tell me
who   or   what
I have to be.
I will be my own person —
make my own decisions.
People come
in all sizes and shapes
with our own
thoughts and beliefs —
creating a wonderfully unique
individual.

Matthew Gaulin, Grade 10
Hudson Falls High School

Falling

Do you see the petals falling slowly?
Little by little,
Piece by piece,
Just like my heart slowly shattering
During the time I spend with you

I didn't know
Being with someone who doesn't love you back
Being with someone who doesn't know about your feelings
Could be so painful
The pain seems to tear apart
My heart my mind
I don't know if I could bear this pain anymore

Petal by petal,
Piece by piece,
Slowly falling
Until they reach the ground

Just like how I'm slowly forcing myself
To forget about this lost love
The memories are slowly fading,
Little by little,
Piece by piece...

Michelle Ruan, Grade 12
Brooklyn Technical High School

Basketball

Basketball is my favorite sport
Get the ball down the court
Sink a basket, win the game
Smile as they scream your name
Dribble to the left and right
Shoot the ball with all your might
For every basket made, every play played
We get some red Gatorade
I'm sad when the season's done
Because basketball is so much fun
I live for the sport
It's not that hard core but when I get out on that floor
Taking over shooting that jump shot
Driving to the hoop it's a different world
It goes by so fast I don't want this hour and a half to pass
Make it last, make it count shoot that jumper, get the rebound
Live for the moment live for the game
It starts now — don't give up, keep on trying
Win or lose
You go home smiling cause in the end it's just a game
But if you try your hardest there's no one to blame!

Laura Phillips, Grade 11
DeSales High School

Tragic Love*

Paradise where Adam and Eve meet,
Lays Bodega and Vera on a never ending quest
Adam and Eve for love
Bodega and Vera for money
Paradise in Spanish Harlem nothing alike

Bodega blindly reaches for the apple
Vera has always dreamt for
The greed from her eyes grows
As she takes a bite of the golden apple
The skies turned gray
What once was a paradise has turned to hell

Everything was destroyed
Risks were better off untaken
As for the love of Bodega and Vera
It came to its tragic end

Genesis Caba, Grade 12
High School for Health Professions and Human Services
*Based on the novel "Bodega Dreams"

Sickness

A sickness,
That plagues all,
Unable to get away,
We look at people who are different with disgust,
With hate,
When we are the people who should be disgusted at ourselves
For falling for the inevitable sickness that hurts others,
For we all are the same,
Even if on the outside we are different,
We let the appearance on the outside judge what's on the inside,
For the sickness has taken over,
Making us as sick as the people we judge.

Jesse Mashaw, Grade 10
Massena Central High School

Assisting a Strange Man to Regain Eyesight

Lights litter a pure black sky
Nights spent basking in a lie
Look to the moon, let out a sigh
Trying is harder than having tried

Leaves falling to a cold wet ground
Leave me to fall, falling down
Look to the trees, look all around
Being up is better after having been down

There's a girl in my bedroom
She's staring at me
She's asking me questions
About life, death, and God
I look to the ground, look to the wall
Look to her eyes and tell her a lie

But I know God.

Samuel Ventura, Grade 12
DeSales High School

Not Enough Time

I sit and watch the time go by.
And wonder why.
The days come and the days go
I've come to realize this goes to show.
Live each day like it's your last,
In the end, time flies too fast.
Growing old and staying friends
Keeping secrets, it all depends.
You only get one life to live
Learn to forget, and how to forgive.

Erica Gross, Grade 10
Heatly School

I Find You

Tears drowning my eyes
My heart punching inside
I try to close the
Box inside of me,
But it won't.
All the memories
Running at 500 mph.
I want to speak,
But a ball in my throat won't let me.
Rain coming out of me,
A huge thunderstorm.
My best friend isn't
Coming back.
My best friend is lost in
The heavy clouds,
And I have to find him
But I find him in myself
On the left side of my body
Where the music comes from
Waiting for me to
Find him.

Ashley K. Rodriguez, Grade 10
Bronx Academy of Letters

S(l)ip-Up

just one taste
just one sip
just one sip won't kill you,

just one sip too many
just one sip too much

just one game too many
just one kiss too much

just one lie too many
just one regret too much

just one more thing I can't take back
just one more quality that I lack

Jenna Fregoe, Grade 10
Massena Central High School

Adultery

My youth is dying,
placed into the children's museum, right next to the broken crayons.
Breath after breath,
shock, aftershock
Then nervous laughter.
The mask is dropped-fallen to the cold cement
The bedspread is stained left lascivious in my haste to clean
The eyes catch one flicker too many
and so lids refuse to rest.
Inhale-exhale
Repeat as necessary.

Hindi Kornbluth, Grade 11
Bat Torah Girls Academy

We Remain Hopeful

We remain hopeful
That the world will change, peace will rain
And everybody will be seen as the same
Racism is just a term, never exercised in the smallest of spaces
Empty court rooms because of peace, no more cases
Where the only lead I need to worry about is from a mistake with a pencil
Where we don't need steel we learn and live using our essentials
Of course it's all a dream, the concept is so soulful
But one thing remains
We remain hopeful
We remain hopeful
That going hungry would never be an issue
Where we can act as men to our women and never leave them with wet tissues
Where we could fall and get back up
Where we can live for one another, instead of grounding, we develop a come up
Hatred among religion is not used now or later
Where we could live life, not worrying, about dead presidents on green paper
Of course it's all a dream, but the concept is so soulful
But one thing remains
We remain hopeful

Nicholas Greene, Grade 12
James Madison High School

I Am the Light

No need to worry, there is a point that all must stop and be still.
It is not the end for any blossom when the light comes shining through.
The mask bearing the allusion of happiness
Breaks away and reveals the real, actual you.
The heart beats fast, yet not at all as you are
Free falling into a deep sea of emptiness and
Your life is exposed for all to see.
No need to worry, there is a point that all must stop and be still.
It is not the end for any blossom when the light comes shining through.
What do we see? There is nothing to recognize.
The mask was your protector, your shield from the outside.
There is a way for the searching eyes to find an answer.
Follow me; I am the light.
No need to worry, there is a point that all must stop and be still.
It is not the end for any blossom when the light comes shining through.

Arielle Glash, Grade 11
General Douglas MacArthur High School

Our Greatest Gift

And on the 6th day He created humans
And breathed life into us
And still that's not enough
The world we live in is always tough
And people tend to be rough
People being used as bombs
14 year olds making the choice to be moms
Women are being degraded by songs
Why? Can't we just appreciate the rights not wrongs?
We should live in the moment and not when it's gone
All people care about is the bill
And eventually that kills
And causes fear and terror
When really we should be making our world better
Just live your life to the fullest
Spit complements to others like thugs spit bullets
Have no regrets
Hold your head up high
With dignity and pride
And do what you need to get by
— Life —

Kayla Tufo, Grade 10
St Jean Baptiste High School

A New Serenity

A deep blue washes over me
As I dive into the never ending waters.
Cold currents glide across my body,
And I fall into peaceful serenity.
My eyes open to see the wonderful things that surround me.
I let my body go as it twists and turns, and I go numb.
Soon I can feel thousands of thoughts and emotions.
I float to the surface and wash back onto land.
I lay in the sand as the water pulls back,
And I let the sun shine over me.
I tell this tale to those who wish to follow —
To take a chance and dive into the water.

Tyler Kundler, Grade 10
Smithtown High School West

I Thought Growing Up Was Fun

I thought growing up was fun?
In the morning I couldn't find my shoes,
The dog threw up on the carpet,
And the shower was cold.
I couldn't find a cab
To go to the job that I am not fond of.
I thought growing up was fun?

The office copier had a paper jam,
I got out of work late.
The city's lights were watching me as I walked home,
When I arrived I noticed it smelled like a dumpster.
My dinner was cold,
I lay down my head to begin this cycle over again.
I thought growing up was fun?

Wil Neves, Grade 10
Massena Central High School

Creation

You tell me that the world
came of itself
arising from one point of matter,
and after a series of reactions,
sparked by an unknown impetus,
became what it is today.
You tell me of energy and matter
and evolution
and that all life sprang forth
from a single molecule.

But tell me now, what is more foolish:
To believe in a theory,
with no proof
other than that a cluster of scientists said it was so,
Or to believe that we were created by G-d,
who out of His infinite love
gave us the breath of life?

I tell you that nothing in this world
can exist without a Creator,
and that the laws of science
are governed by the hands of G-d.

Melanie Wiederhold, Grade 11
Sewanhaka High School

Poverty

I saw an old man on the street.
Why is he sitting there like a deadbeat?
Because he has no money or shelter
Or anybody who will help him either.

What is this wretched thing called poverty?
Poverty means abomination and agony.
Poverty means destitution and homelessness.
Poverty means misery and lifelessness

I walked up to the meagered beggar.
And gave him a dollar.
He thanked me with a half-crooked smile.
But in him is a frown deep down inside.

I knew I did an admirable action.
But that will not solve this predicament.
Poverty is something most people ignore
Because it reminds them of things they abhor.

Is there nothing we can do?
Is there nothing you can do?

Huy Nguyen, Grade 10
Townsend Harris High School

Me, Myself, and I

When you look at me what do you see, in your eyes do I look happy, do I look free?

When you look into my eyes what do you see, do you see you, or maybe you can see the real me.

Do you see the soul that is locked inside these eyes, or perhaps all you can see are my long forgotten sighs.

When you look at my face what do you see, can you see my pain, can you see my fear, or maybe the stain from some long ago tear?

When you look at me what do you see, I know I'm not what you would expect, but than again, you didn't see now my young life was wrecked.

Margaret Cardarelli, Grade 10
Oneonta Community Christian School

What Is Life?

Life starts off as a beautiful flower
After a while it fades and everything seems to be fading and dying
But then something magical happens,
It's raining the flower stretches out and takes in water
Soon the sun comes out and the flower is twice as beautiful
Life is beautiful filled with lovely things and bad things but it gets twice as beautiful after all trials.

Elrene Harry, Grade 12
Environmental Studies High School

Through the Looking Glass

she looks into her looking glass tracing her paths in history from the Great Wall to the Huang He she saw all.

she is a child of the sun, his bearer, his wearer, his heir.

a droplet of THE bamboo leaf that rests in the hands of Guan Yin

she is a product of her country's fields blood, Vein, Grain, Sweat, risen from her people's soil.

she is a child of her people. she is a fallen lighting star from the green valleys of Guo San province.

ASLAN, strong, fierce, unfaltering racing against the winds of time,

across the Great Open Plains of Pandasville to where Blue majesties lay within.

she's her father's daughter, a "ticki ticki timbo" fallen into a stone well

alone, and trapped in reality, not a helping hand in reach dark as the sun. cold as the devil's Hell.

she is a Ginko Baloba bearing bold and proud. a lie, a façade, an act all mixed into a warm duck soup warm and broiled.

she's a child of Siddhartha whose goal is for enlightenment.

her father, her god, her holy one. her life embedded in his hands protected, warm, cozy, NO!

she's blended in a salad bowl there's no way turning back but the dressing apart from the others could stay separated and true.

she is an artwork, a canvas unfinished started by her people, her beloved country, her blood.

ending buried with her grandchildren and children of that and that

each brush, each stroke brew into one into a book of a better tomorrow.

but the sun is still her father. the mountain still flows in her veins.

a lone star in the ocean. cavities form the sugar canes.

surrounded by the city air, she is nothing but who she is.

An American, in The City smiling through her looking glass.

she is what she is, what she wants to be, what she must be. and whether I like it or not, she is she and she is me.

Jessie Pan, Grade 12
Baruch College Campus High School

Black Cat

One minute you're happy, the next you're not.
I bob and weave steering clear of your path.
I can only keep guessing for so long,
I wait wondering what you have in store for me next.
Am I really a "Beast" as you claim me to be?
I'm not here for your sick pleasure.
My heart races as you begin to come near.
I am sitting in this dark cramped space mounted on the corpse of the only one who cared.
As I see the wall collapse I feel the freedom that I surely deserve.

Emilee Smithler, Grade 12
Cato Meridian Sr High School

You

Walking, cool day
Scarf wrapped tightly around my neck
The breeze is thick and doesn't seem to go right through me
Contemplating on the last text message received
Calling him
Such a sudden conversation
Ticklish tears running down my face
Second phone call had made no sense
Wanting more than a few words, wanting a full explanation
Dad's arms squeezing me tightly, reassuring that I'm okay
Best friend calling endlessly
Computer stocked with puppy love comments and pictures
Acquaintances asking what happened?
My heart ripping slowly but definitely surely
Terrible reaction to his new girlfriend
Depressing hours spent wondering
Happy nights spent forgetting
And you're not here denying it all
You, a question without the question mark
A never ending circle that continues to get bigger
A person filled with deceit and lust

Angela Cook, Grade 10
Laguardia Arts School

The Sun Is Setting Right Before Her Eyes

The sun is setting right before her eyes
Youthful ones spend all day under the sun
Mysterious it is how the time flies.

After a while, the truth will turn to lies
Her life which started so early is done.
The sun is setting right before her eyes.

Sympathy brings closer family ties
The burden it brings is over a ton.
Mysterious it is how the time flies.

Helpless, sad and devastated, she cries.
Fragile but determined, she starts to run.
The sun is setting right before her eyes.

When the light is gone, the rich laughter dies
The era of depression has begun.
Mysterious it is how the time flies.

In the end all is heard, a night of sighs
The sound of breathing only comes from one.
The sun is setting right before her eyes
Mysterious it is how the time flies.

Victoria Ku, Grade 11
Francis Lewis High School

Arctic Explorer

I am an arctic explorer with a passion,
I wonder if my men will show compassion.
I hear all the men's pleas,
I see them all falling as if they were struck with disease.
I want to continue this expedition, it is my mission.
I am an arctic explorer with a passion.

I pretend that my men want to continue,
I believe that this isn't an issue.
I touch this icy face of mine,
I feel the sun so far away, no longer does it shine.
I worry if my men will turn against me,
I cry at the sight of what I see.
I am an arctic explorer with a passion.

I understand we must turn back,
I say my ambition is what they lack.
I dream of exploring the arctic, but I have given up this dream,
I hope that this helps heal my team.
I am an arctic explorer with a passion.

Ana Ferreira, Grade 11
Maria Regina High School

Time: Now

sometimes we're meant to pick up
the broken pieces and shattered mirrors
that litter our walk.
and sometimes we're meant to give up
the hopeless battles and useless rejoinders of wit —
less combats and lethal words.
because sometimes,
sometimes,
there is an instance in the eye of the storm
where an epiphany is reached.
and sometimes, we're meant
to take that courageous step *up*
from our self inflicted gloomy doom
in order to see

the dawning moon.

Cynthia Xue, Grade 11
Bronx High School of Science

Breathe

quiet nights and abstract mornings
conversations heavy with meaning
held just before the brightening of the sky,
just before dawn lays its kiss upon the earth.
the heat of the day no longer stifling the body,
oppressing the mind. a cool breeze, opening the
heart and cleansing the soul. peace, no matter
how troubled the thoughts, how tight the throat with
emotion unexpressed. life is a journey, twisting and
full of change, of paths followed and whispered "what
ifs." a world of bittersweet memories, forever striving
for a connection with one other creature on this earth.

DessaRay Hannon, Grade 12
Cicero-North Syracuse High School

We Love You Dru Baby

God had decided
That your time was done.
He took you from this world
So your suffering would be gone.
All of us cried,
Mourned in our own ways.
No one will forget
The best of your days.
You were a great friend,
Everyone knows that is true,
But when we lost you
Our friendship only grew.
I wish I could see you
Just one more time
To say good-bye and let you know
You were a great friend of mine.
Now I know the saying
"God only takes the best" is true,
Because if it wasn't, why did he take you?
Vanessa Stevens, Grade 11
BOCES/LoGuidice Alt Ed Program

My Inspiration

You've been through quite a bit
Yet you never once decided to quit
Don't ever settle for second best
Cause you're not like all the rest
I hope you know I'm proud of you
In all that you have done and will do
The voice that plays inside my head
As I cry in regret for every tear that I shed
You're the reason
And all that I've believed in
The one thing in life that inspires me
Kristy Kent, Grade 12
Depew High School

Direction

Where does the wind blow?
North, south, east, west.
Where do the soldiers march?
Left, right, charge, retreat.
How does a student learn?
Lecture, study, test, repeat.
When does the news report?
Six, twelve, five, and ten.
How does a fencer duel?
Salute, bout, lunge, parry.
Whom do the people elect?
Clinton, Bush, Gore, Cheney.
How does a writer write?
Think, draft, edit, review.
Where does a thinker go?
Words, emotion, vision, forward.
Yang Li, Grade 12
Ward Melville High School

A Living Poem

Every Friday night
You recite words that you normally would not say,
but you still smile
with your eyes — captivating an unfamiliar crowd, with hidden truths.
Your hands firmly structured with mind-boggling fingers hold a chunk
of history,
Smudged with scribbles and scratches, cross-outs and ink stains.
It's always the same thing.

From Friday to Friday
You question the root of forever
and I guess your age.
You mumble 'why?'
and I measure the time I have known you —
One poem at a time.
But your muscular, pale, lifelong body
and detailed face,
makes me wonder who are you — what is your story about?

One Friday to the next
In the eighteenth chapter of my book, I write
a living poem
This is who you are.
Katrina Arce, Grade 12
Baruch College Campus High School

Hands

These hands have been loved.
Wrinkles of skin embedded with the memories of years past
And time worn into the callused palms and fingertips.
The grain of the sand.
The girt of the enveloping earth.
Beneath fingernails lay the secrets and stories
And in every crevasse trickles some forgotten truth.
These hands held when hope was lost
And gently let go when time came to move forward.
These hands have been loved by all that has been touched.
The prick of a pin. The leafy pages of books. The refreshing splash of streams.

But these hands were never loved.
Never held.
Never grasped.
Never embraced.
Hands that never explored the silky strands of some beauty's hair
Or touched the youthful skin of a face in need.
If life could live forever, they'd go untouched,
Growing rougher and harder, as they crumble to dust.
These hands will one day hold a face, but a face of their own
Longing for the love that they never touched.
Kirby Marzec, Grade 12
Clarence High School

No Worries, No Cares

I've got no shoes and I'm running fast
Between my toes is soft, wet grass
I take a fall and hit the ground
I don't bother to get up, I just lie down
Looking up into the sky
The moon glows radiant
And the stars shine bright
The time goes by as I dream away
And before I know, here comes the next day
I've got no shoes and I'm running fast
Between my toes is soft, wet grass
I take a big leap into the lake
I forget my pain and my mistakes
I now forgive and also forget
I take my chances and never regret
Because life is too short to live in the past
So take your shoes off and run too fast

Devan Bariteau, Grade 10
Heatly School

Proliferation of Canvas

African violets fall wildly upon
A painted canvas, swirling
   down a kaleidoscopic
   waterfall of fuchsias
   and sanguine reds,
The salamandrine fires amidst crackling embers
Where the sanctified phoenix arises.
Her wings, as if resting upon turbulent waves
Proliferate the canvas,
The weary brush following its almighty conductor.
Stopping at most immaculate intervals,
It must rest,
It must breathe.
The canvas is a striking arena
Brinded with the marks of battle,
There leaves no air for its fiery magenta lungs.
It's salsa absolute above sweltering oranges and scorching reds,
It's tranquil amethyst waltz in attempt to catch its breath,
They swirl.
The brush possesses tendrils that   lunge   for   more.

Theresa Lee, Grade 12
Sewanhaka High School

Good/Bad

Pride can be negative or positive
it depends on your take on life
pride can lead you to destruction or success
as my grandmother used to say
don't let your pride lead you to ruin,
so what is pride?
is it your enemy
or your friend?
It is neither,
just a stepping stone
in this journey we call life.

Tamoy Coke, Grade 10
East NY High School of Transit Technology

For the Love of God

What would you do?
Going to church isn't mandatory.
Reading the Bible is difficult.
Praying every night is predictable.
These would not give you a pass into heaven.
You try your best to be good,
But then the weak side shows,
The temptations to do wrong grows and
No one knows how to change it.

What would you do?
Reading the scriptures, and
Praying the gospels are what helps.
But at any time,
The devil comes and breaks you down,
And you don't know where to begin again.
Just have faith, God will make it right
If you fight the good fight to follow the way
to salvation, not temptation.

So…What would you do?
For the Love of God????

Ariana Serrano, Grade 11
Bishop Ford Central Catholic High School

Voyage to Hell

It was the day,
The white settlers came aboard our land,
One by one, we were moving closer
To that ship that would keep us banned,
Heavy irons were hung about our necks
We were loaded with chains

I even remember a Negro getting beat
Till his limbs were in so much pain
I felt like running and it was clear, danger was in the air
There was no escape
Not now, not now, not ever
The thought of this, I could not bear

I closed my eyes
I heard the shrieks of pain
I shut them tight, away from the looks of disdain,
We were getting closer now to our voyage to hell,

This could be the end for many of us,
Never returning, never again,
We boarded the ship with fright and fear,
The inevitable thought of death was near.

Dipabali Chowdhury, Grade 10
Townsend Harris High School

Who?

Living with people you know,
But sharing with the ones you don't…
Saying *I LOVE YOU* to the ones that don't care,
And waiting to hear it from the ones that do…
Hugging the fake ones,
And fighting with the real ones…
Drowning people with emotions when they really don't care…
Would you want to be there…?
Or nowhere?

Eliana Perez, Grade 12
Oyster Bay High School

Deadly Silence

Itz like I was put on this world to be misunderstood,
and if I could change it I most definitely would.
But I can't and it seemz like I just realized that.
My dayz are getting darker as this sadness casts over and thatz a fact.
Liez keep being repeated in my head as the tearz fall,
just not understanding any of this at all.
Whatz wrong here? why isn't anything right?
Why is it that I can't make it through the night,
without crying and wishing to just be heard,
how I'm just expected to put my feelingz into 1 single word,
and I'm sick of the fact that no one getz what I'm saying.
I'm sick of the fact everyone thinkz I'm playing.
Cuz I ain't, I'm telling how I feel but apparently thatz a joke,
but the girl inside me has finally awoke.
And she'z ready to be taken for the person she really is and not some fake,
cuz thatz what I've been all this time and I can't take
it anymore so as I end this rhyme with a single tear,
not bein' heard has become my only fear.

Mawia Khogali, Grade 10
Brooklyn Technical High School

United We Stand?

The warring factions of Blue and Red
Fight with words, and this I dread.
Politicians throw blows using rhetoric,
For whom will you vote? You now must pick!
The few things we see are battles of language;
But will bullets soon wage a battle of carnage?
Could this talk lead our country to the next American war?
Will lead soon fly? Will it knock on our doors?
Like North vs South, not too long in the past,
Will Blue fight Red? Will Americans soon clash?
Is blood going to flow from the wounds of men?
Because of political differences, even though we were once brethren?
Blue vs Red, Red vs Blue,
This difference is childish, and all should see it too.
"United we stand" is what we proudly boast
But the lie that it tells I loathe the most!
For this to be true, united we must be;
From coast to coast, from sea to shining sea.
Political differences aren't what we need;
To stand together is what the founding fathers decreed!
So stand together, together indeed!

Carlos Benitez, Grade 10
Townsend Harris High School

The Words That Changed My Life

It's funny,
How seemingly random letters making up meaningless words
Have the power to steal my feeling of security

I would have never imagined in my wildest nightmares.
Those words were not even comprehendible to me
But then the words caught up with me
They caught me off guard

They grabbed me by my neck
They suffocated me
They stung me like a snake bite
And still today I am cleansing my body of this venom

This venom that still runs through my blood today
Is comprised of merely a memory
The memory
Of a single sentence

A single sentence that changed my life forever.
Never should a child have to hear
That they will never see their mother again

Aviva Nassimi, Grade 10
North Shore Hebrew Academy High School

Hockey Dream

You lace up your skates for the millionth time
But this time is different,
Every time the whistle blows
Signaling to do another down and back,
A lifetime of dreams and hard work
All comes down to this.

The adrenaline pumps like never before,
Don't give up now, only 3 more periods
60 minutes to go faster, harder than ever before.
You step onto the ice and your heart skips a beat,
As the crowd roars louder than ever before
Your blades crunch into the ice
Stick hovers over the ice like a hawk, ready to strike the puck.

It's a tie game 1-1
1 minute left in the third period
Your eyes set upon the net with the clock ticking
Top right, perfect shot and the red light flashes,
The water bottle jumps off the top of the net.
Leaping higher than ever before
All your dreams have come true,
Your name will be among the greats.

Ryan Young, Grade 10
Massena Central High School

Fading Dreams

As I gaze out over the river,
This beautiful sunset
Still makes me shiver.
Beauty captured me like a huge fish net,
Woven from the brightest reds
To the darkest gray threads.
Peace within me spreads
With each long passing day.

Slowly horizon colors fade
Turning darker and darker in night skies.
It's time to relive childhood games we played,
All of the things that we wanted to try.
This sunset started with a wonderful feeling
But it slowly transformed me,
Fading colors stealing
All that I wanted to be.

Ashley Devine, Grade 10
Massena Central High School

Missing You

I never thought the day was ending,
But your heart is still extending.
Even though you're above,
We can still feel your love.
Thinking about what took you from me,
Still can make me so weepy.
I'm so sorry that you lost,
And that you had to pay the cost.
In this game, God has made checkmate,
Now you're an angel inside the gates.
I think I'll always need a tissue,
Because I'm going to always miss you.

Chelsea Sherman, Grade 11
Lansingburgh Sr High School

You Are the One I Always Wanted

Thank you for all the times you cared.
You always listened, no matter what I shared.
When it was bad, advice is what you had.
When it was good, you helped me to feel how I should.

Thanks for loving me.
With your love, I feel free.
How it started, we do not know, but together we will grow.
Things are great, with this love I believe in fate.

Thanks for never wanting to fight.
You helped me get through, night after night.
It's good to know that we agree, and it's okay to just be.
Even when I am wrong, you never harp on it long.

Thanks for being you, for staying true.
There are not many I will trust; you are one of the few.
You never would let me stray; it's just your way.
I've got my heart on a string, you are my everything.

Carly Scherer, Grade 12
Mount St Mary Academy School

When You Think...

When you think you're in love,
Everything is great...
You think he's perfect,
You think he's the best.
And that he's different than the others.

You tell him all your secrets,
And things you would never tell anyone.
You trust him with everything,
Eventually...
You trust him with your life.

Then you realize...
You've made a huge mistake...
Turns out he's not so perfect,
And he's just like the rest.

They want you to trust them,
So at the end they can use it,
Not to make you happy,
But to hurt you...
And shatter your heart into tiny pieces,
Pieces no one can put back together...
Kelly Castro, Grade 11
Amityville Memorial High School

Truth

Every heart has a key
And also a beat
As every red rose has a petal
More or less
An ordinary leaf
With no lungs to breathe
And still unique enough to birth a seed
A new flower will arise
And form a garden of these.
Luke Corsi, Grade 12
BOCES/Alt Ed Program

Can't Find My Way

These moments left at present time
make me wonder where I'll find
my one and only love and happiness
that still is lurking in my mind
this fading memory of what we had
has kept me feeling oh so sad
but things change fast
and I can't keep up
all I have left is to just give...
Adam Van Hise, Grade 12
North Tonawanda High School

Where I'm From

I'm from New York City,
From the smell of wet pavement and Riverside Park,
And the bookstores that don't care if you sit and read for an hour
And don't buy anything.
I'm from an apartment on the Upper West Side,
Filled with the sight of my Mom's paintings and the sound of my dad's records.
I'm from write it down, cut it up and sew it back together,
A #2 pencil drawing on sketchbook paper.
I'm from the Mid-Village near NYU,
Where the stores are secondhand and people wear their clothes
Like billboards wear slogans.
I'm from Hungary, Latvia, Alsace-Lorraine and Bohemia,
From artist to chef to psychologist to interior designer to I don't know.
I'm from eating pizza before Seder so I don't starve,
From not even pretending to keep kosher.
I'm from the Lotus Garden and chasing fireflies in the summer.
Wherever I go in the not-so-distance future,
I'll be rooted to this city
Like the trees in the streets.

Jenny Reisman, Grade 10
Bronx High School of Science

Music

The heavy base so hard to pick up
The lyrics that move you away by storm and sea
Emotion and Idea smashed together like a Peanut butter and jelly sandwich
The sounds that oozes closer and closer towards your ears
With the rhythm and beat makes you move your feet
Makes you feel good anywhere you go,
Like how a little kid gets treats in a candy store
Each song played on the radio gets better and better
And to think, sometimes, artists make songs from a letter
As the song ends you can only just wish for an even greater song to come
Like how you would wish on a shooting star
That shoots so high above in the sky like birds do when they fly
From up and down and all around
Music travels around me, like tourists on an airplane

Dia Rogers, Grade 11
Clarkstown High School North

No More

Broken heart, untruthful lies, all she does is wonder why.
Torn to pieces, confused and small, encased by this growing wall.
Air is thin, and hard to breathe, wishing her mind was at ease.
Shortened breaths, pounding heart, doubted from this very start.
Fuzzy vision, racing mind, this is where she draws the line.
Shattered life, she watched it fall, cries for help, no one hears her call.
Passions from pasts burned deep within, she has failed and let him win.
Her body cold and shaking bad, rising anger, it makes her mad.
He isn't the man she thought he'd be, she was blinded and didn't see,
his true side, the sneaky one, her dreams quickly become undone.
Holding on by a thread, she almost feels as if she's dead.
As quickly as their life was built, she goes numb and starts to tilt.
Falling fast to the ground, she doesn't even make a sound.
As she lies there on the floor, she realized that he is no more.

Allyson Wallace, Grade 10
Harrisville Central School

My Uncle, My Friend

The motions of you walking by,
Will capture pictures in my mind.
They say ones like you are hard to find.
The one that you can be near for hours,
And never make a sound,
But know exactly what was intended,
Just by the actions that you've found.
The days we spent, the nights as well
Many stories I continue to tell
The summer was "awesome" just like you said
My feet all sandy, my face bright red.
We sang so loud, the world could hear
I loved knowing that you were near.
Live life to the fullest ability,
Light goes to dark, the day comes to an end
Your more than a memory, my uncle, my friend.
The days were great, we laughed, we cried
These memories will last forever
And never will they die.

Lindsay Kenney, Grade 11
Douglas MacArthur High School

Timeless Treasure

I need not riches nor jewels or gold;
My treasure lies within pages of old.
Stories and heroes shine with window's light,
And play out between my eyes well past the middle of the night.
I travel beyond earthly limits without ever leaving my chair,
To be ridiculed for intelligence, that is my only fare.
Every word is savored,
Every sentence treasured.
With each passing passage,
I surpass the masses,
'Till I reach the end, the pages filled,
And my story still cooling on the sill.

Jennifer Werbitsky, Grade 11
Nardin Academy

A Past Melody

The violin soloist charms the crowd
as his bow gently runs across a string
I think of a time my grandpa was proud
When I too could make a violin sing

I walk outside the concert hall and stop
The city traffic caught in busy time
I can hear the cultured rap and hip hop
Eyes search sidewalks for a lucky dime

I remember the best time of the year —
It was Christmas, and I was with my dad
The love I felt was so sincere
No thing that moment could ever be bad

One chides oneself not to dwell in the past
but cherish the moments that flee too fast

Taryn Teurfs, Grade 10
Baldwin High School

One Chance

As I lie here aimlessly,
Staring into the black abyss of the night,
I wonder what
Has gone wrong with my life.

Everything changing,
Going so fast,
I do not know
How long this will last.

Looking at the stars,
So pure and bright,
I wonder why anything can't
Just go right

Why does everything have to be so difficult?
Why does everything have to be so hard?
Well to shine bright as the stars,
I need to take charge.

Come back to reality,
Face the facts
That you only get one life,
One chance.

Stephanie Parsons, Grade 12
DeSales High School

These Waters

Staring into waters
You can see the memory of the rain.
If you close your eyes
You can feel the droplets
You can reach out your arms,
Desperately trying to catch them
But they will slip through your fingers
Without apology.
Until you cry out in desperation
And tears overflow from between your closed lids.
But they too will slip through all barriers
And fall,
And connect with other waters
Which will flow through the cracks
Of time and space and
Never be halted by solid things
Like your frail and passive body.
So don't feel the flight of the waters,
Open your eyes.
And don't feel the memories like me,
For I have drowned in these waters.

Alanna Lauren Rice, Grade 10
The Waldorf School of Saratoga Springs

The Game with the Wind

It is the last inning as I wait in the outfield, and the game is tied.
The score is two to two and I hope its over soon when I feel a huge gust of wind hit me.
The wind is so physically powerful it can knock over a house, when ping the ball hits the bat.
I look up to see the ball is coming right at me, but it's going over my head.
I start back on my run and as I approach the fence, back, back, back the wind blows ferociously and,
the ball stops descending and falls right into my glove. I look up and breathe a sigh of relief.
Now it is our turn to bat, but rapidly we get two outs.
Then the pitcher loses control, he walks one batter, then another, then another and I step to the plate.
The coach decides to change pitchers,
I think to myself, oh great; I have to face the best pitcher on the team.
I stride to the plate and sense the wind hit my face, I'm geared up to win this game.
The first pitch whizzes by me…strike. I say okay, now I know what he's made of.
The second pitch draws closer and it's low, so I let it go,
but the umpire declares strike and I ask for time in disgust.
I know this is it, the last pitch or last hit. I dig in and focus.
The pitcher winds up and throws, I swing as hard as I can and crack, the ball leaves my bat.
I watch it go, back, back, back, the center fielder pursues it, but then halts.
I recognize this means he's under it and fling my bat down like an angry ape,
but then a gargantuan gust of wind arrives and drives the ball over the fence, home run.
We win, we win, we win. As I round the bases, I look up to thank God for the strength to do this,
and to thank the unpredictable wind for the additional thrust, to help preserve the game and win it.

Cody Nastasia, Grade 11
Sewanhaka High School

War Hero

It's the simple things in life we forget.
If you could save somebody's life, would you do it?
John — the Marine who returns home after being discharged against his will from the war in Iraq,
His will was to be a real soldier and have his fellow soldier's back,
a man who was being held hostage in some kind of death match;
John the Marine wasn't having that,
He alerts the captain the captain gives order to stay back,
but like I said John the Marine wasn't having that
He decided his own way, to save the day, and I mean he took action,
Kick down the door, and rolled in on the floor, saved hostages in the war
Now the world sees him as the hero
but John the Marine knew how much it could mean,
to his fellow Marines.

Malcolm Bonilla, Grade 10
Bronx Academy of Letters

My Heart Is Calling for You

No one ever told me I would feel like this.
Kinda funny, but quite comparable.
I never looked for you.
You came looking for me, but now I can't seem to leave you alone.
I'm sacred to be with you, but I can't run away from you.
When I try my heart starts to call for you and then you appear how funny can that be.
I never taught I could find happiness in someone I barely know.
I have given myself some thought and I realize my heart is calling for you because I let my heart do so.
Boy I can't stop you're amazing at everything you do.
The best thing about you is your smile It draws me to you.
When I see you temptation takes over me.
Gosh my heart is calling for you and I think I'm In love with you.

Angie Laguerre, Grade 11
Midwood High School

Remember

Remember in the days of old
When our dwindling feelings weren't so cold
We would run and jump and laugh and play
But frivolous childhood cannot stay

As we grew our hearts filled with spite
We had our stupid, petty fights
Slowly, gradually we grew apart
You broke my fragile shell of a heart

You came and told me you're leaving today
I fought back the tears, held my feelings at bay
No touch goodbye, no second glance
Our shattered friendship is now filled with can'ts

Long passed memories flash before my eyes
Bit by bit my happiness dies
So much crying throughout the years
I'm drowning in a sea of tears

In my heart you will not be forgotten
In each other's eyes, lost and misbegotten
Christian Gerholdt, Grade 10
BOCES/LoGuidice Alt Ed Program

Make a Difference

Stand out People are starving, people need help,
Set out your priorities, without one being yourself

Kids are failing, students are alone,
Assist at the library instead of going straight home

Kids are made fun of, kids get upset,
Don't wait, take initiative, and ask why they fret

Stand up now, get up on your feet,
And help the frail woman trying to cross the street

The kitchen needs volunteers, and the teams need fields,
It's time we correct these community fears.

Our parks are littered, as swings rust alone,
Plants are withered, and we call this place Home?

We need a cooperative effort to improve the community,
And it all starts with unyielding unity

So stand out, Make a difference, In any shape or form
Because if you act like a rose, you will have no thorns
Jimmy Wisniewski, Grade 11
Sewanhaka High School

Growing Up

As a child you want to grow up,
You want to be big,
You think it's more fun.
You want to do things that big kids can do,
You want to get older,
You want to be cool.

But when you get older you want to go back,
Back to a child when you can relax.
Being a big kid's no fun anymore,
And the responsibilities are making you sore.

So when you're a child don't try too hard to be big,
'Cause when you get older you just want to be a kid.
Jennifer Miraglia, Grade 11
Douglas MacArthur High School

Stars

Unclose that window, let the moon come in
And shed its balm upon unhappy hearts.
Our souls shall see their kind and flee our skins;
And with the moon they'll soar — the magic starts.
Their bliss will take the gentle form of light;
They'll travel joyous, free of sorrow's toll;
They'll shine and give the world delight that night;
The glory of the evening shall be whole.
But no great glory lasts for very long.
The flesh of sleepers summons them to come;
And they cannot resist, though they are strong:
They must return to that unpleasant home.
The sleepers wake, resuming sinful ways:
The souls are in such pain throughout the days!
Georgiya Djibirova, Grade 12
Laguardia Arts School

Talkative Footsteps

Footsteps in the sand
Equal distances apart.
The tale of the journey
Is imprinted in their footsteps.
And, oh, the stories they tell.

They disappear over the horizon
Getting smaller all the time.
And even though they disappear from view
The journey still goes on.

Footsteps in the sand
They speak about obstacles overcome
And triumphs won.
They speak about the journey
They speak about life.

My footsteps in the sand,
They speak all the time,
And, oh, the stories they tell.
Emily Marshall, Grade 10
Massena Central High School

Music to My Heart

You are like a song
You create a melody that
Can't be messed up
You make me feel so new
Every time I press play again
Never will I leave you
Just like a song you will
Always be here in my heart to stay
I listen to you when I'm
Mad, sad, depressed, and stressed
But once I hear your voice
I already feel that you're going
To help me through it
I love your song
Forever no matter what
I love your lyrics I love you
For always being there
When I need you
I love you for your kind of design
To make each beat count
I love your song
Erica Dimanche, Grade 12
Stella Maris High School

Ardor

The kiss dropped off his lips,
As her hands touched his cheek.
All that she knew was spoken through
The blinded gaze they shared.

His fervor she felt,
Through the lingering scent
And the sound of his breath,
Leaving his chest
As her head lay next to his.
Laura Denby, Grade 12
Ward Melville High School

Postcards

From the Leaning Tower of Pisa,
To the ancient Pyramid of Giza,
We'll stroll along the Great Wall of China,
And don't forget the beautiful Barcelona.

Imagine the places we'll go,
For the soft breeze blows,
the blue river flows,
And your lovely face simply glows.

In these little postcard pictures,
Lies our future.
You're different from everyone,
And I know, that you are the one.

Postmarked — 1991
Zi Xiang Zhang, Grade 10
Bronx High School of Science

The Prison I Call Home

These floors have felt too much
I can still feel them shake
I'm surprised the tiles haven't shattered
Along with the red shards of glass stuck to the bottom of my feet

These walls have heard too much
I'm surprised they're still standing
I can still hear them scream
Even under several layers of yellow

This cold concrete angel has seen too much
I can still see the fire in her eyes
I'm surprised she didn't use her wings to hide
The anger that was held in her fists left cracks on her sore fingertips

My tearstained teddy-bear has tasted too much
I can still wipe water off his floppy ears
I'm surprised he never choked on my tears
But I guess he couldn't with his mouth sewn shut

This little girl has felt, heard, seen and tasted too much
I still feel their screaming surfacing my prison floor
I'm surprised I can even sleep here
My heart will always be torn between my two heroes

Heather Leiser, Grade 12
St Dominic High School

Thinking Of

The sidewalks are laced with mistakes of us
Filled with the children who cry at night
And I could only tell you their mistakes against plastic accident chambers
The crumpling hiss mumbling your direct spew
I plant the tears beneath the floorboards
Breathing smoothly across the hardwood
So they will bloom into oceans, crash against the stone dressers
For we've been left with only time to waste
Dieting our moments to keep sane
This is my dilated sculptor's clay
Your sweet growing characters
Regurgitated nothingness, these barren wrists
I am only here to remember
And yet, could you be a spring lily after winters of dust?
Let me in, let me in. Pull me out.
The light of the mind stays black well past dawn
And I've forgotten to tell you what horror lies beneath
Crying between burnt pages
Charred tips, this preliminary undertone
When will the ransom note read another name than happiness?
Blunt and unpracticed, I will never title well

Jenny Rae Bailey, Grade 12
The Beacon School

Ode to Mi Gente

We are hispanics, latinos they say,
We are unique yet alike in our ways.
No matter the country, no matter the place,
Together one culture we all embrace.
We speak a language unknown to all others,
Except for our sisters, brothers and mothers.
Sombreros, ponchos, chancletas we wear.
We have our own style, we have our own flare.
Tacos, mofongo, pernil with rice.
Our food has flavor and undeniable spice.
Salsa, merengue and now reggaeton,
We express ourselves through the words of our song.
Estefan, Cruz, Puentes and Ricky,
You all make us proud of our family tree.
Hermanos, paisanos you are to me,
We all are a family, latinos we be.
Latinos hold high each of your flags,
Don't be afraid to boast and to brag.
Side by side, let's all unite,
Let's stand with pride, we've earned the right!

Jasmine Cotrich, Grade 10
Townsend Harris High School

Your Best Friend

It's a happening, an unrare commonality.
For better or for worse, it's reality.
When things are going bad in your life.
From your job, to all kinds of strife.
Maybe, taxes, your car, or disease.
You look up to the heavens, Oh please.
And then, as if answered by the omnipresent.
There they are, by your side, oh so pleasant.
They're there to let you cry on their shoulder.
And there to remove that heavy boulder.
They make all your problems go away.
They rub your back and tell you, it's okay.
They're with you every step, every stride.
They're with you the whole way, by your side.
They're with you, no matter what, till the end.
No doubt about it, cuz they're your best friend.

Avi Kohn, Grade 11
Yeshivas Ohavei Torah of Riverdale

Ashes

The pit of fire;
A dance of flames
Sparks of new life.
It moves with sudden succession,
Smoke billowing among the treetops
Mingling with the dew of light.
Branches lay tangled and torn
Listening to the crisp whispers of the wind.
A soft drizzle of savory mist emerges from the sky
As the creatures of destruction scamper.
And then emerges
Nothingness.

Jenna Zito, Grade 11
Kings Park High School

Ode to a Vase

Oh vase
In my room at night
You look so beautiful under the moonlight.
With your long curved stripes of blue
And patches of tannish gold.
It almost looks like you never get old.

Sitting on a desk
All day shining down
You're like a glass shining golden-brown light
Reflected from the sun from where you sit.
In the heat I lose my strength;
You help me get better.

My dad used to have you
But he gave you to me
Just to be nice.
Before that
I watched your pattern
For a long time.
I will fix you if you fall.
But I hope you never will.

David Weintraub, Grade 11
Stuyvesant High School

The Night Owls

The night owls watched
As the mice tried clambering,
Climbing, escaping from the world of the real

The night owls were there in the dark
But they could see, and they chose not to

They saw the jackals tear mice apart
Their jagged teeth shining in the moonlight
The man on the moon turned his face

The night owls were there
But they could hear, and chose to ignore

The screams, the pleas, the calls for help,
Dissipated in the woods as if none had shouted

The night owls were there with unchanging hearts
But chose not to feel, turning their faces

The night owls were there
They were just like jackals
Passivity is silent support.

Alex Kaufman, Grade 10
North Shore Hebrew Academy High School

Liberty

As far as the eye could see, bodies were sinking to the Earth.
Men gasped for that last intake of breath,
Boys' voices grew shrill from their agonizing outcries.
For what purpose does mankind kill?
For what purpose does one father slay another?
For a word growing obsolete with time,
A word whose nurturing embrace has long been forgotten,
The sweetest reward:
Liberty.

Yaroslav Yanischin, Grade 10
Townsend Harris High School

Cheerleading

Cheerleading is a way of life, shared by few,
It's working as a team in everything we do.
Cheerleading is rivalry, the competition is what makes you strong,
It is sharing secrets and shedding tears, while learning to get along.
Cheerleading is that ongoing drive to be the very best,
It is patience, and determination, and little rest.
Cheerleading is having poise and charm with every word you say,
It is total dedication every day.
It is always being ready with encouragement or a smile,
Cheerleading is your chance to express your individual style.
True cheerleaders are cheerleaders at heart and that will always last
They pay attention on this moment and forget the past.
Cheerleading is a talent being able to shine on cue,
It is hiding the pain and failure that if only people knew.
Cheerleaders, after all, are real people that sometimes feel down,
But when they're in the spotlight, they must never wear a frown.
Cheerleaders are actresses, always ready to go,
That is why it is my goal for all the world to know.
Not every girl can be a cheerleader, it takes a special kind,
To say "pssh, girl you can only wish that you could cheer like us."

Alexa Elliott, Grade 11
DeSales High School

Tragedy of Virginia Tech

April 16th 2007 seemed like another school day
Little did Professor Livescu know things were astray
In his midst a bomb waiting to explode
A tragic tale about to unfold

The words of forensics was all he could hear
But suddenly another sound rang loud and clear
The sound of the gunshot made its way to his ears
A chilling sensation he hadn't felt in years.

The very few moments, his very last
He held back the gunman bringing safety to the class
Gunshots, they pierced him but still he held fast
Tragedy, it struck him as it had in the past

This Holocaust survivor's old memories started to erase
The fear escaped him and he stared death right in the face.
He told his students to go escape and most of them have fled
But the last blow to the head pronounced this brave professor dead.

Tharmika Sinnathurai, Grade 10
Townsend Harris High School

Columbine

April 20, 1999
A seemingly normal day
Those students were unaware
things were about to go astray

Dylan Klebold and Eric Harris
Their crime changed so many lives
A plan as simple as could be
A bomb no one could've survived

Their bombs, they did not detonate
But their plan would not stop there
Laden with knives and guns
The cry of death was in the air

Into the school they entered
Where shots began to fly
Those students could not foresee
That death was so close by

Down the hallways they came
Bombs thrown amid this disaster
They smiled happy as could be
All through the halls, the sound of laughter

Crystal Wong, Grade 10
Townsend Harris High School

The Bare Scar

I don't know whose choice it was,
to bestow pain onto me,
I thought it was by chance,
In school would I be able to advance?
I'm only a young man,
I have yet to find romance,
I thought it would be bad,
for my parents to see,
my helpless face, beat red,
like I've been stung by a bee,
embarrassed to have this scar,
people will look at me,
but when I was through, it was clear to see,
a 15 year old young man…
a helpless child screaming in pain,
I call out to God,
people look at me as though I am insane,
but they merely see my scar, my humiliation,
my huge worry which seems so blurry,
although they see my scar,
they have missed my complicated life story.

Jonathan Odinsky, Grade 10
Davis Renov Stabler Yeshiva High School for Boys

Our World

The Middle East is suffering, endless nights and days,
But people care more about Britney Spears at the VMA's.
Melting ice caps in the Arctic, pollution in the air,
Global warming isn't real to Bush, why should we care?
The ozone layer is depleting, many forests chopped down,
Starving children, 3rd world, beware when Angelina's around.
Lead poison from paint, recall all Chinese toys,
Michael Jackson on trial for molesting little boys.
Low wages, long hours, subsistence living, communism,
No hope, no future, ever-growing cynicism.
Religious wars, jihads, and fights for the Holy Land,
This has gone on long enough; it's time we take a stand.
In this planetary globe, watch as the chaos unfolds,
And young men and women are growing old and weak,
And far too scared of the powers that speak,
So instead they claim peace in the midst of war.

Robert Wechsler, Grade 10
Bronx High School of Science

A Vow at the End

The war torn country was awash with blood.
Men fought like animals over some meat.
A pair struggling in the knee-deep mud,
And the one on top accomplished his feat.

Looking upon his equal that he caught,
The man did not salute the flag unfurled,
And he hesitated before he shot,
For the puppet in power had destroyed the world.

The sound of a bullet pierced his ears.
The man, vowing again never to fight
Fell without shedding any pain-filled tears.
The brave soldier closed his eyes to the light.

And upon the rising of the new sun,
He took his purple heart, and hung up his gun.

Tess Morgridge, Grade 11
Briarcliff High School

Memories Lost in Darkness

Who can save me?
When you cannot even get a grip on me
And every time we got close we were torn apart
Slowly we began to drift away from each other
I begged for eternal sleep, away from the pain of loss
A place where no one can get to me, because I was trapped,
In my eternal sleep where all I see is the darkness of the heart.
Everything I have done wrong by others' standards
Everything I did wrong and was hurt for it I won't remember
But will I forget the memories of the friends I made
The happiness they gave me.
Would they even want to save me?
Even after the path I have chosen
I hear their cries telling me to wake up
But I ignored them, because I already forgot them.

Emma Troini, Grade 12
Tottenville High School

Noisy

If you're loud
You're annoying to some
But people could be just like you
Some need to be loud
Or you can't be heard
And to be heard
You must be loud

Andrew Dennis, Grade 10
North Tonawanda High School

The Kool-Aid Brigade

I have a group of friends
Who are always a great time.
They always know just what I need
I never have to mime.
I'll start with Ben & Jerry,
They're the coolest of the bunch
But when I don't want dairy,
I'll take Sarah Lee to lunch.
Betty Crocker plans great parties
With so many lovely cakes,
Uncle Ben is always ready,
Though he never bakes.
We also have a club house,
Though it's not a secret lair —
We just have frequent meetings
In my giant Frigidaire.

Rachel Eisenman, Grade 10
Oceanside Sr High School

Raw War Backwards Is Raw War

Innocent blood spilled on the ground.
Screams and gunshots are the only sound.
Lives cut short, nothing to be said,
no time for help, ground is their deathbed.
Loved ones at home have no clue,
what they are about to go through.
No one can save them, made by their choices.
Choosing their own over loved one's voices.
They die with honor and respect,
"What ifs" or "sorrys," are there regrets?
Years from now, the pain will fade,
Amongst friends and family a bond is made.
Memories of the past will guide their lives,
Memories will feel like stabbing knives.
But deep down, beyond the watery eyes,
An unbelievable pride stretches across the skies.
Remember those who died for you to live in their place,
Doesn't matter that you do not know their face,
Although they are gone their spirits soar,
All the lost sours of such raw war.

Kibret Yebetit, Grade 12
Townsend Harris High School

Ocean Experience

Stand at the edge of the ocean water on the beach.
Listen to the marine's whistling wind preach.
It tells of its vast power.
Yet the ocean is kind; do not cower.
The water only licks at the ankles of your legs.
It leaves its mark, dried salt, because it begs.
The ocean begs to be remembered — a brilliant memory in your head.
It wants you to remember each word it said.
It showed you, taught you, both strength and placidity.
Frothy waves to and fro recede.
Showing you no mercy and at the same time offering pity.

Aquamarine oscillating turbulence.
Calmness, smooth and clear.
It may be a bit of a disturbance.
But it is nothing to fear.

Emily Stein, Grade 12
Staten Island Technical High School

Sundance

Show the speckled sun cerulean eyes
and hold your hands a high,
blind yourself; white film orbs cordial with the sky.
Come to rewind life a day before,
where crystalline tears merge with green grass; wispy sentiments collide.
Don't hide behind shattered expression,
but show us the shadows you've cast-off, and scatter all that remain.
Stare into the sunspots for the dark weeps light refracted.
Shoulder all the pain just to turn away.
Keep crying.
And heal yourself again; eyes like the world oblong.
Forward your hands reach, where sympathetic sky appears,
don't play dead, lying there exhausted.
Most importantly,
Listen.
Listen to the spinning record, round and round;
Dance asylum to the amber inferno.
Let the silence ignite you.

Yvonne Dykstra, Grade 11
Warwick Valley High School

A Beautiful and Divine Place

The Milky Way, our galaxy
The sun, a blazing ball of fire, making life possible for our world
Our world, a place created to be our home
Our planet, so beautiful and divine
The sun, created to hold the planets together
The Earth, created to hold us
We, the people, created to live in the image of the Divine
The Divine, creator of the people
The Divine, creator of the Earth
Earth, one mere planet in a collection of celestial bodies
Our duty, to help our home, the Earth, flourish and grow
Our duty to our home, a beautiful and divine place

Erin Geraghty, Grade 10
Staten Island Technical High School

The Holocaust

No one could imagine the horror they went through,
or how many tears they cried.
The Nazis where slowly destroying their country
and quickly taking away their lives.
They were tortured and beaten, destroyed, and defeated,
many died of starvation and thirst.
The prisoners lost their family, their friends, their freedom,
nothing else could be worse.
They were forced to hard labor and tricked to their death,
they were lied to and told they were worthless.
For those who survived I give them respect, for the pain
they went through we will never forget.

Lindsay Frankel, Grade 11
Sachem High School North

Truth Beneath China's Economy

Those large factories,
With long smoking chimneys,
Created scarcity within our lands.
They stole all water
And left us with none.
So much is depended on the water
Beneath the grounds.
We need to feed our wheat and grains,
Our babies and selves.
But it shrinks each passing year.
Lower and lower, the water sank down.
Deeper and deeper, must we dig our holes.
As those cities down there
Expand,
We, farmers up here,
Choke on their growth.

Jessica Li, Grade 10
Townsend Harris High School

We Salute You

We all salute you.
We all salute the great hero.
We salute you for your bravery,
Your valor,
Your deeds.
We all salute the father, the husband, and the son,
But who salutes your family?
What do we tell the daughter?
The son?
The wife?
The mother?
The father?
And all the others that mourn for you?
They'll be told that you died fighting for your country;
They'll be told that you died fighting for a cause;
But what they won't be told is the truth —
The truth that you died fighting to go home —
That you died fighting to see those you love;
But all they know is that you died fighting.
And that isn't enough.

Joe McGarry, Grade 10
Smithtown High School West

Fall

The leaves start to fall;
Baseball draws to an end.
Football is starting up
meaning the wild fans come out.
Tailgating begins and everyone talks about the playoffs.
High expectations for some teams hold up and others fail.
Some teams are long shots,
Others are shoe-ins, and
Some teams aren't given any shot at all.
This is all just talk leading up to the season.
Once the season begins,
The teams start to show their true colors.
Stars start to emerge and expected stars drift out of sight.
Players get hurt and sit out,
But the true players play through the pain.
They don't want to sit out, they just want to play
Not for the money but for the game.
The season grudges on and teams go down.
We reach the playoffs the best teams compete.
The Super Bowl comes and goes,
Football ends and so does the fall.

Vin Corona, Grade 11
DeSales High School

The Stitched Hearts

Two hearts bleeding as a mass
To rot away from each other
Unlikely to meet

The first thumping madly
Torn in half
Seeking companionship
Yet, finding no one

The second beating softly
Ripped in two
From a robber of love
The heart lies in sorrow
From the time it enjoyed

The unlikely turns to the likely

The two meet, unsure of each other
For fear of being hurt again
Yet they feel the connection
The hearts feel as though they found their missing halves
Thus a new heart is born
Stitched together they sit happily
Hoping to never feel the sorrow that they knew before

William Patterson, Grade 12
Fort Plain High School

My Love

You were my love, you were my friend…you held me down through thick and thin, you loved me day, you loved me night even when we would fuss and fight…you took my heart and made me see, just how great love can truly be even though our love was strong everyone around us said it was wrong…in your arms is where I would lay, forever in my heart is where you will stay, I love you now and I loved you then…the only thing I want is to be with you again, but I know its too late and you're probably long gone…but to tell you how I feel I wrote you a song, it's about ten minutes beginning to end…tellin' you you'll always be my lover and friend.

O'Naya McKoy, Grade 11
Geneva High School

negroes 4 sale

To ensure the preservation of a culture would be a lie told by many,
We were brought here 300 years ago, we were child property free then segregated,
To say we are a lost cause would be an understatement
We've divided our groups into subdivisions,
We are broken up people and fragmented individualist,
We came from sun heat and gold, to-over-crowded ships and cooper shackles
Thick strands of bamboo split in half by raw flesh,
Dehydrated tears filled all the faces, it's even shared among the races
From nazi germany, apartheid africa and imperialist america
A party of black panthers with a sprinkle of hippies smoke pipes and reefer
With tough naps and berets — black fist in mid air wanting what rightfully theirs
Lets go back further, the gas chambers are now intoxicated minds only
Hate knew his demise, had to take so much to prove something trivial
A problem found a solution by genocide and executions to complete extinction
The cycle is not broken and free for repetition
Time now to progress not just africans or blacks but the jews, asians and the forgotten.
You see ghettoes are infested the poor have nothin' but drugs, alcohol and hopelessness invested
Assimilation is not an act you engage rather a bug feastin' on your brain i'm lost
We've became intergrationlist to oppressive closed-minded people
We're lost, negroes fo' sale, hope's free

Amanda Green, Grade 12
High School for Economics & Finance

Painting His Love

If I could only paint the days that will follow, after his moment's time.
dims of light that shade the sky, with gentle brush strokes of blue.
Tinges of reds and orange that rest past this Orient moon.
beyond this day, is yet another, another I share with him
blankets of stars that fold over suns, to come to a full night's rest.
I know in the morning, to you I'm adoring
as the rise from east to west.
The strokes of blues, that rest upon reds, that mix together as one
sweeps of black and gray and hues of white that blanket the suns with stars overnight.
To become a medium, a painting, a masterpiece.
Rest in the heavens the greatest artist.
Unto you brings the birth of each new day,
a small piece of heaven not faded away.
The tale of a king born unto a virgin.
The king of purples, silvers and golds.
He descended his only begotten.
The life and the death of a great loving son.
When the people asked him how much he loved us,
He opened his arms, and took a last breath, nailed to the cross, He replied and said THIS MUCH!
To the creator the king Emanuel Gloria in excelsis deo.

Heather DeCamp, Grade 10
Odessa Montour Jr/Sr High School

I Never Believed Fairy Tales Came True

I never believed fairy tales came true,
Until I met you.
I was Rapunzel locked in a tower,
Waiting for love to show its true power.
I never believed fairy tales came true.

Like Snow White in the coffin of glass,
I was frozen in the past.
Awaiting my prince to come and save,
My life with the kiss he gave.
I never believed fairy tales came true.

Like Cinderella at the ball,
He chose me above them all.
As we danced night stars did shine
And I hoped you'd forever be mine.
I never believed fairy tales came true.

I never believed fairy tales came true
But we are proof that they do.
I never believed fairy tales came true.

Cassandra Brooks, Grade 11
Massena Central High School

The Triumph of the 54th Massachusetts Infantry

There was a mighty band of troops,
That had yet to prove their mettle,
To the loudmouths against their race,
Would those rambles be soon settled?

Now time went by as they trained,
Knowing the great expectations,
Always hoping to silence the critics,
And earn at home tremendous ovations.

The African troops led by Shaw,
Now learn their task at hand,
Leading the assault on Fort Wagner,
They can finally make their stand.

Charging at the fort they never give up,
The rain of pain they had to endure,
Yet any terror is left unseen,
They expressed great courage for sure.

While the attack has now failed,
With all the lives that have been lost,
They still keep their heads raised high,
Knowing their glory was worth the cost.

Lawrence Yu, Grade 10
Townsend Harris High School

The Missing Key

The old bureau is weathered and worn
containing memories equally tattered and torn.
I'm not quite sure what secrets it hides.
Maybe Grandma's lace gloves
yellowed with age.
Or photos of my mother's childhood.
Images of her as a young girl at Zore Valley
(Sur Ally as my sister calls it)
with water stains or tears
from too much handling over the years.
Maybe Grandma still has Rocky's old collar hidden away
somewhere in there.
I may never know what's in there.
They key to the bureau has been missing for ages.
…maybe the key is in there too.

Ashley Evans, Grade 12
Clarence High School

Tears of a Rose

Love is a feeling which none can endure,
They give in to the feeling lead by the lure.
They start to go mad as the days pass by,
Their hearts beat fast as they steadily cry.

As tears of sadness fall onto the rose,
Which they hold as a symbol as their love grows,
They start to get old, desires don't fade,
Stronger than diamonds on the grassiest glade.

Their minds are set on their one goal,
To fill the emptiness inside the hole.
The hole belongs to only one feeling,
Which can't be fixed with any type of healing.

As their final days approach though their body may be weak,
Their love is stronger than any diamond shiny and sleek.
Love never fades even after one dies,
Their lover will weep as they say their good byes.

Mir Shajee, Grade 10
Bronx High School of Science

Winter

The ice cold wind blows from the north
Bringing winter to us on swift wings
Autumn's gentle breeze is swept away
As the wind, through window panes, sings

Snow rips across the frozen ground
Scouring the land with ice
But inside I am filled with warmth
As a fire burns brightly in the grate

Desolation and neglect are, in winter, apparent
To many the season is a burden
To me it is a blessing
Filled with comfort and light

John Maher, Grade 12
DeSales High School

Amnesty

Sitting down 'cross from you
I look into your eyes —
A sparkle that makes me
Try to suppress my sighs

It feels as though you can
Read my mind. You must know;
The way I feel; you can't.
My heart, away, you throw

My friends think it insane
That I cannot speak, but
I am no longer well.
Emotions, I must cut.

Stephanie Moronta, Grade 12
Bronx High School of Science

Love

Love, lying like death
Upon the floor of your soul
Sinking into grief

Brittany Augustine, Grade 10
North Tonawanda High School

The Contrast

The core of the heart,
Filled by happy and regret,
Leaves life with a gap.

James Hogan, Grade 12
North Tonawanda High School

Leo: My Grandfather

I will not forget
The times we spent together;
The places that we went.
And my life will go on.
That's what you would have wanted.
That's what I need to do.
I know that this is hard.
I know it won't get easier.
But when the time comes,
I'll be prepared.
I'll face my fears alone,
Although you're there with me.
I'll never let you go.
You'll be in my heart.
The path you chose is clear.
You're wandering alone now.
I cannot come along
No matter how hard I try.
So I will not forget…
You.

Justine Howell, Grade 10
Kings Park High School

Cool, Cool Wind

I think I can I hope I can I dream I can
But is dreaming enough to make me a man?
I think about it every day each and every single way
Thumbing through different combinations and formulas
Dreaming
Color my words so you may wish butter me up and throw me in a dish
I feel and see and do I work and please and woo
I lay beneath the embers of the sun feeling raindrops prance on my tongue
I cry and show emotion I laugh and smile and show devotion
I sing, dance and act I try my best and that's a fact
Cool, cool wind oh blow across my steaming face time will stand still there is no race
Taste the colors of the sky and pry you can be cool and so may I
Blabber, blabber, blabber mindless jabber
Incoherent words touch my tongue no this is not a pun
This could be real
Or just something I perhaps may feel, maybe I'm just trying too hard?
Or I'm becoming charred with confusion
Cool, cool wind oh blow across my burning face
Time will stand still there is no race
But if fire may come and time will not stand still I'll be here ready to embrace
My face

Vincent DeStefano, Grade 12
Clarence High School

Her Miracle

She sits on tiled floor, her purple dress flows around.
Dark brown eyes close to see a miracle that cannot be found.
Those endless moments under stars, if only they could be;
If only she could relive them; if only he would see.

Tears pour down her tattered photo, it begins to fray.
She sets it down beside her, 'til tomorrow it will lay.
One last glimpse outside, as the starry cold night falls.
"Keep your head up high," an angel above her calls.

Tomorrow turns today, sunshine creeps into her room.
"Today is the day," her confidence says, "I will escape my cocoon."
She puts on her two-minute makeup, as sweet pea scent fills the air.
Her fake smile reflects in the mirror, for the one who doesn't care.

Through the hallways she wanders, catches an eye here or there.
She looks out hazy windows, and whispers, "It just isn't fair."
Rushing around the corner, a familiar face approaches near.
An excited expression lights his face as her hair tucks behind her ear.

She pauses for a moment, puts on her brightest smile.
She walks briskly towards him; it feels like the longest mile.
Her mouth opens to say, "Hello," but he just cannot see,
He hugs the girl beside her she wishes she could be.

Nikita Gupta, Grade 10
Massena Central High School

Facts or Opinions
How do I say this?
I really don't know
How should I say this.
Should I just let it go?
But after my Baptism, Communion, and Confirmation
Is it too late to change religions?
Do they have me locked in?
Do they have me trapped?
How do I escape?
Is it too late to fix that?
Is it too late to change my faith?
I ask myself that question every day.
Because I don't want to go to church, and I don't want to pray
But apparently, Jesus loves me anyway.
To stick in this religion,
I need some proof
I have the Bible, but who knows if it speaks the truth
Forgive me, Father, for I have sinned
I don't know if I want to be a Christian,
Science or religion,
Facts or opinions?
Michael Papandrea, Grade 11
Bishop Ford Central Catholic High School

Desire
Does it seem you never get what you truly want,
Desiring something that's unreal,
Your wishes never coming true?
Holding onto something that will never be reality,
Hoping for something to happen,
Not knowing what's next?
Taking the chances, the choices, the opportunity
And was it really all worth it?
Wishing you could change everything
To the way you wanted it,
To the way you hoped it could be,
To the way that felt right?
Does it seem you never get what you truly want,
Desiring something that's unreal,
Your wishes never coming true?
Brian Jacks, Grade 10
Massena Central High School

New York City
Eight AM on the F train:
Jackets and windows are painted with rain.
Bodies shift, uncomfortably close to mine.
Eyes meet, awkwardly with mine.
They are tired and sad.
I wonder where they slept the night before,
what their beds were made of,
and who laid beside them.
A rain drop descends from a tall man's white hair
onto the top of my ear.
It is wet, and startling,
like the morning.
Emily Sussell, Grade 12
Institute for Collaborative Education

Is This Love?
Inside, there is so much I don't know
There are feelings that have decided to suddenly show
I sat outside in the falling snow
Wondering if this flutter in my stomach was joy or woe
They were emotions that I already knew
My heart kept subconsciously thinking of you
I know this is strange but I must make it through
Feelings of agony and turmoil grew and grew
But now I can't see
For there is nowhere for me to flee
And I make a silent tender plea
I let my heart slowly slip into the sea
Eternal night without a star
His voice is distant, but he is not far
We don't reveal who we truly are
I hide my heart to conceal that scar
I think we all hope that we cannot break
Our hearts build a wall so that we cannot ache
A dream we pray we will not wake
Our hearts are all that is at stake

That was my very first mistake

Elizabeth Adams, Grade 10
Ward Melville High School

The Closest Friend
Running in the park, I tripped
I scraped my knee, and the tears started falling
A kiss from Mom made it all better.

Getting ready for my prom
Walked down the staircase
Was blinded with camera flashes
I felt like the most beautiful woman in the world.

I was at my college graduation
Reached for my diploma
Scanned the crowd for my family
And saw the tears well up in my mother's eyes.

I was walking down the aisle, my father at my side
An hour later I hear "You may kiss the bride."
I turn around my mother wraps me in a bear hug
Tears of joy in both of our eyes.

My life went on,
And at each event my mother was there.
She was happy for me, or helped fix my problems.
She supported me constantly, and never took me for granted.
I was lucky to have her, my closest friend.
Christine Olivo, Grade 10
Sacred Heart Academy

Bee

Black and yellow vicious stripes
With dark mysterious eyes that I have
Wings that fly to mischief during the day but not at night.
Sweet tender honey waiting for them at their nest,
While they are buzzing through the skies.
Stingers that seem harmful to humans
But harmless to them…
Sweet yet bitter

Taylor Ackerman, Grade 11
North Tonawanda High School

Analyzing Life Through a Pen

Knowledge is written yet it can't be erased only covered and scribbled out,
This represents uncertainty and doubt
Because to have no scribbles means you know what there is to know about,
And nobody's perfect,
But the key is to make it sound close to perfection
Because writing can be as powerful as a gun,
The pen is mightier than the sword
But those that lead a fight with a pen I pray for them…
A pen is silent so words must be involved,
And those oh so powerful words must be truth because the truth can hurt,
So pens quickly go to work and create a battle on paper
Where subliminal messages lurk,
And people form behind these thoughts
Set in ink, their paper message is sold and bought,
So now red ink vs blue vs black ink,
Marks your association on the dotted line,
And it starts to seem that these words now rhyme
And that is how rap has evolved over time.

Eugene O'Neill, Grade 12
Averill Park High School

The Suffering of My Memories

The day we found out, they said she wouldn't survive.
They said we should spend the last weeks with happiness in our lives.
I didn't want her to leave, I needed her to stay.
Once she would pass, her soul would be taken away.
She didn't know who I was, but I knew she was there.
Even when she was unrecognizable, when she lost her hair.
She raised me to be an adult, but now I am just a kid.
Now I try to reflect on all the good things that she did.
But now she is gone and I must try to carry on.
It will be such a burden because of our close bond.
Life is too short to burden my shoulders with her terrible death.
But I must move on to put life within the soul in my chest.
She was a role model, always being kind.
Trying to do the impossible when she knew there was limited time.
The enemy conquered her beautiful body, eventually taking her life.
Why did she have to pay the price?
This terrible suffering, why did this happen to her?
Why did this mess have to occur?
With open arms God should accept her soul.
Like she did to warm me up, when I was very cold.

David Kaufman, Grade 10
Davis Renov Stahler Yeshiva High School for Boys

My Best Friend

She stood in the doorway,
Her bags packed in the car.
She's leaving me already,
Oswego State seemed so far.
She leaned in to hug me,
This isn't our goodbye
It couldn't be!
There were too many times it was just me and her.
My best friend was leaving
This I was sure.
My mouth was dry, no words would come out
She was out the door
I already miss her, no doubt.
We took one last teary look at each other
At that moment we knew,
We would never lose the other
We became one, never again two.
My sister and my best friend,
I will love her 'til the very end.

Amber Baines, Grade 10
Massena Central High School

The Burden of Love

When I walk past you in the hallways
I pretend not to know
For my pain and anguish I surely will not show
Why do you hurt me so?

Your friends laugh, giggle, and smirk
But I am the only one that you hurt
The days go by so slow
And you don't even know
Why do you hurt me so?

You used to care
You used to always be there
Now your gone, so long
To what used to be
To you and me

Emily Bigelow, Grade 11
Seton Catholic Central School

Untitled

It was late last night when you heard the whispers
Of the mistakes I made, the lies, and the gestures

Your heart begins to beat

Slowly

As the rage from your mind reaches your
Hand
As the words from your mouth punch my
Face

This gives a whole new meaning of saying Sorry.

Mike Richter, Grade 11
Manhasset Sr High School

The Hope of Righteousness

Cruelty spreads like a malignant plague
A disease that is here to stay
It will spread throughout one's heart and soul
And corrupt a mind like a never ending hole
Where is the light in the darkened room?
That will help solve this impending doom
I always have hope in a person to do what's right
Though it may be a heartless fight
There still is love in many hearts
That breeds the light to prevail against dark

Jake Kramer, Grade 10
Harborfields High School

Less Than Useless

Candy to a starving man
Time to a child
Secrets to a monk
The monk hides them
As he sees fit
And locks himself in a cave
As the subject
Unaware,
Peril nears.
To show the secret,
Both cave and monk
Must be destroyed
So thinks the monk
As he picks up his hammer
He swings
Halfheartedly
Running a hairline crack
And as he stares
The wall shakes:
Some things are not worth knowing.

Daniel Mosesson, Grade 10
North Shore Hebrew Academy High School

"Running Away"

People might think that I'm weak
And that I can't confront my fears,
But they are wrong.
I am strong.
And if I need another person to help me move along,
I always have my friends.
I never run away;
Running away will not help me
Grow as a person.
It will only hold me back from reality
And it will destroy little by little my personality.
In my mind
Running away is not an option,
But just an idea that will keep holding me back
If I let it.
But I always try to confront my fears,
Before one day
I'll truly regret them.

Melissa Guillén, Grade 10
Bronx Academy of Letters

Sensitivity

Sensitivity
A mother's touch
To a crying baby
Sensitivity
Holding a newborn
Baby
Sensitivity
The gentle wings
Of a harmless
Butterfly

Danielle Darby, Grade 11
Tri-Valley Central School

If You Are God

If You are God
Should I turn away?
Or do I come towards You?
Do I cry and say You don't listen?
Or do I come thanking You?
Should I scream?
Or should I pray?

God said:
I am the Lord your God.
Do not think I don't listen
I love you,
And I hear you,
And I see everything.

I know when you go through hard times,
I have sent an angel to you.
Therefore, believe in Me.

Jonitha Ninja Theodore, Grade 11
Bishop Ford Central Catholic High School

Believe

Believe that the world
Will be at peace
Believe that world hunger
Will decrease
Consider the world
As a wonderful place
And that no one
Will ever
Be judged by race
Our world is made up
Of envy and greed
If only you believe
Then you can succeed
Hope for the best
Be prepared for the worst
If you believe
The world's horrible future
Can be reversed

Laurena Patarkatsi, Grade 10
Clarkstown High School North

The Country

The clear land bringing a slight breeze
Miles and miles of green grass
Wishing on white, soft and beautiful dandelions
Waking up hearing the rooster and drinking fresh milk every day
Running around in the empty space, hoping you can fly away with the birds
Sitting at the edge of a hill and looking at gorgeous spectrum sunsets
Staring at the roads hoping to see a new face
Chasing the chickens and playing hide and seek
Learning how to ride a tractor before a car
Jumping up and trying to reach the mangoes on a mango tree
Looking at the sky above and counting the stars
Sitting on top of haystacks looking at the passing clouds
Wondering how life would be without the country

Ramya Geddam, Grade 10
W Tresper Clarke High School

Acceptance of Spirit

He created the animals and humans
to the earth and the feeling to love,
Must He stand and accept the good and evil
And guide us from above?
Must He forgive our sins?
And accepts those who sin to heaven?
Why, my Lord, did You forgive us from the beginning?
I think it's time I accept You gave me the hope and faith I need to proceed,
And the guidance You gave me when I was in need,
The power You gave me when I needed to heal
And the punishment when my bad side was revealed,
But through my prayers I pray for acceptance
And through my life, I am always in Your presence.

Gregory Baffi, Grade 11
Bishop Ford Central Catholic High School

Stories

There you are, old house
with your naked, glassless windows
shutters hanging, sighing at the slightest breeze
your faded brown bricks and
your small weak staircase leading
to the tired, groaning door
behind which lie all your stories
How many families have called you home?
How many times has the sun set upon you?
How many lovers shared a kiss on your front steps?
How many ghosts moan within those walls?
How many stories do these amount to?
But look! A naughty hand has painted something
on the side of your face, near the gutter
Bold, red, wicked letters
A word not part of your hidden stories
Yes, there you are, somewhere camouflaged among the shadows
of finer buildings, taller, newer, stronger
I weep, for you have withered as these buildings were born
You are unworthy of the world now, forgotten
And the stories have gone with you.

Kathleen Zabala, Grade 10
Townsend Harris High School

Picnics in the Park

I am from the barrettes,
Extra-large tee-shirts and
Leggings that my mother dressed me in.
The neon colors, reflecting in the pool
After kick line practice and arts and crafts.
I am from the watermelon, and grape juice sips.
From climbing my best friend's monkey bars;
Finding four leaf clovers; pressed butterflies.
The coloring books and ticket stubs,
Stuffed in a box only I can find.
I am from my backyard time capsules,
Still waiting to be dug up.

Gabriella Orlando, Grade 12
Sewanhaka High School

My Difference

I can make a difference by shutting the lights off,
Recycling papers and plastics,
Planting trees.
I can make a difference by walking to and from school,
Stop using fossil fuels.
Not wasting water.
I can help heal the world,
Help mend the damages that have been made.
I can reduce carbon dioxide emissions,
Put a pause on global warming,
Put ozone depletion on hold.
I can play a role in supporting global foundations,
Donating to the causes that matter,
Helping the movement for change.
I can make a difference.

Susan Morrissey, Grade 10
New Hyde Park Memorial Jr/Sr High School

Forgiveness with Lies

I said I was sorry,
I tried to tell you but you never gave me a chance
I said I was sorry,
I was silent and I thought that it
Would be good enough when
I said I was sorry
You never believe there are lies
Inside these tears.
Even though my whole reason was to be with you
Because you are my life.
All the time and you never realized that they were lies,
I cried and said sorry
But you never understood me.
I said I was sorry,
Then when you finally understood that I was sorry
Because of my lies,
You were in pain,
You were really mad
But with your love that you have for me,
You can forgive me and start to ask me why?
But I'm still saying I'm sorry.

Angelica Vega, Grade 11
Brentwood High School

Elaine

Awake, she's awake, it's time again,
She gets up to start her routine and then,
She sighs and another breath escapes.

Smile, she smiles, she plasters a fake smile,
She is waiting for something remotely worthwhile,
But she knows it is not possible.

Work, she works, until she's acquired,
Her dream, but can't you see she's tired,
Is this the dream she expected?

Thin, she's thin, she wants to be gorgeous,
So she decides to pretend, she decides she forges
To be something that isn't her.

Promised, she promised to be so perfect,
She tells herself that it'll all be worth it,
She can't find herself anymore.

Elizabeth Shiang, Grade 10
Clarkstown High School North

Liquid Music

The piano notes drop into the air
She feels their cold rain wet her skin
Selfishly, she drinks the music
Thirsty for everything she has lost.
Her salty tears pour out of the pianist's fingers
Staining the smooth innocence of the keys.
A single ray of light shines on the music
Calling her out of the darkness that envelops her soul
She stares towards the light
Eyes reaching for it, wanting it, needing it.

But her heart holds her back
Weighing her down, she kneels
Closes her lids
And bows her head.
She submits to the music.

Shannon King, Grade 12
Clarence High School

Indigo Orange

indigo city and bright orange looking over it,
families in every color, love is every color,
a spectrum of beauty,
a bloody-nosed child, a loving father,
he would give her the sun if he could,
lace and roses make her feel beautiful,
childish reds and blues,
and artist paints the landscape,
he paints it through his cracked inner-city apartment window,
his window of opportunity,
music and color and instruments with strings,
percussion, the colors come booming from the drums,
el toro, the lovers, umbrella for the sun.

Lauren Halligan, Grade 10
Galway High School

Kindergarten

There was once a time where the only hurt a person felt were skinned knees.
The only race that was known was who ran the fastest.
WAR was a card game. And nothing made a difference.

Kindergartners are known to be immature.
But who is the real immature one?
The adult who can't accept another because of a difference of skin?
Or the child, who likes to play with his food,
Or follow his older siblings because they know no better.
Make a difference by going back to kindergarten,
Play with anyone you wanted.
Even if they were different in their own ways.
Being with someone different meant something more to enjoy.
The innocence that a kindergartner shows puts the "maturity" that an adult "possesses" to shame.
If they can play with anyone no matter how they look, then why can't we treat each other with equality?

The people who teach these kindergartners
Hold tightly to the immaturity that they expel upon people that are different than them.
It is not later that we must make a difference.
It is now.

Make a difference and skip back a couple of years.
To the times of scraped knees and sand castles,
Of acceptance despite looks.

Linda Mathew, Grade 10
New Hyde Park Memorial Jr/Sr High School

Dancing

The music flows through me; like water through the sand.
The rhythm becomes my own; the beat one with the beat of my heart.
Secret instructions, like hieroglyphics on the walls of a vast pyramid.
Possessing a secret message that my body some how knows how to decode. And I move.

My feet have a mind of their own; as if disconnected from my brain.
Fast, Slow — it doesn't matter — the music plays, and I must dance.
To try to stop it would be of no use.
Once my ears hear that beat — my feet start tapping — my fingers start drumming — my head starts bobbing.

Next thing I know, the music has taken over. My body has been possessed.
It is like a magic spell, something I cannot fight.

The music plays. I must dance.

Melanie Graber, Grade 11
Great Neck South High School

Trapped

Why in the world did I dance on a grave? Especially Walt Whitman's grave. Now he's haunting me with his beard and obsession with boys. I'm becoming his cosmos of Manhattan, his scent of drooling armpits. In school, I'm becoming Waltzified, learning Waltz in ballroom, about Walt Disney in history and even a Walter McKay. Water begins sounding like Walter. Crossing the street, the sign reads Walt and Don't Walt. Now I'm dreaming of his beard stabbing me to death, piercing my body like a thousand knives. Every hobo in the street suddenly has a beard like Old Walt, as their eyes lock onto little boys that walk past them. It's getting dark and I know it's about time he comes out of his grave again. I go take a nap beneath the stars, but he still won't leave me in peace, preaching SAT words and definitions into my brain with grandiloquence and hypocrisy. Old Walt is screwing me over, even my poetry.

Nelson Chiu, Grade 12
Stuyvesant High School

Music Under the Door

Silence my ears could not hear
Although the door, its hinges, were there
Melodies from times already spent
Flowed clear and under the door they went

These sounds suddenly reached me
To a place where I thought sounds would never be
Each interval spoke truth to a fact
Not sounds, but his thought, made this place react

Imagine clouds that once covered a vast sky
Which suddenly dissipated leaving vision to these eyes
This brought a clearly driven halt to my position
As I became more than a listener with mediocre recognition

The universal expression eternity carries with time
Mundane moments fall to matters sublime
The one who dare lives when one is not
lives as a companion-attacker of spiritual rot.

Paul Rigoli, Grade 12
Hutchinson Central Technical High School

Thunderstorms

As I watch from my window
Dark clouds race across the sky, blocking the sun.
Sitting on my window seat
I watch as the first raindrops fall gently.
They *ping* on my roof, my sidewalk;
The rain falls simply everywhere.
As I stare outside, the thunder rumbles,
Lightning flashes.
I see my breath fog the glass,
Feel the cold radiate from my window.
The barely restrained violence of the storm is audible,
And the raindrops become aggressive,
Falling to the ground viciously.
And as the storm rages,
I sip my hot chocolate,
And I watch from my window.

Bridget Eng, Grade 10
Oyster Bay High School

Shut Out

Your eyes have shut me out of your mind
You've let go of me like another memory
The cries within are showing throughout
Just let it go and never turn back
The time is dark and without a sound
The feeling is gloomy
Your screams are heard within your soul
It's maybe more than what you see,
This world as you wish
There's more to life than what you imagine.
Just let go
And envision.

Adalene Lam, Grade 10
Plainview Old Bethpage/JFK High School

The Nook

Lounging in the nook cornered in her living room,
She noticed how the colorless sky met the white snow
At a smooth angle in the distance.
Beginning as a dark grey,
Melting into a ragged white,
Reminding her of icicles which reflect the shades
Of a horrible storm.

She imagines the thick, heavy snow
Weighing down the sky, and becoming night.
She watches trees whip ice at the streets,
Clouds throw sleet on her roof,
The wind banging and crashing at her front door.

But she is beautiful, and she feels beautiful.
She loves, and only feels his love.
She dreams, and only dreams for him.

The storming night, sweeps and blows
And she drowns out the whistles of the wind,
Only hearing his voice.
She is within his arms,
And that is her only concern.

Cassandra Schrantz, Grade 12
Clarence High School

Destiny

Untouched, undressed, but alive

When I came out my mother's womb
She never left my side
She loved me dearly and always cared
Stepping into different communities
She was never scared
Not really knowing my destiny
Or why I am me
Searching and finding became my dream
In a political and social world
Being the best I could be
Is what my mother wanted for me
She wanted me to never settle for less
In my decisions I became the best
I learned from my mistakes, turn them around so that
My actions will pave the ground
Because of my choices
That is why I am me
My background is history
Because of the love of my family now I am

Touched, dressed, alive

Joi Wilkins, Grade 12
Commack High School

Black Crow

Dost thou mock me, Sinning Bird
For sins worthy of Black Crow
Dost thou mock me, Grinning Bird
Then thou must mock him also
Thou dost mock me, Sinning Bird
For temptations not denied
Thou dost mock me, Grinning Bird
For sins that lead to lies

Desirae Trumble, Grade 12
Pulaski Jr/Sr High School

As if the Sky Was Falling

We rush our way
through our lives
Never stopping to see
the good things pass by

Never looking out
at the beauty of our time
You don't realize
what you left behind

Place to place
choosing a road
What lies down the other
you'll never know

We run around like
the end is near
Ignoring emotions
never shedding a tear

As if it's the end
you're calling and calling
maybe it's 'cause you think
the sky is falling

Denise Deegan, Grade 10
Stella Maris High School

Hero

Last day to become a hero
I know the time has come
As I march into battle
Beneath the blood stained sun
Images flash before me
Of times happy and sad
As I see my enemies faces
Expression scared and mad
My heart pounds like a hammer
I can almost hear it beat
As I pick up my weapon
And struggle to my feet
I wonder what they will talk of
When someone brings up my name
A son a father a husband
Or a hero in his day

Christopher Costanzo, Grade 12
Earl L Vandermeulen High School

Supplication

A letter of meticulous thought and fornication,
Stamped with the emblem of final justification,
Embedded in the lifting arms of culmination,
Is scorched by the flesh of deaf termination.

Aleksandra Neboga, Grade 11
Laguardia Arts School

Failed Expectations

On Monday you hope by next Tuesday you will be able to forget.
But no, Regret is like a drop of fire
Scorching every emotion, chocking every sound, mutilating the rhythms of the heart,
Leaving behind a rubble of smoke and destruction.

A month after Tuesday your heart returns to its old routines.
Regret withers with time
Black fades to white, deceiving the eyes of its texture and taste
You walk into the morning air cold with freshness from the moist soil,
Transparent of the looming dust of daily grind.
But a spring morning cannot resist the rising of the sun
Spreading light on to all things while drying up the ground you tread
The moisture of the earth vaporizes you sense
The wave of dust encroaches your expectations
Burying your alive under the weight of Regret.

Months later Regret is a reservoir of unshed tears
It collects the daily drop of brine from you eyes
Now, the reservoir crumbles and
Your heart cries out from the beatings of old expectations.
Your mind questions the bleak unknown as it journeys through the sea of bitterness
And you know that the thrashing waves and terrible lightning will never rest.

Jingwen Hu, Grade 11
Brighton High School

How Daddy Died

Lil boy says, "Mama, how Daddy die?"
Mama says, "All you need to know is that he lived."
    "But I heard you and your friend talking and this is what you said…"

Daddy was a hero
He stepped in front of a bullet meant for an elderly woman
Death took him and shook him
He screamed and he wept
Clenching his fists
Soaked with his sweat
Trying to breathe his last breath
Trying to take one last look at the world
But all he could think about was his wife his son
His baby girl
Doctors rushing him into the emergency room
But it was too late he died too soon
Now he's six feet under the cold dirt
Leaving everyone feeling so hurt

Lil Boy says, "Mama when I asked you how Daddy died, that's not what you said,
    But I already knew why Daddy was dead"

Johnkarlo Velázquez, Grade 10
Bronx Academy of Letters

The Way It Feels

Feeling all depressed inside
Wondering why my eyes never dry
The pain begins to run so deep
So I begin to weep

I have a piece missing in my heart
A mystery but don't know where to start
It hurts like my veins are about to explode
And I constantly feel like I can't hold

I wanna explode because the pain runs so deep…
That I can hear my heart beat

And my blood flows through the veins
That wanna explode…
So I sit all day and weep
Until I find that missing piece

But until then it remains a mystery
While I feel all depressed inside
Wondering why my eyes never dry
The pain begins to run so deep…

Ashley Lopez, Grade 10
Bronx Academy of Letters

Playground Sounds

After school I walk to the playground
I sit back in the old familiar swings.
The wind gently moves me back and forth
As kids around me play and laugh.

I close my eyes; the sound of the playground engulfs me.
Sound of children ringing through my ears.
"Higher, higher," one kid says.
Yes, the familiar sounds of the playground.

Hands clapping excitedly
The great game of pattycakes.
But then all of a sudden, a bawl
As one kid falls down to his knees.

Loud bangs against the cheap plastic
As they jump up and down the slides.
Little scurried feet along the pavement.
The creaking sound of swings.

This playground is full of feelings
Feelings that I once used to feel.
Occasionally, I enjoy spending time here
Reminding myself of those memories.

Beverly Mah, Grade 11
New Hyde Park Memorial Jr/Sr High School

Wonders

It's the little things you do,
not everything you say,
that come to mind when asked,
why I feel this way.

What lies beyond your smile,
is something I am unaware.
It would be a lie to say,
I don't miss you when you're not there.

Wishing and hoping,
yes, all of this is true.
It's not the fear of wanting
but longing to be with you.

Your inner thoughts shine through your eyes,
how deeply they do gleam.
If what we are feeling is mutual,
could this only be a dream?

Briana Nussbaum, Grade 11
Douglas MacArthur High School

Just Us Two

Let's say we'll be together just us two.
Whatever happens let's pray we'll always make it through.

I know I may not say it half as much as I should
But when I say I love you
That will always be for good.

When all else fails and there's no one to turn to
I'll be the person that's always there for you

Promise that until the very end
We'll always be together
And always be best friends.

We've held on tight for so long
I never believed anything could be this strong.

Lauren Richardson, Grade 11
DeSales High School

Golden Fall

The leaves are red and yellow
The weather is no longer mellow

I love the sound of the crushing of the leaves
But for others it could be a pet peeve

As I would walk on the wet ground
I love the sound of the loud pound

The air is cold and brisk
On my face I enjoy the cold wet mist

As I look at the sky I can see the grey dark clouds
It is the season of no sounds

Cara Casalino, Grade 11
Stella Maris High School

The Empty Chair
Empty and bare
So lonely it is as I stare
Big and square
Sits my dog's chair

So beautiful and white
I would hold him so close and tight
He was full of life
He was such a delight

Now he is resting
With sorrow, my heart is so bare
But in my dreams
He will always be there

Brielle Hills, Grade 11
Vincent Smith School

Life of the Animals
'Life of the eagle'
Soaring through the woods
Flying over people
Flying over cities
Diving towards the water
Grasping to the fish
Flying for freedom

'Life of the deer'
Ambling through woods
Sniffing the fresh air
Jumping around the woods
Sleeping by the trees
Heading toward the family to become food

'Life of the beaver'
Swimming in the water
Collecting wood for the house
Sleeping with the gang

Scott Farrell, Grade 10
North Tonawanda High School

Time Flies
Wow the time flies!
Almost four years have gone by,
Since we entered high school
As just freshmen thinking we were cool.

Always on the go,
Barely ever at home,
Involved in clubs, sports,
And dances of every sort.

We have created so many memories,
Sometimes followed by apologies.
No matter what has happened,
These are the years we will never forget.

Angie Donadio, Grade 12
DeSales High School

Fear
Everyone has a fear in his or her life.
Whether it is that monster under your bed or something really dramatic.
Fears are not very easy to overcome.
You can grow out of the fear of the monster but,
It is hard to overcome the fear of dying.
You know it happens every day but you never know when it is your turn.
And that is the scary part.

Jessica DelGiudice, Grade 10
Smithtown High School West

I Am the Creature
I am mistreated and misunderstood.
I wonder if there's another like me.
I hear people screaming.
I see people laughing.
I want a friend.
I am mistreated and misunderstood.

I pretend people like me.
I believe the creator will make another like me.
I touch my face and feel my tears.
I feel as if no one understands me.
I worry I'll be alone forever.
I cry because people look down on me.
I am mistreated and misunderstood.

I understand I'm ugly.
I say who cares about looks.
I dream one day people will look beyond my physical appearance.
I hope people can come to see I'm not a monster.
I am mistreated and misunderstood.

Brittney Walter, Grade 11
Maria Regina High School

Engraved Memories
I'm looking at a stone
I remember my moments spent with her
Sending kisses over the phone
Going to the flea market early on Saturday mornings
Couldn't wait for her next home cooked meal
Playing in the swings outside
Her beautiful garden
Helping her with anything I could
She called me her nurse
I remember the hot summers and mosquitos
I remember her always leaving during the night while I slept
I didn't want her to leave
She always told me she loves me
The garden is now dying
The swing is now lonely and rusty
The kitchen is now empty
No one to send a kiss over the phone
I'm standing here looking at a stone with her name engraved in it
My memories forever engraved in my heart

Giavarna Faison, Grade 10
St. Joseph High School

Summer

The impending summer:
sunshine virtually raining down
on us every day,
catching us happily stepping outside,
enjoying the day ahead of us
and what it brings.
We laugh about the past school year,
what was cool, what was fun, what was typical;
we think of only the good memories,
never dwelling on the unpleasant ones;
it keeps us smiling
and makes us content.
Thinking of the stories to be shared
by the bonfire at night under the moonlit stars:
a beautiful evening
too glorious to keep to ourselves.
This is summer.

Dona Yu, Grade 11
Bay Shore Sr High School

The Light vs the Darkness

With every moment of time that's passed,
The day grows near and shall arrive
For what's envisioned upon some minds
The light and the darkness intertwine
The war's begun and now to end
The dark and white lighters now will clash
For once the soldiers rise, all things shall fall.
The master of all good is God
The leader of all evil is devil
The mightiness of masters of both sides
This will confirm who has the stronger will.
The light will overcome the darkness of the world.
Every man and woman choose
Which side that they will be upon for when the time will come.
Everything about this world will become meaningless
Compared to that of needs that each man has.
But to this day, for what is stronger in one's heart?
What have people chosen, light or dark?

Tyler Cho, Grade 10
Townsend Harris High School

Covet

Long-limbed, square-built
Amazonian
Dark-haired, squat, lustrous
Flashing emerald eyes
Generous mouth
Alabaster, but sun burnt in the summers
Lantern-jawed
Sure-footed
Distinct voice, sonorous, but rich
Poised, handsome
Fatherly, sympathetic, magnanimous, best friend
Alas, I have no brother, but
Maybe my son

Jackie Abbatiello, Grade 12
W Tresper Clarke High School

Life Is...

Life is the first winter snowfall —
spectacular, breathtaking, amazing, beautiful;
like the falling snowflakes,
we are unique, special, worthy of life.

Life is the bloom of the first spring flower —
miraculous, wonderful, brilliant, beautiful;
like the petals that open up,
we celebrate our beautiful and creative minds.

Life is the celebrating fireworks of summer —
tranquility, enchantment, excitement, beautiful;
like the colors that brighten the sky,
we shine, glimmer, sparkle.

Life is the crisp autumn air —
refreshing, mind opening, magnificent, beautiful;
like the ever-changing autumn leaves,
we express our true colors: freedom, sovereignty;

the power to be you, the power to be me.

Life is pure magic, thrilling in every way.
Like the four seasons of miracles and joy,
celebrate life —
life is beautiful.

Kaye Bassarath, Grade 12
Clarence High School

I Wish My Love Was Just Enough

I wish my love was just enough
To get you through the day,
To build you up, to make you think,
To help you find a way.
I wish my love was just enough
To show you that I care,
To wrap my arms around you,
And to let you know I'm there.
I wish my love was just enough
To pass the empty time,
To push the pain, to hide the hurt,
To make your life sublime.
I wish my love was just enough
To live as though it's true,
To dance inside a lifetime,
And to dream of something new.
I wish my love was just enough
For you to love me back,
To follow me, to ask for me,
To know of all I lack.
I wish my love was just enough for you.

Andrea Diminick, Grade 11

You
The memories of you stab me right through my heart.
They pierce,
Making me unable to breathe.
When I see you,
I feel my body become a flame,
Ready to burn down anything in its way.
I would rather the earth swallow me
Than have to ever see you again.

Katie Bonilla, Grade 10
Oyster Bay High School

I Can Make a Difference…
I am only one
But yet, I can make a difference
It doesn't matter whether I have money or fame
For all it takes is the power of one
I don't need to make a huge speech or fight in a vigorous protest
I don't need to travel the world or solve social unrest
Just in my own little world, I can make a difference
For all it takes is a smile to begin a friendship
Or a touch to show you care
All it takes is one word to start a movement
Or a heart that judges fair
I may not be able to rally for a cause
Or question national policy
But by being a light to those in darkness,
And guiding those who are mistaken,
I can make a difference with every action I am making
For even if I am only one
I can make a difference!

Jeena Joji, Grade 10
New Hyde Park Memorial Jr/Sr High School

Moving On
When we look into the future things tend to get a little blurry,
But don't be afraid there is no reason to worry.
The past is over and you can't change what you have done,
So look at life as an adventure, filled with surprises and fun.

As you look up at the stars you wonder what time has meant,
So many things could have been better, so much effort better spent.
All those memories both good and bad have gone by so fast
But it's time to move on and not dwell in the past.

Going to college next year seems hard to believe,
There are so many more things that I hope to achieve.
Now is the time to be mature, independent, and free,
The hardest decision will be choosing which university is a match for me.

No matter where I go I will always do my best,
If I work hard and shoot high I am destined for success.
Soon I will bid my friends and family a solemn good-bye,
Always live life to the fullest and reach for the sky.

Robbie Gilles, Grade 12
DeSales High School

At the Coney Island Freak Show

Two demons fought on the pinhead's chest
On a canvas of ink and skin
And he lifted the nail and the hammer, too
And flashed us a crooked grin

And he fit the nail to the hole in his flesh
And tipped his bowler hat
And the tap tap tap of the hammer sang
And purred like a satisfied cat

Then I wanted to scream, but I couldn't avert
My eyes from the dreadful show
And he showed no pain as he hammered away
At least, none that we could know

And the goth girls in anarchy t-shirts
With swastikas carved in their arms
Who had paid their ten dollars to see evil things
Wished they had the performers charms

For he wasn't a self-proclaimed rebel
Of whom we could be forgiving
But he was a beautiful hammering man
Who did this for a living

Mira Gutoff, Grade 12
Huntington High School

Time

We all know our time is coming.
We all know we have to leave this place called Earth.
Time is running out,
And we all rush to do all the things we wanted to do in life.
We all make mistakes, but all that remains
Is the regret of what could have been,
Instead of wishing for what could be better.
In times of sadness, we all become closer
And make up for the times that we lost.
Because knowing that we lost time
Can be like a punch in the stomach.
We all take in a sharp breath,
And realize the bruise lasts longer than the pain.
It stays etched into our memory,
Fading slowly as time goes by.
So let's take the regret we have
Along with the memories
And make newer, happier memories
Because tomorrow
The sun will still shine
And make our happier memories shine in the gray cloudy sky.

Rosa Yoo, Grade 10
Smithtown High School West

The Garden

I can see the garden in front of my eyes
What is between us is not a sweet fragrance
But cold course metal bars
Bars that only want me to suffer
And they do
They keep me
Out of the garden
But they still let me see
What I cannot have
A place full of magic and wonder
Where the water is as clear as air
So crisp so clean so perfectly pure
But I am still so far away
I can taste the water but I am still thirsty
I can see the fruits but I am still hungry
I can see the gate but I cannot open it
All I want is that perfect garden
To spend just a moment in its borders
But no matter how much I want to go
My feet won't allow me

David Gold, Grade 11
Solomon Schechter Middle-High School of Long Island

Hurt

Tears of sorrow I waste today
Feels like my life just fades away
I mark my calendar day by day
Waiting for the pain to go away
In school I'm counting to ten
This painful pressure builds up again
I'm starting to cry because it hurts so much
How I remember your gentle touch
To let it out I must cry
I wish I was still with this guy
I want to forget him but it doesn't work
So I start to think why was he such a jerk?
It's hard to smile when your heart is bleeding
I don't want to admit it but it's him I'm needing
Even though this hurts so badly
I would still do it all again

Diamond Brown, Grade 10
Bronx Academy of Letters

11:24

It's hard to describe what the eye can see
I can only reveal with my pen, my paper and me.
It's almost as if I'm blind yet,
I can see perfectly.
It is my inspiration,
At moments my mind can freeze,
Drop everything
Only breathe.
It calls to my attention,
Like you call to me
Letting me know that,
I can see.

Dylan Payne, Grade 11
Spencerport High School

Anxiety

I try to hold in my heart,
Pouring from my chest,
But it flows and floods
Onto the paper as I write this,
The hole ejecting it,
Burn ebbing around the edges
In hurt
Fear
Worry
Anxiety
Fear of
Rejection
I scream through gritted teeth,
Tears leaking from my eyes now,
Tossing and turning in my bed
As I clutch my aching chest,
Wondering what the next day will bring.

Brittani Doran, Grade 12
Madison Central School

Liberty's Light*

Marching over lives
Lost in the fight for freedom
We must carry on

Ever valiant men
Fighting on for liberty
Never turning back

To here we were led
By the Lady Liberty
She guides us forward

The light of freedom
Can never leave our full hearts
Long as we are one

Shanyce Spain, Grade 10
Townsend Harris High School
*Inspired by Delacroix's
"Liberty Leading the People"

Man vs Wild

The river was calm that morning
It was more pristine than water itself
The jagged peaks of the mountain
Reflected upon this azure glass
A picturesque scene
Fauna living in peace, uninterrupted
Until man reigns down
Speedboats, picnics, noise
This picturesque scene defiled
The azure glass shattered

Ganesh Thippeswamy, Grade 12
Ward Melville High School

My Home*

I am from the midnight skies illuminated by the delicate stars,
I am the soft grass made moist with dew.
I am from the blurs and swirls of daydreamt thoughts,
I am the lazy days and heat from the sun.
I come from a place where silence has more meaning than words;
From bright colors, new ideas, and intricate details,
I am the laughter that signifies happiness.
I am from beyond the trees in the forest,
I am the mist that sits upon the mountains.
I come from a place no one knows quite as well as I do,
I am me.

Kamila Buraczynski, Grade 12
Cicero-North Syracuse High School
*Inspired by "Where I'm From" by George Ella Lyons

I Can Make a Difference By...

Making a difference is not as easy as it seems.
The first step is working together in teams.
Working together to get the job done,
Can be easy and sort of fun.
If one person takes charge, others will follow too.
Facing tough obstacles, and making it through.
Everyone must be smart and strong,
And figure out ways so that everyone can get along.
Making new friends and accepting someone that is not alike,
Could result in a friend that you truly like.
Acceptance is a major issue,
But doing it can be an important breakthrough.
So accept people, for whom they truly are,
And just being a good friend will get you very far.

Dolores Yovino, Grade 10
New Hyde Park Memorial Jr/Sr High School

My Grandpa

My grandpa grew up back when the stock market crashed,
he grew up in a little poverty, but was never spiritually bashed!
As he got older my grandpa went to school and learned a lot,
he did his homework, and put his grades in a good spot!
Later on in his illustrious life of school,
his life would not turn out to be so cool!
You see my grandpa ended up being a drill sergeant in the Korean war,
he lead his troops through battle grounds, into dangers, explosions and more!
There were many nights when his troops and himself could have died,
but he acted on his wits and steered them to safety, with pride!
He never left them alone, and always was the hero, this is true,
he even went as far as to put himself in front, I think it's noble don't you?
As the Korean war came to an end, he got out of the army with a smile,
he knew that the war was over, now he could relax awhile.
My grandpa found the right woman, when he met my grandma, her name was Joan,
he asked her if they could be wed, so he wouldn't have to be alone.
Within the years my grandpa grew older and more wise, along with joan, his wife,
so happy and carefree, he lived a good life.
In the year 2004 he died, months later his wife, my grandma died with love, so
this poem was to amend all of his achievements, his brains, nobility,
and to tell the world, "I love my grandpa!" and I always pray to him above.

Shannon Metcalf, Grade 10
Cincinnatus Central High School

A Cinema Scene

It was a chilly fall day
In a small northern town
We stood under a golden crispy tree
The leaves were all falling down

My eyes brimmed with salty tears
Yours twinkled green against the dull gray sky
It was hard for me to let you go
Seemed impossible to say good-bye…

As we faced that homeward road, I clung to you tight
I didn't want to drive away from you
Into the desolate night

It may have seemed a cinema scene to someone passing by
Lovers' sweet farewell kiss, but I'm trying so hard not to cry
I know I'll see you soon, yet I have so much left to say
I promise to save my love for you
When I see you that near day

Molly Gutschow, Grade 12
DeSales High School

Late for School

I overslept again, I'm late for school
Rush out of bed with a zoom,
Will I make it for homeroom?
Turn on the water; great, it's freezing cold
What else can go wrong? The answer was about to unfold.
I have to get dressed, but there's nothing to wear.
Grab a shirt and jeans; oh, I forgot my hair!
Open my drawer, what now, I'm out of gel.
I have to start running, now my mom begins to yell.
Take off out the door, just in time to grab a bite
The taste of burnt toast, oh, just to my delight.
I can't see the bus, it must have already gone.
Start sprinting to school, running through my lawn.
I can see the school ahead, I'm almost there.
And then I stop, as if in a nightmare.
I see my friend; he says "You want to go play?"
"What?" I said, today is Saturday.

Amit Persaud, Grade 10
Sewanhaka High School

That Morning

I got up that morning all happy and fine,
When I saw the sun pop up and shine,
"What a day it is going to be!
I'm going to school to learn and do good deeds."
But little did I know the horror that happened,
When 9/11 was around the corner.
I tried to run as fast I could —
From fears and my worries.
As I ran, I tripped and fell.
I had to face the painful, malicious truth.
Till this day I can't believe,
The tragedy that fell on New York City.

Sueliz Melendez, Grade 12
Williamsburg Charter High School

That September Day

The air was crisp on that September day,
Streets filled with the usual traffic delay,
Today, I stopped to get a coffee at a corner cafe.
First came the sound and then the cries,
Confusion filled eyes as they gazed to the skies,
But then came the sirens and rush of brave guys.
Fire! Fire! Way up there!
But without any time to say a quick prayer,
One crumbled, no longer a pair.
Upon me came a more horrifying sight,
Men jumping from that great height,
As if they had at all no fright.
Still watching, a tear rolled down my cheek,
But I jerked as a lady let out a shriek,
My husband! As her knees fell weak.
Even worse was yet to come,
The second had now succumb,
Stepped on like a tiny crumb.
Looking down at the cup in my hand,
I simply could not understand,
Ten minutes late, surely it was planned.

Jillian Muhlbauer, Grade 10
Kellenberg Memorial High School

I Can Make a Difference By…

There's nothing that can tell me
What I can and cannot do
If the world can only change me
Why can't I change it too?

For I can make a difference
The world will have to see
It will shine with all my brilliance
A change you will envy

When I think of the world
I dream of a place that can be
I dream of it uncurled
Where all the dreams can live free

A difference is a grand thing
And my imagination goes wild
When I think of what I can do to the world
I feel like an ignorant child

With one little thing someone can do
The difference is for the world and for you
Picking up the garbage and trash that you see
Helps our world prosper, benefiting you and me

Stephanie Wilches, Grade 10
New Hyde Park Memorial Jr/Sr High School

Sailing

It feels as though I was a boat tied to a dock and then suddenly someone came and untied the knot. Every day that passes by I'm drifting away with no one's love, care, or comfort. I'm just slowly disappearing, without a soul noticing me. Once in a blue moon, the wind makes attempts to push me back. BUT then a storm manages to succeed and now I'm floating on rough tides that's pulling me with them FAR, FAR, AWAY. No longer is the dock in sight. At this moment, I'm separated more than before. All I wish for, is that the wind finds a way to stay behind my shields and push me back to MY DOCK.

Christie Haskins, Grade 12
Abraham Lincoln High School

Where I'm From

I am from a big family,
When one holiday party can wake up a whole town
I am from a street full of kids,
If we don't play after school the day feels unfinished.
I am from summers of man hunt every night,
We always beg our parents, "Please, just 5 more minutes!"
I am from long drives to Lake George every August with my family
As a group of almost 20 people we fill restaurants and stores
It doesn't matter if I wander around the hotel; I always bump into a family member sooner or later
I am from watching sports and horse racing with uncles
And watching grown men yell at a game or race on TV, even though they know no one else can hear them
I am from my backyard,
With the shed roof we climbed on without telling mom and the popped water balloons melted into the grass
I am from, "Mom, do I have to?" and "I don't want to clean my room."
I am from home cooked meals and sitting at the dinner table as a family.
I am from eating take-out in front of the TV to watch American Idol.
I am from a loving and caring family,
I am from my home.

Rachel Conley, Grade 10
Smithtown High School West

The Great Mughal Empire

The Mughal Empire is known as the Great
To which many empires could not possibly relate!
Babur set out from Ferghana, his native land,
Where he established his people in India, and began to expand.
Akbar, more commonly known as the Great King,
To which no other emperor could relate a thing.
He was tolerant of both the Hindu and Muslim people
And formed his own religion, Din-e-Ilahi, that differed from the church with the steeple.

As it had been done time and time before
The men of the family fought to become the mighty successor
It started with Babur and ended with Aurengzeb,
With the Great Akbar second and Shah Jahan not far after him.
Though there many accomplishments of their time,
Art was most definitely the prime.
There is the Taj Mahal which still stands until today,
And there were many other artworks that are gone, probably due to decay.

Like every beginning comes with an end
The status of the Mughal Empire began to descend!
When the taxes were reinstated, economy fell, and corruption broke out,
It all led to the fall of the Empire without a doubt!

Aliza Altman, Grade 10
Townsend Harris High School

Daybreak's Eyes

Looking into daybreak's eyes
Cups of coffee in the tears she cries
Deep red smile like the blood in our veins
No sunrise is ever quite the same

Rain falls from daybreak's eyes
Letting go of nighttime's ties
Broken hearted and all alone
Trailing glitter like the sun she's shone

Light streams from daybreak's eyes
No small feat after all your lies
Recovering slowly from the aftermath
"Cover up honey, there's a draft."

Erin Mayer, Grade 11
Floral Park Memorial High School

rain glorious

i didn't know her eyes; they were hidden by the rain.
her sigh sang tired through the mist,
swept from her hood, umbrella echoed,
try to catch her fingers, loose and light, thin and listless
next to mine, clutching and forever reaching,
drawing patterns in her palm
that yields to tracery and fondness.
beseeching silence in november rain, tranquility and calm.
why do you love me in the rain?
(hair curled on dampened sweatshirt framed by lights
on the city street, the darkened lane,
curls coiled around gray eyes that spend nights
lonely on too-white pillows) i love the rain, her unyielding gaze,
we share out like thieves the glory of nights and days.

Mark Chiusano, Grade 12
Stuyvesant High School

Self-Portrait

Looking at the self-portrait I see that
Even after all the troubles
She decided to go on living again
Looking at her now
She erased all her bad memories and
Depends on her good ones
To relax again
To smile again
To laugh again
Even embarrassed and afraid of what people would think
She makes new friends
She trusts again
She loves again
Having all this courage
Enough to share
She faces her fears
And starts living again
Realizing I'm my own hero

Lucelys Popoter, Grade 10
Bronx Academy of Letters

Snowflake

Flakes of white are plowing down,
They pass the trees and hit the ground,
I stand outside, my arms outstretched,
Hoping for my tongue to catch,
A vibrant, vapor flake of white,
That I may be able to meet tonight.

Julie Tortora, Grade 10
Oyster Bay High School

Modern Crusader

Here I stand
Upon the tallest peak
Staring into night's light
The light that shines from the past
I glance into this light, questioning and puzzled
I wonder where my life has gone
I wonder where the world has gone
I wonder where those dreams have gone
The dreams of the people who desired to change our world
Those dreams are gone

Now we stand here
Upon the tallest peak
Staring into the morning's light
The light that shines into the future
We stare into the light understanding and fulfilled
We have discovered a new life for us all
We have discovered a world worth living
We have fulfilled those dreams of our own
The dreams that are pure, righteous, and fair
Those dreams are of God

Sal Rosa, Grade 11
Bishop Ford Central Catholic High School

Sadness

When I'm sad I like to write
My feelings down in black and white,
It helps me to realize what caused the pain,
It helps shed some light,
On what brought this darkness and rain,
It's a feeling we experience from time to time,
Like happiness, depression and loneliness inside,
Sometimes this emotion makes me cry,
Especially when someone close to me dies,
Or when I hear bad news about someone I know,
These are the times my sadness really shows,
Writing gives me some relief,
It sometimes helps when I'm filled with grief,
Other times I try to pretend,
That I'm not really sad and hope this feeling comes to an end,
I guess it's all about life and learning to cope,
I try dreaming and wishing not giving up hope,
That this feeling of sadness,
Will eventually pass,
That I will soon be happy again, at last.

Ashley Maglione, Grade 11
Stella Maris High School

Blameworthy Ember
How do you do it
Stand for what is wrong
Kill our heroes
And leave us helpless
Trying to take it all
When there was too little to be had
Daniel Huenger, Grade 11
Douglas MacArthur High School

Winter Day
White, dusty coating
Snow crackles beneath my feet
Cold reddens my face.
Soft inside layer
Comfort and relaxation
Hood stuck in my hair.
Chalk on the chalkboard
Quiet swish. To my relief
The bell resonates.
Getting off the bus
Cold air whips my face, my hair
Blowing all around.
At my house, I sit
Happy and warm from the fire
My wet socks drying.
Milk pours in a cup.
I stir in the chocolate.
I sip and I sigh.
I go to my room.
Immediately my cold
Head rests and I dream.
Kate Mandracchia, Grade 10
Ward Melville High School

The Dancer's Dance
Soft, slow, and tender,
This feeling will send her.
Peaceful, calm, and flowing,
Into worlds unknowing.

Growing in passion and pace,
Her heart begins to race.
The spirit of it flows,
The pain inside her grows.

Fast and fiery the dance becomes,
Knowing now what she has done.
Moving as the blue birds fly,
Her dance within begins to die.

Winding down the final stretch,
Her breath she now begins to catch.
The dancer's heart is on the mend,
The dancer's dance is at its end.
Katherine Duprey, Grade 12
DeSales High School

Season Dreaming
Winter is my favorite season
All year I dream of winter
I think about it every day
About all there is to do
About all the fun I will have
I sit and wait for the snow to fall
Remembering how good it feels on my whiskers
Remembering the feeling of the snow hitting my face as I ride my snowboard
I feel like the king of the mountain
Free to do whatever I want
Winter is the only season when I am totally happy
Nathaniel Martin, Grade 12
DeSales High School

Blurry
Why can't I save you? Why must you hate?
The sea has decided your fate. Accept.
For the blood shall flow with the river of life even as life departs.
And the ice shall scald all ye broken hearts.
The sun and moon shall develop less
For stars can only shine against darkness
And all the secrets you shall be able to feel
for the pain isn't mine but the tears are real
potential isn't enough but the terror sells
And the salt burns and the blood swells
For she gave the wound by which she died
yet she stares at me now and cries
"death is a debt to nature due
which I have paid
and so must you"
Michelle Currier, Grade 11
Massena Central High School

I Hope You Understand
I hope you understand
that I want to vanish.
I hope you understand
that I am hurting and I am in pain.
I hope you understand
that every single time you ask me if I am okay and I say
I am,
It's a lie.
I hope you understand
that if I outright tell you I am not okay all you can do is convince me that I am.
I hope you understand
that I am mad at you,
not only you but this whole world including myself.
I hope you understand
that I hide everything because I don't want you to know.
I hope you understand
that the tears you have witnessed me shed,
Is all you are going to get to be able to decipher who I am and how I truly feel.
I hope you understand
that my greatest wish is to vanish.
Kisna Palacios, Grade 10
New York City Museum School

Pay Yourself First

Love yourself for who you are,
Believe that hands down you will go far.
Don't expect others to know you first.
Trust yourself and try not to get lost.
"Keep your head up," is what I say.
We all make mistakes, and it's okay.
We are all humans; yes it's true,
But we are also different,
So know who is you.

Allen Archaga, Grade 10
Brentwood High School

A Winner's Mind

No one has a mind quite like a winner,
They hate to lose, even if they are a beginner.
Whether it's sports, a race, or maybe a test,
They always strive to be the best.
Winners will go through many pains and strife
To be at the top of every aspect of life.
Confidence is a virtue in every winner's head,
Hard work and determination is how champions are bred.
Competitiveness is a cause of every person's success,
After hours of practice, winners do things with great finesse.
Being the best does not come overnight.
But when it is accomplished, you will be filled with delight.
Pain is temporary and pride is forever,
Practice makes perfect, but you can always get better.
A winner's mindset can never be exactly repeated,
If you have thoughts of doubt, you have already been defeated.
They go into each day with their head held high,
They believe in themselves so much,
The only limit is the sky.

Brendan Costello, Grade 11
DeSales High School

Blessed

God, you have blessed love,
Blessed the heavens and this Earth,
Blessed the people.
But, our wickedness destroyed everything.
Now there is no love.
Only lies, lust, and loathe.
We strangled trust,
Betrayed friendship,
Shattered dreams,
Murdered,
Everything that made us humane,
We let fear and pride hide the pain,
Yet still hope remains,
No matter what.
Trust may be renewed,
Betrayal subdued,
Dreams caressed.
Maybe that means we are still blessed,
Even today.

Ikadshi Thukral, Grade 10
Plainedge High School

This Is It

What is love?
Love is sunsets.
Love is holding hands.
Love is brown eyes.
Love is soft green grass.

What is love?
Love is parking lots.
Love is walks in the dark.
Love is movies together.
Love is late night talks.

What is love?
Love is June to July.
Love is July to August.
Love is August to September.
Love is September to October.

Love is a feeling,
A connection,
A moment.
Love is when time stops,
And suddenly you realize,
This is it.

Alexandria Cragg, Grade 11
DeSales High School

Shower

Practice is over
The day is done
My legs are sore after the 2 mile run
The nozzle squeaks
The temperature's right
Keeping me warm on this cool autumn night
I slowly step in
Release all control
I've been pushed to the limit
It has taken its toll
The scent is refreshing
Impurities wash away
So do all the mistakes of the day
Time to start over
With each rising day
It's hard to leave though
I wish I could stay
Dry myself off
My work is now done
Tomorrow it starts again
But for now there is none

Margaret Shaffer, Grade 11
DeSales High School

Last Performance
So, she lay with her own essence
the red mixing in her raven threads
Her cheeks matching the blue tinged lips
as her eyes view the dancing dead
She's unaware of the gathering crowd
as day breaks upon her final hour
Flashing stars seem to fade as
the curtains zip around her
The darkness enveloping her is deep
as she stumbles off stage, her breath gives one last frozen sigh
And so her performance is over
her debut as the
Last Performance

Pa'Seana Nelson, Grade 11
Spencerport High School

Otash
Blood, dust, and the beautiful colors of your robes.
Tattered garbage flapping in the wind. Screaming, crying, with no escape.
And the whites of a thousand eyes, that stare hauntingly.
Your throat is as dry as the sand in which you lie,
Your shelter — a heap of sticks and rags. Your food — a handful of okra
Your lullaby is the pitter patter of machine guns
And where each death in America will make headline news,
In counting the deaths of your people, we must round to the nearest hundredth.
Have we become different species, you and I?
You think of life and death, my worries are, shall I turn this poem in on time?
And what would you think of me writing this poem?
Would you be enraged to see, that I have read the horrors of your life,
And done no more than write this poem?
Would you despair to hear, a literary praise describing
The murder of your friends?
For we shall all write our poems of injustice and inequality.
We shall write them "from the heart" and feel that we have empathy.
But when the day is over, and we are warm in our comfortable beds,
Will we have helped the dying people of Otash?
Will we have made the world a better place?

Sojourner Morrell, Grade 10
The Waldorf School of Saratoga Springs

The Black Rose Under the Cherry Tree
A beautiful red rose lay at my feet,
As I sit under the cherry tree,
Cherry blossoms in full bloom start to fall,
As translucent tears from my eyes start to fall onto the ground,
As do the cherry blossoms.
As I flood the rose,
My broken heart cries crimson tears,
Tears that fall,
Fall forever into a blank void,
As the cherry blossoms fall from the trees,
The tears from my heart forever turning
The beautiful red rose that lay at my feet black

Kasondra Alice Reed, Grade 10
Elmira Free Academy

Wisdom

I saw a man walking proud and tall,
   through the crowd in the mall;
His eyes raised,
   empty and glazed;
He held a stick,
   which he walked with;
His son held his hand,
   leading him best he can;
A frightened look on his face,
   like he was the one out of place;
A tear came to my eye,
   as he kept his head high;
But I knew he had twice the sight,
   any many might.

Philip Papas, Grade 11
School at Northeast

Burden

A sewer stirs behind dark-less light
A shadow casts beyond the night
Water drips like facets of stars
Forgotten dreams, we die in cars
Shadowless figures cascade our fright
A creak, a flash, a line of light
We juggle steps and buttons and flames
Birds of the night we never see again
If a noise above can kill our love
We face a burden undreamed of

Matthew Michaels, Grade 12
Clarkstown High School North

Her

My life began one beautiful morning
I heard her voice
The voice of an angel
My ears were convinced
Not long later I saw the face of an angel
My eyes were amazed
They say no one is perfect
But she is
She is nothing less than spectacular
God's gift to the Earth
I thank Michael Fera
He was the reason for living to me
He introduced me to perfection
I fell in love
Deeply
My life will never be the same
My dreams were changed
My goals in life altered by her
There's not a word that can describe her
All I know is
I love Carrie Underwood more than life itself

Zachary Young, Grade 12
DeSales High School

This Closet of Mine

This closet is mine
and mine to uphold.
Staring at it would mean
understanding my mold.

With pink hats and socks,
and green shoes and black.
With skirts with patterns
to make it all contrast.

With leggings and stockings
and silk bands and masks.
With cashmere and feathers
that eyes can catch.

With gold jeans and blue shorts
and purple coats above
all the other knits and frills
with my red scarf and gloves.

With old shirts and ties
with the names of every hue.
If you dare step in
I'll warn it's not for you.

Zhen Li Zhu, Grade 11
Bronx High School of Science

Saying Good-bye

I thought I could get over you,
but you stay on my mind.
I just can't find a way
to let go of you,
you keep my feelings deep inside.
There's no way I can
express them out
unless you're right here by my side.
I can't help but wait
loving you and loving
me at the same time.
You keep my lips from speaking,
all I could do is cry.
Many days I questioned you,
but realized
that it didn't matter to you.
I feel that whatever
I say to you will
help you to survive.
So take my advice 'cause I'm saying good-bye

Ebony Nance, Grade 10
Academy of Urban Planning

I Am Victor Frankenstein

I am intelligent and ambitious
I wonder if I can make a creature
I hear the regret of my conscience
I see something much grander
I want to reach brilliance
I am intelligent and ambitious

I pretend that I did nothing wrong
I feel regret for what I did
I touch this monster, so strong
I worry that I won't be able to get rid
I cry about my mistake all night long
I am intelligent and ambitious

I understand that this is my entire fault
I say that people shouldn't be like me
I dream about William's assault
I try to be responsible fully
I hope I can reconcile for something that's my fault
I am intelligent and ambitious

Kasie Maiolo, Grade 11
Maria Regina High School

I Came to Lead

Words echo in the realm of the world
Whose road I follow.

The winding and twisting length
Extends beyond what sight
Used to be for sore eyes.
And yet, the sunshine, the reflection,
The luminescence of the stone
Is all apparent, too visible, on
Whose road I follow.

Voices sounding, first whispering,
Slightly chanting;
Only miniscule a threat is posed
Before knowing the secrets to
Whose road I follow.
And only then will I embrace
The meaning to the echoes themselves,
And the snaking, not straight road
That leads to no definitive place.

Whose road do I follow?
I do not know.
But I came to lead.

Theodora Koullias, Grade 12
Staten Island Technical High School

My One and Only You

You are my favorite day dream
I couldn't concentrate
Couldn't think straight
You were the only one I could see
You made my heart skip a beat
Put butterflies in my stomach
And made me forget to breathe
You are so beautiful
If only words could say
This is the most alive I've ever felt in years
And you were more than worth the wait.

Stacey Caves, Grade 11
DeSales High School

Playmaker

You've been waiting all day,
And you finally lace up.
You're in warm-ups, the home crowd is already roaring.
When first half is over, the team's only down by 6.
They are all counting on you to make it happen.
As third quarter starts, you're starting to heat up.
Only down by 1 now, your crowd
Is into the game as much as you.
Boston has the ball at the top of the key.
He looks right, then passes left.
You see it coming and jump the pass.
You pick it off going the other way,
Dribble down the court and take off for the big dunk.
Cameras flicker when you throw it down.
You know exactly what the fans
Want to see,
Playmaker.

Taylor Elsner, Grade 10
Massena Central High School

Surviving The Holocaust

As I boarded the train headed for the camp
A terrible stench was in the air and the weather so damp.
My mother and father were shouting my name
I was pushed and shoved until I got on the train.
All we wanted to know was why we were there from the start
Why were these people splitting my family apart?
Parents tried to hold on to their little girls and boys
And I could still hear my mother's voice through all of the noise.
My father was silent and my little sister cried
While my younger brother wiped the tears from her eyes.
The first door to the train was quickly slammed shut
And a terrible feeling pierced through my gut.
We were all very scared, things were not going well
As I was forced aboard the train on the railroad to hell.
What had I done wrong, why was I there?
Why must life be so unfair?
While one of the guards closed the last door
One final teardrop fell to the floor.
I closed my eyes and prayed more than anyone can
But sadly, I never saw my family again.

Anthony M. Troffa, Grade 11
Deer Park High School

My World

By day my life is normal, but at night my dreams are unusual
A flower blooming from the outside, little by little every day you see the true colors,
But eventually this life and place of torture is far from being good
Thinking of the times where the world was nothing but quiet land
The dark shadow was not discovered, it was never ever mentioned.

I guess it is my set to life, can't beat it so I'll join
Thinking of the times when the world was nothing but quiet land
The dark shadow was not discovered, it was never ever mentioned
It is the living crates, which were the one's that made it what it is today
A flower blooming from the outside, little by little every day you see the true colors in,
But eventually this life and place of torture is far from being good
The world is what you do to me, you know how to unpleasant me and carry me in your arms when I fall.
I don't know if I should hang on for long or should I let you drop me when your hands get tired?

Megi Imeraj, Grade 11
The High School of Fashion Industries

Before School

Waking up every morning and doing the same thing I do every day. Brushing, eating, and trying to catch a quick break.
Leaving for school, work.
Where you got to go? I wonder how long I have until I grow up just to get a simple job at a crappy place.
I always ask myself: why does the world seem so cruel today?
People pushing you on the bus, train, trying to get some place on time always with their attitude, I don't even bother because it's just wasting my time.
In a rush gotta go before the bell rings. Because 1st period is always a drag.
I wonder why they ever invented school in the first place. I know it's important but it's just so tiring to get to the classes before the bell rings.
The morning classes are so tiring and then are boring soon you know it you'll be snoring.
But I gotta stay focused.
I gotta stay cool because school's more important then being a fool.

Alisha Noboa, Grade 10
Bronx Academy of Letters

Dear Bugz

Remember in the 8th grade? We used to hang out with each other 24/7
Yeah, those were the good days right? Running in the hallways chasing boys
Sharing secrets with each other mostly about other people though
We were like two cherries connected by one stem wherever one went, the other followed right behind
We were like sisters even though we only knew each other for one year but it didn't matter
We were like a two person music group, without the other artist, it wouldn't be the same
But now that I'm gone a huge part of my life has disappeared
When I left, I left behind all my happiness and most of my life now all I have left with me is sadness
It's like a dark cloud has just appeared over my head and is starting to pour down
When I moved away, I actually cried my eyes out my mother yelled at me
She said that it wasn't that serious but she doesn't know what we've been through together
You know that there's not a day in my life that I wouldn't want you with me laughing by my side
I'm afraid that our friendship will not last that long that it's slowly fading away
Leaving me with nothing to smile about especially when I have my bad days
I wouldn't be able to call you and tell you my issues all that I'm trying to say is that I miss you
I know I probably won't be able to tell you this in person since you're so far away from me
So write me when you get a chance ok
Your best friend no matter what,

Grace Forte, Grade 10
Bronx Academy of Letters

Christmas

Christmas time is drawing near,
It brings great comfort and loads of cheer.
Faraway families reunite,
They cuddle close on Christmas night.
Waiting for Santa to bring all the gifts,
It is one holiday you do not want to miss!
Trimming the tree is one of my favorite things to do,
And hanging the stockings on the chimney too!
The snow falling is a beautiful sight,
Especially when surrounded by Christmas lights.
Christmas is my favorite day,
I hope it never goes away.
Christmas bells ring so proud,
While families bake cookies and sing carols aloud.
Children anxiously await the arrival of St. Nick,
There is no other holiday I would rather pick.
The smell in the house of the evergreen tree,
And putting the angel on top for all to see.
Christmas time is filled with lots of love,
While beautiful angels watch from above.

Megan Lynch, Grade 11
DeSales High School

Lost and Unfound

Raindrops pour down onto earth
Soaking through, bringing tears to rebirth
As wandering souls and rigid shields
Make their way through empty fields

As all defenses fall
All the pain recalled
They'll soar once more

The children's faces looking up
Just wondering what brought them about
All the people walking past are blind
The things that were lost and can't be found

"Ignorance is bliss" they say
But will anyone help these kids one day?
Will they find answers that they've been looking for?
When the people just ignore

Anna Langerman, Grade 12
Laguardia Arts School

Thoughts That Bind

Useless thoughts rush through my head
With all this going on I think to myself why aren't I dead
All these things happening all around me
I just wish I was free
Nothing about me is ever right
All these tears come to me at night
Nothing good can come out of this
It was just a simple kiss
I never did the things you say I did
It's not like I'm a kid
I understand wrong from right
So why don't you fight?
Have I become the cause of this?
From that simple kiss
Useless thoughts rush through my head
With all this happening now I wish I was dead
And now the lesson that I've learned from this
Is that I will never find eternal bliss

Jonathan Pacheco, Grade 11
Urban Assembly Media High School

I Am Victor Frankenstein

I am ambitious and irresponsible
I wonder how great my creation will turn out
I hear horrific hollers
I see the creature as my ruined project
I want to be successful
I am ambitious and irresponsible

I pretend I am not responsible for William's death
I believe I can abandon my creation
I touch the letters of my beloved Elizabeth
I feel exhausted
I worry the creature will kill me
I cry, for my wife has been murdered
I am ambitious and irresponsible

I understand what I've done
I say "Please God forgive me"
I dream of getting revenge
I hope I will succeed
I am ambitious and irresponsible

Elizabeth Kucera, Grade 11
Maria Regina High School

Making a Difference

Picking up trash and throwing it away
You might get caught, but that's okay
Recycling plastic and glass
We're gonna save the rainforest at last!

Cause you're letting people know you care
Letting people know America is rare
Working hard to do something right
Working hard you make America a beautiful sight.

Giving blood and some food
Help the poor, you know you should
Giving a dollar to plant a tree
We're gonna make a difference, just you and me!

And if you do this you will succeed
Also be doing a good deed
So let's fight, fight, and fight to make America the best!
And finally put America's problems to rest.

Neshad Hussain, Grade 10
Elmira Free Academy

Just One

I hold out my hand to the world around
Hoping to find another,
Someone waiting to be found
One simple smile can brighten a day
One drop of trust can open the way
The storm of hate can be controlled
The windy gusts of anger can't uphold
One thoughtful soul can wipe away the tears
One brave mind could chase away the fears
Love can conquer a cloud of hate
One small voice could make the path straight
I can make a difference in a life this twirled
I can make laughter the language of the world
You may think she's too small
She can't do it she can't change it all
But one heart beating with alert
And the eyes seeing all the hurt
Can feel the pain their going through
If only, if only, if only you knew.

Joyce John, Grade 10
New Hyde Park Memorial Jr/Sr High School

Young Poets
Grades 7-8-9

Top Poem Grades 7-8-9

In That Field

the sun is shining,
a shade of orange

a car is left lifeless,
not needed anymore

the wildflowers growing all about,
are like peaceful words that speak out

orange and rusted,
magic is thrusted,
upon this old engine

not knowing why,
laughing to myself
the flood washes over me
remembering memories
deep in my heart,
they now float about

just sitting there for awhile.

Allie Gettino, Grade 7
Camillus Middle School

Top Poem Grades 7-8-9

Don't Forget Grandpa

To My Grandfather,
I remember hearing the news,
I cried right away,
I remember your wake,
On that sad, sad day,
Remember who your family was,
Not by blood but because we cared,
Remember who your family wasn't,
By blood but impaired,
Impaired of the ability,
To value family first,
Impaired of reality,
They knew you'd get worse,
Impaired of compassion,
They only wanted to cash-in,
Impaired of love,
You deserved far above,
Remember our last visit,
Remember how it used to be,
Don't forget Grandpa,
Don't forget me.

Matthew Gilligan, Grade 9
Whitesboro High School

Top Poem Grades 7-8-9

Too Much to Say

Perfect is not so
Perfect after all
It is like putting a square into a circle.

Every day I feel like
Dragging my feet,
But sometimes I feel like flying away.

Sometimes life does
Not make sense
I really don't know why
It is hard enough to be me
But harder not to be me at all.

People say there is something inside me
But I just say it's me as a little person.
Where in life, did I ever go right?
I am always late and always wrong.
Where did I go wrong?

I'm always in a crowded place,
Wishing I were somewhere else
In my own little world, all by myself.
— Just me myself and I.

Michelle Guzman, Grade 9
Bishop Ford Central Catholic High School

Top Poem Grades 7-8-9

Luv

Venus must have blessed her,
Because ever since I saw her,
I was struck by Cupid,
I don't want it to be just my imagination
That we collide,
If my kiss were like a tree,
I'd give her a forest,
If my heart were like water,
I'd give her the seven seas,
If my love were a rock,
I'd give the world,
Her beauty cast a spell on me;
She is the princess of webs
Because my mind is stuck on her
Like a fly to a spider's web.

Jean-Garmel Marcelin, Grade 9
Bishop Ford Central Catholic High School

Top Poem Grades 7-8-9

My Insanity

A paper sits before me, an intimidating blank,
should I write a blissful poem? Or, perhaps a note of thanks?
A beast is acting up inside, tearing up my mind.
It needs a key to set it free, a key I cannot find.

I pray for inspiration, yet none visibly appears.
Could I tell a whimsical tale? Or confess all of my fears?
Time is slowly ticking by, my mind's about to burst!
Nearly an hour floats by, I fear for the worst.

Suddenly I realize the page is almost full!
By writing of my frustration, the beast drops to a lull.
I'm safe from my insanity, at least for one more day.
My relief encompasses my brain and protects it for today.

Kristen McPeak, Grade 9
Maine Endwell High School

Top Poem Grades 7-8-9

I Am

I am young.
Unaware of my surroundings,
Smart, but not wise,
Growing and strengthening.
I am unsure.
Worried about what's unknown,
Knowing, but not all,
Watching and listening.
I am free.
Open to the outside,
Let go, but not untied,
Exploring and investigating.
I am musical.
Creating beats of life,
Composing, but not thinking,
Playing and changing.
I am me.
Different than everyone else,
Great, but not perfect,
Learning and building.

Haley Meltcher, Grade 8
Commack Middle School

Top Poem Grades 7-8-9

The Cave Man

He was always dressed in rags, his pants were tied with a rope instead of a belt,
His two boots did not match, on his nose was the strangest pair of glasses we'd ever seen,
And to us he was the cave man
We taunted him and teased him, we insulted him and mocked him,
We would even throw rocks at him, and to us he was the cave man
His cave was made of trash, there were milk cartons, there were tires,
One piece of junk on top of another that's how he lived
And to us he was the cave man
Whenever we teased him he would run after us and scream,
And we thought it was all a game, we couldn't imagine the pain we brought him
And the shame we brought on ourselves
And still to us he was the cave man
But we will never forget that day
The day the tractors came, and ruined everything
They knocked down the cave he had nowhere to turn
And still to us he was the cave man
We decided to help,
Each day we would bring milk cartons and tires,
Slowly the cave man began to rebuild his cave,
And that's when we realized it, to us he was not just the cave man anymore,
He was our friend.

Ilana Saltzman, Grade 9
Stella K Abraham High School for Girls

Top Poem Grades 7-8-9

Harmony

I want a lake of blue, a sea of green.
Just land, and sea, and harmony.
Yes, harmony, peace, laughter, and love.
Is that what it's like in the heaven above?
I wonder and wish for a life of free.
Just land, and earth, and harmony.
I want to live in a true red land,
With the sky above, and my toes in the sand.
A place for blue, green, and sea.
A land of love, me, and harmony.
The flowers, the sky, the grass of green.
The petals, the blue, the roots of the trees.
All these things, a part of nature.
Do they affect a person's behavior?
The peace, the love, every little thing.
The clouds and the birds, the song that they sing.
A song of joy, happiness, and love.
A place of earth with air that's clean.
That's want I want, a place for me.
I want and NEED a place of love.
Just earth, harmony, and the sky above.

Beth Walters, Grade 8
Hauppauge Middle School

Top Poem Grades 7-8-9

Silver Beauty

Moonlight spills from the night like rain falling from a cloud,
City streets turn silver.
Cat and moon greet each other like a gleam of silver that strikes an eye.
Silent paws splash silver moonbeams in puddles on silver pavement.

City is silent as the two friends tumble and play.
Moon plays hide-and-seek with clouds; cat slips in and out of shadows.
Crickets sing softly, cat purrs in reply.

But the summer night is short,
Silver moonlight soon turns to golden dawn.
Cat must sleep.
He curls his silver back like the sleeping moon.
Twitches his ears as he dreams of his friend.

Alexandra Wang, Grade 9
New York City Museum School

Top Poem Grades 7-8-9

My Hands

The fiery sun beats down on me,
Beats, unsmiling, showing its hate for me.
My body caked, with dirt.
My body aches, with hurt.
My hands, clutching, grabbing, pulling,
I work quickly, as quickly as I can —
Waist deep in water,
My hands, clutching, grabbing, pulling,
I wipe the sweat off my brow,
I stop and look around; only two colors surround me, green and brown.
I wish I could stop
My hands — clutching, grabbing, pulling,
I wish I was the Empress,
Living in the Palace of Terrestrial Tranquility.
Everyone would be able to see,
My hands, adorned with bracelets of gold, and silver and jade.
My hands, soft, small and petite.
But that life is not mine.
My hands, always,
Clutching, grabbing, pulling,
The rice.

Sarah Wu, Grade 9
Townsend Harris High School

Anger

Anger
It's just a twig
You can break one side
But, it's still there
You can never get rid of it
You have to control it
Anger

Jennifer Kroll, Grade 7
Solvay Middle School

Life

When life begins this is how it is:
Life is fun
Life is work
Life is good but sometimes goes bad
Life is boring
Life is sometimes in a rut
But when life ends what happens?
You remember about the people you
helped or helped you, you remember
your friends, you look back to the
good times, you wish to take back the
pain you caused but remember
that little thing, when life begins?
It wasn't so little to that person
that began it.
You need a hint who it is?
She always loved you,
your Mother.

Rrok Ndokaj, Grade 8
St Mary's School

An Ending Road

A sad day
A road that ends
Shattered hearts
Soon will rise again
A teardrop cry
When someone dies
What to expect
From a death
A future comes
Don't want to see
For what to be will be
A voice of sorrow
A box of love
A heart locked up
Never to be seen or heard
The dirt in pile
The person gone
Memories haunt the loved ones
The soul gone with the wind
The laughter still within
The people live, and will love again

Catherine Muhlenforth, Grade 8
Robert Moses Middle School

Stupid Humans

In this world there are many who are thought to be wise,
But much of what they speak is basically lies.
We destroy things around us as if it were a game,
And when our world comes a crumbling, we will know who's to blame.
We slaughter each other because of our differences or for land,
When if we united, our intellect and technology we could expand.
We "terminate" many of our youth,
But if we call it murder they do not wish to hear the truth.
If we injure an animal, it's a terrible crime,
But if someone's starving, people don't have the time.
We spend thousands of dollars on cars, televisions, and toys,
But other places don't have enough money to feed their little girls and boys.
Some say that the Lord is not there,
But if so, the Universe would be bare.
You say that matter can neither be created nor destroyed,
If so, then what is left to fill the void?

Cody Anderson, Grade 9
Holy Cross Academy

Missed Memories

Since I was born I have shed tears about her. I missed her by months…
Why didn't she wait for me? Was there some sort of catch?
Was it said that we could never be together in the flesh?
I can never hold her hands…or give her a hug.
I sometimes question "Would she have liked me?"
I used to think…was it my fault?
Had I not been born I really doubt that she wouldn't be here…
with my family, stopping their unshed tears from ever falling.
Then I blamed God…maybe he didn't like me
doing this wrong just to spite me. Or was he jealous and wanted her back!
Maybe things were just…too good. My family always told stories about her…
Her smile, her personality, her habits,
Not knowing of course that these stories were tearing me apart.
I couldn't join in, I could only listen. Everybody knew how they ended…
because they were there. But I can never say the same.
I would look around looking for some solitude
and see the pictures…of her…that everyone was in,
except for me. But in this sad sorrow I do always feel her presence
Guiding my spirit and leading me softly
But I will never gain these missed memories,
Until the day I meet her, but somehow I feel that she has already met me.

Aiyana Batton, Grade 9
Bishop Ford Central Catholic High School

Eagle Lake

There is a place called Eagle Lake.
We love to go down there for heaven's sake!
I absolutely love swimming in the water,
It belongs to my father, my grandparents, and their daughter.

Eagle Lake is one of my favorite places to be,
I like all the mountains, all and the scenery.
I love it there, and there is no other place my heart would rather be,
All it is, is Eagle Lake and me!

Erik Riley, Grade 8
Holy Cross School

The School System
"Sit down and start your quizzes. Good luck."
Are some student "smart?" I don't think so, maybe they
Just gotta head start.
The school system is whack,
Poor people go to public school.
For what? They don't learn notin'
Rich kids go to private school. Stay educated, get a good job.
The school system is designed
To keep the white kids on top.
While the black kids grab a mop "start cleanin'."
No way, not me,
You buggin' son
I'm gonna go somewhere,
I'm gonna be someone.
I'll invent the next big thing,
I'll discover the next life-saving antidote.
And in the end, all you people
Who put me down
Who didn't recognize, my potential
You gonna recognize and realize,
"I shoulda let that boy fly."
Abdiel Bourne, Grade 8
Nativity Mission School

The Gridiron
A 100 yard field full of grass and dirt
Athletes pacing back and forth
Trying to score touchdowns for their team
The crowd cheering and screaming
The stadium full of light
The crowd watching with full sight
Referees making decisions
Coaches full of excitement from completed plays
The game of football being played in its home
The gridiron!

Daniel Hinson, Grade 9
John Bowne High School

The Starry Night*
Rays of sunlight flashing on me
Stars falling one by one
Standing up so tall I thought I'd never fall
Can't hold on, I'm drifting away
Sun has faded by the day
Out of breath
Everything so silent, so still
Heart is crushed
Throbbing stops
My day has come to an end
As I look above to the sky
I see nothing but emptiness
You have left me in the cold
My mind clouded by darkness
Oksana Yakubova, Grade 9
John Bowne High School
*Inspired by the painting "Starry Night" by Vincent Van Gogh

Snowflakes
Raindrops are usually falling on my head,
Instead, snowflakes are sneaking —
Down from the sky.

Snowflakes sprinkling
Onto every evergreen in sight,
Sparkling in the nighttime life.

Silent snowflakes
Float gradually down the sky
Landing softly on the ground.

Winter wishes are made,
Snowflakes drifting into the unknown,
Sprinkling, sparkling snowflakes.
Meghan Davis, Grade 8
Warwick Valley Middle School

Tech Deck Skateboards
I own about 20 tech decks they're really lots of fun
They keep me busy, all day in the night or in the sun
They are quite the little toy for any boy or girl
Just put them on a table and make them jump and twirl
If you are tired of your other stuff I'll tell you what to do
Just get yourself some Tech Decks they really are cool
Tech Decks are nice Tech Decks are cool
Just watch out for your teachers and never take them to school.
Matt Thompson, Grade 8
Southern Cayuga Middle School

Where I'm From
I am from chicken pox,
to short brown locks.
From little Cinderella,
to my dog Bella.
I am from my two brothers my inspiration.
To my older brother being my main source of transportation.
I am from my best friend Geek-Geek who really wasn't there.
From when I couldn't get the doll and screamed it wasn't fair.

I am from terribly playing my sax,
from when the golfers told me to relax.
From trading in my lacrosse stick.
For my greater pick.
To pretty pink ballet shoes,
from crazy tap moves.

I am from being the best nerd ball.
From my friends picking me up if I fall.
From middle school, to the high school,
from San Diego, swimming in a pool.
To my mom saying no, to saying I have to go.
I am From.
Cathryn Posillico, Grade 9
Harborfields High School

Love of the Game

The squeak of the sneakers,
The painted hardwood.
The sound of a swish,
The colorful uniforms.

Flashes of cameras,
Roar of the crowd.
The beauty of the game,
Love for the sport.

Dedication of the player,
Speed, agility, and talent of the team.
The impatience of the coach,
The bright lights of the scoreboard.

Anthony Blancha, Grade 8
St Mary's School

A New Page

Flip one over
To the next page.
No scuffs, no marks —
Just another chance.
You get to start over
And forget your mistakes.
Try to do better,
Redo things displeasing.
Choices, lifestyle;
Different words on the page.
There's nothing but a shadow
Of the previous page.
Like a forgettable memory —
the future ready to change.

Ivanka Bihun, Grade 8
Most Precious Blood School

My Dad

My dad is my hero
My dad is my friend
My dad was there for me until the end
He will guide me through my life
He will be the bright star in the sky
Watching down on his little angel.

Jillian Callanan, Grade 8
Holy Cross School

Chloe and I

My friend Chloe and I
Will never say goodbye
We are there for each other
Like sisters and brother
We share our thoughts and dreams
About life and what it means
My friend Chloe and I
Will never say goodbye

Elaina Slater, Grade 7
Holy Cross School

The Door

What can come out of that door?
Some people respond and say it's fury, green,
Other say broken sadness,
Or ghosts unknown,
Many simple-minded people respond: just other people,
Deep thinkers mutter: love and fear,
I still, however, cannot see how any of these can come out of that door.

Adam Reichel, Grade 7
Camillus Middle School

My School, My Teachers

Which teacher do I love the most?
Is it Mr. Isola, or is it Mrs. Oakes?
Savvy Mrs. Goldstein, once showed me the math mountaintop.
I'm still climbing every day, thanks to incredible Mr. Cutajar.
Mr. Reinbold taught me to adventure,
In the vast universe of literature.
Mrs. Jasser makes me feel like a curious creature,
In a huge literary pasture.
Mrs. Teoh said, "To science, full speed ahead!"
Smart Mrs. Schrack
Everyday lights the science bulb in my head.
Oh, what would we do,
Without sweet Mrs. Duboff's nuggets of information?
Every day, time spent in Mr. Isola's class is a wonderful celebration.
Mrs. Oakes, my fantastic art teacher, is so very unique.
An artist, an educator, a master of every art technique.
Someday I wish I would be just like Mrs. Sapir.
Helping so many kids by making the obscure, the clear.
My school, P.O.B.M.S., a superfine homestead.
Full of happiness and warmth.
A grandma's house with a warm hearth.

Nidhi Mann, Grade 8
Plainview-Old Bethpage Middle School

Abraham Lincoln and John F. Kennedy

Both studied law.
Both were a part of the military.
Both were name for their grandfather.
Both suffered from depression.
Both could speak French fluently.
Both were married in their thirties.
Both of their wives were previously engaged to someone else.
Both had four children.
Both were related to senators.
Both died on a Friday before a holiday.
Both were concerned with civil rights.
Both were shot in the head.
Both were shot in front of their wives.
Both were killed by people who are known by their three names.
Both assassins were killed before their trials.
Both died while serving as president.

Sonia Seehra, Grade 9
Townsend Harris High School

A Freedom of Silence

In a world where silence is nice,
everyone there has no life.
No joy, no happiness, just sorrow strives there.
No spirit in the morning air
No joy to console you…
But lo' light is here!
No boundaries to adhere!
So speak out in this land of freedom,
And let your voice be heard!

Jordan Yee, Grade 7
Holy Family School

Black and White

It's all gone now
Feeling like there's nothing else to do
You're gone and now
Everything's black and white
I stand in the middle of the field and see what we made
The tree that we created when we were kids
Has grown day by day with our love and care
You're not here and so it has stopped
My life is black and white,
My world
Upside down
Just like our tree of love
I'm just waiting for you to come
So we can make our tree grow once again
I'll wait for you until that last leaf falls

Jennifer Paredes, Grade 9
John Bowne High School

Inside Me

Inside me is the color blue
Like a vast summer sky
It is peaceful and quiet at times;
I am happy.

Inside me there is a bounce of a basketball
Like an unpredictable heart beat;
the "not knowing" what life will bring
but I keep on bouncing.

Inside me is the sound of ocean waves
Like the crashing of words
that can hurt my feelings
Just when it's calm the words crash again
and I am sad.

Inside me there are many questions about my future
Like a book filled with knowledge
The answers I seek will write themselves;
Even if no one knows me in a hundred years
I am a part of history.

Eric Fluty, Grade 7
Schalmont Middle School

8B's Friendship

Now this is a story about friendship
No not just any friendship,
8B's friendship. We got friendship that's good
And friendship that's bad, but it's okay,
Cause we all bounce back. We might feel glad
We might feel mad, but then we remember
The fun times we had. We might argue
We might fight, about a little thing
That isn't right. We may make fun
We may laugh, and we all know
It's just a joke, and we're sorry
If we made you mad, but in the end
We just bounce back. When someone's sad or even mad
We talk to them, to cheer them up.
Even in some classes, we might get tight
Try talking to them, to solve the problem
But you know how people get, they don't talk
About the problem, and then we leave
To let them be, to reflect
And be in peace, but in the end
The next day comes, and we see it as…a memory.

Xavier Moreno, Grade 8
Nativity Mission School

Wow

I'm so excited for it's Halloween night.
I'm ready for candy, funny costumes
And for all who can give me a fright!
There can be some strange people out tonight,
And my parents told me to be careful!
I will try with all might,
For, I know they are right!

Brian Anderson, Grade 8
Christ the King School

Loneliness

Loneliness is blue like sadness.
It tastes like a sour lime with salt on it.
It smells like rotten food and causes madness.
For fun it likes to do nothing but bad things.
While almost everything makes it angry
Everything makes it sad,
But nothing makes it happy.

Loneliness is smaller than you and me,
But bigger than peoples' minds.
Happiness is its enemy,
But nothing can be its friend.
Loneliness keeps its happy feelings in a secret place.
Its favorite place is in peoples' minds.
But it hates to be anywhere else.
Making people feel bad is its greatest success.
Not cheering people up is its greatest failure.
Loneliness makes me feel as sad as a deserted island.

Debora Fredericq, Grade 8
Intermediate School 278 Marine Park

Make Your Own Road

Make your own road
Make every choice you make bold
Choose your own path
Don't follow the crowd
State your decisions clear and loud
For everyone to hear
Who cares what they say
You can go your own way
You'll always be glad
Even if sometimes the plan goes bad
If you make your own trail
Tell your own tale
You will always end up
Satisfied

Sara Beck, Grade 8
Warwick Valley Middle School

Nature

I see an ocean of green trees,
I smell the fresh pine,
This is nature, a beautiful thing,
I can taste the fresh air,
I hear the birds chirping
Nature, it is very alive
Living, breathing, moving,
Like a human itself

Dennis King, Grade 8
Warwick Valley Middle School

The Fall

One solitary apple hung
Upon the apple tree.
A lonely prison inmate
While all the rest were free.

It yearned to look upon the world,
To see beyond its view,
It gleamed but no one noticed.
Of people there were few.

The apple hung and sulked and sighed
For many days and nights,
Dreaming of a different world
Where everything was right.

Until the day the apple fell
The ground was hard and dry
It lay still and thought quite hard,
The apple wondered why.

It wondered why it had to stay
When all the rest could go,
But so is life and so is fate.
Now this the apple knows.

Emma Tomko, Grade 8
Warwick Valley Middle School

Day and Night

Rain and wind,
Day and night.

Day — glum, sterile, dark.
No shine
No shadow
Rainy haze, clouds half-lit,
The whines of trains, the rumble of traffic

Suppressed sobbing of the sky, sighing in the winds,
A lengthy day, how distant is night?
Worn out hours, sluggish moments;
the shackles of time — endless, tireless

Night— dread in my heart, wailing in the city, darkness in the sky
Shadows, winds, murmurs, whispers, deep sighs
In the city, barren room,
Rain-covered darkness, in the shackles of time

All day and night.

Shaharia Uddin, Grade 9
Townsend Harris High School

Winter Wonderland

I wake up in my bed,
I get up, open the curtains,
and wipe the fog off the window…
then, a chilling sensation runs over my body.

I look out the window,
I see beautiful sparkling diamonds falling from the pillows of the sky.
I look down and see a white sheet covering the ground,
and avalanches falling from the pines.

This is something I like to call,
a winter wonderland.

Joseph Cirillo, Grade 7
John Jay Middle School

Taking Things for Granted

Kids these days say, "What do we need parents for?"
Other kids you aren't friends with say, "You should appreciate and think."
You say, "What? You know you're a loser."
They reply, "Yes, maybe to you I am, but I'm only poor."
We need to think our parents could be gone in a blink.
Just because you have perfect parents,
My mom is gone and my dad is a boozer.
After you realize everything you have is good,
Your world could just sink.
You see the kids with foster parents,
I think, "Wow! I'm glad that isn't me."
You sit down and see the kids who live in the hood;
The world ain't perfect, like the boy who gave you a wink.
So be happy with what you have and think about what you say and do.

Shayla Evans, Grade 8
Barker Middle School

Queen

A pointe routine, the Nutcracker ballet
A quiet stage; a peaceful silence
Leotard and tutu with gold accents
She is the queen
Spotlight beams on her
It dances with her
The remaining stage is black
Silence stuns the audience as they watch in amazement
Nutcracker plays in the background
Her pointe shoes move along with the music, as they were one.
So painful, so intense
How does the smile remain on her face?
Longing, wishing that soon I'll be on that stage
One day positions will be switched and I will dance
On that Lincoln Center stage
Queen
Queen
Queen

Ciara O'Sullivan, Grade 8
Baldwin Middle School

Snow Pile

Every winter my neighbor makes
a giant snow pile
that is as big as a mountain
Last year I was climbing up the mountain
as my friend was sliding down
as if he were in a race,
I had my skateboard deck in my hands
and my "snowboard" punched him in the face.

We played king of the "mountains"
after my neighbor had made more mountains
He enjoys watching us play
so he makes the piles bigger.

After that we came in and had tea
then we went back outside to play on the mountains
before we went to his house to play.

Jeremey Campbell, Grade 8
Southern Cayuga Middle School

The Beach

Little brown specks, one by one
As I sit in the water and they cover my thumb.
Warm and tiny,
Soft and light,
When the wind blows, it ruins my sight.
With my bare feet, I gently cross over,
Back to my blanket without seeing a single green clover.
Sitting on my blanket, closing my eyes,
I hear the waves, making faint cries.
Falling asleep alone in the sand,
The waves crash up touching my hand.

Larin Falsetta, Grade 7
Marlboro Middle School

My Hero

He is my hero, he gives me pride.
He always laughed and never cried.
Then the day came when God took him away.
I still remember him every second of every day.
We would laugh and joke to make memories of the time,
never once had he committed a crime.
We would hang out and have so much fun,
but the day is over and reality has begun.

Abby LaDue, Grade 8
Chazy Central Rural Jr/Sr High School

Stranger

I'm sick of being lied to,
Of your not being who you are.
When I look at you,
I see everything that's ever made me smile,
But then, when I look past that,
Deeper into your eyes,
I see all the lies you told.
Every word that left your lips,
None of it was true.
I don't even know who you are anymore,
Or who you've become.
You're not the one I used to know.
You've finally removed your mask,
That shielded the real you all this time.
I began to see who you really were.
You're like a stranger to me.
You were a coward for hiding from me.
I trusted in you,
And all you did was cause me so much pain.
I just want to know why.
Why couldn't you just be yourself? Can you tell me the truth?

Leandra Rivera, Grade 9
Bishop Ford Central Catholic High School

Martin Luther King, Jr.

"I have a dream"
The place to be
The Promised Land he thought it to be grand.
He was born in Atlanta, Georgia
That's where he lived in a large house
His parents, brother, and sister, were there.
King was the youngest person to win the Nobel Peace Prize.
Of the achievement he was proud
He shared the prize money with the civil rights crowd.
In Memphis, Tennessee was King's final act.
He was shot on a balcony.
He left a family behind and could never look back.
The gunman could never silence King's words.
He left them everywhere he had been and throughout the world.
His message was one of peace and love.
MARTIN LUTHER KING, JR. WAS HEARD.

Kieran Gilroy Rock, Grade 7
St Catherine of Siena School

Dogs

Fur, claws
Drool, paws
A man's best friend
Long droopy ears
Crispy treats like Kibbles and Bits
Play with them all day
Ripped pillows
Mommy, please may I have a dog?

John Oliver, Grade 7
Robert Moses Middle School

Flower

Flowers everywhere,
Flowers in the summer,
Different kinds,
Make me wonder,
The colors of the flowers,
Make a person happy!
In them I see
A way of remembering,
So many memories,
Of many celebrations,
Flowers pink, red and yellow,
The sun hidden,
Green grass, flowers
On top of it,
Petals fly in the air,
Flowers, flowers,
You make me smile!

Delia Ladino, Grade 9
John Bowne High School

Happiness

The low microwave drone.
The rice cooker is sputtering
steam is jumping around
the vivid scent is throughout the air.

The water from the sink
is sprinting quickly to drain
making a great noise

The tomatoes are sweet
yet dripping from ice cold wetness.
The cucumbers have a crisp taste.

My mother is making the spatula
tap the dish and
creating a rhythmic beat.

The kitchen is
a great place
filled with happiness,
sunshine and joy.

Saiganesh Ravikumar, Grade 7
Anderson Middle School (P.S. 334)

My Shadow

I walk through the pastures and toil in the fields, and my shadow follows me.
I climb the tallest mountain and gaze at the clouds, my shadow gazes with me.
Out in the open, on desert lands, my shadow trudges with me.
Though I stay at home beside the fire, my shadow sits with me.
My shadow; not a word, nor a sound, or a cry.
Like a ghost, lurking in the darkness…as silent as can be.

Raquel Medina, Grade 7
Ardsley Middle School

Without Friends

Without friends, who would you turn to when you get a low mark on your test?
or who would you rejoice with when the mark is your best?

Without friends, who would you share all your deepest secrets with?
And who could you trust not to tell your secret to anyone else?

Without friends, who would you laugh with when you have a private joke?
or who would you cry with when you feel there is no hope?

Without friends, who would you have fun with even in a boring class?
And who could you trust to make you laugh when you're doing tedious work at home?

Without friends, who would you lean on when something hasn't gone as planned?
Or who could you share the joy with when everything has worked out perfectly?

Without friends, what would we do when we no longer can stand on our own?
And who will always be there just when we need them the most?

Liat Weinstock, Grade 9
Stella K Abraham High School for Girls

My Guardian Angel

I walk down the deserted hill
All alone with no one to comfort me.
Tears of sorrow stream down my face.
I am walking amongst the deceased
In search of Grandma.
Dressed in black, the color of death, pain, and sorrow,
I'm all alone in cemetery with no one to console me.
Full of despair, I collapse on a grave,
A grave marked with a familiar name.
Suddenly, I feel no more sorrow.
My once dull, grey world now filled with colors.
I feel a warm hand on my shoulder.
Spinning around, I am surprised.
Grandma is beside me, a face full of love.
"How I have missed you!"
But she simply nods as she slowly turns to go
Leaving me alone once again.
Still, I am filled with comfort
Because I know Grandma is happy.
And I know I'm no longer alone since my guardian angel is always with me.

Alexandria Jay, Grade 7
Holy Cross School

Stream of Consciousness

Got the ball gotta run
They're coming, coming for me
Can't escape have to escape
Must reach the end zone
Sprinting to the goal
Dodging, spinning
Keep moving your feet
Have to keep going…
…There's no one around now
Just me and the touchdown
Fans going wild Coach going crazy
Only a few more steps…
…But now the pain hits
Legs are on fire heart is pounding
It's all a blur blacking out
Sweat pouring into my eyes
Losing too much body fluid
Can't go on…
…It's right in front of me now
Slowing down can't breathe
No more air lungs are bursting…TOUCHDOWN!

Eric Caliendo, Grade 8
Our Lady Queen of Apostles School

Candy Dandy

Halloween is so much fun,
Especially when there's no more sun.
Some dress up for the night,
While others have a shaving cream fight!

You can see ghosts and witches, who come out to scare,
While some tots dress up with crazy hair!

The night is spooky with black cats,
And the sky is filled with vampire bats.
Some don't think Halloween is so dandy,
But, the children don't care, for they just want some candy!

Eddie Schwartz, Grade 8
Christ the King School

Thanksgiving

T hank You for the sky so blue
H arvest festivals
A nd seasons too!
N othing in the world can compare to
K nowing and understanding You
S ounds and music are a delight
G oing to bed and sleep at night
I n the end means nothing without You!
V ery special days come and pass, but
I n the end they mean nothing without You
N ot only was everyone made by You but
G iving and living through You too!

Victoria Witte, Grade 8
St John School

Bodies

A body is a home
That you live in
When your body is done
And all worn out
Your soul moves to heaven

The body is no longer your home
Just a remembrance of where you once lived
Since you have left
The body looks different
Seeing it is not seeing you

We cannot see your new home
All the way up there in heaven
We will visit you in our thoughts and dreams
And have a spot for you to stay
In our hearts forever

Our souls will reunite
When my body is done
And all worn out
And I'll move up to heaven
With you

Madison Hoffman, Grade 7
West Hempstead Middle School

Her Heart

The heat from the sun beats down on her face
As she walks outside slowly
She keeps her smile as she looks around
Smells of perfume fill her nose
It's spring, it's love
A part of who she is
He's all that runs through her mind
His crystal blue eyes
That resemble the vast sky
The sound of the birds
Sing along with her heart

Nicole Torres, Grade 9
John Bowne High School

Disney

Lines packed to the brim like a pack of animals.
Children running wildly all over this exciting place.
The crowds chatting like noisy hyenas.
The fireworks in the air boom loudly.
Like my mother yelling at me when she's angry.
The great food so sweet and tasty.
The lake so clean and flowing smoothly.
The churros as long as a yard stick.
The chicken so tender and fresh.
Mickey Mouse's hand so magical and special.
The safety bars coming down on my lap for safety.
Wonderful, joyful, and free like no other place before.

Sara Mahan, Grade 7
Our Savior New American School

Family

You pressure me to rise to my full potential
You push me to do my best
You show love and support even when I turn my back on you
You are there when I fall to help me back up
Through your love and affection I see everything I've ever needed right beside me
Although I continue to stumble and fumble through life you stay by my side
The clothes, food, shelter, and love that I wake up to every morning are all possible because of you
Even in the darkest moment your hands are always there to guide me though
You are what keeps me going
You strengthen my weaknesses
You are the twinkle in the dark that whispers "you're almost there"
You are the essence of my soul

Gabriel Mitey, Grade 8
Holy Name of Jesus School

Hope and a Dream

I was young and unaware, she was wise and smart
I was young and did not dare, while she had her way with art
She ran away to pursue her dream and I stayed home with mother
My life deteriorated by each seam and hers was like no other
Some nights I think about my older sister, some I just don't try
At times the tale is too much of a tongue twister, at times I want to cry
Then I read the letter she wrote just before she left
The words she spoke without regret
As she formed our family cleft, when I hear these words I could never fret:
The paths we take, the lives we lead
The hearts we break, the ones we succeed
The journey will be long, the endurance factor will be high
The survivors will be strong, each step will lead us nigh
I can't promise you tomorrow will be a sunny day or that you'll never have a problem
Someone won't always be there to wipe the tears away and some troubles you must solve them
But little sister listen to me, you ought to listen well
Life is nothing without hope you see, it's a tale you should never tell
Hope and a dream set me free, hope and a dream is all you need
I am where I'm destined to be, it's time for you to let both to intercede
One day our journeys will intertwine, only God knows the date
But until then we've both got our places in the grand design, time is of the essence so sister don't be late

Alexis Oni-Eseleh, Grade 8
Most Precious Blood School

Oh We Won't Stop for Nothing*

As they watch us walk and walk trying to get our way for peace and equity,
They stare with angry faces whispering,
When is all this hatred going to stop around here, oh please when will it stop
When will we see smiling faces and equity on Earth?
Just give us a sign, please tell us we're doing fine
They may laugh, they may talk, they may harass us bad but we are determined to get our way
We won't stop, oh believe me we won't stop
We will walk till our feet ache real bad,
We will keep going, marching up these winding roads
Can't you see our posters
They are screaming out to you
Oh please just let us have peace in this world tonight.

Adriana Iaboni, Grade 8
Hauppauge Middle School
*Based on the Civil Rights Movement

Friends

They can be good to have.
They are people who will be there no matter what.
You can tell them your deepest, darkest secrets.
You have sleepovers like every day.
They know when something is wrong just by looking at you.
So I have to ask, "Do you know somebody like this??…"
If you don't, please find one.
They are really great to have.

Brittany Charette, Grade 7
Heatly School

Dreams

God came to me in a dream,
His beautiful ways gleamed.
For every star was placed into his eyes,
And everyone's life was ever realized.
Shown before me in one human being,
The only trick to seeing him was believing.
His shoulders stood stiff and bold,
Looking as if they were carrying my life's road.
His stomach small and tight,
Showing me how he worked all night.
His legs looked strong yet weak,
For still having carried that cross one Easter week.
The shoes/sandals he had,
Scraped his feet showing me he dealt with bad.
Never giving up what I did see,
there was much more about God that puzzled me.
Something stood out of him most of all,
The love that brightened my life to catch me if I was to fall.
Never will I forget this very dream,
That changed my life beyond what it seemed.

Kathleen Westervelt, Grade 9
St Anthony's High School

Christmas Magic

Cold breezes chase each other,
Icicles drip like the steady beat of a drum,
Trees shake off the snow,
Snowflakes spiral downward.

Inside the house a fire blazes,
Good smells fill the air,
While music plays softly in the background.

The Christmas tree bends and shines,
Lights twinkle like captured stars,
Ornaments glitter like water in a stream.

Friends and family come together,
Children laugh and play,
Joyous voices sing out the truth;

Christmas is here!

Taylor Lesky, Grade 8
Warwick Valley Middle School

Racing

Speed
Speed
I have the need for speed
Hearing the motor rumble under the hood
Feeling the vibrations of the car as I race down the track
The smoke from the tires might make me choke
Just the heat from the motor, man that's sweet
Just knowing that one little mistake could mean life or death
Drive around the debris and feel like you're free
Driving past a wreck is like flying through a forest at high speed
Speed
I have the need for speed

Johnthan Burchim, Grade 8
Southern Cayuga Middle School

The Love I Have

Although I wonder why it is
My Mom and Dad couldn't have many kids
I used to ask and sometimes cry
But not anymore for I know the reason why

I've been blessed with parents who live for me
And extra blessed with an extended family.

I never have to worry, I never have to fear
Because the love that I'm surrounded with is very crystal clear.
I've been taught to hold my head up strong
Don't doubt my faith, just move along.

God has been great, I know it's true
I may not have a sibling or two

But what I do have
Can never be replaced
For the love of a big family
Gets rid of the empty space.

Alissa Ferraro, Grade 8
Avon Middle School

Forgiveness

Forgiveness is as hard
As it is to learn Italian
I have to forgive that
My mom and dad are not together anymore
I had to grow up and
Forgive my parents
It's not fun
Growing up with my parents split up
You will have to forgive people
I love both my mom and my dad
But there is nothing I can do
If they are split now
That was the decision

Jamie Cullen, Grade 7
Solvay Middle School

Flowers

Splashes of colors,
Here and there.
Pink, white, red,
Orange and yellow.

Smell them all,
They smell great.
The roses and daisies.
The sunflowers.

There are so many kinds,
You can get them all.
Some common, some exotic.
They come from all over the world!

Now look at your garden,
It is beautiful!
There are tons of colors and
It smells great too!

Emily Dominiak, Grade 7
Holy Cross School

Kittens

They are born blind, deaf, furless,
Later they learn to walk.
Soon they are just little balls of energy,
Shooting around the room.
They're warm, they're furry,
They're just sweet packs of joy.
When they get older, they're less active,
But they're still lovable the same way.

Alex Cherniwchan, Grade 7
St Mary's School

What Is Life?

Is there a meaning or not,
Is life just meant to live,
Or is it meant to die.
Is life like a dove,
Or is it like a raven.

Is life meant for the birds.
Life is about time?
Is it about the past?
About the present?
The future?

Is life worth living?
Is there a love worth loving?
Is time worth spending?

Have you ever wondered,
Have you ever thought,
Why you are here right now?

Krystle Sullivan, Grade 8
William A Morris School IS 61

Thanksgiving

Thanks be to God, for all that he's done
Have a great day and don't forget to give someone a big hug
As we eat we think of the less fortunate who
Are hungry tonight
Now I'm in bed thinking about what happened today
Knowing that I have a very loving family helps me fall asleep
Saturday is another fun day but I feel like I want to help
Giving is my solution!
I give food and help people
A week passes and my friends decide to help
We start by visiting people at the hospital and giving them fresh baked cookies
I feel really good about myself
And want to do more
Never in my life did I feel I would care this much about people
Go and help,
You will feel the same way I do!

Amber Nicholson, Grade 7
Riverhead Middle School

Fearless

So fearless, yet not strong, when you realize you're a mess,
Everything in your head goes wild… the crazy wild but then
again so mild, don't ever give up the fight, because someday
You'll be sure to see the light, you might think your life is
Getting worse, And sometimes you get so mad you just want
To curse, when you think your life couldn't revive itself one
More time, when Bam! It happens, no more crime… then life
Is great and all is well, and you forget you even fell, so
Remember, life goes on no matter who you are, and never forget
You too, are a beautiful, gleaming star.

Breanna Karasek, Grade 7
Camillus Middle School

Under My Kitchen Sink

In my kitchen sits a space.
It is black but a lighted path awaits me.
I know with jaguar-like precision the predictable turns and twists.
Come in! Welcome home! Where have you been?
I enter the neverending and a new dark day has begun.
Doubt and a day's work left behind, finality.
Crawl further still in the cave, I smell my lemon trees
Yes the lemons grow here, but wait, is that jasmine teasing me?

A waterfall gliding down the pipes navigates towards me.
The water flows through me, like a wave pool at a water park,
I see energy that is unharnessed and untarnished
Pass me, and into my gardens. Was that a splash?
Definitely a splash, the intense scrubbing of a sauce encrusted pot.
Peruse my sweet dark vast dominion for evidence of intrusion.
Serenity was not lost, it remains safely tucked here.
Take a last breath of lemon air,
Beg a brief pardon from my latest guest jasmine.
Time to leave this imaginative world, where,
No light is needed here.

Dario Dell'Orto, Grade 7
Iona Grammar School

Me and Sports I Love to Play

There are a lot of sports I like to play
Like football and basketball, hurray!!!!
My favorite would probably be football cause I'm
Really good at it, but basketball is still fun to play
I play wide receiver and cornerback
Plus I shoot and make baskets
I have been playing basketball for four years
And this is my first year playing football
I will be playing next year hopefully as running back
Or a good lineman, blocking and pressuring the
Quarterback is fun on defense
But even better when I tackle the running back
Or the fullback from hitting the hole
Well I hope I can make the basketball team
If I don't I am still playing C.Y.B.A.
I hope to have a good season
And win the next two football games of the season
Peter Richardson, Grade 7
Camillus Middle School

Christmas

When you wake up on Christmas day,
You can't wait to go and play.
It takes you seconds to get to the tree,
And you can't believe what you see.
The boxes are big, small, long, and square,
Wrapping is off as fast as you can tear.
When it is all done and the family sits near,
Let's not forget why we are here.
Joe Stein, Grade 7
Most Precious Blood School

The Sun

Bright yellow rays, fiercely shining beams
A great ball of fire lighting up our sky
The Sun

The sun burns and radiates our Earth
And puts the light into our days

There is no sound within many millions of miles
There is nothing to be heard, but plenty to see

Why does such beauty only reveal half the time?
Why must it give joy when it rises, yet give doubt when it sets?

The Sun, placed in any scenario still shines its way through
It's bright rays strike, illuminating the Earth
Those stunning bright rays

Bright rays
Bright rays
Bright rays
Kiefer Teurfs, Grade 8
Baldwin Middle School

Invisible and Broken

Most don't see the one who hides,
For she hides behind the scene,
She just sits there and listens,
But to no man she will obey,
Because she sees the lies,
That lie in their eyes,
They don't see her when she cries or care if she dies,
For her heart has been broken,
By those who are not to be spoken,
So, she just sits there and cries,
As she morns the death of her broken heart,
She could look at the men,
Who still have a choice,
To mend or break her already badly broken heart,
She will never know which one they choose,
For she still sits there,
Behind the scene,
Watching them,
They can't see she is dying,
Invisible and broken.
Rebecca Campbell, Grade 8
Southern Cayuga Middle School

Space

Heavenly space
Resting upon the earth
Where the planets and satellites lay
The sun shining
Lighting everything in its path
Where the astronauts explore
The stars giving us light at night
The moon giving us light
The night sky lighting the night so we can see
A joyful feeling
A wonderful feeling
Beauty overcoming
Looking from the ground
Reminding us of how small we are
Bryan Kloepfer, Grade 7
Camillus Middle School

The Road to High School

I remember my first day of school.
In kindergarten fun was the rule.
In first grade all day we had to stay.
In second grade we had our First Communion day.
In third grade we sat together in pairs.
In fourth grade our classroom was upstairs.
In fifth grade we started doing book reports.
In sixth grade we got new gym uniform shorts.
In seventh grade our field trip was to Boston.
Now I'm in eighth grade and on safety patrol with Austin.
Nine more months until graduation.
I can't wait for high school…but after vacation!
Rachel Dempsey, Grade 8
Holy Cross School

Beginning of Forever
Does this bone-chilling wind
know its beginning?
Does the uncontrollable ocean
believe in an end?
When would the earth,
turn over, wither
and bend?

I know the beginning of forever,
no matter how long it may be.
Forever
is a lifetime.
We journey on forever.
And it seems
that this
is the beginning of forever.

For me.
Rachel Wong, Grade 9
Bayside High School

The Perfect World
a world with no hate
only things that are great

the weather is warm
there is never a storm

people are talking
and nobody is gawking

there is laughing
and dancing
no one is sad or bad
everyone is glad

friends are never mad
they help you when you are sad

it's summer all the time
the color of the grass is green like a lime

every day would be fun
outside playing in the sun
Elle Swete, Grade 7
Camillus Middle School

Healing
Healing is key when injured,
Mentally or physically,
Think positive,
The difference between good and bad,
And the possibility of what can become,
Soon once again.
Avery Wheelock, Grade 7
Solvay Middle School

Life
The key to life
May just make you stutter.
The shock of
Its aroma may make you
Open and flutter.
Through the arrogant flowers and
Much more to
Come, life will make peace
Within you, for
You are the chosen one.
Jack Schattner, Grade 7
Camillus Middle School

From Chains to Freedom
Chained to flesh, O my soul,
Slave to walls of wanting,
Beat and torn, O my wings,
My heart he is taunting.

Broken now, O these chains,
This One, who gave me might,
He made flat, O these walls,
And let my wings take flight,

Blessed with peace, O my soul,
No sorrow lingers long,
With freedom, O my wings,
His strength will be my song.
Joshua Colón, Grade 8
Our Savior New American School

Spoken
Some people say
Some speak with art
Well I have witnessed this
A young girl
Of about 10
Was the Picasso works spoken
At first was rainbows
Then clouds of gray
Then come butterflies in the sun all day
All became dark
Then swirls of light
Then a yellow and red kite
It all went white
Or so it seemed
But were the clouds of a dream
I then came back
I knew she could
And I knew that she would
Some people say
Some speak with art
Well I have witnessed this
Rachel Baumgarten, Grade 7
Brown School

Oh Boy
You're so cute,
especially in your suit,
you're my close friend,
we hung out one weekend,
you have great style,
and a nice smile,
I like you a lot,
because you're so hot,
so ask me out — why not?
Tiffany Lloyd, Grade 8
Bethlehem Central Middle School

Spring Time
Spring
Spring time
Time for flowers
Time to play outside
Time to run and use energy
Time to play all day
Time for baby sparrows
Time for sun to come
Enjoy the warmth
Spring's coming
Spring time
Spring
Karen Harris, Grade 7
Solvay Middle School

The Song of the Heart
The song of the heart is sung,
Behind the walls within.
Sometimes it shows through,
With glee, guilt or sin.
The song may be joyful,
Filled with love and laughs,
But others may be mournful,
With sorrow and distress.
My heart song is my favorite song,
It makes me feel at home.
But sometimes it screams out to me
"Just leave that alone!"
Sometimes it is sad,
But most times it is glad
The song in my heart soars,
How about yours?
Olivia Tyrrell, Grade 8
Southern Cayuga Middle School

Life
Life is hard like $E = MC^2$.
Life is fun like a roller coaster.
Just don't let it get the best of you.
Just hold on tightly
and keep your hands and feet inside
Joe Emilo, Grade 7
Solvay Middle School

Fairy Tale?

Once upon a time lived a little girl, she was lost,
confused in a lonely world.
All alone she walked all day,
running and running with nothing to say.
She had a home of love and care,
but there were still people she just couldn't bear.
She ran away looking for today,
but in the grass is where she lay.
She tells herself she'll be okay,
but that's another story…

Erin Moreno, Grade 9
St Joseph By the Sea High School

Friends

When you need something
Something you really need
When you're frustrated
And you plead
There are always your friends
When you're frustrated
Or somehow hated
Even though it's over-rated
There are always your friends
If you need someone to spill things to
Like a deep secret in someone's shoe
Who are you going to…who who who?
There are always your friends
Sometimes when you eat some cream
And then you just want to scream
You're mad at some bratty girl
Or criticized by some jerky boy
Who can you talk to?
Friends
Sometimes you just want to have some fun
What should you do? Have some fun with your friends!!!

Zeinab Saleh, Grade 7
Al Iman School

Tribute to Granny

You've lived many years
Seen many things
And worked hard to take care of your family
You've become both old and wise
And with your wisdom you teach
The offspring of the new generation
That will one day rule this nation
With the wisdom told
And they shall tell when they grow old
Granny I hope you live long
To see the new generation grow old
And tell us all that you know
Without you our lives would be empty
We cherish every moment with you
We will always love you

Brandon White, Grade 8
Intermediate School 227 - Louis Armstrong Middle

Colorless Despondency

With a single tremulous roar of blades,
They chopped the vibrant trees that stood
like ornaments, bedecking the emptiness
Of my brown heart.
My blood that was once the
Purest shade of blue, flowing freely through
The landscape as it dispersed its vividness,
Is now a polluted dump scattered with blind junk.
I had given them the ocean which ran swiftly
Through my veins. They stole its color and
Replaced it with a crude substance that is black,
Like the future that I foresee.
They ruptured my bones, the animals,
by demolishing their homes and leaving
Their faiths relentless.
I have warned them many times, asking
The sun to release endless waves of heat.
And ever since this day, blindness is their obstacle
My despondency shall never end. Colorless as I.

Tamara Yunusova, Grade 9
Townsend Harris High School

Christmas

Christmas is a great time of year,
When people are jolly and full of cheer.
It's a time to be with family and friends too,
If you're angry with some one you can start over new.
You can build a snowman out in the snow,
And watch the lights on the Christmas tree glow.
When you put up the lights everyone will know,
Because it sure does put on a show.
Opening up presents here and there,
Everyone's in the spirit everywhere.
Watching Christmas classics on the TV,
And seeing Rudolph go down in history.
Playing in the snow and having a snowball fight,
And looking for Santa as he flies through the night.
So stay up, play games, and have fun,
Make your Christmas the best one.

Jarett Miller, Grade 8
Commack Middle School

Feelings of a Soldier

Draining the feeling
That's the point
That's how I'm living
That's how the man wants and thinks is right
And how I'm living without love
it is just wrong
No matter how you see it
Or how you think it
Life without love
It's just messed up

Cristopher Guerrero Nugent, Grade 8
Baldwin Middle School

Sky

Somewhere in the sky
shooting stars fly in the dark
dark black sky, be life
Sam Schwartzapfel, Grade 8
Hauppauge Middle School

Gossip

Gossip is no respect
Nobody's friend
Gossip is on the phone
At parties
At home
In school
Gossip destroys
Friendships
Relationships
Reputations
Gossip is remembered
Repeated
Gossip is disgust
Disappointment
Dissatisfied
Dishonest
Gossip is like
A big book of lies
That never ends.
Jackie Troy, Grade 8
Southern Cayuga Middle School

Perfectly Pleasing Pies

The warm bread,
The sauce that's red,
The delicious cheese,
Can I have some pizza please?

Sausage, onion, and chicken
Sounds so very lickin'.
Pepperoni, and pineapple too,
I like pizza, how about you?

The great smell,
Who would sell?
It's very tempting to buy,
Those very tasty pies.

So, if you need something good to eat,
Grab this so very delicious treat!
Samantha Louden, Grade 7
Robert Moses Middle School

The Breezes

Leaves fall off the trees,
Jumping into Autumn leaves,
Flowing with the breeze!
Tara Herrera, Grade 7
Christ the King School

Pressure

Screaming yelling never right
Always in trouble never winning a fight
Too much pressure not enough time
Stuck in the middle too much to handle
Need to go somewhere need to find a safe place and fast
Parents fighting sister in need
Things falling apart not enough time to breathe
Depending on friends for all the things I need
No ones caring when I'm in need
Everything is wrong and nothing's the way it seems
People say they care and they promise their not going anywhere
Then they turn around and leave
No one's here and I'm all alone here is where I need you most
I always thought you'd be here I never thought you'd leave
I'm stuck here in this horrible place where no one even cares
But this is the life I choose to lead, and it's hard enough without a fight
Shannon FitzMorris, Grade 8
Our Lady Queen of Apostles School

Life...Is Good

I have to sit and shake if I want a treat,
I wag my tail when it's time to eat.
Everyone's gone, so I'm alone all day,
But when the UPS man comes, I'll bark till he goes away.
My next door neighbor Murphy is getting old and won't romp around,
So, I have to chase my tail and roll on the ground.

Sometimes Jamie will take me for a walk,
But sometimes it's annoying because she really likes to talk.
If I act real cute and tilt my head,
Then Jamie will let me sleep in her bed.
Some of my friends spend their day tied to a tree,
I've got it pretty good, it's a dog's life for me.
Jamie Martin, Grade 7
Camillus Middle School

That Place

Relaxed feeling, that soft touch, oh how I miss that place
That place of friendship and trust
How mysterious its ways are, the feeling of love it brings
When, oh when the waves crash and that sound of Jersey seagulls
My heart pounding of joy and excitement
My love for that place, that place Heaven on Earth
Playing soccer in the sand with special friends, close friends
Or lying in the sand to tell secrets yet untold
Still I hear the ocean calling me home and out of this prison
Calling me to that beautiful place of wonder
I'm waiting and still not there for I am lost without her
for I still hear the giggles with the girls and laughter with the boys
Still we all will not forget that place, oh the wonderful place
Sophia Mocciaro, Grade 7
Camillus Middle School

My Own Work of Art

My life is a canvas, splattered with black,
Dappled in blood and heart attacks.
Dressed in a metallic border shining,
Yeah, that's what I call a silver lining.
And if you look closely
there are faces,
confessions, possessions, and
distant places.

My life is a canvas, hanging high on a wall,
Swinging alone in an empty hall.
And maybe — when I'm dead —
it'll be worth something.
But right now, it's just a canvas,
though somewhat deceiving,
Right now it's the only thing keeping me breathing.

Nicolette Siringo, Grade 9
Oyster Bay High School

At Ease

The three of us are at ease and relaxed
Each of us is very different in our own ways.
We smile in the sun,
With vibrant green grass that flows behind us.
The puffy white clouds reflect in my sunglasses.
The air is still.
Our hair falls straight.
"You two actually look related," says Papa, humorously.
Rachel and I did each other's hair,
On this golden sunny and grand summer afternoon.
We pose, and squint, for the sun is blinding.
The white and yellow flowers in the background,
Seem to pose as well.
This sets the scene and makes the day seem happy.
All three are unique and different,
Yet we love each other the same.
We may not see each other often,
But when we do we rejoice, and praise.

Andi DeBellis, Grade 9
DeSales High School

The Bent Branch

The fragile branch is bent with the weight of
the ice from last night's storm. Silent snow,
gentle drops of rain, necessary and good for
the tree…
    But look at the bent branch.

The fragile back is bent with the weight of
the books from last night's assignments.
Silent words, gentle drops of information,
necessary and good for the student…
    But look at the bent back.

Penina Hecht, Grade 9
Stella K Abraham High School for Girls

Winter Snow

Snowflakes falling freely into the air,
Each one lighting the earth.
I run out into the night,
To see these fresh flakes.
Watching the white snow slowly fall,
It looks like the perfect powder.
The ground more white than it is wet,
Left with trails of thickening snow.
The large white balls of snow,
Are all used to make snowmen.
Kids running out to play,
While yet small puppies are afraid to touch this icy water.
Trails of footprints all through the snow,
And snow angels looking oh so lovely.
Just as the flakes hit the ground,
The green grass starts to disappear.
The bare and leafless trees,
Soon to be blanketed under the snow.

Olivia Jackson, Grade 8
Warwick Valley Middle School

Halloween

Ghosts and goblins,
Witches and warlocks.
Costumes galore on this Halloween night.
Hershey's and Kit Kat's,
Snickers and Smores.
Candy galore on this Halloween night.
Kids in costumes,
Adults with flashlights.
All this commotion on this Halloween night.

Sarah LaJeunesse, Grade 8
St Mary's School

Nature's Life

As I wake I find myself in the rainforest
The longer I stay the more I see
I saw a snake
Next thing I knew I started to quake
The snake and I were unsure of each other,
We stared and studied to see what would happen
We both made the choice to back away for a day
The next thing I knew I was surrounded
By a flock of birds that squawk they left off
All the birds above my head looked like
A big array of colors over my head
The monkeys looked like a crowd dancing,
People and the frog were the crooking band
Rainforest a place with animals and plants
But people say it's scary but I say it's merry
I look overhead when I got lost
In a flash of a bright light
The bright light almost looked like a flaming phoenix
How cool that blue light looks in the night

Brandon Faatz, Grade 8
Southern Cayuga Middle School

Flying
Sometimes I feel
I feel like I can fly
soar above the trees and clouds
but then
I see
my feet
rooted
to the ground
never willing
to let go.
Sidney Cannon-Bailey, Grade 7
Gananda Middle School

365 Days
It has been 365 days since that day,
the day you took your last breath.
The day I cried, and cried, and cried.
The day I never slept.
I've cried 365 tears since that day.
Enough for a pond of sorrow.
Where I drown all my silent sobs,
and bad memories that follow.
I've slept 364 nights since that day,
when my dreams took me back to you.
I could be happy in the world I created.
It was like the old life I knew.
It has been 365 days since that day,
and I just want to go back,
but I keep on moving forward
on this reckless racing track.
Out of those 365 days
I never, ever forgot
the way I loved him,
and how hard he fought.
Kerry Kelvas, Grade 8
Dawnwood Middle School

The Kitten
There was a kitten.
It was abused.
The kitten's owner did not feed her
or clean her kitty litter box.
She ran outside,
as fast as a little rat.
She did not come when called.
He was sad.
He glued pictures of her on paper.
People saw the picture of his kitten.
Two weeks later a girl saw the kitten
she played with her.
She went home.
She asked her mom to keep the kitten.
Her mom said "yes."
The kitten found a new home!
Ashley Felt, Grade 7
Solvay Middle School

The Soul of a Sole
The soul of a sole is
Worn and beat UP,
And
F
R
A
Y
E
D
At the edges.
These soles have seen all of my life.
They were there for the games, the pressure, the pleasure, the pain.
They held me UP.
Yes, the soul of a sole has surely seen it all.
Trampled and shredded, ripped at the seams,
These soles have outlived my childhood dreams.
And now, as I lay them down to rest,
I think about all that we have shared,
And for that deep, weathered, loyal soul of a sole
The end is something I cannot seem to bear.
Diana E. Vlavianos, Grade 9
Oyster Bay High School

In a Meadow
Flowers blooming all around like a colorful tapestry.
Butterflies dancing in the air like little children playing.
The sound of swaying grass as the wind blows.
Like tiny bells, are the chirp of various birds which soar high in the air.
The fragrant scent of flowers like a million perfumes.
The smell of spring, of everything fresh.
Small, delicious berries, sweeter than anyone knows.
The cool, clean air like purified water.
The breeze which ruffles my hair like a river.
The soft, rich earth between my toes.
Relaxed and at peace with not a care in the world.
Kiana Frick, Grade 7
Our Savior New American School

Cycle of Words
What is life?
Life is full of happiness when we are all together
Life is sorrow when we are apart
What is life?
Life is phases and twists
Life is controversy when things don't turn out to be what you want
What is life?
Life is love when you find your kind
Life is affection, what makes up trust
What is life?
Mix irony and a pinch of faith
Life is part of trying and succeeding
What is life?
Life is the treasure which should be treasured
Life is ours!
Ayesha Ahmed, Grade 9
John Bowne High School

Sunset

A fire ball of heat arches over the sky
across the ocean and the land
until it finally dips down into the sea,
cooling itself in the wavy waters.
It turns yellow, orange, pink, and then finally a deep red,
casting its rays of light and happiness to the clouds.
They join in the fun and turn pink and purple,
letting everyone know they're beautiful too.
Then, as the last light falls out of the sky,
the stars come out, dancing and twinkling with glee,
making the whole world sparkle.
Finally, the moon comes up over the horizon,
shimmering and casting a faint glow over everything,
as a hush falls over the world.
She also glides across the sky,
gracing everyone with her beauty.
But as she falls,
the Sun rises, with a never-ending promise.
And it all starts,
And ends,
With a sunset.

Meghan Dorsey, Grade 7
Onondaga Hill Middle School

Never Alone

Walking through the wintery woods
you find yourself scared because it's getting late
and you think you're alone

but in fact you're not alone
but with many other creatures around you
the peaceful blue jay calling your name
the furry little chipmunk offering you some acorns

you find yourself looking around
and seeing the freshly fallen, white snow
and all of the other animals that you
didn't quite notice before

and you find comfort in knowing
you're not alone

Patrick Christen, Grade 8
Warwick Valley Middle School

The Perfect Chocolate Brownie

First, you need to clean your space,
Otherwise, you'll slow your pace.
Then, you must assemble your ingredients,
Of water, oil, eggs, mix, and chocolate chips in obedience.

Next, at last you bake,
For 24 or 26 minutes, to make this gooey little cake.
Then, some chocolate frosting when the cooling is done,
Will help to leave you none.

Cassie Flynn, Grade 8
St Mary's School

Tornadoes

The beating thunder echoes for miles on end.
A flash of lightning like a camera.
Appearing from high in the sky.
The whirling winds go round and round.
Angrily tearing apart the Earth.
"Why can't we stop it?" we ask.
No one knows,
And no one will ever know.

Serena Strozewski, Grade 8
Avon Middle School

The Night

Now, as the sun slowly fades away
Transforming the sky from blue to grey

The clouds are fading and a gentle breeze
Flows through the night with care and ease

The moon shines through the darkened day
As the night whisks all my cares away

From out of nowhere a speck of light
One so small yet so bold and bright

As it twinkles and shines it begins to fly
Gliding so gracefully across the night sky

Its wondrous beauty is a breathtaking sight
As more and more appear throughout the night

The trees are whispering all around
It's such a calming and soothing sound

I look up at the sky knowing that I'm here to stay
I lean back, close my eyes, and dream away

Emily Frazee, Grade 7
Camillus Middle School

Only You

I want to hold you in my arms for a lifetime,
and get the feel of your heart
I would like to melt away in your warmth
Only with you I'm in my right mind
knowing your love is true…
Me without you is like the sky without blue
or Winnie without Pooh,
But one thing I know is that you're my boo
I don't see what these other girls see…
I see your worth and I love you
so much it could make my heart burst
no matter how much you might see me flirt…
Your love is like gravity,
it keeps me down to earth!

Khadijah Guthrie, Grade 9
John Bowne High School

School Today
In math class today,
We learned to divide and add the right way.
I thought it was really fun,
To do the worksheet but, before I knew it I was done.
I thought it was too good to be true,
When all of a sudden I remembered my English homework was due.
So I fumbled through my folder bit by bit.
But the clock was ticking I couldn't find it.
So I run to my locker and there it was right in front of me,
My English homework how could this be?
I grabbed it fast without a second to spare.
Oh No! A wet floor sign, I slip and fall everyone laughs and starts to stare.
I am all wet but, I don't care.
I have about thirty seconds left before being late,
Now I am sprinting I may get there at this rate.
As I slip into class the unfamiliar teacher says, "Who are you?"
And I say, "Isn't this third period English" even though I may get a black and blue,
From falling I still look relaxed but my chest is pounding.
He says "no this is 2nd period Science" he knew I was running by the way I was sounding.
Wow what a day.

Christina Minenna, Grade 7
Robert Moses Middle School

Little Did We Know*
It was a normal day for the country no one rushing, no one in a hurry
Little did we know what would take place that day; little did we know it would turn out this way
Parents kissed their kids goodbye, they couldn't imagine how much they'd cry
Everyone prepared for this brand new day, later on, however, we didn't know what to say

Passengers boarded planes ready to take off, bombers and hijackers prayed to Allah
Secretaries and others took the train to work, little did they know their lives would be jerked
Planes took off, there was nothing left to do if only…Oh if only they knew
Planes were turned around, crashed and fallen, frantic bystanders picked up phones and began callin'

People who were hurt cried, "Lord why me!" People standing by warned, "Come on let's leave."
Police officers and firefighters swarmed the buildings, but they weren't prepared for all of the killings

People and bodies were covered in steel, injured and wounded yelled, "This can't be for real"
Many died from the immense pain, Lord knows there was nothing to gain
It was a tragic day for New York City, the day was filled with smoke, fire and debris
Little did we know how many people would be lost, little did the culprits know how much hysteria they caused

Little did we know how many men fought for their lives, little did we know how many men left behind their wives
Little did we know how many kids became fatherless, little did we know how many lives would become worthless
Little did we know how much help would be sought, little did we know how much help would be brought
"Little did we know" was the phrase of the day, little did we know and little could we say

Brea Baker, Grade 8
John W Dodd Middle School
*In remembrance of 9/11

Why?
Why does it seem frightful to me all these broken and shattered dreams. I fall asleep for one moment and when I wake I feel a flake. A flake of snow that drifted on top of my nose. The crazy thing that hurts the most is why does this snow fall. Why does the tree grow. Why does the stream flow and the reason is because God said so.

Dawn Bodie, Grade 7
Morris Central School

Zen Dog

Zen Dog, dressed for one more picture
If dogs could talk *anglais* he would say
"Why yes, this perfume makes my nose happy."
Zen Dog obediently comes when
Master of the Zen Dog calls
Zen things on occasion, *"When do I get to leave?"*
Zen Dog may be zen,
However, Zen Dog is normal like any other dog.
Being a Zen Dog, a faithful follower
No woof or rawrf
Only doggy smiles and tail wagging.
Zen Dog is magical, some say
Because Zen Dog is in random magazines
Zen Dog is magical
But all diggity dog wants
Is to be free.
Zen Dog, Zen Dog, this is the last picture.
Take care, and I hope you do well
My fondest memory of you will be
Your doggy perfume smell.

Ruby Roth, Grade 9
DeSales High School

Winter

In the frigid air, I shiver in the night
While I wait for the morning sun to bring light.
When I wake up, I see beautiful white snow on the ground,
And a flower nor leaf is to be found.
I wear a hat and scarf because your wind blows cool air,
And you can see gusts of snow blowing here and there.
I also wear gloves and boots because your snow is all wet,
And if you do not, frost bite is what you are going to get.
Winter is a wonderful season,
And everybody who loves it, loves it for a different reason.

Jasmine Newsom, Grade 9
Our Savior New American School

The Opera

Ah, Ah, Ah, Ah, Ah, Ah, Ahhh
It is time to rise and shine
Shake the cobwebs from your mind
Lift up your dreamy sleepy head
Sings the woman by my bed
She is on an opera stage,
Singing me a morning praise
I wish that she would stop the clatter
So I could sleep, it doesn't matter
BEEP, BEEP, BEEP, BEEP, BEEP, BEEP, BUZZ
BEEP, BEEP, BEEP, BEEP, BEEP, BEEP, BUZZ
Then I wake up from my dream
Just in time to hear Mom scream
Turn off the clock, you're late for school
Get out of bed, wipe off the drool

Emily Sliwowski, Grade 7
St Dominic Savio Middle School

'Tis the Season

Snowflakes falling to the ground,
as I sleep safe and sound.
Winter's coming with its joys,
to all the little girls and boys.
Munching on candy canes,
out in the cold.
Putting up Christmas trees,
all looking bold.
But once every year when winter is through,
everyone's faces are all looking blue.
Santa Claus gone,
all presents out of sight.
Snow has all melted,
the sun is looking very bright.
All we have left is that one special date,
when winter arrives, not a day late.

Victoria Lena, Grade 7
Most Precious Blood School

Memories

The canvas of her life
She portrays a smile fake
Watching the world spin faster
Her hands begin to quake
Bewilderment lies upon her
Unsure why she is of hate
Blind by all the shadows
Of her imaginary fate
Her friends — they all left her
But it's really not their fault
She's done some bad things in the past
Putting knowing them to a halt
Used by her beloved
Her crush so far away
Loneliness is her punishment
Yet more thoughts begin to play
When you try to write down feelings
They always come out wrong
Never to be forgotten
Who knew memories could be so strong?

Kate Abazis, Grade 8
Our Lady Queen of Apostles School

The Crying Woman

A crying woman
Stands in front of a building
She has a ring on her left hand
There are four people trying to comfort her
The woman crying has blond hair
And green pants
A man with a Padres t-shirt stands near to comfort
A woman stands close behind with good intentions
The woman crying is clutching sunglasses
The crying woman has a ring on her finger

Tadhg Karski, Grade 9
DeSales High School

Winter
Winter is when I can't skate.
Winter is when I hate.
Winter makes me sad.
When does it make me glad?
CHRISTMAS!
Anthony Lawler, Grade 7
Solvay Middle School

A Moment of Silence
A moment of silence…
For the angels above.
We'll always remember them,
With grace and love.
A moment of silence…
For those who've passed away.
They'll be remembered tomorrow —
They're remembered today.
A moment of silence…
For those who gave their lives.
Their deaths still cut us,
Like jagged knives.
We'll remember their lives,
Not their death.
Remember that we loved them,
Even after their last breath.
So a moment of silence,
We'll all give.
To those who,
In our hearts,
Will always live.
Raven Hicks, Grade 8
Riverside High School

What Is Love?
What is love?
Is it what I'm feeling deep inside
The feeling I've kept in secrecy
For so long
The one that is killing me inside
The one that needs to come out
But isn't sure how
The one that confuses me the most
Are these feelings toward you
Real or fake
Why can't I figure it out?
What is this?
Is it just another heart break
That hasn't come out of its shell
Or is it real?
Will I ever know?
Do I want to know?
Should I know?
Could it possibly be…
Love?
Erika Estus, Grade 8
Westport Central School

Flying Free
I stood there, shaking like a volcano about to explode.
My legs were jelly as I got strapped into the harness.
My stomach began to twist and turn every which way while my eyes
wandered down 1,000 feet below.
My heart was a loud drum beating against my chest.
I began to sit down, waiting to be released off the platform.
Holding on for my dear life, I slowly inched to the edge as
I watched like a hawk for the signal.
Then, the countdown began.
Three — should I really be doing this…
Two — maybe I shouldn't…
One — no turning back now…
Go! — I let go and was suspended in thin air.
Then, whoosh! I flew like a bird.
Shooting down the zip line over treetops, buildings, and friends below,
Up higher and higher until I could touch the soft clouds against my face.
The cool, crisp air stung my bare skin as I sped faster and faster
like lava flowing down a mountain.
I was going like no one could stop me, nothing else mattered.
I was as free as ever, watching the world zoom by.
I was going…going…going…gone.
Hannah Bucklin, Grade 8
Eagle Hill Middle School

Teen Machine
Every single day I open my eyes, I feel the calm reprise.
Then I'm shoved into the fight.
Something in my heart erupts, that something is corrupt —
That something is not right.
Every single day I go to school, forced under a rule.
Forced to do what I cannot conceive.
I can't help but feel that I'm a tool, a blind fool —
What was I made to achieve?
Every single day I'm trapped in the same scene. Becoming a teen machine,
Trying with every breath not to be outdone.
There is a scream in my ears, and all of my fears
Are telling me that I cannot fight what has already won.
Every single night I close my eyes, drown out the cries.
Sweet sleep makes me anew.
With no plans to contrive, I am blessed to be alive,
Dreading that tomorrow this sequence will once more ensue.
Dan LeMar, Grade 9
Oyster Bay High School

Niagara Falls
Niagara Falls looks like a thousand thundering waves breaking on the rocky shore.
It sounds like the rumble of a freight train as it speeds by.
It smells like clothes when first pulled from the dryer.
It feels like the mist of a rain shower on a cool day.
It tastes like hose water when it first splashes out.
Erin Sliwowski, Grade 7
St Dominic Savio Middle School

Best Friend in Disguise

Floppy ears and big brown eyes
She's so cute and adorable
I can't believe she's mine.
She may not understand everything I say
But when it comes to listening
She definitely gets an A.
She enjoys her food, but only with a treat on top
And when she makes a mess, then I grab a mop
When she wants to go outside she means now
Her patience with me I can't know how.
When I get mad she looks at me sad.
I can't stay mad, she loves me and I love her.
When it's time for bed she curls up real tight,
and I may, just might let her in my bed.
I say good night waiting for a new day
I know she loves me because of the look in her eye,
When I see her face we are connected.
Now and forever, I will always love my best friend

Alycia Andolina, Grade 7
Camillus Middle School

Musical Harmony

The sounds go through her mind
Voices are like whispers in the dark
Her eyes are closed, listening intently
Sharp noises, soft noises, they're all familiar
Sunlight pours through the blinds
Making light streaks across the cold floor
She's alone in the room, yet the room is filled
Her imagination takes over the place
The lyrics in the music create her world
She controls them all

Carmen Sheppard, Grade 9
John Bowne High School

Please!

"Crack!" you hear the sound —
as the tree goes falling to the ground

You can hear the birds squawk and trill,
you can feel the leopard's eyes upon you —
as he watches you from a distant hill,

The monkeys are not happy —
for you have just claimed their home

If I could do something;
then I would

So I write this
and beg,
and plead —
PLEASE! lumberjacks —
Stop cutting down the trees!

Natalie Quinn, Grade 8
Warwick Valley Middle School

The Spiffy Looking Duck

He's a funny looking duck,
A rich and wealthy looking duck.
He's wearing people clothes like a guy,
He has a button up shirt and a red bow tie.
He has a diamond on his right hand,
And a cane in his left.
He looks like he is in a jolly mood,
Like he has not a care in the world.
The duck looks like he is doing just fine,
It's like he won't have any problems for a long time.

Alberto Estevez, Grade 9
John Bowne High School

Baseball

Baseball is my dream
I love to play it all the time.
I love our Avon baseball team.
We're all so good and love the game.

I love it when I catch that ball
And throw it to the base, then smack
"He's out" the umpire says.

It's pretty cool when I hit the ball.
BANG!! It's over the outfielders head.
"Slowdown," the ump says "you're already home
And he still doesn't have the ball!"

We won the game,
And we celebrate.
I go home to change,
Just so I can do it all over again.

Doug Yencer, Grade 8
Avon Middle School

Fun Family Trips

Off we go to the patch,
Wind in our face looking back.

Looking around so many things to see,
Running to one place, like to be free.

Gazing in the fields looking for the right one,
Right over there I see that special one.

Bringing it home ready to carve out,
Digging the seeds out and about.

Putting it on the porch
For a happy Halloween.

Then it can glow
With an orange glee.

Alyssa Gardiner, Grade 8
Warwick Valley Middle School

Coco

A brown, black and white beagle
A little speeding dog
Has beautiful brown eyes
An always happy dog
Has crazy floppy ears
When she gets excited her hair sticks up
A perfect little dog

Matthew Richmond, Grade 7
Heatly School

Wrestling

The noise of the crowd
It was so loud
My heart is beating
Then it starts screaming

Stop, stop or
Drop to the mat
What a fight
It gave me a fright

The mat felt like
A bat on my back
It felt so good
The match was finally on

He soon met the mat
With a whack

Then he was on his back
Just like that
Then I heard the ref say
It is a pin

That means it's a win

David Wheat, Grade 8
Southern Cayuga Middle School

Cliché

You're a stereotype.
Cliché.
A generic copy of society.
And I hate it.
You walk alike.
And talk alike.
Dress alike.
Even break my heart alike.
You skate alike.
You write alike.
You sing alike.
You act alike.
You have no identity.
You're a cliché.

Lindsay Weiser, Grade 9
Clarkstown High School North

Mistakes

M istakes happen more than once
I t's okay to be disappointed
S ay we should try harder
T each us life lessons
A ren't always bad
K eep us realizing that no one is perfect
E xist in everyone's lives
S how character if you handle them well

Alana Russell, Grade 7
Dake Jr High School

Misery

I tried so hard
but I can't get you back.
I tried so hard
but misery is following me.
I've tried so hard
hoping one day
you would rescue me.
Until then I'll be here,
at my post, looking for you.
I can't get away from you.
I can't get away from misery.
This is a game to you
but I have tried so hard.
Misery is still with me.
I've tried for so long.
I've tried so hard.
I need you.
I will be at my post.

Maurianna Piccirilli, Grade 8
Windsor Middle School

Curiosity

Money doesn't make the Earth go 'round
Curiosity makes up our world
It makes us take risks with no reward
The lessons we learn are ours to keep
Curiosity cannot be learned
It is thrust unto us from the start
We imagine and philosophize
We wonder about things we don't know
Our ancestors had it long ago
So do we in this generation
Curiosity keeps us going
We keep pondering, striving to learn
It makes up everything, school, labs
    But especially our entire lives
Everyone has it, people, pets
We can't stop until it's satisfied
It's not always good; it can be bad
Curiosity killed a cat once
We're all the same, we have it in us
We're all curious, we're unified

Mason Towne, Grade 7
Heatly School

?P/E/A/C/E/?

Look under the bed
Search in the dark,
    fight other people,
and countries from afar.

Nothing you found,
and nothing you see.
That's helping you fill,
    this desire of need.

But how can you expect,
    to find this desire?
When as you look
    you fuel the fire.

Desiny Smith, Grade 9
Ketchum-Grande Memorial School

Old Barn

In a field brown and old
By the countryside
Around rainy and cold
But when near warmth and sunlight
Mist and sun
Now a rainbow
A beautiful day
In Ireland
The storm has passed
Now it's time to play
Hide-and-seek
Who dares to hide in the barn?
No way!
In your dreams!
I will
Good luck
Count to twenty
I've found you all but one
Where is he?
In the old barn

Amanda Lattimore, Grade 7
Camillus Middle School

Poems

Have you ever thought about poems?
Or how amazing they are?

They are like pieces of your Soul,
They are like music from your heart,

They sparkle in your eyes,
They laugh when you laugh,

Poems are amazing,
Enjoy them in your life.

Marta Szmidt, Grade 7
Robert Moses Middle School

The Hill

The hill I live on has beauty.
With the trees and the flowers blowing in the breeze.
My favorite spot is in my tree
I sit in the tree with the birds to read
And other times I play in the pond
With the geese and my friends
It is quiet and calm.
This is mine!

Erin Sundlof, Grade 8
Avon Middle School

Trick or Treat

The night was cool,
The leaves were blowing.
It was a Halloween night,
And the ghosts and goblins were showing.

I left my house after I was fed,
And hoped to return to my nice warm bed.
There were spiders, bugs, and bats too,
I was so scared I didn't know what to do.

I spotted a vampire wearing a hood,
I ran for safety as fast as I could.
Crazy noise and howling is all that I heard,
As something flew past me like an evil bird.

Then I remembered this night was supposed to be fun,
And it wasn't scary even though there was no sun.
People gave me candy and treats,
Halloween night really can't be beat.

John Garcia, Grade 8
Warwick Valley Middle School

Offense to Defense

Our offense lines up straight.
We know this play is our fate.
Two Twenty-Two, Two Twenty-Two shift GO!
They all launch getting off that first blow.
The tight end gets open,
while we leave the defense moping.
But wait, there's a guy.
Where did he come from, the sky?
Too late, the pass is gone.
They clearly show us brains, not brawn.
In one quick second, offense changes to defense.
Surely we'll see a lot of violence.
The tight end misses the tackle,
as one smart lineman breaks his shackle.
He runs, wraps, and pulls him to the ground.
His face pounds.
Black D! Black D!
That's me.

Bryan Heatherman, Grade 8
Windsor Middle School

Why We Cry

We cry to express our feelings.
We cry because we hope never to die.
Why?

Why are we alive only to die?
Many of us have no reason why.
But we all try,
Try to hide our feelings deep inside to protect our pride.
We fight to protect who we love so we never lose them
But when they die we want to cry.

We're shy because the people we could be with are gone.
So now we cry.

Alex Toréa, Grade 8
Southern Cayuga Middle School

Squirrel

I see a squirrel sitting on the rail,
it was fuzzy, along with the tail.
Looking like a statue,
with a hunch on its back too.
Just sitting there,
while I can't help but to stare.
Its eyes black like a marble,
and a shine of light made it sparkle.
It's like looking into a hole, pitch black,
and the only way out was toward the back.
Listening to the wind passing by making whistles,
and the leaves on the floor sound like bristles.
Thinking to myself why wasn't it moving?
Why wasn't it afraid of me?
Why was it looking at me?
Feeling bad and helpless,
thinking what to do next.
I figured it was shy,
as so was I,
and I thought to myself…
Why?

Henry Castillo, Grade 8
Baldwin Middle School

Follow Your Own Path

As you walk down the hallway,
Do you feel eyes scornfully beam on you?
Glares, stares all day…
FOLLOW THE NEW!

Be your own person.
That's all I gotta say.
You will have more fun.
Be with the right people, MAY YOU, MAY?
Don't copy others to fit in.
OR you will feel the wrath
Of your deadly unwanted SIN!

Jenny Agbo, Grade 8
Warwick Valley Middle School

Stupid Decisions

Stupid decision
Trying to fit in
Always on the outside
Looking in
No excuses
No apologies
No taking it back
Boys will be boys
And that's crap
Consequences were high
Chances were low
Lives were changes
And we all know
If only we could turn back time
Chances are
I would not be
Saying this rhyme

Cody Reeves, Grade 8
Southern Cayuga Middle School

Wishful

Tears run down my face
I wish I could say that's new
I could feel you breathing
Slowly I sleep
Sad. Feel alone. Tired.

Wake up
Run to express the anger
Sprint and fall
Dirty I get home
Cold. Alone. Scared.

Still alone
Shower
Hot water
Almost burning
Hot. Alone. Depressed.

I almost wish I could have started alone
Just so I was used to it
The quiet.
The hurt.
Wishful. Alone. Crying.
Almost wish you were back.

Alexis Corvo, Grade 9
West Islip High School

Death

Stiffness, lifeless corpse
In a casket of sorrow
Heartache spreads through the family
As the beloved one starts
Eternal rest

Michael Hamersky, Grade 8
Warwick Valley Middle School

Life

Life is something to value and cherish,
Life is something to adore and appreciate,
It isn't something that should collapse or perish,
Life isn't something that we can make it's something that only God can create.

Life can be taken away anytime,
It doesn't matter if you're awake or asleep,
Whether you see God's light or see his prime
Life is something that we all wish we could keep.

Life has its ups and downs,
Some people imagine they can rule the world wearing a crown
Everyone has bad days when they frown,
But you eventually turn your frown upside down.

Paul Persaud, Grade 8
Holy Family School

A Summer Day at the Jersey Shore

A beautiful sun setting on the water
Dark blue waves crashing against the shore
The sound of laughter coming from the boardwalk
The cry of birds longing for food like children cry for their parents
The scent of the ocean carrying through the air
The cotton candy that small children hold
The funnel cake from the carnival
The saltiness in the air
The sand that I lay on as soft as a cushion
The freezing water as cold as ice
Every second is a miracle from God

Brianna Fitzpatrick, Grade 7
Our Savior New American School

I'm Sorry, I'm Sorry

His deep blue eyes look at her, her warm brown eyes look back sadly
"I wish I could tell you" she whispers
The cuts and bruises on her back sting as she walks home and opens the door
Her father sits at the table with a bottle of beer
He turns around and says slowly, "you're late."
He gets up slowly, his eyes like piercing darts, she pleads, "Please dad, no,"
But it's too late, he lashes out at her
Helpless, she crumbles to the floor, but he doesn't stop
At last, he gives her one final kick and storms away
Breathless, she sobs in the corner
She looks up and sees her mother weeping quietly at the door
Her mother quietly says, "I'm sorry baby, I'm sorry."
She gets up and runs out of the house
She runs and runs, tears flying off her bruised cheeks
She reaches his door and knocks over and over and over
He opens the door and she falls into his arms
Sobbing, she holds on tight
He looks into her dark eyes and bruised face, kissing away her tears
She looks at the sorrow in his blue eyes that say, "I'm sorry, I'm so sorry"
She asks him for one favor, he says, "anything, anything for you."
She says, "get me out, get me out of this nightmare."

Christine Liao, Grade 9
Shenendehowa High School

In the World of the Smokies

On top of the mountain, you might feel a breeze,
But down below the mountain tops, all you see are trees.

Some trees are old and worn,
While other trees are just being born.

Most animals in packs work as a team,
While guarding those who drink from the stream.

In the World of the Smokies

In all this peacefulness, there is still worry,
You might catch an animal in a ball of fury.

Predators go for the small and weak,
So shelter the little ones always seek.

Many trees die from deadly blight,
And predators still hunt late into the night.

In the World of the Smokies

Christopher Kramer, Grade 7
Robert Moses Middle School

Basketball

I love basketball it's my favorite sport
I like to school people on the court
I like to dribble the ball
I'm so fast you're lucky if you don't fall.

You wanna play me that's fine
Because when it comes to that basketball it's mine
When it comes to basketball I'm the best
I'm way better than all the rest.

When I play basketball I'm unbeatable
When I'm on the court I'm unstoppable.
Basketball's my sport
So if you want to face me, meet me on the court.

Miles McGowan, Grade 8
Avon Middle School

The Move

Painting, fixing, and storing all things,
and missing the happiness
all can bring.
Shuffled around from home to home can
make a person feel all alone.
Sadness and anger can come from this too
missing neighborhood friends
can make you feel blue.
A new house is found from all of these things
like painting, fixing,
and now unpacking things.

Daria DeMauro, Grade 7
Camillus Middle School

I'm Not Perfect

My heart is not pure,
I am not pure,
I have hope,
I have faith,
I love one another,
With all the grace.
No one shall pass me,
And do evil do's.
It isn't fair to hurt others.
While you laugh and play games.
It will break their heart apart,
I only have one dream,
That everyone will be treated the same.

Nimmy James, Grade 9
New Hyde Park Memorial Jr/Sr High School

Winter Blizzard

Winter blizzards come and go,
They always come with lots of snow.
I look out my window; see not a soul,
Can't imagine where they all go.
A blanket of snow has set upon us,
Good thing there is no school bus.
Staring out at the trees,
Pondering whether to take out the skis.
For I would not want a limb to fall on me,
Or an icicle pointy as can be.
We wonder what to do,
So we decide to make a hot stew.
Our blizzard is fading away,
We now have nothing else to say!

Jessica Hillery, Grade 7
Camillus Middle School

I Am Me

I am me
That's who I want to be
I like me as you can see
I am a reader, writer, and published poet
I would like to do many things
But I am not to blame
And I am not ashamed
I would like to be a doctor who does surgery
I would like to be a musician who plays the piano
I would like to be a saint
I would like to teach everything I am good at
Most of all I would like to be remembered
As a surgeon who saved many lives
As an artist who brought life and meaning to paintings
As a great musician whose music brought joy to everyone
I would like to be remembered
For being helpful, thoughtful, and kind
By being me I will do all these things

Ashley White, Grade 7
Queens Gateway to Health Sciences

Life Is Like a Roller Coaster

Life is like a roller coaster,
You've go your ups,
You've got your downs,
You've got your smiles,
You've got your frowns.
You've got to hold on tight,
because it's just one night
because your ride isn't over yet.
Danielle Ciaccia, Grade 7
Solvay Middle School

Fiery Love

The charcoal and wood burns
As the fire warms and learns
The faces of you and me
And to dance happily
It's sacred to the top
As the light begins to drop
Our faces they slowly move
As the candles fires dance to the grooves.
They flicker out and the fire too.
As I move closer to you
In the dark shade
The silhouettes have land
A gentle touch and feeling
To the lips it was appealing
We turn so fast away
But quickly we return to lay
Another Kiss…
Another Kiss…
Kinsey Sheppard, Grade 8
Baldwin Middle School

Art

Art is one of my favorite subjects,
I especially like a lot,
I go outside or in my room,
And pick a favorite spot,
What am I going to draw?
I close my eyes and think,
I paint a picture in my head,
To make my art complete!!
Collin Raimo, Grade 7
Holy Cross School

Stars Are Falling

Stars are falling
In the sky
While I watch them
When I lie
On the cold solid ground
I see them when I finally found
My true love I like to see,
The stars falling above me.
Melissa O'Connell, Grade 8
Holy Cross School

Tiger Woods

Tiger Woods learned golf at a very young age.
He was putting when he was eleven months old.
Tiger excelled at golf, and his parents gave him the most support.
They encouraged him to try hard and not let a few obstacles stop him.

Tiger Woods is part African American, white, and Asian.
There were a few times that he was kicked off golf courses because of his ethnicity.
The owner of a golf course challenged Tiger to a match with his ten year old son.
Tiger beat his son by one stroke. He was only three years old.

Tiger appeared on the *Good Morning America* show at age two.
He had his first hole in one at age six.
Tiger Woods was the youngest player to ever win the Master's Tournament.
He was just twenty-one years old.

On the golf course, Tiger showed courage and extraordinary skill.
At a tournament, he set the club record for the lowest score — fifty-nine.
He was the first person ever to win the four major tournament:
the Masters, the PGA tour, the British Open, and the US Open.

Tiger Woods has tried to become a better person than golfer.
He wants people to become anything that they want to be.
He has started many charities to help people deal with poverty.
Nothing seems to stop him from accomplishing his dream.
Aaron Gialanella, Grade 7
St Catherine of Siena School

Where I'm From

A cool breeze tousles my hair
I rub the sand off my feet and jump into the ocean
I sit on the blanket mind set on the newest Supergirl issue
I harass Dad until he takes me back to the hotel
Where he whines about not getting enough sun
We sit in the airport stuck with delays
I take out my laptop and write for as long as I can
When writer's block takes over I buy a book
I read until we arrive back in New York
I go up to my room my sanctuary and play with Donna my photogenic guinea pig
I upload new photos onto Photoshop and manipulate them until my hands hurt
Dad yells at me for being lazy
I pretend not to hear him and work on my story some more
At night I dream about being a best-selling author
When I wake up I watch the sun rise with Donna in my lap
My best friend calls me to let me know of her latest boy troubles
With none of my own I do my best to help her out
I ponder what the new day will be like
The same as yesterday or new and improved
I go to school and find out I have to write a poem about myself
I smile knowing I hate poetry but I'm ready to take on the challenge
Rachel Silverstein, Grade 9
Harborfields High School

An Ode to the Lion That Stands Before Me

You purr and you growl.
Your breath is quite foul.

I stand so close and motionless,
Just barely feet from your lioness.

Oh no, what's this? I have to sneeze!
I hold my breath to smother the wheeze.

For at any sudden movement you will pounce.
If I have any time, then away I will flounce.

But you are the king from the Sahara to New Jersey,
And now I find myself at your mercy.

Now I need to sneeze at large.
There I go, and now you charge!

Look at me, so scared, a funny sight had anyone seen us.
Oh! Thank goodness, there's an iron fence between us.

Margaret Doyle, Grade 7
Catholic Central High School

Friendship Never Ends

Friendship is a nice thing.
You have to take care of it.
When I am down, my friends cheer me up.
When my friends are down I cheer them up.
When I need help, I ask my friend.
Whenever my friend needs help, I help them.
Sometime I feel like a little mouse, getting run over by giants.
Then when they see me left out, they include me.
If you need some one by your side, find a friend.
Then if you do, take care of each other and look out for them.

Catherine Montreal, Grade 7
Solvay Middle School

Flowers

Flowers flowers,
Oh how I love how they smell,
Even though they don't look as good as a shell,
So if they were put together,
They would make something quite cute,
With all of the looks and smell,
Oh…
Flowers flowers,
Oh how I love to draw them,
As you can see,
They give you ideas just like this one you can see,
Flowers flowers,
Oh how they gave me this idea to…
Write a poem and relax to think about…
Flowers you can see.

Megan Pettit, Grade 8
Southern Cayuga Middle School

What If

What if the does and the deer shot back,
and the trees were at our legs and away they'd hack.

What if we got stuffed and put on fireplaces,
and they had our expressions arranged in scary faces.

What if they littered all over our things,
and sold us in pet stores and clipped our wings.

What if they destroyed our homes and our land
for things of their own selfish demand.

What if we were made into big fluffy coats,
and they were always fishing for us in their big fancy boats.

What if you were crossing the street and you got hit by a bus,
What if nature was hunting us?

Emma Delia, Grade 8
Warwick Valley Middle School

Family

Family is who you go to
When you need them the most,
Not for you to go and brag to or push or boast,
But for you to say "I love you the absolute most."

Respect your elder family,
For they have created you,
And when they say they love you,
Make sure to say, "I love you, too."

Can family be your friend?
Of course they can. Just know,
You cannot take them for granted,
Keep the loving flow.

So when your family tells you,
"you mean the world to me,"
It is not to tease you,
But to show you what you mean.

Romel Williams, Grade 7
Dake Jr High School

I Am

I am Danielle Lee Raynard.
I am a very aggressive athlete.
I am kind to almost everyone.
I am a fun and exciting person.
I am in the 8th grade and some what smart.
I am patient, yet impatient at times.
I am a teenage girl, getting through junior high school
I am immature and goofy with my friends.
I am responsible when I need to be.
I am Danielle Lee Raynard, and I am awesome.

Danielle Raynard, Grade 8
Avon Middle School

The Water Hole

Giant gray rocks, calm running water above; as the water turns rough the rock becomes slippery and down we slide into deep crystal clear freezing water. Water pouring down hitting us as we jump behind the waterfall, we stare in amazement at the beautiful sight.

Drying, we lay spread out on the giant rock, bright sunshine beating down on us, luscious bright green trees surround the rocks; dead brown leaves lie gently on the ground, afternoon approaching, no shadows to be seen.
Peaceful sounds of birds chirping happily, wind hitting the trees as they sway back and forth, the sounds of the rushing water so soothing and relaxing; we're ready to go in the beautiful water again, the sound of us splashing as we jump off the rocks is all that is heard.

Will this beautiful sight stay so clean and untouched forever? This gorgeous sight so amazing to look at. Being here takes away every negative feeling and brings about happiness and comfort.
Amazing
amazing
amazing

Krista Langdon, Grade 8
Baldwin Middle School

Winter

As the Earth slowly changes colors from luscious green to polar bear white,
You know it's winter.
Snow gracefully hitting the ground,
Kids putting out their tongues and trying to catch each snowflake coming from the sky.
Looking out kitchen windows while making hot chocolate with marshmallows,
For the children that can't even feel their hands or feet because they are so frozen.
Watching them all slide down their driveway with gigantic smiles on their faces, never looking happier,
You know it's winter.
Anxiously awaiting the weekends, to build snowmen or have snowball fights with dad.
"Come inside," parents yell out of their front doors,
"NO!" they scream back and take another snowball and throw it at their friends.
The temperature under zero and little bodies shivering inside their jackets,
But yet they refuse to come inside and get warmed up.
You know it's winter.
Little ones stare in amazement at the snowplow coming up and down their streets,
Cleaning up the snow and making huge piles.
The sun starts to go down and the moon starts to come up, the daylight changes into a midnight black sky filled with stars.
Kids getting ready for bed, glancing out the windows, seeing the glistening snow before settling under their warm cozy covers.
Dreaming of their wonderful winter day,
You know it's winter.

Brianne Garcett, Grade 9
Smithtown High School West

The Spring I Was 13

The spring I was 13, my best friends and I were about to have the time of our lives.

Standing in the stalls tacking up our horses, and singing "Hello World." Cutting up apples for our horses and handing them out. Hearing their lips smacking together as they happily eat their apples.

Now all of us are saddled up cantering through the field. We hear the thundering of all our horses slamming on the ground as they run on. I feel the sweat coming off the sides of my horse's legs as he hurries on.

We smell the fresh air hitting us in the face. It feels so chilly. Still, all of us run on kicking up dirt as we go. I start to taste the dust in my mouth.

As we make our way back home, everybody is really tired. We untack our horses, and say good night. I kiss my Sailor on the face and say; you will always be my baby boy.

Rhiannon Faith Madej, Grade 9
Ketchum-Grande Memorial School

Love

The best thing in life to have is love.
Everyone just needs a hug.
A smile can go a long way.
It can turn darkness into day.
Do everything from the heart,
Never to part,
With the feeling of love, love in your heart.
Love will overcome,
Any bad that is done.
Love your neighbor
Love your friend
And this life will never end.

Brianna Condon, Grade 7
Camillus Middle School

Eyes

Memories flashing all through my head,
thinking of the note she left on my bed.
She left; She ran,
Far away, thinking I did not want her to stay.
Independent, brave, determined,
she was.
But she couldn't hold on,
she had to let go.
No one knows where she is,
most likely somewhere alone,
for I called her house and she wasn't home.
And I am the "him,"
who inflicted all the pain.
But I loved her.
But I was vain.
I drove her away,
ran her train off the tracks,
And all I want is to have her back.
But she will not come,
for she is independent and wise,
but one thing I can never forget is her dark brown eyes.

Maria Troisi, Grade 8
Commack Middle School

I Am

I am
Love, Peace, Life
I care about my health and the poverty going on in the world
Patience is important to me
Kindness is important to me
Authenticity is important to me
Love does help everyone
Cruelty is a bad thing, but it can help you
Find out who's true and who's not
No one's getting younger
Live like there's no tomorrow
Dance like no one's watching
This is me

Raquel Cunningham, Grade 8
Hauppauge Middle School

Soccer

Soccer is the beautiful game.
The fans can never be tamed.
The excitement, satisfaction, and disappointment.
We all have our heroes and villains.

It is played around the planet.
Soccer or Futbol, everyone enjoys it.
The tricks, goals, saves all excite the crowd.

"Joga Bonito" is what the Portuguese say.
It means play beautiful.
The rest of the crowd screams Ole, Ole, Ole.
When the home team scores the whole crowd is cheerful.

Taylor Wells, Grade 8
Avon Middle School

Sandy Paradise

I love the sandy warm feeling,
that takes my breath away.
I look out to the ocean's ceiling,
that oh so makes my day.
The creatures swimming swiftly,
can maybe be my friend.
Although they aren't all nifty,
they can still last to the end…
The coconuts are yummy,
but only the right ones.
It all gets to my tummy,
which feels like many tons
Frisbee can be much fun,
many people laugh loud.
The best is in the sun,
when there is a big crowd.
I love the beach altogether,
Everything about it, just works out forever!

Alyssa Danes, Grade 7
Camillus Middle School

Life

For each moment is a day yet begun
to feel another, live a minute undone.
To understand a meaning, to know all the answers,
to be happy and free, by just being me.
To have a thought to do something new,
to rethink and just be you.
To hope to sing for a reason, for
someone to care, and jump for seasons.
Is it possible? Can it be done?
No one really knows unless they've had the fun.
To figure out if it is true or false.
To stop breathing and have no pulse.
That is life full of surprises.
To just live and see you'll never know what'll be.

Erica Maudsley, Grade 9
Cassadaga Valley High School

Love You

L ove dies and opens again
O pen hearts to one
V ows of the heart
E xcellent compassion of feeling

Y ours to hold and kiss
O pen the way
U nited as one

Frances Smieya, Grade 8
St Mary's School

Witnessing Morning

As I open my eyes,
from my sleep.
I hear the birds say,
cheep, cheep, cheep.
As I run out of my bedroom,
and into the hall.
I hear the sun saying,
"Good morning to all."
I see dew on the ground,
As I look around.
I run outside with no shoes or socks,
I looked out for all the rocks.
I hear my mom say come inside,
I said yes but in time.
As I kiss the morning goodbye,
I turn and see the sky.
No more morning but now,
It's noon time.

Brittney Downey, Grade 7
St Mary's School

Life

Skipping, running, jumping
Laughing and playing
Living life completely carefree
Dreaming of being an astronaut,
Or a doctor,
Or even president.
Live out this life,
Chow down on candy,
Shove cake in your face,
Sniff every flower,
Only paint with your fingers,
And eat with your hands.
Wish at 11:11 and hope it comes true
Believe in childish things
Wonder and dream with all your might
Be curious, explore
Dance in the rain
Make up a game for when it's thundering
Have fun and don't let life pull you down
Live like a young child

Camille Pensabene, Grade 7
Camillus Middle School

Heart "Beat"

Put your hand on the neck, put the pick on the strings,
It's time to close your mouth and let your fingers sing.
Express your emotions through the notes that you play.
Sometimes notes speak louder than what you do or say.

From violent to peaceful and everything in between,
Chords and notes are unspoken words for whatever you want them to mean.
Your guitar is a blank canvas for you to make a work of art,
Your painting of sounds comes naturally after you've found your place to start.

The beat of your heart is the beat of your song.
But unlike your heart, your beat forever lives on.
Whether you're the next Jimi Hendrix or you don't own a guitar,
Everyone has music inside of them that lets you know who they are.

Lukas DeSarbo, Grade 9
Oyster Bay High School

Indians and the King

As we watched from the cliff, the bison flocked
As we readied our spears, we saw the beast
A majestic king with a golden mane, his beauty stunned us all

He took down bison
Like they were leaves on the ground
He took down two, four, then seven in an instant
The king, in all his beauty had a thirst of blood

He left a bison for us, he urged us to take it.
We did a roar so loud, we knew he was the Great Spirit
We puzzled the thought of the Great Spirit turning into a mysterious beast.
We praised the Great Spirit for all time

Justin Scharff, Grade 7
Our Lady Queen of Apostles School

Unanswered Questions

What will be ten years ahead?
Will all our jokes and traditions be dead?
Will everything change, or remain the same?
Will you still remember my name?

Will you forget everything we had?
All the good times, the laughs, the cries, the bad
Or will it remain fresh in your mind?
As bright as glass that's just been shined

I don't know about your thoughts, but I know about my own
I know these memories will remain with me, even as I've matured and grown
I'll never forget you — my sister, my best friend
You'll be in my heart, until the end

What will happen in ten years — I have no clue
I just want to still be close to you
What will happen, we'll have to wait and see
But for now, I just want you here with me.

Rachel Zehnwirth, Grade 9
Stella K Abraham High School for Girls

New York, New York

New York City is an amazing place
Whenever I go my heart begins to race
Though there is danger yet a sense of pride
Here's New York you're in for a ride

There's always something to do you'll never get a bore
Unique people showing who they really are
Streets crowded with people and traffic
Restaurants, stores, and hotels galore

Yet some places are very poor
Glamorous shows there called Broadway
Scary and interesting people you'll meet on the subway
Famous people and famous places

Only in New York City you'll have these experiences.

Kaileen Rozanski, Grade 8
Avon Middle School

Deep Down Inside

When I look at her I see

Those small, innocent eyes,
full of comfort

Those small, furry ears,
always alert

That small, black nose,
on the lookout for danger

That small, curly tail,
wagging with joy

But when I look further and deep, down inside,
I see more than small

I see a big, warm heart
always making room for more

Abbey Walters, Grade 7
Camillus Middle School

En"light"ened

John Parker, the richest guy in the state
is so happy he must celebrate.
He calls Thomas Edison to install a light bulb
and invites all the townspeople to show off his gold.
Everyone stares and waits for the lights to turn on,
but the lights don't shine — his pride is gone.
John Parker's full of anger and shame
and calls Thomas Edison to explain this game.
All Thomas says is, "flip the switch on the wall,"
then the lights turn on and everyone has a ball.

JoJo Tawil, Grade 7
Yeshiva Shaare Torah

Ode to Soccer

I run down the huge field
My opponent runs at me like a tiger
I run past him
Then I pass to a teammate
He passes to me
And I get the ball as the glowing sun beats over me
Sweat drips and rolls off my face
Again I pass to my teammate
He passes back to me
I rush towards the goalie net
I get closer to the huge net
I think what will happen if I miss, but then,
I kick that black and white ball
I score, I feel like I have won ONE MILLION DOLLARS!
I walk off the field feeling great

Tristan Hillman, Grade 8
Hendy Avenue School

Friends Forever

Together all the time, friends till the end.
Always telling secrets, on them I can depend.
Sitting around laughing and talking about boys.
Getting so crazy, neighbors complain about the noise!
Singing and dancing, having fun.
Begging our parents to stay even when the sleepover's done.
So much more I'd love to write, but there's no more time.
My mom shut off the light!

Jessica Florio, Grade 8
St Catherine of Sienna School

Basketball Happiness

There's the tip —
Players run up and down the court
Like holiday shoppers
Players shoot and merrily skip
For two quarters these players run
Then the buzzer sounds
They go to the locker room, without noise.

During half time the coach speaks
For no one knows what they talk about,
But the players and layers of wall

They run back out, the crowd shouting
While players take place.
The game is running on
Soon it's the fourth quarter
The game is tied
50-50 when time starts to run out
All the dust is a hurricane
They pass to Clark, who puts up a prayer
Then "swoosh" it goes in
Everyone is happy
But most of all the kid.

Alex Clark, Grade 8
Southern Cayuga Middle School

Anger

Anger is something that lives inside us
You can never lose it
You can only hold it back
Anger is what hurts people
Anger can control people
And you can't stop it
Brandon Parrott, Grade 7
Solvay Middle School

Hurt

You do the dance
you sing the song like a rock star
You have all the memories
of being mauled
by The Spirit Bear,
You're hurt inside
because of what
You've done
are you the only one?
Erica Campion, Grade 7
Solvay Middle School

Football

There is sportsmanship,
running, tackling
as hard as you can
Like football is a game
of physical ability
The yelling of plays
to tackling a mean machine
The sounds of
thump, thump
down the field.
Then the taste of victory
I can feel the sweet
sweat of winning
electrifying as it
tingles down my head.
To me
it's not just a game,
It's life!
Zachery Brimacomb, Grade 7
Dake Jr High School

Birds

Birds flying through the air
Soaring past without a care.
Flapping wings give them a lift
Not knowing of their gift.

Birds flying through the air
Soaring past without a care.
Lifting with barely a try.
You look up and wonder why.
Sean Houlihan, Grade 8
Warwick Valley Middle School

Go

Which way to go
if only I could know
to find the direction
with no exception
you must measure the distance
do not have resistance
there must be one to lead the way
not to the city
but to the bay
with green grass growing
and little boats rowing
I must find the way
seek it today
Mariele Anneling, Grade 7
Bethlehem Central Middle School

Love

Love is so pure
Just like gold.
Love is so innocent
Just like a baby.
Love is something you can't control
Just like something going crazy.
Love can really change you
In ways I can't explain.
Love can change the coldest heart
To the warmest in the world.
Samantha Gumkowska, Grade 7
St Mary's School

Grandpa

Grandpa grandpa grandpa
You were my biggest fan
Cheering me on every time I ran
From base to base
Even when you were sick
I was still your favorite pick

Grandpa grandpa grandpa
Crack! As the ball hit the bat
You watched me like
I was a baseball star and
I was in the World Series

Grandpa grandpa grandpa
As I sit here on the bench today
I can see over that way
Where you sat each and every day

Grandpa grandpa grandpa
It's been 3 years from today
And I miss you
And everything you'd say
Eric Elenfeldt, Grade 9
North Tonawanda High School

The Day

That day was the saddest
Hearing the cries,
Seeing the pain,
Feeling the hurt of losing family
That day
Was when the trees wept,
And the tears seeped,
From my big, brown eyes
That day
Was when my grandpa,
Aunt and uncle
Lost the fight of holding on to life
Although, I shall say
They did not pass the same day
Though my grandpa passed
A day after my uncle
But still they did not pass the same day
That day
Was when I lost
Those who meant a million to me
Those who I love and always will
Michelle Pickering, Grade 8
Sodus Middle School

An Elegant Dance

Spins and twirls, and
dips and bows, tip
toes and curtsies and
beautiful gowns, girls
fly through the air
like delicate birds, boys
with bow ties and black
rented suits, big rooms
with flowers all around,
dancing makes the
world go around
Leah Warner, Grade 7
Dake Jr High School

Dessert

Helado in Spanish
Glace in French
Of all the desserts
Ice cream is the best!

Cake is cool too
It's a wonderful food
I eat it with a drink
And it puts me on the brink
Of heaven

Dessert is my friend
When it comes to the end
Of the day

Phil Linden, Grade 8
Avon Middle School

I Am

I am
Peace, love, joy
I care about the people in my life right now.
Humbleness is important to me.
Loyalty is important to me.
Honesty is important to me.
Lying is wrong, but it can get you out of things.
Live each day as if it was the last day.
When will the world have peace?
The most important thing is our family.
This is me.

Stephanie Torres, Grade 8
Hauppauge Middle School

The Real Me

I like sports,
especially if they're played on courts,
and I get to wear my shorts.

I love my dog; she is shiny and black.
She might look fierce, but she'll never attack.
If you pet her, she will roll on her back.

I love to vacation at Disney World every Spring Break.
My favorite dessert there is chocolate Mickey cake.
Family vacations are necessary for everyone's sake.

To myself I'll be true,
In everything I do.
For my career I have no clue.

Dylan Kyle, Grade 7
Camillus Middle School

Life

Life can only last so long.
Until God takes it away.
While we sing our lovely song.
For art thou leaving us now.
With only sorrow in our hearts.
Its how life goes.
Don't depart for only sorrow in our hearts.
Life slips by so enjoy it well,
while we have it, so don't drown.
You never know you might pass,
so make it last.
You might hate life,
but then other times you love it.
Cherish life,
and your family.
To me I feel like it was just yesterday when my
grandmother picked me up,
and held me in her arms.
God brought you into this world so be thankful.
This is the way of life, so treat it right.

Lourdes Cotton, Grade 7
Public School 3 D'Youville Porter Campus

My Summer Picnic

I went on a picnic one summer day
Much went on that's what I have to say
There was a worm in my apple
And an ant in my Snapple
I got stung by a bee
Of course, only me
I fell in some water
And I lost my only quarter
Then I walked into a tree
And got stung by another bee
That is all I have to say
About my horrible picnic day

Brittany Barton, Grade 7
St John Baptist de LaSalle Regional School

The Summer Sky

It's so big, it goes on forever
with fluffy clouds as soft as cotton candy
The sun hangs there bright and shimmering,
making objects below sparkle
casting a warm glow over the land
There's a peaceful silence, but it's interrupted —
the wind softly blows through the green tree tops
birds slowly fly by
airplanes rumble through the pillow-like clouds
How can it seem so serene, but then so chaotic?
It makes one feel calm and safe
the word comes to mind — freedom
The endless sky
The endless sky
The endless sky

Ferisha Hosein, Grade 8
Baldwin Middle School

Earth

there is nothing at all but darkness Everywhere
but in the middle is this huge form Earth
no light, dark all around except near Earth
the sun reflects off earth and the Beautiful
colors are shown everywhere, the water is Blue
land is Green
clouds are White
no sounds, just a Peaceful
kind of silence Why
would everyone continue to Destroy
it, so they can get to work on time? Beautiful
is the word that comes to mind, the Darkness
around it really makes it look Amazing
it feels so Peaceful
from this view
Peaceful
Peaceful
Peaceful

George Abreu, Grade 8
Baldwin Middle School

The Opposites

Most of the time I am limish green,
Like a lima bean,
Energetic, lively,
Like spring opening up,
But at times I'm a crimson red,
Mad, obstinate,
Obnoxious, mean,
Watch out those in my path!
These both contradict themselves,
But they're both part of me!

Andrew Jones, Grade 7
Our Savior New American School

Mr. Brisk

Leaves fall off the trees.
Getting cold, using jackets,
People feel a breeze!

David Schwartz, Grade 7
Christ the King School

Turkey Day

Thanksgiving is fun
all the people
that you love
come.
You eat, laugh, you
have some fun.
You have stuffed
turkey, chicken,
ham, and mac and cheese.
After our bellies are full
we watch sports,
and movies.
This is why I like
Thanksgiving.

Terell Duck, Grade 7
St John School

Love in a Lifetime

Sometimes… Your life is perfect
Sometimes… It's too crazy to think in
My life is like a story
What comes around goes around
OR
A perfect fairy tale moment
One heart fixes a whole
One love is all you need
Love in a lifetime
And forever
You might see
The stronger your words
The stronger you will be
Love in a lifetime
And whatever it may bring

Alexis Tesiorowski, Grade 9
Henninger High School

Solved

Gas prices and the number of troops being sent to Iraq is going up,
While crimes, terrorism, and abuse leads more people into the death cup.
The days left of the Earth before global warming goes down,
Soon there just won't be any more people around.

The President watches the homeless in the subway,
Sleeping on the dirty floor because their lives had gone astray.
Car crashes and accidents happen with many distractions in the air.
It seems as if the drivers are unaware.

Bacteria going around to every student in school.
Nobody is taking precaution just being a mere fool.
Smaller schools you tell us,
But yet, there has not been any progress.

Illegal immigrants pouring into the nation.
No one seems to do anything not even come to the point of realization.
Genocides in countries, killing the souls of kids.
Their bodies and eyes of hope is the only thing it rids.

Facing discrimination and the occurrence of gangs on the street,
If only for every fight, a gang would stop for good and just retreat.
Minors buying drinks and drugs, soon they'll be like the rest, buying a gun.
If this was all to be solved, then a new world has just begun.

Anastasiya Kachur, Grade 9
Townsend Harris High School

Cross-Country

The hardest part is the start
Once you're on the line there's no turning back
When the horn blows, that's when you run
You try to get out before the others
Once you're a half mile in, you can hear voices
You come out of the wood and in two lines, faces are staring, clapping,
Cheering you on, to help you do your best and help you hang on
Then into the woods you go
But you cheer and encourage your team to do their best
And if they aren't, you bring them along
Once you turn by the bog, you can see the coach
Once you get to her you know what's coming next
Drive, drive, drive the hill
But once you get up the hill your coach disappears
She takes a shortcut to the finish where you will meet her next
After you reach the football field, you see faces
Then you see your coach at the end and the final turn
But once you reach her, you know what she's going to say next
L.A.T., L.A.T., L.A.T. SHE SAYS
After that, you just have to sprint your heart out
Soon after you know it, you have finished the race

Allie Van Allen, Grade 7
Camillus Middle School

Thanksgiving

When everyone gather and sits down at the table,
Every person is willing and able.

I'm in between Grandma and Uncle Pat,
Squeezed in tight,
No room for even a rat.

Thanksgiving prayer is finished with "Amen."
Everyone shouts, "Cheers."

Cheers for good health,
Cheers for all men.

The prayers are done,
The eating begins.

Everyone passes and starts to dig in.

When the dinner is done,
Plates are brought out,
The children get up and run all about.

Until the pies are brought in,
Pumpkin, apple, and cherry,
For Thanksgiving is very merry.

Patty Zick, Grade 8
St John School

A Soldier:

Here comes a soldier
Marching off to war,
Clad in golden armor
Shining in the sun.

He doesn't really want to go
But he knows he has no choice,
For his king has called all the men to help him
Fight this pointless war.

Sweat dripping down his face
Glistening in the sun,
As he marches to the meeting place
Over the next hill.

He leaves a wife, a family
Two children, both girls,
He leaves them behind
To find his fate in battle.

As he comes to the camp he looks up,
Watches the sunset,
And wonders
Will this be his last?

Timothy Beyer, Grade 8
Warwick Valley Middle School

Memories

Looking back at our past,
Why does time go so fast?
My earliest memory is as a little boy at play
Riding my sled on a fine winter day.
Thinking about the tears and the laughs,
Having fun with all our crafts.
Seeing many things go by,
Chasing them as they fly.
Looking back here and there,
Hoping we can hold them as much as we can bear.
Not feeling your warm embrace,
As you reach out to my careless face.
Acting like a flashback in your mind,
Something special that you will find.
There was not one moment in this span of time
That your memory tiptoed across my mind.
Don't be afraid someday we'll meet again,
Memories un-fading until the end.

Marvin Banzon, Grade 7
Holy Family School

The Job of a Fairy Godmother

With a surge of magic,
And a wave of my wand,
To go from tragic,
To a fairy tale.

With a snap of my fingers,
And some fairy dust,
To go from sad singers,
To a dance at the ball.

With a swoosh of my hands,
And some belief,
To go from far off lands,
To a castle.

With a supply of aid,
And some magic words,
To go from a maid,
To a princess.

Gurnaina Chawla, Grade 8
Nesaquake Middle School

What Is Love?

What is love?
What does it do to you?
Do you just wonder what to do?
Is that person ever on your mind?
Is that person one of a kind?
Do you worry what to say?
Are you sad if you don't see them that day?
So I'm asking you what is love?
Cause for me it's all of the above!

Devon Newland, Grade 8
St Mary's School

Life in the Fall
The muddy smell of the grass
The leathery feel of the ball
The quarterback steps back to pass
This is life in the fall

The sound of the helmets that crack
As they feel like they hit a wall
Defense looking for a sack
This is life in the fall

Joseph Boccia, Grade 8
Warwick Valley Middle School

Seasons and Time
Seasons change,
    just like time.

Every spring, flowers sprout.
    Every fall, is very colorful.

Every winter, snow falls.
    Every summer, the sun shines

Every exciting moment, my camera
    remains at home.

Sometimes I have it,
    I take funny pictures.

Every time a song comes on the radio,
    We sing and laugh.

I take these kind of pictures,
    So these moments last.

Seasons change,
    just like time.

Nicole Coyne, Grade 8
Avon Middle School

Jocund Day, Night...
Golden day
Black night
Black night will make him pay
It will surely give him fright
Golden day
Black night
Under bright sky
The boy flies a kite
Under dark night he may die
Until he lives again in the light
Happiness is a warm sun
For the boy lives in fun,
During the golden day
Before he dies, when the day is done.

Sean Toomey, Grade 9
Bronx High School of Science

The Loss of Someone Special
This pain inside is killing me
When I think of you I remember all those
Smiles, all those good times, and all your tears.
I know in life they say people come and go
I just wished you weren't the person who had to go away,
You were so special to me and to everybody
The person who was always happy
It looked like life wouldn't take you away
You weren't the person that had to suffer a lot
The person who didn't have to through all that pain that killed all of us
And I think
Why?
Why God?
Why did you take her away from me?
What did she ever do to you?
And start tearing,
Begin to cry
But I think
She's not dead she's only sleeping
Sleeping so deeply in the arms of our Lord
In His kingdom were one day we will meet again.

Andrea Marca, Grade 9
Queens Vocational High School

Christmas Eve
I see white lights on the tree
The only light outside comes from the glow of the white snow
The smell of burning wood covers the cool air
The warmth of the fire moves across the room
Snow falls softly to the ground
These things aren't noticed, but it wouldn't be Christmas without them.

Mallory Wiederspiel, Grade 8
Warwick Valley Middle School

Turkey's Advice
There are many, many reasons to eat chicken on Thanksgiving...
Turkeys gobble, chickens squawk
Turkeys waddle, chickens walk
Turkeys are big, chickens are small
Chickens are smart, Turkeys know nothing at all
Turkeys are harder to look for
Chickens are easy, just go to the store
Turkeys are hunted
Chickens are plucked
Trust me my friend,
You'll have way more luck
Spyin' a chicken
than eyein' a turkey
If you eat turkey
You're full of mulurkey
Take my advice and eat that
Finger lickin'
deep-fried
CHICKEN!

Abbie Gillespie, Grade 7
CS Driver Middle School

Ready to Cheer

The big golden bows sit pleasantly on top
   of their curly, bouncy, over hair sprayed hair
Eyeliner spills out of the side of their eyes
   just merely because they put it there
Bright red lipstick will bring out their smiles
   on the floor…
The big bright blue mat every team prays
   they won't mess up on
Stunts fly high
   basket tosses hit the sky
Cheers are screamed louder than ever before
   circles are formed as places are called
Girls and their big bows bounce as they are forever
   the number one squad.

Tayler Murphy, Grade 9
DeSales High School

Life's Lesson

We are supposed to listen and do what we are told,
   and to bundle up when it is cold.
To fulfill our dreams with all our heart,
   and to read and write so that we can be smart.
But what some people don't know or teach to others,
   is to follow your heart and love one another.
We know to obey and to teach and learn,
   but we must know to be thankful for what we earn.
Because if we're not and our time is done,
   our last times of our lives will not be fun.
So don't take anything for granted, yourself or your things,
   and to know that what you get is what God brings.

Meghan Graham, Grade 7
Most Precious Blood School

Why Did You Go

You never said you would leave me
Instead you said you would love me forever
But the day you left made me tear
Tear that I won't see you anymore
Or hear your voice again
You didn't even say "goodbye" or "we're through"
You just left me in misery
And making me think you left
Because of me or what I did wrong
Now every time I hear your name
It makes me feel worthless
And unworthy for you and your love
Because every night I think of you
And wish I can see you again
I would tell you "I love you"
Or say that I could change for you
But I missed that chance

I guess love wasn't my thing
Since you took that away from me

Shawn Uy, Grade 9
Fordham Preparatory School

Magnificent and Malicious

Fire is beautiful, it knows no boundaries
Fire is warmth and welcome
Flames lick and lash
Fire is our symbol, signal and survival
Fire is sacred

Fire is deadly, it breaks all boundaries
Fire is destruction and merciless
Flames kill and scar
Fire is our worst enemy, hate and death
Fire is demolition in a beautiful disguise

Fire is magnificent yet malevolent
It brings down life and drags up death
Fire is power, fire is weakness
It deceives beautifully, blindly, secretly
Fire is dreadfully beautiful

Ashley Williams, Grade 9
Marble Hill High School for International Studies

Assaulted Puppy

There was a puppy.
And he was sad.
He was kept in a cage
And was not fed
Tears welled up in his eyes as he whined the whole time
With a smirk on his face his owner abused the puppy.
Then the guy sold the puppy.
The puppy was adopted.
He got fed.
He got attention.
He got every thing he ever wanted.
So the family and
Of course the puppy
Lived happily ever after

Dustin W. Queor, Grade 7
Solvay Middle School

Forbidden Love

Alone at last,
You and I.
Since the last time we talked,
Wow, it's been a while.
My elegant behavior continues to show you,
Just why you chose me.
Seeing you laugh and smile,
Joy fills my heart.
To have to say good-bye,
I think I'll fall apart.
I still love you,
And you love me,
I wish our forbidden love
Was meant to be.

Caiya Moye, Grade 9
John Bowne High School

World Peace

World peace is soon to come
It would feel like all worries are all gone
It would be peaceful, delightful, and very great
The wars will be over soon to be
But right now there are way too much
Just wait till you see, the wars will be over as soon as can be
Don't be too worried, soldiers are there, so brave and very great
They protect us from harm
Soon they will create harmony
World peace is soon to be, so just wait and see!
I know it doesn't feel good to just watch hundreds die in war
But it will soon be over in a blink of an eye
So keep on cheering soldiers on with all your cards from children all around the world
Soldiers feel great with all the little cards to know how much we really do care
That little card is really great to let soldiers be encouraged to fight in war for world peace to be created
So just watch, world peace will come
Just believe me and it soon will come!

Melanie Morgan, Grade 7
Holy Family School

Realize

As I smell the fresh air. Look out the window and stare.
It seems like a maze has me in a daze.
I look around for the ones that I love. It seems I am wondering about the stars above.
I have a fear that no one will be there.
I feel that love starts with a smile, grows with a kiss, and ends with a tear. I feel in the air that the end of this love is near.
I run hopelessly from this pain, and my self-esteem is one thing that I have to regain.
I feel that I can't hide and fear has taken me for a ride.
I try to shake it off; for some reason. It seems like it isn't my time or season.
I look to find the honesty in my soul, sometimes the hate that I have for people turns my heart into coal.
My soul is hungry; I feel that I need to eat, this is something that I want to defeat.
This might be a dream that happened because I didn't realize.
I needed something and didn't know how to ask, it's like I have a job and don't know my task.
In my heart there is a hole. As I search for my soul.

Tiara Carter, Grade 8
John W Dodd Middle School

Friends Forever

Friends are friends forever together 'til the end. You promised me that you would always be my friend.
One day something changed I'm not sure what it was.
I lost you on that day and the reason was because of a stupid fight.
And for some reason, I don't know why, we couldn't make it right.

We went our separate ways. This went on for days and days.
I made new friends and you made yours, but that hole in my heart could not be filled for that hole was only yours.
Times got really tough, my road of life was, oh, so rough.
I needed friends, not the kind you see from day to day, but the kind that will always and forever stay.

Memories were all I had and just the thought of them made me sad.
I sometimes cried wondering how to make it right. I wish you could erase that day and that fight.
Would you please forgive me? I don't know where to start. It hurts me so bad to have this hole in my heart!

I don't want our friendship to totally end. I need you! You are my best friend!
So can we make a promise to stay together 'til the end? A vow to each other to ALWAYS be BEST FRIENDS?

Catherine Auguste, Grade 7
Chestnut Ridge Middle School

Halloween Magic

Halloween is frightening and dark.
Monsters, witches and ghosts prowl around,
Leaving their mark!

Candy, costumes, movies,
Are all a part of the Halloween fun.
But, when you hear spooky sounds,
You know you better run!

Lock the doors, close the window blinds,
Creep around the scary house,
For, you do now know what you will find!

Creaks are the only sounds,
That fills the lonely darkness.
While vibrating noises you hear behind the walls!
Give you goose bumps and a frightening call!

Just remember it is all pretend,
It is only in your mind!
But, is it really?
Well…that is for you to decide!

Kelly Huvane, Grade 8
Christ the King School

Beast

The beast that lies in dark wood shadow lives
as long as it eats the living.
Thus the prey is shy.
As long as the young ones don't cry,
it remains alive; it cannot die.
The shine of the full moon
burns the grass in which it hides.
Its pelt conceals its fearsome claws
that have killed them all.

Of all the beasts that followed this one,
the cats are the greatest, the children of the beast.

Alex Kilgallon, Grade 8
Windsor Middle School

Destiny

Come with me and you will see,
my love for you is everlasting

Nothing can compare to how beautiful you are,
my love for you, is beyond the stars

When you smile the stars will shine
Your laugh is as great as Father Time

Come with me and you will see,
life's greatest adventure, our destiny

Michael Stankiewicz, Grade 8
Most Precious Blood School

Winter

Winter is my favorite season
I like it for so many reasons.
You can play in the snow
As many of you may know.
You can sit by the fire
And watch games that come down to the wire.
You can have fun
And at the end of the day it will all be done.

Courtney Miller, Grade 7
Holy Cross School

Growing Up

As babies
We'd go crazy
We'd cry and whine
This would happen all the time
We'd fall, get a bump
And then get what we wanted.
Turning ages older,
No more crying on your shoulder.
I got more responsibilities
You said you trusted in me
Now I'm even older
And getting ready to move out
Is that what life is really about?
Now I'm getting jobs,
Doing things on my own,
This is the way you have shown
To live life out and to be free
Being the best me I can be
This I wrote, I hope you've read
These are the things you have taught me and said.

Kristen Lonnborg, Grade 9
Stella Maris High School

43 Racers on the Track

43 racers on the track
Dale Earnhardt Jr. leads with a gap.
What's Jeff Gordon doin' takin' a nap?
Now he's in the back of the pack.
Juan Montoya just gave him a smack.

Now there's a caution for debris on the track.
Everyone pits to get some gas
The pace-car is out and off and away
Dale Jr. still leads the way
While Jeff Gordon is in the pits to stay.

Now into turn 4 the pace-car is off.
Away with a roar Dale Jr. takes off.

On the last lap the checkers fly high
42 drivers are now eating pie
While Jeff Gordon has gone to cry.

Julia Leonard, Grade 8
Southern Cayuga Middle School

Thanksgiving

During Thanksgiving,
I eat a lot of food.
I can have anything
that I choose.
From mashed potatoes,
to pumpkin pie
I love this food,
I cannot lie.
During Thanksgiving,
my family comes over.
And most of them,
are much much older.
They travel over a mile,
and stay for awhile,
until the day is done,
and we've had some fun.

Nicole Episalla, Grade 8
St John School

Ice Cream

I love ice cream
it's like a creamy dream,
that chunky Rocky Road,
it's never chocolatey and cold,
it never lasts,
I just eat it too fast,
especially Pecan Surprise,
ooh and Sorbet Sunrise,
don't forget my personal favorite,
the banana split,
the cherries always get lost,
in that gooey chocolate sauce,
don't forget about strawberry,
mmm…yummy in my tummy,
YES,
ice cream is the very BEST!

Hannah Reynolds, Grade 8
Southern Cayuga Middle School

Bullies

Bullies are cruel
They're cars
They use your fuel
To ride all over you

They think they own
The friends they loan
Until they're shown
The no-passing zone

Don't be a fool
Bullies are bad
If you think they're cool
Then you are sad

Elaina Canestrare, Grade 7
Solvay Middle School

Land of Christmas

Snow is white but not as bright as the sun that melts it.
Evergreens here and there. You can smell Christmas in the air.
Jingle bells on the sleigh. Reindeer quietly munching on hay.
Snowmobiles are quite a fright to the little old lady who walks her dog at night.
Snow is falling. Kids aren't stalling to go outside and play.
Today's the day the tree goes up.
My friends are coming and I will say, "What's up?"

Nick Warren, Grade 7
Camillus Middle School

Her Love

Out the door, to the open field to smell the cool autumn breeze.
She sways back and forth in and out of reality.
"Lilah?" she hears from inside that dungeon.
She smiles and runs the other way.
Trying to reach the sun and moon and stars.
She runs till she reaches the weeping willow.
Oh, how many times she had spent leaning against that crying tree.
They cried together.
Lilah and Willow.
She misses that adorable loving boy. She needs him to keep her sane.
But his flame is extinguished, the breath gone from him.
And with that breath went the glow from her eyes, never to be seen again.
In her heart she hears; "Lilah and Ryan" in love, together and apart.

Tori Malin, Grade 8
Warwick Valley Middle School

With You

With you I'm invincible.
In a dream I can't get out of.
On a cloud I can't fall through,
or on the moon defying gravity.
Your smile is priceless.
Brighter than the sun, but can only blind me with beauty.
As perfect as a single red rose,
and as innocent as children playing tag.
Your love leaves me breathless, speechless, and careless.
There's nothing in the world I need besides it.
It's the lyrics to my soul,
and it lets me live without breathing.
With you my heart sings.
Cannot be broken with sorrow.
Although it's bound to be cracked,
its easily sealed with a single kiss.
You make my life a roller coaster.
Ups and downs, happy but scared.
Not knowing where I'm going to end up, but still following the path.
In hopes that when we get back to where we started,
You'll still be right next to me, holding my hand through it all.

Cat Ludwiczak, Grade 9
Briarcliff High School

Attitude

I act how I want to act
I'll never change and that's a fact
My attitude is mine alone
It's mine to use and mine to hone

If you dislike my attitude
Then you mustn't understand the multitude
Of my true emotions
Or my true devotions

If you don't like me then boo hoo for you
Because I'm a swell girl and a good friend too
I'm someone you can depend on
Friends I would never abandon

If you dislike me that's your problem not mine
But I think my attitude is down right fine
If you ask me to change I'll say no way
Because I like to live life

Nicole Whiffen, Grade 8
Southern Cayuga Middle School

Writing for the Worst

The arch of a branch,
The curve of a tree,
The green of the soft grass,
The whisper of the wind,
The crystal blue lake,
The puffy white clouds,
Staring up at the blue sky,
She scribbles out a poem without much meaning.

The rain falling from the sky,
The murky brown puddles,
The gray storm clouds,
The swaying bare tree,
The hard cold ground,
Staring into the fog and rain,
She writes out a poem that means the world to her.

Jamie Shields, Grade 8
Marlboro Middle School

Fiery Orange

A fire at its strongest point
Bright, lively
The aroma of warm, crisp brownies just baked
Fresh, new
The rush of being chased
Frightening, exciting
A spicy potato chip awakening every taste bud
Sudden, hot
The sizzle of boiling water
Noisy, bubbly
Fiery orange.

Becca Leibowitz, Grade 7
Ardsley Middle School

My War

There is a war inside me
Even though my soul's right beside me
How long will this war go on
For as long as I live my life
It is the war of what is right
And it is the war of what is wrong
It is the war of how to live my life
And the war of what is life
Can I really think that this war will ever end
Can I really think that this war is not going to change me
The answer to these questions is simple
The answer is no
This war inside me with my soul beside me will never end
This war inside me that will make me new
And the war inside you will do that too.

Jon Stockton, Grade 7
Camillus Middle School

Basketball

Whenever I'm down or feeling blue,
I can always go outside,
With just a basketball and a hoop.
And dribble and shoot and dribble and shoot.
I can forget about anything bad that happened that day.
Such as a bad grade or getting in an argument.
And when I am done I go back to the real world,
But it does not matter because I know that basketball,
Can cure anything.

Joe McDermott, Grade 7
Camillus Middle School

What Becomes of Us?

I close my eyes and
I take a deep breath.
I am standing on the beach
As I smell the fresh salty air.
I hear the wind roar,
And the oceans crash.
The wind whipping my hair about
And the ocean waves gliding gently beneath my foot.
Every time I stand on the ocean shore,
My thoughts wonder,
They wonder about life.
When our time here is done,
What becomes of us?
Do we live on?
As these thoughts race through my mind,
Time flies by
Minutes, hours,
I do not know.
My mind churns with questions,
And the main one is
What becomes of us?

Samantha Wacha, Grade 8
Warwick Valley Middle School

Outdoors

I open the door
See the green grass,
Feel the dew on my bare feet
I am outdoors.

I smell the red roses
Feel the bark on a tree,
Feel the nice gentle breeze
I am outdoors.

I see the animals
The big brown bucks,
I see the big black bear,
The tiny raccoons,
I am outdoors.

Ryan Parchinski, Grade 8
Warwick Valley Middle School

Death

The Grim Reaper is big and tall
He is not one you will wish to meet
"Death" is his call
Most will think that is not sweet

All he will seek, will fall
He cannot be beat
He cares not if his victims are small
So if he comes, don't go and greet

Oscar Lopez, Grade 9
Upper Room Christian School

So Say Good Night

The moon shines bright
As the morning light
As you sleep
There is no peep
Peacefully in your bed
As the dogs shed
While the cars are driving
You are snoring
As everyone turns out their light
It is no more bright
Except for the moon
Shining in your room
You are dreaming
With no meaning
As you hear the TV's sound
You hear the neighbor's dog hound
As you get tucked in tight
And you say good night
So lay down your head
And go to bed
So say good night

Emily Schillinger, Grade 7
Robert Moses Middle School

Ashes

First there is a spark,
Then a light,
Then the smell of burning wood.

Tress are burning down
And you hear a cracking sound.
Then finally, the fire ends.

Now everything is ashes.
Everything is so lifeless,
Dead, lifeless ashes.

Joe Farrell, Grade 7
Camillus Middle School

Testing Pressure

I study day
I study night
They are going by
The day has come
I sit in class
Expecting to pass
The teacher comes in
Passing them around
Scared and frightened
I might fail the exam
Looking at the question
Makes me go blank
I calm myself
And I take a few deep breaths
There I go answering one
I then go on two, three, and four
Finishing the exam, successfully done
I hand it in
With goals dreams and hopes
A few days later I got my grade
ALL MY STUDYING PAID!

Tuka Almuhaisen, Grade 7
Al Iman School

The Lion

Lion with wings,
the lion of night.
He's stone during day,
alive at night.
His roar is loud
and very deep.
One pounce and you
are dead meat.
He's fast as lightning,
way stronger than man,
Be careful at night,
you're safe all day
But when it turns night,
he's out to play.

Kevin Serrano, Grade 9
John Bowne High School

Snowflakes?

Snowflakes look like sugar in a jar,
Sometimes I wonder what they really are.

Are they sugar?
Are they ice?
Are they something really nice?

Are they circles?
Are they squares?
Or are they just floating in the air?

Isha Chhabra, Grade 8
Seven Bridges Middle School

A Rose

A rose for the living,
A rose for the dead,
We miss the people who are gone,
The people who have left.

A rose for my family,
A rose for my friends,
They disappear so suddenly
Like rose petals
In the wind.

Deanna Ciampo, Grade 8
Maria Montessori School

Good and Evil

Good and evil the ancient war
None may win and none may fall
It continues on through different lives
Sides are growing
Stronger still
Eternally intertwined in battle so fierce
Neither is even able to pierce
Each other in their weakest spot
The dark in good
The good in dark

Brian Sheehy, Grade 7
South Woods Middle School

Native Warrior

A nose so long
Ears that look wrong
Eyes, very small
Face is so tall
Mask shows a call
Call of the wild
Feeling so mild
Work like a soldier
Achieve like a savior
Act like a warrior

Fahmid Ahamed, Grade 9
John Bowne High School

Young Life

When we start off life we don't think very much,
But we start to learn as we grow,
Like how to read and write, and tell time and such,
Playing outside in the winter with snow,
Laughing and having a good time with life as it is,
Until you start school and work very hard,
In grade school learning how soda can bubble and fizz,
And coming home to go out and play in the yard,
Going through Pre-K to fifth grade and learning in between,
Making friends each and every day of our years,
Hoping to not run into anybody nasty or mean,
Using prior knowledge and friends to not have fears.

Ethan Osborne, Grade 7
Camillus Middle School

Anger, the Walk and Talk

If you have something to talk about,
TALK!
If you need to think and cool off,
WALK!
But just don't sit around, or else you'll pay!
Just let go of everything and you'll be okay!

Courtney Honeywell, Grade 7
Solvay Middle School

Same Girl

Same girl
That one girl
I guess I leave her speechless
Same girl
That one girl
The one I want to be with
I don't know what to do right now this girl is on my mind
She's way to shy to talk to me I think I'll give her time
If the sky is the limit than she must be heaven
Cause on the scale one through ten she's three times seven

Kayshawn Macharie, Grade 8
Chestnut Ridge Middle School

Tiger*

Tiger, so mighty his language
In his stripes the colors we all know
But don't know what they mean
They tell a story and pattern for which it was granted
Since tiger cannot speak, it roars with all its heart
Telling us to understand what he has gone through
His family was shot and killed, leaving him all alone
Now he doesn't know what to do
His stripes are his mask, hiding from the world
Not wanting to feel or know
What the past holds from that cold night
When he became one.

Angela Auletta, Grade 9
John Bowne High School
*Inspired by the painting "Tiger" by Ito Jakuchu

Reflections

Multicolored with my friends
Always laughing and starting trends
Yelling and being mad
Making up and being sad

Colorless when there is nothing to do
Sitting around counting by twos
Mom putting me to work and I do my part
Next thing I know I am pushing a cart

These sides are both really me
I hope for you it was easy to see.

Pamela Gaylord, Grade 7
Our Savior New American School

Pizza

Hot sizzling slices of pizza,
Most are served as toasty warm pies.
Pieces of pepperoni are usually placed on top,
To hold the cheese so it doesn't drop.

You can get pizza all over the world,
Even in Paris and Spain.
It comes in all different shapes and sizes,
Like Sicilian that's the one that rises.

Pizza is good, pizza is yummy,
You better make sure it ends up in your tummy,
Because if it ends up on the floor it wouldn't be so funny,
And it would have been a waste of money.

Shane Ginley, Grade 8
Warwick Valley Middle School

Music Is a Poem

Music is a group of words,
Written out with notes.

Music must be spoken with an instrument,
For it to be heard out loud.

Words are just as valuable,
But they must use the mouth.

A musician is no different,
From a poet in disguise.

Music is a rhyming poem,
But with a melody.

There are many different languages,
Used in many different ways.

Just like all the types of songs,
Are sung in different ways.

Thomas McCarthy, Grade 7
Holy Cross School

Autumn Is Here!

Out in the fields
Animals gather
Berries and nuts
The birds are like hawks
And the bunnies are like thieves

Leaves are falling
While birds are calling
Out in the fog
We are chilled
By the ice cold air

I look and I see
Animals swooping down at me
I can't believe I am seeing this
But autumn is here and I can't believe it!

Veronica Jacobson, Grade 7
Riverhead Middle School

The Rain

The sky turns gray
Clouds start to roll in.
The sun starts to hide.
Then the rain falls.
Little droplets of water fall on my face.
While others hide away;
I stay until I am soaked
I try to have the rain,
Wash away my pain.

Christina Manzi, Grade 8
Soule Road Middle School

War

Families crying
People hiding
Gunners marching
Soldiers dying

Sickness
Nervousness
Anger
And violence

Explosions
Gunshots
Death
And wounds

Fire
Smoke
Destruction
And screaming

So what's so funny about war?

Zach Lancette, Grade 7
Camillus Middle School

Far Away Beyond the Earth

Far away tucked in the corner of space.
Where nobody lives and nobody has discovered.
Beyond the earth and universe and farther than the stars so bright.
Beyond the planets and moon.
A magical place out of sight.
A far away place so magical nobody can reach.
A quiet and peaceful and gorgeous place.
A place high above the clouds.
A place where it never snows or rains.
A magical place full of wonders.
Where I have happy thoughts and no worries.
A place to be discovered.
Where I can dream the magical dreams.

Monica Petrus, Grade 7
Camillus Middle School

You Plus Me

Its funny how after someone leaves,
That's when you realize you don't know who you are without them.
They are a part of you, and the people who made you who you are.
They are the air you breathe. They are the air all around you.
They were the only thing worth seeing,
And now that they're gone, you're left blinded.
You're only left with memories, and faded laughter.
I haven't really noticed the missing part until now.
Those hours we spent on the phone…
We didn't have to say a word,
Just being together made our hearts sing.
Your favorite song still plays in my head.
Over and over…it never ends.
When we looked in to each other's eyes,
There was no one else in the world but us.
We were invincible. Undeniably one, and incredible.
But then you started to fade.
Now you've completely disappeared.
There are times, now and again, I think of those days we spent.
The warm summers beneath my apple tree.
You carved our names in it, you plus me.

Suzanne Khalil, Grade 9
Fayetteville-Manlius High School

Confidence

What is Confidence?
Believing in yourself and in the choices you make in life.
Doing what you think is right and knowing that you are certain it is.
What I feel when I am on a mound.
What I feel dribbling down the court.
The key to any successful person.
A feeling no one can describe.
Having a positive attitude in any and everything you do.
Showing that you can make your own decisions.
Having a sense of responsibility.
Knowing that you're a strong-willed person.
That is Confidence.

Santino Figueroa, Grade 7
Our Lady Queen of Apostles School

The Starting Notes
I had the notes
I knew the words
But I could do it
We had rehearsed
We knew what to do
But I kept messing up
At least, that's how I felt
I had told the teacher
I had taken my medicine
I had my water on hand
I felt I was ready
We were set, ready, and started
I was doing fine, so I thought
I walk up and start
The noise starts but
OH NO!
It's scratchy, and hoarse
It's just plain humiliating
My eyes are watery as I walk back
I had just ruined my chance at showing off my skills
I feel HORRIBLE!

Jessy Boyce, Grade 7
Camillus Middle School

True Friend
A true friend is hard to find
Nice and kind
Sweet and gentle
Someone who doesn't tell your secrets to others
Friends are the most important
Part of life
They'll always be there for you
And help you through the worst
Friends are needed
They are bad and good
But there will always be one that's there for you

Alejandra Pineda, Grade 9
John Bowne High School

Survival
Tents for sleeping
Swimming in rivers
The ground for a bed is as hard as a rock
Gathering firewood for the night's use
Cooking food over the campfire
Telling scary stories
Reading a book
Waking up before dawn
Like a kid on Christmas morning
using candles for light
Fishing with lanterns
Dealing with mosquitoes
Burning leaches off my back
This is what I deal with when I go camping

Kyle Scott, Grade 7
Solvay Middle School

March Rain
Let the rain beat you
Let the rain soak your face and back
Let the rain seep through the deep crevices and cracks
The rain is like a sapphire stream
Coursing through the veins of the streets.

Daniel Gibbs, Grade 8
The New York Institute for Special Education

Spooky Night
Halloween is finally here,
Ghosts and goblins is what I fear.
Blinding fog everywhere,
Creeping darkness filling the air.

Trick-o-treaters fill the streets,
Hoping to get a bunch of treats.
Spooks and witches can't wait to scare,
Creeping darkness filling the air.

Jack o' lanterns light the night,
They give children such a fright.
Vampires scream out, "Enter if you dare."
Creeping darkness filling the air.

Cauldrons are brewing,
Ghosts are "Booing."
Tonight is the night to *beware*,
Creeping darkness filling the air.

Francesca Monaco, Grade 8
Our Lady Queen of Apostles School

Thinking of You
I sit on this roof top, as I watch the cars go by
Wishing I was able to jump off and fly

There's a park down the road, I go there to think
I found a rose there once, it was a pretty pink

Oh, it's so cold, I climb back inside
Wrap up in my blanket, wanting to hide

I stare out this window, wishing you were here
Watching the snow fall, haven't seen it since last year

I am so alone, with nothing to do
I sit here tonight, thinking of you

It's bad, oh I know, shame shame on me
But I just can't help it, you're amazing you see

I wish I could just run and break free
From all of these thoughts and what's not meant to be

Rachel Morgan Ciervo, Grade 9
Our Savior New American School

The Grinch

There one was a mean old Grinch near the village of Who he hated the Whos and knew just what to do
"I'll steal the Who's Christmas it'll be nothing but a cinch" said the nasty old Grinch
He stitched up a suit put on his other boot
Then packed up his sled patted his dog Max on the head
and soon was out the door
And speeding off he would go, with nothing to stop him not even the snow.
He arrived in the silent town without even a sound
Then off he went to ruin the joy on which the Who's had just spent
He packed up the boxes and bags, thinking of the Whos as losers and hags
He said to himself "The girls and boys will run for their toys
and not a one will be found then in their own tears they will be drowned."
So he took his large pack cracked his old back
and up Mount Crumpit he went, off to dump it
Then he was on the tip of the peak when he heard a small squeak
It was not crying as he thought but instead the Whos were rejoicing and voicing
their gift of each other, sister and brother, father and mother not a one was in tears.
He thought it over and over and even nibbled on clover
Then against his own mind he turned very kind
and raced down the drop with more than one plop
Down he went with the speed of a wild stampede and no warning would he ever have to heed
Then later that evening he sat down to a feast and he, yes he, carved the roast beast

Riley Shurtleff, Grade 8
Southern Cayuga Middle School

Seasons of Life
Snowflakes.
Falling swiftly into the air of a winter wonderland.
The trees are bricks stopping at once in a moonlight heaven.

The playful air is singing with birds sprouting and flowers calling, it's too good to be true.
The big white clouds are puff, puffing in the wind of the fresh air galore.

Sun blazing and my heart awakens to the phenomenal sunlight that's calling my name.
The water relieves me when the temperature is blazing hot.
Skin is blistering and cooling off is the only option.

Red, orange, and yellow.
Colors are the only option for fall.
The trees are sprouting and branches rapidly moving.
The crisp air has finished the year, a new beginning has started.

Clare Cirillo, Grade 8
John Jay Middle School

Security at Last
Were you scared
When I walked through the door with your life in my hand
Were you scared
When you saw all your faults flash before your eyes when I came to you
Were you scared
When I said another would come to judge you
Were you relieved
When you found out you were already saved from harm and will be when the time comes?

Dillon Harvey, Grade 8
Our Savior New American School

Fly Fishing

Fly fishing for fish is fun.
It isn't something easily done
Fly fishing is an art,
Clearly casting to find that perfect spot.
There are so many flies to choose from,
Some are bought and some are made.
They're hard to see in a lot of shade.
The trout comes along thinking it's food,
The fisherman catches it and is in a happy mood.
After some photos he lets it go,
Hoping next time it will show.

Peter Zajac, Grade 8
Warwick Valley Middle School

Back of the Bus

Back in the day, it was such a fuss
For African Americans to sit in the front of the bus

They tried so hard and put up a fight
To gain that ever wanted right

They went through hardships
Boycotts and strikes
Waiting for the day when it would be all right

Martin Luther King had a dream
But it was forgotten…
Or so it would seem.

Because today blacks are in a rush
To be able to sit in the back of the bus.

Tonisha Husbands, Grade 9
Bishop Ford Central Catholic High School

Food

Food…is a glorious thing,
It makes me dance,
It makes me sing,
It makes me jump up and down,
And twirl around…
And cry with glorious glee,

Food is so delicious,
But food is often unhealthy,
You have to be stealthy to get into the kitchen,
Just to steal some Kentucky Fried Chicken,

While eating, most people watch television,
Although it's bad for your vision,
So while you are eating your fries,
You're really burning your eyes,
Food…is a glorious thing…

Kyle Howe, Grade 8
Southern Cayuga Middle School

Read

When you read a book,
You meet characters like Captain Hook.
Go to places like the Eiffel Tower,
Feel the rain in a light shower.
See the lightning in the sky,
Have many days go by and by.
Fight with a General who has lots of glory,
So go ahead and read a story.

Amy Collins, Grade 8
Holy Cross Academy

Handball

Any normal dry day,
Hot or cold,
I'll be on the courts,
Playing young and old.

The courts are usually crowded,
It's tough to get one free,
But playing someone for it,
Sounds good to me.

There are many types of fouls —
cracks blocks and short.
They get pretty annoying
But they're a necessity to the court.

Handball is the sport I love,
It is what I play and do,
You'll see me on the courts.
You know it's true

Bobby Logozo, Grade 9
Bishop Ford Central Catholic High School

Storm

The boat will tip,
the waves will crash.
The lightning strikes,
and thunder laughs.
All the men will fall;
into the sea.
The waves will swallow,
their deaths will follow.
Upon the deck,
The captain will stay.
He'll wait patiently till the boat over flows,
and when it does, down he'll go.
Down they'll go,
to the bottom of the sea.
Where the sea critter swim,
and the light is very dim.
There they'll lay,
their bones will stay
but their purpose gone

Brittney Ashley, Grade 8
Sodus Middle School

You

Life is so complicated,
but at the end of the day, it's you,
it's you who calms me down.
I can tell you anything.
You would never judge me,
never hurt me,
I'm always trusting in you,
that's everything;
I wish you were to me.
You messed things up
and we can never go back.

Lucy Castillo, Grade 9
Bishop Ford Central Catholic High School

Jesse Owens

A soon to be Olympic athlete
was born on September 12, 1913 in Oakville, Alabama.
At a young age he was discriminated against for his race.
But he didn't give up.
In junior high he started his track career.
His friend and trainer, Charles Riley, helped him train every day.
People said he couldn't do it. But he didn't give up.
In high school he met Ruth Solomon.
He also joined the track team.
People did not like him for joining because he was black.
But he didn't give up. He married Ruth Solomon.
When he broke the world record for the two hundred
and two hundred twenty-yard dash, people thought he got lucky.
But he didn't give up.
He attended Ohio State University.
He went to the Olympics in Berlin and won four gold medals.
People praised him, except a few.
But he didn't give up. He won the hearts of many.
He was named the greatest track and field athlete.
He received the living legend award and is now retired.
JESSE OWENS NEVER GAVE UP.

Vito Mesiti, Grade 7
St Catherine of Siena School

I Am

I am
Family, friends, life
I think family is a lot of value
Friends are important to me
Life is important to me
Pets are important to me
Trust means a lot in life
Lying is bad but telling the truth hurts
Death is sad but inside you're always alive
Hate is a strong word
Live. Laugh. Love
I am

Brittany Clauss, Grade 8
Hauppauge Middle School

Clothes

I love going shopping for clothes,
I never seem to have enough.
I'm losing them faster than I'm getting them.
I'm always growing out of my favorite shirt or pair of jeans.
But clothes are getting more and more expensive,
And that's not just how it seems.
It's true,
And I have no doubt that I like clothes more than you!

Casey DuPont, Grade 8
Avon Middle School

Encountering of the Heart

Was it worth it all?
To lose everything and to gain nothing
You came back
In the same formation
But with your alter ego
You left me bewildered from the beginning
And by the end, you opened me up to new fixations
Explored the deeper meaning
Questioned everything
Overlooked nothing
Tears shed when you abandoned me
-Tears shed-
When I yearned to go all the way
To face your troubles, confusions;
To share the break through, your happiness;
To show passion in the making
-Tears shed-
Not to be here in search of
The One I'm missing
But to be with
The One

Erica Varela, Grade 9
Bishop Ford Central Catholic High School

Delilah

Pretty Delilah with her big blue eyes
And her simple grace
Light blond hair
And her smiling face

Sweet as can be
Just like a flower
Playing with Barbies
Hour after hour

Cute and petite
Such a perfect child
Hardly ever does she go wild

My little sis
A little girl
Will do great things someday in this world

Hayley Martin, Grade 7
Camillus Middle School

Losing a Friend

Losing a friend
Is like losing everything
You feel empty
You feel bare.

When you lose a friend
You want to run and hide
You just want to cry

A hand on your shoulder
For sympathy and care
But you just send them away
Because you know that no one really cares

At the end of the day
You confess
"Yes it was I, who
just lost a good friend."
Stefanie Reichman, Grade 7
Jewish Foundation School

A Hero

Firemen, Police officers, our Parents
All heroes to us

Who is there to encourage us to do the right thing?
A Hero

Who is there to save our lives when we are in need?
A Hero

Who is there to guide us?
A Hero

Who is there to keep us safe?
A Hero

Who is there to love?
A Hero

But the real question is "who are you?"
You are your own hero
Joseph Miraglia, Grade 9
Martin Luther High School

I'll Never Forget You Uncle

I remember when you were around
I loved your smile
But I hated your frown
And you made me believe that life was worth living
But it's hard to see you walk away
You were made for me sent from heaven
you see…
and our memories will always be with me
Nicole Flores, Grade 7
Intermediate School 381

Autumn

Orange color makes it bright.
It fills the night with color and light.
Yellow opens the doors to a whole new world.
Brown can be dull, but always changes.
The wind that blows through autumn's leaves.
It makes me cringe.
It makes me sneeze.
Winter's coming.
Fall's end is near.
The birds they fly, they fly in fear.
Of winter near.
Justine Wares, Grade 8
Warwick Valley Middle School

Team

The game started when Moravia got the ball.
There are people in the stands and there are people in the hall.
People are like animals jumping all around.
There are also going crazy and making a bunch of sound.
We were down by one and Steven scored.
I was just thinking oh good Lord.
Now we're up by two and someone got fouled.
People on the Moravia team looked and howled.
They are 6'2" and we're 5'5".
Take a look at them and look at our size.
We're up by 8 and we had some fun.
We worked together and look at them run.
Tanner McCarty, Grade 8
Southern Cayuga Middle School

Outsider

No one knows why I cry,
Or all the pain I hold inside
The times I've been left alone
The times I felt there was no point to live
Because I know no one truly loves me
I know my mind is dark and lost
I have already died inside
I'm just awaiting to die on the outside
My heart and soul turned black
I see no way to go back
My smile is fake
My laughter is a fraud
I cry and hurt every night
All alone in this cold, dark world
No one understands me
I am always alone
I will never love for love is just a word
No one knows why I cry
It is because of all the pain I hold inside
It is because I will never love another
I will always be alone, an outsider.
Kya Gibson, Grade 8
Intermediate School 383 Philippa Schuyler

Life

Life is a raging fire,
but, it is also a calm lake.
Fire is blown out by the wind,
and turns to ashes.
But, the lake flows into a flat ocean,
and becomes a place to relax,
and release your thoughts.
You can take the fierce fire as it comes.
Or, relax in the warmth of it.
You can enjoy the ocean.
Or, turn it into a raging tsunami.
Life is as it comes.
But you can change it.
Fire can be swayed by the wind.
Water can be splashed by a boot,
but only you can change your life.
Life is to be lived,
and to be lived wisely.
Take your life,
and live it to the fullest.

Rory O'Reilly, Grade 8
Sewanhaka High School

Healing/Healthy

The faster you heal
The better you are
You always want to be healthy
Healthy is good
You can play sports
You can ride your bike
You can play with your friends

Zach Weigand, Grade 7
Solvay Middle School

My Mother

My mother is the best
Whenever I'm sick
She tells me to rest
She'll stand by my side
Til the end
She'll hold my hand and say
Never give up!!!
I truly love her
For all she has done for me
I'll never forget her lullaby song
She'll do her best to make me happy
And to protect me from any danger
My mother is truly the best
No one can underestimate her love
For all she's done was worth the most.
She'll catch me when I fall
Feed me when I'm hungry
Always think of me
And love me forever!

Merna Ibrahim, Grade 7
Al Iman School

Neon Lie

Once you look past the neon lights,
You'll realize this city ain't so bright.

The cold concrete emblazoned with tears —
Tears of struggle. Tears of pain.

A hazy, polluted sky, scavenging scoundrels seeking shelter,
Malodorous trash — dormant in the sun:
Filth

One man's sky-scraped rhapsody, is another's freezing hell.
Starving on the streets; Oh no, — the concrete shows no sympathy!

Beyond the fake, filtered, and phony billboards,
Lies a mechanism — A machine which devours all it desires,
Spitting out the bitter carcass of the lives it has slaughtered.

Yet, naïve souls stand in line.
Dreams clenched tightly in their fists, entering the tunnel of disillusionment.

One by one,
Their nightmare has just begun…

Daphne Lacroix, Grade 9
Oyster Bay High School

Just too Fast

It happened. It's here. It's a new world, a new beginning.
It's happening too fast. It's actually here, and we can't look back.
Now I wonder, what have I done, what do I lack?
Why do we try to be something we're not?
Why can't we understand we're not as ready as we thought?
We try to grasp more than we can understand.
We don't get that good things don't always last.
We're growing up too fast.

Now is the time for fantasy and play.
It's the time we learn and create.
We always think we know just what to say.
But we don't usually know what to do, until the next day.

Why can't we live as Peter Pan does?
He lives in a magical world called Neverland.
It's a world where your imagination is in charge.
Where things have been made from pixie dust and sand.
In Neverland, fairies are your friends and pirates are not.
A world where good always wins and evil is fought.
Why can't we see, that we're not ready.
We're not ready to leave our Neverland.
We're just not ready to let go of Peter Pan's hand.

Myrna Hanna, Grade 8
Holy Family School

A Winter Paradise
Looking up at the winter sky,
The snowflakes coming from way up high.

They glisten as they slowly fall,
I try to look and see them all.

Blankets of snow upon the ground,
It piles up without a sound.

Then, I looked up at the trees,
The branches dancing in the breeze.

A hint of stillness in the air,
Hides the fact that something's there.

Morning doves upon the branches rest,
Begin to chirp while in their nest.

Droplets forming into ice,
What a winter paradise!
Karina Hegedus, Grade 8
Warwick Valley Middle School

School Days
I walk down the hallway and all that I see,
Are people at their lockers or at their seats,
I go to my locker to get all my books,
When all that I see, is a kid that just looks,
He looks around like he's new, what a shame,
He probably doesn't know anyone's name,
So I show him to his class and he runs in a hurry,
Then I see everyone else leave the hall, so I worry,
I look in the bathroom and no one was found,
So I just look around and around and around,
Well, I'm off to science to learn about mass,
Hey! Wait a minute! I'm late to class!!
Jamie Wentz, Grade 7
Robert Moses Middle School

My World
There is a place that I call My World,
where I go whenever I want.
No one is sad,
rather everyone is happy and has a great time.
There is no stress, there are no worries,
because nobody commits any crime.
In My World,
no one is poor, no one is rich,
no one pollutes and no one wastes.
Come join me in my perfect place,
the one that I call
My World.
Dan Ginestro, Grade 7
Camillus Middle School

I Cannot Go to School Today
I cannot go to school today,
Honestly I must say.
My lips are blue, my face is green,
I puke so much that it's obscene.
I fell this morning off the top bunk,
I cannot breathe my lungs have shrunk.
Three striking pains fly up my back,
My fingers are frozen, when I
Move them they crack.
My head feels like it weighs a ton,
And my toes have gone completely numb.
My eyes are puffy and swollen shut,
My knee is bum and nose feels stuffed.
Oh wait!!!
I forgot, we go to a play in school today.
Goodbye Mom, I'm on my way!
Tammy Bieber-Carey, Grade 8
Barker Middle School

Fall
Crunch, crunch
Crunch, crunch
The leaves beneath my feet,
Crunch, crunch
Crunch, crunch
As I walk my way down my street.

Walking into my home
To see a nice warm fire
Is the one thing I want,
The one thing I desire.

Sitting in front of that toasty fire
After that long bad day,
It was the one thing I needed, the one thing I wanted,
To melt my troubles away.
Allison DiPalmer, Grade 8
Warwick Valley Middle School

Snow Season
The snow is white and lush
As it falls in a rush
The wind is blowing hard
As the sun doesn't show at all

The leaves are off the trees
As winter season comes
The white bright snow is as far as the eye can see
As the sun is gleaming among the snow

The winter season is cheerful
The snow is very playful
As the wind sings and cheers
The sun shines very clear
Kyle Sakowski, Grade 8
Warwick Valley Middle School

Rain Drop

Splish, splash,
A droplet of sadness,
An explosion of emotion
A droplet of loneliness,
A shallow rush of wind,
Dropping down,
Racing the speed of sound,
Drip, drop,
Listen to the rain drop,
Plip, plop,
Slow and steady,
Falling to the ground
Shhh…
Be quite…
It's the rain drop…
Splash!

Jenna Farrell, Grade 7
Camillus Middle School

Winter

The snow on the ground
The trees with no leaves
Snowmen all around

Thousands of presents
Under the tree
All of them just for me

Sound asleep
I lay in my bed
Until I hear the birds CHEEP CHEEP
And Santa's sled above my head

I arise out of bed
And go downstairs
What do I see?
All of those presents
Just for me!

Tia Fiorino, Grade 8
Holy Cross School

September 11th

O ffer your heart to our country,
N ew Yorkers became heroes.
E xpress pride in your country.

F orever will we give hope.
O ur nation came to a stop for a day,
R ain fell from the sky as tears.

A ll of us came to support,
L ove went around the world,
L oyalty to our troops.

Chelsey Drew, Grade 7
Udall Road Middle School

Ode to Routine

The Mechanical grinding
of the daily routine.
Blocks the numbing pain
of long thought.
O, to form a geometric pattern
with each rhythmic step and
stop
restless work
and rest.
Keeping the Demons from
eating the soul
and drowning the brain.

Zachary Weiss, Grade 7
Riverdale Country School

You and Me

You and me we are each other
I am you and you are me
We are them and they are us
Yet we are not a part of them
But secretly they want to be a part of us
So who are we?
We are you and me
But when you become a part of them
Who am I?
I am lost
Searching for me
Praying that you come back
Until I find me
And then do I realize
I am only me
Not you or them or us
And that is all that counts

Natalie McLeod, Grade 8
John W Dodd Middle School

Time Tells Me I've Got No Time Left

The clock that I keep
Holds memories so deep,
Reminds me of,
How little time I have left.
The many sunsets I've missed,
The fun times from the past.
Good times
NEVER
Last.

I have missed out on things —
That could've changed me forever,
I've lost my grip on life
But —
I'll be holding onto you forever.

Mariah Cody, Grade 9
Oyster Bay High School

Honesty

Be honest to people
Be honest to yourself
Tell the truth when it's hard
Even write it on a card
But being honest is the main thing
So people are honest with you!

Oksana Sokolik, Grade 7
Solvay Middle School

Friends

Friends: faithful and genuine
Not traitorous or forged
Encouraging and understanding
Never shunning our deepest ambitions.

Friends: faithful and genuine
Not preoccupied or self-absorbed
Always willing to listen
Secure vaults where secrets are safe.

Friends: faithful and genuine
Not fearsome or restrictive
Our shields in everyday battles
Candles in an obscure world.

Friends: faithful and genuine
Not insensitive or callous
Rejoice when we're celebrating
Weep when we're saddened.

Friends: faithful and genuine
Not demanding or judgmental
Accepting of our faults
Stands by us no matter what
Friends: faithful and genuine.

Michelle Stadelmaier, Grade 9
Holy Cross Academy

The Snowflake

Glistens as its first fall,
Wet as it slides down,
Catching a glimpse of the eye,
So beautiful.

White with bumpy texture,
Very superior to its others,
Glancing with an envious eye,
So graceful.

The snowflake will slowly melt,
But never will its presence fade,
It will be treasured by all who sought it,
So spectacular.

Abby Beyer, Grade 8
Warwick Valley Middle School

Winter Days

Freezing air hits your face
As the snow falls softly
Shovels pounding the ground
Snow flies around
Kids running fast through the light snow
Winter days the light leaves fast
You freeze and shiver as the dry wind hits you
Breezes sweep the grounds as the leafless trees sway
That's a winter day

Scott Linzer, Grade 9
John Bowne High School

The Bigger They Are, the Harder They Fall

Trapped in the jungle
Gathering rocks
Digging down deep
To build a fire pit
Creating a tree house with bare hands
Capturing food with traps
Finding a wounded gorilla and
Helping to nurse him back to health
Naming him Paco
Finding food together
Protecting our tree house together
Waking up to Paco's blood on the ground
Anger consuming me, drowning in its waves
Gathering my weapons, flying into the jungle.
Finding a trail of blood
leading to a murderous tiger.
Climbing the trees and surprising him
My spear piercing his back like a hot knife through butter
The tiger slashed my sides, piercing like a thousand needles
Stabbing the tiger twice more to make him crumble.
Thinking to myself, "The bigger they are, the harder they fall."

Alexander K. Miro´, Grade 7
Solvay Middle School

Friends

I have many friends
With many different trends
They come from all around
They never make me frown
We do lots of things together
In all types of weather
We all play football and basketball too
When it rains outside we're all blue
When inside we play games
There's so many that I can't name names
Sometimes we hang at the mall
And while in school we talk in the halls, boy they are small
And at night we talk on the phone
As we gossip away in an impolite tone
Sometimes I have sleepovers and we stay up late
I have lots of friends boy don't hate

Bruce Gilfus, Grade 8
Southern Cayuga Middle School

Chewing on a Magazine

Sweet baby blue eyes
Do you need something to chew?
Does *Sound* magazine
Taste so much better to you?

Pages of *My Chem, Chidos,* and *Paramore*
Soothe the ache in your gums.
Sweet little blonde girl
Enjoy your snack.
Daydream of basses and drums.

Sonja Mellesh, Grade 9
DeSales High School

Halloween

Witches and monsters are everywhere.
Goblins and ghosts give us a great scare!

There are many houses for you to greet,
And to say, "Trick-or-treat!"

You can see spiders and cats creep through the night!
These little creatures might give you a fright.

Halloween is spooky and fun,
Not just for kids, but, for everyone!

Emily Giannelli, Grade 8
Christ the King School

Stars

They are surrounded by darkness
yet I can still see them
They glisten in the night sky accompanied by the moon
Stars shine proudly
even when many don't notice them
They produce much light shining so bright
They can be colored blue, yellow, or white
Even when they are so far
the light still comes through

Stars have a silent noise
So peaceful and calming
It can tame even the fiercest of creatures
I ask you,
Why are you so far away?
And why will you have to leave us one day?

Making me calm and amazed at the same time
makes me sad knowing you have to leave
I wish you could stay
Shine proudly
Shine proudly
Shine proudly

Simran Bhatti, Grade 8
Baldwin Middle School

Summer

The sun was shining
A brilliant gold
It was a perfect day
For young and old

The birds were singing
With a happy air
And rabbits were frolicking
Without a care

Flowers were dancing
Bees merrily hummed
People were laughing
While crickets sung

Children were playing
Games in the grass
After waiting forever
For winter to pass

The day was magnificent
The weather was warm
The people were happy…
Then came the storm
Kathryn Stiadle, Grade 8
Southern Cayuga Middle School

Underneath the Tree

Underneath the tree
Wounded as I may be
I hear sparrows chirping
As I lay underneath the tree
I reflect on what I have done
And many mistakes I have made
And the pain and suffering I have gave
As I lay underneath the tree
Zach Mulholland, Grade 7
Solvay Middle School

Autumn

It is that time of year again,
To get your pencils and your pens.

No more long summer nights,
Or long days flying kites.

Yes, it's that time, back to school,
With shorter days and the air so cool.

You can call it autumn or fall,
It does not really matter at all;

Because you know that summer is done
And 185 days of school have begun.
Brock Schmid, Grade 7
Robert Moses Middle School

Family

I love my family so much and I do have to say, there is a big bunch.
We laugh and we cry especially when we have to say goodbye.
To me they all are heroic
I feel they should know it.
Some save lives,
Others just in my eyes.
They are young and old
Some are funny, some are bold.
Some are short, some are tall,
Some are hairy, some are bald.
Some are clever, some are smart
We are rarely apart.
My family likes to celebrate holidays,
In many different ways.
We love Valentine's, Halloween, Christmas, and New Year's
But St. Patrick's Day is the best, we celebrate with many cheers!
I love my family as different as they are,
I wouldn't trade them for anything not even a brand new car.
They accept me and love me clearly
And I treasure them dearly!
Marita Breen, Grade 7
St Mary's School

My Favorite Spot

Ocean breeze from the big blue seas.
That smell of salt makes me crave an ice-cold malt.
Fishes swimming; frolicking around, you can see them but they make no sound.
My love that I have not seen since last year, is now coming very near.
The day I went to that very beach, a little diamond ring came into my reach.
A romantic proposal in my favorite spot,
Will I ever leave? …I think not.
Serena Mignone, Grade 8
Warwick Valley Middle School

The Sunset

An amazing sunset
While out on a boat stayed with me
And every time I see another one
I am reminded of it
Colors such as red, orange, pink, blue, and every color in between
It was spread across the sky and was unbelievably gorgeous

The sun was out and was fading slowly as the day progressed
It was beautiful
A peaceful silence
The sound of the boat moving against the water
Peaceful silence

Why as beautiful as you are, do you end so quickly?
I felt serene and at peace with my soul because of the sunset's beauty

So Serene
So Serene
So Serene

Sabina Singh, Grade 8
Baldwin Middle School

Snowy Hills

The hills are snowy, and very bleak.
    The hills look frozen, but the water is clear.
The hills are deserted.
    The water shows no sign of movement.

Above the hills, rests two figures
    One a crescent moon
The other a faded star.
    They reflect in the water.

The figures, light up in the dark sky.
    One with a white glow
One with red.
    They look as if they have just switched places.

Now they stay, in the dark sky,
    The moon over the sun
The sun over the moon.
    Both reflecting in the still water.

All is still, nothing moves
    Not an animal to be seen
A sound to be heard
    Besides the swish of the water.

Christopher Darby, Grade 9
DeSales High School

The Victory

Come here, come here to stay
come here to taste the taste of sweet, sweet victory,
    that will just blow you away
Here you'll find joy, excitement and that victory that is here
when you feel this victory, you will know no fear
    Friendships can be made here
But with friendships here, the rivalries are near
    So come here, come here to stay
Come here to taste the taste of sweet, sweet victory,
    That will just blow you away

Kaleigh Churchill, Grade 7
Camillus Middle School

Christmas

Christmas is coming,
    It's almost here.
People will be flying to visit family,
    Kids will go sledding in the snow.
Others will be singing Christmas carols at your front door.
    Others will be decorating their trees,
    While being with their families.
People will be doing some last minute shopping,
    While others are baking cookies to put out for Santa.
So hurry up go to bed because Christmas is almost here.

Elizabeth Senecal, Grade 7
St Mary's School

Magic

Magic is what you make of it, like a fairy tale
Magic can be found in ordinary life.
Simple things like kind words or gestures,
Something that suddenly makes you feel better.
These are all magical moments to hold onto.

Magic is chocolate,
Fireworks on the 4th of July or
A simple hug from someone you love.
A Hallmark card that touches your heart,
A piece of jewelry given especially to you.

Simple everyday magic is the
Things we take for granted.
Like a warm sunny day, or
A simple smile from an ordinary stranger on the street
The love of those who care about you.
Another ordinary day of simple magic.

Abby Katura, Grade 8
Southern Cayuga Middle School

Another Day

Every day I wake up at 6:45,
I say to myself another day has arrived,
    As I leave for school,
    I look up and say,
I wonder what will happen today,
    Will I learn something new,
    Or have no homework to do,
But at the end of the day, it all becomes clear,
That from day one, there was nothing to fear,
What was I to expect from a brand new school,
Expecting the worst would make me a fool,
    This is because, it has been great to me,
    This school holds a great future for me,
        And the knowledge I get,
        I will use wisely.

Joseph Biagini, Grade 9
Bishop Ford Central Catholic High School

Thanksgiving Day

it is autumn:
colorful leaves are falling from trees;
    there is a slight chill in the air;
squirrels are gathering acorns for the winter;
families and friends are visiting each other;
people are gathering around a table of wonderful foods,
    including turkey;
conversations of pilgrims and Indians are being discussed;
there is a brilliant parade being viewed on the television;
people are giving thanks to God for all they have;
    supermarkets are sold out of
turkeys, potatoes, other vegetables, bread, and gravy;
    …It must be Thanksgiving Day!…

Danielle Conte, Grade 7
St John School

Love

Someone to hug —
your arms were
doors wide open.

Our relationship
just like the
stars —
both beyond
woman's reach.

All the giggles we shared
let the salty taste of tears
run down our cheeks.

All the laughs,
the smiles,
the hugs,
the inside jokes,
the hours online,
and the eighty minute phone calls.

Just because
you were the family that
God forgot to give me.
Brittany Garmon, Grade 9
Lansingburgh Sr High School

Responsibility

Responsibility is about,
Availability,
Possibility,
Flexibility,
Sensibility,
Dependability,
Compatibility,
And,
Capability.
Responsibility is about,
Doing everything you can do,
To help all the people around you.
Liz Crockett, Grade 7
Solvay Middle School

I Don't Have My Assignment Done

I'm not quite sure
Why I don't have my assignment done
Instead of a picture with other people
And what I can tell from their faces
From the emotions their faces give off
Here I am with my feelings spread out.
I'm a little annoyed
That I keep forgetting to get this done,
But oh well,
At least it's kind of done.
Kayla Mourey-Allen, Grade 9
DeSales High School

New York City

New York City is very busy
Looking at the tall sky scrapers makes you dizzy
New York City is money earning
New York City is hard working
I can't say that New York City is immaculate
But I can say that New York City is very great
New York City is magnificent
But some people are militant
Some people are ecstatic
Some people are vivid like a light bulb in a dark attic

There are always lots of people crowding the streets
Crowded buses not enough seats
The streets are sometimes wild at night
The police are sometimes breaking up fights

New York City is a mecca for shopping
People love the theaters where the popcorn is popping
New York City's food is very good
There's something for everyone from downtown to the hood
There's no place in the world like New York City
The problems are not itty bitty. That's why it is very busy in New York City.
John Calhoun, Grade 9
Greenburgh-North Castel UFSD REACH Program

The Field Mice Throughout the Seasons

One autumn day in the pasture, the field mice slaved away.
Collecting food for the winter which had come to stay.

Working like bees on a warm spring day, foraging without a thought for play,
For the cold white winter, which had come to stay,

The storm clouds showed the signal, the willows shrank in fear,
The winter that was coming, was finally here.

The mice were falcons soaring, they flew across the grass,
The murderous cold white winter, had come to kill at last!

After months of hiding, the weather spoke of warmth.
The murderous cold white winter, had retreated to the North.

The field mice ran out happily! Chattering and scattering with glee!
For the sweet spring air sang through the breeze, tousling the grass and trees!

The spring flew by with great speed, like an eagle in the air
Then things started to warm up, the heat was everywhere!

As autumn showed its chilly face, the field mice worked again.
For the never ending cycle, had just started once again.
Erik Divan, Grade 7
Riverhead Middle School

Who We Are

We are the shadows cast upon the Earth,
We are the twinkling stars in the moonlight,
We are the trees of the tropical rain forest,
We are the fish of the sea.

We are the flowers in the meadow,
We are the raindrops of the storm,
We are the animals of the forest,
We are the ants of the hill.

We are everything in the universe,
We are unique.

Billie Wei, Grade 7
Intermediate School 187 Christa McAuliffe

Judge

We all judge each other by how we look,
But we really all look the same.
We all have two eyes and two ears,
We do have different names.

We all have a mouth,
We all have a nose.
We all have ten fingers,
And we all have ten toes.

We all have two hands, to help us feel.
Our tongue helps us taste every meal.
We all have a heart,
That helps us with our emotions.
Our brain helps us think,
So we don't eat lotions.

I didn't mention what's inside us,
Because that is not the same.
So why not judge the inside and not cause someone pain.

Aviva Mansbach, Grade 9
Stella K Abraham High School for Girls

The Athlete

The Athlete is good at bat
When he's at the plate he gives it a smack
This Athlete hits home runs
And after the game he gets a hot dog on a bun.

In the Fall the Athlete plays football
The Athlete scores touchdowns
He makes sure he doesn't go out of bounds
And when the game is done the Athlete had a lot of fun.

The Athlete likes to play basketball
It is fun to start in the fall
He works real hard every day
Until the season ends in May.

John Salanger, Grade 7
Camillus Middle School

Gathering

As the wind brushes against the shore,
Gathering, examine makes me want more.
The stripes peach, white, and gold,
These objects not ancient, but very old.

Clunk, as it hits the bucket below,
Gathering, examine they put on a show.
These shells like curtains, with ripples and lines,
These objects move on, from time to time.

You can hear the ocean as some of them say,
Gathering, examine they make your day.
Check them twice before adding one on,
When three in a bucket, they sing a song.

Make sure they are shells and not pieces of glass,
Gathering, examine some may not last.
They may stick around for quite a while,
Search as far, as long as a mile.

Some shells looking somewhat out of place,
Gathering examine puts a smile on the face.
To add to the collection is such a galore,
As the wind brushes against the shore.

Jaclyn Wisniewski, Grade 8
Sewanhaka High School

What Is This One Love?

What is this one love?
Is this one love hatred
Or, is this one love
a faithful blessing that came from above,
Out of the huge opening gates of paradise?
This one love is our world's destiny
by the determination, blood, death,
and the resurrection of our brother.

This one overwhelming love
separates into many particles
for each person's heart.
They change it into many levels.
This one love is the gravity
that keeps us secure by force
and to live on this earth,
as we walk on land and asphalt.

This one love is our father's devotion
and his everlasting fidelity.
This one love is the impeccable fruit of life
The fruit that is luscious
And forever will be.

Medgine Alexis, Grade 8
Walt Whitman Intermediate School

Storm

Thunder sounds like a big box falling off the shelf,
Slamming on the ground,
Then comes the lightning,
Flashing like a camera taking a hundred pictures a second,
Right into the night sky.
When thunder sounds some people think it's because the sky or Mother Nature is mad,
Some people think it's because God and all the angels are having a bowling party,
What's the thunder?
It's the ten-pound ball smashing into the pins at sixty miles per hour,
And the lightning?
Well it's the angels taking pictures of it,
I don't know what I think but if I had to choose?
Well I would pick that Mother Nature is mad at all the pollution in the air,
Making her defenses weaker so she can't fight all the bad storms
Trying to make the beautiful night sky dark and dreary.
The next time your looking at the night sky think why?

Meghan Appleby, Grade 7
Bethlehem Central Middle School

What Is Depression?

To feel unwanted
To think that you're all alone in this world when the truth is you're really not
To feel as if every inch of your body is full of worry and sorrow
Desperate to find an inch of happiness which feels like trying to find a needle in a haystack
To feel as if a black cloud has engulfed you and will never go away
To think that you're the only one who has problems and that no one else will ever understand
To wish that one day you will be cheerful again
To hope that everything will one day turn out okay
That is Depression.

Gaitlyn Malone, Grade 8
Our Lady Queen of Apostles School

Malcolm X

Malcolm Little was born May 19, 1925.
As he grew, he didn't know what was wrong or right.
He had three siblings: Wesley, Reginald, and Yvonne
His father was Earl Little; his mother was Louise Norton.
Malcolm got into trouble as he changed his world view.
He was troubled too.
His father died in 1931, a violent death at the hands of whites.
His anger built up; he was filled with rage; he didn't know what was right.
He began to see himself as a hustler and streetwise.
He called himself Detroit Red in his teenage years, as if he were in disguise.
While in prison Malcolm converted to the Nation of Islam.
Malcolm's goal was unity and a sense of calm.
Malcolm became a minister. Now Malcolm knew in his heart he had to do good.
Malcolm made speeches to the people when he could.
Some were inspired; some were not. Malcolm did not stop.
He kept on trying to spread his word.
His message, one of self-respect, was meant to be heard.
All people have to stand up and earn the respect they deserve.
In 1966, Malcolm was shot dead. As he died, he knew he had tried to live what he said.
Malcolm was a gifted man. Malcolm was one to say, "I'll do all that I can."
He knew it was necessary to make his people proud.

Caitlin Hupe, Grade 7
St Catherine of Siena School

A Letter of Inspiration

As time goes by people die
As people die new lives arise.
Thoughts of getting older might frighten you so.
So take in the great memories as time goes.
Remember NOT think of all the bad things that have happened.
But to remember the GOOD things that are to come.

As time goes by
    As time goes by
        Boy does time fly!

Dykota Hillman, Grade 8
Most Precious Blood School

Friendship

Friendship is never ending
it is long lasting like a piece of bubble gum
To have friendship, you must trust
When you have friendship
You share your deepest, darkest secrets
When you have friendship
You care about that person
Want to help that person
When they need it the most
That is what friendship is

Jenna Wilson, Grade 7
Solvay Middle School

Football

We practice and run,
We practice and run
We work hard to have some fun.
We take the field
To meet the other team
And yet we will not yield

The play is called
We take the line
To block and push through
Each and every time
We make it down the field
With a goal of winning in mind
Sometimes it's not easy
Or is it kind.

We play as a team
To meet our goal,
Winning in mind,
Each and every time.
We play with our heart
From start to end, no matter the outcome,
We're still a team in the end.

George Spezzano, Grade 8
Avon Middle School

I Am Becca

I am Becca
I am an 8th grader at Avon
I am a butterfly ready to spread my wings and fly
I am a train with a roaring engine
I am a cheetah ready to pounce on my prey
I am what I am and that's all I can be

Rebecca Rumfola, Grade 8
Avon Middle School

Heaven's Vision

Trees whistling silently from passing winds
A man in white sleeping on a rock
After a moment wakes up and sees a vision
Seeing two trees merge, forming a cross
Beautiful mountains appear, so tall and blue
He reaches for the sky as something catches his eye
Two glorious angels shimmering with light emerge
A vision from heaven appears to him
A glance of the beauties beyond heaven's gates, he
Believes a message from God sent forth to him
Shining light all over the place, no echo or sound
Palm trees on the far side, light green and tall, a
Sense of serenity fills the man's heart
A vision so vast which never will part
The angels smile upon him, telling him where he will go
Looking through God's eyes of the wonders in heaven
What the future will hold from heaven's vision

Richard Allaico, Grade 9
John Bowne High School

Till the End

Is this how it's going to end?
I thought you said forever,
And ever again.

You have left me alone and cold,
For someone else to comfort and hold.
Is this really the end?

Even though you have been a jerk,
I always think why it didn't work.
Maybe it is because of her.
What if she didn't move here?
Would it be different this year?

I've come off strong but deep inside,
What you did to me again made me cry.
I wish things could go back to the way they were,
Just me, you and others and not her.

But now I guess in the end,
We are just good friends.
I hope we will stay like this,
Till the end.

Shannon Campbell, Grade 8
Avon Middle School

Single Spark

What a single spark can do.
A fan of wind and dryness, too.
It grows in size and in heat,
A monster none should ever meet.
It burns and stops at no one's plead.
What a deed
For the bravest men.
The monster blows past all of them
And never stops.
It crackles and pops.
The water tries to drown it dead,
But it continues on instead.
It rages and grows,
Only God knows
When it will die.
The men will try
To stop its rage
And in another age
They do,
Even with the wind and dryness, too.
What a single spark can do.

Ken Brill, Grade 7
Camillus Middle School

Silent Rain

All was quiet I sat alone,
can't help but think in solemn tone,
the rain was cold the grass was too,
I hoped the sun would shine through,
I sat alone all soaking wet,
I wanted to be home and yet,
I knew the house would be empty,
no family at all could I see,
they all had passed in just one day,
no song to sing no words to say,
I looked up to see no rain fall,
I wondered was there rain at all,
then I realize sadly it's not from the sky,
all the rain came from my eye.

Kayla Jardine, Grade 8
Warwick Valley Middle School

Music

Music is life.
Music is freedom.
Music is passion.
Music is soul.

Music is light.
Music is air.
Music is rock.
Music is roll.

Music is me.

Kelsey Wise, Grade 8
Avon Middle School

My English Project

I couldn't think of a poem, so I wrote this instead
This is probably going to be as boring as bread
Poems are supposed to be about what you want or like
Or even better yet, as said my by uncle Mike,
When you write this stuff, it should come from your heart
But I never took the time to figure it out, take it apart
So all my life I've been a dreamer
I've been a planner, I've been a thinker, and I've been a schemer
Now I've been around New York, been to PA a time or two
And they say many different schools make you smarter, I'm proof that's not true
You know, I've been called all the names in all of the books
Making fun of my name, behavior and looks
But none of them have ever really gotten to me
I mean, I understand them and all; I just never minded them and, let them be
Some people have wondered, and asked how and why
But I'll just laugh and say, I'm just some guy

Nick Harris, Grade 8
Southern Cayuga Middle School

My Liberation

The music that gallops through my veins flows through my fingers.
I sigh, and the wind blows through my hair.
Strumming a tune, my consent to circle clouds.
Tears of bliss well behind my closed eyes.
I am finally free.

The music that gallops through my veins flows through my fingers.
I smirk, and the wind blows through my hair.
Piecing together a melody, my sanction to soar
Tears of bliss well behind my closed eyes.
I am finally free.

The music that gallops through my veins flows through my fingers.
I laugh, and the wind blows through my hair.
A harmony sings to me, my permission to fly.
Tears of bliss well behind my closed eyes.
I am finally free.

Indira Abiskaroon, Grade 9
Townsend Harris High School

The Sound of the Night

In my head, I heard the sound of the night.
I heard the song of the night by hearing the 6:00 p.m. Rush hour.
I also heard people honking stressfully wanting to get home,
Maybe to kiss their children or spouse good night or perhaps just so the
Mashed potatoes don't get cold and soggy.
As I listen more carefully I can hear music playing from Broadway.
I look down the street and I see the dark street but lit by the city lights.
As I look out my window and pay more attention I see a bright shining light
Shining into my room. I see it's my mother! I run, shut the light, close my door,
Lay down and hear my mom walk into the room. I then hear her whisper in my ear,
"I love you." I then feel her squeeze me tight, hugging me and so I say to myself,
I will have a great night, all because she hugged and kissed me,
Good Night!

Toniann Puglisi, Grade 7
Robert Moses Middle School

My Dog

My dog Gabby likes to play.
She is fun and peppy most of the day.
She saves her energy for when I get home.
When I walk in the door I throw her bone.
She runs and jumps happy as can be.
She tires herself out and cuddles with me.
She sleeps for a little bit until we eat.
When she hears a plate clatter, she moves her feet.
She watches me eat until I am done,
She is ready for some more fun.
My dog Gabby is number one.

Jordan Arango, Grade 7
Holy Cross School

The Night of May 14th*

In this night of sweetened dreams
I lie awake without a single image in my head
While the whole world is asleep
I rule the night away.
Don't bring me down, don't say a word
I promise you I won't go on
Without being heard
Like the night sky that's dark
But shines the brightest
Like the millions of tiny bright dots in the night
I will be up there
Here I am saying "I'm not giving up"
So I won't.

Fanelli Mendez, Grade 9
John Bowne High School
*Inspired by the painting "Starry Night" by Vincent Van Gogh

Best Friends

When best friends are close to each other,
They will never leave one another.
When I was young I had a friend,
We grew up and spent our time together until the end.
I dream of her every day in my imagination,
She is somewhere in my heart, waiting at a station.
The times when I cry she always breaks through into my shell,
She is like a flipping coin down my well.
She always tells the truth and never lies,
I can tell from her beautiful eyes.
I opened the window it was a rainy day,
Then she surprises me in a shocking way.
She never ever tries to hide,
Cause we stick together side by side.
When we both have plans,
She lets me take a chance.
She is a diamond in my heart,
Even when her feelings break apart.
Our friendship is like a flower,
that is blooming in the spring shower.
She will be my best friend forever.

Sandy Ismail, Grade 7
Al Iman School

Divorce

A spiteful word Divorce!
It breaks the oath.
It breaks the love.
It kills the dove.
The children are in pain.
Not sure which one to choose.
Their mom or their dad?
The mom who taught them to ride a bike.
The dad who taught them to fly a kite.
The judge is the one to decide.
They have no choice.
Their parents bribing them.
For something that never happens.
Visiting the other in shame for what had happened.
Not sure how to explain to their friends.
That things will never be the same.

Samantha Ribbeck, Grade 8
Barker Middle School

Until That Day

Until that day.
I'll think of you —
the love we shared the memories too
Until that day I'll think of you
I'll try so hard in all I do
Until that day I'll find out why
you had to leave with no goodbye
Until that day
this is so your family misses you more than you'll know.
Until that day you'll be with Him.
Your God your Savior and new best friend.
Until that day I see you there you're in my heart
you're everywhere
Until that day

Erica Layne, Grade 7
Intermediate School 381

Soccer

You walk onto the dewy grass and across the field you see
The fresh painted white lines on the ground
You throw your water bottle down and
Run around the field to look at your fans
Your competition stands beside you
Thinking the same thoughts you are
You walk onto the field and get in your position
Defense
The only thing that stands between you and the ball
Are a couple of players
The referee looks at each team's goalie
Blows his whistle
The soccer game begins

Briana Bariteau, Grade 7
Heatly School

Twin Tower Tears

Crash, burn, boom
Sadness arises in every room
I hear screaming everywhere
Everyone stops to stare
Lost and found
Police looking all around
As I see objects falling
I hear innocent people calling
Panic in their eyes
Ashes falling from the sky
Crash, burn, boom

Caitlin Hawley, Grade 7
Camillus Middle School

Life

Life is a plane ride,
Sometimes it's bumpy,
Ups and downs,
You think it's all over,
Then you soar to new heights,
And the ride is smooth again.

Caroline Spang, Grade 7
Camillus Middle School

Dancing

I breathe
I hear the music.
My troubles leave me
and happiness takes its place.
My feet start to move and
the rest of my body follows.
I stop worrying about the
steps and let the
music take me
on a journey.
There is no one around.
There is no sense of time.
The music stops.
The dance continues in my heart.

Ariana Sepúlveda, Grade 8
Warwick Valley Middle School

One for All

O n that day,
N o one can forget,
E verything lost.

F irefighters and cops risking their lives,
O ur Twin Towers are gone.
R isking lives or losing them.

A ll because of one man,
L osing almost everything,
L ong Island will never forget.

Morgan Leonard, Grade 7
Udall Road Middle School

In My Blood

In my blood
Runs a history from when myths weren't fantasies,
To these endless roads ahead.

My mother's hands, red with the powder of spice and garlic,
Shuffle through piles of cabbages
Blotched with the spicy paste.
It fills the air as I draw in the flavor
Through my swelling nostrils.
I can taste the hotness,
Saliva slowly filling the gaps in my mouth
Just like my mother as a child;
Gazing with her small brown eyes
At her own mother wearing the traditional garment:
Hanbok.
Simple with designs and bright vibrant colors,
My eyes are fixed on the short jacket over the
Long, wavy skirt
Hidden away in the depths of my parents' closet.
My mother took one part of our culture, but abandoned the other.

Even if I do the same,
In my blood runs a history that will never die.

Anne Bae, Grade 9
Townsend Harris High School

Horror in the Himalayas

Down deep beneath the Earth's surface there starts a rumble
Pounding, thumping, roaring.
There's nothing you can do about it.
They flee from their homes, but where can they run?
The great Himalayas are caving in on them.
They are running out of choices and no one can escape.

People are trying to help them.
Although they search the rubble for days,
many people are still trapped — and nothing is really working.
It's a race against the clock.
And we have to find them now — But no matter how hard we try,
No one can undo this natural disaster.

But we can help — Sending money and medical supplies,
Blankets, jackets, and shoes,
And garments to keep them warm for the snowy winter to come.

Down deep beneath the Earth's surface
There starts a rumble — Pounding, thumping, roaring —
There's nothing you can do about it —
And you can't prevent it.

Jake Daneby, Grade 8
Hommocks Middle School

Dreaming

Falling asleep to the soft, soft light
but waking up to the dark of the night.

I think about him and I wish I could tell,
if he was thinking about me as well.

I think about him every day,
he lives so close, but he's so far away.

The smile I get when he crosses my mind,
makes people ask, but they're very kind.

My friends are nosy, but I don't care,
I enjoy talking with them and having something to share.

I dream so much, it's usually about him,
sometimes they come on only a whim.

I wake up from a dream come true,
only to find out that my dream fell through.

It scares me a bit, and it gives me a fright,
I enjoy waking up to the dark of the night.

Margaret Gerwin, Grade 8
St Mary's School

The Raging Storm

Even though the foreboding clouds loomed for weeks,
We couldn't foresee how our lives would transform,
But many lives were catastrophically lost,
In this furious and destructive storm.

Buildings and homes had been left in ruination,
As the young and old were unprotected,
And with the separation of families,
The loss of happiness was expected.

The lightning flashed endlessly,
As the deafening blasts struck fear,
And not one person knew,
When the clouds would clear.

Fires scorched the earth,
Darkness and smoke enveloped the land,
Only those who had power,
Had the strength and courage to withstand.

Those who defend us from this raging storm,
Are not as they were before,
Given that they are wounded and broken,
For these are the realities of *war.*

Frumie Ganeles, Grade 9
Stella K Abraham High School for Girls

One for All

O n September 11, 2001, our nation was changed forever.
N ever to forget the ones who died,
E veryone's hopeful the terror is gone.

F irefighters continue to risk their lives,
O ne by one their names are read,
R eminding us who died that day.

A mericans continue to fight,
L aws were made to protect our lives,
L etting us believe our future is bright.

Nick Aponte, Grade 7
Udall Road Middle School

October

October when the breeze comes your way
the leaves start to fall and all the kids yell, "Hurray!"
The jumping, the screaming, the kids having fun,
The fun will never stop until October is done.

Kids get their pumpkins carving in many ways
from scary to funny, we all smile as we roll off the hay
The pumpkins faces as cute as can be
from scary to happy, we all shout, "Candy!"

It's October 31st, the scariest of all days
Kids dress up in many different ways.
From witches to goblins, they all ring the door,
Kids scream and shout, still wanting more!

Brittany Bamann, Grade 7
Dake Jr High School

No, I Don't Want Your Sympathy

Starts with a stem, then a bud,
It all dies eventually
What about when it's alive? I never thought to ask
It was just another day
My heart, blackened with fear
Why did I set myself so far away?
My shield was up, blocking me from you
I walked away,
that last glance, your pain, a phone call.
It replays in my head,
I should have taken what you had to offer,
Your words
What words? I don't have any of your words.
I have nothing of you,
And I am filled with regrets
And I have broken my heart
Trying to figure out why, why would you leave me?
Your petals may have fallen
But they have fallen deep into my heart
Never will I forgive you
Never will I forget you

Arielle Pearl, Grade 8
Briarcliff Middle School

Saint George and the Dragon
The girl looks sad
That's the only pet she had
The knight is happy
He killed the beast
Now he's about to have a big feast
It's a dark scary night
The dragon put up a fight
The dragon has no hands
So he can only stand
And maybe fly away
But not today
Because he is going down for the count
And now his round is out
Rashawn Rhoden, Grade 9
John Bowne High School

On the River
On the river,
in a boat,
across from my friend,
with a fishing pole,
in front of a fish,
with polka dot eyes,
down the falls,
into a lake,
far from my friend,
without a map,
with no pole,
down some more falls,
out of the boat,
into a village,
of unfamiliar animals,
across from a long necked dog,
aside from a walking plant,
far from an acrobatic pig,
in front of a flipping tree,
behind a dancing raisin,
an animal trainer was found.
Brian Cox, Grade 7
St Mary's School

The Water Is My Tears
Farther and farther we grow,
A river emerges between us.
What happened?
Farther and farther we grow,
A sea grown between us.
Come back!
Farther and farther we grow,
There's an ocean.
I'm losing you.
Farther, farther, and farther.
You're gone. I miss you.
Courtney Balgobin, Grade 9
Sewanhaka High School

Chef Soup
Every day I wake up at dawn
I work at the soup kitchen all day long
I cut and steam vegetables in the kitchen
Pots and pans are what I use
All anyone needs is a bowl and a spoon
Making people happy is my job
Adding the right ingredients
Makes the perfect soup
A pinch of salt
A cup of broth
A handful of vegetables
And last but not least
A teaspoon of love
I guarantee next time you have my soup
You will think it is
Mmm…Mmm…Mmm…Good!!!
Sarah Redington, Grade 9
DeSales High School

Morning/Night
Morning
In the morning —
Tired, boring, helpless
Like a baby
Very slow
Useless

Night
At night —
Full of energy
Want to have fun
Going over the day
Excited
Dennis Rice, Grade 7
Our Savior New American School

God's Thumb
As I climb the Mountain of Truth,
I feel God's power through my body.
The strength gets better as I climb up.
Then an eagle soars above my head.
I can feel his wings drifting in the air.
He's calm.
I start climbing higher and higher.
I hear God's wisdom talking to me.
It's a soft, calm voice.
Then I reach the top of the mountain.
The world is in the vicinity of me.
Then I turn around
I see God's Thumb.
Then I realize something I hadn't before:
I am a spirit.
I am God's child.
Tim Norris, Grade 8
Holy Cross School

The Highway
A dance.
That's what it really is,
Cars turning, speeding.
Someone misses a step.
Everyone stops.
Someone goes too slowly,
The chorus of horns begins.
Cars of all different sizes,
Small and dainty, large and clumsy.
All the cars gliding,
Skates on a frozen pond.
The monitors patrol,
With lights flashing.
A dance.
That's what it really is.
Sarah Fessenden, Grade 8
Southern Cayuga Middle School

The Artistic Chef
The chef's first sight
Fishing ideas,
Piece by piece, put together by
Artistic mind,
Colors splattered onto canvas
Moon really high, working late at night
Creation in mind coming to life
A dream, a wish
Of accomplishment
To please everyone he feeds
Janiri Jerez, Grade 9
John Bowne High School

Who Is Mona Lisa?
Behind her eyes
There's a mystery that lies
You'll see a half smile
If you study her awhile

She looks both male and female
And her face is so pale
She appears very shy
If she's about to cry

Is she expecting a child?
Was her personality wild?
There's a feeling that someone's there
Under the beauty of her hair

Who is she?
What do I see?
It's a mystery
What's left is her history
Kimberlyn Rowe, Grade 9
John Bowne High School

The Life of Sports

When you play a sport you dedicate your time
To make it worth your while.
You play with excitement and enthusiasm.
The thing that makes you smile
The sport you play varies with interest
You play the popular sport
Sports take a lot of time
When you should spend it on homework
Football, soccer, or basketball, whichever you choose
You can do it if you put your mind into what you do
It takes hard work
If you were up to the challenge it would work
Sports are very fun
Especially when you play in the hot sun
Sometimes you may dehydrate
But it is worth your time
Many injuries may occur
But sports prepare you for the future
Now you would know what to do
So next time you will be ready.

Shawn Lebert, Grade 9
Bishop Ford Central Catholic High School

Gandy

The one event that changed my life
was when my Gandy died.
It's not the fact that he didn't say goodbye.
It's not the fact that
I won't get a present from him anymore
on my birthday or Christmas.
It's the fact that he's gone.
The satisfying feeling of his
arms gently embracing me.
The smile that could turn
any frown upside down.
His loud but comforting laughter
that filled the room with warmth.
His great attitude and happiness
to which was very contagious.
Knowing that those things were gone.
Knowing that a little piece of my heart was gone.
Knowing that he was gone.
Nothing can describe that feeling.
That was the feeling that changed my life.

Audrey Owens, Grade 8
Hommocks Middle School

Shooting Hoops

Every day I try harder and harder.
I always put myself to the test.
The more I try, the better I get.
When I shoot and miss, I get mad.
I always try again, and do better next time.
I love shooting hoops with my friends.

Brianna Grammatico, Grade 7
Solvay Middle School

Toward Those Dreams

The land of all dreams,
That's where they were all headed to.
The beautiful world of the States,
Where it's believed Americans had money in their shoes.

The Irish with their potato famine,
The Italians for the endless opportunities.
Looked like everyone was headed to one place,
And that was to Lady Liberty.

Since everyone was getting cooked up in the melting pot,
There had to be some scorching jealousy on other faces.
It wasn't long before discrimination broke loose,
And so much hatred was left behind on their traces.

There were acts and laws for those who were new,
And they all were wondering about all those enchanting dreams.
What happened to all those promises and new fates?
The immigrants realized they were caught up in schemes.

As the years passed by, there was still some hope.
Life can get better if you just have faith.
Those dreams will be fulfilled one day,
All we have to do is wait.

Riya Ismail, Grade 9
Townsend Harris High School

Since You've Been Gone

Since you've been gone,
I can't help but think about you.
I think about you every day, all day.
I miss seeing you hopping around in your cage.

Since you've been gone,
I miss seeing and touching you.
I think about when you use to make me feel happy,
when I was sad.
I just wish I could see you again.

Since you've been gone,
I miss seeing you move your ears,
when you heard a noise.
I miss hugging and kissing you.
I always think about all the great times
we have had together.

Since you've been gone,
I've never forgot you and never will.
You will always be in my heart and dreams.
And since you've been gone,
may you rest in peace.

Angelica Castro, Grade 8
St Athanasius School

Championship Day

Today is the hockey championship.
I'm skating down the ice.
I'm passing everybody in front of me.
I shoot I score!
It's 3 to 4 we need a goal to tie.

Here I go again.
I pass everybody in front of me.
There is five seconds left
I shoot and...
I miss.
We lost.

Connor Vankouwenberg, Grade 8
Avon Middle School

Shadow

I am Shadow, a friend
Days outside playing catch
I am Shadow, an enemy
Lurking ravenously behind you
I am Shadow, a sadness
Will not let go
I am Shadow, a conscience
Sticking to you stronger than guilt
I will not leave
For I am *your* Shadow
Days outside playing catch
Lurking ravenously behind you
Will not let go
Sticking to you stronger than guilt
For I am *your* Shadow
I always follow you

Sean Katko, Grade 7
Camillus Middle School

Dance

The pain, the blisters
Your gain, your sisters
The passion, the love
The fashion, the dove
The joints that are sore
The points are now wore
Flying through the air
Flowers in your hair
Gliding across the floor
Crying because it doesn't hurt anymore
The anger, the tears
The running, the fear
The gratitude, the spear
The attitude, the peers
The leaping yet all I can say
Dance is my passion,
My love
My life

Kennedy Giancola, Grade 8
Southern Cayuga Middle School

Lover in Distress

I did my best, I'm a lover in distress.
I couldn't rest because of this mess, I'm a lover in distress.

Even though I knew it was done, I couldn't have any fun.
And the pain of the past, is like an hour glass.

I lost it all, so I took a fall.
He and I will never be, so pain it causes me.

And I'll know, when I'm as low as I can go.
So take my words and go, because for now they're all I have to show.

And pain of the soul, is a feeling we all know.
It makes us cry, at least on the inside.

But you'll be fine, you will survive.
And so will I, I'm a lover in distress.

Nancy Ascenzi, Grade 8
St Mary's School

Beware

On Halloween Night,
Trick or treaters come to this house in fright.
Knowing something bad might happen.

Beware, caution, and stay out are all around the lawn.
Eggs are all over the house until the crack of dawn.
But after the clock strikes dawn the trick or treaters leave and the eggs are gone.

No one knows for sure where the eggs then go
Because no one lives in this house
But that is the mystery every year when trick or treaters come with fear.

Kaleigh McGraw, Grade 7
Camillus Middle School

My Hero

Most think he is ordinary,
But I think he is extraordinary
He is as normal as any other man you've ever met
He doesn't have any super powers,
But to me, he is the most amazing man I know
He has been through life like most other people,
And has had his fair share of hardships, but he never burdens anyone else
My hero has been very important to me my entire life
He has never let me down,
And always lets me know that he cares and loves me,
My hero has always been there when I needed him.
He battles a disease every day of his life,
But never lets it take over
He is the strongest man I have ever met.
And I am happy to say that I look up to him
More than anyone else
I am happy to say that My Hero
Is my own Father

Lynn Buckvicz, Grade 9
Bishop Ford Central Catholic High School

Heroes

I always wondered who is a hero.
Is it Spiderman, Batman, or Superman?
Is it a person, who sacrifices his or her life for others,
Or a person with superpowers and a cape?

Is it the men and women, who fight at war,
Or is it a firefighter or a police officer?

Today we think that to call someone a hero
They must have given up his life for others,
To have lost a part of them at war,
Or to have died for their country.

Are those persons heroes?

Yes!
But for me being a hero,
Also means to have donated food for the food drive
To support a local charity
To help someone cross the street
When you do all these things and others,
You get the warm feeling inside
And you feel like a true hero too.

Karla Reyes, Grade 7
Riverhead Middle School

Just Wait a Little Longer

Whispering words of content
I sit across a birch tree
As comfort reaches towards me
My soul is embraced with memories
As I think of you

Each throbbing beat of my heart
Blackens a piece of my soul
The leaves of the birch
Curl around me
Crushing the pain your memory has given me

Black dust slowly separates
From each wounding remembrance
The regrets slowly crumbles
Hope fills my mind
You are not gone
Just simply far away

When I close my eyes
Letting go of everything
I will finally be with you

Just wait a little longer…

Ashfia Alam, Grade 9
Jericho High School

They Only Skim the Surface

I see people everywhere
Along these dim-lit halls.
And all I can think of is that
They only skim the surface.
These people walking past are of the superficial kind,
Wearing brand name clothes,
Lying about their lives.
They only skim the surface.

Kelsey A. Shields, Grade 9
Oyster Bay High School

I Just Want…

I just want you to feel the way I do,
to think of me twenty four seven,
to believe I'm an angel from heaven,
to pray for me day and night,
to know you would fight for my heart,
to try your hardest…
to make sure we'd never be apart.

I just want you to be a mess when I'm not around,
and try your best to impress me when I'm in town.
That's what I do,
in fact I obsess over you.
Wish you did too,
I just want you
to feel the way I do,
to have a love…
that's always true.

Nadege Isidor, Grade 8
Chestnut Ridge Middle School

Imagination

I'm thinking of pictures all the time,
While writing poems it helps me rhyme.
Imagination, it's what helps me picture things while reading,
When I'm hungry and thirsty I can see myself eating.
When I'm little I think of games and toys,
I would do anything to fill myself with joys.
Rainbows and fantasies flowing here and there,
I know my unique thoughts are very rare.
My imagination tells me lots of things,
I use it to dream about future goals, jewels, and rings.
Every night I dream fun things that will happen in the day,
But when I wake up I'll see it's not real it's only the sun's ray.
Sometimes I daydream what might happen next,
It's my imagination who tells me how to do my best.
I sometimes can't think of things to do,
But my sense of imagination brings the road to my shoe.
This small world of thoughts has no end,
But it will always supply me with ideas to send.
My sense of imagination always delights me,
They are some times sad and sometimes happy and free,
This is why my ideas are shown out to see!

Syeda Arooba Hassan, Grade 7
Al Iman School

The Foliage

The foliage of the autumn solstice as varying in color as the weather
The beautiful foliage with its wondrous shades of red, oranges, yellows, and greens
Sometimes even purples
The towering trees high above the sky, along the highway, with leaves like a paint pallet
The sun shines brightly like a child's smile, through the small slits between branches
The shimmering rays of light casting shadows across the smooth pavement
Gusts of air blow with the wind creating hollow whistles as each car speeds by
Each engine roaring loud
The honks and beeps of traffic sound
How can something so beautiful be somewhere so hideous?
Why are you in a place people just zip on by?
The warming colors of the leaves
The surprising beauty in the empty barren
The jubilant hues of each leaf
How astonishing these works of nature are
The beautiful foliage
The beautiful foliage
The beautiful foliage

Lucas Eager-Leavitt, Grade 8
Baldwin Middle School

My Soul Surrenders

My soul surrenders to the quiet night.
My mind unable to fight the power of that darkness which calls to me.
A powerful and mysterious voice whispers in the night but I dare not ask his name.
For in the dark, true wonders wait for me.
His voice holds my spirit with a strange new sound.
With his entrancing song, he shows me the darkness of love.
As I listen to his song the darkness consumes me.
Slowly he reveals himself to me.
Only for me to quake in fear.

Anastasia Marie Marcos, Grade 9
Port Chester High School

Sleep

While closing my eyes I think of many things
Rust and heat, God and life, cars, beasts, planes, or kings
But one thing that baffled me my whole childhood career
Was what happened to you while you slept? The ideas were most austere

First that your mind left your body behind and went wherever it pleased
Next that you woke and snuck out unprovoked and followed the wandering breeze
That sleep was a charge up just to refill the cup and help you get through the next day
Or that parents made you sleep, made you count up those sheep so they could spend time their own way

And then my poor mind already all befuddled
Tried to add dream to the mix and things became even more muddled
Were dreams just there to help you bear the time it took to rest
To entertain your sleeping brain 'Cause boredom is a pest
Or memories left over from your night job as a rover just yet to be erased
Things half recollected that your mind half neglected adventures half misplaced

To be right there but unaware seems so very crazy
And the things we see that seem so real but turn up strange and hazy

Sean Byrons, Grade 8
Most Precious Blood School

The Joy of the Ride
Riding on the waves with the
wind in my hair,
Nature welcomes me in the warm summer air.

My thoughts seem limitless and I
feel so free,
There's no other place I would
rather be.

Bouncing off the glistening water
are the sun's rays,
And I'm drawn through the lake
and around the bays.

The force pulls me in like a
cowboy lassoing a steer.
When I'm riding my wake board
everything seems so clear.
Ian Richardson, Grade 7
Camillus Middle School

Christmas
Holidays are so much fun
I like each and every one

Christmas is a blast you see
When snowflakes are falling on both you and me

Icy roads and foggy skies
WOW I can't believe my eyes

Is that Santa in the sky?
Flying up there oh so high
Santa, Rudolph, and the crew
Bringing presents for me and you

Now I have to go back to bed
If my mom catches me, I will be dead!
So I threw the blanket over my head

I wondered what presents I might get
Then I noticed the candle was lit
So I went and blew it out real quick
Hoping soon I would see Saint Nick.

Sara Rocker, Grade 8
Southern Cayuga Middle School

Garden
The wind passes by as my heart starts to cry as I sit in a garden
A garden as beautiful as nothing I ever seen before
But still I hurt inside from something I can no longer remember
As I scream out for the pain to stop
For the wounds in my heart to heal
Suddenly, I realize, the garden is not real
Vanessa Gonzalez, Grade 8
The New York Institute for Special Education

Pulse
A beat pulses through my ear,
a beat that no one else can hear.

The tune of my heart is unique to its own,
you can only see so much by what is shown.

Dive into my rhythm and hear my song,
then you can see where I really belong.

Every person has a melody all to themselves,
only few would know the tune very well.

Those that have truly listened to somebody's heart,
could only then, tell two songs apart.
Hannah Lee, Grade 8
Eagle Hill Middle School

Trick or Treat
I come out on this spooky night
To Trick Or Treat with sheer delight

With ghosts and witches and mummies
And kids dressed up as dummies

I go from house to house to Trick Or Treat
And then I roam the festive street

It's something that's so fun to do
There's always something for me and you

I come out on this spooky night
To Trick Or Treat with sheer delight
Ryan Fitzpatrick, Grade 7
Camillus Middle School

Baseball
Last night I went to bed as the normal kid.
And dreamed sweet dreams as my mother said.
This dream was not like any other.
No friends no family and not even my mother.
My Coach called for me to come over.
"This kid's got nothing" I heard over his shoulder.
I was up next; all eyes were on me.
"Remember, you got what it takes," my father said to me.
"Strike 3 you're out," yelled the ump.
The batter before me was surely in a slump.
I walked up there nervous, not calm or excited.
"Fastball," as I read in his eyes, my team will be delighted.
He let it fly, and I knew I was right.
I swung the bat hard, and the ball went in flight.
I knew it was gone so I took my time getting home.
Stephen Payette, Grade 7
Camillus Middle School

I Need My Glasses

I took off my glasses
I couldn't see a thing,
My eyesight was so blurry
That I tripped over a ring!

My teacher was short
And I was so tall,
The floor was the ceiling
And the ceiling was the wall.

There were clowns, there were monkeys
There were elephants and more
There were lions, there were tigers
All walking through the door.

The words I was writing
Went flying off the page,
They turned into parrots
Who needed a cage.

I forgot where my glasses were
No chance of ever getting them back,
So I sat down on my chair
And my glasses went CRACK.

Elana Schreier, Grade 9
Stella K Abraham High School for Girls

Times Have Changed

Times have changed
Movie stars
And Barbie dolls
TV shows
And everything you know
Clothes from the '80s
Seem so crazy
Clothes from the '90s
Seem so lazy
Time has changed
And people age
But your feelings will
Always stay the same.

Hannah Schmitt, Grade 8
Most Precious Blood School

The Impossible

Gravity is for the narrow-minded,
Hate is for the angry,
Regret is for the self-conscious,
Weak is for the failures,
Deceit is for the bitter,
Revenge is for the jealous

And Impossible is for the
scared.

Shannon Bligh, Grade 8
Oakdale-Bohemia Middle School

The Beauty of Nature

Nature has many great things.
In a tree, a harmonious bird sings.
There are flowers, grass, animals too.
Footprints of animals are a pretty big clue
Footprints of animals come with different times of the year.
Pounding of rain, chirping of birds, and the howl of the wind
Is what you may hear

Charlotte Brunjes, Grade 8
Warwick Valley Middle School

I Am a Child

I am a child who cannot see
Sometimes I wonder "why did this happen to me?"
I can hear my brothers and sisters laughing but I cannot see their face
Not a glimpse or even a little trace
I am a child who is wheelchair bound
Expected to sit and not make a sound
Do you think I want to just watch my life from this chair?
Without knowing what it feels like to skip, run, and jump through the air?
I am a child who cannot speak and let my thoughts flow
My insights and ideas no one in this world will ever know
I tried to speak once but no one heard what I said
I feel trapped in a world where everyone is alive and I am dead
We want understanding not pity, we want to be treated the same
We want people to look at us without thinking "what a shame"
Yes in many ways we are different than you but we are all alike as well
Just like you we have thoughts, dreams and aspirations and to the world
this is what we'd like to tell:
My eyes might seem empty, my face might seem dead
My body might seem distorted, but there are thoughts in my head
I am just as alive as you are and in this world I am here to stay
So let me into your life, don't shut me away.

Adina Hart, Grade 9
Stella K Abraham High School for Girls

After Saints Peter and Paul

Where will we go, after the fall, after the snow.
The exams will be over, so much for the 4-leaf clover.

Friends will break branches, those close will hold true.
No one knows how it all will turn out, the lifelong bout.
But me? I will continue to high school, and eventually college.
Widening my span of knowledge.

Before the long-term goals are set, before the friendship ties are severed,
There is the one moment, right before the final bell where time stands still.
The future is unforshadowed, unforetold, and ripe for our picking.
And after the school of middle, we all will play the life-fiddle.
Streaming notes of our success, and successors.

And still, before it all, one last class, one last walk down the hall.
That hall we know so well. That hall is our rite of passage,
And we must walk through it in full. The trembling we must quell.

Because after all...
Does anyone really know where they are going?

Tom Maleck, Grade 8
SS Peter and Paul School

Chains

Clenching your teeth, you close your eyes
Trying so hard to fly
Pulling desperately at the links
That hold you down until you sink

Keeping you captive in such a desolate land
Forbidden the comfort of a soft hand
Confined to this darkness, you softly cry
Hugging your knees and asking why

The metal begins to carve its way
Into your skin, day after day
So how long will you be caught like this?
Strapped to the bottom of your deepest abyss

When all you can do is silently gaze
Letting your eyes wander through the black maze
A chilling touch fingers your spine
Causing an involuntary shudder and a desperate whine

Cautiously, you give a pathetic tug
While the chains laugh; haughty and smug
Why don't you just give up and behave?
Forget the light and happiness you crave

Hannah Migliore, Grade 9
North Tonawanda High School

My Angel from My Nightmare

He eyes me like an hourglass.
Up and down his eyes balance on me.
He is my savior like a soldier in a war.
We need each other, as if we're both broken.
His hands grow cold as I slip away.
My body goes numb as he comes closer.
My angel from my nightmare.
Yet he is not at all scary.
But comforting and gives security.
Comfort and security, our biggest fear.
Will this fear ever go away?
My angel from my nightmare,
Come and rescue me from this dream.
I need you here I need you now.
My angel from my nightmare.
You're all I need, take me away.
Take me away from this horrid place.
Where the only light shines from your eyes.
And this horrid dream will last no more.
I can't do this all on my own.
Angel from my nightmare…save me.
You're all I need.

Nicole Di Lillo, Grade 8
William A Morris School IS 61

Wilted

The music had died: an empty echo.
Why did you keep swaying?
You were always offbeat, even in silence.
Your rhythm could never be matched;
The earth's pulse not once caught the beat.
If not that, what contamination mothered my adoration?
Was it that smile, blissful, crooked?
The beauty you found in wilted flowers?
Or was I locked in mid-swoon since only you held true
To a dishonest promise made by too many
And meant by far too few?
I have seen a million lies. Each read the same.
Then you auditioned. Claimed a part of my heart.

Maya Fink, Grade 9
Earl L Vandermeulen High School

Winter

Winter is my favorite season,
this is for one particular reason.
It is because I love snow,
and the way it gives off a wonderful glow.
Watching it fall from the sky,
zooms my day right on by.
I also love to build snowmen,
once I built just about ten.
Snowboarding is quite fun too,
I always like to try something new.
One last thing I love about this season,
is when school is let out for a snow-related reason.

Nina Orenstein, Grade 8
Warwick Valley Middle School

The He in She

Their eyes meet, a glance, a smile,
He asks her to dance, she takes his hand,
For that moment, no one is around.
Their minds, bodies, and soul are as one,
They exchange numbers and the story begins.
Five years later, that one night changed their life,
They spend every minute together, it seems perfect,
They even plan their lives together,
Things couldn't be better.
But what goes up must come down,
The bond begins to dissipate,
And it comes crashing down,
But she's left with a small fetus
Without even knowing.
The baby is born, he has everything at his feet,
She provides him with the world and more,
He has the best schooling, friends, clothes, and mother.
She couldn't ask for a better son than he,
Smart, respectful, and gracious,
He is made in her image,
He is she.

Randolph Philpotts, Grade 9
Bishop Ford Central Catholic High School

Lonely

Cole was a lonely boy.
His dad abused him
His mother ignored him
He was an only child
Sent to an island
For beating up Peter
Cole spend some cruel
And lonely days there
Cole thought no one loved him,
Cared about him
He wasn't right

Leslie Santos, Grade 7
Solvay Middle School

Don't Close Your Eyes

I close my eyes
To her pain
Because if I love her
They may not love me
So I sacrifice
Her broken heart
Her scared arms
Her precious life
For my comfort
Is she my responsibility to love?
So I close my eyes

Don't close your eyes
On my pain
Your silence is wasting me
Because I have no need for life now
So why live?
You have closed your eyes on me
So I take this vice
To end my broken life
I close my eyes

Karah Lain, Grade 7
Camillus Middle School

The Laws in My House

Sometimes rules can be a pain
Taking out garbage in the rain

The cat pan smells foul to me
Clean my room then I'll be free

My sister doesn't respect privacy
She comes in my room to bother me

Washing the dishes is my task
Before I go on the computer I must ask

Being the oldest is hard for me
But I do the jobs respectfully

Brandon Duffy, Grade 7
Solvay Middle School

Garbage in the Street

Garbage in the street, without a scrape of meat.
People drive right by, because they think they're fly.
People see the garbage, but they don't see the carnage.
The garbage see the mean, but they still stay keen.
The garbage feels the pain, but the people see a game.
The people see a beat population, but they have no representation.
The garbage see the people they resent, but the garbage stay content.
The people think garbage is a pest, but the garbage think they're the best.
The garbage feel remorse, but the people still give war.
The people say it feels no pain, but the people don't help their strain.
The people say that garbage is free, but the garbage says it's not to be.
The garbage says they like their home, but the people think that isn't so.
The people say the garbage is worthless like clumps of old newspaper.
But as you know the saying goes "One man's trash, another man's treasure."

Kevin Watkins, Grade 8
Southern Cayuga Middle School

All Tied Up

As the whistle blows, everyone goes to the ball.
With the game all tied up, we're determined to win it all.

Both teams wildly kicking, it's a long game,
And I don't think we're winning.
It's been the same since the very beginning.
They play better than us, they have better aim.

Luckily not a single shot has hit its target.
I think we're starting to forget what we're supposed to do when we receive the ball.
Suddenly something seemed to be coming at us as if a giant who's so tall.

It was a flashing and booming cloud and the referee shouted aloud, game over.

Kegan Leberman, Grade 8
Avon Middle School

No One Knows

No one knows
How I really feel inside
Everyone expects me to smile
And that I'm always as happy as I seem to be
And never give a thought whether it is actually an illusion

No one knows
That underneath this smile
I can be unhappy
That I fake the lovely smile that everyone knows
That this very smile is forced

No one knows
Of how I want to scream
And break free of this illusion
An illusion of someone who is responsible,
Someone who is smart and practical and would never cause any trouble

No one knows…of how I really feel…

Heather Mak, Grade 9
Staten Island Technical High School

A Wonderful Woman

When you were young, they were there for you
When you got scared at night
You scurried down the hall to her bedroom
And when you got there, and curled up to her in fear,
You suddenly felt warm and protected.

Now when you look at her, you think she's against you
Because she won't let you go here or there
Or maybe it's because she won't let you have what you want
But the only reason that she seems to be against you is because
She loves you more than the world itself.

This women works all day just to feed her family
and does it with the weight of the world on her back every day.
You might think this is a wonder woman, a goddess or even a
character in a fictional story you read to little kids.
But I know who this so called "Wonder Woman" is,
She is called many names, but one that is known to all…
Mom

Samy Melvin Accorso, Grade 7
Dake Jr High School

I Am Who I Am

I have a habit of mixing up messages,
I talk over other people's conversations,
I have become an expert at hiding my feelings,
I never learn from my mistakes unless I am forced to,
I am not perfect but I like to believe I am,
And yet I say this with a smile,
I like my flaws the way they are,
If I didn't have them I wouldn't be myself,
I am different.

I am contradicting with my character,
I know no better than the person next to me,
But I am open-minded with the world,
I'm curious at everything,
I am strong because I have been defeated,
I am passionate because I know where I stand,
I know what I like and when I want it,
I am not perfect but I am who I am.

Laura Anne Tanzil, Grade 8
Holy Family School

Be True to Yourself

Be true to yourself
Don't always follow what others say
You might want it your way
You don't have to be cool for them
You can be cool in your own way
You don't have to do things you don't want to do
If you do you're just acting like a fool
I'm telling you be true to yourself
Because that makes you cool

Tyler Boyce, Grade 8
Warwick Valley Middle School

Thanksgiving

Turkey and all the trimmings
Having and sharing
Attitude, positive for the ones we love
Neat conversations
Kitchen, the heart of the family
Scrumptious food
Giving to those in need
Ice cream on top of the pie
Vegetables 'cause they are important
Interesting day because it's only once a year
God, always our guiding light

Thanksgiving is a day we all care;
A day we wish to share;
Thanksgiving is forever;
We form bonds that we won't sever

Molly McLoughlin, Grade 8
St John School

Sports

Sports are very very suspenseful
Sports can sometimes be a handful.
Sometimes they're hard
Sometimes they're easy
But all in all they are quite pleasing.

Sports can be very entertaining
Especially when the players on TV fight and start complaining.
Sports are good, sports are fun
They're even better when a prize is won.

Some sports are rough, some sports are gentle
But one thing they have in common
Is they are both physical and mental.

Zach McGee, Grade 8
Avon Middle School

Feelings

Colors, colors everywhere,
Are colors of leaves at fall,
When you can feel the cold, crisp air.
Sometimes you see your breath over all,
You see the gorgeous views from there to here.
Feel all nice and warm inside,
The sight of changes go through like a spear!
Sometimes you want it all to stay.
Stay the same forever and ever,
Too bad there are seasons after all,
But hey! The next season is winter…
My favorite season…better than fall.

Sharon Lee, Grade 8
Warwick Valley Middle School

Wedding

Two rings
That are gold and shiny

Wedding Dress
White and beautiful

Flowers
Are bright and colorful

Church bells
Have a wonderful sound

Perfumes
Have a sweet smell

Family and friends
Feel happy and smile

The bride and groom
A promise to love forever in their hearts
Joseph Holmes, Grade 7
Camillus Middle School

Movies

Cady and I wore ballerina dresses
We made many messes

Throwing popcorn everywhere
In people's faces, in people's hair

People laughing, people staring
People pointing, people glaring

Winning dinosaurs by the dollar
Jackie that ones quite a holler

Launching popcorn at each others faces
We soon got it passed Jackie's braces

Sadly it was time to go
And we missed most of the show
Jessie Karr, Grade 8
Avon Middle School

Anger

Anger
Will always be there
You can do nothing about it.
Anger won't leave.
It will always be there like a shadow
Following you.
Sometimes it will get you into trouble.
Just don't listen to it.
Mariya Olinchuck, Grade 7
Solvay Middle School

A Content Autumn

A soft breeze blowing
A bird quietly crowing
The crunch of leaves under feet
On a smooth, paved street

The trees gently rustling
The leaves dancing across the sky
While the warm sun shines down
On people walking by

A sweet smell in the air,
Of cinnamon and apple pie
And laughter in the distance,
From children everywhere.
Jessica Mason, Grade 7
Camillus Middle School

Fall

Leaves, the colors of
Brown, red, yellow, and gold
Fall from the trees,
Blocking my view for
Only a second.
Then, I can see all
The wonderful colors,
The people, the animals.
And of course the leaves.
Fall, fall the falling leaves
Crashing down like broken dreams,
But then again,
The newborn snow,
(That the leaves are making way for)
Stands for newborn dreams.
Seeping into you
While you lay,
Sleeping,
Dreaming.
Shaina Card, Grade 8
Warwick Valley Middle School

Extant

And if the sorrows of the living
Had not their somber cadence
In their damp hovels of eternity;
A half-spun thread,
Sharp in its finality.
Through the ages
The noise and the music,
Blended within
Were not dark and light,
Light and dark
In the end.
Michael Zhang, Grade 9
Commack High School

Colorado Summer

One summer morn'
a little girl wakes
eyes full of hope
innocence, never fake.

Walks to the meadow,
a field full of dreams.
White balls of fuzz
how perfect it seems.

She plucks one from its stem
the gentlest of touch.
Seeds sail to the sky
with one little puff.

Off into the world,
let the limit be the sky.
One wish can go anywhere
one day might reply.
Gina Hendry, Grade 8
Warwick Valley Middle School

Forgiveness Can Mean Many Things

I'm sorry
I want you to forgive me
Must I gain your trust?
Some say forgiveness is a good thing
I apologize for what I did
The memories still haunt me
It's important you forgive me
Because I'm really sorry!
You probably hate me but
I want your trust back
David Furness II, Grade 7
Solvay Middle School

Papa

You never give in
Even though you are hurt
You try your hardest every day
You never let anything
Get in your way
Even though you can't
See well
You understand our difficulties
You try to help us
Especially with school work
You try to see us
Even though you can't
You are a great role model
You are the greatest role model
You are the greatest
Person in the world
Catie Pfluke, Grade 9
Holy Cross Academy

Rainy

On rainy days I'm stuck inside
Just watching the rain drops fall.
All day trying to find something to do
Watching TV and playing games.
Just letting the day rush by
Wanting to go outside and play,
Yet the rain just gets in my way.
The one thing that I just can't stand is a rainy day.

Jessica Scarcella, Grade 8
Warwick Valley Middle School

Wild Fire

The grief that spreads like wild fire,
We all have it inside.

The death of a loved one,
You must put it behind.

Huddled in a ball won't help,
You can't hide forever.

A shield is on your side waiting for you to fight,
Battle wounds will last,
But life will go on and on.

Soon the flood will come,
And wash everything away,
Your chance to start over.

Kaila Falk, Grade 8
Bethlehem Central Middle School

Christmas

Christmas time,
Oh what joy it brings!
We decorate our house with many jolly things.
And people sing along,
to all their favorite Christmas songs.

Cold snow covers the ground like a gentle blanket.
And our homes are toasty and warm.

Children hope night and day,
that Santa Claus is on his way.
And soon children will play with all their new Christmas toys,
And smiles are on the faces of every girl and boy.

Christmas time,
Oh what joy it brings!
It reminds me of so many wonderful things.
Christmas time.

Holly Signor, Grade 8
Southern Cayuga Middle School

My Life

I am Brenna Donegan.
People call me Brenn sometimes.
I have many friends.
My best friends name is Alissa.
She has the coolest family.
I love to play sports.
And I am very athletic.
I have a dog named Daisy.
2 cats named Luke and Pumpkin.

School is fun but a lot of work.
And I like and dislike some teachers.
I really dislike reading.
But I love English class.
I hate taking tests.
But I love it when you get your test back with a good grade.
I think my life has many ups and down.
But I totally think my life is AWESOME!

Brenna Donegan, Grade 8
Avon Middle School

The City's Song

Morning's soft sounds of the birds and the breeze,
growing increasingly louder as the minutes pass.

Early afternoon brings hustling people and cars honking
as hardworking business people take a break from work.
Everywhere, there's the sound of a construction site —
drilling, hammers, and men chatting.

Later, children are playing outside after a long day at school.
Their parents begin arriving home from work,
and the peaceful sunset begins.

Then the subtle sounds of evening —
the occasional car passes and a dog barks.
There's the soft sound of the trees outside,
gently blowing in the night's wind.

Who says a song has to be a melodic tune, in the literal sense?

Mary Mazur, Grade 9
Bishop Ford Central Catholic High School

Get Ready to Fly

Four men trying to fix an airplane
So they can fly out and have a great time
They look like they're discussing where they're about to go
So when they leave they can talk about it
All dressed in army or navy uniforms
The plane is green and yellow and so big
Four men all alone, look like they are ready for battle
It's dark outside, the ground looks sandy
A red airplane sits next to the yellow and green one
Extra people can go out with them and have some fun

Ukwan Milliner, Grade 9
John Bowne High School

Fall

Gentle breezes pass.
The leaves glide in the current.
Autumn settles in.
Ryan Rossi, Grade 8
Hauppauge Middle School

Promise

Making a promise
Is important to do
Keeping secrets
Helping with chores
Feeding an old dog
Washing a car
These are promises I keep
What promises do you keep?
Nick Filippi, Grade 7
Solvay Middle School

In the Moonlight

As I sit in the moonlight,
I see the stars glistening,
the lake steady.
The wind is whispering to me,
the trees are humming.
I see a girl.
She looks familiar,
she is smiling at me.
I smile back.
I realize just then,
it was my reflection,
still and fragile.
A teardrop falls into the lake.
My reflection becomes blurry.
I wait patiently,
and there it is again,
my reflection, in perfect condition.
That is all you have to do, wait.
On this starry night, I see hope.
Katie Ulloa, Grade 8
Warwick Valley Middle School

Buddy

Buddy is so tall
But his eyes are so small
He is black and brown
One time he almost drowned
He is seven years old
But he is never cold
He is always in a good mood
He also loves to eat people food
He has so much flubber
I sometimes call him Bubber

I love my dog
Roni Scherer, Grade 8
Avon Middle School

Video Games

Hours and hours of entertainment
Never wanting to put down the controller
Palms are sweaty; fingers are twitching, just one more level…
In a trance with the dancing screen,
Concentrating is very keen
The outside world is currently displaced
Until I finish this addicting game!
Ian Potash, Grade 7
Camillus Middle School

Lost

Lord, I need You, now more than ever.
I'm having trouble keeping my life together.

I opened my heart and let You in,
But You seem to have drifted out again.

I reach out to You and all I feel is air.
I know that You're out there, but I don't know where.

So I look for Your face everywhere I go.
My eyes can't find You, so I move on with all my woes.

And then I hear You call me. I don't know what to do.
I slowly crawl in Your direction, 'til I'm standing next to You.

I looked for You everywhere and in everyplace.
My heart focuses better than my eyes though, when looking for Your face.

I couldn't feel You with my hands because we are apart.
When You're in heaven and I'm on earth, I can only use my heart.
Larissa St. Louis, Grade 9
Barker Middle School

Life Is a Roller Coaster

Life is a roller coaster, it has it's ups and downs.
Once you get on there is no turning back.
It starts off slow without knowing what is ahead of you.
Then it speeds ups, going faster and faster.
You seem to get higher, and you look back at the beginning of the ride.
Before you know it, you are speeding down.
You try to stop, but you remember you can't turn back.
you get scared and start to cry, but no one can hear because they are all screaming.
There is nothing to hold on to just a little bar.
You feel like you are going to fall out, but surprisingly you are all right.
You finally fall to the bottom.
Things calm down and you start to enjoy the ride.
You smile, you laugh, and look over to your friend.
You know everything will be all right.
You put up your hands until you see a loop.
You hold on tight, but then you let go.
You get scared, and start to hate the ride as much as you did before.
You go through more loops, twists and turns.
Faster and faster the ride goes.
Sometimes you wish to get off of this ride, but sometimes you want to hold on.
Before you know it the ride comes to an end, and you wish you enjoyed it more.
Claudia Mazur, Grade 8
William A Morris School IS 61

The Day of Thanks

It's Thanksgiving!!!!
The leaves are all sorts of colors red, orange, yellow and green.
There are a lot of things to do.
Go outside have some fun in the leaves.
Help prepare Thanksgiving dinner.
Play football.
Watch football.
Relax with your family and friends.
There are always things to do on Thanksgiving.
Thanksgiving is my favorite holiday.
Celebrate.

Grayson Ross, Grade 7
St John School

Looking for the End

Do you know what it's like?
Walking on that same empty road.
Day after day,
It's always the same, bleak and desolate.
Nothing alive for miles around.
It reminds me of myself.
Maybe something was here once.
But it's gone now.
I guess it doesn't matter anymore.
If I keep going,
maybe something will turn up.
But for now I'll keep walking, staying the course.
I'll give it a try, the same thing I've been doing
For as long as I can remember.
I'm not supposed to be here
I was due to leave years ago.
Falling behind the horizon
Chased by the darkness, the sun dies.
But it'll be back soon enough.
This is my favorite time, the ground falling away with the dark.
And you're left alone with the empty road.

Jordyn Fisher, Grade 8
South Side Middle School

Invincible

They'll break you down, they'll break you apart.
They'll turn things around, and leave a mark.
They'll burn your ego, they'll make you small.
But don't let them win, you've got to stand tall.
They'll stand in all their glory, and leave you in the dust.
They'll take everything you say and do, and turn it into a fuss.
You've got to beat them, you've got to fight.
You've got to stand up for what is right.
Your soul's unbreakable, your heart is made of gold.
Your time is now for you to behold,
The power within, the flicker of light.
The tables have turned, it's your turn to fight.
You're one in a million, you're one of a kind.
You will soar high through the night sky.

Lamia Kadiruzzaman, Grade 8
Dawnwood Middle School

The Truest Lie

You are an angel, from heaven sent
But I still can't believe the way it went
How did it end, before we could start?
How come, you still have all of my heart?

Your voice, your eyes and the smell of your skin
Makes my whole body tremble, of passion within
This is the sweetest torture, poisonous bliss
Still I know, all of my life has come to this

I wish to hold you tight, silence your cries
And whisper to you, the most beautiful of lies
To tell you I love you, over and over, simply because I do
It might be a lie, that coming from my heart, so very true

Having you here with me, makes me feel like kissing the moon
Reaching for the velvet sky, I think I'll be able to fly soon
I'll reach out my hand, and caress every star
So they can bless you, no matter where you are

I love you, and that's the truest of all lies
I'll love you until night fall, and sun rise
I'll love you for today, tomorrow and forever
I'll love you for always, even if we're not together

Melissa Oakley, Grade 8
Robert Moses Middle School

Suspenseful Night

Lay sound asleep in their bed
Slam! They hear a door

Awake they become
Footsteps they hear

They sit up tall
Creek a door opens

They are out of bed
Clip clomp, Clip clomp

There is someone in the house
Hush don't make a sound

911 they dial
When they come the man runs

That suspenseful night
They all had a fright

What could have happened on that very night?

Victoria Burch, Grade 8
Avon Middle School

The Life of the Future S. M. Amey

I see life through no one else's eyes but mine.
I live my life to no one else's standards but mine.
I make a point to love people the way I see fit not the way other people say I should.
I believe what I believe without letting anyone interfere with what I say.
I debate with the best of them no matter how nervous I am.
I make it known that no one runs my life, and I like to play by my own rules.
I am a legend.

People say I am mature for my age, but I know I'm not most of the time.
People say I can be scary when I'm making a point; I just don't like to be wrong.
People say I'm funny, but I'm only funny when I'm not trying to be. I hate that!
People say I'm caring, but I can be so cruel sometimes.
People say I have a great vocabulary and I say, "Microsoft Word's Synonyms help!"
People say I have a great imagination; I just write and say what I feel inside.
People say I'm very creative and I say, "I get my inspiration from things around me."

My friends are my life in the sense that they are my support system at school.
My family is my life in the sense that they made me who I am today.
My dog is my life in the sense that his spirit is with me wherever I go.
My computer is my life in the sense that it has all my written works on it.
My love for music is my life in the sense that I can't stop the beat that runs through me.
My clothes are my life in the sense that they explain I am ordinary, but not normal.
My book is my life and I must keep writing it, I just have to decide when it ends.

Madison Amey, Grade 8
Avon Middle School

The First Snowfall

Strolling past a large, foggy window,
I discover unique shapes of white fairies gently dancing their way down from the gray sky.
My eyes are captivated by the overwhelming beauty of the swirling wind and flakes.
The bare tree branches were shielded with ice as a blue jay scurries out of the way from a smoking chimney.
Layers of white blankets lie upon the frozen ground for miles,
And brightly lit Christmas trees are displayed in windows from a distance.
Everything seemed at peace as I smiled at an ordinary miracle:
The first snowfall!

Lauren Sarrantonio, Grade 8
Commack Middle School

Lost

Being lost is scary
People walk by, many, but pass without thought
You stand still, frozen in time but the clock still ticks
You peel from shock and search around against the clock, walking, faster, faster, not running
You feel tension and anxiety to find the person who keeps you safe
When you're lost, you will obliviously encircle a room, face flushed with terror
All until you stop, slide down into a corner and cry, cry for a long time
Wondering why no one comes up to you and asks if you're okay
Or "Come with me, I'll help you"
And you sit there longer, minutes upon minutes until they're hopeless hours of misery
Not caring about time at all
Tock, your time is up
The doors close, the lights turn off
You are now stuck in a tall dark building
Lost

Odette Colangeli, Grade 7
Holy Family School

Cry No More

Do not cry for me my loved ones
For I am where I want to be

Please do not cry for me I am where I want to be
And that is in heaven and in heaven there is no pain

I am silently watching over you
I see all that you do

Just hold out your arms anytime you need a hug
I send you a thousand kisses to wet your face like the rain

So I ask you one last time
Please do not cry for me I am where I want to be
And that is in heaven and in heaven there is no pain

Alyssa Pappalardo, Grade 7
St Mary's School

Patterson Kaye Lodge

A little lodge; a huge lake
The old white hammock that tells stories of yesteryear
The sun's smiling rays hitting your back
Not a cloud in the sky.
Every worry is gone.
Refreshing pool
Warm hot tub
Old friends; new faces
Summer days: hot and steaming
Sandcastles, water slide, tennis courts.
Summer nights: cool and brisk
Bonfires, hot dog and marshmallow roasts, counting stars
The fishing dock, a photo album, holding many memories
The cross bridge, majestic and worn, holds strong with old age
My home away from home
My getaway

Alexis Parry, Grade 8
SS Peter and Paul School

One for All

O ne day the world was changed,
N ever forgotten, always remembered.
E veryone's lives changed in different ways.

F allen city lying in ashes,
O r a second home to some of us.
R emembered in more than words, but in dreams.

A ll people shocked and surprised,
L ying there the ashes, the memories
L ingering in their minds.

Harry Gonyon, Grade 7
Udall Road Middle School

The First Lady of Jazz

Was known as Mary Lou Williams
Although not much from the start,
She discovered her voice that was enjoyed by millions

Mary Lou Williams
Was born on May 8, 1910
Moved from her birthplace Atlanta to Pittsburgh
Still under the age of seven

Williams' career was pretty hectic
Many bands united
They experimented, worked hard
But all of her bands, eventually divided

Williams became solo for awhile
But soon announced that she had retired
Father O'Brian urged Williams to get back out there
So she sang, taught, and inspired

Mary Lou Williams died May 28, 1981
From a horrible disease known as cancer
She was a legend, an artist, and a woman of deep faith
This is why we still recognize, admire, and respect her.

Ana Castro, Grade 7
St Catherine of Siena School

Steps to Success

Life can be a pain
But living it makes it hard
In life we take baby steps to success
It doesn't matter how old the steps are
Or how long and hard they are to climb
You will always make it if you trust in yourself
You will find many things in your way to success
But don't let these things get in your way
Once you make it in the top you
Will feel so proud but after you're done
You should help others to follow
Your steps you made to success
And the only things you will
Hear will be thank you

Angelica Alarcon, Grade 9
John Bowne High School

Chris Brown

Christopher Brown born in Tappahannock, VA
Stayed away from drugs and gangs.
Started singing at a young age.
While he struggled to stay on track
He found his love for singing
And became known to the world.
He emphasizes staying in school,
So that the world won't be hard on you.
What a great influence on young people today.

Juliana Bernier, Grade 7
St Catherine of Siena School

The Windy City

Can you hear it?
The taxi's horns beeping
The doorman's greeting
The music from street performers

Can you smell it?
Uno's pizza on the corner
Marc Jacobs perfume from Nordstrom
Gasoline from the traffic jams

Can you see it?
The skyscrapers as far as you can see
All the shoppers on the streets
The Bears winning yet another game

There's no mistaking
This is Chicago.

Erin McCormick, Grade 8
Avon Middle School

Guitar Playing

I strum fast
I strum slow
I switch to G
Then back to E
But I just play, play, play

If I could play like Boston
My music would be even more awesome
If I could play like Queen
Then my music would be clean
But I just play, play, play

As I move my fingers fret to fret
I feel a vibe that can't be of threat
When I progress my chords
I feel like a guitar lord
But I just play, play, play

Bradly Rieks, Grade 8
Southern Cayuga Middle School

This Is the Year

This is the year
when peace will finally come to Darfur
and the disembodied hands
of refugees
will reach out
and clasp
the hands
of their saviors
pulled
into
a sea
of blue berets

Jake Sidransky, Grade 8
IS 243 Center School

My Cat Peaches

She's been around for quite some time,
She's ten year old and still in her prime.
All she does is eat and sleep.
She catches mice with one great leap.
When she tries to bring her prey in the house,
We all stop her and say, "DROP THAT MOUSE!"
She never loses in a fight,
She always wins with great strength and might.
She's a tough little cat even though she's thinner,
When she gets in a fight she's always the winner.
We all love and care for her a lot,
I don't see how anyone cannot.
She knows her way around the town,
When she crosses the street she knows that cars will run her down.
Her street smarts are very high,
The way she climbs up trees you would think she could fly.
She never gets lost,
no matter what the cost.

Adam Aliotta, Grade 8
William A Morris School IS 61

Nothing More Than a Father

I always wanted to see you
To see who actually brought me into the world
I used to long for the day to experience your fatherly, caring hug
That day did come
The whole ten minutes wasn't the least bit fulfilling
I realized that you are just some guy who thought he made a mistake
I'm that mistake
We took a single picture
You think one picture can erase the pain and heartache
You think the amount of time that a picture lasts
Can replace the amount of time
That our relationship should have lasted
Where is that picture now?
Like you, it is lost
Because of you, I know who my real family is
The people I call sis, bro, cuz, mom, etc. are my *real* family
All I can call you is my father
Never ever my dad

Tamika Normil, Grade 9
Bishop Ford Central Catholic High School

Anger

Anger is something that you can hold inside of you,
or you can use it on people or things.
This reminds me of this story *Spirit Bear*.
A boy named Cole used his anger on another boy.
Sometimes you can make a choice to hold your anger in and let it build,
or talk to someone about it and get it off your chest.
But that was not what Cole does.
He takes all of his anger out on a boy.
Some people hold all those grudges in,
then take it out on the wrong people.

Michael Fuentes, Grade 7
Solvay Middle School

Uncommon

You've heard of death by Shark,
But never by a Rook.
So I made a list of uncommon animals.
Now let us take a look.
You have…
Crab, Lobster, Goldfish, And more.
Alpaca And Llama, A Wombat A Boar.
There's also Skunk, Turkey and Shrew
Don't forget Sheep. Females are called Ewe.
Porcupines, Penguins, Oryx and Ox.
Raccoon, Pandas, Falcons or Hawks.
Squirrels, Guinea pigs, Hamsters,
Definitely not at top.
Beavers, Cockatoos,
I think it's time to stop.

Luke Sakran, Grade 7
Camillus Middle School

My Amazing Pet Mouse

I am number 1
I rule having fun.
I like to do my best
Not like all the rest.

I've always been nice
While I'm quiet like mice
I do dishes at my house
And then have fun with my mouse.

I went to bed one night,
Then woke up and hit my head on the light.
My eyes went bright
As bright as white, and knew something happened

I looked around and started getting up
When all of a sudden my pet mouse said, "what's up."
And I thought I was dreamin'
Then I looked up and saw
That he was standing there beaming
Like nothing was wrong.

Jacob Quill, Grade 8
Southern Cayuga Middle School

Rising Sun

It looks like someone was confused,
And has dramatic signs from sun up to sun down.
I see a circle and some lines.
It makes me feel confused and worried.
It's a life of confusion.
The picture was yellow, black, and purple, red
Orange and gray.
The picture makes me think about when
I went to kindergarten when school was new,
Trying to conquer my fears.

Bierca Anderson, Grade 9
John Bowne High School

Shoes

All shoes are great
I have nothing to hate

Steve Maddens, Uggs
I want to give them a hug

Sandals, sneakers and pumps
I get goose bumps

Cleats with soccer and softball it's great
It must be fate

I love them all
I want to buy every pair at the mall

Every place I go
I want my shoe collection to grow

The only problem with buying new shoes and cleats
Is that they hurt my feet

Andi Reeves, Grade 8
Southern Cayuga Middle School

Remembering September 11th

O ur lives were forever changed on that day,
N ever will our guard be down,
E ach one of us will never forget.

F ighting for our right to be free,
O nly the strong will survive,
R emember our fallen heroes.

A merica for which it stands,
L oyal and true,
L ive and breathe red, white and blue.

Cassandra Wubbenhorst, Grade 7
Udall Road Middle School

The War Jet

The thunder chief flying through the sky
Taking heavy fire enemy jets behind
Loud sounds of missiles coming up behind
Shaking the missiles and flying into the clouds for cover
Scared and speechless training come into effect
You flip your jet and take charge now you are in control
Now you shoot out 2 missiles and one enemy jet goes down
And shoot at the other enemy jet he shakes the missiles
You let out two more and direct hit the jet goes
You smile and thank God that you are ok
And then you fly the thunder chief home

Christian Latorre, Grade 9
John Bowne High School

Graduation
Graduation is a fun time.
A time to remember what we did.
A time to be with friends.
A time to do fun things.
A time to get many awards.
A time to be free from school.
Andrew Clough, Grade 8
St Mary's School

Friday Night
Throwing toys
And lousy noise
Begin when you can see

For these are the
Two little brats
That I've been hired
To watch for a fee.

The money I make
Or have I made a
Mistake for all of
The things I have
To take

When I see the
Car lights come
Around the bend.
Knowing they will
Probably call again.
Allie Delo, Grade 8
Warwick Valley Middle School

Snowflakes
Snowflakes, snowflakes
In the air
Snowflakes, snowflakes
Flowing through my hair

Snowflakes, snowflakes
Shine so bright
Like this morning's dawning light
Snowflakes, snowflakes
Dance with all their might
Flying 'round like a kite

Snowflakes, snowflakes
Everywhere,
Sprinkling down the mane of a mare,
Snowstorms are light and fair
Snowflakes, snowflakes
In summers are rare,
They are much smaller than a pear,
Something for which I care!
Rachel Quinn, Grade 7
Riverhead Middle School

The Minute and Moment
The minute and moment I opened my eyes,
The minute I closed them slammed shut,
That was when everything rushed by.

The things I used to dream of,
The things I wanted to say,
Then the things I wanted most came from far, far away.
Jessica Boscio, Grade 8
Warwick Valley Middle School

All Growed Up
When she was born,
I knew that every time she cried,
I'd be running to see what was wrong.
I knew that I'd be the one to teach her the alphabet and such,
And I was right!
We'd be quite a sight,
As we danced across the floor laughing,
Paying the world no mind.

Such a short time later,
Only three years really,
But she needs my help no more,
'Cause now she's Little Miss Independent,
Tackling even patterns all by herself.
I feel as if I've been put on a shelf,
Like a discarded old letter.
Even though she's "too big for hugs,"
And no longer afraid of those creeping bugs,
I know that someday I'll feel better,
Because although my baby sister's "all growed up," as she does say,
I know she'll make me proud I was her loving teacher someday.
Peter Jafferakos, Grade 9
Bishop Ford Central Catholic High School

Life
The road ahead of me stretches afar,
I start to advance and ignore all dangers,
As a result, a car pulls through,
I get hurt and fall to the ground.
A helping hand reaches out,
I pick myself up and hold on to it,
I learned from my mistake and keep on walking,
As I keep advancing, the road splits,
Each leading to many different outcomes.
I take the one that fits me best.
No longer a child, as I know I've grown up.
Where the road took me, I'm not sure.
Until there I meet a dead-end in the way.
Took awhile, but figured it out,
A new path replaces the dead-end and a new adventure has begun
The new highway stretched to the sky,
I knew I could do anything, if I tried
The paths I took and take, are mine alone,
As you may already know, this is my life.
Geoffrey Lin, Grade 8
New Hyde Park Memorial Jr/Sr High School

Dream Place

This is a place where nothing goes wrong,
All you can hear is a blue jay's song
This is a place where anything is true
The sky can be purple
The grass can be blue
There can be sun,
There can be hail,
There can be a meadow surrounded by rail,
There can be peace,
There can be love,
There can be a field, covered by doves,
Anything you want is possible in this land,
There can be water,
There can be sand
Oh, I'm up now,
And sorrowful I am,
But I shouldn't be mad,
I shouldn't be sad,
Because tonight I will return,
To *my* wonderful land,
That I like to call, Dream.

Joe Amedro, Grade 7
Camillus Middle School

What's in the Box?

It has been there all my life,
At the bottom of the stairs,
Just sitting; never opened,
And it has never moved from there.

As I sit and think on my basement floor,
My eight year old mind is wondering,
What's in that box? They said to keep away.
But I still want to know more.

What is in that big old box?
That brown, old, chest of old wood,
I want to look in, oh so badly, I do;
But still don't know if I should.

So I crawl quite slowly up to the box,
And open its lid up wide,
I don't think that in all my life,
I could have been more surprised!

Of course, I can't tell you what I found;
And to think it's been here since my birth!
But I'll just give you this one little hint:
There is *nothing* quite like it on Earth.

Sara Penna, Grade 8
Holy Cross School

Outsider

I feel so alone
I feel like a cone
Thrown in the middle of the road
I feel so cold
Like a blizzard in the winter
I feel like an immigrant
Coming to America
As quiet like a spider sneaking upon its prey
My solitude is with me
Every day
I am abandoned and
Alone
On the wrong side of the road
Like a locked up soul

Jacob Merrill, Grade 7
Solvay Middle School

You Might Not Know...

You might not know...
But I saw you looking at me from the corner of my eye,
I know you wrote my name on the wall,
I realized that you stood at the corner just to see me passing by,
I know you thought about me until nightfall,
Back then, I pretended to ignore you,

You might not know...
But at night you hid in the jungles of my dreams,
You had me lost in your thoughts,
I saw your face in every flower under the sunbeams,
Wherever you went, it would turn into sunspots,
And now, I want to tell the whole world, I Love You...

Nazish Khalid, Grade 9
Sewanhaka High School

Darkness

Darkness:
It strives to control us,
To mold us
Into what it wants us to be.
It feeds on our fears,
Our grief,
Our disbelief.
Darkness:
It's every where we go.
Darkness:
It's all we see,
All we know.
Darkness lives inside us.
It knows our every thought.
It slowly controls us,
No matter how hard we've fought.
In the end, the darkness may control some lives I see.
But, in the end, with hope,
The darkness will never control me.

Ariell Morales, Grade 8
Manhattan Christian Academy

Anger

Anger makes you want to hurt others
Eyes squint
Red face
Deep voice
Loud as a marching band
Stomach tight
Fist clenches into a punch
You could be angry forever so
Talk to somebody
Just get out
Away from it
Calm down
Try to forget
Or at least forgive

Danielle Eckert, Grade 7
Solvay Middle School

Autumn

Gray clouds are outside.
The rain taps on the window.
I feel very trapped.

The trees are bare now.
Leaves of different colors
They blanket the ground.

Christine Rienzo, Grade 8
Hauppauge Middle School

At the Beach

Sitting at the beach
Getting a tan
Sitting at the beach
Playing with sand
Splish splash
Lazing on a float
12 year old on a banana boat
Fish here fish there
Running here running there
Running everywhere

Shawn Brown, Grade 9
Upper Room Christian School

Fall Leaves

In autumn
during the night,
outside the house,
near the shed,
by the garden,
on the tree,
with the squirrels,
among the branches,
the leaves fell.

Megan Riley, Grade 7
St Mary's School

My Favorite Person

My dad takes that title,
he's my favorite person.
He is nice every day,
never keeping far away.
We make cookies,
we drink milk.
We do the laundry,
we put it away.
My dad is the best,
on top of all the rest.
We play,
we laugh.
We read,
we watch TV.
Now that I'm done,
I have to say we have lots of fun.

Gabrielle Gagliardi, Grade 7
St Mary's School

Blackboard

A large bright board
Reflecting smirks
In front of me
Like a television
Moments forever printed within
Writings and dreams forever dusted
Showing the memories of old students
The dust shows
Faces of new students who
Stare at the board waiting

Rahil Browne, Grade 9
John Bowne High School

Fulfillment of the Hidden

Watching from the distance
Waiting for the moment to act
A plan in the making
A future remaking
The part that you play
Is that of your creation
You wish for nothing
Destruction and chaos
In the end, time stops
Just for a second
Enough time for your plan to be fulfilled
Who are you?
The person behind the mask
The one with the tainted heart
Even so, it doesn't matter
For when your plan is fulfilled
Nothing will be everything
And you shall be gone from our lives
Living behind your mask

Yogeeta Chatoredussy, Grade 9
Stuyvesant High School

Friendship

Friendship is a pact
And unspoken agreement
That you trust
Help each other out
Be a friend
Believe in you.
Without trust
We would be
Like an empty jar
Used up
Ready for the garbage.

Joshua Dwyer, Grade 7
Solvay Middle School

Beautiful Flowers*

A beautiful flower
Filled with love
A special flower
That someone gives you
It's pretty and pink
With leaves growing all around
One flower standing
Others dying
The signs that it gives
Are very true

Ashley Reyes, Grade 9
John Bowne High School
*Inspired by the painting "Paeonia
Suffruticosa Yachiyo Tsubaki"
by Manabu Saito*

A Single Gift

A single gift,
Treasured by many,
Yet, questioned by some.

It's very common
Usually taken for granted,
Passed from person to person.

It's the most important thing we own,
Yet guarded worse than gold.

Should we not want it,
Why should we not pass the gift on
To some other deserving person?

It is in every land, every ocean,
As big as a tree or as small as a monkey
Each one special in their own little way,

May each of you choose what that gift is.

Jianxiang Shiu, Grade 9
Stuyvesant High School

Christmas Time

Snowflakes — they're white
   Bright with sunlight
Fall to the ground
   Create a mound
     No sound
Around a fire
   Cocoa and pie
They fall outside
   Different shape, size
Marshmallow fluff
   Smooth
     Never rough
Ding! Ding! Bells chime
   As children sing
A baby, a star
   Above his head
A mother, a donkey
   No crib for his bed
Christmas — a time of thanks and cheer
   For a new babe is born as we start the New Year.

Mary Grace Donohoe, Grade 7
Holy Family School

What Is Life?

Life is a very important thing
We must cherish the possessions that it brings
Life is like a bird; it can really pass you by
Take time to look at the stars that are floating in the sky
Life is like an ocean, and we are the fish in the sea.
Angels floating in the sky is what we want to be.
The humming of the bees, the singing of the birds in the trees
If happiness will last forever, than that is what we please
Seasons change from summer, fall, to winter
The path of goodness is what we wish to enter
Life connects with the body, the mind, and soul
Based on how we live our life,
Our paths just might unfold.
How much is life worth on a scale of one to ten?
Once you live your first life you second will never end.
You can choose what to do with your life
Because your life is in your hands.
Once you waste your first life, you won't get another chance
New life is created by life, and the sun creates a new day,
But if new life is created by life then what created life?

Gregory Joseph, Grade 9
Bishop Ford Central Catholic High School

A Scary Night

Candy, goblins and don't forget ghouls,
This is Halloween night and you can act like a fool!
Halloween is both for you and me,
It is the scariest of nights just wait and see.
The Headless Horseman who can give you a fright,
On this Halloween night!

John Ocskasy, Grade 8
Christ the King School

The Circle of Life

When barren ice turns to endless sea,
In the clearing stands a sapling tree.
When snow was still on the ground,
Its branches were empty, its only color brown.

But cold turned to warmth,
With flowers pink and white,
Blossoming and blooming,
Left and right.

As the days grew longer,
The sapling did grow,
Its leaves bright green,
Coming row by row.

Then the autumn swept in
With a chilly breeze,
And the leaves were crisp,
Falling with ease.

Yet winter did come,
And the branches turned bare,
But spring would return,
With its warm air.

Sarah Angle, Grade 8
Warwick Valley Middle School

untitled

where are the lights
that burned your eyes
on that long weekend when
the town was just a heap of dust
and we were just debris
trapped inside remember
it was that weird silver the
kind where when you see
it gleams through you and
it splits your heart in half
and you're screaming until
you realize there's something within
that wasn't there before
something that finally holds
the two magnets of your tarnished soul together
and all of sudden you don't
feel like you're pulling yourself apart
and you don't have to worry
about how much harder you can stretch without breaking
because you know you're broken and that is why
you are whole

Nicole Schreiber-Shearer, Grade 8
New York City Lab School for Collaborative Studies

The Last Treasure

The silent breeze sweeps over the lake
It makes you wonder makes you think

Ten houses built upon a square
But only three a treasure bare

And something special waits behind
These old four walls erased from time

A picture is the only way
To find what's lost and save the day

Two secret treasures have been found
But yet the third shall make no sound

For only children's eyes can see
The hiding place of number three

More than one is needed here
To solve the puzzle the table cleared

For inside that room the treasure waits
For every Smith to take their place
Larissa Orlando, Grade 8
Marlboro Middle School

Family Gathering

Families are outside
For a day of fun.
Children are playing with
One another.
People brought umbrellas for
Shade from the hot beaming sun.
People on land watch others in
The sea on sailboats.
Families make memories
To pass on to the next generation.
Janel Nobles, Grade 9
John Bowne High School

Thanksgiving

In the morning
bright and early
I smell a joyous aroma
mother's in the kitchen
checking the turkey
a great day to share
I hear
the people cheering
for the delicious food
It's a great time
to celebrate.
Happy Thanksgiving
to you!
Gianna Scaletta, Grade 7
St John School

Darkness

Someone turn the lights on.
I hate the darkness where I cannot see.
Help me find an ending because, I don't want to stay in this place.

I think these feelings are obsessed with me.
They follow me everywhere I go…
So don't come close to me.
My pain isn't free to see.
You could get hurt too.

But it seems everyone is losing in the shadows,
As I'm hanging on the edge of reason.
I have NO trust and my ability to rationalize is fading.
I'm so sick of pretending.

Just try living in my head,
With all the thoughts and paranoia that never seem to go away.

If only I could take back all the yesterdays and change today,
I would look at the future with broken fate and lies.
Instead I'd have a warm heart and a peace of mind.
Stasha Cuzdey, Grade 9
Heatly School

Gratitude

Thank you mom for being my friend,
Thank you dad for being there from beginning to end,
Thank you grandma for taking care of me,
Thank you grandpa for showing me things I didn't see,
Thank you auntie for being my second mommy,
Thank you uncle for being my second daddy,
Thank you god-mom for being there for me,
Thank you god-dad for watching over me,
Thank you sister for loving me more and more,
Thank you cousin for always saying "Yeah," "Of course," and "sure,"
Thank you God for letting me be in great health,
Thank you Jesus for telling me to stop second guessing myself,
Thank you everyone for letting me explain,
Thank you for when I need something you give me love as an exchange.
Lenee Brown, Grade 7
Robert Moses Middle School

Home

Home can be where you stay
Or where you dream every day
It's where you smell homemade cookies when you walk in the door
And where you do homework that's such a bore
The saying "I'm homesick" can be totally true
Even if your home is new
Whether you are hanging with friends or having a birthday
You'll always be able to say
"There's no place like home"
And that's why I wrote this poem
Rosie Sovocool, Grade 7
Camillus Middle School

My Mother

If only she could see
What is going on inside of me.
I love her so and I want her to know
So I will tell her.
She is a strong woman
The strongest I know
I keep her near and dear
Because I love her so.
She is the most courageous person
I have ever known to face cancer
At 30 years old she was faced with the decision
To die or to fight
To fight the cancer till she could fight no longer
She fought until it was gone, but it soon was back again
Again she fought till it was no more
Again it came back.
Fighting the never-ending battle of Breast Cancer
With a heart full of hope and a family by her side
Her tools of love and hope are what help her Survive
I love this woman always and forever
She is not only my mother, but also my friend.

Georgianna Raynor, Grade 9
BOCES/LoGuidice Alt Ed Program

Deep Blue Sea

A boy watches from the sand,
while he gathers up some shells.
Admiring the beauty of the ocean,
all of the sights, all of the smells.

Every day when he wakes up,
he walked out on his balcony.
He takes a breath, opens his eyes,
and looks out at the ocean as far as the eye can see.

To him it is a land unknown,
something no one can explain.
A place in which when people arrive,
they may even forget their names.

For when they step into the ocean,
dip their bodies into the water so cold,
they will begin to feel an amazing sensation,
no matter how young, no matter how old.

So as they look at this little boy,
hanging out over his balcony.
They can wonder about what he is thinking,
when he stares into the Deep Blue Sea.

Philip Giacalone, Grade 9
Bishop Ford Central Catholic High School

Someone New

I want to see the space that fills your tiny hands
I know patience is a virtue
But waiting hurts a bit
I've tried and tried and yet I quit
To see your face fill with joy
Will it be a girl? A boy?
Will it be safe, or will I lose you
Sometimes I fear, for both of them
My heart is open, but I feel that maybe I won't see
To get excited, and all for nothing
It might be too late for it to happen
If it's a girl, she'll know her father
If it's a boy, he'll know his father
It will be different, not like me
But, somehow I hope
That it all works fine
To create we

Sua L. Mendez, Grade 9
John Bowne High School

When I Skate…

This is freedom, this is fun.
This is happiness for everyone.
This is joy, this is good.
This is the feeling to be understood.

This is amazing, this is exciting.
This is what you can do to keep life from biting.
This is power, this is pleasure.
This is my version of buried treasure.

On this board, the wind in my face.
It's almost too much to embrace.
In the air, all noises cease.
On this board, my excitement starts to increase.

These vibrations beneath my feet.
As I set up for my trick, I start to feel the heat.
This is not love nor hate.
This is what happens when I skate.

Jake Trashansky, Grade 7
Robert Moses Middle School

The Path of Life

To this path there is a start,
But the journey along takes awhile.
On this path you will meet many people,
Some young, some old, and some wise.
You may come across some obstacles in your way,
Or maybe a ditch or two.
Some days the sky will be blue,
Others it may be grey.
No matter what happens on this path you travel,
You will always have yourself to guide you.

Stephanie Cairns, Grade 8
Warwick Valley Middle School

Unwritten

I walk into a room of forgotten dreams, this is where unanswered prayers,
ungranted wishes, and lost destiny's are kept.
Locked up, never a chance of coming back to memory.
A glimpse of time, a wasted thought, just this once, maybe this time.
I find an old book, yellow and water stained.
I wipe off the layer of dust, clearing away someone's lost future.
A deep breath makes me cough, I spatter someone's whispering words, hoping to come alive.
I open the book, an encyclopedia, it's as heavy as someone's burdened soul. It crinkles and rips.
My gentle fingers slide over the words, hoping to find some meaning, just one piece to life's big puzzle.
I can't connect it, it seems a mystery. I read, I imagine, I dream of my future.
Right as I close the book, a word catches my eye.
It seems as if it's been highlighted, ancient colors swirl, a collage of history.
Hold on to your dreams, they are a part of you, they are your childhood, what you have always wanted to be.
Who you are.

Hunter Miller, Grade 9
Our Lady of Mercy High School

A Letter to the President

Think smart
Become your name
Being ashamed is not a shame
Take a hint
Step into the line
Unwinding the clock, is not unwinding time
Open a door
Create a permanent mark
Turning on the light is not turning off the dark
Look at yourself, and then look at me
And don't forget History is his story.
Don't just know, but understand
That the time has passed for what you could
And, just because you can
Doesn't mean you should
Take a chance
Open your eyes
Because, adding one more death
Is *not* adding more to life

Taina Diaz, Grade 8
International Finance & Economic Development Career High School at Franklin

Grandma Allen II

You are so far away but yet so close that sometimes I just know you're there standing, looking at me.
I just don't know how I was able to move on without you and your precious smile.
I hate this cycle of death, it's like it won't leave my family alone.
I lost you, but I guess that's not enough, and I had to lose more.
It's like a horrible curse that my family is under and I can't figure out a way to stop it.
My grandmother is in the hospital with the horrible monster disease cancer, and she will soon be gone.
I feel like this disease has put a target on my family and will stop at nothing.
Haven't I been through enough pain, enough suffering, and enough loneliness?
I feel like I am a blooming flower in a beautiful yet lonely field and there is no one for miles.
I am all alone and have no one I can go and cry to because no one really knows how I feel.
Sometimes I don't even know how I feel and I try to hide my feelings but inside I feel empty.
I don't know what's going to happen, but I hope things will get better and this cycle will end.
I love you Grandma Allen.

Kristen Matuszak, Grade 8
Oliver W Winch Middle School

Remembering September 11, 2001

O n that one September day, our nation was changed forever.
N o one thought it could ever happen.
E very life was affected.

F riends and family joined together,
O ur entire nation joined as one,
R ecovery has been hard and long.

A lthough many years have passed,
L ives have been lost.
L et us never forget the day our lives changed forever.

Billy Martin, Grade 7
Udall Road Middle School

Best Friends

You laugh together,
You cry together,
Never leave each other alone.
You always support your friend.
You always believe in your friend.
That's the definition of a best friend.

Don't talk about each other,
And always forgive each other.
Never hold a grudge…
Against your best friend.

Help each other with problems,
Love each other always.
You can tell secrets to this person,
Knowing they will be kept.
That would be some best friend

So don't deny or neglect this person.
She wouldn't do it to you.
That's a …
Best Friend..

Sasha Augustin, Grade 9
Bishop Ford Central Catholic High School

The Fumble

On a rainy day in Watervliet
The ground was soaking and so were my feet.
The Trojans played the Cannoneers
The teammates clapped and parents cheered.
The center hiked the slippery ball
Twenty-two players engaged in a brawl.
The carrier got hit, the ball it fell
Adam looked for the ball he could smell.
Then he saw the ball he sought
He dove for it and hard he fought.
He covered the pigskin and held it tight
And Watervliet fell to Trojan might.

Jotham Zak, Grade 8
Holy Cross School

My Years at School

My first bus ride was today.
My first day of school.
I made lots of friends today.
Kindergarten was really cool.

I turned nine today.
All my friends sang to me.
We would one day split up,
But we were only focused on grade number three.

The leaves turned to snow,
And the snow turned to rain.
There is much more I now know,
School made nothing plain.

The end of fourth grade,
My brother's graduation.
I had to wait four years,
Until my eighth grade celebration.

My eighth grade year,
I must say goodbye.
There is much more I now know.
I leave St. Mary's with a sigh.

Kaleigh Cerqua, Grade 8
St Mary's School

Miss Molly

Run, run
Run Miss Molly run
It's Wolfred the Wolf
He chases you
He chases over lakes, over deserts, marsh
He chases over all terrain don't let him catch you
He thinks "Run before you're my dinner"
Run Miss Molly run
He is a hungry tiger he has starved for a week
Run Miss Molly run
Hurry Miss Molly hurry before he catches you
Ahhhh so sad Wolfred caught you
Poor Miss Molly
She couldn't run from him
I had warned her now I mourn for her
Wolfred could run like the wind
He could run for days on end
Now he feasts now he eats
Wolfred the Wolf a good wolf
He loved to run
He is a happy camper

Nicole Jackson, Grade 8
Southern Cayuga Middle School

Shoes

Sneakers for running
Flats and high heels for dressing up
Boots for the winter
Flip-flops for the summer
Sandals for spring
Oh no! What will we wear for fall?

Elizabeth Joa, Grade 7
Edward Bleeker Jr High School 185

I Am Not Lucky

I am not born lucky
I am not taught lucky
It is not lucky that I can walk
It is not lucky that I can talk
I am not lucky to have *ADD*…
I am special, I am me.
It's not luck that brought me here
love to me is always near
I am not lucky to have a mother
I am not lucky to have a father
I am not lucky to have two sisters
I am not lucky to have grandparents
I am happy, didn't you get the point?
My family and I are now joined
But can't you see, can't you see?
I am not lucky to have all that I do
I am not lucky to be who I am
I have learned, I have seen…
I am not lucky, I am loved

Nathan Rok, Grade 9
Suffern High School

A Dime

At a point in time,
    Perhaps long ago,
A dime was a dime,
    Away I could go,
To buy a lollipop
    Could be anytime
A treat I could buy,
    But as time has gone by,
No longer is it a dime.

Kyle Krzemien, Grade 7
SS Peter and Paul School

Softball

I don't care if the fields are muddy,
    there's nothing you can say.
Not even if there's not enough players,
    the other team will still pay.
We have our bats, gloves, and balls.
    We're ready today.
Let's get out there right now,
    I'm ready to play.

Dina Moffett, Grade 8
St Catherine of Sienna School

Peace

The world as we know it isn't peaceful at all.
Gangs thugs and violence at local shopping malls.
Anger and hate towards another race.
War poverty and people discriminate.
How could anyone do such a thing?
The world belongs to a better place.
We need peace.

Mary Howard, Grade 9
Ketchum-Grande Memorial School

Starlight

Gazing
Staring
Looking high
Looking up at the great night sky
Amazed by the glowing dots
Astonished by the new robots
These robots comb the universe
And look for new things for better or for worse
They look at all the text details that most of us don't see
They find new things up in the starlight
that we can look upon and enjoy all night
And in the starlight that special night, I look upon the sky
I see a new world up there
That I can go and let my imagination fly
So now I look and stare
Those final minutes of night
And try to get away and be a kid and dream
Oh, this is the day, that I can look up into that beautiful and dazzling night
And see all that precious starlight

Nick Sabatino, Grade 7
Camillus Middle School

I Finally Realized Why I Love Marlee!

I woke up in my bed and looked around.
Then I saw on the ground, my little sister sitting there,
Looking at me with that little kid glare.
So I got out of bed and then I said,
"Marlee, what's wrong? Are you ok?"
Just then she got up and went to play.
About 5 minutes later I heard a noise
And I knew it wasn't one of her toys.
So I got up and ran into her room and again I saw her sitting there
Looking at me with that little kid glare.
I now knew something was wrong.
So I picked Marlee up and went into my room
And I could tell that she was now sad.
I hugged her tight which I hadn't done in a while until I finally saw a smile
It was then that I knew…
Marlee is more like me than I believed to be true.
Then and there I could see in her eyes
The love and connection nothing could buy.
I looked at her and she looked at me
And finally now I could see, that over time we had grown apart
But you're my sister and I'll always love you from my heart!

Emily Bishop, Grade 7
Camillus Middle School

Sanctuary

I just need a place to recreate myself,
From the beginning,
With out anyone else in my way,
A place to feel safe.
Where I won't be criticized for who I wish to be.
A safe place,
Where I can sleep without the bad dreams
I need my own fantasy.
A place to feel free.
Where I am alive to do what ever I wish.
A free place,
Where the rules don't apply.
I need my own kingdom.
I need to rewrite myself
All the way from the beginning,
Before I give up all my will,
Before it takes my body, my soul.
I need more time.
Every day I fade away without you,
I need you by my side so I'm not lost.
I need my own sanctuary.

Danielle Lipsky, Grade 8
Plainview-Old Bethpage Middle School

my mom

I wish nothing will ever get in the way
But the problem is your to far away
Just so you know
My heart will never let you go

I will always thank God for giving me
The gift of my life
I thank my my mom for caring for me
And making me a better person
I thank you mom so much

Life with out my mom
Is life with out a soul
Life with out a soul is like looking
In an empty bowl

When my mom falls down
I will always be picking her off the ground
And I will always be around

So people out there
Never give your mom a hard time
And I will always thank God for giving me my mom
I love you

Fatme Saleh, Grade 7
Al Iman School

Girl in a Lighthouse

Girl in a lighthouse looking over a town
Girl in a lighthouse looking down
Girl in a lighthouse watching the sea
Girl in a lighthouse watching me
Girl in a lighthouse can't you see?

Girl in a lighthouse standing out
Girl in a lighthouse shall never pout
Girl in a lighthouse has no doubt
Girl in a lighthouse wears a dress
Girl in a lighthouse does not wish to impress

Girl in a lighthouse with matted hair
Girl in a lighthouse just sit and stare

Girl in a lighthouse looking over a town
Girl in a lighthouse looking down
Girl in a lighthouse watching the sea
Girl in a lighthouse watching me
Girl in a lighthouse can't you see?

Alex Williams, Grade 8
Avon Middle School

Nightmare to Reality

Cornering me with a rifle,
I felt I was being stifled.
The gun fell to the floor;
I quickly escaped through the door.
I felt terrified, petrified, then relieved
It was only a nightmare, I couldn't believe.
Back to reality, it was only a scare.
I went back to sleep hugging my teddy bear.

Davey Haber, Grade 8
Yeshiva Shaare Torah

Memories

Crackle,   Snap,
Hisssss!
The sound of the flaring fire comes back to me
as I think of memories of you.
All those times by the fire come from
deep down in my heart. These are the moments I'll
remember for the rest of my life even though I will
have unfortunate, unhappy bad times.
Yippee,   Whoa,

Wow!
The sound of all of our screams come back as
though in a dream. The excitement we endured
is now so unbelievable to think about. How brave
and bright we were. I hope we will always be this
way. These reflections drift through my mind often
and I can only hope they do the same for you.

Elaina Marino, Grade 7
St Dominic Savio Middle School

Fall

In the fall
The leaves blow all around
Whipping and tossing
Like clothes in a dryer
You make piles of leaves
You and your friends jump in
The temperature drops
That means winter is coming

Mitchel Cometti, Grade 7
Solvay Middle School

Hiking Trip

In fall when the trees lose leaves
I go on a hike to the lake.
Even though it's cold
I hold the pain against my chest.
When I get out
I just like to rest in my tent.
Then I give mom and dad a hint
about what I want to do next
That is my hiking trip.

Harry Tucker, Grade 7
Solvay Middle School

Passing

Each passing day,
As we walk down the street.
We see homeless people,
No shoes on their feet.
You don't seem to notice,
You walk without care.
You heighten your pride,
As they lay and stare.
But suddenly you see,
Your fancy black tux.
Your shiny new shoes.
Why not give a few bucks?

Alec Irace, Grade 8
Warwick Valley Middle School

Sweet Victory

3...2...1...0, Yes!
You did it, you won.
You passed the test.

You worked hard,
and you played your best.
The road was long.
The training was tough,
but you battled through
and you had the right stuff.

It's the greatest feeling in the world.
O, sweet victory!

Patrick McMahon, Grade 7
Camillus Middle School

A Day on the Farm

A snowy, white stallion gallops through its pasture,
The wind whipping through its mane.
Nearby chickens peck the ground constantly looking for seeds.
A German Shepherd pup runs like lightning herding in the cattle.
The wind rustles drifting in the scent of fresh yellow roses that hung on
the farmer's dark brown gate.
The red robin sings a sweet, calm melody in the blazing, hot sun.
Light pink pigs roll in the mud trying to stay cool.
The stallion runs past the old Billie goats that are climbing on steep rocks.
Some cows moo as they graze on the grass covered in dew.
The stallion stares at the beauty around it.
It was a day on the farm.

Charnelle Jones, Grade 7
Holy Cross School

Poems

There are many different kinds of poems
One kind of poem is free verse they are pretty easy, personally
You just write about whatever you want
You need syllables in a haiku,
It's first five, then seven, then five
Some poems have to rhyme
But that can be hard at times
It can make people whine
Wait, rhyming is easy, never mind
Couplets are stanzas with only two lines.
They have ten syllables, and they too rhyme
There are tercets or triplets too
They have three lines, instead of only two
A triplet having three lines, you probably knew
And then there are quatrain stanzas
These can be an extravaganza
They are easy once you get the hang of it
To write one doesn't even take much wit
Last but not least there are Epic Poems
These poems are just like stories, but in poem form
I would write one, but they are usually long so I am not going to write one

Jacob Carney, Grade 8
Avon Middle School

Winter Wind

Winters first snowflakes twirl through the air.
People stop and start to stare.
Adults shiver, thinking it a bit tragic
They put up the collars of their coats, but children think its magic.
Icy cold crystals drifting along
Make them think of their favorite Christmas song.
And building snowmen in the cold.
And maybe, if they're bold
Start a snow war, and build a snow fort
Who says throwing snowballs isn't a sport?
But then the sun comes and melts it away
And children all wait for the next snowy day.

Elizabeth Deprez, Grade 8
Avon Middle School

Sunrise and Sunset

As beautiful as a child's smile you dance up high.
Peace seems only temporary.
People change as if leaves in the fall.
We will miss you at the end.
Warm our souls with you kindness we're all in your debt.
You truly are the heat of the sky.

Katherine Cottone, Grade 8
Avon Middle School

The Sunset

Alone in the distance,
A figure so clear,
Such beautiful color,
Life's ever seen,
So vibrant and orange,
So big in the sky,
The sun sits and watches,
As years go by.

It watches us grow,
And it watches us fade,
It helps us come over,
Not so wonderful days.

A friend who will listen and understand,
It sets in the horizon,
With a promise to come back.

I sit and I wait,
For my wonderful friend,
A friend called the sunset,
Who comes every day.

Laura Arrubla, Grade 7
Marlboro Middle School

Eyes

Eyes can help the world to see,
What all people can truly be.

Blue or brown it makes no difference,
Everyone sees the same.

Eyes all come in different sizes.
They give you away and tell when you lie.

Eyes are the windows to the soul.
What do yours say about you?

They show us the bad, they show us the good,
Some are just misunderstood.

Whatever they say, just remember what's true;
Your eyes tell people all about you.

Jennifer Milbouer, Grade 9
Bishop Ford Central Catholic High School

My Brother — My Best Friend

We've known each other
since the day we were born,
maybe even before,
I don't know, but what I do know is
your like the brother I never had
and the best friend I've always wanted

As kids we played tons of games,
games we made up in five seconds
but played like we knew them forever

My question is, where did those days go?
those days of playing and laughing
again I don't know, but what I do know is
you've always been there
been there to help with anything
and to catch me when I fall

Well wherever those days went
they will always be great memories
memories we will never forget
I know no matter what you'll always be there by my side
forever till the end
my brother — my best friend.

Maddy Sulla, Grade 8
Valhalla Middle School

A Very Jewish Christmas

On Christmas Eve I don't decorate a tree
or bake chocolate cookies and pour a glass of milk.
I just sit in my room listening to music.
The day goes by,
the snow softly falls to the ground,
dancing gaily as it drops from the heavens.
As I lay in bed,
I think of all my friends,
jumping joyfully at the idea of new presents.
I finally fall asleep and it seems like only seconds go by.
When I awake it's Christmas,
I'm looking forward to nothing.
There is no lit tree,
Or present prancing underneath.
My friends aren't around,
So I sit with myself.
Later that night I don't eat a feast.
I might go to the movies,
I might just try to sleep.
This is my Christmas as a Jewish lad,
in a constantly Christian world.

Nick Spiegel, Grade 8
Warwick Valley Middle School

Dreamland

I'm living in a dreamland,
Where people come and go,
Usually it moves fast
But when you're in it, it moves slow.
Yea, I'm living in a dreamland,
Where I don't dare wake,
For once I leave this dreamland,
People are exceedingly fake.

Real people
Hide in the shadows.
I think of my dreamland
Where the only people in it,
Sitting by the beach,
Are you and me.

We sit and we watch —
We watch the sun fall,
Fall into its own little dreamland.
I sit and I wonder —
Why is this my dreamland?
Why can't it really be just you and me?
Jen Maucher, Grade 9
Oyster Bay High School

The Storm Flies By

As the storm comes by
the leaves fly by.
Then the water comes pouring
as my heart is roaring
then I looked at the sky to see
the clouds go by.

But during the storm I saw
this dust, it was a golden dust,
it swirled, and twirled and
went through the trees
and went to the sky
all the way up high.
Anthony Raccuglia, Grade 9
Upper Room Christian School

Dreams

The moonlight shines upon my window
Every night the light is upon my eyes
I look up and see the shadow
My dreams have finally arrived
I have been waiting for this day
As long as I could say
My dreams came alive
I said to the shadow
Go ahead and spread your wings
My dreams have finally arrived
Victoria Agostino, Grade 7
St Mary's School

Winter Snow

It is snowing now quite heavily
The heaviest by far
Far away not by my home
The only warmth is in my car

Don't worry now, I don't care
The snow is a beautiful thing
Must love it while it lasts
Because it isn't long 'til spring

The kids are out playing now
Hoping not to get a cough
They are living it up
Because it is their first snow day off

It is cold outside but they don't care
The snow is a beautiful thing
Must love it while it lasts
Because it isn't long 'til spring
Clare Seeberg, Grade 8
Warwick Valley Middle School

Winter

Winter brings lots of cheer
People gather far and near
Oh Christmas is here!
Kimberly Schlosser, Grade 7
SS Peter and Paul School

Thank You Parents

My father is a flight attendant
he has a very interesting job
thanks to him I have seen the world
I have seen the anime in Japan
I sipped tea in London
I basked in the sun on the beach
in Singapore
Thanks to them I have found my calling
I want to become a pilot!!
Marceline Holness, Grade 7
Intermediate School 381

Nature

Leaves come with fall
Like snow comes with winter
Trees comes with soil
Like plants come with water
Storms come with clouds
Like lava comes with volcanoes
With every living thing
Something connects to it
That's the cycle of life
Shaunasee O'Dell, Grade 7
Solvay Middle School

The Window

Today she woke up,
thoughts filled her head
of the boy who's name
shall not be said.
Her grey window
stood next to her bed.
A window of opportunity
he said.
She looked out the window
and all that was there
was a small feather
that fell from an angel's hair.
Peri Zarrella, Grade 8
Linden Avenue Middle School

Raindrops

Rain drops, rain drops
Falling from the sky
But where does it come from
Where does it hide
And why is it coming out
Out of the sky
Is a cloud crying or
Is an angel dying?
Rain drops, rain drops
When do you find time?
To come out and play
When you come down from the sky
Making ripples on the water
And making bigger tides
Having the world on your shoulders
Falling down from the sky
Becky White, Grade 8
Southern Cayuga Middle School

Life Starting Off Small

Skies of blue,
Water so clear,
Makes all flowers
Come to life my dear.
Petals so delicate,
So soft to the touch.
New beginnings, laughter,
Joyfulness and such.

A budding flower
May not catch the eye,
But when it is full of color
You may be surprised.
With all different shades
And sizes to be found;
Flowers can show
Beauty on Earth's ground.
Elizabeth Lepski, Grade 8
Warwick Valley Middle School

I Cannot Go to School Today

I cannot go to school today,
My running nose could fill a bay.
My throbbing body just shivers, quivers, and shakes,
And I'm so exhausted, can't stay awake.

You see, the flu can strike when you least expect it,
My bones are aching, I can hardly sit.
And all of these symptoms have just begun,
Already my fever is a raging 101.

My eyes — red and gritty — I can't see straight,
That Nyquil stuff knocked me out by eight.
Morning came, alarm blasting, I thought I was dead,
And then I fell off my bed and whacked my head.

I tried and tried to get myself dressed,
When all I wanted to do was lay flat and rest.
Was that bus number four that just flew by?
Please don't be mad cause I'm gonna cry.

My clothes are drenched from the sweat and the heat,
An in between sweat comes the chills, ain't that neat.
The homework I missed I promise to do,
If you felt like me, you'd stay home too!
Griffen Raymond, Grade 8
Barker Middle School

My Dead Dog

It was a winter morning
The sun was just rising from the horizon
The family was asleep, the only one up was Edison
He had a bad habit, running in front of cars
He would try to make them stop, but this one did not
I imagine it as Edison dashing, barking in front of the car
The driver was caught off guard
The headlights were saying "Move get out of the way"
But he was bred for herding
The driver scrambled for the brake, yet it was too late
When I woke up that morning I had no idea
My mom and dad were outside
I went out with my brother to see what happened
When I found out I fell to the cold snow
My face was freezing like a block of ice, but I didn't care
My dog was dead
Later when we had to bury him
I was walking beside the sled that had Edison in it
All I could think of was
The night that we both slept on the rug in the living room
I'll always have that.
Chris Ellis, Grade 8
Southern Cayuga Middle School

Christianity

Two testaments; the old and the new,
12 Disciples, faithful and true.
Jesus, the Messiah, a savior to humanity,
Was selfless and courageous, free of any vanity.

The son of God lay on the cross,
Unfortunately, his life was at a loss,
But his generous sacrifice opened the gates to the above,
This was the ultimate gesture of his love.

Today he is worshiped by Christians everywhere,
Whose wrongdoings and sins God chose to spare,
And although he is physically gone, his spirit will always stay,
Because he is honored and remembered on each Sabbath Day.
Louis Calabro, Grade 9
Townsend Harris High School

Lonely and Scared

As days go by
I sit down and cry.
I'm thinking of you
All the time.
I look around
Not seeing you there,
Feeling
lonely and scared.
As time goes by
I sit down and cry.
Thinking to myself
Rewind
Rewind
Go back in time!!
Dayanara Latorre, Grade 9
Bishop Ford Central Catholic High School

Family

Family loves you
Family keeps you safe
Family gives you food
Family gives you shelter
Family gives you money
Family comforts you
Family is always there too
Family makes you laugh
Family makes you cry
Family takes you places, but not all the time
Family is kind
Family is critical, but only for you
Family is patient
Family always trusts
Family always hopes
A real family never fails
But no matter what, family is you.
Katie Rosso, Grade 8
Avon Middle School

Every Time

Every time
That those waves break
I start to think
Every time
Every time
The tropical wind blows
It makes me wonder
Every time
Every time
I step onto the sand
It seems to happen
Every time

Sarah Balseiro, Grade 8
Warwick Valley Middle School

That Girl

She was as beautiful as a sunset,
Like an angel from heaven,
I couldn't keep my eyes off her.

Funnier than a clown,
Sweeter than a chocolate bar,
And a voice like an angel.

When she kissed my lips,
It was like dying and coming back to life,
From the moment I met her,
I knew I would love her,
Forever and ever.

Dylan Riley, Grade 8
William A Morris School IS 61

My Agony

Running from my fears
is harder than it seem.
My body tells me to run.
My mind tells me to stay.
But no matter what I do
It's always the wrong way to go.
I am not afraid of death,
just what comes after.
Will I ever see anyone again
or am I just here to live, love, and die?
I fear nothing other than
the loss of my memories,
the people and thoughts that they hold.
The love I feel is true.
If I died today
for the ones I love,
I would feel no pain
for they have my heart
to pass to others.
Death is not what I fear
just living a little too long.

Jacob Mead, Grade 8
Windsor Middle School

Depression

Depression is almost like a disease.
It is a feeling of emptiness and/or sadness.
Depression changes your mood.
It can make you sad, mad, lonely, or unhappy.
Depression can affect the people around you.
It is a very serious common problem but
It can be treated.

Mina Gilchrist, Grade 7
Solvay Middle School

The Cries from Within

Though I may try my hardest, the pain's still there.
It won't leave the aching heart, that has begun to die,
Behind the mask I call strength, and power.
But through all of the walls of protection,
Are cries for love and happiness.
I am trying to break through.
But for so long, the walls were being broken down,
So I had to build them to be thicker and stronger,
So I couldn't be hurt again.
The soul crying out to you, has been reduced,
To nothing but the remains of the soul weakened by lies and trust.
I know you hear the cries of a broken soul I call me.
And you can't pretend it's not there. Not forever.
You can't ignore the pain you see in the depths of my soul
Pouring out of my eyes, as tears.
The cries from within are not cries that can be covered up for much longer.
My broken soul cannot be put together. Not on its own.
You can hold it together and use love as glue.
Restore the lost pieces of a broken heart,
And stop the cries from within.

Mindy Pollard, Grade 9
Bronx High School for Writing and Communication Arts

My Power and Dream

Follow your dreams you'll reach the stars.
But how does one single person reach so far.
There is no stool, nor is there a bench
To make you grow not even an inch.
I reach for the stars, but only get many clouds in my way.
I go to sleep and dream then when I wake up I try to make it a reality.
I have to go beyond the stars and over the sky.
We all need a boost to get where we need.
We all have a secret power to reach our destination.
Some of us draw, some of us sing, but the power I use is my pen and ink.
With this simple tool, I can make my dreams come true.
The stars shrink down all is good.
I can sail on a cloud and dance with the stars,
Edit my dreams, and sing with the wind
Shine bright and confident with the sun, and read silently with the moon.
Now that I've reached my final destination,
I too must continue this dream,
To see what really comes true.
Close you eyes, and you will see too.

GinaMarie DeCavallas, Grade 7
Our Lady Queen of Apostles School

Remembering September 11, 2007

O n that unforgettable day our city fell,
N ever again would it be the same.
E ven if the days go by, it will always make us cry.

F orget the happy times and triumphs we had,
O' why does this have to be so sad.
R egrets are made past those days; even if it's been 6 years.

A lot of people died on this day,
L et me have one more thing to say,
L iving should be about making things better.

Meagan Chi, Grade 7
Udall Road Middle School

Cheerful Christmas

Christmas, Oh Christmas what a wonderful time of year!
How we live, we laugh, we love, we cheer.

From Christmas trees, to mistletoe,
Look outside! Here comes the snow.

Children waiting for Santa Claus.
Shh…Be quiet…Do I hear reindeer paws?

Presents, Presents everywhere,
Boxes torn without a care.

Through the day,
The children play.

But, as the dark of night draws near,
The children ask their question clear.

Will Santa Claus be back next year?
Do not fear my little dears.
Santa lives in your hearts all through the years.

Victoria Avidano, Grade 7
Most Precious Blood School

My Wind

The wind whispers what is left unwritten
A girl feels a chill and runs in for her mitten
The wind howls horrors soon to be found
The girl is turned and pushed to the ground
The wind talks nonsense usually ignored
The girl sings a song that has long been stored
The wind groans its dirges, a shiver up a spine
The girl runs in as the clock strikes nine

As she listens out her window
The girl perks up an ear
And whispers to herself,
"My wind is here."

Rebecca Sklar, Grade 8
Oakdale-Bohemia Middle School

Roses

A rose is much more than a flower,
Much more than something to look at or smell.
A rose can say a lot.
It shows beauty, and joy, and love
It can show the good or the bad.
It can show happiness or pain.
Make you laugh or cry.
Don't doubt it because it's pretty
Look past that
See what else it hides behind that sweetness.
You can't just see behind something so beautiful
It seems no more or no less
A rose to me shows of sorrow
Of pain and of heartbreak.
People must see beyond the outside beauty
To see past the physical nature.
Everything and everyone has beauty
Especially a rose.
Next time you see a "rose"
Don't just look at its beauty
Look beyond.

Nyjah Ferryman, Grade 9
Bishop Ford Central Catholic High School

Brit

Brit, one of my favorite places to be.
I can feel the excitement pounding in me
as we pull up to the cozy cottage.
Our Georgian Bay adventure begins.

Our first stop, Billy's Island, right across the way.
We laugh and play on that huge rock for the rest of the day.
We wake to delicious scents coming from the kitchen.
And after breakfast we race back to the cool water.

We take a boat to the lucky spot,
Where hundreds of fish are to be found.
Then off to the cliffs we go
Sailing thorough the air, then splash!
Into the water we go.

Next we go to Clyde's hole.
A wonderful fishing and relaxing place.
Tomorrow we will go to Sand Bay,
the only sandy spot in the Georgian Bay.
Where we will knee board and tube the whole day.

As the sun falls and the beautiful sunsets paint the sky
We crawl into bed and wonder what will come of tomorrow.

Myriah Kingston, Grade 8
Avon Middle School

Hushed Renovation…

The absence taunts through my fear…
The eternal desire through craving emotions, soothe the moment in which is vital for joy…
Take away in which the thought of the absence…
Blind and mute so not a soul to hear…
Give it all away…find me…and the burden that scratched across my face will be found…
The raw insides…commit a sense of circumcision…pursued by my loss of desensual thought…
Fallen out of the sudden pulse, grace held without a sound…
Tomorrow is nothing to my eyes…
Twinned was, and never is…now
Thou lay a crest fallen heart, let it die…
Thy breathless flutter; mingle to the opposing absence with pleasure…
Promise?…The truth is a farewell…
Truly…soundless, the absence is soundless…and diminished…dead
Dance around the glade honey replenishment…
Save the sundown for the next farewell to commit…
Soundless is the aura…It's said…
Oppose the soundless absence…
Forward, and gush, daze…and thwart…
Hinder the absence with the meanings apart…

Julie Ortiz, Grade 9
Marble Hill High School for International Studies

I Follow My Own Star

I follow my own star…it leads me the right way and direction to go where I need to go and know what I need to know. I follow my own star…to understand my life, to know what went wrong and how to make it right. I follow my own star…to be who I want to be and to see what I want to see. The dark nights that I've seen would usually make me blind but my future's still in sight cause my star is one of a kind. It's the one that gives me the power to keep holding on, and the one that gives me the strength to keep standing strong. Although my days are hard and although my nights are cold, the star that I follow leads me down the right road. I follow my own star…through the day and through the night, 'cause no matter how hard it gets, it helps me to shine bright!

Breontai Gates, Grade 8
Randolph Academy

Influence

A child growing up at two, watches his brother and "what to do."
Sees him smoke, sees him drink, "It's ok," is what he thinks

That child is now three, and looks at his brother to see
that gun he got from his gang clan, "That looks cool," thinks the little man.

So now the five-year-old child, chills with his brother for a while.
Sees how tough a gang makes him, he thinks, "My brother's like Superman."

Well, when the child is seven, his brother goes to heaven.
A bullet from a gang fight, now he thinks, "That's not right."

This little boy now 43, thinks of how his life would be
if he joined a gang like his brother did, maybe he too would be dead.

"Stop the violence," "Stop the influence,"
preaches the once little man and thinks how violence kills, it really can.

Now he teaches kids like him how to act in a tough situation.
There's only one you in all mankind, so don't let negative influences change *your* mind.

Kristiana Nelsen, Grade 8
Warwick Valley Middle School

Our Souls

Whatever that is mine it is yours,
Whatever that is yours is mine.
For that we shall together shine.
In one night or one year,
Together we will be fine.

Let's take our souls and put them together and combine.
We will become two to one and nothing more,
Because our souls are much alike.
Take my word and have some faith,
That our souls wouldn't end through a stake.

Share your soul and make it grow,
Like a rose to blossom.
For there is much more than you will ever know.
A soul is something special to cherish,
Please oh please I beg don't ever let it perish.

A soul is so gentle and smooth,
Like the wind which is so pure.
Your soul holds all of your sins,
And pulls them through,
Like a beautiful bird that came out of the blue.
Take this advice from someone worthy as you.

Nirwair Singh, Grade 7
Public School 124Q

Dirge of the Wolf

He stands transfixed,
The wolf,
A denizen of the night,
Who roams freely between death and light,
Yet no matter how long the wolf stares,
The moon's silencing beauty cannot be absorbed.
Instead,
He can only howl,
To let go his full emotions.
The waning howl,
Is the wolf's dirge.
Its dirge echoes,
Throughout the dark,
Heard by all,
The song of the night.
The gem of the empty heaven,
Is a reminder of the wolf's,
Suffering and calamity,
And his reasons to live,
So he can continue,
To roam…

Muhtasham Sifaat, Grade 9
Bronx High School of Science

I'm Sorry

I'm sorry that I hurt you
I'm sorry for what I did
I didn't mean to hurt you
After all I am just a kid
I let my anger get to me
Now I don't know what to do
I am stuck here on this island
Nobody here just me
Not even you
I've been on this island for awhile
Surviving on my own
I hope that you will forgive me
As soon as I come home
I know that it's been hard for you
Ever since that day
And I regret it even more
But trust me I have changed my ways
I know that you hate me now
But this shouldn't be the end
Because I have changed my ways you know
So you can trust me and you can be my friend

Jackie Baron, Grade 7
Solvay Middle School

Soccer

Soccer is what I love to do.
It's my passion it's my joy.
It gives me that cool.
I dream about it all night.
I think about it all day.
It has so much rhythm; you don't know what's happening next.
It gives me an adrenaline boost.
I can't wait to grab my gear.
The field is my home.
When I'm in my cleats I feel like I'm floating.
The adrenaline is pumping with the goal in sight.
The cheer of the crowd is all I hear.
The shin guards protect me from all bad kicks.
Your team is your family, your team is your friends.
The celebration never ends after a win!
With the new fall coming a new season comes alive.

Scott Wheat, Grade 8
Southern Cayuga Middle School

The Big Decision

I can't believe it's Halloween.
And for a costume, I'm stuck in between!
Should I be something scary, or, be something funny?
Maybe a vampire, maybe a bunny,
It doesn't really matter, as long as,
I get goodies, and do it with ease!
The candy that I will get will surly be yummy,
And I really can't wait to have it all stored in my tummy!

Nick Del Giudice, Grade 8
Christ the King School

A Changed World

A world that is filled with suffering
A human race that is depleting
The cause is our wasteful lives that are still proceeding
Many are carrying a large diamond stud
For others their lives are a great thud
They need help in the life they drive
So I declare, "I can make a difference by…"
Helping the poor to have food to live
Brightening someone's eyes from the help we give
Sitting with someone who is lonely
Who is living for the sake of it only
Cheering up a person who is sad
Which will eventually make them glad
Standing up against something that is wrong
That it makes us really brave and strong
Even the simplest type of kindness and compassion
Will make a huge difference
A world filled with peace and harmony

Joel Varghese, Grade 9
Sewanhaka High School

In Pakistan

In the land of Pakistan
The shifting sand moves coolly through you.
You feel like the sun and moon clashing
Forming an everlasting peace — not cold.
Hot, hot, hot but nice.
Replaying the sun all day
Until we go inside
We have fun, fun, fun until we leave.
When we are in the airplane going back to America
All I could think of is…
Mom when are we going back to Pakistan?

Aysha Naeem, Grade 7
Intermediate School 381

My Life

I love my life, it's very unique.
I want a wife, and have little feet.

I like school, it's really fun.
Math is my favorite subject, so you better not reject it.

When school starts, we all say hello.
Then we part, and say bye my fellow.

When it's gym time, we laugh and play.
When it's time for work, we play with clay.

The school day is long, can't wait till it's over.
Know it's finally done, now I can go under my covers.

I will pass all my tests, and go to the next grade.
I will know I am the best, and celebrate with Labor Day Parade.

Rochan Morrison, Grade 7
Intermediate School 381

Young Poets
Grades 4-5-6

Note: The Top Ten poems were finalized through an online voting system. Creative Communication's judges first picked out the top poems. These poems were then posted online. The final step involved thousands of students and teachers who registered as online judges and voted for the Top Ten poems. We hope you enjoy these selections.

Top Poem Grades 4-5-6

Looking Through the Window of My Pain

The words you spill from your mouth
drips directly into my heart
burning like acid
ripping me apart
since the start of this pain
it felt like poison in my vein
leaving my conscious stained
but still remaining sane
the cells in my brain
keep my thoughts locked
like prisoners wearing chains
reactions pull me away from this attraction
If we both did the math
you could see the subtraction
how I divided times
giving you less than a fraction
I added my own love
which equals
my heart's satisfaction

Robinson Baez, Grade 6
Intermediate School 227 - Louis Armstrong Middle

Top Poem Grades 4-5-6

The Humpback Whale

Splashing, swerving, diving, plunging into the tranquil silence of vast blue.
Twirling through thousands of bubbly streamers in a roar of gushing waves and spray.
The whales leap, whirling through the briny air
Then back to the salty silence of the ocean.
Sometimes they chase each other,
Splashing and twisting, diving through rings of bubbles
And breaching, just playing.
Then, sometimes,
They swim silently, gracefully, like birds of the ocean
Lost in thought in the endless stretch of blue water
And sometimes they sing, long, haunting melodies
Laced with mystery and beauty. Then they get restless again
And resume their frolicking play leaping, diving, swerving
Skillfully riding the thousands of currents that fill the ocean.
Then, inspired by the joy and energy that sweeps through the salty water,
One may leap into the air, and spin through the wind, flanked by seagulls.
And if you are lucky,
And watch the surface closely, you may see this happen.
If you watch even closer, you can see more humpback whales below that whale,
Who boldly clears the surface. Waiting to welcome that whale
Back beneath the surface to the ocean.

Caroline Carr, Grade 6
Shelter Rock Elementary School

Top Poem Grades 4-5-6

Halloween

The wind is blowing,
Jack-o-lanterns are glowing,
Crowds of people are roaming the streets,
Going from house to house, collecting their treats.
Decorations hung up everywhere
On this street and that street and that street over there.
A pirate! A ghost! A skeleton!
So many witches you could not even count!
And all of these things were out and about!
What street to do first?
Which street to do next?
What streets to avoid?
Which street is the best?
But when your bag's getting heavy
And mom says, "No more,"
And your dad is so sleepy he's starting to snore —
Wait until next year —
There's always more.

Laura Chapman, Grade 4
Bedford Road School

Top Poem Grades 4-5-6

Pencil

The pencil continues to scratch away listening to my ideas
It forms the wrong word
So, it disappears behind now just a memory

My brain is a city and the pencil is the mayor
It makes the final decisions on all my thoughts

As I write words flow in and out of me
I breathe them in
As I exhale them they dance down onto my page

The surface of this page is now full
The scratches on the floor from another pencil,
Look like the message of the Earth to my mayor,
My pencil, my friend.

Victoria Ende, Grade 6
Harold D Fayette Elementary School

Top Poem Grades 4-5-6

Morning Thoughts

When you wake up,
it's a new day.
A time to start over,
when your thoughts get icy gray.
A time for new beginnings,
a time to start brand new.
A time to do some thinking,
for what you want to do.

When you wake up,
warm headstrong joy fills your mouth.
And you sit up,
and rub your eyes, and watch the birds fly south.

You hear the school bus miles away,
and dress in quite a rush.
You jump outside in haste,
just in time to catch the bus.

Celine Gosselin, Grade 5
Transit Middle School

Top Poem Grades 4-5-6

The Tree

In front of me,
    looms a great tree.
        Its green leaves
            and powerful branches,
                lean as far,
                    as far can be.

Up above,
    the sun glistens.
        While squirrels play,
        and bird fly,
            in the shade,
                of the tree.

Then sudden winds,
    sway about
        causing the tree
            to move with excitement.

Raymond He, Grade 5
Public School 162 John Golden

Top Poem Grades 4-5-6

My Snowy Lane

I look this way
You look that
My path's snowy
Your path's flat
You look down your path
That's where everyone goes
My path looks quiet
Like untouched snow
I start to approach the untaken path
I want to explore that snow covered lane
Follow your heart I hear inside me
Go, explore! Make up your own game
I ran down my path
My snow covered lane
I skipped through my forest
I played my own game
I observed all the birds
I climbed all the trees
I laid in the snow
I felt the cold breeze
I took my lane and felt no shame.

Ettienne Sanjamino, Grade 6
Intermediate School 227 - Louis Armstrong Middle

Top Poem Grades 4-5-6

Watching the Water

As I sit on the beach,
The waves go by,
The sun goes down,
I sit and watch the water,
I don't pay attention to anything around me,
I just think,
And watch the water.
As I think the sun is setting,
People are leaving, I stay,
It is now two hours later,
The sun has set the moon has come up,
But still I watch the water,
It is slow and cold,
The water is washing my feet from all the sand,
It is cold but calm,
I stay another hour, I get up,
Just stare into the sunset for a couple more seconds,
It is hard to leave this beautiful sight,
I walk a few steps to get to my car,
Breathe out,
And leave.

Rebecca Simon, Grade 5
Robert Seaman Elementary School

Top Poem Grades 4-5-6

Freedom

Freedom is the aura
of colors at sunset,
or a rolling hill.
It is a cool breeze
kissing my cheek,
the heavens' tears
gently rolling down my face,
or the whispering trees.
It is sitting in a classroom
with a white girl in front of me
and a Hispanic girl behind me.
Freedom is the American flag
waving in the wind,
or silence after the last trigger is pulled,
the last bomb dropped.
It is a cage opened
or a mustang galloping
towards the horizon to the unknown.

Asia Stewart, Grade 6
Bay Shore Middle School

Top Poem Grades 4-5-6

Mankind's Quest

The beauty of nature displays God's wondrous plan.
Too bad it's all crushed by the horrors of man.
All the trees and the plains,
The bushes and reeds,
Are cut down and destroyed,
To fill our selfish needs.
And the creatures that God made,
They deserve mention.
We kill 'em. Do we care? No. We pay no attention.
And the furry white giants that live in the poles?
And how 'bout the ozone and all of its holes?
I'm not done yet, to say there's much more.
You'd think I'd be done, but what about war?
Because God made each one different than the other
We brutally murder our sister and brother.
On Earth there is racism, drugs, mugs and guns.
Yes, we are all sinners, every last one.
Can this deathly world ever live congenially?
I really don't know, why should you ask me?
If you can live in peace, then peace will live in you
And our entire world will become something new.

Casey Vincelette, Grade 6
Bethlehem Central Middle School

Spring

The air is fresh.
The air is cool.
The birds are singing.
The flowers are blooming.
Kids are playing.
Trees get leaves.
Wind is blowing.
Spring is beautiful.

Nirvana Narayan, Grade 5
St Benedict Joseph Labre School

Halloween Night

On Halloween night,
All creatures with fright.
Trick-or-treaters with fear,
Because goblins appear.

Witches with brooms,
Cleaning their rooms,
Bats wearing hats,
And scaring acrobats.

I hate to say bye,
But this is the end my friend.
Now…We…Are…All…
Done!!!

Eric Colvin, Grade 5
Staley Upper Elementary School

Shadows

Shadows are as black as the night,
watching your every move,
Shadows, walking behind you,
Shadows can meet other shadows,
Shadows cannot be stolen,
Shadows are invisible in the night,
But shadows are always there,
Even in the darkest night.

Jesse McKiernan, Grade 5
Public School 41 Greenwich Village

Sounds from the Couch

Sitting alone
On a red rough couch
Cars zoom by
Like fireworks exploding
On a hot sticky night in July
Airplanes overhead,
Like thunder in the sky
Crickets serenade me
Like a Christmas Choir
Sitting softly relaxing my mind
While sounds drift in and out
Sounds from my couch

Colin Lowe, Grade 6
Harold D Fayette Elementary School

Awesome Nature

Awesome autumn
Colorful clouds
Wonderful waterfalls
Beautiful butterflies
Popping pansies
Dazzling daffodils
Shining stars
Lovely leaves
Terrific tomatoes
Frolicking foxes
Isn't nature awesome?

Ariannah Logan, Grade 5
East Hill School

My Wonderful Bear

My bear is wonderful
Her name is Sidney
She is caramel brown
Her eyes are black
She is soft and silky
She is extremely furry
She loves to play
We love to play hide and seek
She never finds me
We play tag
She never catches me
I always find her
I always catch her
She was given to me
By my Auntie
She's special to me
When I tell her my problems
She never answers
SIDNEY IS MY BEST FRIEND!

Brianna Alexander, Grade 5
Public School 203 Floyd Bennett

Leaves Falling in the Night

Leaves here, leaves there
Leaves are falling everywhere
The sun is down
The moon is bright
and the stars are shining
Winter is coming
Animals are sleeping
and the oceans are turning cold
The sun is still sleeping
The wind is whistling
Now is winter
Winter is leaving
Spring is coming
Now it is Spring
and the sun is awake
The moon and stars are now sleeping!

Ken Kopczynski, Grade 5
Bretton Woods Elementary School

Football

See the pro football,
Flying down the turf field.
The quarterback throws it
As it whistles through the air.

Randy Moss cradling
The Wilson football
"Catch me, catch me
I don't want to fall."

Final two seconds,
Final one second
Touchdown?

Pats!
Randy Moss scores!
And spikes the pigskin
To the ground.

Austin Medole, Grade 6
Akron Middle School

Thanksgiving

T ime to spend time with family
H ave turkey and mashed potatoes
A nd some homemade gravy
N ever leave anything on my plate
K ickball is played on this day
S ing and dance around the house
G ive thanks to our family
I love Thanksgiving
V isit our cousins in Pennsylvania
I nterested in all the good food
N ever leave without saying goodbye
G ive hugs and kisses and say goodbye

Justine Velazquez, Grade 5
Northeast Elementary School

The Sky

The sky is blue.
The sky is gray.
The sky is there every day.

Up in a plane,
The sky is there.
Look up, look down,
It's everywhere!

Matthew Anecelle, Grade 5
Cortland Christian Academy

Christmas

White, cold
Giving, getting, celebrating
Decorating the tree
God's Birthday

Bianca Calvanico, Grade 4
Leptondale Elementary School

Magic

Magic is like an illusion
An illusion that becomes reality
From card tricks to rabbits in a hat
Magic amazes us all

Magic expands our minds
Some card tricks are hard
Some are very simple
Some are just plain weird

Turn a coin into $100
Become a pro yourself
From the card trick the fantastic five
All the way to the box of implement

Magic is a gift
If you believe it can happen
So just believe
And you will succeed.

Shawna Maldonado, Grade 5
Public School 105 Senator Abraham Bernste

The Five Senses of Fall

Fall smells like roasted marshmallows.
Fall looks like children jumping in a leaf pile after raking them.
Fall feels like bitter cold weather.
Fall sounds like children playing in the yard.
Fall tastes like turkey, potatoes, and pumpkin pie!!
I LOVE FALL!!

Gabby DeLass, Grade 5
Harris Hill Elementary School

Life Doesn't Frighten Me

I am home alone,
Then, I hear the phone
Who could it be?
Life doesn't frighten me
I hear something fall
I peek downstairs I see a shadow, it's really small
Life doesn't frighten me
A creek, a screech, a frightening noise
I sit there at night playing with my toys
Life doesn't frighten me
The lights begin to flicker
I feel a sudden fright
Then I realize something's not right
Life doesn't frighten me
I hear someone stomping
I shudder, I scream, I hear moans
Then I remember nobody's home
Life doesn't frighten me
I hear a voice and begin to scream
I wake up and it's all a dream
Life doesn't frighten me

Eliza Simons, Grade 6
Long Beach Middle School

Family

Sticks to you
like super glue
and will never
break apart.
Sewn together
forever
until you
pass away.
That will be
a very sad moment
for them.

Sandy Contreras, Grade 4
Public School 152 School of Science & Technology

Flying Through Nature

Pollen flying through the breeze
Going towards a wonderland
In the early spring
Because there is a bear running through the plants

Ryan Weaver, Grade 5
East Hill School

Devastated

Down a curb at midnight
I could do nothing but hope
My white shirt was the only thing I could see now
Everything is a mess

The essence of smoke filled my nose
Cars were destroyed and blasting their alarms
People were crying screaming hard
I followed the cracked and damaged road
Devastation to all
Everything is a mess

6 years after that I remembered this day
Everything was quiet silent
I hoped for the best and it didn't happen
Everything was a mess but 9/11 is no more
But it will always be remembered
As a devastation to all

Sean Isaacs, Grade 6
Bellport Middle School

Jim

Jim is slim.
He looks like a Slim Jim.
He loves to swim but he's too slim so he hangs with Tim.
Tim teases Jim because Jim can't swim.
But people don't like Tim because he makes Jim look real slim.
Tim is way far from slim,
That's why he makes Jim look real slim.
Though Jim eats Slim Jims to stay slim
Unlike Tim who's not slim at all!

Colin Moriarty, Grade 5
Harris Hill Elementary School

Halloween
Jack-o-lanterns lighting up
Freshly cut pumpkin pie
Kids giggling "trick or treat"
Sour Air Heads
Gooey pumpkins
Halloween
Maddy Mieschberger, Grade 4
Belmont Elementary School

Orange
Orange is the hotness in summer.
Orange is a fruit that is sweet.
Orange is the color of happiness.
Orange is the color of Halloween.
Joanne Carnero, Grade 4
Leptondale Elementary School

Fall Actives
Kids jumping in leaves.
Celebrate Thanksgiving Day.
Bare trees everywhere.
Raking leaves for Thanksgiving.
Fall is over, Winter comes.
Anny Flore Luberisse, Grade 5
Northeast Elementary School

Rainbow
I look over my head
To see colors streaming
Going up then coming down
Just like a roller coaster

My eyes follow
Wishing to see the end
Wondering if there really
Is a pot of gold?

Each color imaginable
Is above me
I close my eyes and wish
For whatever I want
Then smile knowing
Why leprechauns
Love to see it
A beautiful sight
Carly Caiazzo, Grade 6
Bellport Middle School

Spring Waterfalls
Spring waterfalls
Changing shapes
Along the beautiful horizon
At the beginning of summer
Because water is amazing
Jordyn Logan, Grade 5
East Hill School

Cats
Cats are fun to play with
They are cute and cuddly
Oh how they are warm and cozy
Sometimes they run outside
It is also fun to chase them
They like to catch mice and birds
Cats also like to cheer you up
I really like cats.
Barbara Dillon, Grade 5
Holy Cross School

Four Seasons
Spring, spring:
It's everywhere,
Gaining leaves in the trees,
Flowers pop up everywhere!
Summer, summer
Ah! A day at the beach,
So quiet and peaceful,
Wind blowing in my face,
Whoosh!
Fall, fall,
Leaves crunching under my feet,
Crunch, crunch!
Laughter of children playing!
Ha, ha, ha!
Winter, winter,
Snow is finally here!
Big, fat, white flakes of cold snow,
Whoosh!
Guess what I hear?
The wind against my cherry red face!
Marion Slater, Grade 5
John T Waugh Elementary School

Truth of the Glistening Sea
As a pirate sails
Across the deep blue sea,
He travels to find
What the truth can be.
The sea sits calmly
Whispering the truth to thee.
His travels tell,
Even fiction can be.

The glistening sea
Stays silent in the dark night.
She tells of a tale of how
The truth can be a fright.
All you'll need
Is a little belief
To discover the truth

Of the glistening sea.
James Schuster, Grade 6
Akron Middle School

Thanksgiving
Thank you for the world so sweet,
thank you for the food we eat.
Thank you for the sky above,
thank you for my family's love.
Thank you for the football games,
thank you for my Grandpa James.
Thank you for the birds that sing,
thank you for the turkey wing.
Thank you for my dog and cat,
thank you for my Uncle Pat.
Thank you for my Grandma Joan,
thank you for this Thanksgiving poem.
Vincent Maffei, Grade 6
St John School

Nature of Trees
Gold light
Beats down on me
I look for the shade
Of my maple tree

Leaves rattle
Slightest breeze
Among the branches
Of the tall oak trees

Dogwoods blossom
In the spring
Pine trees make
Winter sing

Flowers blossom
Trees grow
This is nature
That we know
Hallie Nowicki, Grade 5
Munsey Park Elementary School

Thanksgiving
Turkey here
Turkey there
Turkey everywhere
Gobble gobble gobble
I ate so much
I wobble wobble wobble
Pumpkin pie here
Pumpkin pie there
Pumpkin pie everywhere
Yum yum yum
All that is left is the
Crumb crumb crumbs
Why why why
Did I have so much
Pie Pie Pie
Joshua Pawliczak, Grade 6
St John School

Pointy Building

Oh how that tall pointy thing
in New York City could slice like a million swords!
It's as sharp as a knife at its point
One-hundred sixty four floors await me
The elevator music roars good music
as I put my eyes
to see far off
in the distance

Vivek Hariharan, Grade 4
Concord Road Elementary School

Fading Light

Towards your death there is a light,
a whole dark room with only that light,
you run trying to get it,
every step you take, takes you farther away
the light starts to fade darkness is everywhere,
just a small little bit of light is left,
the light disappears,
only a world of darkness,
is left.

Diego Guallpa, Grade 5
Public School 41 Greenwich Village

Ice Cream

Ice cream is sweet,
Ice cream is cold.
It has a flavor
That you'll never forget.

The softer it is
the crunchier it will get,
from the bottom to the top
the sweetness grows.

Your lips get moist
with your chocolate taste.
A meal you won't forget!

Monica Dieudonne, Grade 4
Public School 152 School of Science & Technology

Love

Love has always existed from the start.
Love has and will always be in everyone's heart.
When you feel love, you feel like you can fly.
Love is a feeling you can't define.
Love is sometimes something that keeps us apart.
Sometimes it is love that keeps people inside a person's heart.
Whether you love someone or something,
Love will always set anyone and anything free.
Love is a feeling that everyone should know.
Love is something inside everyone's heart that glows.
Love doesn't always have to be seen.
Love is something that is, was, and forever will be.

Annika Maniego, Grade 6
Holy Family School

Love

Up there
He looks down on me
My brother too
In my heart
I can hear him saying,
"Take care of my daughter, that's all I ask of you.
Love, your Grandpa"
That will always be in my heart

Joshua Goldman, Grade 4
Norman J Levy Lakeside School

Racism

What does it matter what color you are?
For look, are you different than I?
"Beneath d'skin is all d'same"
Was said by one who knew the ways of kindness
He knew that color did not matter,
It was attitude that mattered — And really,
On the inside you are the same as I.
We both have bones and skin and blood
And even two rounded eyes
If you question my statement, then ask yourself
Why are flowers different colors?
Red, white, gold and green
Yet they are all flowers, are they not?
Life is too short for fighting,
So why make life difficult for others who are different,
When instead you could learn from them.
God meant for us to be friends, so we should not quarrel
Over such an outrageous thing as color,
For instead there could be peace.

Bryan Herbert, Grade 6
Shelter Rock Elementary School

The Tree

What would I be today?
I would be helping people with oxygen.
I'm brown and have leaves, branches, and bumps.
I also have roots and I'm tall.
I have shade under me.
What am I?
I am a tree!

Sherisse John, Grade 5
John T Waugh Elementary School

Summer

Summer is a time to go on vacation
Summer is like a joyful birthday party
Summer is as fun as Christmas morning
Summer has cooking grills and sweltering heat
Dogs, cats, and squirrels
Summer has swimming and sports
Summer is emerald leaves
And aqua skies

Max Ley, Grade 5
Leptondale Elementary School

Stupid Cupid

I hate stupid cupid,
Because of his wings,
Because of his diapers,
And the way that he sings.

I hate stupid cupid,
And now I'm feeling blue,
He shot me with an arrow,
And now I love you.
Rachel Atkins, Grade 6
Canandaigua Middle School

Statue of Liberty/Lady

Statue of Liberty
Green, tall
Stands, greets, informs
Compassion of many years
Lady
Arielle Boyd, Grade 4
Leptondale Elementary School

Life

Up with the sun and
Down with the moon
In with the north wind
Out with the sea
As fast as a cheetah
As slow as a sloth
I am here
I am there
I am everywhere
I am life
Elizabeth Pellegrino, Grade 6
Eagle Hill Middle School

Pink

Pink is a ballet dancer
gracefully dancing
Bunnies prancing
It reminds me of flowers
swaying in the meadow
Especially when I'm staring
out my window
Pink is a girl's best friend
And the latest trend
Pink is graceful!
Morgan Flanagan, Grade 5
Eastplain School

First Sight

Love at first sight,
A glance at each other
For years to come,
They will love one another.
Trevor Ciampo, Grade 6
Maria Montessori School

The Fragile, Yet Fuzzy Panda Bear

Fragile, yet Fuzzy
Munchin and crunchin
On crisp bamboo.

Fragile and Fuzzy
Like hidden giants
Off to a costume party,
Like delightful circus clowns
Yet, sweet as honey.

Fragile and Fuzzy
Pandas look like a lot of fun
They sleep in the night
And play in the sun.

Fragile and Fuzzy
Not all fun and games
With razor-like claws
Just stay away!

Fragile and Fuzzy
The Panda bear,
Very rare
Fragile, yet Fuzzy!
Alexandra Eckerson, Grade 6
Akron Middle School

Glowing Toes and Nose

Oh no I just found out my nose glows
and so do my toes.

Does it show through my clothes?
Suppose everyone knows!

They are glowing as red as a rose.

Oh I wish I chose to enclose
and decompose of those toes!
Sarah Strong, Grade 5
Harris Hill Elementary School

Frame of Mind

So much learning,
so challenging, so grueling,
but I'm gaining knowledge
and I'll go to college.
A healthy lunch of broccoli and cheese,
I would rather eat sweets.
But I'm getting stronger,
bigger and taller.
I must go to bed
and put my pillow to my head
as "early to bed, early to rise,
makes man healthy, wealthy and wise."
Moshe Saadia, Grade 5
Yeshiva Shaare Torah

Ocean

The clear blue waters
pure white sand
in between your toes
as if someone painted a picture
tropical fish
with bright orange and yellow scales
tropical plants all colorful and bright
in the blazing hot sun
as if someone painted a picture
the sound of the waves
crashing
against the shore
on a rocky coast
the sound of boats
as they zoom
and make waves and marks
as if carving the water
the sound of the wind howling
and the crashing of the waves
of the ocean
Rachel Street, Grade 6
Northwood Elementary School

Math

M ath is cool.
A mazing
T eachers made a song.
H ow many do we have?
Jessica Rose Lewry, Grade 4
Granville Elementary School

Summer

summer is…
Hot days in the pool
not worrying about school
that is Summer
Eyan Underwood, Grade 5
East Syracuse Elementary School

Snow

When I fall,
I am beautiful and shiny.
I blanket the green grass,
With specks of glitter.
The children enjoy me,
They love to build me.
Create tunnels,
And throw me.
But for adults I am a labor.
They need to shovel me,
And sometimes even snow blow.
But they even enjoy me,
As they ski down slopes,
Or snowmobile through the trails.
Trista Davis, Grade 5
Staley Upper Elementary School

Autumn's Fall

You walk outside eager to go to the beach
But summer is just out of reach
You lash summer out of your mind
You go on with another thought, a good thought of some kind

While taking a stride
The small smile turns into a one you can see from either side
A thought of the dreams of fall
And there's one that's the best one of all

It's about the color of the leaves
And of course, Halloween
A thought of new friends
And friendships that never end

Making new people feel welcome
Like a new beat of a drum
You can't forget about picking apples
Take a break and drink some Snapple

The sweetness of fall comes along to comfort you
It's so good you wonder if it's too good to be true
No, it's fall everyone feels it too.

Jade Blocker, Grade 5
Munsey Park Elementary School

Friendship

Friendship is like a knot that cannot be undone
Friendship has its own voice
Friendship is about having fun
Laughter and joy in your eyes
Friendship can mean anything
Hate and war I despise
Friendship means the world to me

Kirsten Horvath, Grade 6
Long Beach Middle School

Cooties? Cooties!

"Cooties! Cooties," the children cried,
as the teenagers laughed and the teachers sighed.
"There's no such thing," their parents reassured,
but of course, the children never heard.
So one day when Joe Rein went out on a walk,
he told his mother, "We need to talk."
"There's a deadly disease infesting the school.
It can infect anyone, and it's mighty cruel!
Rumor is it'll make your eyes turn red,
and you will want to dance on your head.
Now I will tell you it's terrible name:
Cooties! Cooties! That's what to blame!"
Joe's mom replied, "There's no such thing, honey!
But your description sure was funny!"
"There's no such things as cooties!," Joe said,
but that night he saw his daddy dancing on his head!

Anna Rusignuolo, Grade 5
Eagle Hill Middle School

The Shore Ghost

Have you even been to the ocean shore
at midnight of all the times.
And saw that wretched flying thing
hovering in the sky.

It will swoop down and bring you up
then throw you to your grave.

It's not a pretty sight to see,
when it does these things to those
who walk along the sea at night.

So make sure you're careful
when you decide to walk at night,
for you may be the next victim
of the monster that lives in the clouds.

Nicky Kinna, Grade 5
Staley Upper Elementary School

Family of Mine

To be a part of a family like mine
is very divine
It is very hard to define
We share love
way above
We sometimes hate and go to debate
but we also love to appreciate
We always share
because we always care
We are trustworthy
because we care about honesty
We connect by showing respect
and also to protect
It's always all for one and one for all
and goes on forever just like how
the Earth is shaped like a ball
We go through ups and downs together
Just like how we should forever
They'll always be there for you like a friend,
all the way to the end.

Mariza Navera, Grade 6
Long Beach Middle School

Kings

You know there are kings right?
There are Egyptian kings, and even Chinese kings.

There's really only one king, the true king. God!
Most importantly he rules with his son Jesus.

Both of them rule the Earth, the sky, and even the sun.
They created a set of rules called the ten commandments.

That's the kind of king I want, don't you?

Lucas Mitchum, Grade 6
St Mary's School

Sunsets

Pink and orange are spreading
From one cloud to another
Some people are getting tired
As the night comes like fire
Some people are getting excited
But some people are wondering
About tomorrow's thundering
Carolina Gazal, Grade 5
Holy Martyrs Armenian Day School

Snakes

I catch snakes by stepping on their tail.
Then I put them in a pail.
They like to smell with their tongue
And bathe in the sun.
Gavyn LeClair, Grade 4
Granville Elementary School

A Scream

In the night, night, night
there seems to be a fright.
You hear a scream
is it a dream?
No.
In the corner of the room
you see a girl
weeping and screaming
and weeping and screaming.
Then she turns around
she has no face!
You scream in terror and disgrace
and then it happens all over again.
Danielle Nicole Silverman, Grade 5
The Albany Academies

Waiting

I stare out the window
waiting for her
I dream of her
coming to me
the way she says hello
in her soft gentle voice
I can tell she's coming
but just can't tell when
she's coming soon
to me
I know
we'll be together again
I picture her in heaven
I hide away from the
darkness
waiting for her
to come home
again
Ashley Taylor, Grade 6
Northwood Elementary School

Global Warming Dream vs Reality

There once was a fairy tale that the earth was full of snow
A silly little tale that it was at least a little cold
Polar bears on the ice that catch fish by the sea
And fish that swam happily by the coral reef
Where birds lay eggs, chirp, and sing inside the spruce trees.
Some diseases ceased to exist like Lyme disease and Leptospirosis
As glaciers stood upon their land and shined miraculously
Even when Romania was known by its winter wonderland scene
Beautiful homes throughout the forest border.
Various fruits hang upon each tree making it look lovely
But we hate to say the hot temperature has put a delay
As the seasons go the winter doesn't seem to show.
The ice is disappearing into the water as well as the polar bears too.
The fish lay dried up on the beach as the coral reef has been bleached
As the western pine beetle damages the beautiful tree the birds have nowhere to breed.
While some diseases vanished, more disease spreaders are famished.
The warm temperatures are tumbling our glaciers into the sea
Romania is now a never-ending fall
The homes are gone and lost in a fire by the dry land
Now this fruit is rotting in the unbearable heat
Global warming is a terrible thing, just look around how it's changing.
Ariana Vallejo, Grade 6
Intermediate School 72 Rocco Laurie

Baseball

The pitcher stares at me
He winds up; he throws.
I swing, "STRIKE ONE!"
Again the pitch comes in.
I take a big swing, "STRIKE TWO!"
The pitcher, with a mean look, nods to the catcher and he throws
"CRACK!!!"
The ball flew high in the air and very far.
It was a HOME RUN!
As I rounded the bases, I heard the crowd roar with joy.
When I stepped on home plate, my whole team came out to celebrate
my heroic hit.
Sam Vercruysse, Grade 5
Harris Hill Elementary School

Nature

The birds singing, the crickets talking
Smells of nature absorb me like a sponge in water
The air cold and moist
I am living in a wonderland of nature
Finding peace within my thoughts, the fighting of my soul has stopped
I open my eyes I witness greenery, the gorgeous red-sun setting
The wondrous sky is a fresh new blue, it tastes like ice cream
Making my mouth watery and
Crickets composing a musical
Ants march in rows, worms hiding in their rock houses
Dark green grass is standing tall like an army ready for battle
The sky grows darker like a true violet-blue
I become the sky and nature.
Brice Vadnais, Grade 6
Harold D Fayette Elementary School

In the Car Today

I see the snow slowly melting,
I see the horses in the field.
I feel the rocks underneath the Jeep.
I smell the skunk that sprayed him yesterday,
      although I will not say.
I look out the window of the front seat
The wonders I see just can't be beat.
Riding in the car,
I'm sure that it can't be beat.
Going up, going down,
I feel like riding all around
In this car, on this day
I feel like screaming hooray.
In the car with my uncle.

Finola Meyer, Grade 5
Munsey Park Elementary School

God's Beauty

When I see a rainbow, my heart
beats harder and harder.   To say the
sky is so beautiful, why not look at it.
Just one more minute.
Never know if it will come back today.
So why not look at the sky. One more
minute to say. The sky is so beautiful today.

Navjot Kaur Pabla, Grade 5
St Benedict Joseph Labre School

Flowers

Flowers are a rainbow of extraordinary colors
They emerge in the spring and summer
just like a butterfly coming out of a cocoon
But sadly fade in the winter and fall
almost like melting ice cream on a hot summer day
As they grow they bring wisdom up to the sky
Like little messenger birds on a path that can only be seen
by those who can see through their imagination

Singing a beautiful song that sounds ineffable
just like little angels in heaven
With the flowers always singing
there is never a gloomy, lonely, or quiet moment
With the flowers always singing by your side
there is nothing to fear and nothing can break through
the lovely sound of the flowers

Geena Cantalupo, Grade 6
Harold D Fayette Elementary School

My Grandma

I watch as my eyes blind with shimmer as I see her
I see her dying I watch as I cry.
I prayed for her not to die because of her cancer.
I have pain in my heart for her but now she's free
she has no more pain as she now watches over me.

Jade Williams, Grade 4
Upper Nyack Elementary School

My Haven by the Sea

As the day grows long it's time for me
to escape to my haven by the sea.
We walk together but alone, my friend and I, the breeze.
I love to feel the warm breeze in my face
and the shocking cold waves splashing around my ankles.
As I finally get to my haven by the sea —
I climb and I climb to the top of my world.
The sun is flashing upon the sea and sparkles
like a thousand stars.
I'm up so high — into the sky, the pounding
waves can't reach me, just the whisper of their spray.
In the distance I see the world rushing away like the tide.
The countries I imagine…in my mind's eye?
Spain, Africa, Italy, where are you?
Oh how I love my peace and quiet…
to escape from the rush of life.
To toss a few shells as a gift to the sea.
I love her and she loves me,
the everlasting sea.

Joseph Earl, Grade 6
Holy Family School

School

S kull has 8 bones to protect the cranium
C ow means California, Oregon, and Washington
H ope to have a successful year in fourth grade
O utgoing teachers who help us learn
O ptimistic students interacting with each other
L uscious words to help us write enthusiastic stories

Emily Gillespie, Grade 4
Helen B Duffield Elementary School

Life

We are all lonely,
At one time, your life,
It is a special thing.
To be alive,
It is great, for one,
I love life,
It is special.
For God gave it to us.
God is important.
I for one am very interested in God.
God is your whole reason you are here.
If it weren't for him you would not be here.
You should pray, listen,
And trust in God.
He is our life,
Our reason to be here.
You, God made me, and everybody.
We are all unique,
Different, and special.
We're like snowflakes, not one is the same.
So that is life a graceful thing.

Luis Vorek, Grade 6
St Mary's School

Girls
Girls, can't live with 'em,
Can't live without 'em.
Cool girls,
dorky girls,
good girls,
bad girls,
beautiful girls,
and ugly girls.
No matter what,
girls are the same
somehow.
And, for guys who say they're
not, boys and girls
are equal,
sometimes.
Like I said,
Girls
Can't live with 'em
Can't live without 'em
Lamar Leacock, Grade 5
Public School 114 Ryder

Chilly Autumn
The leaves turn colors
We celebrate Thanksgiving
I get lots of treats
I like to jump in the leaves
I don't like wearing sweaters.
Katherine Ramirez, Grade 5
Northeast Elementary School

The Darkness of War
War is like a poison.
It will never go away.
I know somewhere in
that darkness there is some light.
And in that light is peace.
Someday that light will
overcome the darkness.
But until then, I wish
the soldiers good luck.
I am still praying for
that light to overcome
the darkness, and lives
would be saved, and the
soldiers would come home
to their families.
Cecelia McAuliffe, Grade 6
Long Beach Middle School

Butterfly
Little butterfly
Floating through the wispy air
Coming to the nest
Adam Castar, Grade 5
Guggenheim Elementary School

Kitten to Cat
Kitten
cute, small,
frisky, jumping, running
playful, wild — dull, lazy
sitting, eating, sleeping
old, fat,
Cat
Mackenzie Aldous, Grade 4
Granville Elementary School

Rainbow
The rain has stopped for a while now
The mist is in the air
Red blends into orange
Yellow blends into green
It is so pretty

Green blends with blue
Blue blends with indigo
And last
Indigo to violet
What do all those colors make?
Well red, orange, yellow, green, blue
Indigo and violet
They come together to make a…
Rainbow
Halle Grossman, Grade 6
Bellport Middle School

Night
The sky is blue
the night sky sparkles
the moon shines above our hearts,
the fish sleep beneath the waves
and its time to go to
our soft sweet beds
Alishbah Saddiqui, Grade 4
New Hyde Park Road School

Give Thanks
As I sit upon my lawn
gazing among the trees
it occurs to me.
That the leaves that change
and fall are a lot like me.
They remind me to
give thanks for those who touch my life.
Embrace the changes as
the colors begin to fade.
So remember as Thanksgiving
is approaching
the leaves will fall
to remind us
be grateful for it all.
Valen Kester, Grade 6
St John School

Big Fluffy Jacket
My big fluffy jacket
All black and white.
It feels so soft
It is so nice.

It feels so great,
I can wear if forever.
I wish I never needed
To take it off.

It is the best
I love it so much.
It is so soft
I wish I never needed
To take it off.
Jonathan Hopper, Grade 6
Bellport Middle School

Spring
I see flowers blooming.
I smell honey in the flowers.
I hear bees buzzing.
I taste honey.
I feel flowers.
SPRING!
Alyssa Pennington, Grade 4
Belmont Elementary School

Fall's Process
Kids jumping in leaves.
People raking the fall leaves.
Kids pumpkin picking.
Kids help their mom baking pies.
People get their sweaters out.
Leon Hope, Grade 5
Northeast Elementary School

What Is Poetry?
Poetry is
life
Poetry is
death
Poetry is
strong
Poetry is
sweet
like the fragrance
of a flower
hmm…
Can't you smell it?
Poetry is
right there
Poetry is
you.
Autumnsarah A. Foster-Pagett, Grade 5
Public School 114 Ryder

Autumn

Red, green, yellow and brown are swiftly falling down,
These are our leaves dancing to the ground!
Our leaves are changing from green to brown,
And are scattered all across town!
The sounds of crinkling, crunchy leaves in bunches,
Leave our trees with naked branches,
In the care of Mother Nature!

Paula Telyczka, Grade 6
Christ the King School

Seasons

Summer has gone, fall has come
The leaves are changing and school has begun
The winter will soon be here and we will say Happy New Year
Then spring comes and school is done
Then we go back to summer and the fun has again begun!!!!

Alyssa Marshak, Grade 5
Guggenheim Elementary School

My Family

My mom is as sweet as honey,
made from the best bees ever.
My dad shouts like a lion,
roaring at the sky.
My cousin runs,
like a rocket blasting off in full speed.
My other cousin,
is very slow but she is really smart.
That's all I can say today,
but hope to write very soon!

Anthony Martinez, Grade 4
Magnet School of Math, Science and Design Technology

My Cream and Sugar

Sailing, rocking back and forth
Feeling light like a feather, holding a baby
Eating cream chicken from a flowery bowl
Grandma and grandpa in Hawaii
Water laps at the beach
Grandparents' house during Christmas
Warm baked cookies, soft comfy beds
Light white clouds hugging me
Spending weekends with grandma, baking, eating cookie dough
Choosing a perfect Christmas tree in New York City
Combing grandpa's white hair, crawling into bed with them
Early in the morning under their soft snug blankets
Watching "Road Runner" and "Tom and Jerry"
Cartoon friends in the morning
Strolling to church with them, roaming at Rockefeller Center
Shopping for a Christmas dress in Macy's
Snowing on Christmas at grandma and grandpa's house
Picking up grandma at the train station
Walking down their hallway every single weekend
Falling asleep to the city noises

Rachel Kessler, Grade 6
Harold D Fayette Elementary School

Christmas Tree

Big and large like a giant.
Tall and lit like a star at night
You can barely see a star on top
Smelling as good as apple pie
All covered in lights
Beautiful and delightful
Covered with pine needles like a porcupine

Taylor Garrett, Grade 5
Edward J Bosti Elementary School

Dashing

Dashing dashing down the road
Going fast as I can
While people watch me do the race.
My dad and mom are clapping, so is everyone.
As soon as the race was done I was hungry.
So I got some hot dogs and it cheered me up.
I could not wait for the next race.

Curtis Sloley, Grade 4
Public School 69

Monster Sisters

We are like animals that fight
over prey on a warm summer's night.
We act like big monsters
That will give children a fright.
Although I look like them,
We are nowhere alike.

However, they're the ones
That I grew up with and look up to,
These monsters could look mean and scary,
But they're my sisters no matter what.

Adrianne Croce, Grade 5
Edward J Bosti Elementary School

The Ocean

The ocean waves were twisting
and turning during the day.

But at night the waves gently
get lower and the ocean is peaceful again.

As you look out to the moon
it is the most beautiful thing.

The moon shines onto the ocean
and the waves make the most beautiful sound.

When day returns the ocean has visitors,
the visitors go into the ocean, the visitors go far out to sea

The ocean does this every day,
The ocean will never go away.

Keriann Tenney, Grade 5
Edward J Bosti Elementary School

Page 229

To Fly
As I sit and watch
The clouds go by,
I wonder what
It's like to fly.
To be soaring
In the air
And come down,
whenever you care.
Cara Waterson, Grade 6
Holy Cross School

My Brother
Eddy has black eyes.
He has big eyes
He is cute.
I like my brother.
Eddy likes me back
Eddy is funny to me.
He is my best brother.
Edgar Rojas, Grade 4
Public School 148 Ruby Allen

Snow
White as clouds.
Soft as pillows.
Bitter as the freezer.
Builds snowmen and snowangels.
Fun as carnivals.
Kids having fun outside with the snow.
Going sleigh riding down the hill.
Having snowball fights with your friends.
Snow is the best thing there is!
Kyle Endlekofer, Grade 5
Edward J Bosti Elementary School

Sea Cucumber
Who am I?
I'm a slimy, creepy, oozy
echinoderm.
I am a sea cucumber.

I dwell in the midnight zone,
I bury myself in the sand,
camouflage on rocky walls,
diversity is who I am,
there are over 1,250 species of me.

I hope you like music,
Erik Satie described me in a song,
maybe I can help you find a cure,
I am used as medicine,
please don't eat me,
although I taste great in soup.
I am a sea cucumber.
Ryan Lennon, Grade 6
Shelter Rock Elementary School

Fall Is Falling
Pine cones are ignored
Squirrels throw acorns to ground
Crisp leaves also fall
You will rake up those items
And you will fall on them, too!
Ivette Garcia, Grade 5
Northeast Elementary School

Christmas Day
I woke up at seven
and the ground was white.
The snow is falling
and is a beautiful sight.

The lights on the tree
are nice and bright,
and the presents I see
are such a wonderful sight.

My family wakes up
and we gather together,
to enjoy a Christmas
that we will remember forever.
Alyna Thayer, Grade 5
Staley Upper Elementary School

Basketball
Basketball
Big, round
bouncing, flying, rolling
always playing with happily
winning, scoring, playing
orange, hard
ball
Brett Dufore, Grade 5
East Syracuse Elementary School

Pup to Wolf
Pup
Gray, white
Playing, clawing, dog related
Claws, small — big, black claws,
Tearing, ripping, scaring,
Vicious, old,
Wolf
Jonathan Fisher, Grade 4
Granville Elementary School

Brothers
Brothers
fun, funny
playing, fighting, laughing
has fun all the time,
My friends
Jaime Calcagno, Grade 4
Leptondale Elementary School

Dream Horse
What is that figure?
In the distance
It is a horse, a stallion
Running next to my train
I wish I could ride her now
But no, she is simply the snow
The snow is her body
A blue jay in the distance is her eye
I smiled and thought to myself
She is just like in my dream
Emily Marks, Grade 5
Granville Elementary School

Autumn Leaves
Red, yellow, and brown
Changing colors all around
A beautiful sight
Lovely swirls,
Making trees bare.
CRUNCH!
That's why I love leaves
so MUCH.
Alexa Stegmeier, Grade 5
Edward J Bosti Elementary School

The Ocean
Waves crashing everywhere
O the ocean I adore
Children building sand castles
O the ocean I adore
Long moonlit walks on the beach
O the ocean I adore
Footprints in the sand
O the ocean I adore
Combing the seashore for seashells
O the ocean I adore
Sea oats blowing in the ocean breeze
O the ocean I adore
Relaxing at the beach
O the ocean I adore
Dolphins jumping everywhere
O the ocean I adore
O the ocean how I love thee
Laura Enzinna, Grade 6
SS Peter and Paul School

Football
Football, football it's a hard hitting sport.
The Colts, the Patriots playing so hard.
They know what they're doing,
Unlike the Buccaneers.
Please, oh please, don't let the Colts lose.
There were doing so good and now
They are starting to snooze.
Joseph Resnick, Grade 5
Edward J Bosti Elementary School

Parents

My parents are very special to me
Without them I could not be
They work day and night that's why I cannot sleep,
I think about them every day, even when I play.

Merima Siljkovic, Grade 5
Public School 2 Alfred Zimberg

Something Called Life and Love

I beat and burn I curl and turn,
I shiver and shiv I love and live,
What I make right is something called life,
I make, take, and fake smiles,
Well sometimes it's worth while,

You know I don't care
If it is nice or fair,
People don't know if I'll ever go,
I will walk to and fro,
I will never go.
On the river of life and love,
I will row...

Fatima Livan, Grade 6
Immaculate Conception School-Stapleton

Tree Falling

Leaves fly through the air,
Red, yellow, green and brown,
Falling from the trees,
And covering the ground.
There are plenty enough
To make a big pile,
Where we'll jump, giggle
And smile.
The trees are empty and look very mean,
The leaves cover the grass, I see no more green.
The leaves are gone,
I won't shed a tear,
Because I know they'll be back again next year!

Emily Papa, Grade 6
Munsey Park Elementary School

The Wind

The winter wind is like a race car,
Zooming down the track.

While the summer wind is like a feather,
Floating freely in the air.

The autumn wind is like a tiger,
Hunting down its dinner.

While the spring wind is like a rollercoaster,
It's slow when it goes up the tracks,
And zooms down fast.

Chris Halleran, Grade 4
Shelter Rock Elementary School

I Like Fall

I like fall,
but I love
when the leaves change colors to orange, red, and
yellow because it reminds me of magic.

I like fall,
but I love
to rake the crunchy leaves and jump in them because
it makes me feel like I am flying.

I like fall,
but I love
Thanksgiving because I eat a lot of food. Turkey is
my favorite part of the Thanksgiving feast.

I like fall,
but I love
going to haunted houses. They are very scary and fun, too.

Joshua Gonzalez, Grade 5
Northeast Elementary School

The Beach

I love the beach.
Like dipping my feet in the sand,
Or building a sandcastle with my bare hands.
Pretending to be a mermaid in the water,
Or buying ice cream for a quarter.
Little fish swimming on the sea floor,
Or buying bait from a store.
But there is still so much more!

Sarah Altreche and Victoria SanFilippo, Grade 5
St Mary's School

The Castle

I wake up
In the castle
The golden sun rises
I leap out of bed
As the sun shimmers through the window
It is silent outside
I go down stairs to get some breakfast
I am served by a waiter
Some cereal with milk
After I finish my soaking cereal
I go to the fire place
To watch the flames burn the wood
Making a sweet smell in the air
Just then I see a flock of geese
Heading north for the winter
They are swooping up and down
Soaring through the air
Then I hear a little noise
Saying get up or you'll be late!
It is my mom and I was dreaming

Austin Pieniaszek, Grade 6
Northwood Elementary School

rocks

rocks are…
white and grey or green or blue
many different colors for you
they don't move off the ground
oh how I love them
that is rocks!

Josh Jasniok, Grade 5
East Syracuse Elementary School

The Sun

A torrid burst of sun
forcing me to fasten my eyes shut
like a seat belt on a roller coaster
a thousand daggers piercing my skin
as tears pour down
my lobster red face
Sunburn.

Michael Roberts, Grade 4
Norman J Levy Lakeside School

Triumph

Left Saturday
Drove to airport
Fly to Florida
Land
Drive to boat
Get key cards
I went to my room
I'm a roomie with my sister
I explored the boat
Ate lunch
We went swimming
I took a shower
Ate dinner
I ordered room service

Benjamin Schoen, Grade 4
Public School 69

My Mama

brings me to el parque
she buys me cosas
My mama
I love her much
she feeds me la comida
I am always with her
mi mama and me
te ciaro mucho.

Luis Fernando Moran, Grade 5
Public School 148 Ruby Allen

Bats

They sleep in the day
They fly in the moonlight sky
They swoop down for bugs

Jaime Majano, Grade 5
Northeast Elementary School

A Fishy Treat

I put it in, I take it out
It flips and flops all about
A salmon, a salmon I have caught
Just remember it's caught not bought
But I think salmon tastes really bad
So I give it to my dad
My dad says that's really kind
He says he's glad I didn't leave it behind
Dad cuts it up on the seat
He is making a fishy treat
Right now it looks like something mushy
He is making a box of sushi

Natalie Haines, Grade 4
Granville Elementary School

Winter

Winter is cold.
Winter is pretty.
Winter brings snow that is fun to play in.

I like to ski.
I like to skate.
I also like to play.

The winter snow is cold
when it touches my nose.

The cold snow makes my hands cold
When I build a snowman.

This is winter.

Gabriella Dybas, Grade 5
William B Tecler Elementary School

Silly Kids at School

Silly kids at school
That everybody thought was cool
He made it to college
And got some knowledge
And never went back to that school

Sabrina Pawlikowski, Grade 4
Granville Elementary School

Places

When I go places I feel an emotion.
I get to see nature
I get to see the world that I am in.
When I touch my heart
I can hear and feel it pounding
boom-boom-boom boom after boom.
When I touch my heart
I can see everything in Queens.
Stores, train stations,
super markets and deli groceries.

Jeffrey Linares, Grade 5
Public School 148 Ruby Allen

The Leaf

I saw you hang on trees so tall
And when wind blows I see you fall.

I see a lot of you all around
Like city folk walking all 'round town.

O leaf that when you fall, I rake
O leaf in bags the garbage men take.

I've seen you fall on people's heads,
And fill up every flower bed.

How I miss you in the cold weather,
But in spring you're light as a feather.

O leaf that when you fall, I rake
O leaf in bags the garbage men take.

Justin Dantzler, Grade 4
Public School 124Q

Burning Sizzling…

Burning sizzling…
Hot!!
I am the burning touch
mixed personality

Burning sizzling…
Burning wood as I touch it
mixed with oxygen
destroyed by water
don't want to mess with me

Burning sizzling…
Injuring anything flammable in my path
many irresponsible people
blame me for their mistakes

Burning sizzling…
My role model is the sun
I will burn any living thing
blow on me and I will come back
I help I hurt
I am fire.

Jonathan Laird, Grade 5
Public School 114 Ryder

Outside

Birds chirp
Trees stand
Flowers bloom
Wind howls
Butterflies fly
Bees hum
Have fun!

Marissa Saloman, Grade 4
John T Waugh Elementary School

Spring

Birds come
out of their nests,
polar bears wake up.
It's almost like
the bell is ringing,
"Ding, ding, ding,
it's spring."
Flowers blossom —
the sweet smell
like butterscotch,
full of joy!

Theresa Banatte, Grade 4
Public School 152 School of Science & Technology

Apples

Apples are like chewing gum,
Pounding your mouth with a rum-pum-pum.

They give my mouth a crisp feeling,
Just like the chilly crisp snow.

Some are very sour,
Like old Granny Smith.

But some are rather juicy,
Like the beloved Golden Delicious.

While all the other apples
Are very luscious indeed!

Kailey Singh, Grade 4
Public School 124Q

Jackie Robinson

At first a little baby,
he didn't care about the color of his skin.
Born in 1919
in the South
where little Jackie
learned that some people hated him
because he was black.
He did something amazing.
It wasn't just that he was gifted
at baseball.
It wasn't just that he became the first black
to be inducted into Major League Baseball.
He was always a gentleman,
even when people insulted him
with racial slurs.
Jackie stayed focused on the game.
He always tried his best.
He was Rookie of the Year
and a National League All-Star.
He made man proud — not just his people —
all people.

Sujith Varghese, Grade 6
St Catherine of Siena School

Broken Heart

Yesterday was just a normal day.
I was going downstairs to play.

I was having fun with my dog,
But the very next day was a disaster.

My dog was nowhere to be found!
We then found him lying on the ground.

He looked really still,
That's when we knew that he had been ill!

My lovely dog,
Was now looking as still as a log.

That was when we noticed that he had died.
I was so upset, that I cried and cried.

At last we called the vet.
I had just lost my favorite pet.

That was the worst day ever,
I would never forget this appalling day. *NEVER*

Cindy Do, Grade 5
Public School 176 Ovington

It Is Winter

It is winter
And
There is warm love in the air
As the kids go out
Into
The cold frosty air so that they feel like snowmen
Others stay in and put on the heat
And
Drink hot cocoa
And they are toasty warm
Burrrr
The people say as they take out
The sleds
And
The hills are covered
With a delicate blanket of snow
Until
It melts away
It is winter

Kerri Buckley, Grade 6
Harold D Fayette Elementary School

Black

Black is the color of the dark midnight sky,
Black is as dark as a shadow,
Black is as cool as a spring breeze,
Black is fast and fierce.

Dana Porcaro, Grade 4
Leptondale Elementary School

Dancing

When you dance, you stomp your feet.
You follow the rhythm,
You tap to the beat.

Dancing makes your body move.
You shimmy and shake,
You get in the groove.

Dancing is the very best.
It makes you feel full of zest.

Angela Alcamo, Grade 5
St Joseph Hill Academy

Night

Night,
is when
the sun
goes down.
Night is
when you
have sweet
dreams.
Night is
when all
your hopes
go down.
Night is
when the
day ends.

Taylor Cioffi, Grade 4
Public School 69

The Sun

Shining with all its might.
Yes, in fact the blazing,
Brilliant sun is very bright.

It warms you
Like a crinkled blanket.
The flaming rays shoot
Like a ruffled net.

Boy do I wish
I was the licorice sky,
With all the shapely
Planets and bright stars.

Acting like siblings.
"Hello," they'd greet me.

Though my wishing dream
will never…

Be mine.

Bailey Apholz, Grade 6
Akron Middle School

Sweet Home Ronkonkoma

My neighborhood is where mischievous middle school kids hang out at 7-11.
My neighborhood is like a book; you never know what is going to happen.
My neighborhood is the precious smell of pumpkin pie wafting into the air.
And it is where the amber sunset turns into lunar light that is as bright as
A flashlight in the midnight sky
And it is where I splash in my pool like a tidal wave on the beaches of Miami.
And it is an elegant, glorious place to call home.

Alex Deger, Grade 4
Helen B Duffield Elementary School

Pillows

I like a new pillow.
It seems soft, silky and fluffy.
I sleep soundly with it at night.
I fluff it in an attempt to make it more comfortable.
I feel warm and — safe — in and around it.
I will not throw it away when it loses its extra batting.

I like old pillows too,
I don't wear them out or use them too much,
They are etched into my heart,
I can have a pillow fight with them and I know they will still keep me safe and warm,
They lay under my heart and wait for my head's arrival,
They love me for who I am,
They know me inside and out.

You know it's a funny thing…
Family is like a pillow.

Ileah Scheck, Grade 6
Nesaquake Middle School

Storm

A wolf in the forest runs to his cave
Hiding from the approaching rain as the autumn wind rushes
Making leaves fall to the ground, ruffling his fur.
Clouds come out, covering the sun
Darkening the sky
The air becomes cold.

Rain falls
He sees a rabbit run to her hole
A bird flies to his nest
The grass becomes wet as if it were night and the rain was dew.
He hears other animals running from the storm
The wolf creeps out of the cave, letting rain fall on his head
He stands outside his cave. The rain runs into his eyes
And the forest appears blurred like a reflection in the water.

He heads back to his cave and lies down to sleep to the sound of the rain.
As he wakes up the wind stops, the sky brightens and the air warms.
Animals creep out to see why it is quiet again.
The wolf barks joyfully as he dashes from his cave.
The ground soft and wet under his feet.
The storm is over.

Delaney Palma, Grade 5
Harris Hill Elementary School

All Together

Thanksgiving
The turkey is in the oven
The cranberries are in a dish
Soon the guests will arrive
On this cold, rainy, November day.
Through the turkey, the stuffing,
The cranberries, and the mashed potatoes
The pumpkin pie and coffee
We all laugh and talk
And have a good time —
Something to be thankful for
Tomorrow it will be time to prepare for Christmas
But for now, let's just enjoy each other's company.

Victoria Smith, Grade 6
St John School

Thoughts of Fall

Red, orange, yellow, green and brown
Falling from the trees and coming down
Now I smell the pumpkin pie
I will share it with friends and I
Christmas cookies, Halloween candy, Christmas morning
All these holidays we are enjoying

Raymond Hart, Grade 5
Bretton Woods Elementary School

My Colors

White,
Is the soft, fluffy snow on a cold winters day.
Blue,
Is the ocean rubbing against your body like a relaxing massage.
Pink,
Is all the love on Valentines Day that I can give you.
Black,
Is the frustration I feel when I don't get what I want.
Green,
Is all the money you have filling up your pockets.
Red,
Is my mom's car speeding to get to work on time.
So what do your colors mean to you?

Danny Pace, Grade 6
Mahopac Middle School

Study!!

"Study, study, study"
That's what all parents say,
They say "study, study, study!"
When there is a test the next day.
Everybody knows that our brains sometimes ache!
Please try to give us kids a break!
Because of all this studying,
When we play we are weak!
So why can't we have tests every month
instead of every week!

Emily Walsh, Grade 5
Dickinson Avenue Elementary School

Green

Green is the color of a bright, lit up Christmas tree,
Leaves smell green,
Grass is green bushes and trees too,
Green is like a spring sprinkling down rocks,
I look green when I get sick of eating,
Green is fresh cool air on a high mountain peak,
Green is when I think of emeralds in caves,
That Is Green

Paul Lombardi, Grade 5
Eastplain School

Blooming Flowers

In my garden,
I see flowers,
Blooming everywhere,
In every different name,
Like petunias, blue bonnets and sunflowers.
Flowers are blooming everywhere!

Indranie Sharma, Grade 5
St Benedict Joseph Labre School

Yellow

What is yellow?
Yellow is the pollen, in the center of a flower,
Yellow is the cool lemonade, when it touches my lips,
Yellow is a banana, one of my favorite fruits,
Yellow is a tweety bird, chirping on TV,
Yellow is Homer Simpson, in Springfield,
Yellow is the rays of sun that shine in the morning,
Yellow is the pencil I write with in school,
Yellow makes me think of a Labrador,
Yellow is a bee, buzzing in the spring air,
Yellow is Spongebob, frolicking down in Bikini Bottom,
Yellow is the color of my cousin's blonde hair,
and a canary singing in the morning,
Yellow is the color of my highlighter, inside my desk
But most of all, Yellow is what it is, a color.

Alexander Kromer, Grade 5
Eastplain School

Ambition

Ambition is necessary to accomplishment.
Without any ambition to gain an end, nothing would be done.
To win anything, we must have the ambition to do so.

Taylor Zaccarine, Grade 5
William Street School

Winter

W ill or might, snow
I s very cold outside
N ever scorching out there
T oo cold for mosquitoes to bite you.
E very day we might wear coats against
R aving winds.

Owen Zeng, Grade 4
Public School 152 School of Science & Technology

The Tide
The tide comes in and takes me away
My mind sails off almost every day
While I lie on the beach
I dream and fly away.
I just have to get away
If it's the last thing I do
I really can't stay here
But I really want to
Elaine Minew, Grade 6
Intermediate School 72 Rocco Laurie

Fire
Hot crackles
Moves in different motions
Spreads as fast as lightning
Exotic
William Harris, Grade 4
Campbell Savona Elementary School

Fall Breeze
I see a fish in a clean cloud.
I hear the cars driving by.
I feel the wind in my face.
I feel the wind in my heart.
I see an airplane making art.
I feel the sun on my cheeks.
It feels good.
I see the trees moving side to side.
Inviting me to come.
And swing on their graceful branches.
April Noe, Grade 6
Amherst Middle School

yellow
yellow is the color of
the leaves in the fall.

yellow is the petals on
a sunflower.

yellow is the pollen inside
the sunflower.
Jessica Esposito, Grade 4
Leptondale Elementary School

Baseball
Baseball
Stealing bases like a starving fox
Roaring crowds
Hitting a homer as far as Mars
Pitching as fast as lightning
Turning double plays
Hitting batters
Sorry!
Danny Strick, Grade 4
Concord Road Elementary School

Grassy Fields
Green grasses
Flowing in the wind
Watch as it touches
The side of your face

Blue sky
Up above.
Clouds so nice
And fluffy

AHH a truck
Coming to me
Oh, no it's gone.
And I am too.
Conor Devlin, Grade 6
Bellport Middle School

God's Ocean Moment
The waves
proceed to move
closer and closer
to shore
their journey ends
at shore
then
go back
next
another set
of waves come
struggling to catch up
with the first
then I wonder
"What's the idea?"
"Going back and forth?"
I then
discover what's happening
God is just creating
an ocean moment
Tristen Jones, Grade 6
Northwood Elementary School

The Bear
In my house all alone,
I hear a roar.
I scream a loud tone,
Running down, down, down,
To see who or what is there.
To my surprise,
I see with my two eyes, a bear,
I hear a familiar voice, voice, voice.
As I run, run, run,
I realize it's Halloween,
and it was my dad — Chad, Chad, Chad
Brianna Hart, Grade 5
The Albany Academies

Fall
I play in the leaves
Because it is fun.
I jump in the leaves
In the November sun.

I like to play
And ride my bike.
On a cold fall day
I go on a long hike.

When I dive in the leaves
It's my friends that I call.
There are no more bees
And we have a ball!

Our shirts — in we tuck
When we play tag.
We pack our leaves up
In a big bag.

Fall is a busy season
But it's best
That is the reason
I get no rest.
Alissa Lasher, Grade 5
Marie Curie Institute

Life
Life is a world of wonder,
Life is a world of sight,
Life is a world of everything,
Everything from wrong to right
Haley Jacobs, Grade 5
Dickinson Avenue Elementary School

Football
Football
rough, difficult
tackle, kick, run
big good hard hits
touchdown
Cameron Beauford, Grade 5
Most Holy Rosary School

Christmas Season
C an't wait to open presents
H ardly any sun
R eindeers fly to the chimney
I can hardly wait
S itting by the tree
T hinking about what I got
M agical things to come
A nxious to see what happens
S weet cookie smells
Ciarra Jae Olivera, Grade 5
Northeast Elementary School

Basketball

I like basketball,
It usually starts in the fall,
You don't play on a field you play on a court,
After all, basketball is my favorite sport.
To be MVP you have to practice a lot,
But in the summer practicing is way too hot.
There are many great players like Jordan and Kidd,
They work hard in their careers like Shaq did.
I practice very hard to be the best player I can be,
Maybe someday you will play against me.

Alexandra Helou, Grade 6
Holy Cross School

Love

Through time and space,
comes something that you can't explain.
Is it something that you can hold on to,
or is it something that slips through your fingers?
You don't really know a speck about this thing
until it happens to you.
Then, at that moment, you realize
it's something you can hold on to as long as you please,
but sometimes it disintegrates
and turns into tears on your fingers.
Then you know that this thing is love.

Heather Kalish, Grade 6
Pleasantville Middle School

Winter Days

A blanket of snow is covering the ground
Except for the whistling wind, there is no sound.

The trees are covered with snow instead of leaves
Is this real or am I in a dream?

Above, the blue sky is like a crystal shining bright
The distended white clouds are a brilliant white.

As the sun smiles, its gleam reflects off the snow
With the blink of an eye, this whole scene may go.

Kirsten Back, Grade 6
Harold D Fayette Elementary School

The Egyptians

The Egyptians make us work day and night
We were captured like birds in plain sight.
We work from morning to noon
All we eat is a ration of soup
The Egyptians may have crippled us
But our pride will not turn to dust.
We will stand tall and proud.
We will be heard loud around,
From Babylon to Jerusalem
The Wailing Wall will answer our call.

William Koganov, Grade 6
Intermediate School 239 Mark Twain

Poetry and Me*

Poetry is a song you recite
It's words that take flight
It's a flower that blooms
Or scary tales from the tombs
It's a voice from your heart
From the soul's deepest part
Poetry's the place where imagination flies
Poetry's the place where boredom dies
Poetry can make you happy or sad
Poetry can tell of the good or the bad
Poetry can be in verse or rhyme
Poetry can tell of today or past time
Poetry can be read in many different ways
It's where one tells a story and there the story stays
From Shakespeare to Hughes
To Cummings and Frost
Poetry's one of my favorite places
Where I can get lost

Grant Schietinger, Grade 6
Shelter Rock Elementary School
*Dedicated to my 3rd grade teacher, Mrs. Mass

Leaf of Mine

Leaves are spinning all around
leaves are falling on the ground
Different colors, different shapes
leaves are just all over the place.
So many kinds
I can't possibly find
the perfect leaf of mine.

Helena Roth, Grade 6
Intermediate School 227 - Louis Armstrong Middle

Gates Hall

A wonderful scene appears on the theater stage,
A choir group perfectly on tune,
Sweat dripping off people's cheeks,
The tap of a hammer, Bang! Bang! Bang!

The doors open with sunlight pouring in,
The wind rushing against our faces,
Tiredness fills the air,
The piano beat going faster and faster,

And suddenly it all stops,
Now all you can hear is your heart beating and the fans running,
Fresh fruit set out in a wooden basket,
We move to the fruit but to me we're going in slow motion,

Water being gulped like a drowning cat,
Peaches are pig food,
All the sudden I gained a whole lot of energy,
I jumped up on stage and danced until I fell over,
My heart was racing and I was filled with excitement.

Kasey Winder, Grade 6
Sodus Intermediate School

A Thankful Heart

I have a thankful heart,
For my mom and dad.
I like to go for hikes with Dad;
Mom's smile always makes me glad.

I have a thankful heart,
For my happy home.
I love my brothers,
And my furry dog Sam.

I have a thankful heart,
For going to my school,
Science, penmanship, and library.
I try to obey each rule.

I have a thankful heart,
For my country — the USA.
I am thankful for our soldiers;
They keep us safe every day.

Brandon Buchanan, Grade 4
Cortland Christian Academy

It's Snowing

It's snowing it's snowing winter's here
Autumn is over so we cheer!

We drink hot chocolate
And marshmallows too,

And here are some greetings
Especially for you!

Allyson Bates, Grade 4
Webster Montessori School

Long Beach

Long Beach is the waves that run.
Run down and up through the sun
The moon that shines in the light night
Can sometimes scare you with fright
The waves run through the moonlight
And through the sunny light
Long Beach is quiet through the night,
But is crazy and fun in the light.
Long Beach is where I live
And Long Beach is my community.

Tara Costello, Grade 6
Long Beach Middle School

Colby

C ares about fish
O rganizes his clothes
L oves doing homework
B oys are mean to me
Y u-Gi-oh! *Gx* is my favorite show

Colby Lewis, Grade 4
Granville Elementary School

Racism

We may be different on the outside,
But we are all the same on the inside.
Without different races the world would be uniform.
Without different colors, there would be no diversity on the planet.
If you look at everyone on the planet at the same time,
You'll see that we are all unique in our own special way.

Grace Halio, Grade 6
Shelter Rock Elementary School

Television

I just love television.
It's so fun to watch.
All the comedy and action.
Game shows and reality shows.
The comedies make you laugh out loud like a feather tickling you on the face.
The action is so intense you could cut it with a knife.
All the money on the game shows make you wish that you were there.
And the reality shows are so cool you watch them every night.

I love that big box in the middle of my living room.
Feeling the remote in my hands and just flicking through the channels.
My family fighting over what show to watch.
(My baby brother screaming because of the fighting over the remote.)
Television's just great.
It gives me something to do.
I bet *you* have a television.
Don't you?

Matthew Moon, Grade 5
Harris Hill Elementary School

New York Is the Best Place to Be!!!!

Lights flashing everywhere makes you wants to stop and stare.
At night the lights shine so bright putting different cultures in the spotlight.
People walking every which way, going to see different shows on Broadway.
With all the different places to shop you will never ever get a chance to stop.
I love New York it's the place to be, someday you'll see it the same as me.

Brianne Garcia, Grade 6
Our Lady of Good Counsel School

Writing a Poem Is So Stressful

Writing a poem is so stressful.
You don't know when to start or stop.
The ideas in your head overflow or deflate.
Writing a poem is so stressful.
I have one due tomorrow.
The teacher says, "It better be perfect."
If I don't write a good one I guess I'll have to borrow.
Writing a poem is so stressful.
I need one really soon.
I feel like my paper is cloth and my pen is a bull.
I could get an A on the one in my head, but it's about a little spoon.
Writing a poem is so stressful soon I've got to be done.
Oh, look here…
I've got one!

Landy Erlick, Grade 5
School of the Holy Child

Winter Is Here

Winter is coming
I can't wait
I can't wait for the snow to fall,
I can't go and play,
I have to stay in,
Because I am sick,
I watch through the window,
And start to cry,
Why oh why can't I go outside.

Semina Radoncic, Grade 5
Public School 105 Senator Abraham Bernste

Winter Scenery

The fireplace glow and warmth puts,
heat on my body as the coldness disappears.
Snow gently falling, drifting down to the frosted land.

As my brothers leave in layers to go outside,
I feel this chill run through me.

I look outside to see snow cover the lawn,
My brothers laughing, covered in snow
and their cheeks rosy, red.

My brothers come inside asking for cocoa.
I ask if I could have some too.
My brothers and I sit down to have cocoa.
Holiday music is all you hear throughout the house.

Joanna Bryant, Grade 5
Edward J Bosti Elementary School

Visiting Heaven

Imagine as you get to the top of a skyscraper,
you realize that you've gotten yourself into a caper.
You keep going up until you reach heaven,
now you've reached floor nine hundred sixty-seven.
You climb all the way to the roof,
and then you feel a really good feeling and poof!
You look down and see
people so small and tiny.
Then you see God, the big guy, and notice that you are in
the castle in the sky.

Jaime Reuter, Grade 5
St Joseph Hill Academy

Smithtown Lacrosse

L osing because you gave up is not an option
A nswering with a goal is the way to win
C ross checking your opponent to the ground
R ough housing is the way of the Bulls
O ur high schools are competitively amazing
S mithtown East and West are a threat to beat
S coring at will against their opponents
E xpect the best from the Big 7 champs

Logan Greco, Grade 6
Great Hollow Middle School

Alone on a Plane

I go onto a plane excited for my destination
I sit down with an exclamation!
Wondering how long it will take.
Thinking about staying awake.

Bing! Seatbelts on,
Just about to yawn,
Time to go,
Having my iPod, staying on the down low.

In the air,
Can't wait to get there,
Bump!
Thump!

Turbulence, oh no!
Hey, just go with the flow,
Don't be a coward,
It's only an hour!

Almost there,
I think I see a flare!
I'm finally here!
I'm in the clear.

George Tsourounakis, Grade 6
Intermediate School 227 - Louis Armstrong Middle School

The Wind's a Thief

The wind's a thief,
It steals the leaves from the trees,
And robs the things we value most,
It slams the door furiously,
And with its strength, it can even create a hurricane.
The wind can be a warm breeze,
But when it's sad,
it makes you mad,
because it sets its emotions free!

Kalliopi Kapetanos, Grade 4
Shelter Rock Elementary School

Science Is...

S peculation
C reatively learning everything we can
I nvestigating the unknown
E xploring the universe
N ew species all around us
C ompletely astounded by our world
E verything, and anything that comes to mind

Hope means life
Life is inspiration
Inspiration leads to future
Future is our world
The world revolves around science!

Albert Kim, Grade 6
Shelter Rock Elementary School

Music!
Loud and low
How high can it go?
Hard and soft
Like Rap music does
Rock and Jazz and many more
Pop and Hip-Hop
R&B, as slow as it can be
Classic is for me.

Sotiris Papa, Grade 5
Public School 2 Alfred Zimberg

Family
sitting around a fire
on a cold winter's eve
with loved ones around you
you don't want to leave

telling old stories
and having lots of fun
it's much better when
you're there with everyone

telling funny jokes
and laughing along
you might even start
to sing a happy song

it might be a holiday
or a special birthday
as long as they're there
it could be any day

playing fun games
you always share
it's the right thing to do
because it shows you care

Arielle McManus, Grade 6
Long Beach Middle School

Flowing Lava
Flowing,
Tumbling,
Melting,
Crashing like waves,
Master of destruction,
Glowing red and black.
Falling
Down,
Down,
Down,
The steep sloping surface
Until it sets
And stays hard and black.

Lauren Dorobiala, Grade 6
Akron Middle School

Soccer
Kick! Kick!
Mud everywhere
Gooey, slimy, wet
Trying for a goal!
Score! Score!

Joyful faces all around
Boot that ball all day long!
Sun beating on your faces
Wet, hot, sticky, and red

The goalie hit the dirty old stained ball
And then watched it fall.
Falling like a fish covered in sweat,
Wishing to finish the game and win.
Yeah! We scored!

Cassie Carlson, Grade 6
Akron Middle School

Rats!
I hear a pit-pat, pit-pat, pit-pat.
The rats are staring and glaring,
glaring, glaring, glaring.
The rats are scaring.
They have no laws,
they have sharp claws.
Oh why me,
for can't you see,
the rats are going to eat me.
Suddenly cats march in,
the battle they'll surely win.
They go to war,
let their spirits soar
forever more.

Mary Bischoff, Grade 5
The Albany Academies

Winter Day
Watching the snow,
Waiting to go,
Outside and play,
On this winter day.
Winter is short,
But has many sports,
On the hilltop we stay,
On this winter day.
Sledding down the hill,
What a thrill,
We sing and play,
On this winter day.
I just have to say,
On this winter day,
Snowball fights are fun,
Even in the sun!

Emily Leone, Grade 5
Eastplain School

Kittens
When asleep soft and silky
When awake dreamy and milky
Purring purring
When you hold them
They grab your arm
As they drift
Asleep

Zach Saklad, Grade 4
Concord Road Elementary School

Just Because
today is not a holiday
it isn't even your birthday
but still i thought i'd like to send
a little message to my friend

you make me laugh and make me smile
you ease my troubles for a while
when clouds are thick and skies are grey
you put some sunshine in my day

you're really thoughtful, sweet and kind
a friend like you is hard to find
i know i've told you once or twice
that i think you are really nice

but a person who is as great as you
should be told more than i do
and so i send these words with great love
why did i send them…just because

Rachel Kull, Grade 6
Intermediate School 72 Rocco Laurie

Zebras
White with black stripes,
Or black with white stripes.

Up on a hill running so cheerful,
Sprinting a plain leaping so graceful.

Here is a predator
Looking for something to eat,
Better do something
Before on them he starts to feast.

Back to a spot grazing for grass,
If another predator should come,
An alarm will sound.

But after all that,
Still one question remains,
White with black stripes,
Or black with white stripes.

Adrian Ross, Grade 6
Akron Middle School

Seasons

Fall, winter, summer, and spring
Which one is your favorite? Mine is spring.
Mine is spring because you start the countdown
For summer vacation; so let's have a celebration!
No more school! No more homework that's why
I like spring most of all.

Nathan Burroughs, Grade 4
Cortland Christian Academy

Dream

I had a dream
Just like Martin Luther King, Jr.
But it's not about freedom
Everyone told me to do what I have to do
And keep trying
Some people said
I would fail
My father said to try my hardest
And never give up
So I did
And now I completed
My dream.

Anthony Rodriguez, Grade 6
Graham Elementary and Middle School

The Moon

The moon is like a night light
The brightest thing in the nighttime sky
We need it and we love it.

Its source comes from the sun
The sun is the brightest thing in the solar system.
That's why the galaxy is called the solar system.

The ray of the sun gives the moon light
So we can see in the dark.
Moon, what would we do without you?

Chiedu Moses Mbonu, Grade 5
Munsey Park Elementary School

Thanksgiving

In our family,
The Thanksgiving meal,
Is a big deal.
My sister and I arrive early to help prepare,
the food which we all will share.
When the family gathers we have a crowd.
Sometimes the noise gets rather loud.
Please pass the turkey, and the gravy,
Leave the cabbage, red and wavy.
Skip the lettuce, and tomatoes,
I'm waiting for those mashed potatoes.
Thanksgiving is lots of fun,
For old, for young, for everyone.

Mary Zick, Grade 6
St John School

I Am a Tree

Swoosh the wind brushes my hair back and forth
I wiggle a bit
My only friend is the squirrel that lives inside me
Rocking back and forth
My leaves start to fall as they brush upon the ground
I am bare, with no leaves to cover me
My bark is peeling, I'm withering away
I'm as cold as a snowflake
Soon my time will come
And a seed will be planted
Right over my remains
Another generation of oaks will grow
The cycle will go over and over again
For I am a tree

Nicholas Ponzio, Grade 6
Harold D Fayette Elementary School

Proud to Be Trini

Where else can you go
to hear the best calypso?
Where else can you play
mas in the street all day?

Where else can you listen to Bunji Garlin,
De girls dem darlin,
or, Machel Montano,
De king of calypso?

Where else can you eat
Tamarind balls so sweet
Crab and callaloo alone,
strew chicken down to de bone?

Dem Trini like dey carnival
cause dey like plenty backanal.
Yes I live like an American
but I'm really proud to be Trinidadian!!

Niesha Hunte, Grade 4
Public School 235 Lenox School

Family

Family is like something you can't describe
All you can say is that it is all about love,
caring and they're always by your side.

Family is someone really close like
Ms. Panoff to the Yankees
Family is people who sit with you at dinner.

Family is people you can get good advice from.
Family is cozy and warm.
When I hug my family I feel so warm.
It's like drinking hot chocolate and it's going down your throat.
Having a family is a good, warm feeling.

Karla Campos, Grade 6
Long Beach Middle School

My First Day of 6th Grade

Nervous not knowing what to do,
Bent down to tie my shoe. I thought to myself whatever,
But finally things turned out to be better.
Now I know everywhere to go, thanks to the teachers
For telling me I'll know. So this is my poem about my first day
Of 6th grade, it's already starting to be one big parade.

Paulina Karekos, Grade 6
Canandaigua Middle School

Skates, Rays, and Stingrays

A barbed tailed fish,
Who fears the Bull Shark,
With a pancake body,
That has razor sharp teeth to crush Mollusk shells,
A fish that will eat its own species just to live,
The coolest fish in the sea,
Except that it killed Steve Irwin,
An animal that is threatened,
That is as tall as a six-foot man,
But won't hurt you until you make it feel threatened,
My favorite ray in the sea.

Joseph Blando, Grade 6
Shelter Rock Elementary School

Fall

As I wake up to the birds chirping loudly.
Chirp, chirp, chirp, chet.
The fall leaves crunch beneath my feet.
Snap, crunch, crunch, snap.
The wind sings a song slowly but lovely.
Whoosh, whoosh, swish, whoooo.
It comes to be my favorite season, fall.
The wind blows gently across the tree tops.
It makes a calming noise.
The chimes blow a sweet, sweet song.
The colors of the trees bring joy to my heart.
Nothing is better than sitting with your family by the fire,
Watching with a cup of warm tea in your hands.
I bet you think it should be summer all the time,
But I think it should be fall.
My sweet, sweet fall.

Kathryn-Ann Conroy, Grade 6
Great Hollow Middle School

When I Close My Eyes

Stars twinkle in the night sky.
As I close my eyes I wish for a pony.
I want a car,
I want to travel very far,
I want to be a princess
And live in a magical kingdom with trolls and fairies,
But right now,
I close my eyes and dream of being
Me!

Rebecca Rivera, Grade 4
Magnet School of Math, Science and Design Technology

Through Tired Eyes

The world looks through tired eyes
The tired eyes that look upon
The wars and famines
Disasters and drought

The world's tired eyes
They need change
They need to see a few hearts
Just a few hearts that have a mind to change

To change the way the world is now
To purify the souls
The souls of those
That are cold hearted

A change of heart is all that is needed
To refresh the tired eyes
The tired eyes the world looks through

Emily Faso, Grade 6
Harold D Fayette Elementary School

Mommy Kissing Santa Claus

I awaken and it's Christmas night,
as I open my eyes I see someone in sight.
I turn on the light the person is wearing red and white
when I came closer I knew who it was so I took a pause,
I saw mommy kissing Santa Claus.

Somuto Mokwuah, Grade 6
Immaculate Conception School-Stapleton

Hot and Cold

Hot
Fire, red
Burning, sizzling, roasting
Warm, sweat, ice, fog
Shivering, raining, sneezing
Wind, snow
Cold

Mahir Alam, Grade 4
Public School 108 Cpt Vincent G. Fowler

The Sweet Wind

The wind can be a
A funny monkey playing through the trees,
A bully when it hits you and you fall over,
A king because it is powerful.

What can the wind sound like?
A parent screaming for help,
A whistle — loud in your ear,
A song — so sweet.

If you use your imagination,
What will come?

Emily Golway, Grade 4
Shelter Rock Elementary School

My First Day of Fun

My first day of fun
Kids are the spreading wind
Rollercoaster like a soaring bird
Splashing pools and roaring slides
Sparkling sky, shimmering rides.

My first day of fun
Screaming toddlers like caged monkeys
Laughing friends are hysterical hyenas
Rushing water and pattering feet.

My first day of fun
My favorite ride the screaming eagle
Controlling me, spinning, flipping, turning
In my brain making me fly
The adrenaline, the excitement.

My first day of fun
It's over, my heart is pounding
My heart adjusting to my blood
The great smile when I exit
Through the tall black gates
My first day of fun at Sea Breeze.

Jeffery Stratton, Grade 6
Sodus Intermediate School

Science Is…

Science is plants that grow,
Observing the first fall of snow.

Science is measuring the mass,
Learning about liquids, solids and gas.

Science is dissecting animals,
We also learn about all kinds of mammals.

Science is about the water and air,
What is happening to our Earth just doesn't seem fair.

Hannah Press, Grade 6
Shelter Rock Elementary School

Hopes and Dreams

As beautiful as a rainbow
As bright as the sky
With the vision of an eagle's eye
There lie your *hopes* and *dreams*
Safe, but forgotten as it may seem
You can dream anything
You can dream pans or pots
And in your head there is
ONE little spot
And in that one little spot
There lie your *hopes* and *dreams*
Safe, but forgotten as it may seem

Samantha Lion, Grade 5
Sunquam Elementary School

Life Doesn't Frighten Me

I had a fear one day
That I knew would never go away
Life doesn't frighten me at all

I saw him there every night
He truly gave me a fright
Life doesn't frighten me at all

He watched me as I slept
And heard every time I stepped
Life doesn't frighten me at all

I would turn on the light to see if he was there
It always turned out that he was just a glare
Life doesn't frighten me at all

My closet is now always closed
So he will never be exposed
Life doesn't frighten me at all

Now that I'm older I know nobody's behind that door
But I still close it tight, just to be sure
Life doesn't frighten me at all

Melissa Rubin, Grade 6
Long Beach Middle School

Stranger

Yesterday you were a stranger to me,
But today, we're as close as can be.
Your hand, I'll never let go,
Afraid you'll melt like snow.
Together we can fly,
Soar way up high,
Like birds into the sky.
With you my fears seem small,
Because together we stand tall.

Navida Rukhsha, Grade 6
Intermediate School 227 - Louis Armstrong Middle

Fall

Hot juicy turkey, tastes so fantastic!
Turkey with gravy will pop taste buds!

Some leaves are translucent and some are opaque
Some are red and yellow.

Raking leaves is hard work.
After, it feels like I got frostbite.

When Hanukkah arrives
I get two amazing presents.

My cold, green murky pool disappears
Saying goodbye to fall as we cover it.

Stephen Silver, Grade 5
Edward J Bosti Elementary School

The Porcupine Fish
A small, slow swimming fish,
Looks like a tasty dish,
Easy to catch, I believe,
Hurry now, my prey might leave.

I cannot eat that little fish,
It has filled itself with water,
Now it's far too big to swallow,
And far too slow to follow.
It has long, sharp spines,
And its eyes are very big and scary,
This little fish is not so tasty after all!
Madeleine Quinn, Grade 6
Shelter Rock Elementary School

Yankees
Jeter at shortstop
Philips at first
When the Yankees lose I want to burst

Up comes A-Rod at the plate
Here comes a homerun
Open your eyes before it's too late

Another World Series
It's gonna be great
Before you know it they'll have 28

Mattingly, Berra, Posada, Jeter
And Mantle too
Just a handful of the greats
Mariana Palella, Grade 6
Holy Cross School

A Better Place for All
I didn't really die
I just went away.
To a place that's so much better
A place where I can stay.

You think that I still am
Just around the bend.
So you stand at the corner
And wait for your pain to end.

What if someone told you
That there was no end to sorrow.
Would you still go to bed, thinking,
"He'll be back tomorrow."

When you next see me
I'll show you the way
To a place that's so much better
A place where you can stay.
Allison Franz, Grade 6
St John the Baptist School

The First Day I Went to 4th Grade
I was so nervous
like a mouse
I felt like
squeaking
squeak, squeak
and hiding
under my chair
When I walked
into the classroom
everyone was
looking at me
I felt like a monster
roar, roar
I thought everyone
was going to
talk about me
I heard whispers
here and there
and you know
they thing they were saying
was a sweet hello.
Lucero Depeña, Grade 4
Public School 148 Ruby Allen

Day or Night?
I'm very tired, I need to sleep.
I try, I twist, I turn — there's a creak.
I get tired — is it dark? I'm too weak.
It's like my eyes are eating my day.
I'm mad, sad, tired, not gay.
When I awake, I hear crickets.
A train worker yells, "Anymore tickets?"
My mother says to stay in bed.
"I just woke up," of course I said.
Well it's late, I took my guess.
I fall asleep, I drift, I fly, I'm not a mess.
Anna Gerwin, Grade 6
St Mary's School

Winter Fun
Sweat hibernates like some animals,
The grass gets covered with cushioning
white cloud-like snow.
Snowmen look human.

The attachments to a tree trunk
become leafless.
Trees become as white as an
old man's head.

Hot cocoa steaming, about to
be guzzled down;
winter fun has just begun!
Anthony Avgi, Grade 5
Edward J Bosti Elementary School

Brothers*
Brothers have a piece of mind,
And they are always kind.

Brothers,
The only other choice.

Brothers are always there for you,
To make sure all your wishes come true.

Brothers,
The only choice.

Imagine, no brothers,
No only other choice.
Mackenzie Vojtko, Grade 5
Whitney Point Intermediate School
In memory of my brother, Alec Vojtko

Mouse
There was a boy.
Who had a toy.
His favorite was a mouse
That lived at his house.
And brought him great joy
Alyssa Gebo, Grade 4
Granville Elementary School

Survival
Food and water are the key to life
Shelter and trust too
For without these simple things
Survival will be tough for you

As time goes by
Maturity comes too
Bringing knowledge and courage
As it passes through

As the journey ends
You will miss the tension
Of living alone
And working for food
You will find you're not the same too
You're all grown up
See how much a little journey can do.
Christopher Harragan, Grade 6
Shelter Rock Elementary School

Cute Wormy
Wormy, wormy
So little and squirmy,
So slimy,
So tiny,
What a cute little wormy!
Symone Maracle, Grade 5
John T Waugh Elementary School

Softball

Crack! Goes the bat as it smashes the ball.
You run, run, run, hoping you will get a home run.
You feel the ball as it hits your well-worn glove.
You catch, you throw, and slide to home.
Just play and have some fun!

Cassidy Chainyk, Grade 5
Holy Cross School

A Peaceful World

I dream of a peaceful world.
Where kindness, respect, and love fill our hearts.
Hate and war would be no more.

Michael Malinowski, Grade 5
Staley Upper Elementary School

The Flag, Our Country

Through the air we see our country,
We see our flag,
We look at our flag,
To see the stars and stripes,
To see how much our country has grown,
And how much we have accomplished.
We raise our flag high in the sky,
To show the world,
Who our country is,
And what the world should be and what it should look like.
The sky loves our flag the best,
Because it is always flying,
With dignity and pride.
Our flag is like a lion,
Strong, proud, and rich with dignity,
A lion goes "roar, roar, roar,"
And the flag goes "swish, swish, swish."
This is our flag,
With red and white stripes,
Blue with white stars,
This is our country.

Colin Bayer, Grade 6
Harold D Fayette Elementary School

Thanksgiving

Thanksgiving is such a happy time of year.
Eating together with all of the family here.
Eating turkey, stuffing and pie,
so much food piled so high
It is like an awesome day in the sun,
Hearing all of the voices at the table having fun
While everyone is stuffed,
we calmed down and are to tired to be roughed.
We play games after dinner
Best of all we always have a winner.
We will miss our relatives but
we say our good byes and off they go
That was the best Thanksgiving I know.

Vinnie Gagliardo, Grade 5
Harris Hill Elementary School

The Bright Sun

The bright sun
shining in my face
I sit under a tree looking up at it
while reading my book
I wonder
Will I ever touch
That yellow sun
which shines all day?

Nope, I guess not!

Zachary Johnson, Grade 4
Magnet School of Math, Science and Design Technology

The Piano

The piano is fun to play
Even on a rainy day
It makes you feel good inside
And makes you look good on the outside
The piano is a big instrument but it has a beautiful sound
You can touch the keys softly, you don't have to pound

Julia Pettit, Grade 5
Holy Cross School

Upstate, New York

Camping is so marvelous,
Rocky areas are so colossal,
Mountains are large and sharp,
Trees wee to immense,
Grass as lovely as a flower,
Merry animals take a stroll,
Lakes and rivers petite to massive,
That is the end of my superb camping trip.

Courtney Hickey, Grade 5
Edward J Bosti Elementary School

Summer

Congrats, congrats you're out of elementary school,
Now you can relax in your own heated pool,
Run around and meet new friends,
Live some freedom until time ends,
You can score a touchdown or rob a homerun,
And go outside and enjoy the sun,
Relax at the beach, watch the waves go by,
Enjoy the summer, don't let time fly,
Create some athletic, fantastic games,
Don't let your house go up in flames,
Never relax, don't stop playing,
Some people are out of church, not praying,
Free at last no time to rest,
No more taking some vocabulary test,
September has come so back to school,
Listen up kids this is your #1 rule,
Your #1 rule is to raise a quiet hand,
Look over there, it's the Jonas Brothers Band

Zack Stein, Grade 6
Intermediate School 72 Rocco Laurie

Time to Pass

Spending time wondering what to write.
Spending time taking a bite.
I can't wait 'til the night.
I cannot wait 'til the sun is bright.

Hayleigh Shaw, Grade 4
Granville Elementary School

War

War is a puzzle of darkness
Confusion and pain
Both equal and hate
With a bit of of light
Anything can change
From enemies to friends
From vengeance to peace
From fear to happiness
All this can be designed
With a bit of light.

Juan Jose Duque, Grade 6
Long Beach Middle School

Love

Love is a blossoming flower.
The shining sun
And a blanket of snow.
Love is a beautiful pure heart.

L ovely
O ptimistic
V ery beautiful
E xciting
Love is me
Love is you
Love is everything!

Glory Estevez, Grade 6
Intermediate School 77

Butterflies

They   have
Many   talents,
Coming   from
Their   land
Waving back at you,
Shooting for the stars.

There is no doubt about them
While they rush past you.

Nothing to say about them
With their flowery scented wings

Just waving back at you,
Shooting for silvery stars

Rayna Sundown, Grade 6
Akron Middle School

My Dad

My dad works
At a metal shop.
It's called
JK Peris
He works
On a laser.
A laser is what
They use to cut metal.
His basement
Is very big and loud.
His office is
Also very big.
He has a big
Hole in the shop.
It leads to the
Next building.
At least one
Person bleeds a day.

Lucas Peris, Grade 4
Hendy Avenue School

Autumn Comes

Autumn comes,
Leaves fall.
August, September,
October, November,
All enveloped in a cloud
Of falling history
When
Autumn comes.

Tom Sheridan, Grade 6
Bethlehem Central Middle School

Thanksgiving

T hanking
H appy
A ll happy
N o one is mad
K issing all day
S miles
G iving to others
I nside playing
V ery merry
I nside eating
N o madness
G o home after eating

Devin Cohan, Grade 4
Granville Elementary School

Hope

Hope is like a leaf in the wind
Or a balloon in the sky
Hoping to go somewhere
But going wherever the breeze takes it

Eli Husiak, Grade 5
Public School 41 Greenwich Village

Summer

Summer's fun
Summer's cool
Come on!
Let's get in the pool

Summertime is made for fun
Summertime is for everyone
Summertime goes really fast
Before you know it's in the past

Summertime comes ones in a year
That's when everyone cheers
All we want is summertime
School's out so that's fine

Taranpreet Kaur, Grade 5
Public School 124Q

Dragons

Dragons fly so high,
Dragons soar so low,
Dragons blow their flame so big,
It could be good or no.
They could be evil so be aware,
If they are just please don't stare.
They could be good,
Hip hip hooray,
If they are you can soar away,
Up,
Up,
Up,
And away!

Chantala Murphy, Grade 5
Harris Hill Elementary School

The Rainbow

first a splash of red for every rose
a stripe of orange for every burning fire
a line of yellow for all the gold
a bar of green for the treetops
a segment of blue for the ocean
a piece of violet for the night sky
there are a lot more colors
without these though there wouldn't be

Nahshon Williams, Grade 5
Public School 114 Ryder

Highway

The road is empty,
empty like a big brown box
nothing but straight lines.
Road is black as the night sky
drifting off the road
like a quiet, slow, cold dream.

Elliot Ma, Grade 4
Public School 69

My Cat
There once was a cat that was lazy
Now that we got him I was crazy
His name became Skrachy
And he was very sassy
Now I like him because he plays with Daisys
Nathaniel Waugh, Grade 4
Granville Elementary School

Monkeys!
My favorite animal,
Outstanding,
Never ugly and always cute,
Living in the jungle and swinging from the trees,
Enthusiastic animals and happy as you please,
Hey, look at that monkey,
He really swings like the breeze.
Olivia Segota, Grade 5
Dickinson Avenue Elementary School

Autumn
Crack, crack, crack,
stepping, and crunch, crunch, crunching
the leaves, while walking.
The sky is getting darker,
and the owls have taken the chirping bird's place,
coo, coo, cooing in the midnight shadows.
The cold, crisp air I'm breathing in,
I truly, feel the season of autumn.
Yelena Khajekian, Grade 5
Holy Martyrs Armenian Day School

The Beauty of Kindness
The beauty of kindness
Can only be compared equally
To the beauty of a rose
The petals are
Good deeds
The stem is
All the kind things that we've done
The leaves are
The thanks we give when kindness has been thrust upon us
And the thorns are
The way we protect ourselves from acts of cruelty or selfishness.
Allyson Geiger, Grade 6
Woodmere Middle School

Christmas Day
Down the stairs you go
Happy and excited
You sit and wait to open presents
Excited, you wait to see what is inside the box
Look inside the box
It is something that you really wanted
All the waiting is worth this day of joy
CaiLi Wachtel, Grade 4
Sacred Heart School

Four-Wheeling in the Deep Dark Woods
Fast, dark
Disrupting the quiet
Of sleeping animals.

Flying through the weeds
Fast furious.

Covering me
In a coat of mud.

Climbing steep hills
Traversing around ponds.
Four-wheeling
In the woods.

Rubbery, rubbery mud
Squiggling around.
Trying to grip my tires.

ATV's.

Fun.
Wet.
Messy.
Doni Roehling, Grade 6
Akron Middle School

My Grandpa
My grandpa was loving, caring, and thoughtful.
Even though he died
he's always in my heart.
He always said he was next,
but I did not believe him.
My grandpa made the best tea and crackers
before I went to school.
When a car tried to hit me,
he would raise his cane,
and say STOP!
and yell at that guy in the car.
When I went home,
he made the best omelet.
that melted in my mouth.
My grandpa is ruler of the world in my eyes.
But most of all
he is my grandpa.
Jada Warner, Grade 5
Public School 203 Floyd Bennett

Anger
Anger is another person inside of me
That only comes out when I'm mad
When I'm mad the kernels inside me start to pop
The bad thing about anger is that you make some bad decisions
But all you can do is learn from them
Layla Said, Grade 4
Norman J Levy Lakeside School

My Brother Went to Boston

Where is my brother? He is not here. Where is my brother? He is far from here. Before he left I touched his face. I hear his voice saying goodbye, I see him walk out the door, about to take the trip of his life. He's going to Boston. The smell of his cologne fades away as he leaves. I taste my food it doesn't taste the same, it tastes dull. It's quiet I can still hear him laughing at the breakfast table. I just want him to know that I love him and can't wait until he comes back.

Autumn Bush, Grade 6
Immaculate Conception School-Stapleton

October 25, 2007

Born in a star in the desert at noon you fall from the moon and past the sun you land in your mother's arms.
The stars look down at you and the bees ring bells and the heavens watch you through your life.
It's like having an invisible sword everywhere you go.
It is like a dream.

Kenneth Petty-Merring, Grade 4
Upper Nyack Elementary School

A Great Birthday Party

My party was fun with festivities and games. My parents sang "Happy Birthday to You…". I saw the birthday cake in front of me. I could see its fire and I made a wish and woosh! I blew out its candles making my tenth wish for my tenth year alive. Then the party stopped as a party pooper stopped it. Then my expression changed rapidly as if I am in a mood swing. Then everyone got out of the room as if they disappeared from my life. Then I fell asleep in my bed. It was as soft as mashed potatoes. It was a great birthday.

Jose Rodriguez, Grade 5
Public School 148 Ruby Allen

Cookies

I enjoy eating, there is nothing like coming home from school, and
Smelling the familiar scent of chocolate chip cookies baking.
I can almost taste them, the crunchy buttery outside and gooey center with lots of melted chocolate, Yum!
I enjoy the sight of the cookies lined up on the cooling rack.
I even can hear the timer ticking just waiting to take out the next batch, and ding it's done.
Be careful! The cookie tray is very hot right from the oven; I think I will go now to get some milk to go with my cookies.

Dylan Malone, Grade 5
Harris Hill Elementary School

All Together

Waiting for the doors to open
Waiting for the door to success
Walking through the halls
More doors opening
But not quite ready to be pushed out in to the big world
Some of us are checking out each door while some of us are choosing carefully
Some of us are racing by while some of us are taking it step-by-step
It doesn't matter what we chose just that we're moving along, getting along all together!
Oh yah!

Autumn Grimins, Grade 4
Hendy Avenue School

Home Sweet Home

My neighborhood is where a rich, sweet coffee scent wafts gracefully through the air.
My neighborhood is a quiet, peaceful place to gently relax on the soft, cool grass and have a picnic.
My neighborhood is where friends greet each other with happiness to say "Salutations."
And it is as elegant as a blue bird singing its cheerful song along the street of Louis Kossuth.
And it is a marvelous place to see pumpkin colored leaves falling from the chocolate brown trees.
And it is a superb place to call home!

Alexandra Fazio, Grade 4
Helen B Duffield Elementary School

A Masterpiece in the Making
Light on the page of *darkness*
My pencil leading me through a jungle of lines
There, That's It!
The beautiful words make the paper shine

B-L-A-N-K
My mind goes empty
Like a sky without the clouds
But the ideas come to me like a sunrise on the horizon

Thoughts running
Racing through my head
I grab one
And examine it piece by piece

I let the words *flutter* through my head
Words appear on the dark page
The words form into sentences
There, a Masterpiece

Emily Dolan, Grade 6
Harold D Fayette Elementary School

Winter
W inter is cold
I gloos are fun to build
N othing in the air, only the smell of burning fireplaces
T aking snowballs and turning them into snowmen
E ating hot chocolate
R unning up a hill to go sledding

Samantha Hoffman, Grade 5
Guggenheim Elementary School

Life Doesn't Frighten Me
In this house I'm all alone,
It's so quiet I hear every moan.
Life doesn't frighten me at all

A creep, a step, a noise I hear,
I feel myself crawl right up into fear
Life doesn't frighten me at all

Those little bedbugs used to give me a fright,
I thought they would attack me all through the night.
Life doesn't frighten me at all

I hear the thunder, I hear the rain,
I hear a knock on the window pane.
Life doesn't frighten me at all

My brother's food allergies give me a scare,
Thinking of what he might do on a dare.
It's a scary feeling knowing he can die,
Sometimes I ask myself why, oh why.
Sometimes life does frighten me.

Lindsay Ricci, Grade 6
Long Beach Middle School

Ocean
A waft of salty sea air
Enters my nose
The sand is all between my toes
Clinging on to me like glue
The ocean is trotting to me
And away from me
Like a loved one moving on
The sun is letting darkness take over
The sun is moving downward
The sun
The sun
The sun is letting darkness take over
It is a big war
Darkness declares himself
The king of the heavens
The ocean CRACKS!
Like glass falling on the floor
And trepidation enters my body
And it is worse than a woman's shrill cry of pain
I walk away leaving my footprints in the
Sand

Kelsey Cotton, Grade 6
Harold D Fayette Elementary School

The Side of My House
The side of my house where no one finds me.
Tall trees bend and shade me from the sun's bursting light.
There,
I share secrets with my best friend.
There,
I remember my past when my grandpa died.
I always think my grandpa is seeing me when I'm alone.
There,
I am in peace.

David Bungo, Grade 4
Norman J Levy Lakeside School

Moving
Sharks are sharks swimming in the water.
Snakes are snakes slithering on the ground.
Kids are kids and we all have something in common,
Moving all around.

Dylan Jurnak-Lefflear, Grade 4
Granville Elementary School

Joy
Joy is happiness.
Joy is love.
Joy is freedom.
Joy is friendship.
Joy is what helps us have fun
and enjoy our life.
Without joy, life would be sad and miserable.
Joy.

Christopher Cioffi, Grade 5
Eastplain School

Fall…
Hooray Hooray Fall is here today
Summer days fade as Fall approaches
Say good-bye to the
smell of roses
Hooray Hooray Fall is here today
it's time for Trick or Treating fun
days go by as fast as they can
as pumpkins lit on Halloweens night
Hooray Hooray
Fall is
here today!
Alyssa Khan, Grade 4
St Benedict Joseph Labre School

A Taste of Summer
Hot summer's day
Morning comes
Through the strawberry curtains
Lettuce hills
And blueberry lakes
Cinnamon beaches
And frothy waves

Noon brings lemon sun
And orange rays
Trees of wisdom
And cherry flowers
With wind that tastes like berries

Then comes dusk
Heavier on the tongue
With a white chocolate moon
Behind cotton candy clouds

Hot summer's day
Melting
Into cool summer's night
Anna Blech, Grade 6

Unique Autumn
Whistling wind whipping around
Acorns tumbling to the ground
Songs of birds in a round
These are all Autumn sounds

Crackling fire I love so much
Wrinkly leaves fun to touch
Squirrels dashing up the trees
Turkey's ready…I'll have some please!

People skating on the ice
Leaves are changing…it looks so nice
Snow starts falling down, down, down
Autumn's gone…put on a frown
Sean Gatta, Grade 5
Edward J Bosti Elementary School

When I Grow Up
When I grow up
I want to be a teacher
When I grow up
Can't no one tell me anything!
When I grow up
Just wait until I grow up
I'm going to be me!
Ny'Kee Tucker, Grade 6
Graham Elementary and Middle School

I Am
I am intelligent on the inside
and strong on the outside

I can reach for the skies
to reach my goals

I am just one human trying
to make a living out there

If I just believe in myself
I can achieve anything

If anybody asks you who I am
just stand up tall and look them
in the face and say:

I am a mountain, I am an ocean,
I am the EVERYTHING.
Victoritchy Hector, Grade 5
Public School 203 Floyd Bennett

Many Faces of the Wind
The winter wind's a tyrant,
rich with greed,
ugly and frightful,
robbing your gold,
acting mean.

The spring breeze is a whisper,
quiet and calm,
soft and silent,
mild and serene.

The summer wind's a kitten,
purring in your lap,
playing with a ball,
taking a nap.

The fall wind is a prankster,
stealing your hat,
giving you a bad hair day,
just like that!
Adonia Low, Grade 4
Shelter Rock Elementary School

Friends Moving
"Good bye!" They say,
"I'll miss you!" I say,
my heart felt like
a puzzle with missing pieces,

Without them, I'll have no fun!
I thought,

Watched car drive away
and cried.
Giulia DiBenedetto, Grade 4
Public School 69

I Am
I am tall and active,
I wonder why the sky is blue,
I hear the wind blowing
I see the heavens open
I want to be a teacher
When I am older,
I am tall and active,

I pretend I am a teacher,
I feel the hot blazing sun,
I touch the clouds,
I worry about tests,
I cry when I get hurt,
I am tall and active,

I understand math,
I say you get what you get
and don't get upset,
I dream about being a teacher,
I try to do the best I can,
I hope I do well in school,
I am tall and active
Olivia Benevento, Grade 5
Eastplain School

Happy Holidays
Happy, happy holidays!
A time where there are no bores
Place after
Place, the spirit is spread
You should join

Happy Hanukkah and Merry Christmas
Oh, and look at that blanket of snow!
Leaving each house with peace and joy
I feel it too
Days where a family lights a Menorah
Another decorates a tree
You should join
Simply no time like the holidays
Rebecca Leibowitz, Grade 5
Ardsley Middle School

Horses + Me

"Check your diagonal, heels down!"
Riding my chestnut brown horse, Calvin
My instructor, Leigh, calls out to me
Breathing in horse smells all around me
I love their warm scent
Hot, sticky air all around
As I trot, I struggle to find a helpful breeze
One leaf takes the first step, turning a rich yellow
Cascades on my head to remind me that fall is calling
Leaves, like people all different, unique, but exist in one world
Ponies, like Tinkerbell, trots by
Ready to take children for rides on the beach
Clip-clop, clip-clop Tinkerbell is fired up to go
Purple ribbons in her mane, all dressed up
The last gentle leaf dances from the sky
My lesson is over, I'm as sad as a baby
Whose pacifier has been taken away
Without horseback riding,
Life is like
The season without fall…
SIMPLY IMPOSSIBLE!

Danielle Aglio, Grade 6
Harold D Fayette Elementary School

Stars

There are so many stars
some are red, blue, yellow too
have you ever seen a star?
They are beautiful.
Have you ever seen a shooting-star?
If you do, make a wish
so, it can come true!!!

Santiago Zamora, Grade 4
Magnet School of Math, Science and Design Technology

Blueberries

Sweet, delicious blueberries
You can find them anywhere.
In bushes, in trees, and stores in Tennessee.

You can pick them, you can lick them,
But be careful, they might have worms.
Don't forget if you squish them,
Some blue wet juice might come through.

They are fresh, they are sour,
Don't forget they give you power.

They are fruity, they are mellow,
They're very nice fellows.

Sweet, delicious blueberries
You can find them anywhere.
In bushes, in trees, and stores in Tennessee.

Bailey Clouse, Grade 6
Akron Middle School

Science Is

Science is, cooking.
It is flipping the onion bits in the pan,
chopping up cloves of garlic,
sautéing mushrooms in a skillet.
It is searing a flank steak,
hearing the oil sizzle and burst out of the wok,
watching the water boil.
Science is all of these things,
but most of all, science is cooking.

Aaron Tabibzadeh, Grade 6
Shelter Rock Elementary School

Heaven

Heaven, is there such a place?
Where everyone has a cheerful face,
Angels voices high and low,
Everyone's steadily on the go,
The father listening to all his sinners,
But no matter what, he calls us winners,
The faithful carrying out the news,
Some so sad they cause the blues.

Heaven, is there such a place?
Angels busy for the holiday race,
Waiting for a baby's birth,
Although it takes place on earth,
They have to have the choir rehearsal prepared,
The holy ones aware,
Hatred flows in the air,
But not when the father is near.

Heaven, is there such a place?
You may believe that you may,
But to this very day,
I believe in my father in every way.

Shannon O'Rourke, Grade 6
Intermediate School 227 - Louis Armstrong Middle

The Sunny State

North Dakota is a land of plains and plateaus.
The Peace Garden State
Makes the 39th state.
Come to this sunshine place,
Where you will find wide-open space.
North Dakota badlands have a lot of sand.
The Shoshone, Sacagawea made her home
On the prairies where the buffalo roam.

The Red River Valley has porcupines.
They might be poisonous but we don't mind.
The sunflower fields have lots of bees.
They like the nectar from the sunflower seeds.
North Dakota is really great.
It is like a perfect state.

Amarilys Cintron, Grade 4
St Andrew School

Alone

I feel alone when no one
but no one
cares
No one listens
No one understands
No one takes time out
for me
to see what's going on
No one pays attention
They ignore me
I feel as if I'm invisible
No one loves me anymore
It's just me, myself, and I
Not one helping hand
to support me,
care for me,
love me
I'm messed up
sad, so sad

Kyla Formey, Grade 5
P.S. 203

A Place Where I Can Go

The rich sand in my toes
Oceans roar in front of my face
Kites high in the air
Feeling melancholy

Fresh air in my lungs
Sideways crabs
Shells along
The shoreline

The beating sun
Decorative towels
Swimmers and surfers
Floating away

Jayne Hommel, Grade 6
Long Beach Middle School

The Beautiful White Doves

Coming down as little white rocks,
lighting up the December night,
turning into a liquid as it impacts
on the ground,
turning into circular balls in
a snowball fight,
it makes its nest on bare, brown trees.
a beautiful sight, oh yes it is,
it comes down as swift white flakes,
and into a glove,
because snow is a
beautiful, white
dove

Kalif Jeremiah, Grade 5
Public School 114 Ryder

Immigrant

I'm on a ship to America.
The breeze is salty and is burning my eyes
Down under the deck in the steerage huddled together in one room.
When I reach America, I'll feel so happy to be in my new country, unknown
Are the struggles I will face.

Dwight Chase, Grade 5
Public School 152 School of Science & Technology

If I Were in Charge of the World

If I were in charge of the world
There would be soccer and baseball
No other sport that's all there would be

If I were in charge of the world
There would be more
Knitting in math classes and more recess

If I were in charge of the world
School would be shorter
And especially, no homework!

If I were in charge of the world
There would be parties all day
And no such thing as too much or too little candy on Halloween night

If I were in charge of the world
There would be no such thing as cavities
Or dentists
And there would be more fun activities

If I were in charge of the world
There would be no such thing as chores or taking out the trash
Anyone who disobeys their parents could still be in charge of the world!

Alice Donnelly, Grade 6
Shelter Rock Elementary School

The Bright Night

The bright night is alive, with the secrets hidden among the stars.
The night is like a wide open prairie, made for everyone.
It's like a miracle, with lights strung from planet to planet.
Like a silk blue cloth covering the world, filled with beautiful lights.
Everything seems so perfect in the sky.

Emma Anderson, Grade 4
Upper Nyack Elementary School

Halloween

Kids in costumes running while crushing fall leaves
Green faces from witches flying in the air on brooms
Ghost making spooky noises in an abandoned house
Kids playing hide and seek during the spooky night
Adults scaring people while wearing costumes
Cool, foggy weather on our faces
Bad smells of witches boiling their poison soup to give people fill the air
Sad because the day is over

Junnette Checo, Grade 4
Northeast Elementary School

The Rose

Oh, beautiful rose!
The prettiest in the garden,
When I walk by you,
Your aroma fills my heart.

Jessenia Mejia, Grade 4
Magnet School of Math, Science and Design Technology

Life Doesn't Frighten Me

Ghosts outside try to come to my door
I don't pay attention to them any more
Life doesn't frighten me at all

Awake I stay in my cozy bed
Stories of vampires don't mess up my head
Life doesn't frighten me at all

Black cats follow me home from school
I'm not scared — I just stay cool
Life doesn't frighten me at all

A full moon glows above the deep dark bay
"How are you tonight?" I say
Life doesn't frighten me at all

Flying monkeys soar in the sky
I wave my hand and say bye-bye
Life doesn't frighten me at all

Night time creatures get set to come out
I don't freak and I don't shout
Life doesn't frighten me at all

Claire Fleming, Grade 6
Long Beach Middle School

My Sister's Blister

My sister has a blister.
It's on her biggest toe.
You can't help not to look at it.
It's red and almost glows.

She shouldn't have worn those high heeled boots.
She knew they were too small.
They rubbed so much against her toe,
But she wanted to look tall.

We took her to the doctor
When the blister got too big.
The doctor said, "Don't wear those boots,
And do not dance a jig."

She could be very pretty
As everybody knows,
If it wasn't for that blister
On my sister's biggest toe.

Audrey Flint, Grade 5
William B Tecler Elementary School

9/11 — Complete Confusion

The sound of an airplane above
People running for their lives
The sound of screams showering New York
A spurt of rocks from every crash
A cloud of smoke from every cry
People jumping off with hope in their eyes
The distant sound of sirens
Every face wearing a mask of hope
Every child silent in awe
Complete confusion

Nisreen Abdelaziz, Grade 6
Intermediate School 77

The Grass

I saw you waving to the trees
And heard you singing soft to me
And smelled your wonderful hair
Like me smelling a sweet, sweet pear.
O grass that is so smooth and green
O grass, most awesome thing I've seen.

In winter covered with white snow,
In spring you're eating the snow very slow.
I smell your wonderful soil
Like a baby about to be spoiled.
O grass that is so smooth and green
O grass most awesome thing I've seen.

In fall you're piled up with leaves
I heard you chatting to the bees.
All times, so sweet
Each time we meet
O grass that is so smooth and green
O grass most awesome thing I've seen.

Jillian Irving, Grade 4
Public School 124Q

Racism

Don't ever be racist,
can't you see?
It's just really not fair
to everybody.

Like people for who they are on the inside,
beneath their skin,
not for where they're from or what their religion is,
but what's from within.

Color doesn't matter,
black or white,
we should work together
and all unite!
Unite against racism!!

Alexandra Lambadarios, Grade 6
Shelter Rock Elementary School

Fly
Let your worries fly —
Woosh!
As fast as a jaguar
Under the night sky
Let them
Be free
Let all your worries
F
A
D
E
Away
And start
A brand new day.
Julia Alfarone, Grade 6
Harold D Fayette Elementary School

Oh, Winter
Winter, winter, snowy winter
One of my favorites
Oh, winter
Winter has us warmly dressed
Please Santa, give me the best!
Snowflakes falling
Smiles drawing attention
Winter makes me say "HOORAY"
One thing I would like to say
"Please give us a snow day!"
Kate Atkinson, Grade 5
Eagle Hill Middle School

Proud Being a Girl
I'm proud of being a girl
Going out
Having fun
That's what it's about
Hosting or being invited to sleepovers
Telling secrets that can never be told
To anyone else
Talking about boys
Giving makeovers to each other
Going on shopping sprees
Wearing cute clothes
Obsessing over shoes
Wanting the latest stuff
Putting on makeup
Being me
Being free
Being who I want to be
Being a girl
I am proud
I'll say it loud
I'm proud to be a girl!
Laura Belle, Grade 5
P.S. 203

Summer
Summer fun,
Summer sun,
Summer play,
On a warm day.

I go to the beach,
I swim in the waves.
I make a sand castle,
On a warm summer day.

Summer fun,
Summer sun,
I love when summer has begun.
Alyssa Turo, Grade 5
William B Tecler Elementary School

My Shoulder
I walk alone on this dark and scary
night, night, night.

Because everyone was giving me
a fright, fright, fright.

I hear a voice calling my name,
it gave me a scare.

I start walking fast, fast, fast,
but the voice is getting
louder, louder, louder.

I scream my way home

I freeze at the door to
find a hand on my shoulder

I turn around with a chill, to realize
it was my brother giving me a scare.
Ellie Daly, Grade 5
The Albany Academies

Forever Sister
You and Me,
Me and You,
will always be together.
Friends will come,
And friends will go,
But you always have your sister.

You and Me,
Me and You,
will always love each other.
Friends will come,
And friends will go,
But you always have that steady love,
from your forever sister.
Gabrielle Murphey, Grade 6

Him
I miss him so so much
I don't know where he is
He's either getting chemo
Or sleeping in his bed
I'm visiting him soon
She's been taking care of him
I'm sure he'll be all right
When I snuggle up with him
Madison Landau, Grade 6
Long Beach Middle School

Fall
The leaves change colors
Winds get very cold in Fall
I see the trees blow
The kids go pumpkin picking
Kids jump on piles of leaves
Adrian Rodriguez, Grade 5
Northeast Elementary School

Nature's Deer
Deer
Prancing by
In the open field
At the crack of dawn
Because the hunter is in the woods
Faith Thomas, Grade 5
East Hill School

Life Doesn't Frighten Me
People call
In the hall
Life doesn't frighten me

My locker is a mess
Please give me less tests
Life doesn't frighten me

So hard for me
To be exactly what they want me to be
Life doesn't frighten me

Getting up before the sun
It rises to make light for everyone
Life doesn't frighten me

Yummy food at lunch
Crunch, crunch, crunch
Life doesn't frighten me

With a clock in the room you can tell
The gateway to freedom is the bell
Life doesn't frighten me
Jamisen Beechler-Ernst, Grade 6
Long Beach Middle School

Alabama

I lived in Alabama
I always will be true
I lived in Alabama
After what I say you'll want to too

The sun is always shining
The sun is shining hot
I hear the coyotes whining
From light to dark

I lived in Alabama
I always will be true
The problem is I miss it much
The problem is I moved

Hannah Ann Robinson, Grade 6
George Grant Mason Elementary School

Life Doesn't Frighten Me at All

Spiders, roaches, slugs
And all those other bugs
Life doesn't frighten me at all
Icky, icky boys with lots and lots of cooties
They're weird, disgusting and odd looking
They just give me the snooties
Life doesn't frighten me at all
Stinky, green old spinach lying there for weeks
Staring me right in the eye
It just gives me the creeps
Life doesn't frighten me at all
Bad weather conditions coming at me soon
It doesn't hit in the morning but just the afternoon
Life doesn't frighten me at all
Black cats and broken mirrors
Just give me the fears
I'm not that superstitious and neither are my peers
When a Stranger Calls
And then Thanks for the Ride
Hide and seek, please don't peek
Life doesn't frighten me at all

Hannah Scelfo, Grade 6
Long Beach Middle School

Change

Colors of leaves transform
From green to red and earthy brown

Hot sticky weather, slowly turns to frosty white
A lone leaf flutters and falls from an oak tree

No one is outside, people huddled in houses
Great changes can and will happen

Even our state of mind changes

Dalian Moya, Grade 6
Harold D Fayette Elementary School

Friendship Wings

Friendship is like a butterfly
With two hand-like wings hinged together
They never fall off or break apart
They don't care if they are different colors or patterns
No
They just fly on together
Forever and ever

Caitlin Begley, Grade 6
Shelter Rock Elementary School

Soccer

S occer is my favorite sport
O utstanding
C reated by Brazilians
C razy
E verybody who likes soccer must practice to get better
R eally fun

Riley Bartlett, Grade 5
Harris Hill Elementary School

Fall

Lots of trees
with lots of leaves
And one by one
the leaves fall
soon all the leaves are on the ground
and people come and go
playing in the leaves
soon the leaves get picked up and carried away
for a winter wonderland to fall on the ground

Daniel Probst, Grade 5
Bretton Woods Elementary School

Water

The rush of coldness hitting your skin
So cold it gives you goose bumps
You want to jump out, but it pulls you in saying
"Come on in, it's fine"
You start to jump around and get used to the coldness
When suddenly someone calls you and you realize
You have to get out
Dreading every moment of it, you walk out and dry off

Bethany Frank, Grade 6
Most Precious Blood School

Autumn

Many things happen in the season of Fall.
The leaves change colors and start to fall.
We have our Autumn Fair,
Bringing all fun and fresh air!
School and sports return, giving us new insights.
Halloween and Thanksgiving give us trick-a-treating,
Filled with candy, friends and family delight!
Oh, so many good memories, let us always remember!

Emily Keane, Grade 6
Christ the King School

Eggs

Butter, mutter
Need a cutter
For the butter

Yellow, scrambled
Sizzling hot
Pan, fan and almost canned

Warm and fluffy
Toast is crusty
Starting to look a little rusty

Eggs and toast on the dish
Jelly and a swish
Fine time to dine.

Taylor Nikolevski, Grade 5
Harris Hill Elementary School

The Beach

As the big wave
Rolls toward the shore
The soft sand under
My feet stuck in my toes

CRASH finally it has
Reached the shore
Salty water hits
My face cold and wet

The water slowly
Rolls away toward the big blue bowl
As I wait for
The wave to come to me again

Amelia Veitch, Grade 6
Bellport Middle School

Werewolf

Do you hear the eerie howl,
Werewolf,
Do you sense his presence,
Werewolf,

He is getting closer,
Werewolf,
Can you see him yet,
Werewolf,

He can see you,
Werewolf,
He can smell you,
Werewolf,

Run, run, run,
From the werewolf.

Sheldan Clute, Grade 5
Whitney Point Intermediate School

The Woods

The woods is my favorite place to be.
I saw the woods the next age after three.

The smell of a burning fire
Is my only desire.

My first sight of the woods
Was the only thing I could
Focus my mind to see

The only place
I want to be
Is in the woods
Only me.

Giancarlo Luca, Grade 6
St Mary's School

Cold Fall

The apple pies are baking
They're really worth waiting
The swimming pool is closed
Ice cream shop has froze
The air is nice and cold
The hot cocoa is nice and warm
The teachers are in their cars
The heat is nice and blowing
and the bears are in their caves
they stay there all day

Christine Downey, Grade 5
Bretton Woods Elementary School

The Creamy Peacock Ocean

Swoosh, swoosh
Back and forth,
Porcelain waves flowing,
Streaks of sunlight filter through.
The salty smell
Of the rushing delft sea
Racing to cover my sandy toes
Envelopes me right away.
Plain, deep aqua on top,
Underneath more colors
Than you can imagine
Dashes of rose, of lemon, of lime.
Wait! Does anyone know
What time is it?
5:00! Oh no!
I'm going to be
Late for dinner,
That's enough time
At the ocean for now.
But I'll be back tomorrow
To see the sapphire blue flow in and out.

Tori Schlosser, Grade 6
Akron Middle School

An Angelic World

I have always wanted an angelic world.
Full of pansy butterflies,
Full of lemon sun,
Full of happy people.

Did you ever want an angelic world?
Not full of horrible things,
Not full of despise,
Not full of sour people.

Did you ever want an angelic world?
Everyone is blissful,
Everyone is gleeful,
Did YOU ever want an angelic world?

Samantha Ziarniak, Grade 6
Akron Middle School

Wrestlers

W atching wrestlers is so cool.
R ock is so great.
E ach wrestler is not a fool.
S lam is an awesome move.
T omb stone is too.
L oving it and coming to it.
E ven though it's violent.
R ay is so wicked.
S ome people won't be silent.

Ricky Baker, Grade 4
Granville Elementary School

Sun

Sun
blazing yellow
shining on me
so warm and cuddly
light

Katie Anderson, Grade 5
Most Holy Rosary School

Life

Life get one
Live it well.
Have lots of fun.
Don't be sad.
You only have one.
Live it well.
Don't be mad or sad,
Just live your life.
Rich or poor.
Be good not bad.
Money can't buy love.
Just live your life.
Remember life
Get one.

Theresa Guthrie, Grade 4
Public School 48

Candy

Candy is so sweet.
It's like a yummy treat.

Candy is so good.
We eat it in our neighborhood.

I would eat candy all day long.
Someone told me "Now that's just wrong."

All the sour ones are so cool.
But the peanut butter ones just make me drool.

But chocolate is the best.
I think it's better than all the rest.

All the candy in the world would make me glad.
As long as none of them are bad.

I love candy big or small.
In fact I love them all.

Chris Abrego, Grade 6
Long Beach Middle School

Up There (Blue Sky, Black Sky)

Blue and black,
Both in the sky
Right up there so high,
Right there in the sky.

White clouds look like cotton,
Gray clouds all forgotten.
We ignore them when they appear,
We say hi to the cotton clouds when they're near.

Blue and black, black and blue,
At night we don't have a clue.
Clouds cannot be seen,
You will have to have eyes that are keen.

It's there all through the year,
It's always up there.
No matter what place you are in,
It's always up there.
Here…Up there.

Taylor Greaves, Grade 5
Public School 203 Floyd Bennett

Spring

In spring flowers change color
just like the weather.
It's great to see leaves fall from a tree.
And feel the air in my hair,
It is a wonderful feeling
When spring brings new colorful things.

Edif Diaz, Grade 6
Immaculate Conception School-Stapleton

Friends

Friends are there at times when you are sad.
They make you laugh so you feel well.
If you are happy friends make you happier.
They make you smile on a regular basis.
Friends support you when you are nervous.
They give you a lot of confidence.
Friends are always there when you need it and even if you don't.
Friends are important in your life.
Friends.

Samantha Manalastas, Grade 6
Great Hollow Middle School

Ocean Life

The ocean is so bright
That you will love
The animals that swim
Their way through the cool water
That rushes through your face.

Swim on the mighty dolphins,
Watch the fishes try to find
Their way home,
But the shark does not let them.

So, go to the ocean,
See strange creatures,
And watch the whale
Push water out of his big hole.

Angelko Gonzalez, Grade 4
Public School 152 School of Science & Technology

The Rocky Secret

"?????"
It winds through the forest,
It's a home to many living thing.
It's a view no one forgets;
Its rocks can be a trap to people passing through,
It can trap its own boarders.
Sometimes it's almost empty,
But usually it's full.
Once you set foot in it you cannot leave.
It's the Delaware River!

Alta Sora Bukalov, Grade 6
Bnos Malka Academy

Fall

Fall is the time of year,
When everyone is howling for all to hear!
Leaves of red, yellow, orange and brown,
Are scattered all over our town!
Father is busy raking,
While Mother's delicious pumpkin pie is baking,
Giving us all a treat for the taking!

Danielle Ashworth, Grade 6
Christ the King School

Friendship

Friendship is about:
    Staying close no matter what
    Getting through tough times
    Doing anything for your friend
    Never giving up on a friend
    Calming each other down
    Not being afraid to tell the truth

A friendship will never die because:
    You always stick up for each other
    You know when to stop

A friendship is strong because:
    You care about each other like family

A friendship would die without:
    Laughter

Zoe Louis, Grade 6
Shelter Rock Elementary School

Mommy

I Love You
I know I get on
your nerves
and I am sorry
You are too
loved to be
disrespected.
You struggle
and
It seems
that I
don't
appreciate
it but
I do.
So I wrote
this poem
to let
you
know
I Love You

Tatiana Hill, Grade 5
Public School 114 Ryder

My Flag

My flag
it waves
and waves,
Nothing can stop it.
Not even snow
Not even water
It waves
but never stops.

Safa Bader, Grade 4
Public School 48

Halloween

Spooky costumes in the night frightening people
The color black and purple can be seen on children dressed as witches
I hear the sound of leaves crunching when people walk
I smell pumpkin pie fill the air
Children trick or treating into the spooky night
Adults give out candy to children dressed in costumes

Kyanda Bailey, Grade 4
Northeast Elementary School

Christmas

Once the sun goes down, the moon comes up
Everyone is talking, everyone is smiling
I feel the coldness in the air, the air so crisp
I know it's Christmas

Once the lights turn on the Christmas tree
Everything is gentle and calm
Everything is in the right place at the right time
I know it's Christmas

Once everyone arrives, the chatter begins
I see the family being loving and caring
Everyone seems to be in a great mood
I know it's Christmas

Once everyone sits down to eat, we all say our prayer
Then, rush to get the food my family made for us
We eat and get so excited to open our gifts
I know it's Christmas

Once we all get our gifts, we all say thank you
Everyone is playing, trying on, or putting away our gifts
It gets so loud in my living room from everyone talking
I know it's Christmas. Everyone knows it's Christmas, when the love is turned up a bit

Kimberly Halloran, Grade 6
Great Hollow Middle School

Charming Cedar Avenue

My neighborhood is where you smell dazzling cedar chips dancing in the air.
My neighborhood is where you hear a delightful baby bird chirping each morning.
My neighborhood is where you see rain preciously touch the spellbinding ground.
And it is leaves dropping gracefully from fall trees.
And it is where squirrels swiftly get ready to hibernate.
And it is an inviting place to call home.

Matthew Peleti, Grade 4
Helen B Duffield Elementary School

A Friend

A friend is when you're close with someone you are always with,
And remember to keep them close,
Trust them to keep your secrets safe inside,
Someone who you love and care for and they do the same,
A good-hearted person who is a great role model,
Friends help you as if they are your tour guide to guide you through life.

Kalah Johnson, Grade 6
Shelter Rock Elementary School

A Night in My Backyard
At night in my backyard
The wind dances around the trees.
At night in my backyard
The crickets sing.
At night in my backyard
The birds are in their nests sleeping.
At night in my backyard
Adventures await until morning.
Without all this —
At night in my backyard
Would be plain old boring.
Melissa Pierre, Grade 4
Public School 152 School of Science & Technology

Life Doesn't Frighten Me at All
When I try to go to sleep at night
I hear noises and get a fright
Life doesn't frighten me at all
Then I try to go to sleep
But I hear a peep
Life doesn't frighten me at all
Then I hear another footstep coming toward my door
It's starting to pour
Life doesn't frighten me at all
I hear another peep
So I take a quick peek
Then I see a mouse
Running through my house
Life doesn't frighten me at all
The door opens quickly and I think it's my mother
It turns out to be my brother
Life doesn't frighten me at all
I finally get to sleep
But only for an hour
It's already morning and I have to take a shower
Life doesn't frighten me at all
Chelsea Shoshana, Grade 6
Long Beach Middle School

My Boat
On my boat,
I see waves,
And birds flying,
And fish swimming

The sun is warm,
The water is cold,
We wave to the people that
Are riding their boats and swimming.

As we arrive to the beach,
The boat stops bumping up and down
As we touch the hot sand, and head for the water.
Jeannie Muglia, Grade 6
Bellport Middle School

My Haunted House
My little house is filled with ghosts.
It is quite a fright,
At the stroke of midnight,
When ghosts come out,
You give a shout.

The clock is ticking, you better run,
Oh this night will not be fun.
You hear a scary sound,
Of footsteps that go pound, pound.

So if you like ghosts and ghouls,
Then my house is perfect for you.
Here, you can take it,
I don't care!
Because tonight, I'll be sleeping anywhere,
BUT THERE!!!
Amber Knight, Grade 5
Staley Upper Elementary School

City Street
Walking down a city street,
Watching as the grey clouds turn pink.
People walking all around,
Through puddles,
Into buildings,
Green lights blinking,
Taxi horns blaring.

Dad and I stop to give a homeless guy cash to buy some food,
And as he says thanks,
We walk away,
Heading towards Carmines.
We get a table and sit down to eat and drink.

By the time we walk onto 31st Street,
It is dark,
But the city that never sleeps is still
Making tons of sounds.
A man is playing a sax and his buddy on the drums.
I'm sad to say I have to leave,
But Penn Station here we come!
Gina Marie Falk, Grade 6
Bellport Middle School

The Fall Leaves
I see the leaves on trees
I also see leaves fall from trees
I hear leaves going "crack"
I also smell leaves on the ground
My brother and I have leaves all over us
My brother and I jump in leaves
I like to have a leaf fight with my friends
I like the Fall because there are a lot of leaves
Zach Reardon, Grade 5
Bretton Woods Elementary School

Fall
Leaves fall everywhere
Pumpkins carved on Halloween
Jump on piles of leaves
Squirrels get ready for winter
The trees are dying quickly
Erik Andrade, Grade 5
Northeast Elementary School

Safari Sights and Sounds
Long grass
Calm lions
Giant giraffes
Weird trees

Hear a lion roaring
Strange bird calls
Melissa yelling

Fierce lions racing the jeep
Colorful birds
Flashing cameras

I wanted to go again
I lost my camera
I was sleepy
Dad is a sleepy bear
Mom is like a cat cleaning herself
Daniel Graham, Grade 6
Sodus Intermediate School

Friendship
Helping each other
Sticking together
Doesn't matter what race
Can develop over time
Always there for each other
How special it can be
Important to have friends
Everybody's different
"Beneath d'skin is all d'same"
James Farrell, Grade 6
Shelter Rock Elementary School

A Little Voice
All alone in the dark,
I hear a little voice.
I look around, but nobody is here.
I hear the little voice
again, again, again.
The wind is howling and growling
I turned around and I saw
what the little voice was.
Then I screamed, screamed, screamed.
Rachel Carney, Grade 5
The Albany Academies

Big Brothers
Big brothers
get on my nerves
talking on the phone
sounding like a

bee hive

"Bla bla bla"
that's all I hear
every day
and night
Christian Dumadag, Grade 4
Public School 69

Flowers
Each flower has
a special seed,

That makes each
one grow about,

No matter what the seed is,
it's sure to sprout.

So fairly enough
the flower will grow.

I wonder if it will
be row by row?
Maryam Banire, Grade 5
Public School 114 Ryder

Winter Wonder Christmas
Snowflakes falling
Down from the clear white sky
Awaking really early
To see such a sight like this

Coming down the stairs
Seeing PILES and PILES
Of these wonderful presents
As I get ready to jump into them

The lights on the tree
Are shining back at me
With its wonder of a smile
Winking with excitement

I hear the sounds of
The people still and asleep
But, I wonder when they will
Wake and see all the presents
Already surrounding
ME!!!!!
Sarah Clahane, Grade 6
Harold D Fayette Elementary School

T-shirt/Coat
T-shirt
short, cool
biking, dirt biking, skateboarding
soft, comfortable soft, puffy
Zipping, warming, velcroing
warm, long
Coat
Maxwell Arieda, Grade 4
Granville Elementary School

The Pest
I have a pest
His name is Drew
He's not the best
But he will do
He has a big mind
There's no other
He's one of a kind
He's my brother
Daniela Gazal, Grade 5
Holy Martyrs Armenian Day School

Green
Green is the color of a glasses case
Green is the color of leaves in summer
Green is the color of camouflage
Milton Peraza, Grade 4
Leptondale Elementary School

Alexander
Alexander
Nice intelligent
Son of Todd
Loves family very much
CRAZY!
Alexander Chichester, Grade 4
Hendy Avenue School

The Voice
It's a cold October night
There are many things afright.
I walk and walk and walk
I hear a voice it starts to talk.
It sounds like nails on a chalkboard
Now I'm scared I charge forward.
I run and run and run
I'm hot as a fresh baked bun.
I scream, scream, scream
The fog is as thick as cream.
The voice drops down to a whisper
I see my sister.
I'm home again and the voice is
gone, gone, gone.
Courtney Breiner, Grade 5
The Albany Academies

Football

I love to play football on a Sunday.
I like to play cyo and travel.
I love to play games with my sister.
I would like to help people
who are unable to do things for themselves.
This makes me happy.
I enjoy helping other people.

Mileidy Mata, Grade 5
Marie Curie Institute

Jaguar

Deathly hunter
Great swimmer
Black spots all over
Its eyes glow in the dark
They also gleam in the sunlight
Their teeth stain red after the kill
One of the best hunting cats of all
Its homes are in the jungle and in zoos
Dwells by its prey as it comes in for the kill

Jackson Smith, Grade 5
Harris Hill Elementary School

Fall

The summer breeze has left
and the fall winds have arrived
The leaves turn from green to yellow and churn to red
Leaves hanging and then dropping off trees
drifting away into the big blue sky
Good-bye my friend, summer, I'll see you next year
I'll miss you as you float gently and softly
into another part of our
World!

Angela Lin, Grade 6
Harold D Fayette Elementary School

Winter

Winter time is a fun time any time,
Morning time, day time, or night time.
Winter can be a great time.
Winter time is absolutely a fun time.

In the morning time for my brother and me
It is sled time.
In the day time for my cousin and me
It is snowball fighting time.
In the night time for my family and me
It is watching the stars twinkling time.

Winter time is a memorable time.
It is skiing, tubing, ice skating, snowmobiling,
Or even walking in the woods time.
Perhaps even drinking hot chocolate time.
For me, winter time is a fun time.

Erica Russo, Grade 5
William B Tecler Elementary School

Love

What is Love?
Is it an Emotion?
Or a spell?
How do you feel
When you're in love?
Are you happy, nervous,
Or sad?
I'm confused
I think I know what love is!
I think…
It's a spell of
Emotion
A feeling that
Cannot be broken
Love is a spell of
Emotion
Am I in love?
I…I don't feel it?!
Did I change?
I'm so confused about what love is
Do you know?

Annchloe Chery Theodore, Grade 5
Public School 114 Ryder

Chanukah

All the family at my house
Playing games and telling stories.
Light the candles and watch them glow.

Spin the dreidels and let the gelt flow
Eat chocolate and other sweets
Eat apples and honey, amazing desserts.

With all the family while staying up late,
Until the candles go out with the contest of whose stays lit.
The winner eats the rest of the chocolate pile.

It is the best holiday of the year
Maybe for you and definitely for me
Chanukah is great every year!

Matt Morgan, Grade 5
Harris Hill Elementary School

From Anna

F antastic
R arely plays with her brothers and sister
O dd, and clumsy
M ad that she thinks she's fat

A fraid to express her feelings
N ot perfect
N ot good in school
A fraid to tell her parents that she can't see well

Charity Warner, Grade 5
Harris Hill Elementary School

Candle

Darkness
Fills the room
Except
For that one light
The scent
Of cinnamon
Fills the air
The flickering flame
Is so relaxing
As the wick
Burns down
The sight of it
Is hypnotic
The warm, comforting, heat
Melts
The maroon candle
Till it's no more

Sarah DesGrange, Grade 6
Northwood Elementary School

Werewolf

Large teeth, scary sight,
Comes out on a full moon night.
In the night he comes with a howl
He will hunt you down
Without a prowl
Although he has no feelings for his prey
He is tortured every night and day
This is my tale
For the night,
But he just might
Be on your trail.

Drew Brueckl, Grade 5
John T Waugh Elementary School

Friendship

Friendship is what you need,
Friendship runs us all,
Friendship keeps us going,
Friendship helps us be strong.

James Pelzel, Grade 5
Whitney Point Intermediate School

My Sister

My sister
is as
tall as
a
giraffe
my sister
runs fast
like a cheetah
when she runs the only sound
you hear is ZZZip, ZZZip, ZZZip

Enyan Liu, Grade 4
Public School 148 Ruby Allen

My Red Rose

When I see you, my little world appears.
When you smile, my world seems brighter.
When you hold my hand, the sun shines bright.
When I hear your voice, my red colored rose blooms.
But when tears fall from your beautiful face, my world darkens,
Everything seems as though it was never there.
When you let go, everything falls apart.
When your smile becomes a frown, my world almost disappears.
When your voice stops my rose turns black and bleeds tears.
When you're gone my heart sinks and shatters,
Tears fall from the edges of my broken heart.
When you're gone there is always one place
I know I can always find you,
Even when there's not one speck of you left,
There's always my red colored rose.
Even when it dies there will always be you,
And my red colored rose, and my little world known as
My heart.

Skylar Trotta, Grade 6
Munsey Park Elementary School

End of Bright, Sunny Days

Baseball fields are closing, no longer throwing footballs,
now fiery, bright red leaves are crashing on the ground
Shiny, BBQ grills are closed, it's getting chilly
No more pool that's silly
The river calmly, peacefully slithering down
Winds whistling and swishing back and forth
Now a smell is no longer here the perfume of summer or
fragrance of spring because it's fall
Pale dark days as summer swimsuits are packed up in drawers alone
No more bright sun shines and easy breezy summer days
Back to homework and school
Tasting tart, sweet, and even bitter Halloween candy,
mummies, ghosts and vampires everywhere
Then Thanksgiving comes and the ovens are ready to have a
juicy, tender turkey and mouthwatering mash potatoes
And even yummy, delicious stuffing
So now fall is almost over and winter's here
and then we sit around a warm, toasty fire and
drink creamy milk or eggnog
and even a chocolaty hot cocoa

Annalisa Myer, Grade 4
Helen B Duffield Elementary School

Roses

How beautiful and gracefully the roses grow.
They sway in the wind and go so slow.
In the morning they bud again but when the night falls they fall into a deep dark sleep
where they dream about the things we would never imagine roses dreaming about.
Back and forth they go.
How gracefully their colors form into this beautiful rose.
Rose, Rose, Rose how they form this beautiful thing that confuses almost everyone.
They call it the beautiful elegant rose.

Caroline Smyth, Grade 6
Woodmere Middle School

It's Springtime Again

The rain is falling.
The flowers are blooming.
The tulips are growing.
The shrubs are showing.
It's springtime again.

Khaleed DeFreitas, Grade 4
Public School 152 School of Science & Technology

Hiding from the Real You

You are hiding from the colors of your heart,
The sun will still shine but you're in the darkness,
hiding from the light,
hiding from the good,
hiding from your real self.
You live the life people want you to live,
not the life you want to live.
Going down the other road,
not the one your heart tells you to.
You end up lonely,
depressed,
sorry for yourself.
You only look at the bad, never the good.
You realize how stupid you were as a kid.
You wish you could go back, redo it,
all of it.
Hang out with your real friends,
do what you wanted to.
Wishin' you would have been the real you.

Alexandra Cipolla, Grade 6
Holy Family School

On Its Way

I looked out of my slippery, damp glass window,
All fogged with crispy, silver snow.
My heart fills with joy,
As I know it's time to go.

I grab my tomato mittens,
And my almond scarf and hat.
As I slide across,
The licorice spiked mat.

I open the ragged sandy closet,
To be all set.
I steal my gritty, dank sneakers,
That give me the icy cold creepers.

I run outside
To become bewildered.
My lungs gobble in
The splendid lukewarm, buttercup sun.
Now I know
That spring has come.

AudreyRose Saviola, Grade 6
Akron Middle School

The Autumn Wind Is a Joker

The autumn wind is back again with a new personality.
He calls himself the joker.
"Come and play," he seems to say.
"I've got myself some jokes."
He'll grab my hat when I run outside.
What a joker he became.
He swirls the leaves around and around my legs,
Uh oh, it reached my head.
Then he steals the jewels off the autumn trees.
The rubies and golden treasures twirl around in the air,
Waiting to be tossed again.
He seems to say "okay,"
It's time for me to go,
And return some other day.

Elizabeth Harris, Grade 4
Shelter Rock Elementary School

Teddy Bear

My teddy bear, oh my teddy bear.
I love to take care of you my teddy bear.
Your fur is so soft and fluffy,
And you are so cuddly, teddy bear.
Your fur is white like a cloud,
I might get you dirty, and then clean you again.
Because you're too pretty to keep dirty.
I will love you always, because you are mine, my teddy bear.

Dakota Andersen, Grade 5
Staley Upper Elementary School

Fall

Thin green leaves blowing in the air,
Calm breezes rustling my sandy blond hair,

With a snowy white cat stuck high in a tree,
Old and ugly, scared as can be.

Lime green apples smushed on the lumpy ground,
With a mulberry ball, bumpy and round.

A long black rope tied to an old brown pole,
Miniature worms scurrying to a hole.

Thin green leaves blowing in the air,
Calm breezes rustling my sandy blond hair.

Chris Mayrose, Grade 6
Akron Middle School

I Drove a Golf Cart

You see me scared, I see water,
I see trees, I see grass, I see rocks,
I see cottages, I see birds flying too!
I hear birds cheeping,
I hear rocks crushing when the cart rolls over them,
I hear people cheering for me.

Jacob Datthyn, Grade 6
Sodus Intermediate School

Horse

Fun, joyful
Riding, caring, pretty
Horses are very fun animals.
Hannah Gould, Grade 4
Granville Elementary School

Buzzing Bees

Buzzing bees
Getting pollen
Somewhere in the meadow
Early in the summer
Because they need to make honey
Jacqueline Reinhart, Grade 5
East Hill School

Stars

Look in the sky
You see a million stars
You see the glow
That reflects on your eyes
And your house windows
The stars are like flashlights
Flickering on and off
Every second
And like a glowing Crystal
The stars are ineffable
And they lose their sparkle
When the sun comes out
And the stars throw in the towel
Then everything is gone
In a flash
And you wait
And wait
Till tomorrow

Stars

Sammy Hijazi, Grade 6
Harold D Fayette Elementary School

Ants in Pants

There once was a man from France
Who had lots and lots of ants
When he went to the market
With some ants in his pocket
The ants in his pants made him dance
Kyle Olivieri, Grade 5
Guggenheim Elementary School

Autumn Is Here

Autumn is here now
We start to clean up the leaves
When we're done, we play
Now we start to wear sweaters
At last, it is Thanksgiving.
Diana Cosajay, Grade 5
Northeast Elementary School

Birthday

Birthday is an
exciting day
eating, playing, and enjoying
I wear my new sneakers on this
Special day
Stefan Hutchinson, Grade 5
Most Holy Rosary School

Friends

Friends are nice.
Friends are people you can trust.
Friends are cool.
Friends are helpful.
Friends are fun.
Friends are funny.
Friends are always there for you.
Friends are very careful.
Julie Namsaran, Grade 5
St Benedict Joseph Labre School

Christmas

C heerful
H appy
R eindeer
I get presents
S anta Claus
T oo much fun!
M istletoe
A family gathering
S aint Nick is coming tonight
Julianna Marchese, Grade 5
Sacred Heart School

Life Doesn't Frighten Me at All

Very scary mummies
That's not really funny
Life doesn't frighten me at all.

Great big superstition
Skeletons with wide ambition
Life doesn't frighten me at all.

Scary big green witches
My they've got twitches
Life doesn't frighten me at all.

Large white ghouls
They're just big fools
Life doesn't frighten me at all.

Monsters in the dark
Frightening sounds in the park
Life doesn't frighten me at all.
Megan O'Connor, Grade 6
Long Beach Middle School

War

Don't you wish
war was over?
Don't you wish
it never was here
Don't you wish
we could all just wake up
from this bad dream
that puts us in fright and fear?
It makes us want to cry
and makes us want to run
from all this fighting and craziness
and those big stupid guns
But those people in that craziness
and fighting with that gun
makes me proud to be a U.S. citizen
I just wish they could come home
Shannon Horgan, Grade 6
Long Beach Middle School

Betsey and Denny

I just came inside,
A sunset orange fluff ball comes by,
A coal black one follows her trail,
I hug them both,
They're the best in the world,
I stroke their silky fur,
Soft as a pillow,
Fluffy as a cloud,
They're mine and forever will be,
For all of eternity
Yael Scholle, Grade 4
Concord Road Elementary School

Rollercoaster Wind

The wind is like a rollercoaster,
Going up slowly like a slug,
Stopping, turning.
Going down like a wild running horse.
Squeaking, whooshing,
Up and down.
Around in circles,
To the ground racing,
Speeding by,
Then it ends,
And we say good-bye.
Grace Hanford, Grade 4
Shelter Rock Elementary School

Autumn Times

Kids jumping in leaves.
Halloween festivities.
Leaves are turning red.
Everybody in sweaters.
People making pumpkin pies.
Sindy Diaz, Grade 5
Northeast Elementary School

What's in the Sky?
It is round,
Rounder than my face.
Brightly it stands
And shines,
What a beautiful sight to see,
The sun.

Denice Griffith, Grade 4
Public School 152 School of Science & Technology

Victory
My team tells me to take the shot,
It's all up to me now to win the game.
It's raining hard now,
The rain is dripping down my face.
The soccer ball is covered in mud,
I keep spinning it in my hands.

I step up to the goal,
The goalie is ready to go.
I set the ball down in the mud,
As I back up I hear the crowd is silent.
I tap my shoes in the mud,
I remember to take my time.

I know anything is possible,
I learned that every time I try something new.
I start to run,
As soon as my foot hits the ball, I watch it go through the air.
Swish goes the net as the ball goes in the goal,
The crowd cheers.
I am proud of myself,
I have lived my dream.

Sarah Jane Phillips, Grade 6
St Mary's School

In the Cemetery
I see grey tombstones
    everywhere.
There's not
    a living thing —
nowhere in here.
I hear noises
    everywhere.

In here, I hear
    wolves howling.
I hear owls hooting in
    the Oak tree
    with no leaves.

Then, I see daisies
    blooming next to the cold stones
And I hear robins
    sing in the clear, blue sky.

Stephon Salmon, Grade 6
The New York Institute for Special Education

Friendship
You can tell a friend any secret.
Be confident that they will keep it.
You fight with them when they tell your secret.
You trust that they will not do it again.
You care about them and they are so special to you that
    you can tell them your deepest, darkest secret.
You go on adventures and far away places with them.
You enjoy them and agree with them.
You can do all these things with them.

Elizabeth Lainez, Grade 6
Shelter Rock Elementary School

Liberty
Liberty, oh Liberty,
Please don't go.
You aren't a foe.
Stay and love for we love you;
Stay just a year or two 'cause we love you.
Year by year, day by day
I say to myself she'll come back and play.

Joni Mitsinikos, Grade 5
Munsey Park Elementary School

My Poem
is a tiger pouncing in my dreams.
is a bird singing in my breath.
is a teardrops melting down and endless pit.
is a snowflake falling on my smile.
is a clown dancing in the mirror.
is a horse chewing apples off my hands.
is a warm blanket covering my soul.
is rain falling from the sky.
is a tree growing in the palm of my hand.

Julian Kiesel, Grade 4
Upper Nyack Elementary School

I Wonder Why
Seems like a distant memory,
so far away, yet so close.
I feel like reaching out and hoisting myself into it,
Just to get a little glimpse of what I left behind,
for what seems like an eternity.
What kills me the most though,
is knowing that I can never have it back.
Not now, not ever, no one can.
When I think of the bouncy hot dogs,
and scratched up knees,
I wonder why it never bothered me when I had to leave.
And now knowing I've missed so much,
and can never have it back,
I wonder why I didn't ask,
to stay some more and see,
what life could truly be.

Adrianna Duggan, Grade 6
Munsey Park Elementary School

The Little Artist

Once there was a boy
Who was small and shy,
Then he grabbed a paintbrush
And some paint
And started to become alive.
As he painted he kept thinking
About what he should paint
Next with the blue or the red,
But he answered that question every time.
When he finished his masterpiece,
He felt bigger because
He thought if he can paint that,
He can do anything.

Molly Cantwell, Grade 6
Holy Cross School

Two Towers

Thud, thud, thud, thud.
Hearts collapsed on the spot,
When two identical buildings arose in a blazing fire.
A white jet collided with glass and stone.
Terror and sorrow, loomed heavy over the heads of the people
Who stood there, helpless, wishing they could do something.
Immeasurable cries were heard
As a loud BANG signaled defeat.
When the blaze arose twice its size
All hope was lost. Brave heroes fought off the blaze
And the blaze captured their lives.
A tear scorched its creator's cheek.
Darkness and pain floods
Floods the souls of the people that were present.
Thud, thud, thud, thud.
Hearts collapsed on the spot
When two identical buildings
Arose in a blazing fire
And on that day…
On that dark day…
All hope was lost

Lucas Hoffmann, Grade 6
Nesaquake Middle School

Christmas Colors

Red, green, silver, white.
These colors are a sight.

Red is the color of Rudolph's nose.
Green is the color of my Christmas tree.

Silver is the color of Christmas bells ringing.
White is the color of snow glistening.

Christmas colors are so nice.
As they shine it's such a delight.

Sarah Sciorilli, Grade 5
Staley Upper Elementary School

I Don't Know

I don't know what to do;
I have to write a poem that is brand new.

Maybe I should write a poem of stew or a cow's moo;
Or a fiction story about Kung fu.

I don't know what to do.

A baby's first sound which is "goo;"
Or a scary story with a ghost that yells "boo."

Maybe about the Outback with a talking kangaroo;
I got it, a witch with voodoo.

I don't know what to do.

Wait a minute; did you just say I got an "A?"
Wow! Phew!

Ricky Tegtmeier, Grade 5
Pleasantville Middle School

It's Fun

Children playing basketball at the park
noises coming from the trees Whoosh, Whoosh,
Whoosh falling leaves falling on the floor
brown, green, yellow, and orange Autumn is
my favorite time of the year

Jorge Ramirez Rivera, Grade 4
Public School 148 Ruby Allen

The Sun

I saw you heating up my pool,
Too bad I have to go to school.
I heard you'll make the temperature rise
Like a boiler of big size.
O sun you shine gleamingly,
O sun you shine so beautifully.

I saw you make the lights go out
And heard you coming, you make me shout.
I smelled your lava, burning hot,
When I'm in school, and working (— not!)
O sun you shine so gleamingly,
O sun you shine so beautifully.

Ashley Waith, Grade 4
Public School 124Q

My Cat

I have a very fat cat.
He is fatter than a 1,000 pound rat.
His name is Max.
He spends his days on the living room mat.
He chewed up my little Babe Ruth bat.
We discovered he was a beaver.

Abigail Munger, Grade 4
Granville Elementary School

Life Is a Rollercoaster on the Track of Dreams

Life is a rollercoaster on the track of dreams,
there are ups and downs.
My friends are there for the ride,
they stick by my side.
Sometimes the track gets broken,
and with our hearts we mend it back up.
The rollercoaster doesn't end,
it keeps going.
Sometimes our lives go too fast,
or we are feeling down.
Our friends help us up,
and we continue the ride.

Sarah E. Brablc, Grade 6
St Mary's School

Yellow Flower

The yellow flower in the dark ocean blue vase
Just stands there
Each petal shown equally
Making it eight inches wide
As it stares at the people
The people stare back
Each wondering the same
How did it get so big?
Hidden behind the petals and vase
Is a slim, jungle green stem
It struggles to hold up the heavy flower
A week has passed and the flower starts fading
Soon it will die
Not all flowers live long in a vase
Others will bloom
Stand and stare
But no flower will be as big
Or as beautiful
As my yellow flower.

Melissa Colopietro, Grade 6
Northwood Elementary School

Thoughts

I sat up stick straight. My feet flat on the floor
I don't know what to think
The past raced through my mind like wild stallions running
free across the grassy plains.
My emotions are hard to figure out. I don't know how to feel
happy, sad, excited or scared
It was as if my entire life was caught on video and plugged
into my head, playing over and over again, the same song
never ending, never ceasing
The world around me felt as if I could never die
and if I were never born
As if I was visiting for a few moments from another planet
and then I would return, back to where
I truly belonged.

Colleen MacBride, Grade 6
Harold D Fayette Elementary School

Shooting Stars

Whish!
    Whish!
There it goes by,
Make a wish,
It may come true!
Tails so elegant,
Disappearing into the black starry nights.
So beautiful
    So majestic
Here comes the wishing star!

At night sleep tight
As stars soar above you.
It dances so gracefully
Like a beautiful ballet dancer,
Balleting across the countless night.

Sprinkling their magic through the window
Showering upon you while you sleep.

The wishing star always there
To cheer you up in your dreams
Always here to rock you to sleep.

Crystal Zheng, Grade 5
Public School 205 Alexander Graham Bell

Untitled

It's dark and light,
perfect weather for flying a kite,
I wish I could but I couldn't escape,
I was walking through when I saw
a huge, terrifying, 20 foot long snake!
It snapped it's jaws and darted for my feet,
jumped over it's head and grabbed onto a tree,
it sank it's teeth into my leg,
then I had to wear a peg,
I was running through the grass and trees,
then I saw some chimpanzees,
they looked confused and somewhat scared,
then they saw I was not prepared,
they started running towards me,
then I realized that this was crazy.

Jack Markham, Grade 5
Honeoye Falls-Lima Manor School

Me

Part of me is orange
Which means I am helpful to others
I am friendly to my classmates
I am friendly because I pick up papers for others
Part of me is black
Which means I am brave
I am brave because I like to drive four wheelers
I like to ride mopeds and golf carts too.

Steven Wright, Grade 6
Alexander Middle/High School

Memories

Your smile, your laugh, your voice,
Slowly reappears into my view.
A memory of good and bad,
The significance of you.

Time is ticking away,
The clock's hands are spinning fast.
Only wishing for one thing,
Only wishing for you to last.

Your voice, very raspy,
A tube attached so you can eat.
A picture of you forms in my head,
A race I wish you could beat.

Please cross the finish line first,
Or at least let it be a tie.
I will really miss you,
And never will want to say…
Goodbye.
Brianna Licari, Grade 6
Nesaquake Middle School

Fall

Leaves changing colors
The kids jumping in the leaves
The wind blew the leaves
The kids went picking pumpkins
Halloween is kids best thing
Mariana Martinez, Grade 5
Northeast Elementary School

Zupan/Great

Zupan
Wild, kind
Walking, laughing, teaching
Mr. Zupan teaches his kids
Great
Kristin Emanuele, Grade 4
Leptondale Elementary School

Figure Skating

Twirling through the air
The breeze in my face,
I love to skate, skate, skate.

Gliding on the smooth ice
Spinning 'round and 'round,
It's such a wonderful feeling.

All the people watch me
Doing twists and turns.
I just love to skate.
Genevieve Dominiak, Grade 5
Holy Cross School

Snow

Snow is as cold as ice
It is as soft as a rabbit
CRUNCH, CRUNCH goes the snow
When I step

In
It
Seeing the snowballs fly
Across the sky
Now I smell the hot cocoa
Tasting it as it warms my tongue
Now my warmth
Is regained
Julia Neugebauer, Grade 6
Harold D Fayette Elementary School

Monday

Mondays are the worst!
I hate them I hate them so much!
After a nice weekend comes Monday!
You stay up so late during the weekend.
Then Monday!
Monday is the worst the very worst!
Everyone is so sleepy.
Mondays are the very WORST!
Brian Zuk, Grade 4
Hendy Avenue School

West Indian Manatee

Looking in the sea water,
Seeing something that looks like a rock,
Grazing in a position that seems to lock.
Eating a huge amount of sea grass,
It's grazing time never seems to pass.
Algae growing all over its back,
Being more quiet than a falling tack.
Living in an estuary or the sea,
The West Indian Manatee
Tommy Gaffney, Grade 6
Shelter Rock Elementary School

Oreos

Black and white
It's just so good, and round.
Who knows, I might need milk.
To dip it and enjoy.
I love it!
It is chocolatey goodness
It is what kids enjoy!
I should share so I need some more
…CRUNCH!
It's another good thing
OREOS!
I can't get enough.
Casey Banks, Grade 5
Public School 148 Ruby Allen

Life Doesn't Frighten Me

When I'm on the field
I get hit hard I wish I had a shield
Life doesn't frighten me at all
When I'm awake at dark
All the dogs are loud with their bark
Life doesn't frighten me at all
When I'm home alone
I'm scared to the bone
Life doesn't frighten me at all
Right before my test
I felt my heart beat on my chest
Life doesn't frighten me at all
I was on stage about to speak
Suddenly I was feeling weak
Life doesn't frighten me at all
The bear was looking straight at me
It was so big it was hard to see
Life doesn't frighten me al all
Not me
Not me
Life will never frighten me
Ben Steinberg, Grade 6
Long Beach Middle School

Soccer

Kick and run,
It's really fun!
Muddy cleats
run to the beat!
Get the ball back —
I don't care, just attack!
We won the game —
we are going to be in the Hall of Fame!
That's our game, it's what we do,
You should join in too!
Haley Gusew, Grade 5
Dickinson Avenue Elementary School

The Speeding Wind

The wind is a race car,
Speeding down the street,
Heading to the finish line,
And doesn't keep itself neat.

The wind is like a rollercoaster,
Going down from high,
As fast as the speed of light,
Not to ever deny.

Wind is like every
Fast thing in the world.
Wind is as strong,
As a truck being hurled.
Jeffrey Chin, Grade 4
Shelter Rock Elementary School

Beneath D'skin Is All D'same
Dark chocolate, white chocolate,
They taste the same,
So why should it be the color
That makes you want something more?
Underneath a tangerine and a plum,
Is the same juicy center that everybody loves.
Skin is but a color.
If everything was pitch black,
You wouldn't be able to tell somebody's race or religion,
So does race really matter?
If we all just linked hands, around the wide world
We'd see that diversity is good.
Look inside somebody's heart for friendship and love
We're all people.
We're all different on the outside.
But "Beneath d'skin is all d'same."

Alexia Mate, Grade 6
Shelter Rock Elementary School

New York City
Walking off the crowded train is like entering a new world.
The noise of the people fills the air,
People scattered here and there.
Cars are lined up in the street like packed sardines,
Honk! Honk! Taxis are clearing the street.
So many people, thousands of feet!

Everywhere I look there are different sights.
There's the Empire State building as high as the sky.
Rockefeller Center is too exciting to walk by.
Signs boasting Mary Poppins and the Lion King,
All shining like it's opening night.
Walking down there is a vision in lights.

Traveling through glorious Times Square
I am squinting to find my way.
The train station is just a short walk away.
I reluctantly make my way on the train.
When I finally get home I breathe the fresh air,
It smells nothing like New York or anything there.

I get ready for bed thinking about my day,
I reminisce as I unpack.
And I realize I can wait to go back.

Catherine O'Gara, Grade 6
Great Hollow Middle School

Life
Life is a long road, a hard road,
For some a road of sorrow and despair,
And for others a road of joy and splendor.
Life is more than we realize,
Life is all we know, and yet,
We know nothing of it.

Zachary Cohen, Grade 5
Public School 6 Lillie Deveraux Blake

Summer
Summer begins. Summer ends.
You better have fun with your best friends.
Singing, dancing, and having fun.
Does it matter what you do? So just believe in you.
Is summer the start of something new?
I think so.

Summer is awesome. Summer is fair
So don't be scared. Give off a flare.
Summer is great. Summer is the time to appreciate.
Summer comes only once a year. Will it begin next year?
I believe so.

School is around that corner there,
To me school is a nightmare.
Getting up at seven A.M., be prepared.
School is tomorrow. Go if you dare.
Summer has ended.
Boohoo!!!

Mackenzie Soika, Grade 6
Akron Middle School

Me
I am an athletic person who likes
to play different sports
like soccer, basketball, lacrosse and much more
Who am I?

I am a person who wants to be
an artist when I grow up
Who am I?

I am a person who has hobbies
Like sports, drawing, cooking and reading
Who am I?

A person who is trustworthy
hardworking and
has a positive attitude
Who am I?
I AM ME!

Olivia Belinsky, Grade 6
Shelter Rock Elementary School

Light
"Oh Naya please turn on the
light on this dark creepy night!"
"No no no, no light in the midnight!"
Finally my brother went to sleep.
I get scared to the bone thinking
I am alone
"Oh brother turn on the night light!"
"Uh, uh, uh, no light in the midnight."

Naya Fitzgerald, Grade 6
Immaculate Conception School-Stapleton

Pittsburgh Steelers

The Pittsburgh Steelers are the best.
Although them Cowboys are a pest.
They have won five Super Bowls.
The Steelers are just on a roll!
They've already won 7 games.
They do not feel any pains.
My favorite player is Jack Lambert.
He practically never got hurt.
The Pittsburgh Steelers are the best.
To me they're better than the rest.

Jack Lawatsch, Grade 5
Harris Hill Elementary School

Teachers

T hey're at school
E very weekday,
A t 8:00 am,
C hanging ways to
H elp you.
E very moment, they are
R ight there to make you
S marter than before.

Daniela Londoño, Grade 5
Public School 2 Alfred Zimberg

Ocean

The ocean's waves crashing
Are like a song calling to you.
The sea foam is like a blanket
Covering mother nature's creations.

Night stars as a light
To guide the creatures' way.
Shining so brightly
In the night sky.

The birds chirping all day.
Owls chirping at night.
Like a peaceful angel
Singing a song.

Megan Muhlenforth, Grade 5
Edward J Bosti Elementary School

The Great One

She's the Great One,
Or it seems.
Her name is Danie;
She's kind of mean.
I don't like her,
And she doesn't like me.
But we both know.
We'll never gain:
Perfect harmony.

Andrew Gazal, Grade 5
Holy Martyrs Armenian Day School

Fall

Kids jump in the leaves
The leaves are changing colors
Raking leaves in fall
Pumpkin picking at farms fields
Some chilly weather also

Angel Ortega, Grade 5
Northeast Elementary School

What Is Love?

Love
It's the thing
that parents
thought they knew about.
It destroyed
their friendship.
Love is a mistake
to some.
Not to all.
Is love a big red heart?
Does it deal with marriage
or kissing?
What is love?

Marsha Jean-Pierre, Grade 5
Public School 114 Ryder

Winter

Cold winter has come
Snowflakes are starting to fall
Snow like a blanket

Katherine Fernandez, Grade 5
Northeast Elementary School

The Night Bird

Their shining talons in the night
Make them look like stars in flight
Widespread wings and shining beak
I wonder what it is they seek?

They are probably hunting for prey
But they must get back before the day
For they are nocturnal, you know
But at night, they seem to glow.

We often think of them as wise
They soar upon the open skies

Snowy, Barn, and Great Gray,
Spotted, Saw-Whet, Sooty, I say!
There are too many owls to count!
Some are large and some are stout.

Elf, Short-Eared, Great Horned, too
I've seen an owl — have you?

Summer Moran, Grade 6
St Mary's School

Penguins

Penguins walk funny
Penguins can swim very fast
Penguins slide on ice

Carlos Maltez, Grade 5
Northeast Elementary School

Alex

Being silly is why Alex was born.
He does not like to eat corn.
He is nice and neat.
He has little feet.
That is the story and it is done.
It was very, very fun.

Alexander Burch, Grade 4
Granville Elementary School

Ghost

Ghosts are scary
Ghosts are white
They can see you,
in the night

Haunted houses,
filled with ghosts
they live in cities
or on the coast

Like Santa Claus,
they know when you're
asleep and they
know when you're
awake, but if they
try to scare you,
and say boo
you'll know that
they are fake.

Jessica Joseph, Grade 5
Public School 114 Ryder

Halloween

When the moon is bright
On Halloween night
Black cats are all around
Crossing the silver white ground
What a night for a fright

Tara Cook, Grade 4
Granville Elementary School

Dogs

Dogs,
loyal, playful
playing with me
always man's best friend
canines

Katie Barry, Grade 5
Most Holy Rosary School

My Family

My family is like a treasure
You will never want them to go away
Your family cares about you
They also keep you safe
That's why you love them
That's why you respect them
They are your only best friends
They will never leave you alone
Sometimes we could get mad
But we know how to say sorry
The next day when you are sad
They will try to cheer you up
When you are sick they will do the best for you
So remember you love them respect them
And care for each other in your family
That you are a group of

Kristel Garces, Grade 6
Long Beach Middle School

My Time to Shine

The stage manager tells me I'm up next,
I'm up next to dance my heart out.
Ok! This is it! It's my turn now,
it's my turn to shine.
I get on stage with the curtain closed,
the crowd is silent.
The music starts and the curtain opens,
everyone's eyes are on me.
The spotlight shines on my colorful costume,
I start to do my dance.
I see my friends in the audience,
all smiling.
The dance is done,
Everyone claps.
I am happy and proud.

Nicole Stamas, Grade 6
St Mary's School

Saphiria

Saphiria, your shimmering scales so bright,
Will you fight with me tonight?
With the Urgals we will win,
Let the great battle begin!

Together we will be victors
With my crimson blade,
With your silver claws and amber flame,
Let the great battle begin!

Watch the evil enemy fall before my blade,
Oh no, here comes the Shade.
With the Urgals we will win,
Let the great battle begin!

Noah Diebel, Grade 6
Akron Middle School

Thunder

When I hear thunder lightning appears
Scarier
than I could ever imagine
thunder
Scarier
than lightning
Listen to the
thunder
You'll be all right
it's just
THUNDER!
THUNDER!!
THUNDER!!!

Pavia Quamina, Grade 4
Magnet School of Math, Science and Design Technology

What's on the Inside Is What Really Matters

Color is not what I see
Friends is what I want to be
Your outside does not matter to me

I don't care if your clothes are in tatters
The inside is what really matters

We may be tight
We may never fight
But open your eyes and see the light
Realize that discrimination is not right

I don't care if you are black, white or even polka dotted
Even if your skin is purple spotted
Let's just be friends
"Beneath d'skin is all d'same"

Stephanie Rohn, Grade 6
Shelter Rock Elementary School

The School Cook

The school cook never makes good food.
You may see some fried fish eyes waiting to be chewed!

See some brownish, gooey salad moving toward the door,
Hear some students scream, shaking in horror.

Even sometimes you'll smell something in the school,
And believe it or not, but rats won't even drool.

And when he makes some bread,
You'd wish that you were dead.

These little greenish, glowing things he wants you to chew,
Oh my goodness, you would swear it was a witch's brew!

So if you're buying lunch today, I think he is making muck,
I only have one thing to say and that is, "Good luck!"

Antonio Alvarez, Grade 5
William B Tecler Elementary School

Baseball/Running
Baseball
Awesome, hard
Batting, pitching, catching
Feel good when you hit a home run
Running
Brian Gabino, Grade 4
Leptondale Elementary School

Fear
Somewhere,
Deep within our souls,
Lies a shadow,
It hides around every corner,
It slithers around every mind,
Into the darkness,
Into the air,
Into nothing,
The growing,
Fading,
Shadow.
Alli DePuy, Grade 5
Eagle Hill Middle School

Playing by the Orchard Tree
Playing by the orchard tree,
Imagining swimming
Like fish in the sea.
We will swim
Like we are free.

No fishing poles to catch us,
Hiding in minuscule holes.
We are not animal fools,
But we can really be cool.
Playing by the orchard tree.
Andrew Robinson, Grade 6
Akron Middle School

Vacations
Vacations can be…
long
short
exciting
entertaining
warm
cold
luxurious
tiring
breathtaking
and even a little weird

But they're always
FUN!
Jake Gulemi, Grade 5
Dickinson Avenue Elementary School

Sitting and Wondering
I sit wondering,
Where they are,
No phone calls.
No e-mails.
No packages.

I sit alone,
Still, no sign of them.
No anything.
I wish they'd call to talk to me,
And not leave me here alone,
And on my own.

I wish that they'd look at me,
And say I love you,
And not have to lie,
I still sit her wondering why.
Allix Freer, Grade 5
Whitney Point Intermediate School

Friends
Friends are brothers and sisters
They work together
They're nice to each other
And love each other
Friends are brothers and sisters

I love them
Reanna Grassi, Grade 4
Public School 69

The Dream
I saw an image,
From the mountains to the plains,
From the river to the desert,
From the beach to the highway
Under the boardwalk
And over the bridge
Sitting on the hillside
Up above
The image was a dream
A dream of life
Yasmine Resnick, Grade 6
Long Beach Middle School

Myself
I am 7 years old
I am a boy in third grade
I have 2 friends
Danny and Luis
I also have a sister
Her name is Margarita
I love to play soccer
It is my favorite sport
Santiago Reyes, Grade 5
Public School 148 Ruby Allen

War and Peace*
War is a terrible thing
hear the peace bells ring
in war there are guns and knives
peace is in bright blue skies
war has a lot of violence
peace is quiet and harmless
in war people die
peaceful turtle doves fly
war is a barrier blocking peace
but one day peace will
destroy the barrier
and the world would
be a better place
Max Esformes, Grade 6
Long Beach Middle School
Dedicated to Mrs. Panoff

Alone
Screaming, yelling, arguing
Alone I want to be alone
Fussing, huffing, frustration
Alone, Alone, Alone
Kicking, fighting, crying
Alone, please leave me alone
And now I am finally alone
But now I'm starting to think that alone
is a little too lonely.
Juleen Burton, Grade 5
Public School 203 Floyd Bennett

Mystery
Spooky,
Scary,
Clues
that you can find.

Detectives,
clients,
there are suspects,
that hide behind
mysterious
intelligent
good
and fun
to read!

I
love it,
We
love it,

Because
it's mystery.
Dorothy Mai, Grade 5
Public School 48

Jesus

My name is Rason
and I like to play.
But I always take time to pray
to my Savior.
The one who did me the favor.
He protects me,
directs me forever,
forgave me.
For there is no shame.
His name is Jesus.
And he remains the same.

Rason Jones, Grade 5
The New York Institute for Special Education

Fall

Oh fall,
Oh fall,
why your leaves must fall,
the colors can't be beat,
orange, purple, red, yellow,
some are green and very mellow,
there's also brown that falls to the ground,
some are crunchy,
some are straight,
some hold on forever,
while the wind must blow,
some say if you catch one it's good luck,
they're big,
they're small,
Oh fall,
Oh fall,
why your leaves must fall!

Gabby Leavitt, Grade 6
Plattekill Elementary School

Snow

I think snow days are very nice
Filled with friends, cocoa, and ice
When it snows I make snow angels on the ground
Hanging with my friends and fooling around
Having no school all day
Giving me time to play, play, play
I love knitting scarfs to wear
How they look I don't really care
My grandparents come to visit for a while
I'm so happy, I can't help but smile
The snow slowly melts away
Getting smaller day by day
I don't get sad because it will snow again
And when it does you'll see me grin
When winter and snow goes away, I say goodbye
I don't get sad and you know why
I love every season
I'm a loving person and that's my reason

Lucy Yang, Grade 6
Long Beach Middle School

The Missing Car

It was like
it was yesterday,
I can remember
the smooth seats,

the breeze
that came from it.
The smell
of sweet honey —

Where did it
all go?
Am I dreaming
or is this real?
I will never know.

Angie Dutes, Grade 4
Public School 152 School of Science & Technology

One by One

A
beautiful
day in the sky
when one bird passes by.
Then comes two then three and four then
came one more. They fly in packs
with twigs on their backs
with worms in their
mouths and chirps
in their house.
They ate
all the food and all in the mood
for happy singing with the
whole crew. They sing in the
morning when everyone is snoring.
Until the sun rises up in the sky above.

Courtney Dunning, Grade 6
Immaculate Conception School-Stapleton

Grandparents

My grandparents mean the world to me.
They are special, kind, and so friendly.
They get me gifts all the time.
I am so lucky that they are mine.

When they come over it is always a lot of fun.
I am always so sad when the day is done.
If they lived with us that would be great.
I would not have to ask them, could you stay late?

My grandparents mean the world to me
When they come over it is always a lot of fun.
I am so glad to be able to call them mine.
Whenever they're near me, I know I will be fine.

Ashley Martin, Grade 6
Harold D Fayette Elementary School

Alone

A lot of people,
Don't like being alone.

But I don't mind,
Because I'm all on my own.

Nobody in this world,
Can change my world except me.

I want to see,
What I can be.

A lot of people,
Don't like being alone.

But I don't mind,
Because I'm all on my own.

Natalia LaMorta, Grade 5
Public School 2 Alfred Zimberg

Am I Just a Slave

Who am I
Am I just a slave
Do you wipe me and work me
Cause of my skin color
Don't I have a right
I think I am a human being too
Am I just a slave
I'm a young lady who should
Get treated respectfully
I will make a difference
You'll see

Ashley Houston, Grade 5
Public School 114 Ryder

Questions

Why do I do that?
Why am I here?
these are the
hardest questions
to hear.

Why am I in trouble?
I don't understand
Why is everyone
screaming at me?
I didn't do a thing
Why, why, why
I ask myself
Will I ever
know when
to start
and when
to stop

Gina Leon, Grade 5
Public School 148 Ruby Allen

The Spooky Spooky Night

I was walking home in the night
until I saw a shadow that gave me such fright.
I started running, running, running
then all of a sudden, I heard a familiar voice, and I screamed!!
When I got home I called for my mom, but heard nothing.
Then I called for my dad, and still heard nothing.
The house was dark, and I saw something that looked like a ghost.
I felt like crying.
I was so scared.
Then all of a sudden the lights turned on,
and the thing that I saw, it was gone, gone, gone.

Sanchi Saitia, Grade 5
The Albany Academies

Friendship

Friends are friends, people you love.
Friends are like the water you need to swim in the pool of the world.
Like the pages in the great book of life.
Like the batter of the cake that is happiness.
As a wise person once said,
"To thine own self be true"
be true to friends, too.
If you don't want friends, you don't get friends,
but you also don't get to be happy.
No matter what, love your friends,
and they will love you.

Bridget Lavin, Grade 6
Shelter Rock Elementary School

A Pool in Florida

Sunscreen before the pool
walking to the seats on the warm tiles
Jumping in the cool fresh water
all my cousins coming in the pool

Walking to the seats on the hot tiles
going to the pool with my sun screen
all my cousins coming with me
we have fun racing in the pool

Going to the pool with my sun screen
running when they push me in
we have fun racing
Matthew, Ricki, Emily and Ross all my cousins in the pool

All we do is have fun while the cold water is running down our shirts
Shooting hoops at the other side of the pool
The love of the refreshing pool
Jumping in the cool refreshing water

The love of the refreshing pool
Shooting hoops at the other side of the pool
The cold water going down our shirts
Sunscreen before the pool

Maxwell Gilberg, Grade 6
Briarcliff Middle School

A Special Place in My Mind

A special place in my mind.
Where everyone is very kind.
It's my imagination, my very thoughts.
Everything's great. Including foods in metal pots!
From impossible to possible —
Dull to bright.
It's a really great place —
It sure is a delight!

Karuna Hadai, Grade 5
St Benedict Joseph Labre School

Stars

Stars Are…
Shining and glistering in the sky
Carrying wishes through the night
Up there so very high twinkling in the sky
Little lights in the sky shining every night every sky
That's what stars are!

Ryan Woodruff, Grade 5
East Syracuse Elementary School

Autumn

Autumn leaves falling,
All of them swirling down,
Like when close friends go,
And when smiles turn into frowns,
Autumn leaves too old to live,
Like our loved ones,
Tears fall just like leaves,
Until the trees have none,
The trees are lonely and bare,
Like our aching hearts,
But as the trees grow new leaves and heal,
So do our hearts.

Maishah Salam, Grade 6
G J Ryan Jr High School 216

Friendship

Friendship is a mushy, gushy melody
With all its beats and turns,
It's a never-ending song
That is ten trillion pages long.

If friendship were a movie
It would be a mixture of all types,
Mostly a comedy that would
Become the film of life.

Friendship is a gift so
Beautiful and rare,
That only true friends can share,
A gift so important you can only have care.
Friendship is a story you never want to end.

Rhiannon Catalano, Grade 6
Shelter Rock Elementary School

My Cat, Tiger

Tiger. She has the color of a tiger.
Tiger. She is always at the head of my bed.
Tiger. She is always at the sink for water.
Tiger. She is always near people so she can be pet.
Tiger. She is always coming home if she wanders away.
Tiger. She is mine.

Nadina Espinosa, Grade 4
Woodward Parkway Elementary School

The Penguin Who Wanted to Fly

There once was a penguin who wanted to fly,
Fly fly fly like the birds in the sky.
He told his friends, they said
Why why why?
They couldn't understand his dream to fly.
Then one day he flew to the sky.
The other penguins were jealous,
So they started to cry.
Many penguins have had the ambition to fly,
But not many can reach the sky.

Christopher Keane, Grade 6
Munsey Park Elementary School

My Friend

I have a friend that none will believe,
Every night she likes to sleep with me,
When I've come home and have had a bad day,
She always knows and wants to play.
Unlike my friend some people are pests,
But she's my friend and one of the best.

Maria Dewey, Grade 5
Whitney Point Intermediate School

Friends

They stick together.
No matter what.
Sometimes you drop them.
Sometimes you don't.
Whatever they do.
They care for you.
They've got your back.
And they know you're not whack.
The point is.
Friends don't care about how cool you are.
It's how nice and kind you are.
That's what matters to friends!

Anthony Faranello, Grade 5
Eastplain School

Make, Make, Make

Make a toy and you'll be filled with joy.
Make a play and it will be a wonderful day.
Make a fair and breathe the fresh air.
Make a door and you're done with your tour.

Xiu Xiu Li, Grade 6
Public School 131

Me
Tasnim
nice, helpful, trusted
I admire my dad
For fun I play outside
Favorite color is blue.

I love to read
I help people in need.
People help me
and I help them.
The book I love is
Charlotte's Web.

I love my life
and forever it will be.
Tasnim Islam, Grade 5
Public School 2 Alfred Zimberg

A Tree in a Park
The playful kids can climb me,
My rough skin is bark.
I'm reddish brown,
Living in a park.

Designs of swirls and twists,
Happy when the ominous sky rains.
When logging companies cute me down,
My ancestor life drains.
Brian Hulshoff, Grade 6
Akron Middle School

Shooting Star
There was a girl,
Who went outside.
One night,
She saw a light,
That looks so bright.
It looks like a shooting star.
She made a wish on
The Star that was so amazing.
Her wish came true!
Isabella Chittumuri, Grade 5
St Benedict Joseph Labre School

This Is the End
This is the end
It's game over
The ashes of life have faded
The staircases to heaven are open.

I have lived,
And I have managed.
But nothing can now
Depart pieces of a broken spirit.
Harpreet Singh, Grade 6
Harold D Fayette Elementary School

A Fruity Sky
The sun is a yellow lemon,
On a blueberry splattered wall.

In the morning,
Grapefruits and oranges
Come to claim them all.

At night a deep purple plum
Covers the ebony sky,
As if to say goodnight.

Blackberries come on a rainy day,
They do not look far away.

On a good day,
A juicy fiery apple
Will keep the doctor away.

Red raspberries and pomegranates,
Go and end the always changing day.

Every day,
A new fruit comes,
And blows them all away.
Leah Bisson, Grade 6
Akron Middle School

Friends Are the Best
friends help when
you are down
they pick you
up
from
the
ground
when you're sad
they
make
you
glad
they turn your frown upside down
when you cry they
make
you
smile
Emily Mercado, Grade 5
Public School 148 Ruby Allen

Tony
T oo smart
O n time
N ever too bad
Y ork mints are his favorite
Anthony Arbuckle, Grade 4
Granville Elementary School

Queen
"Queen"
Demanding, beautiful
Protects the people
Special to our country
"Crown"
Alivia McNally, Grade 4
Hendy Avenue School

Fall Season
I feel breath on me
October is a nice month
Fall is my favorite
I put pumpkins in my yard
I love this season so much
Samuel Turcios, Grade 5
Northeast Elementary School

Crabby Dumanni
Every day when I go to school
I alone think I am cool.
Everyone makes fun of me
Because I know how to ski
They all agree that I am a fool.
Dumanni Williams, Grade 4
Granville Elementary School

Life
Life is an amazing thing,
without it, I don't know what I'll be.
I can do a lot of things with it.
I can fulfill my dreams.
I will swim in streams.
I will fly in the sky.
I will make world peace.
I will stop a great beast.
I will help other people
because all I need is Life.
Caterina Gioino, Grade 5
Public School 2 Alfred Zimberg

Soda Jerk
Soda Jerk, Soda Jerk
the clerk that likes
to flirt. Rootbeer
float? That has to
be a joke, if you're
talking to him. Ice
tea? He won't be
nice. He'll give you
a riot if you ask
for a diet. Soda
Jerk, Soda Jerk,
the clerk that
likes to flirt.
Samuel Huntington, Grade 5
Sacandaga School

The Island

From running with the buffalo,
To swimming with the mermaids in the sea,
And watching the monkeys, thinking,
Why do they always copy me?

I feel the cool breeze blowing,
I hear the ocean waves crash,
Never wanting to leave,
And wishing to stay here on every eyelash.

I'm hoping to stay on the island,
The one I am attached to so much,
I have no clue, should I stay or go,
At home there's nothing from here I can touch.

As soon as I know it,
I'm back in my bed, what hit,
A tornado, a hurricane, a tsunami,
It must have been a dream, or was it?

Alexandra Majka, Grade 5
Eagle Hill Middle School

Christmas

The moon is up.
The night is cold.
The wind is passing through.
The Christmas tree standing
Tall and proud
In the middle of the living room.

The lights on the tree shone
As bright as stars.
So bright it lit up the room.
Stockings are being hung on the fireplace.
Carols are being sung.

My parents put out a plate
Of cookies and they
All went to bed.
As darkness falls, the house is so still,
Through the chimney comes Santa,
And his bag of presents too.

Ava Lam, Grade 6
St Mary's School

Garden

Mrs. Bosi's garden looks nice and bright,
All her plants grow in the light.

Flowers, vegetables and plants all around,
Grow as tall as can be up from the ground.

There are many colors red, yellow, white and green,
Come to P.S. 205 and see what I mean!

Joseph Giordano, Grade 4
Public School 205 Alexander Graham Bell

The Big Oak Tree

I had a rough day,
There's no where to stay,
Where no one is around.

I've heard of a place,
A very special place,
Where no one can call my name.

Oh I had a rough day.

The place is called the big oak tree,
Next to a calm river,
I read my book and fell asleep,
With the big oak tree.

I had a rough day,
But there is a place to stay,
Where no one is around.

It is called the big oak tree,
And when the wind comes it talks with me,
I have so much fun with the oak tree.
And when I'm done the tree sings to me,
And he says goodbye and maybe tomorrow will fly.

Victoria Studer, Grade 5
Whitney Point Intermediate School

Snow in Summer

I was surprised to see a white layer on the ground
And snowflakes falling round and round
When I went to bed it was a summer night
And when I woke up it was a cold sight
I wonder what happened over night
Then I thought something wasn't right
I looked up on my calendar and found out it was December 9th

Diandra Burton, Grade 5
Guggenheim Elementary School

Survival

Survive on a tiny cay
a mountaintop
or the Sahara Desert.
Your goal is to be rescued
and in the meantime stay alive.
You need water, food, shelter and
the ability to maintain a constant body temperature
alone you might go mad but
with too many people there won't be enough food.
Therefore, you must survive with only a few people.
Being rescued is the main challenge.
Build a fire to attract an airplane,
shoot a flare if you have or
just wait and pray that you will survive.

James Haber, Grade 6
Shelter Rock Elementary School

Page 277

Winter

Snowflakes shine in every yard, winter fires go on, animals start to hibernate, ponds freeze everywhere,
Things are happening that we don't know
Winter jackets are fuzzy and warm, there's people cuddling in every house
Hot chocolate burns your tongue Ouch it stings, you get a huge glass of cold water, take a sip, it's too cold, I start to shiver
I think I'll just take a minute and sit by the fire
Time to go outside, build a snow fort, make snowballs, get in a fight
Come inside, time for dinner, Mom's homemade baked potatoes and steak, delicious tastes in your mouth
Brush your teeth, disappear into bed, I'm ready for another fun day to arrive

Laurie Yaeger, Grade 5
Transit Middle School

A Child's Blessing

"Come here my friend, a story I'll tell."
Said my fine Grandpa, so nice and so swell.
"What is it this time?" I asked Gramps with glee.
"Is it fairies and princes? Or how 'bout that big bee?!"
"No, no" said Gramps with a grin on his face, "Guess again, my small pal, guess again!"
"Is it dragons that live in a magical place?" I asked. "Or maybe the beast in the den?"
"Not neither, my child, for this story is true, it is not wild, nor mild but as plain as the morning grass' dew.
You're old enough now to think about life."
"What Gramps?" I asked, "And how?"
"What gift will you bring to this world of strife?" Grampa said so seriously that I began to wonder…
A doctor! A cop! A garbage man! Perhaps experiment with thunder! I thought all these over 'till my head spun like a top.
"Gramps!" I said, "Oh Gramps! I think not like the others, I don't skateboard on ramps!
I don't play those games, but I love to do music! Oh I'm just not the same!"
I thought and I thought, and then thought some more. Then said with distinction: "My choice is,"
I told Grampa, "it can be bought, but it is meant to be cherished. I am going to bless the world with my words!"

Teagan Faran, Grade 6
Transit Middle School

Winter Nights

The brisk air awakes your soul as wild wind howls through distance,
Cotton soft puffs dancing down from heaven,
Bare dressed trees sparkling from a distance, so bright it lights up the night with continuous glimmers.
Down below your eyes lays a path of milk, covering the city with a deep pale sigh,
You smile as you sight such view.
For, it is another snowy night on another winter night.

Christine Xu, Grade 6
Intermediate School 187 Christa McAuliffe

My Lovely Neighborhood

My neighborhood is where birds chirp loudly to wake me up in the bright morn
My neighborhood is going to the delightful Helen B. Duffield with the enthusiastic Mrs. Alway
My neighborhood is the place where I hear cars come by and the loud train
And it is officially the finest place to learn how to ride my blue, shiny scooter
And it is where whistles are as loud as a small dog barking in the afternoon
And it is a sensational place to call "home!!"

Christina DeSimone, Grade 4
Helen B Duffield Elementary School

Autum

Autum leaves changing color make my heart flutter. Pumpkin pie spices too are just some of the great food. People share laughs and rakes. Autum is a time to enjoy other people's company and hang out. Picking out pumpkin and apples too makes everyone glee instead of goo. This is why I love autum so even when the wind blows hard. The cool crisp leaves fills me with glee.

Michelle Carpenter, Grade 6
St Ann Elementary School

Outside at Dark

As I wander outside into the cool crisp air
It caresses my face like soft silk
And I can feel the stillness,
Silence, it smells like an autumn's eve
Cars chug and zoom making their final roars for the night
Farther away they drift into the black, fainter still
Closing my brown eyes,
I begin to dream the night away.

Christopher Losak, Grade 6
Harold D Fayette Elementary School

Star Lab

Zenith is the top of the sky
So far away, so way up high
The moon has not one shape but shadows around,
We can see from below on the ground.
Red stars are cool, blue are hot
We cannot touch them, no we cannot.
Under the Orion Belt is where the new star nursery shines
It glows and gleams so many times!

Paige Amendolare, Grade 4
Helen B Duffield Elementary School

Why?

Why do I hurt so much? Why is it bad?
Why would I do these things to me?
Why do I cry so so much? Why? Why?
Why do I think so much? Why? Why?
Why do I do so much? Why am I sad?
Why does it seem so hard? Why is it bad?
Why do I cry?
Why do I hurt?
Why do I feel?
Why is it me?
Do you care?
Why is it sad?
Is it me? Why?
What happened?
Should you
be here?
WHY?

Christine Akinwunmi, Grade 6
Immaculate Conception School-Stapleton

Banana Plant

Banana plant so LARGE and BIG
You are like a "tree."
Your "leaves" are HUGE
Your stem is brown, green.
The sun shines on you.
The water pours on you.
Then you grow, grow, grow,
Banana plant so LARGE and BIG and *beautiful*.

Judy Kim, Grade 4
Public School 205 Alexander Graham Bell

The Sky

The sky is blue.
The mountains are white like a shining bright star.
It is puffy like a bright light.
The cloud like a cotton candy.
The wind goes sssss!
It looks like an ice cream on a cone and a skeleton on a stone.
The vampire cast with evil lights and thunder frights.
The rain goes BOOM! BOOM! BOOM!
Combines everything it would make a tornado.
WISSSS! It goes. WISSSS! It goes.

Kayra Chobot, Grade 5
Public School 148 Ruby Allen

Life Doesn't Frighten Me at All

I tried to go to sleep
But then I got the creeps
Life doesn't frighten me at all.

I broke something, that's bad
I knew my parents would be mad
Life doesn't frighten me at all.

When I would get sucked out in the ocean
Everything would come back to me in slow motion
Life doesn't frighten me at all.

I didn't feel good that day
I don't like feeling this way
Life doesn't frighten me at all.

I see strange people everywhere
Sometimes it gives me a scare
Life doesn't frighten me at all.

In the dark at night
Sometimes there's a fright
Life doesn't frighten me at all.

Krista Heidenfelder, Grade 6
Long Beach Middle School

A Painful Bite

One very spooky Halloween night
I had a big fright.
I heard moaning and groaning
then I got a bite.
A hurtful painful bite.
I was thinking ow, ow, ow.
Then I heard a bark, hiss, meow.
What was it a dog, a snake, a cat?
After that my hat blew away
I chased it and chased it,
but that was that.
I still wondered, wondered, wondered
what had happened after I got that painful bite.

Yasmina Sultan, Grade 5
The Albany Academies

Halloween

I see witches and ghosts flying around
I smell chocolate candy bars
I hear music from the haunted house
I taste candy corns
I touch buckets to put candy in
Halloween

Brenden Rogers, Grade 4
Belmont Elementary School

Wizard Wind

The wind is a wizard,
Bending tree tops at will,
Twirling snowflakes in the air,
Blowing your umbrella away.

He waves a magic wand,
And whispers breezy stories,
He howls scary tales,
And chills your weary bones.

He tickles children's faces,
He spins people around,
Steals their hats for fun,
And laughs out loud.

The wind is a wizard,
He whistles, he screeches,
He whispers, he roars,
He is beyond control.

Joshua Benabou, Grade 4
Shelter Rock Elementary School

Dogs

They are brown
The are white
They are friendly
They are playful
They are man's best friends
They are dogs

This is what a dog is like
I want one so bad that I
Would beg and beg forever.

I keep on asking for one
My parents say someday.

I want a dog so bad.
So whenever I come
Home and have nothing to do.

I'll finish my homework
So I can play with my dog.

Christopher Becker, Grade 4
Hendy Avenue School

Nature's Tomatoes

Tomatoes are plump and fat
Hold them carefully, so they don't splat,
The garden is their habitat
Now go and set them on the mat!

Marie Key, Grade 5
East Hill School

Soccer

When I got the ball
And passed it to Cole
I hoped he'd score a goal
But the funny thing is he didn't shoot
Instead he decided to scoot
So we lost the game
But we learned what name
To not send to
In the end
Cole!

Brooke Stanley, Grade 4
Granville Elementary School

Prejudice

Shipwrecked and scared
Alone with just each other,
Two very different people
One prejudiced by his mother.

The black man toils
Works hard for their survival,
The young white "boss" boy argues
He sees them both as rivals.

But time teaches a great lesson
In love and understanding,
It erases the young boy's prejudice
True gratitude it does bring.

The old black man is buried
On the small deserted cay,
The young boy that he cared for
Is rescued there one day.

The lesson that the boy had
From the time he was lost at sea,
Would change his life forever
A new person he would be.

Kent Schietinger, Grade 6
Shelter Rock Elementary School

Beach

Hot sand
Running, swimming, building
Marvelous and astonishing place
Seaside

Olivia Trunfio, Grade 5
Most Holy Rosary School

Arpita

She's so good
She's always in a nice mood,
She cares about everyone
She watches TV commercials!

She likes to help
She likes being an actor.

She is nice
    like mice.

She is my friend
    Arpita!

    I call her pitabread
    I call her pitapie
And I call her my
        Best Friend!

Arpa Paul, Grade 5
Public School 148 Ruby Allen

Pure Bred German Sheppard

Tan, black, fury
Loving, caring
Hungry, huge, protective
Biting, barking
Graceful, strong
Dog

Matthew Myer, Grade 4
Granville Elementary School

Colors

Red is for rose
and the color of my cheeks
Blue is the soft music or
the feeling when you're down
Brown is a bear and
the color of my skin
Black is the color of my TV
and my mother's car
White is the color of the paper
I write on.
gold is the color of the gold
in the pot.
Green is the clothes the leprechaun
wears when he guards the pot of gold
The gold and the leprechaun are
at the end of the rainbow
Waiting for someone to see if
they
    can
        find
            them

Alexis Nunez, Grade 5
Public School 114 Ryder

Sky Blue

The sky blue is a wonderful world —
Like being under the sea
or under the comfort of blue bed covers
Like being on the green grass
looking at the sky while the sunsets
as you fall asleep under the horizon of the
sky blue.

Jovani Lorenzo, Grade 5
Northeast Elementary School

Friendship

Friends are always there for you,
If you're happy or even blue!
Through thick and thin they're by your side,
That's what friendship can provide.
Standing up for each other is what it's all about,
Friends are there for day in and day out!
Through good times and through bad,
Friends are there for you when you're sad.
Good friendship can last through anything,
There are so many memories that it will bring.
Friendship grows more and more,
If you're rich or even poor.
Friendship has its ups and downs,
But true friends will always stick around!

Kelsey Connolly, Grade 6
Shelter Rock Elementary School

Boo!

High in the sky
a witch flies by.
Up in the moon
whistling "who,"
On her broom,
flies across the moon.
The moon is going up.
Boo is popping up.
Trick or Treat,
up in the sweets.
Another thing
coming your way
is a big
Boo!

Marijah Alicea, Grade 5
The New York Institute for Special Education

My Name!!

Xavier…exploding with uniqueness beyond control
Xavier…a name with not a meaning — but…
my soul what I represent — me
Xavier…a sheep not with its herd but on its own path to victory
Xavier…making you bawl and bellow for your way out!
Xavier…my name — a unique name — me —
the heart inside — the feeling you can't see!!

Xavier Brathwaite, Grade 5
Public School 203 Floyd Bennett School

The Way the Wind Can Be

What can the wind be?
a hawk,
a wild horse,
a glacier.

How can the wind feel?
harsh,
fierce,
strong.

How can the wind sound?
like a howling wolf,
a waterfall,
a frustrated sea.

The wind is a spirit that lifts you off your feet.
Use your imagination and let the wind carry you away.

Michelle Marcisak, Grade 4
Shelter Rock Elementary School

Global Warming

Roses are red violets are blue,
The world is in danger what will you do.
In a couple of years we could all be drowned,
We need something we need something found.

Winter will stop coming,
Animals will die out.
Hummingbirds will stop humming,
We will all go crazy no doubt.

Roses won't be red and violets won't be blue,
If you keep polluting we will die out because of you.
We can make a change if you give a hoot,
Every one join together and let's not pollute.

Andrew Dudziec, Grade 6
Our Lady of Good Counsel School

Autumn

Autumn is the season we often call Fall
The leaves all change their colors and begin to fall.
Yellow, orange, red and brown
Swirling through the air they fall to the ground.

O what a lovely sight to see
The colorful leaves under the trees.
Blown by the wind they fall into a heap
Into which we children run and leap
Jumping running and having fun
The air is chilly because of the fading sun
Soon the trees will be leafless and all bare
Letting us know that winter is near.

Kathleen Pierre, Vanessa McClymont, Nikita Streeks,
Brandon Telesford, Truel Polite and Neigel McLean, Grade 5
John Hus Moravian School

What Is Clear?
Clear is the color of glass,
Clear is air,
Clear is the color of water,
Poland Spring bottles are clear,
Clear is what fills your lungs,
Clear is the color of sanitizer and
the color of your nails,
Clear is not fear,
Clear you see it every day,
Clear is glass.
Brooke Palladino, Grade 5
Eastplain School

My Teacher's Mrs. Sini
My teacher is Mrs. Sini
my fourth grade teacher

Blond golden curls to her waist,
twinkling eyes on a dancing night,
sparkling lips bright and light
Every walk makes music

Nothing more than tender heart
JuYoung Lee, Grade 4
Public School 69

Summer to Winter
Summer
Hot, sweaty
Playing, running, jumping
Pool, lemonade, ice rink, hot chocolate
Sledding, skating, skiing
Chilly, frozen
Winter
Cindy Claros, Grade 5
Northeast Elementary School

War, Peace, Family and Friends
I wish this war would stop now
Bring peace to the world
Throw all the guns and knives away
And say the war is gone
And peace is now here
Go home and say,
"Hey the war is gone."
Now forget it
You're home in a bed
Having home cooked meals
And you are with
your family and friends
They are happy to have you back
So you can do anything
So you will keep
the friend and family door open.
Heather Weinstein, Grade 6
Long Beach Middle School

Life Doesn't Frighten Me at All
Spiders on each wall people I've never met right down the hall
Life doesn't frighten me at all.

Darkness and footsteps fill the room what could be behind me or whom?
Life doesn't frighten me at all.

Lightning storms in the air sounds of thunder everywhere
Life doesn't frighten me at all.

A car slowly drives next to me to get away I have to flee
Life doesn't frighten me at all.

Creepy monsters fill my dreams all around me I hear their bloody screams
Life doesn't frighten me at all.

All around I feel a chill like some nearby is about to kill
Life doesn't frighten me at all.

I have a secret that I hide I will never reveal what I truly feel inside
Life doesn't frighten me at all.

As I walk away feeling petrified but I say
Life doesn't frighten me at all.
Melissa Lukinsky, Grade 6
Long Beach Middle School

Snow
Snow is white and cold and some animals hibernate in the winter.
The snow is deep and the snow will melt when it gets hot.
And in the winter you can snowboard and make snow forts and have a snowball war.
Ice hangs off the roof, they are dangerous.
Chad Vaughn, Grade 5
Staley Upper Elementary School

A Day in My Life
I'll always remember when I stepped on the field
People could see that I needed a shield
Whenever I picked up that big heavy bat
I thought to myself run to that big white mat
Sometimes I needed to remember to hit the ball and not the tee
But alongside I could hear my parents say, "It's ok, Katie, you're only three!"
At the end of the game I was very mopey until…
I got my big blue trophy!
Katie Margherio, Grade 6
Shelter Rock Elementary School

Halloween
Bats flying in the dark night sending a chill down the spines of children
Dracula black cloak shining in the moonlight
The laughter of children getting candy
Adults handing out candy to the trick or treaters
Cool breezes blow leaves into the mask of children
Stuffed from the candy that I collected
Jason Melgar, Grade 4
Northeast Elementary School

Baseball

Baseball is so much fun.
I try so hard to get a run.
I swing my bat with all my might
Trying to knock the ball clean out of sight.
Around the bases I go with speed
Hoping nobody will stop my deed.
I fall and slide into home plate
And now I know it was all fate.
The sun goes down, we all go home.
I guess it's time to end my poem.

Brian Chamberlain, Grade 6
Holy Cross School

Water

Glistening on a domed web
Frozen on the ice cap of Mount Fuji
Falling from the welkin,

The sign of salvation in Africa
Prosperity in Egypt, when the Nile inundates
Dripping down the sides of the Three Gorges in China,

Misting up windows on a frosty morn
Delicate as a feather
A Tsunami in Indonesia,

I wonder,
If it is the same water,
As the water in my bathtub.

Bram Wang, Grade 5
Ardsley Middle School

The Nothing

Why NOTHING?
What about the NOTHING?
What's the NOTHING got for me.
I know. Nothing!

NOTHING is all around you
In the trees, in the bees
In the whales, in those snails
NOTHING!

NO.
What is life if it's not to be lived.
I don't want NOTHING.
I want SOMETHING!

Don't look at me like that.
'Cause I know you.
Who's on the phone, it's the nothing!
Leave me alone, you NOTHING.
Leave me alone!

Edwin Jacobellis, Grade 5
The New York Institute for Special Education

Shh…

Shhh…they'll hear you,
Topaz tigers creeping along the forest floor.
Shhh…they'll hear you,
Lingering for an evening meal.

Shhh…they'll hear you,
Clambering in and out of trees.
Shhh…they can see you,
Now you might be…
The next meal!!

Sidney Kolo, Grade 6
Akron Middle School

Ugly Little Anglerfish

Ugly little anglerfish swimming north and south,
Searching for his prey with his wide hungry mouth.

Deep down in the twilight zone with his beady little eyes,
Ugly little anglerfish searches for a mate to claim as his prize.

Although his mate is much larger than he,
Ugly little anglerfish is soon filled with glee.

On the tippety top of the food web they will stay,
Two ugly anglerfish searching for their prey.

Amelia Conner, Grade 6
Shelter Rock Elementary School

This Paper

Umm…this paper looks tasty,
Of course it's white,
I was getting SOO hungry,
That I took the first bite!
It was SOO good that it didn't fill me.

Then a few minutes after,
I remembered my essay had to
Be five pages long,
Before I knew it,
My homework was Gone!!

Kalid James, Grade 5
Public School 152 School of Science & Technology

Shaquille O'Neal

Shaquille O'Neal a hero to many.
He achieved so much and helped so many.
By the age of thirteen he was six foot eight,
A giant to some but an inspiration to many.
He helped black Americans to follow their dreams.
Shaq also did so many other things.
He did some shoot offs and games.
With some players like Kobe and Iverson.
He showed black Americans how to follow their dreams
So they could also succeed and live what they believe.

Caterina Giglio, Grade 6
St Catherine of Siena School

Grown-Ups

What is a grown-up?
They sometimes have fear in their eyes
Some grown-ups can have a good job
Can dress up sometimes
Having to go to college to be a teacher
That is a grown-up!

Chelsea McBain, Grade 5
J M McKenney Middle School

The Whirl of Hurl

The click of the belt
My frightened eyes
Large gulp
And shaky hands
Swoosh!
It caves down deeper and deeper
My stomach in knots
With eyes full of fear
We blast up!
My arms hang on for dear life
My hair blows every which way
The intense shriek
Of the others around me
At last, it halts
Everyone is shocked
Getting off
Dizzy as if the place were spinning
Looking back
Relieved that I survived
Yet knowing
That I'd encounter it again

Julie Vu, Grade 6
Northwood Elementary School

Candy/Fruit

Candy
tasty, good
yummy, colorful, big
sweet, sour — healthy, food
cold, good for teeth, different colors
small, excellent
Fruit

Briana Prieur, Grade 4
Granville Elementary School

Yellow

Yellow is like
the hot burning sun.

Yellow is like
a beautiful sunflower.

Yellow is like
my favorite fruit — a yellow banana.

Jacqueline Flores, Grade 4
Leptondale Elementary School

My Best Friend

My best friend is nice
She is like a mini mice
Even though we fight
We still stay tight
We call each other every day
Mostly in the month of May

My friend's name is Keanna
She looks like Breanna
She makes me laugh
She makes me cry
But she is really a sweet pie

Taranpreet Kaur, Grade 5
Public School 124Q

Clover

You were a bird,
You had horrible times,
You liked to chew on my dad's hat,
I wish you were here.
You were cheerful and healthy,
Out of the great times I've had,
You were the best.
I don't know if you are still out there,
You flew away on New Year's day,
And my parents even cried.
You were gone without warning,
And now you are gone forever.

Emily Fiorenza, Grade 5
Whitney Point Intermediate School

My Soul Chills

Autumn chills my soul
Wearing sweaters is so warm
Jumping in a hill
Pumpkin picking is so nice
Seeing leaves fall in air

Hilcia Argueta, Grade 5
Northeast Elementary School

Birds

Birds are turquoise blue
As blue as sapphire.

Birds are crimson red
As red as strawberry colored roses.

Birds have feelings
Like you and me.

But when they go out for the day
They have no way
To lock their house with a key.

Deegan Lotz, Grade 6
Akron Middle School

The Beach

Sunny warm place
My reading
relaxing
loving spot
I love the Beach
because…
I get fantastic
warm
wet
sppllaaassshhh!

Lauren Hernandez, Grade 5
Public School 114 Ryder

Fall and Halloween

You pick red apples
You watch tree leaves change colors
Halloween pumpkins
Make your costumes real scary
Halloween's a scary night!

Anthony Wills, Grade 5
Northeast Elementary School

Best Friends Forever

Staying up talking all night.
When you're sad they make it all right.
There to catch you when you fall.
Standing by you through it all.
Friends.
More like sister.
Always together,
Best friends forever.

Ashley Mascolo, Grade 6
Long Beach Middle School

A Stressful School Day

On your way to your locker…
Plop!
Everyone stops…
A shoelace can do *so* much!

Wait a minute! The locker's jammed!
The janitor is on duty in the lunchroom,
This is…
The day of doom!

We had THAT for homework last night?
Are you sure you're right?
There goes my grade…
My parents' happiness will swiftly fade.

Can this day get any worse?!
I hope not…
But,
It probably will!

Mimi Sillings, Grade 6
Briarcliff Middle School

My World

In my world,
Nobody can be harmed

In my world,
There is peace

In my world,
People can be what they want

I wish my world could be reality,
But the world we live in
Has little peace, people can get harmed,
And people can't always be what they want

I hope someday I can make things right,
But I can't always make it my way

In my world, everybody wins
In my world, everything is right

Iain J. Bopp, Grade 6
St Mary's School

Halloween

Orange pumpkins waiting to be carved
Red blood on scary costumes
Leaves crumbling and crunching
Delicious smells of apple pie floating through the air
Children scaring everyone
Adults playing tricks on kids
Cool swirls of wind blowing against my body
Sad because no more candy will be given out

Desiree Vasquez, Grade 4
Northeast Elementary School

Blue

Blue is the color of the shimmering water,
Blue is the color of my eyes,
Blue is the color of a juicy blueberry,
Blue is the color of my pants.

Anna Smith, Grade 4
Leptondale Elementary School

Marigold

Shining in the sun like the color of gold.
When it is rainy, it is orange instead.
Yellow like the sun and some red too.
It's a beautiful sight for me and you.
It's not so high that it can't touch the sky.
Red like rose and shimmering in the light.
The color is normally very light.
It smells so sweet and it is surely a treat.
It smells like a rose as it is to a daisy.
Marigold, marigold you are so light.
It has seemed to make me very bright.

Joelle Desrosiers, Grade 4
Public School 205 Alexander Graham Bell

My First Time Swimming

I see people swimming in the water,
I see long white bleachers,
I see locker room doors closing,
I see little kids wearing floaties,
I see the water splashing from the diving board,

I hear the water splashing
I hear people talking,
I hear people screaming as loud as a lion,
I hear people going off the diving board,

I am swimming in the pool,
I am playing with my uncle and brother,
I am talking to my brother,
I am going under water,
I am going off the diving board,

I wanted to keep swimming all night,
I wanted everyone to stay and swim,
I want to go in the deep end again.

Jessica Daniels, Grade 6
Sodus Intermediate School

New York City

When I am in New York,
I hear the police cars' sirens screaming
And the sirens of the fire trucks.
People are singing softly
Others are talking loudly.
The music I hear is pumping
Very, very loud.
The ice cream truck comes with ringing bells
And children run squealing to catch it.
At night, dogs bark
As you walk by.
In the morning,
People honk their horns to get to their destination.

Nancy Banger, Grade 4
Public School 124Q

The Wind Is a Bully

The wind is a bully,
Pushing, pounding and shoving at the waves,
Yelling mean names at the leaves,
Pummeling all the houses like crazy,
Destroying and tossing around everything in its way.

The wind is a bully,
So destructive and strong,
The waves are at the mercy of the wind night and day.
The wind is a bully because it has no pity
For anything that is in its path,
So I suggest you stay away!

Tucker Quinn, Grade 4
Shelter Rock Elementary School

spring

spring is a time for flowers
you can just sit and watch for hours
also there's lots of rain
if lightning comes sometimes pain

the birds fly so high
you can see them in the sky
spring is a time for farming
spring is just so charming

spring is the time when bees come out
if they sting you might let out a shout
spring is a time to go outdoors
I hate when it pours
Jonathan Fannetti, Grade 5
East Syracuse Elementary School

The Wind Is a Cheetah

The wind is a cheetah,
So fast and so slick,
Ferocious it is,
It will claw at everything it can reach.

The wind is a cheetah,
Black blotchy spots,
Sharp claws,
A slim body,
And a wispy tail.

The wind is a cheetah.
Alexander Haber, Grade 4
Shelter Rock Elementary School

Winter

Winter is coming
Winter is cold
I see some snow
Ho Ho Ho

The ground is white
Oh what a sight
I see reindeer
they're here! They're here!

I am so delighted and so excited
my heart is pumping oh so fast.
this is a moment that
will totally last

I'm getting on my snow suit
hat and coat too!
I'm so excited
How about you?
Dianne Guzman, Grade 6
Long Beach Middle School

Graveyard Shadows

Graveyard shadows
Upon the night wall,
Shadows, shadows,
I see them all.

Looking around
This place at night,
I'm full of terror
Dread and fright.

See the creepy ghost
Floating there,
Don't go near him,
If you dare.

He tried to chase me
Through the dark night
I ran so fast,
He was out of sight.

Suddenly I stopped
Without a sound,
The ghost was
Nowhere to be found.
Brooke Favale, Grade 6
Akron Middle School

Friends

F un to be around
R ight by your side
I ntelligent
E very day they are there
N ot mean
D elightful
S o nice

Kayla Bogdan, Grade 5
William B Tecler Elementary School

Jailene

Jailene
wise, silent
climbing, running, skipping
fun to talk with
sister
Jailene Pineda, Grade 4
Northeast Elementary School

Explode

Poems are not easy for me to write,
When I write I feel like I might
EXPLODE!
Because it makes me very mad,
And all my poems are very bad,
So please don't assign this again!
Caitlin James, Grade 5
Whitney Point Intermediate School

Fish

Fish
smooth, swift
swimming, flopping, sleeping
misunderstood to people's view
fishing
David Siegel, Grade 5
Most Holy Rosary School

Kangaroos

Jumping and jumping
Leaping so high,
Kangaroos are hard to describe.

They come in all different sizes.
This huge animal is
The biggest natural threat.

But when they come to you,
Kangaroos are the cutest
Things yet.
Mardi Mangus, Grade 6
Akron Middle School

Wind

As the wind whispers,
whoosh, whoosh,
a cold spear of wind
passes through you,
if you close your eyes
you will lift off and fly,
you feel weightless
as you soar through the sky,
the clouds blow away,
you leave the wind behind,
you start to fall,
you're falling, falling,
you start to land,
you open your eyes,
whoosh, whoosh,
the wind whispers.
Jesse Noppe-Brandon, Grade 5
Public School 41 Greenwich Village

Chocolate

Dark, milk, and white
A tasty treasure
That melts in your mouth
So rich and warm like a hot summer day
Staring at me
As tan as a teddy bear
It runs down my mouth
While it starts to get warm
I love chocolate
Daniya Mathew, Grade 4
Concord Road Elementary School

Life

Life is a beginning
Life can be short or long
Life is easy and hard
Life can be funny or sad
Life is sweet and sour
Life can be an adventure
Life is simple and complex
Life can be a task or an enjoyment
Life is a gift that is given

To have lived a good life, the *final goal*!

Courtney Sutton, Grade 6
SS Peter and Paul School

The Colors of the People

What are the colors of the people?
Are they blue or red or green, yellow, orange, purple?
Are they white or black or silver and gold?
They are many colors, all shapes and sizes.
We all may look different,
But on the inside we are all the same.
What makes you better than me?
What makes me better than you?
We are all mothers and fathers, and sisters and brothers.
Don't we all believe in the same color red?
Red is on the inside,
The color of our hearts,
It doesn't matter what we look like,
But the colors of our attitude.
I'm feeling blue like a teardrop
Well, I'm feeling green with envy.
I'm feeling red like a red, red rose,
And I'm feeling yellow like the sun!!!
We all have different color skin,
But what really matters is the
Color of our feelings for one another!!!

Keagan Hanley, Grade 6
Shelter Rock Elementary School

Papou

His memory lost, his slate wiped clean,
I remember him, but he doesn't remember me.

My family and I go to visit,
He doesn't know the difference.
I remember him, but he doesn't remember me.

I sit and reminisce of the times
He took me to the park and played with me.
I remember him, but he doesn't remember me.

His memory lost, his slate wiped clean,
I remember him, but he doesn't remember me.

Andreas Balasis, Grade 6
Ronkonkoma Jr High School

Pets

My pets are cool,
My pets are strange,
My pets are great in every way.

I have two geckos,
A dog, a ferret, a parrot too,
Three cats, and man how they act like they own the land.

I would also like to add,
I have two little sisters,
And a pig of a dad!

Kaitlyn Hamm, Grade 5
Staley Upper Elementary School

Snow Snow

The snow falls down on a wintery day
little flakes in the sky floating
down to the ground sinking and melting.
cold shiver go inside get covered and get warm
close your windows look out and say goodbye to summer
hello winter

Jeton Gashi, Grade 5
Public School 105 Senator Abraham Bernste

Ice Cream Colors

We have ice cream the best in town
Let us begin with chocolate and brown
Now, let us scoop some bubble gum pink
It is sweet and yummy the best some we think
There is ice cream minty and green
It is the creamiest I have ever seen
Yellow ice cream is lemony and tart,
From the very start!!!
Scoops of blueberry would make my day,
Look at all this hip, hip hooray!
Red ice cream is strawberry delight,
Look at all these scoops of ice cream, what a heavenly sight!!
Vanilla white is a popular flavor,
It tastes very good like ice cream craver,
Purple ice cream gives me a kick,
It's really good and yummy until the last lick!!
Ice cream, ice cream what a sensation
We love ice cream just any combination!!!

Magdalena Szostek, Grade 5
Public School 176 Brooklyn

The Dragon Fish

Dragon fish have sharp teeth,
And if you were a fish you would not want to meet.
Phosphors shine like glow-in-the-dark balls.
The barble bounces as it gnaws on food
(HAW HAW HAW)
The dragon fish is a bizarre creature
Eating anything but fish.

Wilson Ni, Grade 6
Shelter Rock Elementary School

Fall

Trees are getting bare
Leaves change to different colors
Start wearing sweaters
We get to go trick or treat
We get to buy our costumes
William Alfaro, Grade 5
Northeast Elementary School

Blue

Blue is the color of a bright sky
in the summertime
Blue is the color of a blue jay
chirping in a tree
Blue is the color of waves rolling
in onto the coast
Blue is the color of the flag
of New York
Aeden Lebron, Grade 4
Leptondale Elementary School

My Beautiful World

I'm in my classroom,
I look outside,
I look around me,
I'm now on my bike.

I pass a house,
I pass a tree,
I see how wonderful,
This world can be.

I pass a park,
I pass a school,
I see some boys,
Who think they're all cool.

I wake up,
In my mirror I see,
My beautiful world,
And how it's with me.
James Cioffi, Grade 5
Eastplain School

Snowmobiling

S uper fast
N ice
O ver snow
W ent in a blizzard
M akes tracks
O ther way
B uy a new one
I llegal to drive on roads
L ike snow
E mpty gas tank
Dylan Daigle, Grade 4
Granville Elementary School

Eraser

On the tip of your pencil
You replace me when I run out
I vanish your mistakes
I hide what you don't
Want people to see or know

You blow away my shavings
As I delete your mistakes
I used to be yours
But now my shavings
Are covering the Earth
Rebecca Greenstein, Grade 4
Norman J Levy Lakeside School

Remember the Good Times

We go through good times,
We go through bad times,
We go through happy times,
We go through sad times,
But the thing that matters most
is we all go through times together.
Rebecca Rouillier, Grade 5
Staley Upper Elementary School

Nature

Nature is so beautiful,
Colorful leaves whistling,
Wet wood sizzling,
Kids jumping in the leaves
Yelling because they're wanting
To be in their now closed pools.
Blowing and swirling
Branches to the ground,
Raccoons, skunks, and deer
Out prowling around
Summer is done
Autumn is about.
Ashley Crawford, Grade 6
Akron Middle School

The Stars

I saw you yesterday at night
But never see you in daylight.
I never hear you in the sky
Like packs of foxes that are sly.
O stars I see you every night
O stars, do you see me in daylight?

I saw you dancing in the sky,
Dancing, dancing, that's no lie.
Like the sun shining in daybright.
O stars I see you every night
O stars do you see me in daylight?
Quinton Chung, Grade 4
Public School 124Q

The Park

In the park
In the dark
My dog begins to bark.

I hear something
But don't know where
It is coming from!

People say it comes
Out in the dark.
I sit and listen
As the sound gets louder!

I decide to run
And to never go,
Into the park
In the dark ever again.
William Coleman, Grade 5
Staley Upper Elementary School

Life Under the Blanket

I walk through the desolate streets.
Holding the sun around my neck.
I see men out in the tundra,
They stare at me with eyes of coal,
With merry smiles,
I grin back at them with delight.

I gaze at the light sprinkle of sugar
glaring in the moonlight.
Everything is silent except for
the naked trees dancing in the wind.
This is what lay under the
Earth's winter blanket.
Thomas Schaller, Grade 5
Edward J Bosti Elementary School

Mother

Mother, always there for me.
Mother, I set my secrets free.
Mother, watch me play.
Mother, what can I say.
Mother, cook and clean.
Mother, look at me.
Mother, like a dove.
Mother, full of love.
Tina Maria Kouridakis, Grade 5
Public School 2 Alfred Zimberg

Yellow

Yellow is the color of the sun
Yellow is the color that makes you happy
when you're sad
Yellow is a very bright color that I like
Emmalee Nott, Grade 4
Leptondale Elementary School

Jane Cooke Wright*

Born on November 30, 1919.
Jane was a very bright girl.
She solved many problems that people couldn't unfurl.
She went to college.
She had a lot of knowledge.
But Jane wanted something more.
This was bigger but not a chore.
She established a cancer research foundation
And found something that swept the nation!
The foundation discovered many anticancer drugs.
They got a lot of hugs.
Jane worked on giving everyone medicine doses.
Then her father died of tuberculosis.
She was very sad.
But she kept going on.
She told people about the cancer treatment in many countries.
Now everyone sees
How an African-American can help the world.

Kerry Losert, Grade 6
St. Catherine of Siena School
In memory of my grandpa who died in 2005.

What Has Happened?

The world has changed from bad to good,
People afraid because of skin color,
Why would anyone do this?
No one knows,
Seeing everything fade in the darkness,
Makes me wonder,
WHY?

Looking around and thinking of what has changed,
People joined and not afraid,
Watching happiness grow,
Seeing them realize that it doesn't matter,
The color of one's skin,
They have realized what it really means,
The real thing that matters is one's inside.

Tara Belinsky, Grade 6
Shelter Rock Elementary School

The Beach

Hot sun on my back
Beating down on me like a bully
Sand between my toes
Like a crumbled cookie
Long walks on the beach with my dad
Picking up shells and throwing sand at each other
Broken seashells pricking my feet
Like pins and needles
Seagulls swooping down
Stealing french fries and leftover lunch
Ocean waves crashing down on me like a tumbling building
Waking me up to amazing sights of the beach.

Lauren Grama, Grade 4
Norman J Levy Lakeside School

The Mountain

I see the mountain big and tall
You must be the biggest of them all!
Made of dust and snow and rocks
You remind me of a pile of socks!
O mountain wherever I go,
O mountain you stalk me so.

Oh mountain, sometimes you block the sun.
Sometimes it seems like the hills are your sons.
O mountains how did you get so tall?
If someone fell off they would fall, fall, fall.
It seems that forever, I am gazing at you,
But now it is time to bid you adieu!

Kerry Kublal, Grade 4
Public School 124Q

The Water

I saw you whoosh upon the rocks,
And heard you crash like falling blocks.
I smelled the salt as your waves rose in the air,
And ate salt taffy at the fair.

O water that shines in the daylight,
O water, what a beautiful sight!

I saw you crash on the shore,
And scare the birds as they soar.
I heard you pass by on the sand,
And heard you rumble like a rock band.

O water that shines in the daylight,
O water, what a beautiful sight.

Nicholas Singh, Grade 4
Public School 124Q

Why Can't I Be You?

Soccer Ball	Both	Football

Oh,
I wish I was you.

Why me?
I want to be you.

Because you can fly,
and I am kicked on
the ground.

But you can roll,
as far as you like.
Where as I have to be
carried, day and night.

We are cool in
our own way.
We're both balls,
so let's have fun.

Audrey Moylan, Grade 6
St Mary's School

Night Fall

Rain taps on my balcony window,
As music rushes through my veins.
I can see the colors of the song in my head.
I lay gently on my pillow
I look at the clock 12:00 A.M.
Can't fall asleep
I listen more to let these words soak into my life
The way I think
I breathe in and out
Fall softly to sleep,
Into the never-ending sky of dreams.

Jen Fitzsimmons, Grade 6
Harold D Fayette Elementary School

Nature

Nature —
Crimson flowers, tall grass, oak trees.
It's all around us,
Floating in the midnight breeze.
Nature —
Breakable, breezy, beautiful,
All the crunchy leaves changing colors.
Now I hear someone scolding the birds,
It is nature's stern mother.
Nature —
Lemon yellow, flame red, forest green, hazel brown,
The buzz of crickets talking all around.
Nature makes you turn your frown upside down.
Nature —
Capture the sweet scent
Floating in the midnight breeze.
Oak trees standing as tall as GIANTS!
Nature —
Respect its breathtaking beauty,
Ruin nature,
Regrets only.

Jenny Komosinski, Grade 6
Akron Middle School

Dream

Dreaming is believing
My mom would always say to me
When she tucked me into bed
And kissed me goodnight.
That's when I would
Always start dreaming.
But now I'm older
I tuck myself into bed
And now I think about school and cool rock bands.
When I get older
I'll say dreaming is believing
When I tuck my children
Into bed.

Egan McCoy, Grade 6
Holy Cross School

Family Is a Great Thing

Your family is there for you all the way,
Aunts, Uncles, and cousins who want to play.

Holidays, parties, and celebration are full of love,
Then at night we sleep peacefully under the stars up above.

In the morning the sun was so bright,
Then my heart got full of light.

My two brothers are so fun,
We play outside in the sun.

At dinner we talk,
Then sometimes we go out for a walk.

Win or lose we still cheer for each other,
That's why I love my family.

Stephanie Marino, Grade 6
Long Beach Middle School

Santa Is Coming

Christmas is just around the corner
So Santa and his reindeers are crossing all borders.
Brining toys for everyone,
So they can have laughter and fun.

Hear how his sleigh bells are ringing
As he glides over the snow.
His reindeers are running happily,
And Rudolph's nose is all aglow.

With a ho! ho! ho! He comes late at night
To see if everyone is tucked in tight,
Then in the stockings or under the tree
He will leave a gift for you and for me.
So come on Santa we welcome you!
We hope you will make our dreams come true.

Mikhail Charles, Grade 5
John Hus Moravian School

When I Look at the World

When I look at the world, I see a whole bunch of people
I see rainbows, flowers, blue skies, and a lot of love.
But it isn't always like that
When I look at the world I see negativity
I see war, pollution, broken laws, and hate.
I think everyone is equal
And should be treated with respect
When I look at the world I see many things,
But mostly you and me.
I see green grass ready to wither away
And smoke rising each day.
The world is a great place,
But needs love and care just like everybody.

Katelyn DiDonato, Grade 6
Great Hollow Middle School

A Beautiful Place
Feel the soft silky sand between your toes
Feel the sun shine softly upon your nose
Beautiful sunsets that catch your eye
Before you know it, time goes by
The world is such a beautiful place
Too bad we all can't get along as one human race
Danielle Williams, Grade 6
Great Hollow Middle School

School
School is cool,
But some kids think it's a drool.
There is math, science, and spelling.
Math is fun,
But some kids prefer it done.

I like science,
But my friends don't.
I kind of like reading and English.
Some kids say "who cares," or "whatever,"
But I don't because I listen to my teacher and they don't.
Lauren Impicciatore, Grade 5
Staley Upper Elementary School

Global Warming
The glaciers in the arctic turn into water,
This is happening because it's getting hotter,
I can hear the animals cry,
No more food or water they'll slowly start to die.

The world needs to unite,
The world must work together,
To stop this disaster,
Now or never.

If plants have no more oxygen to give,
We will have nothing to breath on and live,
In a few years Global Warming will have dried out our lakes,
So we have to stand and do what it takes.
Mehdi El-Hebil, Grade 6
Intermediate School 227 - Louis Armstrong Middle

Butterfly
I catch a butterfly in my hand,
It tickles my fingers and crawls up my arm.
It is linear on my shoulder,
I feel like a pirate with his parrot.
I catch a butterfly in my hand,
It tickles my fingers and crawls up my arm.
Its wings make me joyful because of the spots.
They form a smiley face and it looks happy.
I catch a butterfly in my hand,
It tickles my fingers and crawls up my arm.
Kelly Nola, Grade 6
Intermediate School 72 Rocco Laurie

Life Doesn't Frighten Me at All!
As I go to sleep,
I feel hands on my feet.
I hear noises all around,
My heart starts to pound.
Life doesn't frighten me at all.

Walking to school,
Never seems cool.
Cars passing by,
People walking past me.
Chills run through my legs,
It feels as if I am beating eggs.
Life doesn't frighten me at all.

Playing my violin on the stage which is bright,
Missing one note could be quite a fright.
Life doesn't frighten me at all.

Life is full of surprises and mysteries,
But what ever happens…
Life doesn't frighten me at all!
Marisa Heller, Grade 6
Long Beach Middle School

Life
L ife is unfair
I n so many ways
F ading happiness to sorrow
E ventually, sometimes life can be fair.
Leslie Castro Gil, Grade 4
Public School 152 School of Science & Technology

Life Doesn't Frighten Me
I don't like to be home alone,
It chills me to the bone.
Life doesn't frighten me at all.
Have you ever seen those
Really scary masks on Halloween?
They make me want to scream!!!
That doesn't frighten me at all.
Snakes are so innocent and small
How can I be afraid of them at all?
Life doesn't frighten me! Not at all.
I get clumsy when it's dark outside
My feelings get all jumpy inside.
Life doesn't frighten me at all.
Sometimes I wish dark, scary towers
Were lightened up into neon colors for hours
That doesn't frighten me at all.
All the creaking noises in an alley way
Make me never want to stay.
Life doesn't frighten me at all
Life doesn't frighten me at all
Not me, not at all.
Nina Tassiello, Grade 6
Long Beach Middle School

Jailbreak

Shortly after midnight,
The people in the jail,
Were sitting very quiet,
While the moon was pale.
I heard the sound of a lock rattling,
Creak!
Came the noise from the
door, door, door.
There was a fight in
the dark of the night.
Those people were seen no
more, more, more.

Carissa Wei, Grade 5
The Albany Academies

The Feelings of the Battlefield

The battlefield may seem
Like a horrible place
Sometimes it is
Sometimes it's not

The soldiers know
The feelings of the battlefield
Because they experience it
Since we do not experience it
How can we judge it?

On the battlefield
You could be shot down at any second
You could be killed,
imprisoned by the enemy,
or injured

What are the feelings
of the battlefield to you?

Brenden Donlon, Grade 6
Long Beach Middle School

My Plump Pumpkin

My pumpkin
Is plump and strong
But inside it's
gooey
And spider webby
It's like a scavenger hunt
Looking for all
Those beautiful precious seeds
I grab for some
And all the guts
Come oozing down my finger
My mouth starts to water
As I clean
All of those beautiful seeds

Tobie DiCesare, Grade 6
Northwood Elementary School

Fun at the Park

When I go to the park,
I'm all sparked up,
I love to run in the sun,
it's so much fun,
when I play on the swings
my ears ring,
because I go to the sky
so very very high,
at the end of the day,
I go home and I remember this fun day.

Rebecca Levy, Grade 4
Shaare Torah Elementary School

Friends

A person to rely on
Who is always there
Someone to comfort you
And will always care

When you feel down,
When you feel sad,
A friend will always be there
Even if you're mad

When you cancel out on the plans,
Your friend will understand
You can make up for it
But that is no command

You sign your cards and letters
As best friends to the end
You won't regret it
Until the end, you and your friend

Patricia Hannett, Grade 6
School of the Holy Child

Scared

I'm so scared
my life is frozen
sitting, waiting
nothing happening
fear in my eyes
want to hide
finally my fear drifts away
and once again
I can dance

Julia Reisner, Grade 4
Norman J Levy Lakeside School

9-11

On 9-11 I was afraid.
All I could do was watch and pray.
For all the men and women that died.
Think of all the tears that are cried.

Tyler Massa, Grade 5
Staley Upper Elementary School

Start of Fall

Crunch, crunch
I hear fall leaves crackle under my feet
Brown and crunchy
Perfect for raking up
And jumping in

Bright colors all around
Red, orange, and yellow
The trees dressed up in autumn apparel
It looks like a forest fire

Geese are leaving
Flying south for winter
But if I were them
I would much rather stay
And watch the earth
Transform to fall

Rachel Saur, Grade 6
Bellport Middle School

I Love My Cat

I love my cat
when he dresses in
his black and white tuxedo.
He asks me to dance
with that twinkle in his eye
like the beautiful night sky.
We dance until dawn
then I bawl out a yawn
  I climb
  into bed
  while
he purrs me
a soft lullaby
that gets softer and softer
that pulls us gently
  to sleep.

Sarah Miller, Grade 4
Concord Road Elementary School

The Fall

Fall
All the leaves colors
Red, orange and green
The colors are so beautiful to me
Leaves remind me of butterflies
How they change the leaves
The colors all rearranged
All the leaves in a pile
But only for awhile
Then fall will be over
Man, I will be so sad!

Taesha Lillard, Grade 6
Graham Elementary and Middle School

Red

Red is the bursting lava from a volcano
Red is the burning heat of the July sky
Red is the color of my big eyes
Red is the beautiful color of the summer sunset

Tyler Masterson, Grade 4
Leptondale Elementary School

Survival

When I think of surviving
On a small island I can use
My sharp knife to cut down all
The green coconuts hanging on palm trees.
I can drink the water inside the coconuts
And can build my house with palm trees and rocks.

Surviving is hard but I will work
First I would gather all
The sea grapes and wood to burn
Because there might be aircrafts or boats
The black smoke will look like small clouds
Then the rescuers can come and take us back home.

Sunwoo Hong, Grade 6
Shelter Rock Elementary School

All About Me

Forgiving, friendly, kind, and caring.
Relating to my brother, Dereck.
Caring about my family, my dog and my animals
Feeling loved and cared about,
Needing more safety.
Giving love,
Residing in Manhasset.

Wilfredo Castellon, Grade 6
Shelter Rock Elementary School

It

When I woke up this morning what did I see?
Creepy eyes that stared back at me.
I went for the shower and what did I hear?
Grunting and growling that sounded way too near.
I went down the stairs;
I froze.
IT was right there!
IT was just standing there right in my way.
Knowing it wouldn't be easy I had to get away.
When I passed IT it was just the crack of dawn
I looked back,
IT was gone.
I didn't want to, but I had to go upstairs.
I didn't want to, but I had to brush my hair.
I went to the door; IT was in there.
Horribly, I knew nothing more.
My feet wouldn't move me, I just stood in the hall.
The door slowly opened, IT was mom after all.

Mara Bengry, Grade 6
Northwood Elementary School

Little Night Lights

Little night lights in the sky are the little stars.
The big night light is the moon.
In the night the stars are all twinkly.
They're shining bright through the night.
In the night the moon is shining brighter than the little stars.
In the night the moon comes.
In the morning the sun comes up and it rises.

Sarah Torres, Grade 5
William B Tecler Elementary School

Winter Vacation

Winter vacation, winter vacation,
It is a great sensation!
All the ice and all the snow,
Its temperature is really low!
Sledding, skiing, we can play,
We could even do it all day.
You can also have a snowball fight,
You should give it all your might!
When you're sledding, when you're turning to the right
You should remember to hold on tight!
Winter vacation, winter vacation,
It is a great sensation!

Matthew Tibo, Grade 6
Holy Family School

Family Still Loves You

Feels like no one loves you at all,
Everybody just blows you away.
Haa! Family loves you.

I tried so hard to make lots of friends
But some are not real friends
And I lost most of them.
Still! Family loves you so much.

Family loves me and I love them back.
They are irreplaceable.

Benedith Bruno, Grade 4
Public School 152 School of Science & Technology

West Virginia

Mountains in West Virginia are very high.
Let's go explore the caves.
You may even see the underground coal mine.

You should come and go white water rafting.

The cardinal is resting in the Sugar Maple tree
Rhododendrons sway in the wind
The Blue Ridge Mountains are very high and pretty.

You may want to come in the winter so you can go skiing.

Emily Garofalo, Grade 4
St Andrew School

Butterflies

A monarch butterfly is my favorite.
Their wings are many colors.
You see them mostly in the summer,
After they have turned from caterpillars.
Have you ever tried to catch a butterfly?
It can be fun, but you must be quick!
They flutter from flower to flower.
And fly very high in the sky.
Beautiful fly, fly away.

Emily McCloskey, Grade 5
Staley Upper Elementary School

Grandpa

Old, wrinkled
eat soft food, sleep a lot, not active
yell a lot, can't walk that much
tell stories a lot about old times

Andrea Gines, Grade 4
Leptondale Elementary School

Friends

There for you through the good and bad
Helping you when you're down and sad
Laughing at all your jokes…
Even if they're not funny
Friends are forever

Having sleepovers every night
BFFs are really tight
When people talk behind your back
Friends are with you through the fight
Friends are forever.

Kerri Murdy, Grade 6
Long Beach Middle School

School's Here Right on Time

School's back again
Come to learn
I'm all set for school again
Just in time to learn something new!!
I hate to see the school year end
When I just began something new

Caroline Waldman, Grade 5
Guggenheim Elementary School

A Time to Cry

I am Sad
I hide in my house
I am Sad
Because my great grandma
Is in the hospital
…I Cry…
And wipe my tears with
My sleeves.

Halle Marks, Grade 4
Norman J Levy Lakeside School

'Twas the Eighth Night of Hanukkah

'Twas the eighth night of Hanukkah, when all through the apartment
With the candles burning, not in a compartment
The children were nestled all snug in their beds
While visions of potato latkes danced in their heads
With Rabbi Jim in his 'yamaka, and I in my cap
We just settled our pray books for a long winter nap
When out on the lawn I heard a great crash
So I tore open the shutters and threw up the sash
When, what to my wondering eyes should appear,
But a giant menorah, with shining things that were not clear
With a tall middle candle, so lively and quick
I knew in a moment it was more than a stick
When I heard on the roof, something not fireproof
Down the chimney, a wooden dreidel came with a poof
A bundle of toys he flung on his back looking like Santa when he opened his sack
His stem resembled a pipe one holds in their teeth
And his body could be wrapped in a wreath.
He spoke not a word, but went straight to his work
Said the blessing over the candles, then spun with a jerk
Then I heard him exclaim as he flew out of sight
"Happy Hanukkah and to all a good night!"

Travis Amiel, Grade 6
Briarcliff Middle School

The Trumpet

The trumpet is cool, just like the wind
It dances with its notes, just like my feet,
when I listen to it, it sways the music inside me
Sometimes I listen
Sometimes I don't,
But the trumpet sings out loud and clear
Whenever I think about playing the trumpet,
I start to play with my lips and the notes come out dancing and running.

Dylan Langan, Grade 6
Harold D Fayette Elementary School

Halloween

Jack-o'-lanterns with candles inside look creepy.
Black the color of witches hat and broom, fly past the full moon
The smell of delicious candy coming from children's candy bags
The sound of a tiger's roar echoes into the night
Moms decorating their homes with ghosts and spider's webs
Children trick-or-treating during the night
A sudden breeze blowing the mask off the children
Exhausted from running from house to house to collect sweet candy

Roxana Turcios, Grade 4
Northeast Elementary School

The Mirror

When I look into the mirror, I see my smile
When I look into the mirror, I see my mom
When I look into the mirror, I see a snowflake falling down into my hand
When I look into the mirror, I see the moon
When I look into the mirror, I see the snow.

Cyrus Shirazi, Grade 4
Upper Nyack Elementary School

What Is Purple?

Purple is the color of the walls,
Purple is the flowers blowing in the wind,
And the wild butterflies flying in the sky,
Purple is the teddy bear I hug at night,
And the soft carpet between my toes,
Purple is my teacher's favorite color,
And a cover of a book,
Purple is a color of the sunset,
And a color of a pen,
Purple is wonderful.

Kayla Staheli, Grade 5
Eastplain School

The Wolf Wind

The wind is like a wolf,
He creeps around the trees,
You can hear him stalking in the forest,
and howling in the middle of the night.

The wolf is very fierce,
You can feel him push you down,
Sometimes you can feel him scratch your face,
and prowling around your house.

Michelle Cao, Grade 4
Shelter Rock Elementary School

Basketball

B ouncing the ball up and down,
A im for the basket.
S hoot and make a point.
K eep your elbow in,
E ye contact with the hoop.
T hen get ready,
B alance yourself,
A nd then follow through.
L oud cheering fans are happy.
L oud fans roar louder because we won the game!

Amanda Thornton, Grade 6
Thornton Home School

Frogs

I have never met a frog I haven't liked.
Frogs are great, frogs are good, frogs are helpful.
Frogs live in many parts of the world.
Frogs eat many bugs in your garden.
Frogs come in many colors, shapes, and sizes.
Some frogs are poisonous and some are not.
Frogs are great swimmers and climbers.
Some frogs have big eyes.
And some do not.
Frogs have long legs.
Frogs sleep in logs and on lillypads.
Most frogs live near water.

Ryan McGovern, Grade 5
Staley Upper Elementary School

Ausable Chasm

You are eroding second by second
Running water with white foam and popping bubbles
Your giant walls make an enormous shadow
Above you a GIANT TREE CONVENTION
Millions of them
With leaves that rustle on a lush pillow
Once one piece, you are now two
You are the brother of the Grand Canyon
Both of you
Eroding and eroding
And
Voila!
You're gone
Never again to be noticed

Jack Rosenzweig, Grade 4
Norman J Levy Lakeside School

The Social Studies Test

Social Studies will seem boring
You'll think you need a rest
But once you get an A on a test
You seriously won't be snoring
First you'll be so tense
Your mind would not be able to think
But soon, as quick as a wink
You'll be thinking so intense
When you finish the test you'll be full of relief
You'll think you got everything wrong
But when the teacher says 100%!
You won't even have any belief
So, if your next door neighbor Kate Lomorrow…
Makes fun of you, don't make up a plan and plot
Oh! No! I just forgot…
You have another social studies test tomorrow!

Venkatesh Ramkumar, Grade 5
Park Road Elementary School

Winter

cocoa as light as the first snowfall
the stars dive into a pool of light
and the night sky drifts away

Woof! Woof! Woof!
your dog pleads and begs to go outside
but the request is denied

the calm snow covers your town
like a blanket for us all

the snow, still, a block of frozen ice
as if it was a temperature that was oh so precise

the snow will be blocked by the Iron Gate
but the snow knows its fate

Naami Islam, Grade 6
Harold D Fayette Elementary School

Christmas

Santa Claus
Freshly cut Christmas trees
Bells jingling
Christmas cake
Wrapping paper
Christmas
Ryan Zdenek, Grade 4
Belmont Elementary School

The Sun

The beautiful sun
Warms the earth with shining rays
That bright ball of fire
Vladimir Ignatov, Grade 5
Dickinson Avenue Elementary School

Friendship Is…

Something that you share
An unbreakable bond that connects
A special feeling
Secrets to keep
Having sleepovers
Enormous amounts of fun
Lovable
Trusting each other
Enlarging your feelings
Rocking out loud!
Unbelievable times
Someone that you can always depend on
Kindness that spreads
A tingly feeling in your heart
HUGS!!!
Kellsey Mone, Grade 6
Shelter Rock Elementary School

A Long Time Ago

A long time ago an airplane would be a
Bird flying across the sky.

A long time ago a car would be a
Wooden carriage.

A long time ago a tire would be
A stone circle with a hole in it

A long time ago a motor would be a
Powerful horse.

A long time ago there was no
Pollution or wars,
It was just
Me, you,
And the beautiful
Clean world!
Lydia Anaka, Grade 6
Akron Middle School

The Fall

I am walking down the street.
I see all the leaves of different colors,
They crunch as I walk by.
I see my friend, I say "Hi."
I can feel the crisp, fresh air,
The breeze blows through my hair,
I feel free
And I see
All that God has made to be.
Veronica Ruiz, Grade 6
Holy Family School

Pink

Pink is the color of a blushed face,
being embarrassed
Pink is the color of a pencil eraser,
helping your mistakes
Pink is the color of a flamingo,
standing in the water
Michael John Savini, Grade 4
Leptondale Elementary School

The Whispering Wind

What can the wind be?
a joker,
a thief,
or it can be a very soft breeze.

What sound can the wind make?
a whisper,
a whistle,
or a parent screaming at their child
when he isn't listening.

How can the wind feel?
Like a very soft blanket,
A very cold chill,
or like it can blow you off your feet.

The wind can be all sorts of things,
It can be a terrible cold day or very hot,
The wind has a mind of its own.
Fred Hallett, Grade 4
Shelter Rock Elementary School

Halloween

Scary houses
Fresh pumpkin pie
Kids saying "trick or treat"
Sweet candy
Soft costumes
Halloween
Gabriella Serp, Grade 4
Belmont Elementary School

Chad and Rudi Johnson

Armed and dangerous,
Charging and anxious
To get into the end zone.

Spin, juke,
Grin don't fluke,
Glare don't stare.

Running fast
Plowing through
Blockers and safeties
To get into the end zone.

Armed and dangerous,
Charging and anxious
To get into the end zone.
Trent Barszcz, Grade 6
Akron Middle School

Kasiya Is the Best

Kasiya's my friend
who help's me when
I'm sad, she puts
my frown up not down
She sings a song to
make me glad, she's
my friend Oh Kasiya
my friendship will never
end.
Emily Mercado, Grade 5
Public School 148 Ruby Allen

Football

Football is the greatest sport,
You can have lots of fun.
Like destroy someone
Or run up and down turf.
Carrying the pigskin
From 50 yards to 50 yards
Putting up six points
For your team
Whoops!!
Now you're on defense,
Hit the QB like a freight train.
Make sure
He doesn't get up again.
Yes!
Now you're on offense
Give it to your running back
He will run someone over
Like a steam roller
Yeah!!
Now you've won!
The season has begun!
Danny Sansanese, Grade 6
Akron Middle School

My Blanket of Teddy Bears

I love my pink, and white blanket
It might be small to you
but it keeps me warm at night
It makes my sister laugh when
I show it to her
When I sleep over at anybody's house
I bring it with me
My mother always says to give
it a break for once
That blanket smells like Johnson's
Baby Lotion
That blanket is very special to me
My love for that blanket is the most high love
I've EVER HAD

Brittney Martin, Grade 5
Public School 203 Floyd Bennett

Autumn Playground

Fall is here, Winter is near,
Red and gold everywhere!
All the apples looking their best,
Giant pumpkins taking a rest!
Mr. Scarecrow is putting on a show,
Flapping, swaying, happy there's no snow.
Bunny rabbits playing in the meadow,
Hidden in grass turning yellow.
I rake all the leaves into a mound,
And then fall back onto the ground.

Joaquim Braganza, Grade 4
St Benedict Joseph Labre School

Unmistakable

In the darkest of times
all we have to do is hope.
Hope for a loyal trustworthy companion.
Even when life's darkest shadow hovers over you,
the reality is that the dominant light of friendship
will shatter through the gloomy overcast.

While dwelling in a shadowy place fear takes over
Darkness surrounds you as you struggle to evade the dread.
Out of the black,
a crack of light seems to appear as you survive through it all.
The hardest times,
become the most wonderful memories.

For however long darkness reins,
The lights of the most powerful dream of the world
always seem to reappear.
Underneath it all, the multicolored banner of earth
stains the importance of existence,
to hope for the light of friendship
in our darkest hours,
to demolish the murky overcast.

Josephine M. Tannuzzo, Grade 6
Shelter Rock Elementary School

Family

The warm family hugs,
The happy family laughs,
The way your mom cooks,
The way your dad laughs,
The way your family loves you.
It makes people so happy
to know someone cares
about you feelings,
and your life.
I love it so much it makes me want to cry
The way things go wrong again and again,
but that's ok 'cause they'll go right again.
Soldiers don't get to see their family
but I hope they know it's ok
'cause we love them happily
The whole world is one
BIG HAPPY FAMILY!!!!!

Arielle Roulston, Grade 6
Long Beach Middle School

Falling Leaves

Leaves are falling in so many colors
Red, green, yellow, orange and brown
Leaves are dangling from the tree up above
As they dance down
From the tree up high
They make a sound
When they touch the ground
plop, plop, plop
But then I listened to the wind
As it groaned at the leaping leaves
So I went inside
To get a cup of steaming hot chocolate
For the roaring wind

Anthony Andersen, Grade 5
Bretton Woods Elementary School

Fall Is Back!

Leaves, leaves
Falling down
Here and there and everywhere
There is scarlets, oranges and yellows too
The wind in the air is going through my hair
And the trees are almost bare
Crunch, crunch
A lot of the leaves are on the ground
Jumping in the piles of leaves
the wind is whistling through the sky
The leaves are like a tornado
Wishing and wishing in a circle.
At night the wind makes me shiver.
Winter, winter is almost here
I'm going to miss fall so much!

Lauren Kim, Grade 5
Bretton Woods Elementary School

A Leaf Is There

Big, medium, and small,
Everywhere on the ground,
Some green, some orange,
Wind blowing the leaves off the trees
One round one square
Different shapes everywhere
Curvy end, pointy tips,
Real big, real small
Every step I take,
A leaf is there!

Naivee Font, Grade 5
John T Waugh Elementary School

Twinkling Stars

Twinkling in the night,
They shine like diamonds
Wishing they would stay
They have to
Disappear

Karen Jan, Grade 4
Concord Road Elementary School

Santa

Nice and jolly
He's got lots of holly
with cookies to share
with his reindeer so rare
and flies to bring toys for Molly
Austin Kingsley, Grade 4
Granville Elementary School

Rainstorm

The sky is turning gray
I think a storm is coming
The smell of the rain fills the air

Rain starts falling down
Then a big bang and crash
The ground shakes under my feet

Lightning strikes
Everything lights up
The rain is pounding down
The wind is picking up speed
Emily Salamone, Grade 6
Bellport Middle School

The Beach

Waves crashing against the rocks
Tumbling down to shore
Kids screaming
Seagulls flying
Seaweed hugging the sand
As jellyfish wash ashore.
Jessica Romano, Grade 4
Norman J Levy Lakeside School

The Best Neighborhood

My neighborhood is a wondrous sight, tons of friends to give a spooky fright
My neighborhood is super silly so don't sit on your couch and watch *Free Willy*
My neighborhood is criminal-free, except for the teens that come out at three
And it is spellbinding on Halloween and Thanksgiving
And it is amber in the sky, a beautiful glimpse for you and I
And it is time at 9:00 for us to sleep and in the morning get woken up by
Our noisy, annoying alarm clocks

Alexis Plateroti, Grade 4
Helen B Duffield Elementary School

The Mermaid Song

Deep under the sea mermaids softly sway.
Swirling their tails in crystal array.
They bounce and dive and softly sing their chiming songs of crystal kings.
Swirling with pearls swimming with fishes softly whispering highly toned wishes.
What would it be like to whisper in water?
What would it be like swirling and curling with a soft silver tail?
The figure of beauty elegance and grace is a mermaid.
Flowing hair loving face.
Swirling happily in deep waters or shallows this is a mermaid.

Ashlyn Perez, Grade 5
Calvary Chapel Christian School

Best of Luck

We have the best of luck when we are joining hand and hand.
We have the best of luck when we find money in the sand.
But not all the best of luck can come in a material gift.
We can get the best of luck when you are down and I give you a lift.

Christine Meore, Grade 6
George Grant Mason Elementary School

Softball

A softball is yellow and red, bright and easy to see,
You wear a helmet over your head, so you will not get hurt,
A uniform is of fluffy cloud white pants, rosy red socks and shirts.

You grab a bat and helmet, head onto the field,
You get into position, the catcher kneels,
Looking into the pitchers eyes, get ready for the pitch,
Bat behind head, the pitcher throws a windmill,
You begin to feel a thrill.

Swing…you miss the ball, the catcher yells,
"STRIKE ONE!!!"
Swing…you miss again! The catcher yells,
"STRIKE TWO!!!"
Got to make this one!
The pitcher winds up, "CRACK!!!"
The ball goes soaring through the air like a bird,
First, Second, Third base, the bases pass by,
Can I make it home? Better find out,
"HOORAY! HOORAY!"
Softball is so much fun!

Britney Swarthout, Grade 5
Harris Hill Elementary School

Babe

My horse Babe is beautiful.
I love her.
She is really nice and she has a lot of pink equipment.
She loves treats and grain.
Babe and I love to barrel race. She is fun to be around.
Babe has only bucked me off her back once; that was horrible.
Her saddle came undone and she just bucked me off.
I took grand champion in open twice.
I also took reserve champion in youth twice.
Babe is not friendly when it comes to other horses.
Babe loves to get pet and ridden.

Naomi Garrick, Grade 5
Granville Elementary School

The Power of You

The help of others can only take you so far
but if you want to go all the way
it only takes one person…you,
If you have a secret you'll always know
only one person knows…you,
And if you cried last night
no one will know except…you,
If you want to change
the only person who could help you is…you,
Yes, other people can help you through life
but the main help is the power of you.

Taylor Lillis, Grade 5
Public School 2 Alfred Zimberg

United with Snow

The trees are bare,
The ground is white,
Through the window I stare,
During the still and quiet night.

The kids don't mind
They get to skip school.
Soon you will find,
That is really cool.

The squirrels hide,
Amongst their tree,
The birds now fly to the other side,
From the snow they are free.

The malls are closed,
The holidays are near,
Which is supposed,
To erase all fear.

What is this MARVELOUS thing you ask?
It is Christmas, Hanukkah, Kwanzaa, United with Snow.

Connor Buckley, Grade 6
Harold D Fayette Elementary School

Baseball

Baseball is an awesome sport,
There are baseballs of any sort,
There are a million different teams,
When they pitch the ball can't be seen.

There are vendors everywhere,
People yelling from here and there,
They are selling soda and hotdogs,
When their team loses they will sob.

Look at that player's homerun,
Oh man, this is so much fun,
The cheer of the crown is as loud as a lion's roar,
They're praising the team they came for.

Tyler Obrock, Grade 5
Edward J Bosti Elementary School

Pencil

As I move my pencil across a blank white page,
my work grows in beauty
my personal thoughts appear on paper,
my words powerful in emotion
My pencil is my tool, my secret weapon.

Randy Hernandez, Grade 6
Harold D Fayette Elementary School

Science Is…

Science is fun because it's all around,
I see it I feel it and can even study it in sound.
I learn about the Earth in Geology
Then learn about living things in Biology

The Wii and GameBoy are my favorite technology,
If my mind goes crazy, I might need Psychology.
When I stare up at the sky I learn about Astronomy,
I dream about dinosaurs and experience Paleontology.

When I look at fire or a lightning bolt,
I know that there's physics in them both.
Light, heat and fire,
are all types that I admire.
They're a mix of chemistry and physics too,
Sometimes I need medicine when I go achoo,
See…science is around me in everything I do.

Kyle Bentley, Grade 6
Shelter Rock Elementary School

My Five Winter Senses

I see the snow falling from the sky and the children sledding
I hear the laughter of a family enjoying each other
I feel the cool wind brush my neck as I walk outside
I smell the hot cocoa coming out of a window
I taste the snowflake that falls upon my tongue
If I use my senses I can tell it is winter

Allison May, Grade 6
Woodmere Middle School

How Do We Know?

The sun, the moon, the land, the sea,
All of these were meant to be.
But how do we know
That this won't all end.
And how do we know,
if our friends are our friends.
How do we know,
That God is real?
And how do we know,
that a seal is a seal.
How do we know,
That life isn't a dream.
All of these questions,
Have answers.
But the four words,
That always get me are,
How do we know?

Aashishpal Singh, Grade 5
St Benedict Joseph Labre School

Caterpillar

Creeping, crawling on the ground
use your furry little gripper feet,
Crawling, creeping all around.

Munch, munch, munching
Crunch, crunch, crunching.

Up an old oak tree
On a large, green leaf.
Eat that leaf,
Use that tree,
To become
A beautiful butterfly.

Elizabeth Wager, Grade 6
Akron Middle School

Grandpa's Snore

What is wind?
A wild horse,
A racecar driving crazy off course.

How can the wind feel?
A shiver,
So cold it would make you quiver.

How can the wind sound?
A lion's roar,
Or maybe my grandpa's snore.

The wind can be many things,
In fact, the wind might have wings!

Thomas Clejan, Grade 4
Shelter Rock Elementary School

Skating in New York City

Skating in New York City.
Ollies, indys, heelflips, kickflips.
Riding, buying, trucks, decks too.
When you buy these things
You are tempted to buy two.
When you get home
Your mom asks where you've been.
And you definitely do not want that grin.
I went to my room not making a sound.
Snuck out and skated around.
When I got home my dad was there.
You're grounded for life!
NO skating anywhere!

Austin Leggio, Grade 5
Edward J Bosti Elementary School

My Name

It means "Wealthy Friend."
It's like the number five.
My name is of English origin.
It's the name of my father,
even though he's Spanish.

My name is as green as a lime.
It feels like leather.
It smells like roses.
It tastes like meat.
My name is fun.
It means "Good Life."
It is Edwin.

Edwin DeJesus, Grade 5
Public School 2 Alfred Zimberg

Cheese

Cheese is yellow
        like a banana
it is squishy
        it is soft
it melts
        really fast
I love cheese.

Enzo Pavon, Grade 4
Public School 148 Ruby Allen

Seasons

Fall is a colorful season.
Orange, red, brown and green.
But no dark colors,
Like black, blue, purple and gray.
Winter is not colorful.
All you see is white snow.
It's very cold,
With clear blue skies.
These seasons are all enjoyable.

Eric Ramsunder, Grade 5
St Benedict Joseph Labre School

Puffer Fish

When a puffer fish puffs,
Their life is quite rough.
It means they might be eaten,
It's like they've just been beaten,
Their life might swim away.

Although their skin is smooth,
When they get in a groove,
The fish in their mouth,
Won't be able to move.

Their stomach is stretchy,
And they are quite tetchy,
But still we love puffers.

They might have been used,
to hijack a plane,
and there isn't a single one,
in upper Maine.
But we still have
awe for their skills

Zachary Winn, Grade 6
Shelter Rock Elementary School

My Best Friend Kate

K atelyn
A 9 year old girl
T he cool cat
E very day styling

C ool clothes
R un fast
A n active person
Z ac Efron
Y ear round

C ool
O utside all the time
O wl is her favorite animal
L azy no way

Larissa Prevost, Grade 4
Granville Elementary School

Max

Max is my dog,
He is a hog.
He eats all day,
And sleeps all night,
He snores and snores,
And when he wakes,
He eats and eats,
My dog Max he is a hog.

Cheyanna Frost, Grade 5
Whitney Point Intermediate School

It's Not Worth the Pain

Black or white,
There's no need to fight.

We are all the same,
It's not worth the pain.

In God's eyes,
It's not kind to criticize.

We're made out of blood, yes, it's red!
It's the word "racism" that I dread.

Why should we be in a separate place?
We don't live somewhere out in space!

Freedom should ring for both you and me,
So we could all live together happily!

Benny Borgognone, Grade 6
Shelter Rock Elementary School

Summer Days

Sizzling sidewalks burn my feet,
ripe pink watermelon tastes so sweet,
sun is shining in every which way,
another typical summer day.

Waffle cones pile up high,
bright blue skies make me cover my eyes,
my surroundings seem to say,
another typical summer day.

Loud laughing fills the air,
the dazzling sun shimmering down on my hair,
families splashing in the bay,
another typical summer day.

Vanessa Rijo, Grade 6
Munsey Park Elementary School

The Mako Shark

I'm blue/gray on my back
I have a showy white belly that looks like a pillow sack
My skin is rough like sandpaper
Who am I?
The Mako Shark of course
Reaching up to speeds of 22 miles per hour
I can leap 20 feet out of the water with great speed and power
I am known as a sport fish
Who am I?
The Mako Shark of course
My mouth is as large as it can be
So I can eat the fish swimming in the sea
Razor sharp teeth fill my mouth to a tee
Who am I?
The Mako Shark of course…so beware!

Ryan Kiess, Grade 6
Shelter Rock Elementary School

Lady Slippers

Light pink petals on a beautiful flower
Little yellow bugs are on it
Leaves are about 10 cm long
One bud is about to open,
Most of them are small.

White holes on the leaves
Little black and white ladybug on one of the buds
The buds are fuzzy and soft
There was also spider webs on the flowers
The flowers are 1 in. long and they are soft too.

Leaves have caterpillar holes on them
It makes me feel like the beautiful person
That I know I am.

It has ants on the stem
The stem is green and very tall
Little brown things in the center of the flower
It smells like my mom's perfume.

Taylor Pristupa, Grade 4
Public School 205 Alexander Graham Bell

Boring

I was looking outside on a sunny day,
Thinking, just thinking of a way to go outside and play.
Hearing my teacher talk on and on,
I'm watching a man mow the lawn.
The teacher won't stop talking on and on.
My friend is talking about a boy named James.
While I am thinking about the big school games.
My day is going to be the best,
But of course the teacher ruins it,
By handing out a test.

Rebecca Snyder, Grade 5
Whitney Point Intermediate School

Why I Love Fall

I go out and play
And jump in the leaf pile.
My dogs want to play
And they make my sis smile.
I go around to places with mom, dad, and sis.
I see so many faces,
The girls I want to kiss.
And when my day is over
It's time for some rest.
I buy a clover
Because I am the best!
But I want it to end
So summer comes fast.
And I'll visit Puerto Rico again!

Mashland Santiago, Grade 5
Marie Curie Institute

The Computer

The computer helps in many ways
No matter what some people say
You can play games and type too,
Those are my favorite things to do.
The computer can do many things
It's almost like they are kings.
The computer helps in many ways
No matter what some people say.
Julie Miller, Grade 5
Holy Cross School

December

In the month of December,
Everything is white.
There's also hardly any light,
But it's all such a sight.

Many children laugh and play,
And dream of Santa's sleigh.
On Christmas day there's presents.
Hurray! Hurray! It's Christmas day!
Kathryn Fulghum, Grade 5
Staley Upper Elementary School

Monkeys

Monkeys are fun to watch
While lying on a dock
Looking for a rock
Putting on their socks
And walking on rocks
Michael Ritchie, Grade 4
Granville Elementary School

Sports

S ports
P owerful
O n school days sometimes
R acing
T ouchdowns
S acks
Kristopher Prevost, Grade 4
Granville Elementary School

Sand Pipers

Little birds prancing
Little birds dancing
Running by the shoreline
In and out you go
What are you looking for?
I will never know
I like to watch the way you move
It always fascinates me
How much you move all around
Being chased by the morning sea
Rosie Roggeman, Grade 6
Most Precious Blood School

Fall Is Here

Fall leaves, yellow, orange, red
Flying in the sky
Watching them pass me by
The wind blowing in the air
As it shivers through my hair
No more green leaves or fleas from dogs
The shadow won't be seen for awhile
from the groundhog
Children playing in the leaves
Happy as can be
Giggling through the leaves
As parents come and scream
They can't wait until tomorrow
To do it all again!
Marlayna Myrthil, Grade 5
Bretton Woods Elementary School

Miss You

There's a girl,
She sits alone,
Waiting for someone to hear.

She cries all night,
As long as day,
She thinks she's all alone.

But someone hears,
She wonders who,
She wonders who it could be.

A man she knew,
Who's been gone,
For work mother tells her.

She won't listen,
She's just a kid,
She misses him.
Katelynn Warner, Grade 5
Whitney Point Intermediate School

Poppies

Changing Seasons
Golden poppies smile in the sun
Butterflies flutter craving fun
Ladybugs laugh and fish swish
Cicadas only hiss!
The sun sets, its getting colder
The bugs will die, they won't get older
A blanket of snow falls to the ground
Not a peep, not a sound
A cold tundra of blanket and snow
No plants — nothing grows!
Isabel Kingsepp, Grade 5
St Joseph Hill Academy

Fall

The time of year
Where I notice
The season's changed
The fragile leaves
Crackling
At every step
Some trees
Now bare
When they used to be
Green and full
I can smell
The crisp
cool air
The lawns
Are more colorful
With less green
More orange
And red
It's fall
Justine Deleguardia, Grade 6
Northwood Elementary School

Green

Green is the grass in day
Green is the color of an apple
Green is the color of leaves in summer
Rachel Rivera, Grade 4
Leptondale Elementary School

Birds

Iridescent Hummingbirds,
Buzzing in the
Sizzling summer.

Screaming Blue Jays,
Raucous crying in
The waving trees.

Cherry colored Robins,
Nesting in the
Dark green bushes.

Ash Grey Doves,
Cooing silent shushes.

Darting Canaries,
Shooting slight flashes
Of lemon yellow.

Birds are so noisy singing
At dark midnight.

But so pretty
During the shining bright.
Drew VanBuren, Grade 6
Akron Middle School

Hannah Montana

H annah Montana has a nice voice
A nd she also has beautiful clothes
N ice jewelry and hair
N ice looks and songs
A nd she also has cool best friends
H annah's dad is Billy Ray Cyrus

M iley is her real name
O nly 15 years old
N ew song coming out
T welve is how old Miley acted
A nd Miley has two sisters
N obody's Perfect is one of her greatest hits
A wesome!!

Hailey Knowles, Grade 4
Granville Elementary School

Divorce Stinks

Divorce, divorce,
Sometimes it's easy, others it's hard.

When my parents got divorced,
It was a time I could not ignore.

Yelling, screaming I can't ignore,
Even when I close my door.

Sometimes I get confused, others I'm okay,
But today I still deal with this problem.
Maybe someday I will be set free.

Rachel Geary, Grade 5
Staley Upper Elementary School

F.R.I.E.N.D.S.

F riends are there for you when you need them.
R iding down the road is what we like to do.
I ce cream is our favorite thing to eat.
E very day is a new day to have fun with each other.
N othing can stop us from having fun on a new day.
D oing exercises every day is another thing we like to do.
S ometimes we fight but we end up forgiving each other.

Yuluisa Garcia, Grade 5
St Benedict Joseph Labre School

Marigolds

Marigold, marigold, tell me why,
You go outside in the winter and never cry,
Not only winter, but summer too,
And never, ever, go to the pool.
Orange, green,
Not mean,
You are strong, my marigold.

Erica Lou, Grade 4
Public School 205 Alexander Graham Bell

Black

Black is the color of the cow's spots
Black is the answer to when you cry and you scream or fight
Black is slow and gloomy
Black is as dark as the night sky
Black is a burn shirt, or black jeans

Kristie Dagostino, Grade 4
Leptondale Elementary School

Friends and Family

Friends last for a lifetime
But family last forever
Nothing can be more satisfying
than the smiles on their faces.
Nothing would be fun without never coming to an end.
Friendship's door always opens, never closes.
Friends and family are the best
every time you're sad, they always have your back.
They will never leave you
as long as they love you and you love them.
Friends and family are the best people
to talk to because they understand.
They're good listeners and easy to talk to.
Friends last for a lifetime.
Family lasts forever.

Tasiaha Castro, Grade 6
Long Beach Middle School

The Senses That I Have

The sounds that I hear
Are yelling through my head.
Now I feel my way to my bed.

My mom made this wonderful cake,
And it tasted great!

In the winter, I feel the icy ground
Beneath me as I skate
Happily around and around again!

I can see over miles of sea,
In the water on a boat,
Some people are having fun,
While drinking some tea.

Now I can smell my grandma,
Baking her delicious cookies!
My mom smelled it too,
And ran to the kitchen for a better smell.
Then all the kids came in all muddy and ready to eat!

The sounds that I hear
Are yelling through my head.
Now I feel my way to my bed.
Then awake another day using my five senses.

Dakota Earle, Grade 6
Akron Middle School

Dogs
Black, white, brown, gray
All day
Run and play
Catching Frisbees in the air
Getting mud in their hair
Big or small
Short or tall,
We love them all.

Rachel Youngers, Grade 6
John T Waugh Elementary School

Me
I'm beautiful like an actress
my cheeks are red like roses.

My eyes twinkle like the stars
my head is the size of planet Mars.

My hair is black
my nose is flat.

My arms are strong
my feet are long.

My name is Saiyara!

Saiyara Mumin, Grade 5
Public School 2 Alfred Zimberg

Big Tree Little Tree
You a tree?
Yep
Hundred year old?
Sure am
50 feet tall?
You tell me
Been shot at?
Once or twice
Gotten climbed?
Tons of times
Drinks water?
Every day
How'd you get so wise?
Asking questions

Jake Kramer, Grade 6
Bellport Middle School

Cat
Cat's fur is soft as a baby's cheek.
Cats run as fast as cheetahs.
Their fur is silky as my brother's hair.
Cats hear even better than my dad
When I play and talk at bedtime.
Touching my aunt's cat make me sleepy.
Meow!

Ryo Inoue, Grade 4
Concord Road Elementary School

The Rain Dance
I feel the soft chair under me
While my mom is singing to no one
I hear the tapping of rain on the window next to me
TAP!!
TAP!
TAP!
BOOM!!
The thunder starts to argue with the lightning, interrupting the rain's dance
FLASH!
The lightning answers back in a hard flash
Flavors in my mouth from a moment ago, are dancing on my tongue
The sweet smell of chicken fills my nose like a cup of water
I hear a distant conversation
The rain is still tap dancing happily in a rhythmic beat
TAP!
TA-TAP!
The leaves start to sway in the wind to the beat of the rain dancing
The tapping is fading, like it is moving away to a different town
TAP!…TAP!
It is gone.

Ally Marcello, Grade 6
Harold D Fayette Elementary School

Thanksgiving
Family, friends, and neighbors people you see that day.
Turkey, corn, and mashed potatoes, things that come your way.
You stuff yourself and stuff yourself with stuffing, potatoes and yams.
That is just a start at my Gram's.
Some of us flop on the couch when we're done.
Some of us play games.
We laugh, we talk and have some fun.
Just when you thought you couldn't eat anymore!
The pies, cakes, and ice creams are coming through the door.
After having your Thanksgiving dinner you can't wait till next year for more!

Alexandra Lam, Grade 6
St John School

Cheerleading
cheerleading, black white and read as the color shine,
while the cheerleaders are in the blue cloudy sky,
high V low V touch down broken T all of the arm moves,
while you do your cheer and dance you listen too,
the crowd screaming very loud on the high stands,
the coaches stand there with happiness watching us to the cheer,
but, first while you are waiting for them to say "ok" you stand there silent,
and the crowd waits till it starts, A team B team and C team,
all 3 Penfield teams shine together,
when all of the cheers and all of the competition are done we have the big one,
we are in Niagara Falls and we are all sparkly and ready,
then we started,
we hold up our signs and say GO BIG RED,
then the crowd starts to say it with us,
and before you know it there is a wave shouting
GO BIG RED!!

Lindsay Gamer, Grade 5
Harris Hill Elementary School

Football Season

Football flying through the air,
Referees calling plays,
Crowds chanting,
Smelling fresh cut grass,
Players yelling "Hike!"

Football flying through the air,
Players running yard-by-yard,
Different jerseys all around,
Cameras flashing.

Football flying through the air,
Little boys yelling, "What does that mean Dad?",
Referees blowing whistles,
Players gulping down Gatorade.

Football flying through the air,
Players gasping for air,
Lots of muddy cleats,
Happy and sad faces as the game comes to an end,
Empty seats fill the stadium.

Katie Foley, Grade 5
Edward J Bosti Elementary School

My Friend

I imagined you at the park today,
I love to see you run and play
And heard you having fun today,
Like when the little kids come out to play.

I see the blue sky,
Oh, how I wish we could fly!
Oh my friend, I'd love to see you again
Oh my friend, our friendship will never end.

Tori Hennings, Grade 4
Public School 124Q

Christmas Time

C is for Christmas the season of love
H is the heavenly babe that was sent from above
R is for the righteousness that His birth brings
I is for Incarnate, He came as a man
S is for the star that they followed that night
T is the three wise men with their gifts aright
M is the manger where Jesus was born
A is for the angels who told His birth in song
S is for the shepherds who spread the news around.

T is Thanksgiving that the Christ had come
I is the innkeeper with no room at his inn
M is for Mary the mother of God's son
E is for everlasting life that we have won.

Let the joy bells ring for it's Christmas time
Vincent Estridge, Grade 5
John Hus Moravian School

Walking in My Neighborhood

I see people kill.
I hear people curse.
I smell people smoke.
I feel bad things because the 'hood' is bad.
I walk into drama.
I walk into where people are killed.
It makes me feel sad.
I wish I was never born.
I wish for world peace.

Malaysia Gardiner, Grade 6
The New York Institute for Special Education

Life Doesn't Frighten Me

I once had a fear
That was always very near
But it didn't frighten me at all

I'd hide and I'd scream
But it would never come out of my dream
Life didn't frighten me at all

It would try to open the door
As I would be screaming more and more
Life didn't frighten me at all

It would never fade away
In my dreams it would always stay
Life didn't frighten me at all

Then I opened my eyes
It was just a dream, a bunch of lies
Life didn't frighten me at all
Jessica Shreck, Grade 6
Long Beach Middle School

Life Doesn't Frighten Me

When I'm asleep at night, I have scary dreams.
All of my dreams give me the screams.
Life doesn't frighten me at all.

Even though the doors are locked, I am all alone.
Sometimes when I'm sitting home, I hear the ringing phone.
Life doesn't frighten me at all.

Creaking doors and squeaking floors.
Life doesn't frighten me at all.

Strangers are scary and so is bloody Mary.
Life doesn't frighten me at all.

Everyone seems so tall, but I feel so small.
Life doesn't frighten me at all.
Samantha Walsh, Grade 6
Long Beach Middle School

Girls

Make up
Teddy bears
Parties and more
That's we we girls do adore
We are fancy we are cool
But most of all, we girls do rule
Samantha Maizer, Grade 5
Public School 48

Snow

The snow is so fluffy,
It makes my nose stuffy.
Touching it feels cold,
Making my hands bold.

You can make it into a brick,
it's cold when you lick.
You can make it into a snowball,
it freezes into a cold ball.

This is why I chose snow,
My last name is Lowe.
I made this in school,
Which is very cool.

Outside it is snowing,
It's hard to get going.
The snow is very deep,
I need to go to sleep.
Nicholas Lowe, Grade 5
East Syracuse Elementary School

The Library

Books, books, books,
Rows on shelves,
Stacks on tables,
Running through them all,
I don't know which one to pick,
Scattered all around me,
Decorating the room,
I feel so good to be in this place
It's so nice to be here,
People saying shh to me,

I like it so much,
It's not that tough,
Find one that is right for you,
Just choose one good enough,
It's easy like 1+1,
To me I like them all,
There are lots of books you see,
Some are just right for me.
Gabrielle Gorgy, Grade 4
Public School 69

Science Is...

A bird flying from a tree,
saying something unknown to me,
moss on a log,
home to a hog,
this is what science is.
Rumbling in the bushes,
right behind our tushes,
making us run with fright.
It was only an owl,
who gave us a scowl,
for this was his home tonight.
Andre Clejan, Grade 6
Shelter Rock Elementary School

Trees

Trees have grown so tall
strong enough to hold us all,

Climbing up
Oops! Don't fall

A nice spot to take a rest
Trees are just the best!
Meg Farrell, Grade 5
Most Holy Rosary School

The Big Race

I was in a big race,
There was sweat on my face,
I was racing my class,
Luckily I wasn't last.
There was a tree that fell down,
My teacher's hair got stuck in a frown,
So now I knew I could win it,
I ran as fast as I could.
I got to the finish line,
And I yelled in pride!
Gabe Shrauger, Grade 5
Whitney Point Intermediate School

Tigers

Roarrrrr!
Went the hungry tiger,
On an arctic winter night.

As the frightened animals heard,
They scattered in fear.
Darting through the thick, dark woods,
On a frigid winter night.

Roarrrrr!
Went the attacking tiger,
As the polar woods cleared,
Nothing in sight.
Joseph Sarow, Grade 6
Akron Middle School

Barkley

B is for being a good dog.
A is for alerting us when there's danger.
R is for reading with me.
K is for killing if you had to protect me.
L is for lying with me after a game.
E is for doing exactly what I say.
Y is for you just being you!

This is a poem for my dog.
Everyone liked him even a frog.
He died in '06
Because he was sick.
Ophelia Pierre, Grade 4
E J Russell Elementary School

Christmas

C ool presents
H oliday fun
R ockin' around the Christmas tree
I cy ground
S nowing down
T errific presents
M erry Christmas
A ny present is cool
S anta comes
Alexis Hill, Grade 4
Granville Elementary School

Candy

Candy is the best!
They taste as sweet as a thousand sodas.
Some melt in my mouth. Yum!
Some taste crunchy.
I can hear them talking in my mouth.
Crunch! Crunch! Crunch!
They smell so good that
My taste buds go to heaven.
Candy has all the colors of the rainbow.
They can be as small as mice,
Or as big as trees.
YUM!
Derick Chan, Grade 4
Concord Road Elementary School

Science Is...

Tadpoles being born so small,
Trees' leaves falling off in the fall.
Light bulbs light up so bright,
Gas rising up from a pot,
preparing dinner at night.
Mixing chemicals at a lab,
The miles on a taxi cab.
Gabriella Scaramucci, Grade 6
Shelter Rock Elementary School

Star Lab

To watch the sky is lots of fun
By day we see mostly the sun.
But when it gets dark is when, I see the most
The moon and the stars float by like a silvery ghost.
Night after night after night it's mostly the same,
All the constellations I try to remember their names.
It's hard to imagine all the stars in my vision,
Are far far away from our solar system.

Marc Wangenstein, Grade 4
Helen B Duffield Elementary School

Baby Joey

So tiny, warm and soft
Big brown eyes and chubby cheeks,

Goo goo ga ga!

I like to hold him in my arms,
Sometimes I feed Joey!

Goo goo ga ga!

He likes to play peek-a-boo.
He can almost sit up now!

Goo goo ga ga!

Joey, Joey he's so fine, he's mine, mine, mine!

Morgan Cox, Grade 4
Hendy Avenue School

A Different World

Everything has colors,
So show your respect for others.
Everything is moving with time,
Nature's set all upon a vine.
Respect the world with all its glory,
Because it gave you your life story.
Wake up to the colors around you,
For life just became brand new.
Live your life through other people's eyes,
So give some care before you die.
All different people of different races,
Come out of the shadows and show your faces.
There should be no more war,
Because there's so much more to live for.
We should live in a world without fear,
So we shouldn't have to shed a tear.
Pick up one friend or two,
And ask them to come with you.
So all the world can live as one,
Before the day's work is done.

Meredith Wilshere, Grade 6
Munsey Park Elementary School

Christmas Time

It's cozy inside, so I run outside
In a blanket of chilly snow
I make snow angels while jingle bells jangle
Tomorrow will be Christmas day
I've been waiting all day, to see Santa's sleigh
And the reindeer, oh my, it's bedtime
I must get the cookies and milk
I set them out and ran upstairs
And got in my pj's made of silk
I cuddled in bed and looked out the window
By golly, I said
It was Santa, the reindeer and the sleigh
Then I went down stairs, to meet that jolly fellow
And I saw him eating cherry Jell-O
He quickly spread the presents
And was gone in a flash
I took a glance at the presents
Remembered I'll be back so,
I ran upstairs very fast
I went to bed happy, it was Christmas at last!

Natalie Brueckner, Grade 5
Harris Hill Elementary School

Mom's and Dad's Cake Recipe

711 cups of love
3 cups of happiness
4 cups of sweet honey
7 to 8 cups of strength and confidence

If you put that all together, you get a wonderful
Mom and Dad cake recipe.

Alexandra Garand, Grade 5
William B Tecler Elementary School

Our Four Seasons

Our four seasons are
Winter, spring, summer and fall.
In winter, we play in the snow.
In spring, we play outside and have fun.
So much fun!
In summer, it is hot out all day.
And in fall, we pick apples and play in the leaves.
Our four seasons are so much fun.

Nikki Berrin, Grade 5
Robert Seaman Elementary School

My Balloons

Two balloons so pretty and fine,
I got them both as a present from a friend of mine.
One was black; the other was orange and bright!
They kept me company on a scary Halloween night.
One night I let go of their strings,
Oh dear, my balloon friends blew—
Up to the midnight moon they flew.

Camie Perez-Segnini, Grade 6
School of the Holy Child

Who Will Find Me?
In this barren land will someone please take me, care for me, love me
Someone has left me here, crying alone, unnoticed by the real world
I am lost, fear is with me,
For what I know is gone and all that's left is me
Many people on this Earth have not seen me in a long time
Everyone loved me, but that was a long time ago,
Those who were with me probably don't remember who I was or what I was like.
War has pushed me to the side like the mother pushing away the runt of the litter,
WAR has locked me up in a cage, I am peace, who will find me?

Sophia Wojnovich, Grade 6
Eagle Hill Middle School

Thanksgiving Day
I love Thanksgiving Day
It is a day when most families gather to pray
It is a festive time of year
Everyone is filled with love and cheer
We give thanks for all our blessings from up above
This is a day of pure love
People come from all countries and states
When you walk through your neighborhood look around you'll see different license plates
It's a day when food is plentiful and people willfully share
It's a day of humbleness, gracefulness and care
So now I've shared why I love Thanksgiving Day
And once it's over I know that Christmas is well on its way!

Darriele Jefferson, Grade 6
St John School

I Love Fall
I like fall but I love how the leaves change colors to orange red and yellow. They look different.
I like fall but I love to rake the leaves and jump in because they feel as soft as my bed.
I like fall but I love going apple picking. The apples I like to taste are sour.
I like fall but I love going trick or treating with my friends. We get lots of candy.

Aristides Joya, Grade 4
Northeast Elementary School

My Fun Spot
My neighborhood is a dazzling place to watch the amber sun sink into the horizon.
My neighborhood is the best place to record hilarious memories.
My neighborhood has the most fantabulous elementary school, Helen B. Duffield.
And it is where kids fly on their glowing bikes at night.
And it is where children scream with joy as they play like they just pulled a mischievous stunt.
And it is where on Halloween the houses are the spookiest I've ever seen.
This is the wonderful place I call home!

Brandon Moore, Grade 4
Helen B Duffield Elementary School

Animals
Ape's doing their thing swinging from vine to vine as night falls over the sleeping zoo. Imagine you with the animals as you lie in the green cold and damp grass but you don't care you are with the animals now you're one of them.
Monkeys everywhere here and there, to us they're just monkeys but to you he's your uncle. Lions roaring in your ear like a bunch of blue birds saying "Welcome home, brother." Sun is here you're up and ready when night falls, back where I was but now I say bye to the animal zoo.

Zakiya De Roche, Grade 5
Public School 41 Greenwich Village

Geraniums

Geranium is so pinkish.
Geranium is so pretty.
Geraniums look like butterflies flying.
Geraniums are so pretty.
Geranium's leaves looks like flowers.

Amy Ko, Grade 4
Public School 205 Alexander Graham Bell

Halloween Frights

The Halloween fright
Is only during the night
But you will hear screams
From across the streams
You will hear trick-or-treaters party for candy
Like they do when the beaches are sandy
The wolves howling
And the rain storms showering
With a great fright there was no light
But it was during the night
Don't be afraid, it's only Halloween
But it's just the start of the scene.

Daniel Furtado, Grade 6
George Grant Mason Elementary School

Thanksgiving 2007

Lights dulled down,
Candles lit,
Grandma, Grandpa, aunts and uncle,
Mother, Father, Son, and Daughter,
We gather together,
We gather together in prayer for the sake of giving,
We remember that we all love living,
Thanksgiving, Thanksgiving,
Give a loud cheer,
Thanksgiving, Thanksgiving,
It's the time of year!

Megan Farrell, Grade 6
St John School

Ability

Imagine soaring over seas of mint-green grass,
Or over fields of turquoise water.
Imagine feeling the cool, smooth breeze,
Of the air against your feathery face.

Imagine the clamor of fellow geese,
Whistling through the morning sky.
Imagine the squawking of your friends
As they soar through the air beside you.

Imagine the impact of you and your friends,
As you land gracefully back on earth.
Finally, imagine waking up one morning,
And having the ability to do all of these things.

Trevor Foster, Grade 6
Akron Middle School

Food Fanatic

I love food
It puts me in a happy mood
I eat Ring Dings
And also Buffalo wings

I love food
It puts me in a happy mood
I never take a break
When I am eating steak

I love food
It puts me in a happy mood
I love cookies, brownies and even cakes
Especially the ones my mom bakes

I love food
It puts me in a happy mood
I will eat
Until I am numb all the way down to my feet

Aidan Meade, Grade 6
Harold D Fayette Elementary School

The Old House

On an old lonely street,
There's an old lonely house.
Every now and then you'll hear a shriek,
From the old, old house on the old, old street.
When you step inside the door,
A horrible creak will haunt you forever more.
The stairs will creak 1-2-3-4,
Keeping perfect time,
As if a melody or rhyme.
The wind will hallow,
A ghost will bellow,
A witch will cackle,
A skeleton will rattle.
And you will run, run, run
With a terrible fright
To all the ghosts' delight.
Then you hear a moan
And you will never be alone.

Elizabeth Cassidy, Grade 5
The Albany Academies

Me

Natalie is like the clouds, gentle and kind
Tall and thin, with blonde hair and brown eyes,
Studious and hardworking,
Striving towards anything she chooses to take on,
Spunky and friendly,
Extremely caring about others,
This is her definition.

Natalie Stefan, Grade 6
Shelter Rock Elementary School

Never Met
Grandpa's Birthday
Never met
Died when I was born
Named Bill
I'm named after him
Mom's dad
Was doctor
Wanted to go to cemetery
Mom wouldn't let me
Grave always dirty
In the corner
Was Jewish
Heard he was a nice guy
Simon Lambert, Grade 4
Public School 69

A Dream
At night I heard a noise,
It sounded like a bunch of boys,
They laughed and sang and played,
Just like on a summer day,
I knew it was a dream.
I felt peaceful, not mean,
I was on a never ending rainbow of joy,
Only because I heard a boy,
A dream can be bad,
And make you feel very sad,
But then a thought will pick you up,
The thought of happiness and luck,
That was my dream late last night,
It didn't give me one little fright.
Kayla Schwartz, Grade 5
Robert Seaman Elementary School

From Smoke to the Lighter
A man sits on a bench,
smoking a cigar.
Smoke rises from his nostrils,
as he peers into his newspaper.
Back to the lighter.

His jacket reeks from the stench
of the cigar.
Four yellow teeth left in his mouth.
Back to the lighter.

His lungs blacken,
his wheezing intensifies,
his strength wanes.
Back to the lighter.

The next day,
there is no man on the bench.
All that remains is the lighter.
Ikey Shuster, Grade 6
Yeshiva Shaare Torah

Gone
I didn't know you were gone
Until 10:00
I didn't start to know it
Until it hit me in the heart
I really didn't understand
Until after a week
But I want you to know
I miss you

I miss your smile
I miss your big heart
I miss the feeling of love when I see you
I miss how we were so close
I'm sorry you had to go
I miss you

If I had one more day
The only thing I would do
Is spend it with you
I miss you Nonna
Gabriella Verdone, Grade 6
Nesaquake Middle School

Hailey
I have a niece named Hailey,
who drives me crazy daily.
Her visits are brief,
but I still need relief.
I don't mean to sound cold,
'cause she's only 3 years old.
When she goes home after,
I can still hear her laughter.
I'm glad my niece Hailey,
comes to drive me crazy daily.
Adam Schuh, Grade 6
SS Peter and Paul School

My Friend
My friend Giovanny
plays with me
My friend Giovanny
has black hair
and brown eyes
We will always
be together
at lunch time
we play uno
Giovanny
and
me
best friends
forever.
Juan Sanchez, Grade 5
Public School 148 Ruby Allen

Running
I like to run
It is fun
I came in first
I did it in reverse
I go so fast
I never come in last
If you want to win
You have to beat me
You won't win
I'm too fast
You'll see!
Zachary Hurst, Grade 4
Sacred Heart School

El Salvador
E njoyment in school
L arge houses

S peaking Spanish
A ction
L ots of family members
V alleys and mountains quiet
A ll people own animals
D irt rising in air
O ranges growing on trees
R oosters crowing
Edgar Moreno, Grade 5
Northeast Elementary School

Wind
I am the wind,
The wind is me,
With no sun to be seen,
I am a cold breeze,
I pulse in a steady beat,
I give chills to creatures below.

I search for flying prey,
As I close in,
I realize,
I am nothing to these graceful creatures.

I push through them,
I feel their pulses,
Changing with every moment,
There is difference,
I feel…moved.

The sun comes out from its hibernation,
I become a ray,
I provide warmth to creatures below,
I am now the sun's faithful servant,
I am the wind,
The wind is me.
Eric Ravens, Grade 6
Harold D Fayette Elementary School

My Dog

The dog chases the leaves,
But never catches a leaf.
The leaf soars in the wind
And floats gently to the ground
Like a soft, fluffy feather.
Then he loses the leaf
And goes after another,
But he can't ever catch one
Because he uses his paws.
I wonder why he doesn't use his mouth?
He probably thinks he'll swallow it fast.
Maybe he should just chase my soccer balls —
He probably needs to take a nap
In his dog house.
When he wakes up
He should eat
And chase some squirrels
Or just sit on my lap and cuddle with me.
I love my dog and he loves me.

Artemi Jadribbinski, Grade 5
Dickinson Avenue Elementary School

Winter

When it snows, it is a special treat.
The way it covers everything nice and neat.
It is soft like a pillow when it's touched.
Even though it's cold, I like it so much.
The trees without leaves are bare
Standing without a care.

Sledding, snow angels and snow ball fights.
Picking what to do takes all my might.
Fires inside with hot cocoa to drink.
I cover myself with my blanket that is pink.
The twinkling lights and a Christmas tree.
Does everybody like winter or just me?

Brittany Proseus, Grade 5
Harris Hill Elementary School

Christmas Day

Christmas is coming, get ready for it
By putting up your tree and decorating it.
It was Christmas Eve night
And the lights were shining bright.
Nothing was stirring, all was still
The snow was falling out on the windowsill.
I fell into a deep, happy sleep
With thoughts of Santa my mind did creep.
When I woke up, what did I see
Presents under the tree for my family and me.
It was a beautiful morning, the start of a new day
As we celebrated our Christmas day.

Gabriella Nouri, Grade 5
George Grant Mason Elementary School

Day and Night

Day
Light, bright
Shining, twinkling, sparkling
Glow, glitter, black, shadow
Freezing, frightening, scaring
Dark, cold
Night

Rhea Ramsaywack, Grade 4
Public School 108 Cpt Vincent G. Fowler

The Rain Forest

Trees bristling in the wind,
like hair blowing back while
a person stands in front of a fan.
Animals jumping around like
a pack of wild dogs.

Rain forests across the world
are dropping like flies.
Pollution is growing rapidly.
It is a new fad.

The river's water is as blue
as a clear, summer sky.
Every day another rain forest
is murdered by pollution.

Boom! Another tree drops to the ground.
The world's rain forests are dying.

Tony Novotny, Grade 5
Edward J Bosti Elementary School

Emotions

You love them.
You hate them.
Say to you are strong,
They promise each other,
No demands.
Emotions is a way of words.

Alexander Moore, Grade 6
Immaculate Conception School-Stapleton

Blue

Blue is like a hungry great white shark,
Blue is like raindrops coming down
from the dark blue sky,
Blue is like a pen that has a lot of blue ink,
Blue is like a blueberry rolling off a plate,
Blue is like a boat, that is far out at sea,
Blue is like a person's eye color,
Blue is like bubble gum that is sticky
and chewy, and juicy in my mouth,
Blue is like a dolphin, jumping out from sea,
My favorite color is blue.

Samantha Sanacore, Grade 5
Eastplain School

My Sacred Place
My sacred place
My pillow
Where bad thoughts
Blow away like a dust of wind
And happy thoughts of my future
Come in to cloud my imagination
Night after night
Forever
My dreams for my future
Lior Lampert, Grade 4
Norman J Levy Lakeside School

Puppies in the Moonlight
Deep in the night,
under the moonlight
So bright,

My black and white puppies
Howling in its yellow glow
Just like wolves in the
Deep, deep snow.

Listen to my
Puppies crying,
"Give us a blanket,
And let us come in!"
Claryssa Swiezy, Grade 6
Akron Middle School

Ocean Water
Dark blue water cold as ice
Fiercely crashes against rocks
Boom
Danger
It sprays my face

Farther away is a swimming hole
Where little blue fish hang out
Seagulls chirp
And kids laugh and play
Campbell Block, Grade 4
Norman J Levy Lakeside School

Sounds of Thanksgiving
Whoosh, the leaves rustle
Clank, the moms bustle
Slam, the door opens
Step, the family comes in
Sniff, the turkey sniffed
Tie, the babies bibbed
Chomp, the food is gone
Roar, the TV is on
Sigh, the family sighs
as they sadly bid goodbye
Stephen Kim, Grade 5
Bretton Woods Elementary School

A Definition of Me
A definition of me, well, I'd have to see.
I have long wavy golden brown hair and I am very tall.
This is perfect when I play center in basketball.
Cooking, fishing, and swimming are so much fun,
But when I play tennis, soccer, and basketball I always have to run.
Determined, polite, generous, and intelligent
Are four words that describe me best.
In medical school if I pass the test,
I want to become an endocrinologist.
This is a perfect definition of me!
Georgia Xenophontos, Grade 6
Shelter Rock Elementary School

Me!
Samantha is cool
Samantha is fun
Samantha enjoys fun in the sun
If you like her, you know it's true
because she's always there for you

This girl has got this fire,
lit in your desire.

If you see her you will see
the astonishing beauty of she.

She is your friend when you need her
She's your pal when you believe.

All I have to say, there is no possible way to have this much grace,
but she will put a smile upon your face.

This girl is cunning,
This girl is amazing,
she is blazing, she is me!

Samantha Lamour, Grade 5
Public School 203 Floyd Bennett

Letchworth State Park
Letchworth is awesome!
Letchworth is worth going to.
I like Letchworth cold, warm, rain, snow, hail, thunder and anything more.
It's so much fun!
Letchworth camp fires are the best.
You stay up 'til 'bout twelve o'clock.
There are flashlights shining everywhere you look.
While you hear the wolves howl in the distance.
There are tons of hiking trails including The Canyon Walk and Wolf Creek.
On a Saturday night we're always carving pumpkins.
When it is pitch-black we always play Ghost in the Graveyard.
There is no place like Letchworth, not one single one.
Every year I always look forward to Letchworth State Park.
Nick Nichols, Grade 5
Harris Hill Elementary School

My First Ride on the School Bus to Go to School

I had to sit with other people.
I got to say hi to the bus driver.
On my way to my classroom, I saw other classrooms.
I saw other teachers and kids.
A principal was a giant mountain.

I was hearing kids talking like monkeys.
I also hear the pledge.
What else do I hear?
People saying, "Hi. How was your summer?"
I am saying, "Hi." to other people.
I'm playing with other kids and teachers.
I'm also doing really fun games and other fun stuff.
I'm also doing certain things.

When they said it was time to go,
I did not want to leave school.
It was so much fun!

Courtney Mayo, Grade 6
Sodus Intermediate School

Trees

Trees
Tall, brown
Living, growing, providing
They provide earths oxygen
Budding, breathing, shedding
Colorful, large
Saplings

Jake Gerace, Grade 5
East Syracuse Elementary School

The Sun

Every morning when I see the sun rise,
It makes me think and gives me a surprise.
It burns itself and gives us light
It takes out the darkness and makes the world bright.
The sun is great and important for our life.

Anam Hashmi, Grade 4
Public School 48

The Wind Is Like a Spirit

The wind is like a howling spirit
who bounds upon the restless sea,
and pounds the sea with its mighty fist.
The waves go pale and turn cold as ice with fright.
It does graceful spins and makes trees lose their autumn leaves
in the presence of the spirit.
It dances across the desert,
Turning grains into sandstorms.
It brushes the clouds with its ghostly fingers.
When the wind dies down,
the earth falls silent
and the spirit is no more.

Emma Carr, Grade 4
Shelter Rock Elementary School

Friendship

A friend is like a rope that will never break,
Having one is like a piece of chocolate cake.
Some are better than others and we all know that's true,
When friends are around you'll never be blue

Friends are the ones who stand by your side,
Although it may be like a roller coaster ride.
Though we all know it's the same in the end,
And great friends will not be pretend.

Life is too short to not have friends who are the best,
If they're pure and true, you'll never have to give them a rest.
Decide to be kind,
And many friendships will bind.

Melissa Lee Lombard, Grade 6
Shelter Rock Elementary School

My Home

My home, full of love,
always together, morning,
afternoon, and night.

My home, comforting,
joyful, and fun.

My home, I love my home,
unforgettable moments, and thankfulness.

Nowhere is as great as my home.

Christina Chase, Grade 6
Long Beach Middle School

I Will Leave

I will leave…
Your voice calling, and eyes watching me,
and the shadow I knew, vanishing,
I will leave my windows
With light pouring in like rain,
and the gray clouds in the sky,
I will no longer feel your warm breath
on my neck…
I   will   leave

Phoebe Holland, Grade 4
Upper Nyack Elementary School

Growth

G rowing up to become a mature male or female
R emembering the past like it was just yesterday
O pening the doors to a new beginning
W aiting for another year to be another year older
T he time of your life you enjoy forever
H appy you're old enough to do what you desire

James Ball, Grade 6
St Mary's School

The Mirror

I hate mirrors,
Mirrors are mean.
They copy your movements
And do whatever you do.
This is why I don't like mirrors.
They like to play around with you.
But the only reason I like mirrors
Is because they help you see how you look!!!

Fariha Tanha, Grade 6
Public School 131

The Best Stranger

He was tall with glasses
Bright blue eyes
This stranger took me by surprise
I didn't know him and I didn't know why
But seeing this stranger almost made me cry
He never visited, so we saw him
My real grandpa that's who it is
The best stranger I'll ever meet
Not gone forever
Only 3 hours away
Very sweet

Jackie Gropper, Grade 6
Long Beach Middle School

As Days and Weeks Go By

As days and weeks go by,
It is just like butterflies.
Just as they go flying by,
Sometimes boring and very sad
And other times, they are not so bad.

As days and weeks go by,
It is just like a bird in the sky.
When you turn and look back,
They have already gone by.

As days and weeks go by,
It is like a bear chasing a deer.
Neither you know the deer can see them coming,
Even when they are near.

Charles Cheema, Grade 5
Cortland Christian Academy

My Mother

Is a golden dewdrop on a summer day.
It blooms like a flower.
It warms my heart like the sun.
It is like laying on a fluffy cloud high up in the sky.
It feels like hot chocolate in winter.
My mother's poem.

Joshua Deen, Grade 4
Upper Nyack Elementary School

Imagine a World…

Where you could fly without wings
Where you could walk on water
Where you could walk the whole world
Where kids could drive six and up
Where you were friends with everyone
Where your dreams will come true
Where everything was play
Where everything is free
Where you could have parties nonstop
Where no one could boss you around
Where you could be anything you want to be
And life never comes to an end…

Sydney Gropack, Grade 4
Norman J Levy Lakeside School

Friendship

Friendship is a special bond you share with someone.
It can help any day become happier.
When you are down,
a friend always comes around
to play and turn the day
in a different way.

Friends treat each other
with respect
and watch each other's back.
No two friendships are the same.
Friendships exist
all around the world.

Chase Hampton, Grade 6
Shelter Rock Elementary School

My Precious Sign

God, please give me a sign.
Let it be lucky, let it be mine.
Give me a clover, a number four.
Unlucky days let there be no more.
Give me the magic from you right now.
Tell me where, tell me how.
Give me the eyes of a hawk.
Let it be secret, like a lock.
Help me be focused, like a snake.
Let me be gentle, like a lake.
Then I look closely, Oh my dear!
I can't believe I see it right here!
My four leaf clover so precious and rare.
Thank you, God, for answering my prayer.

Avery Charette, Grade 6
Fabius-Pompey Middle/High School

Green

Green is the green grass blown by the wind
Green is the leaves that are on the trees
Green is the frog that hops on the land.

Tyler Fuentes, Grade 4
Leptondale Elementary School

Science Is...

An interesting subject,
Making electricity with many wires to connect.
Dissecting owl pellets to see their prey's bones,
Everywhere, including our homes.
Measuring earthquakes around the world,
Observing which object turns to mold.
Learning all of the eight planets,
What will happen if we put together a coin and a magnet?
Nature with beautiful trees and flowers,
Earthquakes shaking homes and towers.
The sun affecting the Earth,
What kind of teeth are in a mouth?
The ocean with many plants and animals,
Many groups of animals like mammals.
Studying different kinds of stars,
An exciting subject.

Kana Takeda, Grade 6
Shelter Rock Elementary School

Stunning Autumn

Summer has vanished and
fall has just begun
Leaves falling like tiny snowflakes
Bright red leaves
as red an exquisite Robin
Ducks quacking like noisy whistles
Leaves on the ground as crunchy as dull cereal
Huge Cardinals soaring through
trees to migrate for the winter
Delicious pumpkin pie fresh
from the burning oven
Yellow leaves showing
their abundant lemon skin
Animals getting ready for hibernation
and I am getting ready for the chilly winter!!

Sean Gambardella, Grade 4
Helen B Duffield Elementary School

The Thing

The thing is walking through the night
But please don't worry, it won't bite
Creeping, crawling to the door
Tell me right now if you want more
Piddle, paddle, piddle, paddle
There it is on the doorstep
DING DONG!
Creek, crack, creek crack
Went the door
Splat! Went the candy that landed on the floor
BOOOOOO!
AHHHHHHHHHHHHHH!
Happy Halloween!

Edward Eisenman, Grade 6
Boardman Elementary School

My Guardian Angel

My Guardian Angel flies
within the air
going through the earth
with gentle care. Her wings flap.
Her eyes tap.
I love you angel
and that's a fact.
Her eyes are like crystals
Shining in the light.
She flies with beauty
So gentle and tight.
She has a great mind.
She only works for the good
She only works for the kind.
You can see her fly gracefully above.
She is my Guardian Angel that I know and love.

Jennifer Croce, Grade 5
Edward J Bosti Elementary School

What the Voices Tell Me

I walk outside into the Halloween night,
hearing voices that do not sound right.
Voices that say kill, kill, kill,
So I run up the spooky hill.
The air is as cold as snow!
I keep low!
The fearful footsteps sound close
they are right behind me.
Clomp, clomp, clomp, clomp
clomp, clomp, clomp!
I look behind me nothing's there.
I look all around
then to the ground.
Suddenly, I feel an icy hand on my shoulder,
A creepy chill goes down my spine.
I am not going to survive this time.
Suddenly, I fall and wake up beside my bed,
I look at my door it's creaking open.
Voice tell me,
"It's time for Halloween!"

Cara DePan, Grade 5
The Albany Academies

Life

It is a force.
It pounds.
It throbs.
Within us it lies.
It allows your heart to beat.
It is a journey with many miracles.
Why do we go against each other when we
are bound by the same power to this Earth?
It is one of many mysteries.
Life.

Leo S. Tulchin, Grade 5
Pleasantville Middle School

The Beach

Waves crashing
boats dashing straight across the water
surfboards riding the waves
crabs and lobsters swimming at sea
seashells buried in the wet sand
kids playfully yelling
ice cream trucks singing
and people talking
to the beat of the ocean waves.

Brittany Scalli, Grade 4
Norman J Levy Lakeside School

The Woods

The woods of my backyard
Go swish swish
When the wind blows
Like a dream in the sky
Blowing blowing
Around around
Every thing I do in the woods
Is like a dream in the sky

Alexis Wheeler, Grade 4
Hendy Avenue School

Fairies

I see those little pixie things.
They have no tails but they have wings.
They use their wings so they can fly,
in their fairy world across the sky.
They can fly almost everywhere.
But for me it's so not fair!

Sarah Salameh, Grade 5
Public School 2 Alfred Zimberg

Dreams

Slowly forming after dark
Night falls I begin to wake
I am anything you think of
When your head hits the pillow
Stories are my brain
Thoughts are my heart
I am love
I am fear
I am loud
I am quiet
I am what you think of
Slowly fading away
Morning comes, I begin to sleep
Waiting for the night to fall
Where I
The dream
Forms…

Laura Pugliese, Grade 6
Nesaquake Middle School

N.Y.C.

New York City
as fine as it can be.
So many lights,
you need sunglasses just to see.
Singing in the theater,
Broadway shows at night.
It gives me such delight!
Home of the Big Apple,
potato and Snapple.
George Washington's home
skyscrapers and domes.

Rebecca Steiner, Grade 5
Edward J Bosti Elementary School

I Love Nugget

Nugget is my dog and I love her.
Her fur looks like a chicken nugget.
Her bark is as loud as thunder.
She's soft as a blanket.
She sheds like a tree in fall
She's crazy like a drunk driver.
She jumps on you like a lion
Pounces to get its food.
Nugget acts like a lot of things
But she is my dog and I love her.

Alessandra Ponzini, Grade 4
Concord Road Elementary School

Dream

I woke up one morning in the sea,
And then I notice it wasn't me
I had big jaws,
I had very long claws
I look like a freak,
I had a very long beak
And then I had a funny feel,
My body was turning into an eel
I swam up to the shore,
I put up my beak and began to roar
Then there was a mysterious fog,
I started hopping like a frog
Then I began to yell,
I was running and then I fell,
I slowly lift up my head…
I then found myself in bed.

Faith Titilawo, Grade 6
Intermediate School 218 J P Sinnott

Fall

The sun was so bright
September is a great month
Leaves are falling down
Some people love fall today
My friend and I love pumpkins

Nicole Guzman, Grade 5
Northeast Elementary School

Mighty Siberian Tigers

Powerful beasts
Hiding in the dark jungle.
Strong claws,
Enormous teeth,
Massive feet, and razor sharp claws.

Stalking its prey,
Largest tigers on the earth,
Their stripes are like a thumbprint,
No two are exactly alike.

Ready to leap
Hunting by day and night,
Sneaking close to its prey.
With explosive leaps.

Playing rough,
The ferocious hunter,
Most endangered animals on the earth,
Let's hope it's not too late.

Derek Edgar, Grade 6
Akron Middle School

Dogs and Cats

Cats will lick and clean themselves,
While dogs run and play,
Cats will sun bathe themselves,
While dogs hang out all day,
Cats will take a snooze
under the very warm sun,
While the dogs play around
while having fun,

Cats do this and,
Dogs do that,
But why do you think that is that?
Dogs are different,
Cats are too,
But both are different,
And that is true

Emma Distler, Grade 5
Robert Seaman Elementary School

I Promise

I will treat people fairly,
Protect every individual's rights,
Respect others,
Offer help to those in need,
Make time to listen to others.
I will work hard to do my best,
Share everyone's ideas.
Everyone's voice counts.

Breana Mattice, Grade 5
William B Tecler Elementary School

Missing You

I'm missing you
Why did you have to go?
I remember when I saw you
It's not fair that you left me!

Now everybody misses you
I'm missing you
Your mom's missing you
And your dad's missing you

Now that you're not here
I'm crying for you
All the night and days I still miss you

I'm missing you I'm missing you
I love you so much
Now you're in a better place
And no one can take
The pain and love I'm feeling for you
Love you Derhia

Adriana Garcia, Grade 5
Public School 105 Senator Abraham Bernste

Halloween

Haunted houses covered by spider webs
Witches with purple hair casting spells
Orange pumpkins decorating the stairs of neighbor's homes
Witches crackle in the middle of the night
Children trick or treating with their costumes on
Parents dressed up waiting to scare trick or treaters
Leaves crunching as I walk down the foggy block
Feeling of happiness while trick or treating with family

Maria Baca, Grade 4
Northeast Elementary School

Pure Feathers

As light as a feather, with bones so hollow,
A lemming she is desperate to follow.
She glides down with a powerful whoosh,
And the lemming scatters to the nearest bush.
With a beak so fierce, and talons so strong,
This unfortunate lemming will soon be gone.
Her talons pierce the lemming's skin,
Now her babies will be not so thin.
With another whoosh she flies away,
Happy that she caught her prey.
One last whoosh she soars down low,
With glistening feathers of pure white snow.
She survives through the great amber skies,
Over the clouds and hills she thrives.
No other owl has a beauty so rich and fine,
This snowy owl is superior to divine.
"Goodbye! Farewell snowy owl!" I say,
I hope to see her another day.

Celia Rosa Acuna, Grade 6
Munsey Park Elementary School

My New York

Leaves falling from the trees,
everywhere I look are colors,
the birds are chirping and squirrels getting nuts.
As the white fluffy clouds are starting to block the blue sky,
and the yellow sun.
This is my New York.

Isaiah Townson, Grade 4
Hendy Avenue School

I Am From N.Y.C.

I am from the lullaby of police car sirens
And the honking of peeved drivers
I am from the banging of the subway
BOOM, BOOM, BOOM, BOOM
I am from the big tall sky scrapers that write in the sky
And the luminous blinding lights
Of Broadway

I am from the tight cramped space
Of the apartment
The misty foggy smell
Of N.Y.C.

And the friendly door men who greet you
And become your best friend
I am from the banging street players
And break dancing freaks
I am from all the noisy street fairs
And parades
And the big wide world of
N.Y.C. waiting for me
I am from the concrete jungle
I Am From…New…York…City

Nicholas Hine, Grade 6
Pleasantville Middle School

Me

Listen to me, do you hear me?
I'm sitting here talking
and you're just ignoring me
Am I a different person
that you see in me
or is it that you don't like me?
I yell your name
and you just walk away
I say hi while you're around
but you just look around like
you don't see me
Am I so invisible
that you don't look at me
'cause I'm standing right in front of you talking
but you don't listen?

Chelsea Semple, Grade 5
Public School 203 Floyd Bennett

Colombia

C an't wait to go there again!
O cean is crystal blue
L ove to visit family
O ut all the time
M ountains
B ring home souvenirs
I ce cream melts quickly!
A lot of rain

Amanda DeLorenzo, Grade 5
Northeast Elementary School

Dogs

He likes to run and have fun,
He looks small but he is very tall
And a very good dog
Not a bad dog at all
When I call the dog's name
He is always playing
He loves his ball and never
Looks to crashing in the wall

Hillary Williams, Grade 4
Granville Elementary School

Fireworks

They go up and down,
Left and right,
And most of all
They're always bright.

Crash, bang, boom!
Colors go flying in a zoom.
Then the sky goes black.

Jean Elizabeth Stevens, Grade 5
William B Tecler Elementary School

Autumn

Autumn
So cool and cold
The nights grow longer
And stories are told
Days grow shorter
Leaves race to the ground
Time for bed
Make not a sound

Daniel Hucks, Grade 4
State Road Elementary School

My Teddy

My teddy has one eye
And a rubber tie
A patched up ear
So listen here
I had to throw him in the trash
And then he turned to ash!

Marisa Langlois, Grade 4
Granville Elementary School

Basketball

Thump Thump
Music to my ears
Beats of my heart
just a sound
to you
It's my rescue
It's my hopes
It's my dreams
It's my everything
You don't have to understand it
It's my game
It's mine mine mine
First everyone's there
Now they're not
Just me
in the zone

Jenna Brown, Grade 6
Northwood Elementary School

Puppies

Cute as a newborn baby
Snuggles with you when you feel scared
Barks to protect you
Has fur so soft

THAT'S PUPPIES

Arrienne Martini, Grade 5
East Syracuse Elementary School

Coffee

Coffee is so sweet
and
sour…
It is nice with
a hot
juicy bagel

Coffee is so
relaxing
that at work
you feel
the creamy taste
inside your heart
boom, boom, boom
when you're bored
and you feel that you
have no friends
think about coffee
that creamy taste that runs down
your throat making a sizzling sound
It sounds like a hot pot of coffee
SSSS. SSSS Hmmm coffee.

Hakeem Bakare, Grade 5
Public School 148 Ruby Allen

Joy of Life

CONGRATULATIONS!
A baby is born.
The mother's heart
swells with joy
as she holds her small,
cuddly bundle
swathed in blankets,
blinking and staring
under the light;
the skin smooth as gel.
This is the gift of life.
A pure soul
has entered this world.

Daniel Abadi, Grade 6
Yeshivat Shaare Torah

Disappearing Flower and Bee

A flower, a flower,
So pretty I might stare at it for an hour.
A stem, green leaves,
Watch as it disappears
Through my sleeves!
A bee! A bee!
One day I knelt on it with my knee.
So sorry. Sorry, Mr. Bee.
He didn't accept my apology.
Of course, when I got home,
I told my mom, "Youch!
I got stung by a bee!"

Benjamin Hellert, Grade 4
John T Waugh Elementary School

Scuba Diving

Under the quiet water
In the depth of the cold ocean,
I see all the underwater motion,
All of the creatures swimming around.

While I try to swim
All the way down
The loud waves crash
Above my head.

While the big white shark
Swim already fed,
Under the water I hear the scuttle
Of all the stunned fish
Swimming by.

Under the dark water,
Pushing me down,
Leaning against the chilly dark ground;
I look at the bright sun beaming down
Under the water.

Sabrina Kolo, Grade 6
Akron Middle School

Life Doesn't Frighten Me

Monsters, ghouls, and scary old fools
Life doesn't frighten me at all.

Mutants, creatures, and other bad features
Life doesn't frighten me at all.

Aliens and beasts will make you their feast but
still life doesn't frighten me at all.

Goblins and ghosts should scare me the most
but still life doesn't frighten me at all.

These aren't scary except for missiles or bombs,
the only thing that really scares me is my mom.

Daniel Hanson, Grade 6
Long Beach Middle School

No One

No one knows what's deep within,
No one knows what keeps you in.
There's no one around that knows the real you,
The real you within your heart,
So listen to what you think
And say what you like
'Cause no one knows you,
the way you know yourself.

Jacheem Taylor, Grade 5
Public School 105 Senator Abraham Bernste

The Macy's Thanksgiving Day Parade

Anxious faces in crowded places,
Waiting in anticipation for the start of all the action.
People young and old,
Looking on with satisfaction.

The atmosphere is full of cheer,
Waiting for the floats and balloons to appear.
Choreographed holiday dance numbers,
Skilled acrobatic tumblers.

Commercials, there are a plenty,
I really wish there weren't so many.
Kermit the frog is an old time favorite,
He'll fly by fast so try to savor it.

When you see Santa on his sleigh,
You'll know that Christmas is on its way.
Santa sitting tall and proud,
Children stand on tiptoe in the crowd.

Maybe next year I'll appear,
As a face in that crowded place.

Guy Zoutis, Grade 6
Most Precious Blood School

Blue

Blue is the color of the sky in the morning,
Blue is the color of the rain in spring,
Blue is the color of the waves in the ocean,
Blue is my favorite color!

Ashley Wohlrab, Grade 4
Leptondale Elementary School

Black

Black is the color of my room,
And so is my new Zune,
Black is the night sky,
And the pupil in my eye,
Black is a wonderful color,
Black is the color of sadness and hate,
Black is an IBM ThinkPad with Windows Vista,
Black is the color of my room,
And my new Zune.

Brian Testa, Grade 5
Eastplain School

The Home Run

The pitch was fast,
It was lightning coming my way.
I swung my bat like a mini Babe Ruth,
BOOM!

The ball flew overhead,
And into the blue of the sky.
The boy on second was now rounding third,
The ball had almost hit a bird!

I'm now rounding second,
With one run in.
The ball has now touched the land,
I'm now rounding third.

The outfielder got the ball,
I slid into home.
When I looked up,
I was being covered by a dome.
HOME RUN!!

Michael DiCocco, Grade 6
Harold D Fayette Elementary School

Beautiful Washington

Walla walla onion, and sweet cherries too,
The Willow Goldfinch singing its tune.
Washington's Mountains reach the clear blue sky.
Volcanoes cascade look like tears when you cry.

The Western Hemlock gives you shade.
Mining, space equipment, and lumber are made.
Forests and pines, there are all different kinds.
The Evergreen State has its own shape. I know it is GREAT!!!!

Zulmary Cruz, Grade 4
St Andrew School

Sports

S occer is fun.
P oker is hard.
O ur team plays football.
R obert is good at baseball.
T eamwork is good to use.
S occer is when you kick a ball in a net.

Andrew Matteson, Grade 4
Granville Elementary School

Florida

Florida
Hot relaxing
Surfing the waves
The beautiful sandy beach
Vacation

Conall McCurn, Grade 5
Most Holy Rosary School

Dear Butterfly

Dear little butterfly,
Was the trip fun?
I like your tongue.
Why are you buzzing around?
What? I can't understand you.
No! Do not fly away!
Oh, well, bye, bye.
P.S. I was not done with you!

Anna Thomas, Grade 4
John T Waugh Elementary School

Life Doesn't Frighten Me at All

When I got on my waveboard
I hoped I did not get hurt
That I could not afford
Life doesn't frighten me at all

On my ripstick
I can be quick
Life doesn't frighten me at all

When I was playing judo
I felt like I was on Pluto
Life doesn't frighten me at all

When I was in camp
We went on a hike
I told them I would rather ride my bike
Life doesn't frighten me at all

When I was in the ocean
The water was in motion
Life doesn't frighten me at all

Darran Byrne, Grade 6
Long Beach Middle School

Christmas Time

Christmas is getting closer and
closer each day.
Christmas trees, Christmas lights
Christmas decorations
on each and every house.

Children dashed outside
to play with the snow.
Kids chuckled at each other
when they got hit with snowballs.

When the children trotted in
they smelled the delicious
hot chocolate air in the kitchen.

Erica Davis, Grade 5
Edward J Bosti Elementary School

My Brothers

M ine Forever
Y ours Truly

B est Friend
R esponsible
O thers Are Caring
T here For You
H elps You When You Need It
E xciting
R espectful
S pecial

Adrianna McRae, Grade 4
Hendy Avenue School

Night Time

Nothing is darker then nighttime.
I see the stars shining in the sky.
Getting darker every minute.
Hours go by and it doesn't get brighter
The street lights peering into my room

Time is fast at night.
I can hear the trees Crack, Creek, Crack.
Morning is far away.
Every day has nighttime.

No one hates nighttime.
I love nighttime.
Going to be morning soon.
Having dreams.
The darkness is getting brighter.

The morning has come.
I can't open my eyes it's so bright.
My mom says "time to wake up."
Every day has nighttime.

Joey Lizzi, Grade 6
Harold D Fayette Elementary School

Stars

Stars are bright in the dark sky
Stars are popping at dusk
Stars are shooting in the shadowy sky
Stars are always sparkling yellow
Stars shine my way in a dark pathway

Evan Bershadsky, Grade 5
Northeast Elementary School

Christmas

White, cold
Visiting, unwrapping, decorating
Santa is coming soon
Jesus' Birthday

Donny Wilkinson, Grade 4
Leptondale Elementary School

My Brother

Freddy is tall
just like a giraffe
he plays like a monkey
and he jumps
like a squirrel
he fights like a dog
rough, rough, rough
he's my big
brother
and
I
love
him
so
much!

Marcos Carangui, Grade 5
Public School 148 Ruby Allen

My Heart Is Empty

My heart is empty,
My grandpa died,
And I'm not happy,
He was the only one,
Who was nice,
To give me food,
My heart is empty,
When I look at the sky,
I see him,
When I cry I see him,
My grandpa is gone,
My heart is empty,
It's not fair,
I need him back,
God can't take him,
Just like that.

Farha Laskar, Grade 5
Public School 148 Ruby Allen

Ode to Christmas

The day you come my mouth drops.
I cannot believe you are here already.
When my mom gets ups,
I run like a race car down the steps.
All of the presents are around the tree
like a huge ball with bows.
Me and my brothers and sister run
like raptors we tear those right up.
But when we're done you should see the mess.
We have to play after we pick up.

Andrew Harvey, Grade 4
Hendy Avenue School

Sweet Tooth

Candy is sweet
Candy is sour
It melts in your mouth
Or sticks to your teeth

I'd like a chocolate bar
Or gummy worms
Maybe some Swedish Fish
Or some cookie crumbs

I hate candy for…
Giving me cavities
And crooked teeth
My mom got broke
When she paid for my new teeth

Joanne Fu, Grade 5
Public School 205 Alexander Graham Bell

Peace

Peace is not a place without noise or trouble
It is a place of joy and still be kind in your heart
For that is what keeps you alive

Jonah Weintraub, Grade 4
Upper Nyack Elementary School

Shannon Alive

When I'm happy I'm like a giggling toy,
and when I'm excited I like to annoy.

But when I'm grumpy I'm like a sleeping bunny,
and when I'm sad nothing's funny.

When I'm calm I'm like sand,
and when I'm brave I get up and stand.

But when I'm nervous I'm like a runaway train,
and when I'm angry I could move to Maine.

There are a bunch of feelings in all living things,
sent to us by God to tug at our heart strings.

Shannon Saar, Grade 6
Intermediate School 72 Rocco Laurie

The Sunset on a Beach

I am sitting here on this day
Waiting
And I see the waves
Flowing to shore
The water hitting my feet
Cleaning the sand from my toes
Everyone is in the water
The sun
Beating down on me
The sun
It calms me down
The temperature is rising
Crash!!!
The waves knocking people down
Like a wrecking ball knocking down a building
The sun is dying out
Trying to stay alive
The night is near
Goodbye sun

Bryan Bristoll, Grade 6
Harold D Fayette Elementary School

Christmas

Snow is white
Christmas is merry
A pair of warm gloves I always carry.

The Christmas tree I decorate
With lights, ornaments and lots of candy canes,
And I go to bed early waiting for that
Special day.

Then I heard a noise.
Must be that Santa is coming!
Can't wait to open my presents
On that special morning.

Yeana Cordero, Grade 5
Staley Upper Elementary School

My Song

My song is a garden of truth
My song is a fountain in the clouds
My song is a garden of memories
My song is on dew drop on the grass
My song is a miracle on silk
My song is a snow fall in summer
My song is a star at noon
My song is a never ending wing of sadness
My song is a rose in the desert
My song is a stray moonlight
My song is a moon shining in the day
My song was a copy of nothing

Leah Brand, Grade 4
Upper Nyack Elementary School

Wind

As it slowly moves
I watch the trees whistling
Clearly through the air
Caitlyn O'Connell, Grade 6
Great Hollow Middle School

The Moon

I saw you stroll up to the sky,
And heard you say, "Oh sun, goodbye."
You come upon us oh so calm —
Like a mother's warm and loving palm.
O moon that guides us very bright,
O moon that shows her face at night.

I saw you at night, a ghostly sight,
Then you didn't appear on starry night,
Like a hole in the sky;
Only stars to guide.
O moon that guides us very bright
O moon that shows her face at night.
Aleisha Ramlatchan, Grade 4
Public School 124Q

Football

Football is the sport
You love to play.
Except for when it rains
Because you slip and you fall.

Wearing jerseys with
Your name on the back.
After you put it on, game on.

Then you stretch
And exercise your muscles.
Then coach gives deceiving plays,
For everyone who hustles.

Remember cheaters don't win.
Have fun even if you don't win.
Matthew Coiro, Grade 5
Staley Upper Elementary School

The Beach

The beach is really big
It's where the fishies swim
The beach is a sandy place
That's where I like to play
The beach has lots of rocks
Big as big red blocks
The beach is my place to stay
No one can take it away
The beach is my home
That's where I like to roam
Elizabeth Baldeo, Grade 6
Long Beach Middle School

Life

I have a life, and I love my life.
My life is like a dandelion sprouting from rich green grass.
Sometimes my life is like a ferocious lion ripping the skin off a deer.

I love my life even when it is good and turns ferocious.
Sometimes, I am on my backyard thinking of life,
and how I came to be, placed in this big world where
all they do is kill, kill, kill.
Why don't they stop and think about life how precious it is?
My pumping heart keeping me alive.

Why, why, why, do I sometimes feel like leaving this world,
but I have nowhere else to go so I have to spend my life here.
Olabode Shoniregun, Grade 5
Public School 161 The Crown School for Law & Journalism

Life Doesn't Frighten Me

Midnight: Friday the thirteenth, this day will surely bring bad dreams,
I still haven't open the door, but I hear something squeaking on the floor.
Life doesn't frighten me at all.

I'm not afraid of being attacked by cats, even though the floor is filled with rats.
I shut my eyes and turn my head, my thoughts were speeding far ahead.
Life doesn't frighten me at all.

To climb the tallest mountain high, watch the Thunderbird fly.
I hide inside the rocky cave, I feel like prey and I'm still brave.
Life doesn't frighten me at all.

To play with dragons in the park, the world became Jurassic Park.
I found an Allosaurus tooth, you wouldn't believe it but this is the truth.
Life doesn't frighten me at all.

I saw some weird sparks on the sky, and creatures' shadows walking by.
They were wearing scary clothes, I don't want to get too close.
Life doesn't frighten me at all.

It's like Halloween, with a dreadful scream.
I wish it was tomorrow, it makes me feel so much sorrow.
Life doesn't frighten me at all!
Billy Watson, Grade 6
Long Beach Middle School

Watch Me Fly!

Watch me jump 2 feet high
And see my life go flashing by
An Olympic rider is my goal to be
Horses are my life you see
You will see me in a newspaper
With my trusty steed
With a blue ribbon on his bridal,
When you watch us canter you will think it's so beautiful like a recital
When I come to claim my prize after the show,
I will be hugging my horse so tight as if I were a bow.
Christine Murphy, Grade 6
Great Hollow Middle School

My Family

Whether your family is big or small,
your family will love you the most *of* all

They're here to protect you,
and they're there by you side

They just want to help you
and be your guide

They're here when I need them
and I'm there for them

I'm stuck with my family
until the end

Caity Fischer, Grade 6
Long Beach Middle School

I'm So Thankful

T hanks for my parents, teachers, and friends.
H erald in the holidays.
A lleluia Christmas is coming!
N o more naughty. Only nice.
K ickoff time. Not football! Shopping!
S ervings, BIG servings of yams, stuffing, and ham.
G reen bean casserole? Not in my house!
I love this time of year!
V isitors from far and near.
I n the kitchen, in the basement, all over the house.
N oisy, happy, a reunion of friends.
G reat, special friends. I'm so thankful.

Chase McFarlane, Grade 6
St John School

Colorful Leaves

Firebrick red, sunshine yellow, bear brown
Colorful leaves leaping by.
Strolling in leaves
Crunch, crunch, crunch
Jumping and raking
Fun, fun, fun
Waiting till the shadow fades away
Then spring comes its way.

Holly Chen, Grade 5
Bretton Woods Elementary School

Yellow

Yellow is the color of a sunflower's petal
glistening in the sun
Yellow is the color of the school bus
as I wait on the corner in the morning
Yellow is the color of my favorite apple
the golden delicious

Darragh Connolly, Grade 4
Leptondale Elementary School

School Days

My teacher Ms. Jernigan
is such a special creature

The first thing I do
is make sure I greet her

I leave my class room
toward my path

As I take my time
going to math

Can't wait to get to
science to transform my clay

Into a wonderful shape
that I create on my tray

Then social studies which is last.
I enjoy learning about the past.

Paulina Hernandéz, Grade 6
Immaculate Conception School-Stapleton

Kittens

Kittens
Furry things
Licking their fur
Happy, excited, energetic, joyful
Soft.

Laurie André, Grade 5
Public School 161 The Crown School for Law & Journalism

Winter Time

It is a winter day
There is no school today
Hooray, hooray!
It's Christmas Eve, yay!
Time to bake cookies and gingerbread,
Snow men too!
Snow angels, snowballs
There's so much to do!
It's cold outside so I run inside
I have some cocoa and eat some pie.
I sit by the fireplace and watch TV
I have a feeling someone's watching me,
So I look behind the tree, oh golly gee
It was the big guy himself all plumpy and red.
Hello, I said
Then he jumped in the air
I must have gave him a scare
Then he looked back at me and smiled with glee
Oh my, Oh my, you startled me.
I must be on my way I have to go to Norway
To make sure all the children get presents on Christmas day!

Abby Bourcy, Grade 5
Harris Hill Elementary School

Winter

Winter
snowy white
sledding, skiing, tubing
preparing for the holiday
snowflakes
Jenny Vazquez, Grade 5
Most Holy Rosary School

Home

I love home it's great, great as can be.
Home is the place to be.
My comfy room and comfy bed.
So why am I here at school instead?
I love my house so warm and cozy.
My house is so big I love it so much.
So why am I here and not there?
At school at the end of the week.
I want to go home!!!!
Cassandra Honey, Grade 5
Pleasantville Middle School

Green

Green is the color of leaves
Green is the color of grass
Green is the color of my eyes
Brayan Reyes, Grade 4
Leptondale Elementary School

My Friends and I

My friends are all so special
In more than just one way.
In every situation
It's they who save the day.
They're each a glowing gem,
A character so unique,
Always standing by my side
When I'm feeling weak.
Together we can laugh,
Or shed our tears and cry,
When summer months arrive,
How we dread the word "Goodbye."
Joy Bibi, Grade 6
Bet Yaakov Ateret Torah

Dogs

Dogs are cute
Dogs are sweet
They make my heart skip a beat
They are playful
They are rambunctious
But they are very loving
Dogs are energetic
And they won't regret it
So dogs are the perfect pet
Jessica Furlong, Grade 5
Holy Cross School

Snow Angel

Shine bright,
Fluffy white.
Winter Dream
In the sky.
Fly around
But with no
Wings.
Now that's the
Gift of winter.
Amanda Wells, Grade 6
Rocky Point Middle School

Should I or Shouldn't I...

Gift Card
Hard decision
Me or my sister
Thoughts running through my head
Thinking
She's been so nice
so very very nice
My cute little sister's
big brown eyes
looking up at her big brother
How could I choose another
Finally, I came to a decision
A very big decision
I would share
She was so happy
I felt great to see her smile
Even for a little while
I will surely do it again
cause she's my little friend
Zachary Gorgone, Grade 5
Eastplain School

Autumn

Beautiful leaves changing color
Yucky rain
Pretty birds singing beautiful songs

Delicious apple pie
Jumping in a big pile of leaves
Autumn
Corinne Sikorski, Grade 4
Belmont Elementary School

Nature's Sunlight

Sunlight
Bursting over the horizon
In autumn's wonderland
When the new day dawns
To follow nature's plan
Mackenzie Stock, Grade 5
East Hill School

Softball

I see my fans yelling my name
I also see softballs, softball gloves,
Bases, other team players, and
The hot yellow sun in the sky
Also the umpire, and silver bats

TING, the ball hit the bat
Flying through the air
SMACK! Right in my glove
The batter is OUT!
The coach yelling, throw the ball!

The balls are being hit with bats
The balls are flying through the air
Hitting people's gloves
People are running to each base
First, second, third, and home again

Softball is like baseball
Baseball is softball
The only difference is the size of the ball
Softballs are bigger
Baseballs are smaller
Shaondel Hall, Grade 6
Sodus Intermediate School

My Rabbit

My rabbit is so, so, cute
with his furry nose his
brown spots remind me of
chocolate how sweet he is
Goalas, Goalas is his name he
jumps on me with no pain
Goalas, Goalas you're my love
Jackeline Robertson, Grade 4
Public School 148 Ruby Allen

Breath

Take a deep breath,
Smell the air
The pine cones,
The peanut butter
And jelly sandwiches
Mother has made for us.
In the cold;
Inhale and exhale
To see your breath.
Feel the warmth of your breath.
Breath is special
You can see it, hear it, and feel it.
It is like your world.
If you don't breathe you don't live.
Just imagine,
Our world started as a single breath.
Daniel Maldonado, Grade 6
Harold D Fayette Elementary School

Monday

Grudgingly I lift my feet
6 am SHARP
Sore eyes and aching muscles
I hate Mondays

Tired and stiff
I live to sleep
I long for my rest
I hate Mondays

The absolute WORST day of the week
No friendly faces brighten this morning
Grumpy, grouchy and irritable
I HATE MONDAYS!

Samantha Vallarella, Grade 6
Nesaquake Middle School

Christmas Eve

Walking past houses,
Watching them light up
and sparkle.

People delivering gifts
to their relatives.

Rockefeller Center
crowded with people waiting
to see the lighting of the tree.

Little sisters and brothers
in bed
trying to stay up
waiting for Santa to come,
only to slowly fall asleep.

Christina Allen, Grade 5
Public School 152 School of Science & Technology

Friendship

Friendship is many things
Friendship is hanging out together
Playing video games
Having fun

Friendship is playing sports together
It's practicing
Helping each other

Friendship is backing each other up
Sharing secrets
Helping each other
Friendship is cheering each other up
It's telling each other jokes
Keeping each other out of trouble
These are just some things that friendship is

Ryan Miller, Grade 6
Shelter Rock Elementary School

Christmas

C hristmas brings fun and joy.
H ave you gotten everything you want for Christmas?
R emember what you got last Christmas?
I love when family comes for Christmas.
S o many children love Christmas.
T he day that we get presents is Christmas.
M aybe you will get everything you want.
A t Christmas you get up and open your presents.
S o have a great Christmas.

Steven J. Rodriguez Jr., Grade 5
William B Tecler Elementary School

Who Is It?

Bang, bang on the door,
Who could it be?
Is it the mailman, Den
Or my aunt Sally?

Who would come
This late at night
While I eat and hum
Under the kitchen light?

Who is it?
Who could it be?
I don't know
But I must see.

Who is it?
Who do I see?
Oh, my mom and dad
And my sister, Molly.

Oh, silly me!

Sadia Rahman, Grade 4
Public School 152 School of Science & Technology

Racism

Blacks and whites, are they a different kind?
They are different colors as you might find.
One is dark and one is light,
But in our world they used to fight.
This world we had, we soon realized,
The white had been worshipped and the black penalized.
When World War II came everyone saw,
The death of the Jews from the Nazi's great paw.
The power of racism is something to fear,
But why can't this feeling just steer clear.
For the damage it can cause is just too great,
For everyone to bear and yet still drag their own weight.
Racism is just a destructive term,
To try to explain the damage that it can affirm.

Matthew Schaeffer, Grade 6
Shelter Rock Elementary School

Friendship

F un
R eally nice
I nsane
E ndless fun
N ever mean to me
D ependable
S mart
H appy
I s so funny
P retty much that's what friendship is.

Natalie Vogel, Grade 5
William B Tecler Elementary School

Thanksgiving

T hankful for everything
H elpful to the homeless
A pple pie
N egative for broccoli!
K ind to my family
S adness if my relatives don't come
G iving people money
I give my family turkey
V acation for this day
I share stuff with people
N ice to my sister
G reat day

Edgar Garcia, Grade 5
Northeast Elementary School

Winter Days

The first snowfall
Like many of all
Waking up with a cold chill
While I walk around the house
half asleep still
Walking out to the cold outdoors
Going to bed at ten
Waking up and doing it again

Sadie Hulslander, Grade 5
Eagle Hill Middle School

Stealth

Stealth water ride
in a tube
up down
like a skateboard ramp
on a 40 ft. drop
I see my freaked out shadow
the sun's reflecting
off the ramp
Stealth
what a ride!

Zach Eisner, Grade 4
Norman J Levy Lakeside School

My Brother

He likes to read books with me
His favorite color is green
He likes to play cars with me.
He likes to go to school.
His favorite pet is a dog,
He likes to go to the zoo to
see the animals
His name is Vaggelis he's four
years old and
    I
       love
         him

Erick Peralta, Grade 4
Public School 148 Ruby Allen

My Best Friend and I

My best friend and I,
Are cool with each other.
We always share secrets
with each other.
We love one another
And care about one another.
Nothing would ever tear us apart.
We always care about people.

Amanda Siles, Grade 5
St Benedict Joseph Labre School

A Day by the Pond

I sit by the pond
trying to think,
of what to do.

I wonder and wonder
nothing comes to mind,
not even one little thing.

I just sit there and watch
another day go by,
when I sit by the pond.

Taylor Clink, Grade 5
Whitney Point Intermediate School

The Silent Angel

A girl named Angel walks in the hall,
Nobody can see her.
She speaks beautiful words,
But nobody hears them.
In class she raises her hand,
Mrs. Fisher doesn't choose her.
A new girl comes into her school,
Her name is Crystal.
Angel and Crystal become friends,
They play and sit together.
This Angel is no longer silent.

Camille Saltys, Grade 5
William B Tecler Elementary School

Fall

My friends I dial
When I need clothes for fall.
I walk many miles
When I shop at the mall.
I love the fall.
It's the start of school.
I have a ball.
My fall clothes are so cool!
I make pumpkin pie
And pumpkins I carve.

Mikayla Noack, Grade 5
Marie Curie Institute

Bill

Bill gets the chills
Because he is ill
While he is watching the Buffalo Bills

Bill has a friend named Mike
And they like to ride their bikes
While they are flying kites

At the end of the day
Bill likes to lay
On his bed made of hay

Nick Poehlmann, Grade 5
Harris Hill Elementary School

The Woods

When I am at my aunt's
Oh boy oh boy,
How I have so much fun!

I go into the woods
All day long.
I never heard
So much sounds.

When the wind blows,
You stop to hear
The swishing leaves from near
To your fragile ear.
Rocks tumble
And your heart,
Filled with fear.

Birds are crowing loudly
Caw, caw, caw…
At the end of the day.

Oh how I love the woods…
Hope you can come someday.

Khemwattie Balram, Grade 4
Public School 124Q

The World of the Sea Turtle

Sea turtles are strong swimmers.
Eating habits grow as they age.
Adapted to living in the ocean.

Tiger shark is a predator.
Unborn babies are in danger of being eaten.
Reproduction is crucial for their survival.
Leatherback is the biggest turtle on Earth.
Loggerheads have powerful jaws
that lets them crack open hard shells.
Eating is a big part in their daily life.

Gerson Melara, Grade 6
Shelter Rock Elementary School

Hammerhead Sharks

This animal is very weird,
And it is greatly feared.
It uses its head to smack its prey,
So it can eat three square meals a day.
It lives in warm waters and
It relocates itself from season to season,
With great reason.
It does not want its home to be warm,
If shark went to college they would never be in a dorm.
After reading this poem you will agree,
The hammerhead shark is the last thing
you would want to meet under the sea.

Liam Whalen, Grade 6
Shelter Rock Elementary School

Mystery

Do stars travel by
shooting each other
into the sky?
Does the moon give off its light by
sprinkling glitter
with all of its might?
Do clouds drift away
without bashing together
or having a say?
Does the sun turn yellow and bright
by stealing extra color
from the clouds at night?
Well…
Humans travel by
Train or car
Humans give off light by
Being who we are
Humans drift away
In our dreams at night
Humans turn yellow and bright by
Halloween's light

Chloe Long, Grade 5
Public School 205 Alexander Graham Bell

Life Doesn't Frighten Me

Creepy living dolls
I saw them crawl
Life doesn't frighten me at all
Noises coming from my bed
Trying to block them out of my head
Life doesn't frighten me at all
Disgusting bugs
Do not make me shrug
Life doesn't frighten me at all
Ghosts and graveyards, goblins and witches
Don't make me have twitches
Life doesn't frighten me at all
Scary zombie clowns following me around
Leave me alone don't answer the phone
Life doesn't frighten me at all
Walking through an empty grave trying to be extra brave
Shutting my eyes looking for a place to hide
Life doesn't frighten me at all
Looking downstairs there's nothing there
I woke up and I was just dreaming
Life doesn't frighten me at all

Allyson Peysner, Grade 6
Long Beach Middle School

Snowboarding

I want to snowboard.
Really snowboard.
Not just sit on the board and glide,
but ride down the mountain swiftly.
I'd see trees topped with white snow.
I'd taste the strawberry gatorade in my mouth.
I'd hear the growling of the wind.
I'd smell the ginger.
I'd feel proud!
I want to have hot cocoa.

James Carlino, Grade 4
Magnet School of Math, Science and Design Technology

Racism Hurts

How do you think it feels
To be judged with no appeals?
To be living in this nation
To be living with discrimination.
Dark as chocolate, white as snow,
What's the difference?
I don't know.
Some people have way too much pride,
Though we are the same inside.
It's not your fault, it's not fair,
We can't choose the color of our skin or our hair.
We all have hearts that can be hurt,
Please don't treat others like dirt.
No matter the color of your outer frame,
"B'neath d'skin is all d'same."

Abigail Powell, Grade 6
Shelter Rock Elementary School

Embarrassment

Getting in trouble in class
Is like being in a room with no exit
Walking into the girl's bathroom
When you're a boy is EMBARRASSING!
People laugh at you
People call you names
Dodging everyone
The day feels like forever
Finally finding a friend —
A safe zone!

Joseph Cancro, Grade 4
Norman J Levy Lakeside School

Cream

Cream is the warm liquid in coffee.
Cream is the color of a moist biscuit.
Cream is the delicious color of vanilla.
Cream is the color of a flower seed.
Cream is the color of Autumn leaves.

Olivia Milner, Grade 4
Leptondale Elementary School

The Beach

I hear the waves crash
The wind blows on my face
The sound between my toes
This is my happy place

The roaring of the water
The crack of the shells
The children and their laughter
The lifeguards as they yell

Bathing suits and sandals
Playing till the day is done
Volleyball and surfing
Leaving when there's no more sun

Tomorrow will be another day
To have fun in the sun
and all day we shall play

Sarah Colletti, Grade 6
Long Beach Middle School

Wrestling

W atery as sweat
R ough move
E xcellent kick
S trong in the ring
T alented move
L ong legs
I nteresting move
N asty blood
G round fight

Devon Clark, Grade 4
Granville Elementary School

What Friendship Really Means

I think that friendship is the fun part of life.
You have someone watching your back,
Make sure you are in a good mode,
You can talk to them,
and they will still be your friend,
I think that friendship is the fun part of life.

I think that friendship is the fun part of life.
If you did not have friends,
Who would tell what you missed in class when you were absent?
Who can you talk to without people falling asleep on you?
Life is boring without friends
I think that friendship is the fun part of life.

Eddie Peterson, Grade 6
Shelter Rock Elementary School

My First Rock Climb

Rocky wall, bright beautiful birds,
Humongous trees getting smaller like ferns,
Tightly spun rope hooked to me,
Dazzling bright blue sky

Birds chirping like fire alarms
People cheering
Birds flying above my head
Rocks crumbling off the wall as if they are crumbs from a cookie

As I climb further and further the top gets closer and closer
Finally I made it
I'm at the top
I yell in excitement and start down

Robert Sovie, Grade 6
Sodus Intermediate School

A Wonderful Fall

Leaves falling
Firebrick red, goldenrod yellow, bright orange and emerald green
It's the greatest sight I've ever seen
Swish, swish,
Whistle, whistle
The chilly wind blows
There are five different eye-catching scarecrows
There are bright sparkling amazing sights
The sky is pitch black
It's already night
My mom shouts, "It's time to come in."
I go in the house and breathe in the smoke I see
I really wish that it could be
That wonderful attracting smell that could make your day
It's nice warm hot cocoa so I drink it all the way
I close my eyes and drop my head
So I jump into my nice, warm cozy bed!

Charles Bellini, Grade 5
Bretton Woods Elementary School

Nature's Gifts

Walking through the open forest
Tasting the crisp air filling my lungs
Rich colors pulled me closer to the enormous trees
The sweet smell of nature flowed through my body
I could float away in happiness
It was like a painting
Almost too good to be true
I heard a call
The call of a brilliant bird soaring through the air
Gliding effortlessly
Leaning against the rough bark of an ancient tree
As strong as an army, yet as weak as paper
Realizing that my serene world would soon end
It was coming
Winter

KellyRose Yaeger, Grade 6
Cahill Elementary School

Shadow

As I, myself decrease the light,
and set about my evil plight.
A shape will creep up on the wall,
and reach for you, you cannot call.
You are alone, there's no one here,
I fill you up with cold and fear.
You're stuck in here, there's no escape,
I am a shadow.

Paddy Decimo, Grade 6
George Grant Mason Elementary School

My First Time at the Skatepark

My first time at the skatepark,
I saw skateboards,
My rollerblades,
A couple of rails,
A bench,
Skateboarding is like rollerblading!

I hear wheels rolling,
Crashing,
Clanking of wheels on the ramps,
Skateboards crashing really hard into the wall,
Skateboards breaking in half,
And grinding.

I am rollerblading on a smooth surface to skate,
I am thinking "WOW,"
I said "Next time I'm going on the ramps!"
Skateboarding is skating!
My sister forced me to leave,
I wanted to stay,
I was there for hours to come,
I finally leave at 8 o'clock,
I can't wait to go again tomorrow.

Justin Guerra, Grade 6
Sodus Intermediate School

Christmas Carol

Days getting dark,
Days getting colder,
Days getting white,
Days getting older,
Star on top of a tree,
Gingerbread houses and candy canes,
Snow flying fast,
Faster than speeding trains,
Kids singing Christmas carols,
"La de da…,"
Hats, scarves and coats.
Children laughing, "Ha, ha, ha…,"
The bells going "jingle, jingle, jingle,"
Waiting for old Kris Kringle,
Opening presents all day long
That is the end of my Christmas song.

Ariel Petrinich, Grade 6
Intermediate School 227 - Louis Armstrong Middle

My Day

Breakfast is on the way as I pray
I'm hoping to have toast because I like it the most
Munch munch as I crunch on my brunch
Potato chips and pretzels too
Eating snack is fun to do
Waiting for lunch as we learn
My stomach tosses and turns
Ding-dong went the bell
Running to lunch I almost fell
I opened my lunch box and said
Hooray for the food I got today
Running right home by the end of the day
Waiting for dinner it's on its way
I heard the salmon sizzling
And the broccoli fizzling
Good night to everyone
The food is now done

Brenda Hazan, Grade 4
Shaare Torah Elementary School

Winter Day

It's frigid out here in the woods.
Everything is still.
There is no breeze coming from anywhere.
But I feel frost in the air.
I feel free.
Free as a bird.
It feels like I had escaped from all of the commotion.
Trees have no leaves.
They look dull.
As I walk, I leave footprints in the snow.
It is milky white on this winter day.

Steviemarie Otto, Grade 5
Edward J Bosti Elementary School

Black Looks Good on Everything

Black looks good on nice cars
Black looks good on your hair
Black looks good on your shoes
Black looks good on your clothes
Black looks good on your hats
Like I said, black looks good on
Everything.

Zachary Alibrandi, Grade 5
Public School 2 Alfred Zimberg

The Ocean

Sometimes flowing fast
Soft and silky
Sometimes it's rippling,
Splashing against the
Castles formed in the sand
Disappearing from the shore.

Gaurav Uppal, Grade 4
Concord Road Elementary School

Leaves

Leaves, leaves high in the tree,
Changing colors as we can see!
Leaves, leaves coming down,
Red, orange, yellow and brown,
Covering the ground,
We watch them fall.
Gently they become a colorful ball!
Leaves, leaves here and there,
Leaves, leaves are everywhere!

Brittney Perez, Grade 6
Christ the King School

I Love My Mom

I love my mom
Very much

We both have fun
Times with each other

I love that mom
Like a beautiful star

We play board
Games together

My mom is a special
Person to me

We also play hide and
Go seek and jump rope

But most of all my mom
Loves me like I love her

Bianica White, Grade 4
Hendy Avenue School

Delightful

I love winter it's filled
with delight
Ice cream ice cream
with a cherry on top
What a wonderful
delight
Tea, tea
you are so sweet
to me
What a treat
What a delight
they help you when
you're down
but
the truest
of friends
They will always
be around.

Tiana Bryant, Grade 5
Public School 148 Ruby Allen

Thinking of You

As I sit here and think of you
My heart goes wild and crazy,
Flutters like a butterfly,
And dances like a daisy.

You make me happy,
You make me smile,
You make me dance the jitterbug
When I'm walking down an aisle.

I really don't like school
But I'll come here every day
Cause when I see you smiling face
It makes my heart shout HOORAY!!!

Pamela Edwards, Grade 5
Staley Upper Elementary School

Parent

You never understand them
always nagging you
"Do your homework
and
make sure you
study!!"
What can you do?
You love them
and
they're annoying
but
they are still your parents.

Melissa Essor, Grade 5
Public School 114 Ryder

Leaf

Drifting down to Earth,
In the crisp autumn air.
Wearing vivid colors.
Graceful as a swan.
Swaying in the wind,
Back and forth,
Back and forth.
Until hitting the ground, silently.

Andrew Rosenfeld, Grade 4
Concord Road Elementary School

The Monster

There's a monster under my bed
It wants to eat me up.
It would start with my head
To make sure I don't wake up.

Can you get it for me?
So I don't get eaten?
If you do I'll give you a penny,
Depending on how it gets beaten.

There's a monster under my bed
It wants to eat me up.
It would start with my head
To make sure I don't wake up!

Catherine Dawes, Grade 4
Public School 124Q

Spring

Rain drops,
Plop, plop.
Cars pass by,
With kids sighing.
Flowers bloom,
While dogs get groomed.
Rain stops,
Kids come and play.
Rain starts,
Kids run home.
Rain stops again,
Kids jump,
On puddles…
Jump!
Jump!
Jump!

Ellen Kim, Grade 6
Intermediate School 77

Lion

L aying in the shade
I ndependent
O range
N oble

Samantha Mavris, Grade 5
Harris Hill Elementary School

Joy Is a Park

The trees are branches
that branch out our family

The trees leaves are a quilt with
a pattern fro every season

The flower petals are bees
flying in the wind

The animals that are running
here and there seem to be scattered seeds everywhere

The grass is a blanket that
you lay on and see the sky

Joy is a park, every summer
and winter day

Carmen Diaz, Grade 6
Immaculate Conception School-Stapleton

Marriage

Marriage is for people
Who love each other.
But people don't...
Always marry for a partner.
Some people do it for
Many other things.
Also sometimes marriage does not last long.
Divorce is hard for kids...
And the couple.
Divorce is when
One or both people in the couple decide to split.
So people try not to divorce.
Because it will leave
The kids hearts broken.

Breeanne VanValkenburgh, Grade 5
Staley Upper Elementary School

Science Is...

Problems to solve,
chemicals that dissolve.
The metamorphosis of a common house fly,
how free-flying birds glide through the sky.
Asteroids, planets, and our bright yellow sun,
that shines our way 'til the day is done.

Observing the world, experimenting and such,
using sight, sound, smell, taste, and touch.
Hydrothermal vents found along the ocean floor,
a home for fish, clams, and much more.
The roaring waves of the glimmering sea,
exploration and discovery for you and me.

Priya Alagesan, Grade 6
Shelter Rock Elementary School

Blue

Blue can be lots of things
But never yellow, red, orange, brown, or green.
Blue is the sky but not the rain
It smells like blueberries
Blue can be other things too.
It can be silk or my clothes,
Blue is the color I dream of as I doze.
But always remember, blue is not just a color
it can be silk, clothes, blueberries, or the sky
but never yellow, red, orange, brown, or green
Blue is Blue.

Nicole Natale, Grade 5
Eastplain School

Friendship

Friends help you through the ups and downs
They laugh with you, cry with you, be crazy with you
Playing like you're three years old brings back memories

Have sleepovers
Staying up all night talking
Secret telling and keeping is what they're good at
Friends are the ones you can trust

You have fights
But you get over it
They talk with you when something isn't right
Talking through the night
Until you get over the problem

You have UNFORGETTABLE memories
Always having fun together
You have boxes and boxes of those pictures
From when you played babies

True friends
True hearts
That's all that counts
In life

Melissa Dorogoff, Grade 6
Shelter Rock Elementary School

Winter

Wind blowing
Snow on the way
White as feathers
Coats to keep me warm
Christmas tree with lights and
Presents waiting to be opened.

No violets in the hard ground
Colors of red and blue not to be found.
When spring arrives
Hopefully violets will come alive.

Bianca Batista, Grade 5
Public School 105 Senator Abraham Bernste

Leaves in the Fall

Many colors. Many shapes. Many sizes.
If you look around you will see them up and down, falling and swooshing around. When the wind picks up they are playing tag, running as fast as they possibly can. Running up and down your street like children who have just been released into the wild. If you see some in your neighborhood watch them fly about. If you step on top of them you will hear a crunch, crunch from underneath your shoe. Watch out cause one may land on your head and you will have a brand new hat. If you try to dodge them and when you think you missed them all guess again. They may cover your lawn, but they make tools to pick them up and see your bright green lawn again. Your branches may be bare but soon they will be covered with white, soft, icy snow and will make your town look pretty. Their beautiful colors will amaze your eyes and you never see one the same shape or size.

Rachel Siggilino, Grade 6
Great Hollow Middle School

What Is Life?

Is life just a privilege for you and I? Is there a reason each day why we laugh or cry? Is life just a game and we are the players? Is life the reason we have skin with many layers? Does life reset for us after we die? Or do we just live forever up in the sky? What will happen when the sun burns out? Will we be gone without a doubt? What would happen if there was no life?

Krystyne Josepher, Grade 5
Viola Elementary School

Baseball

Nothing makes me happier than the feeling of my leather baseball glove on my left hand. The bright sun is shining, and a cool breeze is blowing the scent of springtime all over me. As I make my way to the dugout, the sound of kids talking and laughing gets louder and louder. Then I hear my two most favorite words, "play ball!" I eagerly make my way to the batters' box where I ready my bat and watch the ball. It's a fastball down the pipe so I swing as hard as I can. It's a hit, "Quick! Run to first base!" I hear my teammates cheer! Running with all my might I see the ball go over the fence, it's a home run! I stepped on first base, then second, then third, and then home plate where I leaped into the opened arms of my entire team waiting to greet me. Looks like it's going to be a great baseball season!

Luigi Ragusa, Grade 6
St Francis of Assisi School

The Way I Feel

When I am excited, I am as hyper as an energetic three-year-old
When I am sad, I am like a lonely strand of wheat tossed by the wind in the large meadow
When I am annoyed, I'm as furious as a bull being teased by a Spanish matador
When I am sleepy, I am like Sleepy the dwarf coming back from an endless mining session
When I am happy, I am as warm as a freshly baked gingerbread man.
When I am bold, I am like an eagle soaring alone through the blue sky.

Julia Abbondanza, Grade 4
Helen B Duffield Elementary School

I Love Fall

I like fall but I love my mom's sweet potato pie and her pumpkin pie. It is like eating a cloud.
I like fall but I love to make funny and scary jack-o'-lanterns because it is fun.
I like fall but I love going pumpkin picking because my dad's brother has his own pumpkin patch.
I like fall but I love going to Halloween parties and wearing costumes to make my brother scared.

Danny Garcia, Grade 4
Northeast Elementary School

My Life Is Like Poetry

I have never been a poet, but my life is like poetry. About 5 years ago when I was 7 years old it was Christmas Day, we didn't have much. She brought me paper and a pen. I wrote and wrote till there was a story. When I was 8 me and my sister went to foster care. When we got close we had to leave foster home to foster home, tear to tear. Now that I'm home I'm feeling well and my life will never again be a living hell. This is coming from the soul. Some people get rid of the pain with drugs, I get rid of mine with stories. With three thousand dollars I would pay my mom back for everything.

Miriyam Matthews, Grade 6
Charles Carroll School Public School 46

Jesus

Jesus is the prince of peace
He is the provider of all providers
Jesus is the king of kings
He is the Alpha and Omega
Jesus keeps me up when I am down
He turns my frowns all around
He is my God forever
When I lie he will know
And it will most definitely show
Our help for today
Our hope for tomorrow
Red and yellow black and white
We are all precious in his sight
He makes us bright in the light
Day and night angels are in sight
Lord you protect us you make us holy
Without you there is no me
You protect me you guide me and show me the way
And when you do this I don't have to pay
So I say thank you for helping me out
And because of you I will never pout

Olapeju Oladitan, Grade 5
St Mary's School

Red

Red is the color of the fiery sun.
Red is the blood from all of the people who died in war.
Red is the color of your eyes when
you play video games too long.
Red is the color of the horizon.

Ronald Daly, Grade 4
Leptondale Elementary School

My Great-Grandfather Just Passed Away

My heart is a deep hole
with a bear hibernating
because my great-grandfather
just passed away.

My great-grandfather just passed away
he lived in China and got a heart attack
he was laying on the couch
we found him dead
I can't believe he passed away
without telling me he is dead
he was the best
we always play with a ball
he passed away without telling me
I still have the ball in my hand
I could never forget he gave me a beautiful
necklace with my name and his name written in Chinese
with a heart locket with his picture and mine
now it's a deep hole
with a family of bears hibernating.

Nicole Chan, Grade 4
Public School 69

Halloween

Witches, vampires, and goblins too,
they all come out to say boo.

On this holiday in the night,
kids dress up to have a good fright.

Girls and boys in costumes
going house to house, door to door.

Never knowing what's in store.
Who will answer? Who will it be?

Maybe a ghost, let's wait and see,
it's a person happily handing out treats to you and me.

Ricky Drake, Grade 6
St Mary's School

Ring

Endless circle,
Never stops,
Symbol of love,
Joy comes to this passionate circle,
Tears, joy tears,
Smiles, some frowns,
I do's, some I don'ts,
Never breaking or splitting apart,
Meaning importance,
Closeness,
Dear to a person,
Beginning of a new life,
New relationship,
Sometimes puppy love triggering its way up,
Special and meaningful,
This endless circle,
Never stops,
Going on,
And on,
And
On

Dana Bruno, Grade 6
Intermediate School 227 - Louis Armstrong Middle

I Am

I am the soul of the music you hear in the wind.
I am a cloud floating in heaven upon Earth.
I am the GODS of Rome fighting in battle.
I am the very medicine that heals the wounded.
I am the rose petal falling on the floor, from the flower girl.
I am the energy that gives people the drive to go on in life.
I am a golden light in heaven.
I am whatever I want to be.
I am what I am.

Hudson Cianni, Grade 4
Upper Nyack Elementary School

The Rainbow Last Week

I love rainbows
A gleam in my eye
The sparkle of
The yellow strip of color
I can picture
The gold pot so shiny
And so rich
I smell
The warm, wet air
Of the washed up rain
The puddles splattering
Against the hard pavement
I hear
The birds call
Waking from a morning nap
I feel
The wind brush against my face
The rainbow appears
Deep inside my heart
I take in that beautiful sight
and pray for the next rainbow to come

Josh Crocetti, Grade 6
Northwood Elementary School

Football in the Fall

My name is Alexander Lotman
And I play football.
I'm on the Purple Juniors
We start in the fall.
My teammates are Terrence Kretser,
Anthony and Chance.
Our uniforms are heavy
With purple tops and purple pants.
After the game
We are tired and hot.
Our legs are lame,
But sleep I will not!
I go out with the team
To celebrate.
We have a party with ice cream
Because our team is great!

Alexander Lotman, Grade 5
Marie Curie Institute

Things I Love

I love the trees' smell
That blows in the wind,
And I love the wind itself.
Also, I love the grass that is so soft.
I love the birds singing
And the people laughing.
That is what I love.

Kathryn Hechtel, Grade 5
John T Waugh Elementary School

A Halloween Night

It's a beautiful fall day
The birds are singing
The leaves
Iridescently colored
Everything is perfect

It's almost time
for Halloween night
Pumpkins to carve
Scary ghosts
Creepy goblins
Unique costumes

Little kids are frightened
by everything
They're just craving
their sweet candy
to eat in the following weeks
it's just a perfect
Halloween night

Jack Dixon, Grade 6
Northwood Elementary School

Hot to Cold

HOT
Drippy, sweaty
Burning, steaming, boiling
Flames, fire, icicles, ice cream
Freezing, shivering, licking
Windy, icy
COLD

Katharyn Granados, Grade 5
Northeast Elementary School

The Tiger

The tiger,
Tangerine and ebony
With a creamy colored stomach,
Stalks its prey.

A helpless, defenseless doe
With an ivory and cinnamon hide,
Grazes on the luscious green grass.

SUDDENLY
The wild tiger pounces.

The frightened doe
Feels a sharp pain
In its scrawny neck
And falls with a *THUD*!

The fearless tiger
Eats his meal viciously.

Andrew Wallace, Grade 6
Akron Middle School

My Mom

My mom and me
are stuck together
like the clouds
up in the sky
letting the sunshine through
we love each other
so much
we don't know what to do

Evelyn Juncal, Grade 5
Public School 148 Ruby Allen

Roller Coaster

Up, down
Or side to side
Faster, faster
I love this ride
OH NO!
We're slowing down
Can't we go for another round?

Kaylee McFadzen, Grade 5
Dickinson Avenue Elementary School

Ocean

The brilliant blue waves
crash on the elegant beach.

Seagulls soar up in the sky
looking for delicious fish.

The towering waves
are so beautiful.

On top of all of it
the exquisite sunset is
a magnificent sight

Brianna Snyder, Grade 5
Edward J Bosti Elementary School

My Brother

My brother is cool,
He is a cool fool.
Dirt bikes he races,
He sees a lot of smiling faces,
When he races.

Philip Myer, Grade 4
Granville Elementary School

Summer

Fun, heat
Swimming, playing, games
Hot, warm, happy exciting
August

Nicholas Kandaras, Grade 4
Hendy Avenue School

The Sea

The fish live in the sea
It's the most peaceful place to be
Divers explore the coral reef
The air starts to run out so they make it brief
The divers have a race
They take in the marvelous place
Down in the deep blue sea
Is the best place for me

Brigid Neumann, Grade 6
Holy Cross School

Leaf

Autumn leaf whisping around.
Going up, going down.
In the night, in the day.
Soaring through the wind, gliding in the path.
Autumn leaf, Autumn day.
When the sun goes down
the leaf is still around.
At dawn it goes on its way
to fly through the day.
On its way, on its way.
To a new home today.

Annie Laura, Grade 5
Edward J Bosti Elementary School

Puppies

Puppies are so little and cute
They eat everything in sight
and that's when you say don't take a bite
Puppies are the world of dreams
Playful and jumpy
That's what they are
Puppies are bundles of love
Chasing cats that's what they do
Then sleeping on a couch like a great big king
Chasing their tail like they just can't stop
Puppies are so cute
I love…
Puppies

Savannah Andrasko, Grade 4
Upper Nyack Elementary School

Merry Christmas To A Soldier

Santa's coat is red
His reindeer are brown
It's Christmas time, wipe off that frown.
Your family will be happy forevermore
That you are in battle
Trying to end this war.
So we'll try to support you in the war
Because when you fight you give us more.

Sean Olin, Grade 6
Perry Elementary/Middle School

Families Are the People Who Love You No Matter What

Families are the people who love you no matter what
They are the ones who protect you,
Care for you, provide you with a warm home
Families are the people who love you no matter what
They always want you to try your best
and try new things
Families are the people who love you no matter what
Even when your mom is yelling at you,
Your dad is telling you to be quiet — he's watching a game,
Your sister is telling you how stupid you are
And your brother is kicking you and pulling your hair,
You will always know that
Families are the people who love you no matter what.

Melissa Ward, Grade 6
Long Beach Middle School

Love

Love is when you feel all good inside.
It's someone you trust deep inside.
I would always say I love you to show a sign of love.
It shows that you care for someone you love.
You would never do something to harm your loved one.
You would lose their love maybe never get it back.
Love is an important thing.
Love someone and you'll get loved back.

Skylar Pagliuca, Grade 6
St Catherine of Siena School

Martin Luther King Looked to the Sky

Martin Luther King looked to the sky.
He often sat and wondered why.
"Why can't we be clouds,
Floating above, mighty and proud?"
He asked, "Why is the way people are treated so unfair?"
He looked back up into the air.
He thought of freedom,
How everyone should have some.
He saw rainbows, birds, and rain.
He wished no one had any pain.
He saw the bright future light
He thought everyone should have the right
To be equal, black or white.
He never gave up on us;
He worked so hard for justice!

Jacob LaFerriere, Grade 5
Sacred Heart School

Winter

W indy days
I nside, drinking hot chocolate
N ever leave the house without proper clothes
T ake care of your hands
E ntertain my family
R eally cold!

Julio Sanchez, Grade 5
Northeast Elementary School

My Dad

My Dad is the best dad.
He makes me happy, he makes me glad.
Sometimes he even makes me sad,
When I've been bad.
When he is mad he is a crab.
When he is glad he is the best dad.
But no matter what he is, he's My Dad.

Christopher Casadei, Grade 5
Staley Upper Elementary School

School

School is very easy
School is very hard
School is a happy place
We might as well have fun

We always have tests
We always have work
Most of us pass the tests
While some fail
But we are still proud of ourselves

We love when
We have recess
We jump up and down
But then we come back in

At the end of school
Some of us are sad
Most of us love school
We never want to leave!

Jamie Levine, Grade 5
Guggenheim Elementary School

The Color of My World

The sky is orange, the floor is green.
The walls are blue, the sun is pink.
My shirt is purple, my pants are yellow.
My hands are red, my feet are white.
My hair is peach, my eyes blue.
The colors of my world may be weird,
the colors I see are me.

Mashiyat Chowdhury, Grade 5
Public School 2 Alfred Zimberg

Mr. Sun

I'm hotter than an oven,
I'm shaped like a lemon,
But I'm a thousand times bigger,
I'm as yellow as a banana,
Mercury is my neighbor,
I heat the earth,
Be careful,
I might BURN you!

Jad Chaar, Grade 4
Concord Road Elementary School

Life Doesn't Frighten Me at All

Playing soccer on the field using my sister as a shield
Afraid they will kick me I pray they will let me be
Life doesn't frighten me at all

The ball was coming so fast it zoomed right on past
The other team running after us my coach was making a big fuss
No, life doesn't frighten me at all

The 8th graders were bigger and meaner my team was smaller and leaner
We tried to be brave, but that didn't work especially when the captain called us a jerk
No, life doesn't frighten me at all

Back and forth we did run that was not my idea of fun
I finally found the ball but they pushed and shoved and I did fall
No, life doesn't frighten me at all

Blocking the goal is harder than it looks I would rather be home reading a book
It's more difficult in the rain there's no reason not to complain
No, life doesn't frighten me at all

There are many sports I enjoy playing but soccer is my favorite I am saying
The wind swishing by the bright blue sky
No, life doesn't frighten me at all

Samara Rynecki, Grade 6
Long Beach Middle School

My Brother and I

My brother and I have a special bond
That flows and flows through my arms
I am his rock and he is my grass that grows and grows way too fast
I love him and he loves me and together it makes Aeden and me.
Our love is infinite. Infinite to me and if we fall it will never be broken.
My brother and I have a special bond that will stay right in my heart.

Candace Marshall, Grade 5
Public School 114 Ryder

Christmas Day

"Thump thump" it is eleven at night when I hear a sound,
as I sit and wait for the red guy to come down
with a tumble and a crash and the tree falling down.
I sneak down stairs to see what is going on,
I notice all the cookies were gone with no presents,
Santa was nowhere to be found.

So when I went back upstairs,
I found Santa lying in my bed.
I looked in his eyes to see if he was awake,
but no, he was snoring like he was in an earthquake.

So I woke him up and showed him the door.
Then he said, "Just wait till you wake up, with no presents on the floor!"
So I went back to bed
wondering, *"What have I done?",*
and thinking "presents," I will have none.

Mackenzie Maring, Grade 5
Harris Hill Elementary School

Marigolds

Orange like an orange
red like a rose
that's a perfect marigold
More than 6 petals, exactly 23
this annual flower seems as tall as a tree
They come in bunches
for all to see
My marigolds
are so pretty to me

Jaclyn Dortch, Grade 4
Public School 205 Alexander Graham Bell

The Dolphins

It jumps, it dives
Like a gentle wave against the sky
The graceful strokes
The gentle splash
Too bad it's gone in a flash

But here she is, back up again
And look she brought a friend!
Together the show is better then before!
As they raced next to a boat and against the shore
Their swimming is so wonderful you can't get bored

And hear their song?
It isn't long
But short, low and synchronized
Their strokes and songs die away
I hope the dolphins will come back and play!

Emily June Kehrli, Grade 6
Harold D Fayette Elementary School

The Tragedy of 9/11

It was 9:30 when the first tower fell.
Was it war? Nobody could tell.
Nobody knew what it meant.
Did two countries have an argument?
Everyone scared, panicked and running from danger.
Nobody knew who did this, who was that horrible stranger.
Fire and smoke in the air.
Confusion and danger roaming everywhere.
Lots of people losing lives.
Women losing husbands, men losing wives.
Nothing will ever be the same.
We will never forget our heroes' names.

Patricia Okuniewska, Grade 6
Intermediate School 77

Moon

When the moon sings it's a dream I never knew.
When the moon sings it's like a new beginning.
When the moon sings it's like a snowflake in winter.
When the moon sings it's a night of peace.

Kaylee Bayer, Grade 4
Upper Nyack Elementary School

A Midnight Run

I run and jog through the dark, black, night,
with only the moon guiding my way.
Sitting on a still wooden bench I stare,
stare at the rippling reflection of the sky.
Laying in the soft mowed grass I rest,
rest with my eyes wide open,
my hands behind my head and look,
look for all the possible constellations in the winter, night, sky.

Arianna Vetrano, Grade 5
Public School 41 Greenwich Village

Aboard

It has been months
Since I boarded this ship.
I don't have a room for myself
Like I did before I came aboard.
I sleep where cargo used to be —
The room is very crowded.
We have little fresh air
And eat fairly stale and salted food.
The boat, which is make out of wood,
Rocks on the stormy waters.
And the fear of burning ourselves
And the boat makes us huddle together.
All I can do is wait for the trip to end.

Alexandra Simon, Grade 5
Public School 152 School of Science & Technology

The Four Seasons

They stand superior in the neighborhood, they are the trees,
During the summer they have bright, green leaves.
Soon summer will be gone and next is fall,
The leaves detach from the trees so tall.
They fall to the ground.
They circle round and round.
Next will be winter, the leaves are dead.
I know soon they'll be back above my head!
Spring gives me a smile, though it took awhile.
Nature promises to repeat its four seasons next year.

Keiran Carpen, Grade 5
St Benedict Joseph Labre School

Family

From the laughs and the cries
even from those dirty lies.
My family will always stick together.
From the name calling it gives us great shame.
But when things go good there's no one to blame.
So when things turn out great
And there's no one to hate
There will be no debate
This family is great!

James Spinelli, Grade 6
Long Beach Middle School

First Day of School

The first day of school gives me the creeps
butterflies in my stomach
trying to make new friends
can't wait till school ends
tick-tock-tick-tock
only one more hour of school
can't wait to jump in the pool

Ryan Lubrano, Grade 4
Public School 69

Me

My hair is black,
My eyes are light brown,
I am very messy and silly,
I am very hyperactive.

I love Tae Kwon Do,
Jabbing a punch into my opponent's chest,
I am powerful.
I block one punch and kick it away,
I send him flying with a kick,
I love Tae Kwon Do.

I like to play video games,
I am a gaming freak!
I play for hours on end,
The flashing lights reflecting off my eyes,
The CPU player goes flying,
Super Smash Bros. is the game,
I have won.

These are my traits,
My favorite hobbies,
This is all about me!

Shreesham Mukherjee, Grade 6
Shelter Rock Elementary School

The Outstanding Autumn

Glowing trout struggling to swim up stream
Dazzling slow moving water glitters
in the sunlight
Crunching leaves sound like fire wood
being burned
Ducks gliding across the freezing fall water
Devouring my Halloween candy
when I finish
Trick or treating
Shimmering leaves slowly
fall down from Autumn's trees
Fall is almost over and winter is near
We sit around the comfortable fire
until next year

Nick Curry, Grade 4
Helen B Duffield Elementary School

Life Doesn't Frighten Me

Starting the middle school in September
Lots of things I had to remember
Life doesn't frighten me at all.

Walking through the hall
I felt very small
Life doesn't frighten me at all.

It was very hard walking to all of my classes
I was so confused, I thought I needed glasses
Life doesn't frighten me at all.

Taking Spanish
It's like English has vanished
Life doesn't frighten me at all.

A lot of new friends
The fun never ends
Life doesn't frighten me at all.

All of the things for all of the days
Middle school is like a maze
Life doesn't frighten me at all.

Hunter Rogoff, Grade 6
Long Beach Middle School

Blue

Blue is the color of my eyes
Blue is the color of my shirt on November 5, 2007
Blue is the color of my brother's room
Blue is the color of the water that falls

Nicole Detoro, Grade 4
Leptondale Elementary School

Standing in Iceland

Standing in the cold,
Icicles hanging from my nose,
Waiting for an animal to hurry by like a speeding car
Looking up I see a glowing glacier,
It's so close it looks like a painting.
I start to run inside,
But stop,
To gaze at the scenery.
Once again I am standing in the cold.

Matthew Levy, Grade 4
Concord Road Elementary School

Candy

Crunchy, sour, jumbo and good
Bars, sticks, circles and gold
Skittles, Twix, M and M's and Hershey's
Yummy, Yummy in my tummy!
Rainbows, chocolate, delicious and sweet
Yummy, yummy in my tummy!

Kristina DeLeonardis, Grade 5
Guggenheim Elementary School

Cooking Extravaganza
Bubble, Bubble, Bubble, POP
I hear the sound of a boiling pot
When I hear this I run to the stovetop.

Chop, Chop, Sauté, Sauté
I am so overjoyed
That I want to shout
HIP-HIP-HOORAY!

When I am in the kitchen
I want to smile
Even though cooking
Sure takes a while!

Time has past and still not done
Then I look to the right and scream
"THIS IS NO FUN!"

To the right of me
Are dishes piled so high
Now the only words that come out of my mouth
Are "Oh my, Oh my."
Gabriella Librizzi, Grade 6
Harold D Fayette Elementary School

Friendship
Friends
One of life's beauties
Friends are like guardian angels
They always have your back
Friends can be any age or have any color skin
Looks and popularity don't mean anything
They pick you up when you are down
They will always include you
They don't talk behind your back
And force you into things
Not all friends are true friends
But the ones that are
Lead you to a great future
Matthew Wysota, Grade 6
Shelter Rock Elementary School

Christmas
Christmas is the best time to put up all the lights
The children will be happy when Santa comes at night.
While church bells are ringing, the people will be singing,
And all around is joyous and very, very bright.

Jolly Santa comes with a loud ho! Ho!
I know there are lots of kids who'll want even a yo-yo.
But with thousands of little boys and girls all across the world.
I hope the toys will be enough or Santa will be in a twirl.
Kevin Morrah, Grade 5
John Hus Moravian School

Summer Thoughts
Summer thoughts so free, so grand
Throughout summer they're in your hand.

Making a home in your mind
You can never leave them far behind.

When fall breezes start blowing in
Your summer thoughts grow oh so thin.

Throughout winters snow and wind
Your summer thoughts stay warm within.

Until spring grows older and warm winds blow
Your summer thoughts still move slow.

When summer days come around
Your summer thoughts are newly found.

Never in summer's heat and sun
Are your summer thoughts not having fun.

Summer thoughts so fun, so bold
They are thoughts that you will always hold.
Brandon Kunick, Grade 5
Victor Intermediate School

The Changes That Happen During Autumn
Weather changes cold
Spending time with family
Enjoying the time
Staying on the bed all day
Feel the cold air coming through
Jailene Rivera, Grade 5
Northeast Elementary School

My Love
Early in the morning, I think of you,
    Nearly every minute, you are on my mind.
I fear the day you might forget me
    I shed tears at being left behind.

You are as sweet as a pear,
    As tough as a bear.
My love for you will never tear,
    Like steel,
It will wear and wear.

    My love is pure from the start
The proof's in our heart,
    Our biggest part.
That's why,
    When I call you,
I say it twice,
    Once with "dear" and once with "heart."
Sophie Auguste, Grade 6
Graham Elementary and Middle School

Happy Thanksgiving

First: Make the food and set the table
      Patience
      Hungry
      Fun

Next: Have your family and friends come to the table
      Run!
      Quickly
      Run!

Then: Say a prayer, and give thanks for what you have
      Pray
      Believe
      Amen

Finally: Eat and have a Happy Thanksgiving
      Eat
      A stuffed face
      Sleep

Allison Pinto, Grade 6
St John School

Twister on Tuesday

Whooooooo!
The wind is starting to
   blooooowwww!
It waas a stoorrmyy Tuuesdayyyy!

The twwiiisstteerrr iisss ggoing toooo
   bloooooww!
Leetts gggett ggoing!
   Aaaahhhh!

Luma Aldwiri, Grade 4
Public School 69

The World Around Us

The light is around us
Brightening up our paths
With each step you take
You will make many mistakes

Each of those mistakes
Will make you ache
So keep those brakes on, watch out
And you'll never be in doubt

Onaid Zari, Grade 6
Intermediate School 227 - Louis Armstrong Middle

Dog

I once had a dog
Who sat on a log
He saw a fish
And made a wish
That he could eat a frog

Nicholas Jones, Grade 4
Granville Elementary School

Love

Love, Love, oh sweet sweet love.
How art thy love…
How I wish we could travel away beyond the seas.
We would go over the mountains and fly away.

With every heartbeat your heart makes,
my soul grows stronger.
The shine of spirit and the beauty of your wings,
makes love grow everywhere.

The sweet sound of your voice is delightful.
How I listen to your heavenly voice.
Every kiss you make,
makes my voice sing.

All love is not my love.
Everyone else has there own love.
Love is in everyone,
big or small.

No matter different,
love will always be love.

Amanda Nervais, Grade 6
Intermediate School 381

Juggling Names

Lazy ran alone.
Then fell and struggled.
Luckily Fell kindly helped him up.
Lazy Ran was thankful, but puzzled.
Unfortunately Puzzled took it offensively.
Offensively luckily liked his name being used.
While Used didn't.

Jonathan Ancowitz, Grade 4
Hebrew Academy of the Capital District

Index